# The Economics of Nonprofit Enterprises

and Andrei Shleifer (2001), 'Not-for-Profit Entrepreneurs', *Journal of Public Economics*, **81**, 99–115.

MIT Press Journals and the Massachusetts Institute of Technology for article: Marc Bilodeau and Al Slivinski (1998), 'Rational Nonprofit Entrepreneurship', *Journal of Economics and Management Strategy*, **7** (4), Winter, 551–71.

Oxford University Press for articles: Anne E. Preston (1988), 'The Nonprofit Firm: A Potential Solution to Inherent Market Failures', *Economic Inquiry*, **XXVI**, July, 493–506; James M. Ferris and Elizabeth Graddy (1994), 'Organizational Choices for Public Service Supply', *Journal of Law, Economics and Organization*, **10** (1), April, 126–41.

RAND for articles: Henry Hansmann (1981), 'Nonprofit Enterprise in the Performing Arts', *Bell Journal of Economics*, **12**, 341–61; Richard Steinberg (1986), 'The Revealed Objective Functions of Nonprofit Firms', *RAND Journal of Economics*, **17** (4), Winter, 508–26.

Sage Publications, Inc. for article: Richard Steinberg (1993), 'Public Policy and the Performance of Nonprofit Organizations: A General Framework', *Nonprofit and Voluntary Sector Quarterly*, **22** (1), Spring, 13–31.

University of Chicago Press for articles and excerpts: Susan Rose-Ackerman (1987), 'Ideals versus Dollars: Donors, Charity Managers, and Government Grants', *Journal of Political Economy*, **95** (4), August, 810–23; Charles T. Clotfelter (1992), 'The Distributional Consequences of Nonprofit Activities', in Charles T. Clotfelter (ed.), *Who Benefits from the Nonprofit Sector?*, Chapter 1, 1–23, references; Mark McClellan and Douglas Staiger (2000), 'Comparing Hospital Quality at For-Profit and Not-for-Profit Hospitals', in David M. Cutler (ed.), *The Changing Hospital Industry: Comparing Not-for-Profit and For-Profit Institutions*, Chapter 3, 93–112; Laura Leete (2001), 'Whither the Nonprofit Wage Differential? Estimates from the 1990 Census', *Journal of Labor Economics*, **19** (1), January, 136–70.

University of Wisconsin Press for article: Estelle James (1993), 'Why Do Different Countries Choose a Different Public–Private Mix of Educational Services?', *Journal of Human Resources*, **28** (3), 571–92.

Yale University Press for excerpts: Henry Hansmann (1987), 'Economic Theories of Nonprofit Organization', in Walter W. Powell (ed.), *The Nonprofit Sector: A Research Handbook*, Chapter 2, 27–42; Richard Steinberg (1987), 'Nonprofit Organizations and the Market', in Walter W. Powell (ed.), *The Nonprofit Sector: A Research Handbook*, Chapter 7, 118–38; Burton A. Weisbrod (1998), 'Institutional Form and Organizational Behavior', in Walter W. Powell and Elisabeth S. Clemens (eds), *Private Action and the Public Good*, Chapter 5, 69–84.

Every effort has been made to trace all the copyright holders but if any have been inadvertently overlooked the publishers will be pleased to make the necessary arrangement at the first opportunity.

In addition the publishers wish to thank the Marshall Library of Economics, Cambridge University, the Library of the University of Warwick and the Library of Indiana University at Bloomington, USA for their assistance in obtaining these articles.

# Introduction

*Richard Steinberg*

Nonprofit organizations present the analyst with a slew of puzzles. To an economist conditioned to think in terms of objectives and constraints, even the mathematical definition of the beast is a problem. What is a nonprofit organization? How does this definition shape the elaboration of objectives and constraints?

What are those objectives, or as Dennis Young put it in the title of his 1983 book, 'If Not for Profit, For What?'. Organizational founders choose whether to pursue their personal objectives through creation of for-profit firms, nonprofit organizations ('nonprofits'), government agencies, and other structures. Why do some entrepreneurs choose the nonprofit form, knowingly sacrificing their right ever to receive financial returns from the organizations they start? Why do entrepreneurs in some industries choose one form (nonprofit or for-profit) or the other exclusively, whereas in other industries a mixture of organizational forms stably coexist?

For-profit firms obtain most of their revenues from the sale of goods and services. Some nonprofits that Hansmann (1980) labels 'commercial' do the same. How, if at all, do commercial nonprofits differ from for-profit competitors? Other ('donative') nonprofits obtain most of their revenues from donations, which for-profit firms never do. Are these donations part of an exchange process between nonprofits and donors, and, if so, what services are the nonprofits selling? Does the nondistribution constraint determine why donations are made to nonprofits but not for-profits, or is this difference due to laws and regulations that favor gifts to organizations taking one form and not the other? Finally, some nonprofits obtain their revenues from both sources – sales and donations. Are there interactions between the two that affect the pricing and fundraising decisions of nonprofits?

This book brings together some of the most important articles on the topic of the economics of nonprofit organizations. The topic attracted a few early works (Tullock, 1966; Newhouse, 1970; Feldstein, 1971; Pauly and Redisch, 1973), but the subject lacked coherence until Hansmann (1980) articulated an economically useful definition: A public or private nonprofit organization is one restricted, by law or internal governance mechanisms, from distributing residual earnings to individuals who exercise control over the organization, such as officers, directors, or members. As we will see, this 'nondistribution constraint' affects the organization's entry and exit decision, market for control, costs of obtaining resources, form of managerial compensation, and characteristics of those who chose to work for the organization. By this definition, government agencies are arguably nonprofit (depending whether control inheres in government officials or the electorate), but I shall reserve use of the term 'nonprofit' for private agencies in what follows. Hansmann's definition provided something that economic modelers could build upon, and the pace of progress has accelerated since then.

In a real sense, I regard this book as volume II on the subject. Rose-Ackerman edited a book in 1986, entitled *The Economics of Nonprofit Institutions: Studies in Structure and Policy*, which contains many important earlier works. Although not compiled for the Edward Elgar series of reference collections, it has stood the test of time and serves this purpose. Rather than reprint most of the articles appearing in the 1986 volume, I will refer to them in this introductory survey. For those unable to obtain the Rose-Ackerman volume, I include two surveys of the earlier literature prepared around that time (Hansmann, 1987, and Steinberg, 1987, reproduced here as Chapters 1 and 2). In addition, you might want to read James and Rose-Ackerman (1986) which builds on the edited volume but references many other early sources and Rose-Ackerman (1996) for a perspective that complements the present volume.

The literature on nonprofit organizations developed in three waves. The first wave of articles asserted some plausible objective for a nonprofit organization possessing monopoly power, then derived the implications of that objective for organizational behavior. The second wave looked more broadly at the role of nonprofit organizations in a wider economy as they compete or collaborate with for-profit firms and government agencies. The third wave begins development of integrated theories in which the objectives of nonprofit organizations emerge endogenously within an environment potentially containing organizations from other sectors (for-profit and government). This description of the intellectual development of the field is constructed after the fact. Some 'first-wave' articles continue to be written, and elements of the third wave can be found in some early articles. However, the 'wave' metaphor does provide a useful framework for thinking about the development of the field and is employed here despite its shortcomings. Following description of each wave, I summarize two strands of literature that do not fit naturally into this framework: intersectoral comparisons of performance and analyses of public policies toward nonprofit organizations. Each of these strands began atheoretically, but have gradually grown to incorporate insights from the second and third waves. For example, Grabowski and Hirth (2003) build on Hirth's (Chapter 14) second-wave insight that there are competitive spillovers from nonprofit to for-profit nursing homes. They then estimated for-profit performance through regression analyses that account for the nonprofit market share.

## The First Wave: Asserting the Objective Functions

Articles in the first wave asserted that nonprofit behavior results from a variety of plausible objective functions. Most of these articles start by confronting economists' predisposition to regard profit maximization as the universal goal of organizations in market economies. We now understand their arguments as immediate corollaries to Hansmann's (1980) nondistribution constraint. Those in control of the nonprofit are prohibited from receiving the financial surplus generated by their decisions, so departures from profit maximization have a low opportunity cost to nonprofit 'owners'. This same nondistribution constraint, if fully enforced, makes it impossible for nonprofit owners to profit from transferring their ownership rights to others, removing the market for control that disciplines departures from profit-maximizing behavior by publicly traded for-profit firms. How then is this freedom to pursue other objectives used?

Two early articles developed the idea that a nonprofit organization might want to maximize its budget, rather than the charitable services it provides. Tullock (1966) argued that the managers of donative nonprofits prefer to maximize the size of the budget under their control, rather than the amount they expend on charitable services. This is because larger budgets bring more prestige and higher financial compensation to nonprofit managers. To maximize the budget, the organization would seek to maximize gross donations, rather than net-of-solicitation-expenditure donations received. In contrast, a service-maximizing nonprofit organization would seek to maximize net donations, as this is the sum left over for providing charitable services after campaign expenses are accounted for. Niskanen (1971) argued that commercial nonprofits also seek to maximize their budgets.

Steinberg (Chapter 18) recognized that one can distinguish these alternative objectives, for donative nonprofits, by looking at the 'marginal donative product of fundraising' (the increment to donations produced by an incremental dollar spent on solicitation). Estimates of marginal donative product then reveal the objective underlying the fundraising decision. He found that US 'health' nonprofits reveal themselves to be budget maximizers, whereas 'arts', 'education', and 'welfare' nonprofits act as service maximizers. Khanna, Posnett, and Sandler (Chapter 19) conducted a similar exercise using a panel of UK nonprofits. They found that 'health' and 'overseas' charities act like service maximizers, whereas 'religion' organizations act like budget maximizers.

Newhouse (1970) argued that nonprofit hospitals maximized a combination of quality and quantity, and this work inspired similar approaches for other kinds of nonprofits (James and Neuberger, 1981, or Hansmann, Chapter 10). This objective is plausible because managerial prestige depends upon both. Further, many nonprofits state that their goal is to foster tastes for merit goods (goods like opera appreciation that, in the organization's opinion, consumers do not want as much as they should). Others argued that nonprofits maximize the net income per member of a controlling group of agents (Pauly and Redisch, 1973) or the nonpecuniary income of owners (Migué and Bélanger, 1974; Borjas, Frech, and Ginsburg, 1983). Malani, Philipson, and David (2003) provided a model that nicely nests many of these alternative objective functions, highlighting their points of agreement and disagreement on comparative-static behavior.

Weisbrod took the mission statements of many nonprofit organizations more seriously, suggesting the label 'bonoficing' for the objective function of organizations 'whose goals include distributing outputs to "needy" or to "deserving" persons regardless of ability to pay, as well as treating underinformed consumers "fairly," even at the expense of profits' (1988, p. 143). Bonoficing might include goals such as preserving plants and animals in a botanic or zoological garden or advancing the state of scientific research knowledge about a disease. James examined the comparative statics of nonprofit organizations that care positively about some outputs, negatively about other outputs (which are produced only if they are sufficiently profitable, enabling the cross-subsidization of favored outputs) and not at all about still other outputs (which are produced whenever they generate positive profits). Finally, Holtmann (1983) asserted that nonprofit organizations maximize social welfare.

## The Second Wave: The Role of Nonprofit Organizations

First-wave articles looked at the behavior of individual nonprofit organizations, assumed to occupy specified market niches without competition and, often, without explanation. The next step was to consider other actors who might compete or collaborate with nonprofits and try to identify the niches that will be filled by nonprofits. These other actors include other nonprofits, government agencies, for-profit firms, and sometimes others (such as the family, informal associations, cooperatives, and worker-managed firms). Why are some industries exclusively nonprofit, others exclusively for-profit, and others mixed? Are nonprofits particularly good at certain types of activities? Does the presence of nonprofit organizations in a market improve the performance of government agencies and for-profit firms?

Two nonprofit roles have dominated the literature to date. Weisbrod (1975) emphasized the nonprofit role in the provision of public goods, and Hansmann (1980) emphasized the nonprofit role in correcting market failures due to asymmetric information. Each of these roles is discussed here, followed by a summary of the much scanter literature on other roles played by nonprofit organizations.

### *The Role of Nonprofits in Providing Public Goods*

Weisbrod (1975, 1988) noted that most nonprofits provide public (nonrival and nonexcludable) goods as part of their output mix. For example, although the food, clothing, and shelter that charities provide to needy individuals are consumed by the recipient, altruists are each made better off when anyone helps the needy. In addition, poverty creates external costs that are eased in a nonrival and nonexcludable way by the efforts of charity. Education enhances the earning power of students (a private gain), but a more educated citizenry enhances the quality of democratic processes (a public gain). Advocacy simultaneously produces public goods for supporters of the cause and public bads for opponents. Religious institutions arguably foster development of social capital (resources that inhere in community social organization such as trust and authority), another public good.

Economists are familiar with the reasons why for-profit firms do not provide pure public goods, and usually think of government as the institution of choice for public-good provision. Weisbrod (1975) reminded us that a consensus on the level of governmental provision of public goods rarely exists, as Lindahl taxes are impractical and Tiebout migration is limited. Weisbrod focused on Bowen's theory that the median-preference voter is decisive, but whatever level of public-good expenditure is selected by political processes, some would like to see more spent. These 'high-demanders' donate to nonprofit organizations that supplement governmental provision of public goods. He does not explicitly model why high-demanders make donations to nonprofit organizations rather than free-riding or donating to for-profits, but suggests many reasons developed formally in later works such as Bilodeau and Slivinski (Chapter 7). Note that Weisbrod does not try to explain the nonprofit share of public-good *provision* because his theory says nothing about government-financed contractual provision by nonprofits. His 1975 theory explains that share of public-good provision *financed* by donations.

James (Chapter 11) put Weisbrod's theory (and several others, discussed later) to the test, exploring the reasons why different countries chose a different mixture of public and private education at the primary- and secondary-school levels. She assumed that both the type of public education and expenditure on that education are determined by political processes. When preferences for either the type or level of education are more diverse, dissatisfaction with public schools will be higher and, consequently, we should see a larger share of education provided through privately financed private education. This is precisely what she found. Controlling for government subsidies to private education, the private share grew with measures of the heterogeneity of tastes, particularly with measures of religious heterogeneity.

When provision of a private good produces beneficial externalities (nonrival and nonexcludable), for-profit firms will sell that good, although they will not provide the optimal quantity. Preston (Chapter 9) showed how the presence of nonprofit organizations in a market can improve this situation. More specifically, she considered a model of product differentiation in which outputs differ in their ratio of private to public benefits. The equilibrium product spectrum when nonprofits are excluded from the market supplies a limited range of alternatives. When nonprofits and for-profits coexist, the equilibrium product spectrum is broader and Pareto-dominates the for-profit only equilibrium. Her results are particularly strong in that she does not rely on an organizational objective function that incorporates public benefits. Her managers maximize their financial compensation by maximizing the organization's budget, which they accomplish by providing an output mixture that considers both donor and purchaser preferences. Her results are weaker because they depend upon donor knowledge of the ratios of public to private benefits at each organization. Although expecting that most donors are so well informed is unrealistic, her results provide useful insight for a world in which a few key donors are well informed and managers value both financial compensation and the provision of socially beneficial outputs by the organizations they control.

Rose-Ackerman (Chapter 6) also looked at nonprofits that produce public goods differing in some characteristic. That characteristic could be aesthetic (as in abstract versus representational art), ideologic (as in the religious character of a private school), or technical (as in the teaching philosophy of a private school). In contrast to Preston, Rose-Ackerman's managers care about that characteristic, and the manager's preferred value for that characteristic may not match the value preferred by the organization's donors. A compromise is struck on the characteristics of the public good, and the terms of that compromise depend upon the other financial resources available to the manager. Lump-sum government grants allow the nonprofit manager to move closer to his or her ideal level of the characteristic, and grants with strings attached can move the manager closer to the donor's preferred level.

Eckel and Steinberg (1993) assumed that nonprofit managers value two job attributes – private-benefit perks and the public-benefit perk of using their job to provide public goods. The nonprofit organization sells a private good and uses the net proceeds to cross-subsidize these two job attributes. Equilibrium public-good provision then depends on the manager's marginal rate of substitution between these job attributes and on the competitive environment. If managers value public-benefit perks sufficiently, then nonprofit monopolies provide an attractive way to finance public-good provision. This institution is attractive because the welfare gains from incremental public-good provision can outweigh the deadweight loss from monopoly. Further, if the incremental excess-burden of feasible taxes is sufficiently large, nonprofit monopolies would dominate governmental tax-financed provision of public goods.

Nonprofits also provide excludable public goods, especially in the realm of 'high culture' (operas, symphony orchestras, art museums, and the like). For-profit firms are generally willing to provide excludable public goods, but may under-provide them and will over-exclude (that is, keep some consumers that place positive value on the public good from consuming the good in order to protect its pricing structure). High-culture goods typically enjoy high fixed and low marginal costs and face limited consumer demand. In this situation, single-price for-profit monopolies would not produce the good at all, and price-discriminating for-profit monopolies would be unable to solve the demand-revelation problem. Hansmann (Chapter 10) showed that donations to nonprofits serve as a form of 'voluntary price discrimination' enabling production of the good in question. In a similar model, Ben-Ner (1986) showed that the nondistribution constraint allows nonprofits to solve the demand revelation problem and that the control of nonprofits by customers and donors leads to a superior set of discriminatory prices.

*The Role of Nonprofits in Situations of Asymmetric Information*

A major strand of the literature argues that nonprofits are more trustworthy than for-profits in certain situations of asymmetric information. Arrow (1963) was the first to recognize this argument as it applies to health care organizations, where the quality of services provided is hard for consumers to verify, even *ex post*. In such situations, he argued, the profit orientation of for-profits interferes with the trust relationships needed to support provision of high-quality care. Nelson and Krashinsky (1973) made a similar argument with respect to day-care providers, and Hansmann (1980) extended the argument to all kinds of nonprofits. He labeled situations where 'owing either to the circumstances under which a service is purchased or consumed or to the nature of the service itself, consumers feel unable to evaluate accurately the quantity or quality of the service the firm produces for them' (Hansmann, 1987, p. 29, Chapter 1) as ones involving 'contract failure'. In situations of contract failure, the consumer is unable to write an enforceable contract, and recognizes that for-profit firms will short-change him/her on either quantity or quality in order to distribute larger dividend checks and avoid takeover bids. Consumers turn to nonprofit organizations because the nondistribution constraint provides some assurance that these motives will not come into play.

Contract failure certainly applies to collective efforts to finance public goods. For example, if one individual asks an organization to provide food for starving residents of a far-off nation, he will find it difficult to find out whether two aspects of the contract have been complied with. First, finding out whether these people have been fed at all would be difficult, as hiring a trustworthy observer in a foreign land would be costly. More fundamentally, as long as the organization spends at least as much on total food aid as that individual paid for, the individual will be unable to tell whether his money added to food provided or to the dividend checks distributed to the organization's owners. Nonprofit organizations are not legally able to enrich their owners and so provide a more trustworthy vehicle for purchasing this service. This point, while clear in Hansmann's informal treatment, is well formalized in the work of Bilodeau and Slivinski (Chapters 7 and 8 and discussed below).

Hansmann was less confident that contract failure explains the role of most nonprofits in commercial markets, but argued in Chapter 12 that the model works well for at least one kind of commercial nonprofit – the mutual savings bank. Although mutual savings banks distribute financial surpluses to their depositors, they are properly classified as nonprofits rather than consumer cooperatives because those receiving the distribution enjoy no control rights over the use of the bank's assets. They were established at a time when for-profit commercial banks did not take deposits from individuals. Hansmann explained the failure of for-profit banks to enter this market as a consequence of contract failure, when lightly regulated banks had the incentive and opportunity to speculate wildly with other peoples' money. When commercial banks became better regulated, beginning in the mid nineteenth century, the nonprofit advantage shrank and was entirely neutralized by legislation passed in 1933. Since then, no new mutual savings banks have been founded, but most of the existing ones persisted.

Weisbrod and Schlesinger (1986) argued that contract failure also applies to nursing-home markets. Contract failure applies here because some aspects of nursing care are hard to observe (such as whether the enfeebled elderly residents receive appropriate medication and are always treated with respect), because the person receiving residential care is often not the person deciding on the provider (the decider may be the children or the resident's insurer), and because transferring the elderly to another facility is difficult if post-purchase experience proves that the promised quality of care is not being delivered (due to 'transfer trauma' or 'transplantation shock'). However, proving the extent of contract failure by for-profit firms is no easy task.

If detecting less-than-promised quality were easy for the researcher, it is likely that the consumer would also be able to detect this departure and so contract failure would not occur. In response to this dilemma, Weisbrod and Schlesinger found two subtle differences in quality that are consistent with Hansmann's ideas. First, although there was no difference between nonprofit and for-profit nursing homes in the frequency of complaints to regulatory authorities about matters covered by the regulatory code, the frequency of complaints raised against for-profit homes on the typically hard-to-verify aspects of quality not covered by the code was substantially higher. Second, although there was no difference between the sectors in the share of residents possessing a doctor's prescription for sedatives, the staff of for-profit nursing homes administered these sedatives four times as frequently as did the staff at religiously affiliated nonprofit homes. Weisbrod (Chapter 21) and Kapur and Weisbrod (2000) provided additional evidence on nursing homes and two other long-term care industries where contract failure is expected to be especially severe because of the consumer lock-in effect – psychiatric facilities and facilities for the mentally impaired.

Chillemi and Gui (Chapter 13) formalized one way in which contract failure can persist in the face of experiential learning. In their model, consumers can eventually find out whether the promised quality or quantity was delivered, but there is a substantial lag between service purchase and quality verification. For-profit firms choose whether to maintain a reputation for trustworthiness or behave opportunistically for a short-term gain. A good reputation is more valuable when the price markup over costs is large. In competitive markets, it is not possible to raise prices sufficiently and for-profit firms behave opportunistically. In less competitive markets, for-profit firms will charge a high price and maintain the promised level of quality. Thus, either for-profits or nonprofits can be trusted in noncompetitive markets, but the latter are trustworthy at a lower price.

Nondistribution of profits removes one motive for nonprofits to shortchange their donors and customers, but there are others. Nominally nonprofit organizations may want to violate the spirit of the nondistribution constraint, taking advantage of their privileged information to increase their nonpecuniary perks. Alternatively, nonprofits may cheat donors or customers in order to better subsidize a mission-related output that is not highly valued by the donor/customer pool (e.g., Steinberg and Gray, 1993). Three articles amplify why nonprofits may nonetheless act in a trustworthy fashion much of the time. First, Handy (1995) argued that board members will monitor the performance of their organization because, in effect, they post their reputation as collateral.

Second, Ben-Ner (1986) analysed the incentives of donors and customers to monitor and control performance, arguing that the identity of nonprofit board members is at least as important as the nondistribution constraint in solving problems of contract failure. For-profit firms are controlled by 'supply-side stakeholders', investors who care far more about the financial returns resulting from their investment than about the creation of a product that they intend to consume. In contrast, nonprofit organizations and consumer cooperatives are controlled by 'demand-side stakeholders' or 'patrons', who supply funds but are primarily concerned with consuming some output resulting from those funds. Supply-side stakeholders want high prices and less-than-promised quality (in order to cut costs and so increase profits), and can be expected to behave opportunistically to further those objectives in cases of asymmetric information. There is no such problem with demand-side stakeholders in control, for these owners want what all consumers want – low prices and promised levels of quality. Because nonprofit outputs are collectively consumed, a demand-side stakeholder serving as the manager will, in pursuing his own interest, generally advance the interests of other patrons. Thus, parents may be somewhat assured if their child is cared for by an organization that does not distribute profits, but they are far more assured if the owner's children are also cared for by the same organization. In placing the emphasis on patron control, rather than nondistribution, Ben-Ner serves to explain a wider class of organizations that includes both nonprofits and consumer cooperatives.

Third, following a suggestion made by the original Hansmann (1980) article, Handy and Katz (Chapter 15) argued that the self-selection of managers into the nonprofit sector can help to solve contract failures. They developed a formal model in which managers (and other key decision makers) differ in both their ability and their devotion to a nonprofit cause. Although ability is somewhat observable (through costless tests that are admittedly imperfect), the nonprofit board can only learn a manager's devotion by hiring him or her for a period of time. They analysed two strategies that nonprofit boards might take – one designed to promote self-selection by managerial devotion and the other designed to promote self-selection by ability. The first strategy allows the firm to hire its manager for less and, of course, will attract only devoted applicants. The second strategy has a lower chance of erroneously hiring a low-skilled manager but is more likely to hire an indifferent one. They showed that the first strategy is better if (a) testing errors are small, (b) the applicant pool has a large share of devoted and productive candidates, (c) the productivity of the low-skilled applicants is low, and (d) the productivity of highly skilled but less-devoted applicants is high.

Chapter 15 illustrates how positive selection can help nonprofits to 'get more by paying less', but does not quite get them to the desired conclusion that managerial self-selection helps to solve contract failure. Their discussion of fringe benefits hints at how they can go that last step – if nonprofit managers value the quantity and quality of the output they produce, these count as part of managerial compensation and can result in the self-selection of managers that donors and clients can trust. By harmonizing the interests of patrons and managers, this kind of selection can achieve the benefits suggested by Ben-Ner's (1986) model of patron control. When combined with insights from Bilodeau and Slivinski (1996) about entrepreneurial self-selection on the basis of a preference for public goods and from Slivinski (2002) on the effects of compensation on moral hazard, we have the promise of a more complete analysis in the near future.

Two articles consider contract failure in a coexistence setting, where for-profits and nonprofits both persist in long-run equilibrium: Hirth (Chapter 14) and Handy (Chapter 17). Hirth (Chapter 14) presented a remarkably rich set of results that emphasize the interaction between the two sectors. He considered a world in which quality comes in two levels – high (the promised level) and low (less than the promised level). Consumers come in two types – informed (able to observe prices and whether quality is high or low at any particular supplier) or uninformed (able to observe prices and whether an organization is labeled as nonprofit or for-profit). Uninformed consumers estimate the average quality at each type of supplier, but do not know the specific quality of any firms in the market. There are two types of nonprofit organizations – honest nonprofits and 'for-profits-in-disguise' (a term coined by Weisbrod, 1988). As the name reveals, for-profits-in-disguise pretend to be nonprofits, obtaining the nonprofit label from legal authorities but distributing profits to their owners. For-profits-in-disguise attempt to benefit from the good reputation of nonprofits by selling low-quality services at a high-quality price.

In Hirth's model, the nondistribution constraint is imperfectly enforced, and this is what allows for-profits-in-disguise to exist. More stringent enforcement of the nondistribution constraint increases the cost of production at for-profits-in-disguise, but not at honest nonprofits. Depending upon how stringently the nondistribution constraint is enforced, three equilibrium configurations are possible. When there is strict enforcement, all informed consumers buy from for-profits, which charge a lower price than nonprofits in equilibrium. Uninformed consumers turn to nonprofits, which are all honest as for-profits-in-disguise do not find it profitable to enter these markets. The most interesting result is the competitive spillover benefit, where the presence of honest nonprofits improves the performance of for-profits. Specifically, the customers of forprofits are more likely to be informed when a nonprofit alternative accommodates some of the uninformed, and this makes the for-profits more likely to supply high quality. The nonprofit sector can ensure that only high quality is provided in both sectors even if it is not large enough to serve all the uninformed. Thus, the presence of a few nonprofits in a mixed-sector market can entirely solve the problem of asymmetric information.

If the nondistribution constraint is moderately enforced, honest nonprofits will 'limit price' in order to make it unprofitable for for-profits-in-disguise to enter the market. At this lower price, honest nonprofits lack the capacity to serve all the uninformed customers, and so honest nonprofits will employ waiting lists and other nonprice rationing devices. There is still a positive spillover benefit from having nonprofits in the market.

Finally, if enforcement of the nondistribution constraint is weak, honest nonprofits cannot survive competition from for-profits-in-disguise without special help. Tax breaks and the like do not suffice for this purpose, because they are granted equally to honest nonprofits and for-profits-in-disguise. Volunteer labor could supply the needed cushion, as on-site volunteers would have an easier time distinguishing honest nonprofits and would be unlikely to continue offering their services to a for-profit-in-disguise. In this case, there could be either domination by honest nonprofits or coexistence of honest nonprofits and for-profits-in-disguise. Regardless, some informed consumers would patronize honest nonprofits, and the competitive spillover benefit is eliminated.

In Hirth's model, all consumers are alike and all would prefer to purchase high quality if the prices of high and low were set at their respective marginal costs. Thus, there is an identity between 'high' and 'the promised level' of quality. In reality, tastes differ and some might prefer to buy low quality even if fully informed. Hirth sketches an alternative model where tastes differ and everyone is fully informed. Then, nonprofits would choose their niche depending upon their objective function and for-profits would accommodate all residual demand. The two sectors would behave differently, but this is a matter of specialization rather than market failure – if nonprofits did not exist, for-profits would supply the same mixture of high and low quality as supplied by the two sectors when they coexist.

Hirth was silent, however, on what would happen if tastes differed in an asymmetric information framework. Handy (Chapter 17) hints at some of the answers here. She builds on Weisbrod's (1988) suggestion that the outputs include both easy- (type I) and hard-to-observe (type II) characteristics. Consumers' marginal rate of substitution between type I and type II characteristics will vary because their tastes differ and because they assign different probabilities to their ability to recognize and purchase their intended level of type II. With diverse tastes, it is not surprising that some consumers will choose nonprofits and some for-profits and this is what she finds. However, she hints at a variety of complications and institutional features that would have to be incorporated before confronting this prediction with data. What is really needed is a model that combines Handy's ideas on consumer diversity with the rich structure of market interaction in Hirth's (Chapter 14) model.

### *Other Roles Played by Nonprofits*

Clotfelter (Chapter 5) began the scant literature on the role of nonprofits in the distribution of income. He carefully delineated the pathways by which nonprofits serve to redistribute income, paying special attention to the counterfactual (what would the distribution be in a world that lacked nonprofits). What is surprising, however, is how little is known about the extent to which charitable organizations (let alone other kinds of nonprofits) help the poor. Steinberg and Weisbrod (Chapter 24) elaborated on the mechanisms individual nonprofit organizations can use to redistribute income, including: sliding-scale fees and other forms of price discrimination; rationing by waiting, eligibility rules, or product quality dilution; and client recruiting strategies. They showed how nonprofits with distributional objectives would use these mechanisms differently from for-profits, and hint at some of the side-effects relevant to the choice of technique.

Testing for these differences is complicated with existing data, if for no other reason than that the various sources of nonprofit revenue (from fees, dues, and donations) are expected to interact. For example, Kingma (1995) found that Red Cross health and safety training classes had large negative impacts on donations, whereas an exogenous increase in donations reduced commercial profits. Studies of nonprofits more generally suffer from data limitations, but two fine studies included here strongly suggest the importance of revenue interactions: Schiff and Weisbrod (Chapter 26) and Segal and Weisbrod (Chapter 20).

James (1986, 1989) proposed that nonprofits play a role in shaping preferences (particularly religious preferences). She noted that many nonprofits have been founded by religious bodies, arguing that perhaps this represents a conscious strategy to obtain converts. Young people in school, sick people in hospitals, or needy people in shelters are especially vulnerable to proselytization. This is why, she suggested, schools and universities, hospitals, long-term care facilities, and homeless shelters were often started by religious bodies. The competition for converts is fiercer where there is religious diversity. Thus, the finding in Chapter 11 that private nonprofit educational institutions have a larger market share in religiously heterogeneous societies is consistent with the religious proselytization theory as well as Weisbrod's model of public-goods provision by nonprofits.

Although James's work on nonprofits' role in inducing preferences has stimulated much admiration, few have, as yet, taken up the call to advance the analysis. There is also little formal economic analysis of advocacy organizations (such as the Sierra Club, National

Organization for Women, National Rifle Association, or the Heritage Foundation) which, whether they inform or alter preferences, illustrate an important societal role played by nonprofits. There is also little on social marketing – nonprofit efforts to get people to practice safe sex, moderate their drinking, appreciate environmental amenities, and stop child abuse.

## The Third Wave: Integrated Models

Second-wave articles emphasized the demand side – why people would like to give or to buy from nonprofit organizations. Third-wave models also incorporate a supply side, seeking to understand why anyone would start a nonprofit organization that played the roles demanded. Ideally, both the entry decision and the choice of objective functions would be integrated into one model of how nonprofits behave among other organizations.

James's (1986) theory of religious proselytization discussed above has elements of both the supply and demand side, as does Ben-Ner (1986). However, the first article that developed both the supply and demand for nonprofit organizations is Ben-Ner and Van Hoomissen (Chapter 3). This article repeated the variety of existing theories of the demand for nonprofit services, then argued that nonprofits arise to meet that demand when the benefits of formation exceed operating plus transactions costs. Transactions costs include the need to (a) identify and assemble a collection of willing stakeholders, (b) determine whether collective demand is sufficient to cover costs, (c) organize production decisions, (d) induce stakeholders to reveal their preferences truthfully, and (e) establish a governance mechanism to insure stakeholder control against free-riding, agency problems, and the like. Potential entrepreneurs compare the net benefits to establishing a 'self-provision coalition' (either a new nonprofit or consumer cooperative) with the net benefits of lobbying government to fund the service in question or regulate alternative providers. Although this chapter is informal, it is richly sprinkled with considerations that formal modelers should incorporate.

In my 1993 paper (Chapter 4), I argued that there was a need for formal integrated models for the purposes of public-policy analysis. Ideally, I said, a model would do four things: (a) properly incorporate the legal constraints that define an organization as nonprofit, (b) demonstrate how the postulated objective function emerges endogenously within the regulatory and competitive environment specified, (c) specify how the relevant competing organizations (for-profit, nonprofit, and governmental) would emerge endogenously and (d) specify the information structure under which agents operate. I think the second criterion is particularly important for policy analysts. It is not enough to uncover the organization's current objective function and verify that this objective remains viable following regulatory change. Some policy changes will allow the nonprofit to accomplish a different set of outcomes. In the long run, this implies that the founders of organizations will consider the nonprofit option in a different light, and may incorporate different objectives into the organization's charter and bylaws (Young, 1983). In addition, managers and workers will sort themselves into the sector on a different basis (Hansmann, 1980). Thus, the short-run effect of policy changes (while the organizational objective function remains constant) differs from the long-run effect (after the objective evolves). Eckel and Steinberg illustrated this point in more detail in an unpublished paper in 1994, although published work deriving general results would be quite welcome.

A remarkable series of articles by Bilodeau and Slivinski provides an integrated model of how entrepreneurs that value the provision of public goods would found and support nonprofit organizations. Their 1996 article concentrates on the self-selection among nonprofit entrepreneurs. Their 1998 article (Chapter 7) showed why such an entrepreneur would rationally choose to constrain his future possibilities to receive profits. Their 1997 article (Chapter 8) analysed the endogenous emergence of one type of market competition among nonprofits. An unpublished article by Bilodeau (2000) analysed the participation of donative nonprofit organizations in commercial markets that also contain for-profit firms. The common framework employed in all these articles shows considerable promise as a platform to build a general and integrated theory of donative nonprofit organizations.

Their basic approach considered a three-stage game of complete information, where the players care about the quantity of some pure public good. One of these individuals self-selects to play the entrepreneurial role and considers whether to start a nonprofit or a for-profit organization with an initial investment of effort and a 'seed donation'. Following this initial investment, other players simultaneously choose how much to donate, and then the entrepreneur decides whether to make an additional donation, positive or negative. The game ends when total donations are used to produce the public good. If the nonprofit form is selected, the entrepreneur cannot make a negative donation (that is, withdraw some or all of his initial investment) at the third stage. This assures the second-stage donors that their contributions will not be expropriated by the entrepreneur. In the first stage, the entrepreneur makes a large donation so that second-stage donors do not expect to get anything more from the entrepreneur in the third stage. In this way, the entrepreneur does not allow second-stage donors to free-ride off his expected largesse. Entrepreneurs choose to constrain their future options to receive profits because it is in their self-interest to do so. The nondistribution constraint serves as a credible commitment device that results in an equilibrium where they can enjoy a larger quantity of the public good with a smaller personal contribution.

The second Bilodeau and Slivinski article (Chapter 8) considered multiple public goods, and whether a single 'united fundraising organization (UFO)' or rival charities would be created. They assumed away many factors that explain combined campaigns (which are covered elsewhere, notably, in Rose-Ackerman, 1980) in order to focus on the issue of preference mismatch. If, for example, a donor cares only about one of the two public goods supported by a UFO, the diversion of 50 per cent of his contribution to the other public good is equivalent to a doubling of the effective price of giving. However, that same donor is glad that 50 per cent of the contributions of others will go to the public good he supports, even though other donors may not like that public good. On balance, total contributions go down if fixed-percentage allocation rules are used by a UFO that provides two mutually substitutable public goods. Simple donor designation plans (where the donor declares that his contribution is to be used to support only some public goods) do not overcome this problem, as the UFO can undo any designation by reallocating its undesignated funds. However, if the UFO credibly commits to allocate a fixed share of unrestricted funds to each member agency, donor designations become effective and total donations go up.

Bilodeau (2000) extended the approach to commercial activity undertaken to provide more resources in support of a public good (what is generally referred to in the policy debates as 'unrelated business income' to stress the lack or relation to the organization's mission). However, the Bilodeau and Slivinski approach has not been extended to purely commercial nonprofits. The closest we come to an integrated theory of commercial nonprofits is Chapter 16 by Glaeser and Shleifer. They formalized Hansmann's ideas on contract failure in a model that incorporates the decision of the initial entrepreneur about whether to form a nonprofit or a for-profit organization. For them, a nonprofit organization is one that distributes benefits to the owners of the organization as perquisites, rather than cash. This 'softens' incentives to deliver less than the promised quality to the customer, so that nonprofit quality is higher.

Specifically, an organization sells a unit of a private good that has noncontractible attributes. Noncontractible attributes are qualities that may be known to both the buyer and the seller, but cannot be objectively measured so that third parties (such as the courts) cannot determine whether the terms of the contract have been broken. The product in question is privately consumed, but entrepreneurs nonetheless care about quality for either ethical or reputational reasons. A term consistent with either of these concerns is inserted into the cost function, and entrepreneurs maximize profits after accounting for both pecuniary and nonpecuniary costs.

Any expenditure as cash has higher value to entrepreneurs than that same expenditure as perks, so that all else equal, entrepreneurs prefer to found for-profit organizations. However, consumers will pay a higher price to an organization that is trusted. If the price they are willing to pay is sufficiently higher, the trusted organization can finance higher quality and a more than compensating increase in the volume of perks. They closed the model by showing that, by committing to the nonprofit form, the entrepreneur sends a credible signal that she can be trusted. The soft incentives provided in the nonprofit form reduce the gains to shortchanging consumers on quality without reducing the costs, so the equilibrium quality level will be higher.

I am not certain that soft incentives capture the essence of what is distinctive about nonprofit organizations. For example, for-profit firms subject to a profits tax also face a softening of incentives, as do firms governed by rate-of-return regulations. Nonetheless, as the first integrated model of a commercial nonprofit organization, Glaeser and Shleifer's analysis may form the foundation for a more satisfactory model, particularly if Hirth's insights in Chapter 14 can be incorporated in this framework. Ultimately, we would want to extend the analysis further, to endogenize the choice between founding a commercial or donative nonprofit, a process begun by Bilodeau (2000).

## Intersectoral Comparisons of Performance

Hundreds of studies have attempted to compare the performance of nonprofit and for-profit organizations when they each provide similar services. Most of these studies have focused on hospitals. However, many studies of nursing homes, mental health care, and day care centers and a smaller number of studies of employment counseling and placement, drug and alcohol treatment programs, arts organizations, recycling centers, and mortuaries also exist. Most consider the competition between generic nonprofits and for-profits, but some distinguish types within each sector (secular versus religiously affiliated, chain versus independent). Some studies also compare government direct provision with the various forms of private provision. The various studies have focused on diverse measures of performance – efficiency, pricing, input use, quality, and quantity, provision of charity care, sharing of information, and provision of other community benefits. In this book, we include an important essay on quality differences in long-term care facilities (Weisbrod, Chapter 21), an example of the best that the hospital studies have offered to date (McClellan and Staiger, Chapter 23) and a variety of methodological warnings to emphasize the extreme limitations of our progress to date (including Pauly, Chapter 22, and parts of Weisbrod, Chapter 21, and Hirth, Chapter 14).

Rather than summarize each individually, I wish to emphasize these methodological problems. First, any differences in performance may result from the strategic choices of organizations, and need not inhere in the organizations themselves. For example, Pauly noted in Chapter 22 that the finding by some studies that for-profit hospitals have lower costs of production may simply represent the fact that for-profits choose to locate where operating costs are expected to be lower (and hence profits higher). Second, organizations produce a multiplicity of outputs, and if some (for example community wellness education, medical training, and research) are not incorporated in the empirics, costs will be wrongly attributed to the others. A large number of unused hospital beds seems like a source of inefficiency if we look only at medical care currently provided, but the picture changes if we consider the option value of extra beds in times of disaster or epidemics (Holtmann, 1983). Third, differences in output quality may be subtle. As noted before, for-profits do not exhibit contract failure for attributes that are easy to measure – only for those that are hard for the buyer, the courts, and regulators to observe. Finally, observed differences are neither necessary nor sufficient indicators of market failures. In Chapter 14 Hirth emphasized the intersectoral spillover benefits, where the presence of a few nonprofit organizations in a mixed market raises the quality provided by for-profits. No difference in quality would be observable, yet social welfare is improved. Conversely, in his full-information model, quality differences between the sectors reflect nonprofit choice of a niche and have no consequences for social welfare.

A very nice empirical study by Leete (Chapter 25) looked at the differences in wages paid by nonprofit and for-profit organizations. If nonprofit workers derive utility from the output they produce, this counts as part of their total compensation and their monetary wages will be correspondingly lower. If, on the other hand, nonprofits distribute their financial returns to line employees (as permitted under nondistribution because line employees are not in control of the organization), then nonprofit wages will be higher. A variety of other factors are also relevant, and Leete analysed many of these. The patterns of wage difference by nonprofit industry and occupation allow one to explore a variety of theories about the role and functioning of the sector.

## Public Policy

This volume barely touches on public policy toward the nonprofit sector for several reasons. First, this book is designed for an international audience, whereas much of the literature covers the specific policies of specific countries. Second, this book is designed for the coverage of enduring issues in the nonprofit sector, and much of the literature concerns proposals of the moment. Third, there was simply not space to cover everything. I cover two issues that are likely to cross national boundaries and endure – policy regarding the coexistence in commercial markets of nonprofit and for-profit organizations, and policy regarding government contracting with private agencies (for-profit and nonprofit) for service delivery. I neglect other issues of enduring cross-national significance – the proper treatment of donations in personal income tax systems, the proper treatment of nonprofit entities in entity tax systems, the adaptation of antitrust policy to nonprofit combinations in restraint of trade, the regulation (or not) of fundraising, the restriction (or facilitation) of nonprofit accumulations of capital, and the design of operational definitions for the enforcement of the nondistribution constraint (particularly when nonprofits convert to for-profits). Steinberg (2003) provides a brief survey and evaluation of these literatures. Many articles included here have something to say about these issues, but none treats them comprehensively.

Schiff and Weisbrod (Chapter 26) examined nonprofit efforts to generate profits from 'unrelated business income' to cross-subsidize their charitable mission. For example, a nonprofit museum might sell artwork reproductions through mail catalogs, or a university might sell computers to the general public through its bookstores. Concern has been raised, in a variety of countries, about whether this kind of commercial activity by nonprofit organizations is fair, proper, and socially efficient. These concerns are particularly acute when nonprofit organizations receive a variety of tax breaks or subsidies not granted to their for-profit competitors. The 'destination of income' test that regards any such activity as proper provided all the net proceeds are spent on the charitable mission of the organization has gradually been replaced in most countries (other than Australia) by a 'source of income' test. Thus, current US policy applies the 'unrelated business income tax' to the unrelated business income of nonprofit organizations, presumably to place nonprofits and their competitors on a 'level playing field'. Schiff and Weisbrod provided an important first analysis of the underlying policy considerations. They adapted James's (1983) model, regarded unrelated business as a neutral or disfavored activity used to subsidize a favored activity, estimated the relevant parameters of that model, and commented on the economic efficiency of various policy alternatives.

James (Chapter 27) summarized a variety of articles that, following Schiff and Weisbrod, regard unrelated business as a disfavored activity pursued by nonprofits seeking to cross-subsidize public goods. She contrasted this application of her theory with an alternative hypothesis – that nonprofits engage in commercial activities to increase their total revenues. She offered two rationales for the alternative theory. First, nonprofits may wish to distribute their surplus, either as allowable perks or secret cash distributions. Second, nonprofit managers may enjoy the power and prestige that stem from governing a larger organization. Under the alternative theory, commercial revenues need not cross-subsidize public goods. She found that the first approach adequately characterizes the behavior of universities, museums, and zoos in some of their activities, the alternative approach characterizes behavior in hospital conversions or university biotechnology and computing partnerships, and both approaches seem to play a role in social service and public broadcasting organizations.

Governments around the world contract with private agencies, for-profit and nonprofit, to deliver social services. Problems of free-riding and nonmarketability of outputs are overcome through government finance, and problems of monopoly and bureaucratic dysfunction are overcome through private provision, at least in theory. In practice, serious and interesting questions of policy design intervene. How does competitive bidding work when contract failure is suspected? Should bids be adjusted for differences in taxable status or other differences between nonprofit and for-profit bidders? These questions were developed in more detail, and tentative answers were suggested, in my 1997 paper. When are nonprofit organizations selected as service provider? To what extent do economic efficiencies, rather than political factors, determine this choice. These are the issues raised and first answered by Ferris and Graddy's pioneering work (Chapter 28).

## Conclusion

Although gaps remain in each of the three waves of nonprofit theorizing, it is fair to say that we now have a rudimentary understanding of the role and behavior of nonprofit organizations within a broader economy. In my opinion, here are some top priorities for future research. First, our current integrated models are static. We need to better understand the life cycles of nonprofit organizations. What are the impacts of governance structures and environmental factors on the evolution of the organizational mission? We need multiperiod models of fundraising and the giving decision. Second, we need to better understand the distributional aspects of nonprofit organizations. The theory of price and non-price rationing by nonprofit organizations is underdeveloped, and empirical work on this subject is almost nonexistent. Third, we need to develop more encompassing models for public policy analysis, and to obtain estimates of many key behavioral parameters needed for this purpose.

## Acknowledgements

I thank Marc Bilodeau, Cyril Chang, Jacques Defourny, Benedetto Gui, Femida Handy, Henry Hansmann, William Harbaugh, Richard Hirth, Renee Irvin, Estelle James, Michael Krashinsky, Andreas Ortmann, Susan Rose-Ackerman, Todd Sandler, and Dennis Young for suggestions on what to include; Susan Rose-Ackerman, Avner Ben-Ner, Estelle James, Al Slivinski, and Burton Weisbrod for helpful comments on this draft, and the Myer Foundation and Queensland University of Technology's Centre of Philanthropy and Nonprofit Studies for supporting the most pleasant and productive of surroundings while I completed this work.

## References

Arrow, Kenneth J. (1963), 'Uncertainty and the Welfare Economics of Medical Care', *American Economics Review*, **53**, 941–73.

Ben-Ner, Avner (1986), 'Nonprofit Organizations: Why Do They Exist in Market Economies?', in Susan Rose-Ackerman (ed.), *The Economics of Nonprofit Institutions: Studies in Structure and Policy*, New York: Oxford University Press, pp. 94–113.

Bilodeau, Marc (2000), 'Profitable Nonprofit Firms', Indianapolis, IN: IUPUI Department of Economics.

Bilodeau, Marc and Al Slivinski (1996), 'Volunteering Nonprofit Entrepreneurial Services' , *Journal of Economic Behavior and Organization*, **31**, 117–27.

Borjas, George J., H.E. Frech III, and Paul B. Ginsburg (1983), 'Property Rights and Wages: The Case of Nursing Homes', *Journal of Human Resources*, **17**, 231–46.

Chillemi, Ottorino and Benedetto Gui (1991), 'Uninformed Customers and Nonprofit Organization: Modeling "Contract Failure" Theory', *Economics Letters*, **35**, 5–8.

Eckel, Catherine C. and Richard Steinberg (1993), 'Competition, Performance, and Public Policy Towards Nonprofits', in David Hammack and Dennis Young (eds), *Nonprofit Organizations in a Market Economy*, San Francisco: Jossey-Bass, Inc., pp. 57–81.

Feldstein, Martin (1971), 'Hospital Price Inflation: A Study of Nonprofit Price Dynamics', *American Economic Review*, **61**, 853–72.

Glaeser, Edward L. and Andrei Shleifer (2001), 'Not-For-Profit Entrepreneurs', *Journal of Public Economics*, **81**, 99–115.

Grabowski, David C. and Richard A. Hirth (2003), 'Competitive Spillovers Across Non-Profit and For-Profit Nursing Homes', *Journal of Health Economics*, **22**, 1–22.

Handy, Femida (1995), 'Reputation as Collateral: An Economic Analysis of the Role of Trustees in Nonprofits', *Nonprofit and Voluntary Sector Ouarterly*, **24** (4), 293–305.

Hansmann, Henry (1980), 'The Role of Nonprofit Enterprise', *Yale Law Journal*, **89**, 835–901.

Holtmann, A.G. (1983), 'A Theory of Non-Profit Firms', *Economica*, **50**, 439–49.

James, Estelle (1983), 'How Nonprofits Grow: A Model', *Journal of Policy Analysis and Management*, **2**, 350–66.

James, Estelle (1986), 'Comments', in Susan Rose-Ackerman (ed.), *The Economics of Nonprofit Institutions: Studies in Structure and Policy*, New York: Oxford University Press, pp. 154–8.

James, Estelle (1989), 'Introduction', in Estelle James (ed.), *The Nonprofit Sector in International Perspective: Studies in Comparative Culture and Policy*, New York: Oxford University Press, pp. 3–30.

James, Estelle (1998), 'Commercialism among Nonprofits: Objectives, Opportunities, and Constraints', in Burton A. Weisbrod (ed.), *To Profit or Not to Profit: The Commercial Transformation of the Nonprofit Sector*, New York: Cambridge University Press, pp. 271–86.

James, Estelle and Egon Neuberger (1981), 'The University Department as a Non-Profit Labor Cooperative', *Public Choice*, **36**, 585–612.

James, Estelle and Susan Rose-Ackerman (1986), *The Nonprofit Enterprise in Market Economies, Fundamentals of Pure and Applied Economics 9*, Chur, Switzerland: Harwood Academic Publishers.

Kapur, Kanika and Burton Weisbrod (2000), 'The Roles of Government and Nonprofit Suppliers in Mixed Industries', *Public Finance Review*, **28**, 275–308.

Khanna, Jyoti, John Posnett and Todd Sandler (1995), 'Charity Donations in the UK: New Evidence based on Panel Data', *Journal of Public Economics*, **56**, 257–72.

Kingma, Bruce R. (1995), 'Do Profits "Crowd Out" Donations, or Vice Versa? The Impact of Revenues from Sales on Donations to Local Chapters of the American Red Cross', *Nonprofit Management and Leadership*, **6**, 21–38.

Malani, Anup, Tomas Philipson, and Guy David (2003), 'Theories of Firm Behavior in the Non-Profit Sector: A Synthesis and Empirical Evaluation', in Edward L. Glaeser (ed.), *The Governance of Not-for-Profit Organizations*, Chicago: University of Chicago Press, pp. 181–216.

McClellan, Mark and Douglas Staiger (2000), 'Comparing Hospital Quality at For-Profit and Not-for-Profit Hospitals', in David M. Cutler (ed.), *The Changing Hospital Industry: Comparing Not-for-Profit and For-Profit Institutions*, Chicago: University of Chicago Press, pp. 93–112.

Migué, Jean-Lui and Gerard Bélanger (1974), 'Toward a General Theory of Managerial Discretion', *Public Choice*, **17**, 27–47.

Nelson, Richard and Michael Krashinsky (1973), 'Two Major Issues of Public Policy: Public Policy and the Organization of Supply', in Richard Nelson and Dennis Young (eds), *Public Subsidy for Day Care of Young Children*, Lexington, MA: D.C. Heath and Co, pp. 47–69.

Newhouse, Joseph (1970), 'Toward a Theory of Non-Profit Institutions: An Economic Model of a Hospital', *American Economic Review*, **60**, 64–74.

Niskanen, William (1971), *Bureaucracy and Representative Government*, Chicago: Aldine Publishing Co.

Pauly, Mark P. and Michael R. Redisch (1973), 'The Not-for-Profit Hospital as a Physicians' Cooperative', *American Economic Review*, **63**, 87–99.

Rose-Ackerman, Susan (1980), 'United Charities: An Economic Analysis', *Public Policy*, **28**, 323–48.

Rose-Ackerman, Susan (ed.) (1986), *The Economics of Nonprofit Institutions: Studies in Structure and Policy*, New York: Oxford University Press.

Rose-Ackerman, Susan (1996), 'Altruism, Nonprofits, and Economic Theory', *Journal of Economic Literature*, **34** (2), 701–28.

Slivinski, Al (2002), 'Team Incentives and Organizational Form', *Journal of Public Economic Theory*, **4** (2), 185–206.

Steinberg, Richard (1997), 'Competition in Contracted Markets', in Perri 6 and Jeremy Kendall (eds), *The Contract Culture in Public Services*, Brookfield, VT: Ashgate Publishing Co., 161–80.

Steinberg, Richard (2003), 'Economic Theories of Nonprofit Organizations: An Evaluation', in Helmut Anheier and Avner Ben-Ner (eds), *The Study of the Nonprofit Enterprise: Theories and Approaches*, New York: Kluwer/Plenum, pp. 277–310.

Steinberg, Richard and Bradford H. Gray (1993), '"The Role of Nonprofit Enterprise" in 1992: Hansmann Revisited', *Nonprofit and Voluntary Sector Quarterly*, **22** (4), 297–316.
Tullock, Gordon (1966), 'Information without Profit', in *Papers on Non-Market Decision Making*, Charlottesville: Thomas Jefferson Center for Political Economy, University of Virginia, pp. 141–59.
Weisbrod, Burton A. (1975), 'Toward a Theory of the Voluntary Non-Profit Sector in a Three-Sector Economy', in Edmund Phelps (ed.), *Altruism, Morality, and Economic Theory*, New York: Russell Sage, pp. 171–95.
Weisbrod, Burton A. (1988), *The Nonprofit Economy*, Cambridge, MA: Harvard University Press.
Weisbrod, Burton A. and Mark Schlesinger (1986), 'Public, Private, Nonprofit Ownership and the Response to Asymmetric Information: The Case of Nursing Homes', in Susan Rose-Ackerman (ed.), *The Economics of Nonprofit Institutions: Studies in Structure and Policy*, New York: Oxford University Press, pp. 133–51.
Young, Dennis R. (1983), *If Not for Profit, for What?*, Lexington, MA: D.C. Heath and Co.

# Part I
# Survey of Earlier Literature

# [1]

# Economic Theories of Nonprofit Organization

HENRY HANSMANN

Serious work on the economics of the nonprofit sector began only in the early 1970s. This timing probably reflects, in part, the recent growth in the size and scope of the nonprofit sector. Until the 1950s, the sector was largely composed of traditional charities that received a substantial portion of their income from philanthropic contributions. Consequently, economic theorizing about the nonprofit sector, to the extent that it was undertaken at all, focused primarily on philanthropic behavior (for example, Dickinson 1962).

By the late 1960s, however, the character of the nonprofit sector had begun to change noticeably, its structure and performance assuming obvious importance for public policy. This change was most conspicuous in health care, particularly in the hospital industry. The implementation of Medicare and Medicaid in 1965 completed a process of evolution through which nonprofit hospitals were freed from dependence on charitable contributions and came to be potentially profitable institutions deriving virtually all their revenue from patient billings. Large publicly held business corporations owning chains of for-profit hospitals emerged for the first time. Simultaneously, hospital cost inflation appeared as a serious policy problem. The hospital industry in general, and the role and behavior of nonprofit hospitals in particular, thus became the subject of serious economic inquiry. It is not surprising, then, that the first efforts to develop economic models of nonprofit institutions focused almost exclusively on hospitals (for example, Newhouse 1970; Feldstein 1971; Lee 1971; Pauly & Redisch 1973).

A number of individuals provided helpful comments on an earlier draft, including Avner Ben-Ner, Eugene Fama, Estelle James, Michael Jensen, Richard Nelson, Susan Rose-Ackerman, John G. Simon, Richard Steinberg, Burton Weisbrod, and Dennis Young; I am grateful to them all. If the work of these or other authors is nevertheless mis- or underrepresented here, the responsibility is mine. I am also grateful to Walter Powell for his thoughtful editing.

Change was conspicuous in other parts of the nonprofit sector as well, however. Higher education, for example, underwent enormous expansion in the 1950s and 1960s and then fell into serious financial difficulty in the early 1970s. The live performing arts exhibited the paradox of constant fiscal crisis in the midst of rapid growth.[1] The day-care and nursing home industries, which had scarcely existed before World War II, became enormous. These industries—and many others like them—were all characterized by a mix of nonprofit, for-profit, and governmental firms, thus raising questions as to the relative functions and behavior of these three types of organization. Moreover, because all these industries received large and growing public subsidies, an understanding of their underlying economics was of obvious relevance for purposes of policy. The resulting prominence of such industries has led, over the past fifteen years, to the development of a substantial body of work concerning the economics of the nonprofit sector in general.

The economic theories of nonprofit organization appearing in the literature can conveniently, if somewhat artifically, be divided into two types: theories of the *role* of nonprofit institutions and theories of their *behavior*. Theories of the first type address such questions as these: Why do nonprofit organizations exist in our economy? What economic functions do they perform? Why, in particular, are nonprofit firms to be found in some industries and not in others? Why, among those industries in which nonprofit firms are found, does their market share—vis-à-vis both for-profit firms and governmental firms—vary so radically from one industry to another?

Theories of the second type address such questions as these: What objectives are pursued by nonprofit organiza-

1. The fiscal problems of the performing arts were documented by Baumol and Bowen (1965, 1966) in work that helped bring particular attention to the economics of that industry.

tions? What are the motivations of managers and entrepreneurs in the nonprofit sector? How do nonprofit organizations differ in these respects from for-profit and governmental organizations? How does the productive efficiency of nonprofit organizations differ from that of for-profit and governmental organizations? In what ways are such differences attributable to the special characteristics of the nonprofit form?

Ultimately, of course, questions of role and questions of behavior cannot be separated. To understand why it is that nonprofit firms arise in one industry and not in another, one must understand something about the firms' characteristic behavior. Nevertheless, economic theories of nonprofit institutions have tended to focus primarily on only one or the other of these two broad areas of concern, and thus the division will be employed here as a means of organizing the literature.

In this survey I shall focus primarily on firms organized as "true" nonprofits—that is, firms that are formally organized as either nonprofit corporations or charitable trusts. These organizations are all characterized by the fact that they are subject, by the laws of the state in which they were formed, to a constraint—which I shall call the "nondistribution constraint"—that prohibits the distribution of residual earnings to individuals who exercise control over the firm, such as officers, directors, or members (Hansmann 1980, 1981d). Note that nonprofits are *not* prohibited from earning profits; rather, they must simply devote any surplus to financing future services or distribute it to noncontrolling persons. Theories of the nonprofit firm are, then, essentially theories of the way in which the presence of a nondistribution constraint affects a firm's role or behavior. I shall not deal here, except for purposes of comparison, with cooperatives (producer or consumer), which are discussed in chapter 24, or with mutual companies, such as mutual insurance companies or banks; such organizations are empowered to distribute net earnings to their members and thus are not formally subject to a nondistribution constraint. Also, except for purposes of comparison, I shall not discuss public enterprise, but shall rather confine myself to private nonprofits.

## TYPES OF NONPROFIT ORGANIZATIONS

The organizations that populate the nonprofit sector are structurally rather diverse. For ease of reference, I shall adopt here a classification scheme offered elsewhere (Hansmann 1980) under which firms are distinguished according to (1) their source of income and (2) the way in which they are controlled.

Nonprofits that receive a substantial portion of their income in the form of donations will be referred to here as "donative" nonprofits; firms whose income derives primarily or exclusively from sales of goods or services will be called "commercial" nonprofits. The Red Cross is an example of the former; most nonprofit hospitals and nursing homes today would be in the latter category. The term *patrons* will be used to denote those individuals who are the ultimate source of the organization's income. Thus, in a donative nonprofit the patrons are the donors, whereas in a commercial nonprofit they are the firm's customers. In the case of nonprofits that have both donors and customers, the term comprises both.

**TABLE 2.1 A FOUR-WAY CATEGORIZATION OF NONPROFIT FIRMS**

| | Mutual | Entrepreneurial |
|---|---|---|
| Donative | Common Cause<br>National Audubon Society<br>Political Clubs | CARE<br>March of Dimes<br>Art Museums |
| Commercial | American Automobile Association<br>Consumers Union[a]<br>Country clubs | National Geographic Society[b]<br>Educational Testing Service<br>Hospitals<br>Nursing homes |

*Source:* Adapted from Hausmann 1980.
a. Publisher of *Consumer Reports*
b. Publisher of *National Geographic*

Firms in which ultimate control (the power to elect the board of directors) is in the hands of the organization's patrons will be referred to as "mutual" nonprofits. Other nonprofits—including, in particular, those in which the board of directors is self-perpetuating—will be called "entrepreneurial" nonprofits.

The intersections of these two two-way classifications yield four types of nonprofits: donative mutual, donative entrepreneurial, commercial mutual, and commercial entrepreneurial. Table 2.1 gives some examples of each type.

The boundaries between the four categories are, of course, blurred. Many private universities, for example, depend heavily on both tuition and donations for their income and thus are to some extent both donative and commercial. Also, university boards of trustees commonly comprise some individuals who are elected by the alumni (who are past customers and present donors) and some who are self-perpetuating, with the result that the universities cannot be categorized as clearly mutual or clearly entrepreneurial. The four categories are, then, simply polar or ideal types, offered for the sake of clarifying discussion.

## THE ROLE OF NONPROFIT ORGANIZATIONS

Several theories have been advanced to date to explain the economic role of nonprofit organizations. These theories are sometimes competing and sometimes complementary.

### The Public Goods Theory

The first general economic theory of the role of nonprofit enterprise was offered by Weisbrod (1974, 1977), who suggested that nonprofits serve as private producers of public goods (in economists' sense of that term).[2] Governmental entities, Weisbrod argued, will tend to provide public goods only at the level that satisfies the median voter; consequently, there will be some residual unsatisfied demand for public goods among those individuals whose taste for such goods is greater than the median.[3] Nonprofit organizations arise to meet this residual demand by providing public goods in amounts supplemental to those provided by government.[4]

Weisbrod's theory captures an important phenomenon. Many nonprofit firms provide services that have the character of public goods, at least for a limited segment of the public. This is conspicuously true, for example, of those donative nonprofits (such as the American Heart Association, the National Cancer Society, and the March of Dimes) that collect private donations to finance medical research. As originally presented, however, the public goods theory left two questions open. First, the services provided by many nonprofits do not seem to be public goods but rather appear to be private ones. This is true especially of commercial nonprofits, whose share of the nonprofit sector has increased impressively in recent years. For example, the appendectomy performed in a nonprofit hospital, the child care provided by a nonprofit day-care center, the education provided by a nonprofit preparatory school, the nursing care provided by a nonprofit nursing home, and the entertainment provided by a nonprofit symphony orchestra are all difficult to characterize as public goods in the usual sense. Second, Weisbrod's theory stops short of explaining why nonprofit, rather than for-profit, firms arise to fill an unsatisfied demand for public goods. What is it about nonprofit firms that permits them to serve as private suppliers of public goods when proprietary firms cannot or will not?

2. A public good, in the economists' sense, is a good that has two special attributes: first, it costs no more to provide the good to many persons than it does to provide it to one, because one person's enjoyment of the good does not interfere with the ability of others to enjoy it at the same time; second, once the good has been provided to one person there is no easy way to prevent others from consuming it as well. Air pollution control, defense against nuclear attack, and radio broadcasts are common examples of public goods.

3. Logrolling and other devices, of course, often lead to establishment of government programs that cater to supramedian demands. Consequently, the median voter model should probably not be taken too literally here. Nevertheless, extremely intense or idiosyncratic demands for public goods are unlikely to be fully satisfied by governmental programs.

4. Weisbrod's theory has recently been illustrated and refined, with an emphasis on welfare considerations, in a formal model developed by Weiss (1986). In that model, Weiss demonstrates that, while a Pareto superior allocation of resources might well result when high demanders of a public good supplement public production with privately financed production, this is not a necessary result; it is possible that, even where there is cooperation between the public and private providers of the public good, the welfare of the high demanders will be lower when they can undertake supplemental private production than when they cannot. The reason for this result is that the low demanders, foreseeing the incentive for the high demanders to supplement public production with their own private production, might vote to support a substantially lower level of public production than they would otherwise and free ride on the private production, which will, as a consequence, be larger (and costlier to the high demanders) than it would be otherwise.

### The Contract Failure Theory

The elements of a somewhat different theory of the role of nonprofits were set forth in an essay on day care by Nelson and Krashinsky (1973; Nelson 1977), who noted that the quality of service offered by a day-care center can be difficult for a parent to judge. Consequently, they suggested, parents might wish to patronize a service provider in which they can place more trust than they can in a proprietary firm, which they might reasonably fear could take advantage of them by providing services of inferior quality. The strong presence of nonprofit firms in the day-care industry, they argued, could perhaps be explained as a response to this demand. Similar notions had been hinted at in an earlier essay on health care by Arrow (1963), who suggested in passing that hospitals may be nonprofit in part as a response to the asymmetry in information between patients and providers of health care.

The theme advanced by Nelson and Krashinsky was fleshed out and generalized in an article by Hansmann (1980), where it is argued that nonprofits of all types typically arise in situations in which, owing either to the circumstances under which a service is purchased or consumed or to the nature of the service itself, consumers feel unable to evaluate accurately the quantity or quality of the service a firm produces for them. In such circumstances, a for-profit firm has both the incentive and the opportunity to take advantage of customers by providing less service to them than was promised and paid for. A nonprofit firm, in contrast, offers consumers the advantage that, owing to the nondistribution constraint, those who control the organization are constrained in their ability to benefit personally from providing low-quality services and thus have less incentive to take advantage of their customers than do the managers of a for-profit firm.[5] Nonprofits arise (or, rather, have a comparative survival advantage over for-profit firms) where the value of such protection outweighs the inefficiencies that evidently accompany the nonprofit form, such as limited access to capital and poor incentives for cost minimization (see below). Because this theory suggests, in essence, that nonprofits arise where ordinary contractual mechanisms do not provide consumers with adequate means to police producers,

5. The emphasis in the text here is on the role of the nondistribution constraint as a direct bar to opportunistic conduct on the part of a nonprofit's managers. The nondistribution constraint might also, however, serve the same function through indirect means by screening for managers who place an unusually low value on pecuniary compensation and an unusually high value on having the organization they run produce large quantities of services or services that are of especially high quality. A simple model along these lines is offered by Hansmann (1980, Appendix). Data that lend some support to such a theory are presented, in the context of public interest law firms, by Weisbrod (1983). Young (1983; this volume, chap. 10) discusses screening for entrepreneurs at length, exploring a rich set of personal characteristics for which nonprofit firms might serve as a screen.

it has been termed the "contract failure" theory of the role of nonprofits (Hansmann 1980).

### Donative Nonprofits

Although the contract failure theory has its roots in the work of authors (Arrow 1963; Nelson & Krashinsky 1973) who are primarily concerned with the role of commercial nonprofits, its most obvious application is in fact to donative nonprofits (Hansmann 1980; Thompson 1980; Fama & Jensen 1983a).[6] A donor is, in an important sense, a purchaser of services, differing from the customers of commercial nonprofits (and of for-profit firms) only in that the services he or she is purchasing are either (1) delivery of goods to a third party (as in the case of charities for the relief of the poor or distressed) or (2) collective consumption goods produced in such aggregate magnitude that the increment purchased by a single individual cannot be easily discerned. In either case, the purchaser is in a poor position to determine whether the seller has actually performed the services promised; hence the purchaser has an incentive to patronize a nonprofit firm.

For example, individuals commonly contribute to CARE in order to provide food to malnourished individuals overseas. A for-profit firm could conceivably offer a similar arrangement, promising to provide a specified quantity of food to such people in return for a contribution of a given amount. The difficulty is that the purchaser (donor), who has no contact with the intended beneficiaries, has little or no ability to determine whether the firm performs the service at all, much less whether the firm performs it well. In such circumstances, a proprietary firm might well succumb to the temptation to provide less or worse service than was promised.

The situation is similar with public goods. If an individual contributes to, say, a listener-sponsored radio station, then, unlike the situation with CARE, she is at least among the recipients of the service and can tell whether it is being rendered adequately. What she cannot tell is whether her contribution of fifty dollars in fact purchased a marginal increment of corresponding value in the quantity or quality of service provided by the station or simply went into somebody's pocket. A for-profit firm that operated such a radio station would have an incentive to solicit payments far in excess of the amounts necessary to provide their programming. In situations such as these, the nonprofit organizational form, owing to the nondistribution constraint, offers the individual some additional assurance that her payment is in fact being used to provide the services she wishes to purchase.[7]

As this example suggests, the contract failure theory is complementary to the public goods theory described above. Indeed, the public goods theory can be seen as a special case of the contract failure theory. For the reasons described by Weisbrod, there may be residual demand for public goods—such as noncommercial broadcasting—that is unsatisfied by government. Yet even if individuals are prepared to overcome their incentive to free ride and will donate toward financing of a public good, they will have an incentive to contribute to a nonprofit rather than a for-profit firm because of the monitoring problems just described.

We have been proceeding here on the implicit assumption that the donors to the nonprofit firm will be private persons. In many cases, however, the government is an important donor, and in some cases it is the only donor. Sometimes government donations are direct, as in the case of grants made by the National Endowment for the Arts to nonprofit performing arts companies or (now discontinued) Hill-Burton Act capital grants to nonprofit hospitals. In other instances, government donations are indirect, as in the case of tax exemption or reduced postal rates for nonprofits. Regardless of the way in which such donations are made, however, the government is often subject to the same problems of contract failure that face a private donor: it cannot easily determine directly whether its donation is being devoted in its entirety to the purposes for which it was made. Consequently, the government, like a private donor, has an incentive to confine its subsidies to nonprofit rather than for-profit firms, and it commonly does so. And this, in turn, creates further demand for the services of nonprofit firms.

### Commercial Nonprofits

The contract failure theory can also help explain the role of commercial nonprofits. The types of services that commercial nonprofits commonly provide—such as day care, nursing care, and education—are often complex and difficult for the purchaser to evaluate. Further, the actual purchaser of the service is often not the individual to whom the service is directly rendered and thus is at a disadvantage in judging the quality of performance: parents buy day care for their children, and relatives or the state buy nursing care for the elderly. Finally, the services provided by commercial nonprofits are commonly provided on a continuing long-term basis, and the costs to the recipient of switching from one firm to another are often considerable. Consequently, purchasers are to some extent locked in to a particular firm once they have begun patronizing it, and thus the firm, if unconstrained, is in a position to behave opportunistically.[8] For all

6. Fama and Jensen (1983a, 342) seek to distinguish their briefly sketched theory of donative nonprofits from that offered by Hansmann (1980). The difference, however, is difficult to discern.

7. The same arguments presumably apply to situations in which individuals donate their own labor or other goods or services in kind. If a volunteer were to donate his services to a for-profit hospital, for example, he might find it difficult to determine whether the result was in fact an equivalent increase in the services rendered by the hospital without a corresponding increase in price or whether, alternatively, the owners used him as a replacement for labor they would otherwise have paid for and thus simply increased their own profits. Consequently, individuals generally volunteer their services only to nonprofit organizations.

8. Ellman (1982) offers useful terminology for making distinctions between different forms of contract failure. On the one hand, there are problems of "quality monitoring," which involve situations in which the consumer can determine whether performance took place but has

these reasons, patrons might have an incentive to patronize a firm subject to a nondistribution constraint as additional protection against exploitation.[9]

Where commercial nonprofits are concerned, contract failure is presumably a less serious problem than with donative nonprofits. Consequently, it is not surprising that commercial nonprofits nearly always share their market with for-profit firms providing similar services. For example, roughly 20 percent of all private hospitals, 60 percent of all private day-care centers, and 80 percent of all private nursing homes are for-profit enterprises (Hansmann 1985a). If the contract failure theory explains the presence of commercial nonprofits in these industries, then the presence of both types of firms may reflect some division of the market: patrons who are reasonably confident of their ability to police the quality of the services they receive patronize the for-profit firms, whereas those who are less confident in this respect patronize the nonprofit firms, perhaps paying a premium for the service on account of the productive inefficiencies associated with the nonprofit form.

Although this theory is plausible as applied to most types of commercial nonprofits, it does not, interestingly, seem particularly persuasive when applied to hospitals, which constitute (in terms of GNP) the largest class of nonprofit institutions. There are two reasons for this. First, the hospital itself does not provide the patient care services that are the most sensitive and difficult to evaluate—namely, the services of the attending physicians. Rather, the physicians are usually independent contractors who deal separately with the patient. The hospital itself is largely confined to providing relatively simple services such as room and board, nursing care, and medicines. Second, the patient herself does not order the hospital services she receives; rather, they are ordered and monitored for her by a skilled and knowledgeable purchasing agent, namely, her physician. Consequently, it is not at all obvious that the nondistribution constraint offers the hospital patient any special protection that she would clearly be lacking without it.

Why, then, are hospitals nonprofit? It may be that, if we allow for a little historical lag, the contract failure theory in fact explains it. Until the end of the nineteenth century, hospitals were almost exclusively donative institutions serving the poor; the prosperous were treated in doctors' offices or in their own homes. The nonprofit form was therefore efficient for the reasons of contract failure discussed above with respect to donative institutions in general. Then, however, a revolution in medical technology turned hospitals into places where people of all classes went for treatment of serious illness. Subsequently, the development of public hospitals took from the nonprofit hospitals much of the burden of caring for the poor. Finally, the spread of private, and more recently public, health insurance made it possible for the great majority of patients to pay their hospital bills without the aid of charity. The result is that today—which is to say, since the appearance of Medicare and Medicaid in 1965—most nonprofit hospitals have become more or less pure commercial nonprofits, receiving no appreciable portion of their income through donations and providing little or no charity care. The continuing predominance of nonprofit firms may simply be the consequence of institutional lag and of the various subsidies and exemptions that continue to be available to nonprofit but not to for-profit hospitals (Hansmann 1980, 866–68; Clark 1980). Indeed, since the late 1960s there has been substantial entry of large for-profit firms into the industry.

### Contract Failure as an Agency Problem

In essence, the contract failure theory views the nonprofit firm as a response to agency problems. In situations like those just described, the purchaser (donor) is in the role of a principal who cannot easily monitor the performance of the agent (here, the firm) that has contracted to provide services to her. Consequently, there is a strong incentive to embed the relationship in a contractual framework, or "governance structure" (Williamson 1979), that mitigates the incentives of the agent to act contrary to the interests of the principal. The nonprofit corporate form, with its nondistribution constraint, serves this purpose.

It is worth noting, in this respect, that the relationship between the donors to a donative nonprofit firm and the managers of such a firm is analogous to the already much analyzed agency relationship between the shareholders in a publicly held business corporation and the managers of the corporation (see, for example, Jensen & Meckling 1976; Fama & Jensen 1983a, 1983b). The purchaser of a share of newly issued stock in a widely held business corporation, like a donor to CARE, is in no position to see for himself how the management is using the corporation's funds in general, much less what use is being made of his own marginal contribution to the corporation's assets. The shareholder is simply turning over funds to the corporation's management to be combined with other such funds and used however management chooses, subject only to the general constraints that (1) management will seek to obtain a reasonable rate of return for the shareholders on their contributed funds, and (2) management will take for itself no more than reasonable compensation for services rendered. These two constraints are precisely parallel to those that bind the management of a nonprofit firm, differing only in that, in the case of the nonprofit enterprise, the first constraint is replaced by one

difficulty judging the quality of the goods or services delivered. On the other hand, there are problems of "marginal impact monitoring," which involve situations in which the consumer can judge the quality of services performed by the firm but has difficulty determining whether the quantity or quality of services produced is higher than it would have been if he had not contributed. Commercial nonprofits presumably arise primarily in situations in which quality monitoring is a problem. Listener-supported broadcasting, in turn, presents a clear problem of marginal impact monitoring, and charities like CARE seem to involve both quality monitoring and marginal impact monitoring problems.

9. See Williamson (1979) for analysis of other contractual and organizational devices for mitigating opportunistic behavior in long-term complex transactions.

calling for management to devote the corporation's funds to the purposes specified in its charter. As in the case of the nonprofit firm, these two constraints are imposed upon the management of a business corporation by the terms of the corporation's charter and the legal framework in which that charter is embedded. Moreover, it is the second of these two constraints, which is effectively a nondistribution constraint, that has the more bite of the two; the very forgiving "business judgment rule" that the law applies to the decisions of corporate management makes the first constraint a largely nominal obligation.

In short, in the business corporation as in the nonprofit corporation, the only real contractual check on the behavior of the corporation's management is embodied in the nondistribution constraint imposed on management by the corporation's charter. The difference between the two types of corporations lies primarily in the class of individuals in whose favor the nondistribution constraint runs: the patrons (customers) or the investors of equity capital.

There are, to be sure, some important differences in the way the obligations of management are enforced in these two types of firms. The patrons of a nonprofit firm lack the mechanism of the derivative suit to enforce the nondistribution constraint against management. Rather, in most states only the state attorney general and/or the tax authorities have the right to bring suit in case of managerial malfeasance. Further, only in the case of mutual nonprofits do the patrons have any voting rights. And finally, patrons in both commercial and mutual nonprofits lack the advantage of a market for corporate control[10] as a means of sanctioning management.

Easley and O'Hara (1983) have sought to capture the contract failure theory in a formal model, treating it as a principal/agent problem. In this model the manager of the firm (the agent) has sole knowledge of the firm's level of output, the firm's cost function, and the extent to which the manager's own effort exceeds some minimal observable level; a customer of the firm (the principal) knows none of these things but can only verify that the manager has expended the minimal level of effort. The authors interpret a for-profit firm as one that contracts with the customer only in terms of price and output, the firm (or rather its manager/owner) promising to produce a given level of output in return for a given price. In this model, such a for-profit firm will produce no output (since the customer cannot observe it); rather, the manager will simply pocket the whole purchase price, expending no effort and using none of the purchase price to cover other costs of production.

A nonprofit firm, in turn, is interpreted as a contract that specifies (1) the amount of compensation to be received by the manager, (2) that the remainder of the purchase price is to be devoted to other costs of production, and (3) that the manager is to expend at least the minimal observable level of effort—all of which features of the contract are assumed to be verifiable by the customer. Easley and O'Hara show that this contract will result in a positive level of output in those cases in which the manager's minimal observable effort level (together with the other inputs acquired by the firm with that part of the purchase price that does not go to the manager as compensation) is sufficient to produce such a positive level of output. Thus, in this model, the nonprofit firm performs more efficiently than the for-profit firm, since the nonprofit produces a positive level of output in at least some cases, whereas the for-profit firm always produces zero output.

What is most interesting about this result is the nature of the assumptions necessary to establish it. In order for the nonprofit form to perform more efficiently than the for-profit form when output is unobservable, it is not sufficient simply to put a verifiable cap on the manager's compensation; the manager's level of effort and her use of the remainder of the purchase price must also be observable. In short, in this model the nonprofit firm involves policing inputs rather than outputs. If inputs were also completely unobservable, the nonprofit form would do no better than the for-profit form; both would always produce zero output.

This model probably captures the essential features of reality. In effect, the nonprofit corporate form is a device whereby the state (via the tax and corporation law authorities), on behalf of the customer, undertakes a certain minimal level of policing of inputs and of managerial compensation.

Note that an entrepreneur (or manager, in the model) will presumably submit herself and her firm willingly to such policing when she realizes that otherwise she will receive no patronage at all (and when the return permitted her by the nonprofit form is greater than her opportunity cost). It is in this sense that the nonprofit form is essentially a contract voluntarily entered into between a firm (more accurately, those in control of the firm) and its customers.

## Empirical Tests

Weisbrod and Schlesinger (1986) have undertaken empirical work to test the contract failure theory as applied to commercial nonprofits, using data on Wisconsin nursing homes. These authors used consumer complaints to regulatory authorities as a proxy for quality of service. They found that nonprofit nursing homes are the subject of significantly fewer complaints than their proprietary counterparts, and they interpret this result as tentative support for the conclusion that nonprofit homes are less likely than proprietary homes to exploit the information asymmetry that exists between the homes and their consumers. These results must, however, be

10. The "market for corporate control" refers to the process whereby one business corporation can acquire effective control of another (the target corporation) by purchasing a majority of the target's stock, generally through a tender offer to the target's shareholders. Where the target corporation has been managed inefficiently in the past, such an acquisition opens the way for the acquiring corporation to replace the old management of the target with new, more effective managers, thus raising the value of the target's stock and producing a profit for the acquiring corporation. The mere threat of such a takeover, it has been suggested, may be an important incentive for the management of business corporations to perform with reasonable efficiency (Manne 1965).

interpreted with caution, since consumer complaints are a very indirect measure of quality of service, and the authors' regressions do not control for price or cost of service.[11]

Indeed, it is not obvious that the contract failure theory implies that, in equilibrium, nonprofit firms will exhibit a higher quality/price ratio than their for-profit competitors. If, as suggested above, patrons sort themselves among the two types of firms according to their ability to police the quality of service they receive, one would in fact expect to find, ceteris paribus, a lower quality/price ratio in nonprofit firms (since patrons of nonprofits are paying a premium for the added protection they receive). Yet such an effect may be obscured in empirical data by the fact that nonprofit firms, but not for-profit firms, have the benefit of tax exemption and other explicit and implicit subsidies, and these will tend to create an offsetting reduction in the cost of service.

In any event, the contract failure theory is a theory of consumer expectations, not of actual performance. Individuals who are uncertain of their ability to monitor quality might patronize nonprofit firms in preference to for-profit firms in the belief that the nonprofits are most trustworthy, yet be mistaken in that belief. An incongruity between performance and consumer expectations that persisted over the long run would, however, require some explaining.

Some efforts have been made to test the contract failure theory as applied to commercial nonprofits by determining, through surveys, whether patrons in fact believe that commercial nonprofits are more to be trusted than their for-profit competitors. The results are thin and ambiguous, though arguably somewhat supportive of the contract failure theory (Newton 1980; Permut 1981; Hansmann 1981a).

### Subsidy Theories

In most industries in which they are common, nonprofit firms benefit from a variety of explicit and implicit subsidies, including exemption from federal, state, and local taxes, special postal rates, financing via tax-exempt bonds, and favorable treatment under the unemployment tax system. It is often suggested that such subsidies are in large part responsible for the proliferation of nonprofit firms (for example, Fama & Jensen, 1983a, 344), particularly in those industries in which nonprofits compete with for-profit firms.

Given the structure and administration of these subsidies, however, there is reason to doubt that they have had much effect in determining the industries in which nonprofits have and have not developed. In general, the scope of the subsidies seems to have adjusted over the years to include the new industries into which nonprofits have proliferated, rather than vice versa (Hansmann 1980). On the other hand, it seems reasonable to expect that the presence of these subsidies has had an impact on the overall extent of nonprofit development in those industries in which such firms appear.

11. The regressions do, however, control for the certification level of the home—that is, whether the home has been certified as a "skilled," "intermediate," or "personal and residential" care facility.

An empirical study using cross-sectional (state-by-state) data on four industries in which nonprofit firms and for-profit firms compete—hospitals, nursing homes, private primary and secondary education, and postsecondary vocational education—in fact provides tentative evidence that the availability of state property, sales, and income tax exemptions has a significant effect in enhancing the market share of nonprofit firms vis-à-vis their proprietary competitors (Hansmann 1985a).

### The Consumer Control Theory

There are some types of nonprofits—in particular, some types of mutual nonprofits—that do not seem to have arisen in response to contract failure.

For example, it appears that exclusive social clubs, such as country clubs, constitute a distinct exception to the contract failure theory (Hansmann 1980, 1986). In such organizations, the patrons seem as capable of judging the quality of services as they would at, say, a resort hotel. The nonprofit form is evidently adopted here simply as a means of establishing patron control over the enterprise. Such control serves the purpose of preventing monopolistic exploitation of the patrons by the owners of the firm. The source of such monopoly power in social clubs is the personal characteristics of the members of the club. A substantial part of the appeal of belonging to an exclusive club lies in the opportunity to associate with the other members, who presumably have qualities or connections that make them unusually attractive companions. Consequently, if such a club were for-profit, its owner would have an incentive to charge a membership fee high enough not just to cover costs but also to capture some portion of the value to each member of associating with the other members. That is, so long as individuals who would make equally desirable clubmates were insufficiently numerous to populate a number of competing clubs, the owner of a proprietary club could charge a monopoly price to each member for the privilege of associating with the other members. Thus the members as a group have an incentive to exercise control over the club themselves to avoid such exploitation. Exclusive social clubs, under this view, therefore play an economic role that has more in common with that of consumer cooperatives—which, as discussed below, typically seem to be formed to cope with problems of simple monopoly—than with that of other types of nonprofits.

Ben-Ner (1986) takes a broader view of the role of patron control, arguing that *most* nonprofit organizations are formed primarily in order to provide consumers with direct control over the firm from which they purchase goods or services. He points, in particular, to three possible circumstances in which consumers might desire to have direct control over a firm rather than simply exercise control via the market. The first is contract failure (asymmetric information about quantity or quality of output), although Ben-Ner focuses on consumer control as a means of eliminating the information asymmetry rather than on the nondistribution constraint as a means of curtailing incentives for the firm to exploit that asymmetry. The second circumstance is that in which the firm is a monopolist and, although product quality is easily observable, there is a broad range of potential quality levels for the product, only one of which can be chosen. The problem here is that market signals alone may lead the firm to choose a quality level that appeals to marginal rather than average consumer evaluations of quality; direct consumer control could mitigate this problem. The third circumstance is that in which the firm produces price-excludable collective consumption goods. In such a case, consumer control might lead to a superior form of price discrimination, and thus higher aggregate welfare, than would control by profit-seeking investors.

Ben-Ner gives few examples of industries in which these factors constitute important sources of the demand for nonprofit, as opposed to for-profit, enterprise. Moreover, the few examples he does offer—such as the performing arts—may be better explained by other theories (see Hansmann 1981b). Consequently, although the factors examined by Ben-Ner may possibly play an important role in some industries, it is not obvious that they have broad application.

In developing his theories, Ben-Ner does not distinguish between nonprofit organizations and consumer cooperatives, but rather suggests that his theory explains the appearance of both types of firms. As the following section suggests, however, these two organizational forms generally seem to occupy distinct economic niches, and thus we need a theory of role that distinguishes between them.

### Nonprofits versus Other Forms of Limited-Profit Enterprise

Nonprofits are not the only common form of profit-constrained enterprise. Privately owned public utilities typically operate under a form of price regulation designed to permit them no more than a competitive return on invested capital. Limited dividend companies, which are restricted by contract or statute to a stated maximum rate of cash return on equity, are common in the construction and operation of publicly subsidized housing. Producer and consumer cooperatives are constrained by the cooperative corporation statutes to pay a return on capital shares that does not exceed a specified percentage rate. And finally, cost-plus contracts, which provide for no more (and no less) than a stated rate of return to the seller, are common in situations such as defense procurement.

One might be tempted to suppose that all such forms of limited-profit enterprise, being so similar in form, must play similiar economic roles. In fact, this is not the case. To be sure, limited-dividend companies do seem to occupy a role similar to that of donative nonprofits: in particular, they seem to be used by the government as a means of ensuring that public subsidies are passed through to housing consumers rather than accruing entirely to developers. Regulated utilities, however, are a response to the potential for pricing abuses that accompany natural monopoly, a role that nonprofits seem rarely to play. (Indeed, the industries in which nonprofits are commonly found are almost all characterized by a substantial number of competing suppliers.) Consumer cooperatives also generally seem to represent a response to monopoly. Like public utilities, and in contrast to nonprofits, they usually sell only simple standardized goods and hence do not typically seem to arise as a response to contract failure (Hansmann 1980; Heflebower 1980). There are exceptions, however. For example, mutual life insurance companies—which are formally structured as consumer cooperatives—originally arose in large part as a response to contract failure in the insurance market (Hansmann 1985b).

Cost-plus contracts, in turn, commonly serve as a device for shifting risk to the purchaser when *both* parties face ex ante cost uncertainty. Easley and O'Hara (1984) argue that a particular form of cost-plus contract—the cost-plus-variable-fee contract—may arise not exclusively as a risk-sharing device but also or instead as a response to situations of information asymmetry in which producers know more about cost of performance than consumers do. They are careful to distinguish this situation, however, from the type of information asymmetry concerning quality of performance that seems to give rise to nonprofits.

### Nonprofit versus Governmental Enterprise

As the preceding discussion suggests, most work on the role of nonprofit enterprise has focused on the choice of the nonprofit versus the for-profit form of organization. In particular, this has been true of the work that has sought to explain the development of nonprofits as a response to contract failure, subsidies, or a need for consumer control to counter monopoly power. Relatively little work has been done to date comparing and contrasting the role of nonprofit and governmental enterprise. This is unfortunate because nonprofit firms typically operate in industries in which the organization of firms as governmental entities is a serious alternative. In fact, in the United States, governmental firms have a significant share of the market in many industries in which nonprofits are common, including hospital care, nursing care, primary and secondary education, and postsecondary and vocational education. Moreover, many of the activities that in this country are performed in substantial part by nonprofits are performed in most other developed countries almost exclusively by governmental firms; health care, higher education, and the performing arts are conspicuous examples.

An important explanation for this gap in existing theory undoubtedly lies in the fact that contemporary economic theory offers a much more coherent view of the role of for-profit enterprise than it does of the role of governmental enterprise, and thus the proprietary form of organization offers a much firmer basis for comparison than does governmental organization. Nevertheless, there has been some useful work illuminating various aspects of the relationship of nonprofit and governmental enterprise.

To begin with, Weisbrod's work on the public goods theory (1974, 1977), discussed above, suggests that nonprofits tend to serve a gap-filling role vis-à-vis governmental enterprise, meeting some of the supramedian or idiosyncratic demand for public goods that is left unmet by government provision. This theory leads to the prediction that the market share of nonprofit versus governmental firms will be larger in those jurisdictions in which demand is unusually heterogeneous. Lee and Weisbrod (1977) have sought to test this implication with respect to hospitals using cross-sectional (state-by-state) U.S. data. In particular, they regressed nonprofit hospitals as a fraction of total nonprofit and governmental hospitals against various proxies for heterogeneity of demand, including variance within the population in age, education, income, and religion. The results are mixed, but arguably mildly supportive of the theory. James, whose work is discussed in chapter 22, has also tried to test this implication of the public goods theory by exploring the relative shares of nonprofit and governmental provision of services in several foreign countries and seeking to correlate these relative shares with the apparent heterogeneity of the populations involved. She too finds some support for the theory.

Further considerations bearing on the choice of nonprofit versus governmental organization are offered by Nelson and Krashinsky (1973) and by Hansmann (1980). For example, governmental firms have the advantage, through use of the taxing power, of more reliable access to capital and to operating revenues (especially in the case of public goods). Also, governmental organizations are usually linked by an organizational chain of command to the central executive of the government in order to provide the government with the requisite degree of information and control. This chain of command can serve as an additional mechanism for ensuring accountability in situations of contract failure. On the other hand, it also imposes a degree of bureaucratization that can make governmental organizations more costly and less flexible than their nonprofit counterparts. The private nonprofit form of organization has the corresponding advantage that it permits the development of a number of independent firms and thus promises greater competition and responsiveness to market forces. Moreover, a nonprofit firm can be more easily tailored to serve a narrow patronage, since it need not respond to the interests of the public at large. These and other factors that might affect the relative market shares of governmental and nonprofit organizations are explored in a cross-national context by James in chapter 22.

Further questions involve the relationship between governmental action and donative nonprofits. Governmental policy can affect the amount and direction of activity undertaken by donative nonprofits in various ways. Much attention has been given in recent years to exploring, both theoretically and empirically, the extent to which the charitable deduction incorporated in the personal income tax serves to encourage larger donations and the way in which these increased donations are distributed across different types of charities (Feldstein 1975; Clotfelter & Salamon 1982; Jencks, this volume, chap. 18). Less well explored, but of equal interest, are the ways in which direct government grants to nonprofits, or governmental provision of services in competition with those provided by nonprofits, may affect, positively or negatively, the amount or types of activity undertaken by nonprofits. Similarly, it is of interest to inquiry why it is that governments in some cases provide services directly and in other cases provide the same or similar services by means of grants to private nonprofit organizations (see Rose-Ackerman 1981; James, this volume, chap. 22).

### The Role of Donative Financing

Another set of interesting questions concerns the role of donative financing. The contract failure theory provides a potential explanation for the fact that donatively financed organizations are almost universally organized as nonprofits: by definition, donations involve payments that, though usually intended to be used for specific purposes, are not made with the expectation that they will be used simply to finance private goods for the donor. Consequently, the donor is very likely to experience difficulty in overseeing the use made of his donation and feel the need for the kind of protection afforded by the nonprofit form. In itself, however, the contract failure theory does not explain why it is that some services are donatively financed and others are not. To be sure, some services—such as redistribution to the poor or the provision of public goods—must by their very nature be donatively financed if they are to be provided privately at all. But in the case of some services that are commonly provided by donative nonprofits, it is not obvious that either redistribution to the poor or the production of public goods is involved. In such cases, closer consideration sometimes suggests that donative financing has arisen as a means of coping with special types of market imperfections that are peculiar to particular industries.

#### Price Discrimination

It is interesting to inquire, for example, why donative financing plays such a large role in the high-culture live performing arts. The services provided by such organizations, after all, are seldom rendered to the poor and are not easily characterized as public goods whose benefits spill over to individuals who do not pay the price of admission.

One likely explanation is that donative financing in the performing arts serves as a form of voluntary price discrimination, the need for which is dictated by the unusual cost and demand structure in that industry (Hansmann 1981b). In the high-culture live performing arts, fixed costs (primarily those of preparing a show prior to the first performance, including the cost of rehearsals, costumes, and stage sets) are a large proportion of the total costs of a production; once a production has been staged, the marginal cost of adding another performance to the run or of admitting another person to the audience for a performance that has not sold out is relatively small. This is, of course, in part a reflection of the fact that the potential audience for the high-culture performing arts is limited, even in the largest cities. It appears that, as a consequence, for many productions there is no single ticket price that can cover total costs. If costs are to be met, some form of price discrimination must be employed so that high demanders pay more than low demanders for a given performance. Transferability of tickets, however, puts limits on the amount of price discrimination that can be accomplished through ticket pricing. Yet *voluntary* price discrimination has proven possible here: ticket purchasers with unusually high demand for performing arts productions can simply be asked to contribute some portion of the consumer surplus they would otherwise enjoy at the nominal ticket price—and, interestingly, a large proportion is in fact willing to do so.

The audiences for the popular performing arts such as movies and Broadway theater—in contrast to those for opera, symphonic music, and ballet—are large enough so that fixed costs can be spread widely, and thus fixed costs are low relative to marginal costs. Consequently, price discrimination is unnecessary for the viability of such productions, and they are usually produced by for-profit firms.

Although the performing arts seem to offer the best illustration of voluntary price discrimination, this may also be part of the function played by donative financing in other parts of the nonprofit sector, such as museums (which also experience fixed costs that are high relative to marginal costs), higher education, and health care.

### Implicit Loans

The substantial role of donative financing in private education raises similar questions. In part it may serve to finance public goods or the provision of education to the poor. These explanations do not seem compelling, however, in the case of private primary or secondary schools or in the case of four-year private colleges, many of which emphasize teaching rather than research and have (at least until recently) served almost exclusively the relatively well-to-do. Further, such explanations do not entirely square with the fact that donations come largely from alumni of these colleges.

An alternative explanation, more consistent with such phenomena, is that donative financing in higher education serves at least in part as a system of voluntary repayments under an implicit loan system that has arisen to compensate for the absence of adequate loan markets for acquisition of human capital (Hansmann 1980). Many individuals for whom the present value of the long-run returns from higher education exceed the cost of that education are unable to finance it out of their own or their family's existing assets. If these individuals could take out a long-term loan against their future earnings, then this would be a worthwhile strategy for financing their education. Yet, since an individual cannot pledge human capital as security for such a loan (owing to laws against peonage, among other things), lenders will offer an inadequate supply of such loans. Private nonprofit schools provide a crude substitute for such loans. They supply education to many students at rates below cost, in return for an implicit commitment on the part of the students that they will "repay" the school through donations during the course of their lives after graduation.

### Option Demand

Weisbrod (1964; Weisbrod & Lee 1977) has argued that donations to nonprofits may in part reflect what he calls "option demand." In particular, he suggests, this may help explain why hospitals are organized as donative nonprofits. "An individual's uncertainty with respect to demand for hospital services that may become critical to life means that he will be willing to pay a sum to secure the physical availability of those facilities in the future. An option demand may be said to exist for stand-by capacity, which is capacity in excess of the expected level of utilization" (Weisbrod & Lee 1977, 94). Of course, the mere fact that future demand is unpredictable need not in itself lead to market failure. Simply because one's own future demand, or even the entire market's future demand, for personal computers, four-bedroom apartments, or penicillin is uncertain does not mean that for-profit producers will supply them at an inefficient level. Some reason must be given to explain why for-profit firms, in the face of uncertain demand, will provide an inefficiently low level of capacity. One such reason has recently been offered by Holtmann (1983), though Holtmann makes no reference to Weisbrod's earlier option demand theory.

Holtmann develops a model in which demand is stochastic and in which a producing firm must choose its price and its maximum capacity level (which will subsequently represent a fixed cost for the firm) before the level of demand is revealed. The socially efficient behavior for the firm is to select a capacity level for which marginal expected (social) benefits equal marginal expected costs, and then set price equal to marginal cost. Such a policy will, however, produce negative returns for the firm regardless of the level of demand that subsequently materializes, and hence it will not be chosen by a for-profit firm. Without developing the point formally, Holtmann suggests that a donatively financed nonprofit firm will choose a lower price and larger capacity level than will a for-profit firm, and hence will come closer to the social optimum. Hence, Holtmann intimates, donative nonprofit firms might arise to meet the ex ante demand for capacity that for-profit firms will leave unsatisfied.

### Other Motivations for Donating

There are, to be sure, many other reasons for donating besides those surveyed here. For example, donations to performing arts organizations may often be a form of conspicuous consumption (a type of signaling). Donations to one's alma mater may in part be inspired by a desire to maintain its institutional prominence in order to ensure that one's own degree will retain its status or quality. And donations to performing arts organizations, local hospitals, and one's alma mater may in part be, in effect, dues for membership in a club—the club of active supporters of the institution involved—which may be valuable for companionship or contacts. I have focused here on voluntary price discrimination, implicit loans, and option demand—in addition to the familiar functions of redistribution and financing public goods—simply because these are functions served by donations that (1) are frequently overlooked, (2) come to light most clearly when nonprofits are examined with an economist's special facility for appreciating the functions and limits of markets, and (3) have been explicitly developed in the existing economics literature.

#### Why Not Free Ride?

We would also like to understand why, and under what conditions, individuals make contributions rather than succumb to the temptation to act as free riders in situations such as those just discussed. The contract failure theory, after all, suggests only why it is that, *given* that an individual wishes to make a donation, he is likely to direct that donation to a nonprofit rather than a for-profit firm; it does not explain why individuals are willing to make donations in the first place. Yet the question is obviously an important one: Americans *do* donate a substantial portion of their income to nonprofit organizations; moreover, they commonly make such donations in response to impersonal (for example, through-the-mail) appeals. At present, most of the wisdom we have on this subject focuses on aggregate phenomena and especially on the responsiveness of donations to changes in income and in price—in particular, tax incentives. (The available data and theories are surveyed in chapter 18.)

### Demand-Side versus Supply-Side Theories

The various theories of the role of nonprofit enterprise that have been surveyed here are all essentially demand-side theories. That is, they present reasons consumers might choose to patronize nonprofit firms in preference to for-profit firms in particular industries. To date, much less systematic work has been done on developing supply-side theories that help explain why there is a supply of nonprofit firms in particular industries, and whether the current distribution of nonprofit firms across industries can be explained at least in part on the basis of differing conditions of supply. This is not to say, however, that there has been no work at all in this area; chapter 22, for example, offers some important observations on supply. Moreover, the behavioral theories discussed below also offer some insight into these issues.

## THE BEHAVIOR OF NONPROFIT ORGANIZATIONS

The theories of the role of nonprofit organizations just surveyed are all based on the assumption that nonprofit firms are—or at least appear to their patrons to be—bound by a nondistribution constraint. This constraint, however, is consistent with a variety of forms of behavior on the part of nonprofit firms. Therefore, commitment to one of these theories of the role of nonprofit organizations does not necessarily involve commitment to a particular theory of the behavior of nonprofit firms, and vice versa. Moreover, many of the early efforts to model the behavior of nonprofit firms—especially hospitals—were developed without concern for the reasons such firms developed and survived. Consequently, the behavioral models of nonprofit organizations developed to date have been to some degree disconnected from models of the role of such firms.

### Optimizing Models

Following the neoclassical tradition, most models of the behavior of nonprofit firms have been optimizing models, typically focusing on firms in a particular industry. Hospitals have been the most common subject.

Choosing the maximand has been a problem in these models. In contrast to the case of the for-profit firm, there is obviously no reason to believe a priori that profit maximization is a reasonable goal to impute to the nonprofit firm. Most commonly, nonprofit firms have instead been assumed to maximize the quality and/or quantity of the service they produce. The first of these goals might seem reasonable for a nonprofit firm run by professionals who derive strong satisfaction from doing craftsmanlike work, independent of the needs or desires of their clientele. Quantity maximization, in turn, might be imputed to managers who are empire builders or who are altruists of a type that seeks to serve as broad a segment of the public as possible. Models of nonprofit firms that pursue one or both of these goals have been developed by Newhouse (1970) and Feldstein (1971) for hospitals, James and Neuberger (1981) for universities, James (1983) for nonprofits in general, and Hansmann (1981b) for performing arts organizations. Lee (1971), in contrast, presents a model of a hospital that maximizes (or, more accurately, satisfices) not output but rather its use of certain inputs.

Models of nonprofits that seek to maximize their budgets have also been common. Presumably budget maximization might be chosen as a goal because it enhances the apparent importance of (or justifies a higher salary for) the firm's managers or, alternatively, because it provides the preferred trade-off between quality and quantity maximization. Examples of budget-maximizing models have been offered by Tullock (1966), who considers a purely donative nonprofit, and Niskanen (1971, chap. 9), who considers a purely commercial nonprofit. Hansmann's previously mentioned paper on the performing arts (1981b) also models the behavior of a (partly donative and partly commercial) nonprofit budget maximizer.

Each of these optimizing models is employed by its author to some degree to explore the welfare implications of the type of behavior the model postulates. For example, Newhouse (1970) emphasizes that the quality/quantity-maximizing firm in his model will usually exhibit productive inefficiency when contrasted with the performance of a for-profit firm operating in an environment free of market failure. Hansmann's performing arts model assumes that the firm is operating under conditions of contract failure and that it must adhere to the nondistribution constraint; the model then explores the socially optimal objective function for the firm, *given* this constraint. It turns out that quantity, quality, or budget maximizing may or may not constitute efficient behavior for the firm, depending on the structure of consumers' preferences and the way in which donations respond to firm behavior. In Tullock's model (1966), the budget-maximizing donative nonprofit overspends considerably (from a social welfare point of view) on promotion: at the margin, it spends more than a dollar in promotional expenses in order to solicit an additional dollar in donations.

Pauly and Redisch (1973) offer a model of a hospital that is operated to maximize the financial returns to its affiliated doctors. This is not the same thing as profit maximization for the firm. Rather, since doctors do not receive payment directly from the hospital but instead bill patients separately, this theory implies that hospitals will bill patients only enough to cover costs and will procure inputs that enhance the physicians' productivity. Pauly and Redisch then develop an explicit model of the hospital as a Ward-Domar-type producer cooperative (with the physicians as the worker/owners) and thus predict for a hospital the same behavior that characterizes other models of this type—behavior that involves considerable inefficiency in the short run in the form of perverse supply response. Since the work behavior and compensation of hospital-based physicians do not follow the simple fixed-effort and equal-sharing rules assumed in this class of producer cooperative models, it is not clear that in fact we should expect perverse supply response to be an empirically important phenomenon in hospitals. Nevertheless, the general view of hospitals as serving indirectly the financial interests of doctors may capture an important aspect of reality.

### Productive Inefficiency

Optimizing models of the types just surveyed implicitly assume that the firms involved minimize costs. Another line of behavioral theory has argued that, whatever objectives nonprofits may pursue with respect to quantity or quality of output, they are inherently subject to productive inefficiency (that is, failure to minimize costs) owing to the absence of ownership claims to residual earnings (Alchian & Demsetz 1972; Hansmann 1980). This argument is clearest when applied to entrepreneurial nonprofits, which constitute the great majority of financially significant nonprofits. Those who control such organizations—whether the managers or the board of directors who appoint the managers—are unable, by virtue of the nondistribution constraint, to appropriate for themselves the net earnings obtained by reducing costs, and thus they have little pecuniary incentive to operate the organization in a manner that minimizes costs.[12] Of course, it could be that the managers of some nonprofits derive substantial utility from having the firm produce large amounts of output and thus have a desire to minimize costs that is independent of the income they derive from the firm. And there is reason to believe that nonprofit organizations tend to attract more managers of this type than do for-profit firms (see Young 1983 and chapter 10 in this volume). Nevertheless, nonprofit managers in general might be expected to indulge themselves in various perquisites of office—including some forms of nonpecuniary income as well as a more relaxed attitude toward their duties—to a greater extent than do their counterparts in for-profit firms. Clarkson (1972) presents empirical results comparing the behavior of nonprofit and for-profit hospitals that provide some support for this view.

It is almost certainly true that nonprofit firms are productively inefficient in the sense that, in the absence of subsidies or a substantial degree of market failure of some type (such as contract failure) in the product market, they will generally produce any given good or service at higher cost than would a for-profit firm. If it were otherwise, we would expect to find nonprofit firms operating successfully in a much broader range of industries than is actually the case. As emphasized in the preceding discussion of the role of nonprofits, nonprofit firms seem to have survivorship properties that are superior to for-profit firms only where particular forms of market failure give them an efficiency advantage sufficient to compensate for their failure to minimize costs. Thus, in general we do not find nonprofit firms producing, wholesaling, or retailing standard industrial goods or agricultural commodities (such as machine screws or cucumbers) for which contract failure is not a significant problem.

### Supply Response

Empirical work (Steinwald & Neuhauser 1970; Hansmann 1985a) indicates strongly that nonprofit firms tend to respond much more slowly to increases in demand than do their for-profit counterparts. For example, in those industries populated by both nonprofit and for-profit firms, such as nursing care, hospital care, and primary and secondary education, the ratio of nonprofit to for-profit firms is much lower in markets in which demand has been expanding rapidly than it is in markets in which demand has remained stable or declined.

One likely explanation for this phenomenon is that, in comparison to for-profit firms, nonprofit firms are constrained in their access to capital. Unlike for-profit firms, nonprofit firms cannot raise capital by issuing equity shares; rather, they must rely on debt, donations, and retained earnings for this purpose—sources that, even in combination, offer a less responsive supply of capital than does the equity market.

12. In mutual nonprofits, ultimate control is by definition in the hands of the patrons of the organization, and the patrons have an incentive to have the organization minimize costs. If the organization has many patrons, however, transaction costs and free-rider problems may prevent the patrons from exercising effective authority over the firm's management, thus leading to poor incentives for cost minimization in these firms as well.

An alternative explanation for nonprofits' relatively poor supply response points to problems of entrepreneurship. Owing to the nondistribution constraint, nonprofit entrepreneurs are unable to capture the full return that can be gained by establishing a new firm or expanding an old one in the face of increased demand. Consequently, their incentive to undertake such entry or expansion is limited relative to that of entrepreneurs in the for-profit sector.

At present we cannot say to what extent each, or either, of these explanations accounts for the relatively poor supply response exhibited by nonprofits. There is empirical evidence that nonprofit firms are sometimes capital constrained (Ginsburg 1970), but we do not know precisely how this translates into supply response. And entrepreneurship in the nonprofit sector presents an even more elusive problem. Young (whose work is surveyed in chapter 10) has undertaken case studies of nonprofit entrepreneurship that indicate, as one might expect, a substantial range of motivation and behavior. He describes a set of personality types into which nonprofit entrepreneurs can be divided and suggests that certain of these personality types are selected for disproportionately by particular types of nonprofit firms. Not surprisingly, some of these personality types are inconsistent with a strong emphasis on expansion of services.

James in chapter 22 notes that, particularly in countries other than the United States, both the entrepreneurial initiative and the necessary capital for founding a nonprofit institution, such as a school, are commonly supplied by an existing organization that is already well established and well financed—such as a major religious sect. This observation underlines the importance of both factors, though it does not clearly indicate which is generally the more important bottleneck.

### Income-Generating Behavior

To the extent that a nonprofit seeks to provide a service of a quantity or quality that cannot be supported by market demand, some form of subsidy must be found. One source of such a subsidy, evidently commonly used by nonprofits, is cross subsidization: one service is produced and sold by the nonprofit at a profit, which is then used to finance provision of another service that is more highly valued by the firm. The net returns earned on the subsidy-generating service may result from the fact that the nonprofit firm has some degree of market power in providing that service or from the fact that the nonprofit firm has lower costs than its competitors owing to tax exemption or some other form of governmental favor. James (1981, 1983) illustrates this form of behavior with a simple model of a multiproduct nonprofit firm that places different degrees of (either positive or negative) utility on the quantities of the various products it sells, and then determines price and output for the full set of products in a fashion that maximizes utility to the firm while meeting a breakeven constraint. Harris (1979) presents a model of a nonprofit hospital illustrating how cross subsidization can be employed to compensate for distortions and inequities in health insurance coverage and offers empirical results suggesting that to some extent hospitals behave consistently with this model.

Another way to raise funds to pay for services whose production provides positive utility to the firm is to solicit donations. To be sure, as suggested earlier, we can view donations simply as a price that is paid by persons who wish to finance provision of services for third parties. In this sense, then, donations are not a subsidy, and efforts to increase donations are simply efforts to market the firm's goods—that is, a form of advertising. Nevertheless, donation-seeking behavior presents some interesting questions, especially from a welfare standpoint. In particular—depending on one's assumptions about donor information and behavior—nonprofits may have an incentive to expend inefficiently large amounts of funds on solicitation, as Tullock (1966) suggests. Since theoretical and empirical work on donation-seeking behavior is surveyed in chapter 7, however, the issue will not be addressed further here.

### Patron Control

The discussion so far has proceeded largely as if all nonprofits were entrepreneurial nonprofits whose management is constrained in its behavior only by market forces and the nondistribution constraint. However, many nonprofits (namely, those we have called mutual nonprofits) are ultimately controlled, at least formally, by their patrons. Thus, it remains to ask whether, and how, patrons influence the behavior of mutual nonprofits through the exercise of their voting power—that is, through voice rather than exit, to use Hirschman's now familiar terminology (1970).

The only general theoretical treatment of this subject is offered by Ben-Ner (1986; this volume, chap. 24), who sees patron control as the principal raison d'être for nonprofit firms and thus devotes considerable attention to the possible behavior of customer-controlled firms. He focuses in particular on coalition formation among customer-members, arguing that high-demand customers can frequently be expected to dominate the firm and to set price and output parameters that maximize their own welfare while exploiting other customers to the extent permitted by competition.

A more narrowly focused treatment is offered in Hansmann (1986) of social clubs, colleges, hospital medical staffs, and other membership organizations in which the personal characteristics of one's fellow patrons (or employees) are an important factor in the utility derived from membership. A simple model is presented to illustrate the way in which member control interacts with competition to determine the size, fees, and membership characteristics of individual clubs. In that model, each individual is assumed to be characterized by a unidimensional variable denoting "status." Individuals join clubs in order to associate with other individuals, and the value of a given club's membership as companions is given by their average status: the higher the better. Assuming limited economies of scale (in terms of membership size) in the operation of clubs, and assuming that a given club must charge all its members the same fee, free formation of clubs in this model results in roughly the pattern we see in reality: that is, a system of member-controlled clubs that are usually smaller than the size that minimizes average cost per member, and that are exclusive and stratified in the sense that the highest-status individuals will be in a single club of their own, the next highest will constitute the membership of a second club, and so on.

## CONCLUSION: SOME POLICY APPLICATIONS

The theories concerning the role and behavior of nonprofit firms discussed above are of interest simply as a matter of positive social science. They are also of interest, however, from a policy perspective. Indeed, the most pressing current problems of policy concerning the nonprofit sector cannot be resolved intelligently without adopting one or another point of view concerning the role and behavior of nonprofit firms. This is not the place to consider policy problems in detail. But for purposes of illustration and as a means of providing some perspective on the theories that have been surveyed here, we shall look briefly at some examples.

As suggested earlier, the most dramatic development in the nonprofit sector in recent decades has been the rapid growth of commercial nonprofits. The appearance of large numbers of such firms, which derive their revenues largely from fees for service and commonly exist in competition with for-profit firms providing similar services, has brought with it some of the most difficult problems of policy that currently involve the nonprofit sector.

### Tax Exemption

One important set of issues, for example, concerns tax exemption. At present, most nonprofit firms are exempt from taxation (including sales, property, and corporate income taxation) at the federal, state, and local levels. These exemptions were relatively unproblematic when they were first established many decades ago: most nonprofits were simple donative charities that provided either public goods or aid to the poor, thus offering a substantial rationale for public subsidy. In any event, the potential tax liability of the organizations involved was often quite small. Yet the scope of these exemptions has been extended to keep pace with the expansion of the nonprofit sector, so that today large numbers of commercial nonprofits are also exempt. And it is not obvious that the arguments for exempting traditional charities carry over to commercial nonprofits such as nursing homes or health maintenance organizations.

It is difficult to rationalize tax exemption for commercial nonprofits on the simple ground that the basic service they provide—nursing care for the elderly, day care, hospital care, or whatever—is for some reason worthy of subsidy in general, since that argument would seem to call for exempting not only the nonprofit firms in the industry but the for-profit firms as well. Of course, the exemption might be confined to nonprofit firms even under this rationale on the theory that the nondistribution constraint ensures that the subsidy will actually be passed through to consumers (see the general discussion of government "donations" above). But, in industries like those in question, in which firms simply sell goods or services directly to consumers, it would seem that competition among competing firms would go far toward ensuring the same result for for-profit firms. Consequently, the exemption seems more easily justifiable if it can be established that nonprofit firms in the relevant industries offer a type of service that is different from that offered by their for-profit competitors and that would be undersupplied without subsidy.

A possible argument along these lines is that nonprofit firms provide services that have more of the character of public goods than do the services provided by for-profit firms in the same industry. Yet, as we have observed in discussing the public goods theory of nonprofits above, it is not at all obvious that this is the case for commercial nonprofits in most industries. An alternative possibility is that commercial nonprofits are in fact a response to contract failure and that they offer a higher degree of fiduciary responsibility toward their customers than do their for-profit competitors—a quality that is of special service to that subset of customers who do not trust their own ability to look out for their interests in the market. Yet even acceptance of the contract failure theory as applied to commercial nonprofits does not necessarily resolve the question of exemption. For we must ask why it is that customers who want the special protection of the nonprofit form cannot be left to seek it out and pay for it on their own. Do such customers constitute a class that is specially deserving of a subsidy? Or is it the case that such customers will myopically undervalue the special protection afforded by nonprofit firms and thus need a subsidy to encourage them to patronize such firms? Or is the subsidy provided by the exemption best justified as a way of compensating for problems of supply response among nonprofit firms that would otherwise develop too slowly to meet demand? (Note that the latter justification is persuasive only if the problem of supply response is primarily the result of lack of capital rather than lack of entrepreneurship.)

The object here is not to offer a resolution of these issues.[13] Rather, it is simply to emphasize that, if one is to take a thoughtful position on whether to continue or revoke the exemption for commercial nonprofits in any given industry, one must necessarily think carefully about the role and behavior of the firms involved.

### Outlawing For-Profit Firms

In recent years considerable attention has been devoted to abuses in the nursing home industry involving shoddy patient care and shady finances. These exposés have brought proposals from several prominent quarters for public policies designed to eliminate for-profit nursing homes (for example,

13. For further theoretical and empirical discussion, see Hansmann (1981c, 1985a).

by denying them licenses) on the theory that for-profit homes are the source of most of the abuses and that the industry would perform better if it were composed only of nonprofit firms (Etzioni 1976; New York Temporary State Commission . . . 1975). Indeed, such proposals have not been confined to the nursing home industry; public measures disadvantaging or outlawing for-profit as opposed to nonprofit firms have been enacted or proposed at various times as well for aspects of medical practice, legal practice, and higher education.[14]

To accept such proposals, it seems, one must accept strongly the contract failure theory of the role of nonprofits. Indeed, one must presumably believe not just that existing nonprofit nursing homes serve a fiduciary role toward their customers but that even those customers who currently patronize proprietary nursing homes need the protection of the nondistribution constraint and were misguided in choosing a for-profit rather than a nonprofit provider.

Further, to accept such proposals one must also believe that outlawing proprietary homes will not have a significant effect on the character of nonprofit homes—for example, by forcing profit-motivated entrepreneurs to utilize the nonprofit form, thus creating a group of nominally nonprofit firms that actively seek to evade the nondistribution constraint.

And finally, before implementing such a proposal, one must consider the problem of supply response. If one goes no further than simply outlawing for-profit homes, then there will presumably be a long period of excess demand for the services of the remaining nonprofit firms. Thus, many of the elderly may simply go from having poor service to having no service. If capital constraints are the chief cause of poor supply response among nonprofits, this problem might be remedied by governmental provision of loan or grant capital to nonprofit firms. If, on the other hand, the supply response problem has its roots in the lack of incentives for nonprofit entrepreneurship, then capital subsidies in themselves might be unavailing, and the problem, if remediable at all, must be dealt with through more complex policies.

Thus here, as with tax exemption, intelligent policy must necessarily be based on a sophisticated understanding of the role and behavior of nonprofit firms. Recent work on the economics of nonprofit organizations holds the promise, at last, of yielding such an understanding.

14. For a more thorough discussion of such policies see Hansmann (1981d, 548–53) and Young (1983, 141–44).

# REFERENCES

Alchian, Armen, and Harold Demsetz. 1972. "Production, Information Costs, and Economic Organization." *American Economic Review* 62:777–95.

Arrow, Kenneth. 1963. "Uncertainty and the Welfare Economics of Medical Care." *American Economic Review* 53:941–73.

Baumol, William, and William Bowen. 1965. "On the Performing Arts: The Anatomy of Their Economic Problems." *American Economic Review Papers and Proceedings* 55:495–502.

———. 1966. *Performing Arts—The Economic Dilemma.* Cambridge, Mass.: MIT Press.

Ben-Ner, Avner. 1986. "Non-Profit Organizations: Why Do They Exist in Market Economies?" In *The Economics of Nonprofit Institutions: Studies in Structure and Policy,* ed. Susan Rose-Ackerman. Oxford: Oxford University Press.

Clark, Robert. 1980. "Does the Nonprofit Form Fit the Hospital Industry?" *Harvard Law Review* 93:1416–89.

Clarkson, Kenneth. 1972. "Some Implications of Property Rights in Hospital Management." *Journal of Law and Economics* 15:363–84.

Clotfelter, Charles, and Lester Salamon. 1982. "The Impact of the 1981 Tax Act on Individual Charitable Giving." *National Tax Journal* 35:171–87.

Dickinson, Frank. 1962. *Philanthropy and Public Policy.* New York: National Bureau of Economic Research.

Easley, David, and Maureen O'Hara. 1983. "The Economic Role of the Nonprofit Firm." *Bell Journal of Economics* 14:531–38.

———. 1984. "An Information-Based Theory of the Firm." Unpublished manuscript; Cornell University Department of Economics.

Ellman, Ira. 1982. "Another Theory of Nonprofit Corporations." *Michigan Law Review* 80:999–1050.

Etzioni, Amitai. 1976. "Profit in Not-for-Profit Institutions." *Philanthropy Monthly* 9:22–34.

Fama, Eugene, and Michael Jensen. 1983a. "Agency Problems and Residual Claims." *Journal of Law and Economics* 26:327–50.

———. 1983b. "Separation of Ownership and Control." *Journal of Law and Economics* 26:301–26.

Feldstein, Martin. 1971. "Hospital Price Inflation: A Study of Nonprofit Price Dynamics." *American Economic Review* 61:853–72.

———. 1975. "The Income Tax and Charitable Contributions." *National Tax Journal* 28:81–97, 209–28.

Ginsburg, Paul. 1970. *Capital in Non-Profit Hospitals.* Ph.D. diss., Harvard University.

Hansmann, Henry. 1980. "The Role of Nonprofit Enterprise." *Yale Law Journal* 89:835–901.

———. 1981a. "Consumer Perception of Nonprofit Enterprise: Reply." *Yale Law Journal* 90:1633–38.

———. 1981b. "Nonprofit Enterprise in the Performing Arts." *Bell Journal of Economics* 12:341–61.

———. 1981c. "The Rationale for Exempting Nonprofit Organizations from Corporate Income Taxation." *Yale Law Journal* 91:54–100.

———. 1981d. "Reforming Nonprofit Corporation Law." *University of Pennsylvania Law Review* 129:497–623.

———. 1985a. "The Effect of Tax Exemption and Other Factors on Competition between Nonprofit and For-Profit Enterprise." Yale University, Program on Non-Profit Organizations Working Paper no. 65.

———. 1985b. "The Organization of Insurance Companies: Mutual versus Stock." *Journal of Law, Economics, and Organization* 1:125–53.

———. 1986. "Status Organizations." *Journal of Law, Economics, and Organization* 2:119–30.

Harris, Jeffrey. 1979. "Pricing Rules for Hospitals." *Bell Journal of Economics* 10:224–43.

Heflebower, Richard. 1980. *Cooperatives and Mutuals in the Market System*. Madison: University of Wisconsin Press.

Hirschman, Albert. 1970. *Exit, Voice and Loyalty*. Cambridge, Mass.: Harvard University Press.

Holtmann, A. G. 1983. "A Theory of Non-Profit Firms." *Economica* 50:439–49.

James, Estelle. 1983. "How Nonprofits Grow: A Model." *Journal of Policy Analysis and Management* 2:350–65.

James, Estelle, and Egon Neuberger. 1981. "The University Department as a Non-Profit Labor Cooperative." *Public Choice* 36:585–612.

Jensen, Michael, and William Meckling. 1976. "Theory of the Firm: Managerial Behavior, Agency Costs and Ownership Structure." *Journal of Financial Economics* 3:305–60.

Lee, A. James, and Burton Weisbrod. 1977. "Collective Goods and the Voluntary Sector: The Case of the Hospital Industry." In Burton Weisbrod, *The Voluntary Nonprofit Sector*. Lexington, Mass.: Lexington Books.

Lee, M. L. 1971. "A Conspicuous Production Theory of Hospital Behavior." *Southern Economic Journal* 38:48–59.

Manne, Henry. 1965. "Mergers and the Market for Corporate Control." *Journal of Political Economy* 73:110–20.

Nelson, Richard. 1977. *The Moon and the Ghetto: An Essay on Public Policy Analysis*. New York: W. W. Norton & Co.

Nelson, Richard, and Michael Krashinsky. 1973. "Two Major Issues of Public Policy: Public Policy and Organization of Supply." In *Public Subsidy for Day Care of Young Children*, edited by Richard Nelson and Dennis Young. Lexington, Mass.: D. C. Heath & Co.

Newhouse, Joseph. 1970. "Toward a Theory of Non-Profit Institutions: An Economic Model of a Hospital." *American Economic Review* 60:64–74.

Newton, Jamie. 1980. "Child Care Decision-Making Survey—Preliminary Report." Unpublished manuscript; Yale University, Program on Non-Profit Organizations.

New York Temporary State Commission on Living Costs and the Economy. 1975. *Report on Nursing Homes and Health-Related Facilities in New York State*. N.p.

Niskanen, William. 1971. *Bureaucracy and Representative Government*. Chicago: Aldine Publishing Co.

Pauly, Mark P., and Michael R. Redisch. 1973. "The Not-for-Profit Hospital as a Physicians' Cooperative." *American Economic Review* 63:87–99.

Permut, Steven. 1981. "Consumer Perceptions of Nonprofit Enterprise: A Comment on Hansmann." *Yale Law Journal* 90:1623–32.

Rose-Ackerman, Susan. 1981. "Do Government Grants to Charity Reduce Private Donations?" In *Nonprofit Firms in a Three-Sector Economy*, edited by Michelle White. Washington, D.C.: Urban Institute.

Steinwald, Bruce, and Duncan Neuhauser. 1970. "The Role of the Proprietary Hospital." *Law and Contemporary Problems* 35:817–38.

Thompson, Earl. 1980. "Charity and Nonprofit Organizations." In *The Economics of Nonproprietary Organizations*, edited by Kenneth Clarkson and Donald Martin. Greenwich, Conn.: JAI Press.

Tullock, Gordon. 1966. "Information without Profit." In *Papers on Non-Market Decision Making*, edited by Gordon Tullock. Charlottesville: Thomas Jefferson Center for Political Economy, University of Virginia.

Weisbrod, Burton. 1964. "Collective-Consumption Services of Individual-Consumption Goods." *Quarterly Journal of Economics* 78:471–77.

———. 1974. "Toward a Theory of the Voluntary Non-Profit Sector in a Three-Sector Economy." In *Altruism, Morality, and Economic Theory*, edited by Edmund S. Phelps. New York: Russell Sage.

———. 1977. *The Voluntary Nonprofit Sector*. Lexington, Mass.: D. C. Heath & Co.

———. 1983. "Nonprofit and Proprietary Sector Behavior: Wage Differentials among Lawyers." *Journal of Labor Economics* 1:246–63.

Weisbrod, Burton, and A. James Lee. 1977. "Collective Goods and the Voluntary Sector: The Case of the Hospital Industry." In Burton Weisbrod, *The Voluntary Nonprofit Sector*. Lexington, Mass.: Lexington Books.

Weisbrod, Burton, and Mark Schlesinger. 1986. "Ownership Form and Behavior in Regulated Markets with Asymmetric Information." In *The Economics of Nonprofit Institutions: Studies in Structure and Policy*, ed. Susan Rose-Ackerman. Oxford: Oxford University Press.

Weiss, Jeffrey. 1986. "Donations: Can They Reduce a Donor's Welfare?" In *The Economics of Nonprofit Institutions: Studies in Structure and Policy*, ed. Susan Rose-Ackerman. Oxford: Oxford University Press.

Williamson, Oliver. 1979. "Transaction-Cost Economics: The Governance of Contractual Relations." *Journal of Law and Economics* 22:233–61.

Young, Dennis. 1983. *If Not for Profit, for What?* Lexington, Mass.: D. C. Heath & Co.

# [2]

# Nonprofit Organizations and the Market

RICHARD STEINBERG

Many people believe that nonprofit firms, unsullied by considerations of profitability, provide needed social services in a trustworthy and efficient fashion. Others deride nonprofit firms, believing that without a profit motive there is little incentive either to produce services in an efficient manner or to accommodate the desires of consumers. Believers in the first school of thought are likely to stress the advantages of publicly subsidizing nonprofit firms through grants, tax exemption, deductibility of donations, and exemption from onerous regulatory requirements. They may even propose that for-profit firms should be legally prohibited from providing certain services (such as day care or nursing homes). Believers in the second school wish to remove subsidies, arguing that they promote unfair competition that worsens the overall quality of service provision.

This chapter reviews the relevant literature and argues that the behavior and performance of nonprofit firms cannot properly be understood by looking at firms in isolation. Nonprofit firms compete with one another in the markets for donations, membership, clients, and sales. The nonprofit sector as a whole competes with the for-profit and government sectors in the markets for skilled labor, sales, and reduced (or zero) cost service provision. This competition is often tempered by intrasectoral cooperation (in the form of united fund-raising organizations and buying cooperatives) and intersectoral transfer payments (corporate donations and government grants). Overall, market structure seems to determine both behavior and performance.

Of course, one cannot analyze the impact of market structure without a clear understanding of the relevant facts. Unfortunately, consistent and complete data sets for determining the market structures of various nonprofit industries do not exist. Further, there are definitional issues to be resolved. The next section of this chapter summarizes our current understanding of these market structures.

On the surface, nonprofit and for-profit firms appear to possess very different internal structures. Nonprofits receive donations and conduct fund-raising campaigns, unlike for-profits. Workers at nonprofit firms often donate their time—indeed, the members of the nonprofit firm may be required to pay dues if they wish to continue with the organization. Nonprofit foundations and united fund-raising organizations appear to have no structural analogues in the for-profit world. And yet, as the third section of this chapter argues, these differing internal structures perform similarly in the production, marketing, and distribution of services.

Although several theories of nonprofit firm behavior have been proposed, certain types of behavior would not survive inter- or intrasectoral competition. The fourth section examines some implications of market structure on the conduct of nonprofit firms and summarizes some empirical tests of these implications.

The market structure is thus found to be an important determinant of performance by nonprofit and for-profit firms. Although this structure may be regarded as fixed in the short run, in the long run it is determined by the inherent advantages and disadvantages of the nonprofit, for-profit, and governmental forms as well as by tax and regulatory advantages conferred upon the different sectors. Several studies have examined the importance of these factors in determining the nonprofit share of output, and these studies are summarized in the fifth section. Using these empirical results, the government could indirectly improve overall market performance, altering the nonprofit share by employing these tax and regulatory levers.

Space considerations preclude discussion of other impor-

I would like to thank Avner Ben-Ner, Paul DiMaggio, Henry Hansmann, Walter Powell, Susan Rose-Ackerman, Gladys Topkis, Cecile Watters, and Charles Weinberg for a number of valuable comments on drafts of this chapter.

tant regulatory issues. For example, when should nonprofit firms be exempt from antitrust legislation? How should nonprofit incorporation laws be structured? Should cross-subsidization of services by nonprofit firms be regulated? Formal analysis of these issues is just beginning,[1] and considerations of the issues raised in this chapter can only help such analysis.

## MARKET STRUCTURE

In many industries, nonprofit firms compete not only with other nonprofits but with for-profits and governments in both input and output markets. A consistent set of data characterizing the three-sector structure of industries containing nonprofit organizations does not seem to exist, but evidence from a variety of sources has been compiled in table 7.1. The shares of employment, revenue, enrollment, and facilities owned by nonprofit organizations vary enormously across industries, though (perhaps because of definitional inconsistencies in extant data sets) there seem to be no empirical analyses of cross-industry differences in nonprofit share. Shares within each industry vary enormously from state to state and among metropolitan areas.[2]

Economists like to classify market structures by the ability of the firm to control price. Thus, a perfectly competitive firm is unable to affect the market price (or is ignorant of its power to do so) and selects only a production level. A monopoly, on the other hand, can select any price/quantity combination that consumers are willing to purchase. Oligopoly is an intermediate case, where firms may have control over price, depending on the reactions of competitors.

The price control framework is clearly inadequate for many markets containing nonprofit firms. For one thing, not all nonprofits charge a price for their charitable output. For another, nonprofit firms can sustain prices that are below market equilibrium levels if their patrons and donors are willing to subsidize losses to obtain some social goal (H. Schlesinger 1981; James 1983). Thus, even firms in competitive situations have some freedom to choose their prices (though they cannot charge higher than market rates).

How then are we to characterize market structures? A completely satisfactory approach has not been offered, but Feigenbaum (1980b) suggests that traditional indicators of the distribution of firm sizes (such as the Herfindahl index[3] or the concentration ratio) can be used to characterize the economic power of nonprofit firms. Table 7.2 summarizes the market structure of several nonprofit industries, utilizing the four-firm concentration ratio—the share of total market revenues received by the four largest nonprofit firms in the relevant (local) market. By this measure, country clubs are reasonably competitive, whereas museums are somewhat monopolistic.

Certain ambiguities beset the concentration ratio index. Does the relevant market include competing government and for-profit firms? Presumably, the answer depends on whether the outputs of the different sectors are sufficiently similar, so that consumers regard them as one good (technically, the intersectoral cross-price elasticity of demand must be sufficiently high). No one seems to have estimated such cross-price elasticities of demand, though several researchers have examined differences in quality across sectors (Johnson 1971, Rushing 1974, Bays 1977, Kushman & Nuckton 1977 for hospitals; Titmus 1971 for blood; Kushman 1979 for day care).

Second, there is a problem defining the geographical extent of the market. Do hospitals compete for the same patients when they are located in the same metropolitan area or only when located in the same neighborhood?[4]

Third, there is a problem defining the appropriate measure of economic size. Do we wish to include donative revenues and membership fees or only sales revenues? How do we account for endowments in defining market structure? On the descriptive level, any arbitrary resolution of these difficulties will do when the details of index construction are spelled out. However, if theories of market structure and firm behavior are to be tested, or procompetitive policies are proposed, case-by-case resolution of these difficulties seems necessary.

Though all three sectors compete in the same markets, they do not all play by the same rules. The market structure is not complete without a description of the regulatory environment. Government is defined by its monopoly of legitimate coercive power, and governments can obtain resources in any fashion supported by a majority of citizens and allowed by the relevant constitutions. Governments set the rules of competition, and they have set different rules and regulations for the nonprofit and for-profit sectors.

Nonprofit firms are granted exemption from the corporate income tax if they refrain from earning too much unrelated

1. See Hansmann (1981a) and Ellman (1982) on nonprofit corporation laws; Rose-Ackerman (1980) and Bartlett (1982) on united fundraising organizations and antitrust laws; "Antitrust and Nonprofit Entities" (1981) on antitrust laws and other types of nonprofit firms; Rose-Ackerman (1982a) and Giancola (1984) on protecting for-profits from nonprofit competition; White (1979) on protecting nonprofits from for-profit competition; and Joseph (1975), Harris (1979), White (1979), Clark (1980), Caulfield (1981), James (1983), and Bays (1983) on regulating cross-subsidization by nonprofit firms.

2. For example, Hansmann (1982) cites evidence that the percentage of nongovernmental hospital beds in nonprofit hospitals in 1975 varied from a high of 100 percent in Minnesota to a low of 32 percent in Nevada.

3. The Herfindahl index sums the squares of the market shares of each firm in an industry. It obtains a maximum value of 1 if the industry contains a single firm and declines with increases in the number of firms or with increased equality in shares among a given number of firms.

4. Marketing researchers worry very much about the appropriate definition of a market and have suggested various methods for dealing with these and other problems. See Day, Massy, and Shocker (1978) for definitions appropriate in an antitrust context, and Day, Shocker, and Srivastava (1979) or Urban and Hauser (1980) for definitions appropriate for marketing managers seeking to identify competitors and untapped market niches. These definitions need modification when applied to nonprofits.

business income (I.R.C., §501). They can receive tax deductible donations if they refrain from too much political lobbying (I.R.C. §170). They are often exempt from local property and sales taxes (Hansmann 1982) and face differing standards of antitrust regulation ("Antitrust . . ." 1981; Bartlett 1982). They receive special treatment with respect to Social Security (42 U.S.C. §410 (a)(8)(b) 1976), unemployment insurance (I.R.C. §§3306(b)(5)(A), (c)(8)), the minimum wage (19 U.S.C. §203(r) 1976; 29 C.F.R. §779.214 1979), securities regulation (15 U.S.C. §77c(a)(4) 1976), bankruptcy (11 U.S.C.A. §303(1) (West Supp. 1979)), copyright (17 U.S.C. §§110, 111(a)(4), 112(b), 118(d)(3) 1976), and postal rates (39 U.S.C.A. §3626 (West Supp. 1979)). Yet nonprofit firms also face many of the same regulations as for-profits, though their response to regulations may differ.

**TABLE 7.1 SECTORAL COMPOSITION, BY INDUSTRY**

| Industry | Measurement Basis | NP Share[a] | FP Share[a] | G Share[a] |
|---|---|---|---|---|
| Health Services | | | | |
| Short-term and general hospitals | Facilities[b] | 53% | 12% | 35% |
| | Beds[b] | 62 | 8 | 30 |
| | Expenditures[b,c] | 65 | 7 | 27 |
| | Employment[b,d] | 66 | 6 | 28 |
| Psychiatric hospitals | Facilities[e] | 18 | 26 | 56 |
| Chronic-care hospitals | Facilities[e] | 29 | 7 | 64 |
| Homes for mentally handicapped | Facilities[f] | 38 | 46 | 16 |
| Nursing homes | Facilities[f] | 34 | 61 | 5 |
| | Facilities[g] | 18 | 82 | N.A. |
| | Beds[r] | 20 | 69 | 11 |
| | Employment[h,i] | 24 | 76 | N.A. |
| Education | | | | |
| Elementary and secondary education | Enrollment[q] | 10 | 1 | 89 |
| Secondary | Revenues[k] | 14 | 3 | 83 |
| Postsecondary[l] | Revenues[k] | 20 | 33 | 47 |
| Higher education | Enrollment[j] | 24 | N.A. | 76 |
| Social Services | | | | |
| Day-care centers | Facilities[n] | 14 | 52 | 7 |
| | Facilities[m] | 43 | 57 | N.A. |
| | Enrollment[n] | 63 | 27 | N.A. |
| | Employment[h,i] | 56 | 44 | N.A. |
| Individual and family services | Employment[h,i] | 96 | 4 | N.A. |
| Legal services | Employment[h,i] | 2 | 98 | N.A. |
| Culture and entertainment | | | | |
| Theater, orchestra, and other performing arts | Employment[h,i] | 26 | 74 | N.A. |
| Radio and television broadcasting | Employment[h,i] | 5 | 95 | N.A. |
| Art museums | Revenue[o] | 65 | 5 | 30 |
| Research | | | | |
| Research and development | Expenditures[p] | 15 | 72 | 13 |
| Basic research | Expenditures[p] | 67 | 18 | 15 |

a. Where government share is not available, nonprofit and for-profit figures are shares of private-sector activity. When for-profit share is not available separately, private-sector share is reported in the nonprofit column.
b. Source: American Hospital Association 1981. Federal hospitals were not apportioned between long and short term, and all were included above.
c. Excludes new construction.
d. Full-time equivalent.
e. Source: National Master Facility Inventory, U.S. National Center for Health Statistics 1980.
f. Source: *Survey of Institutionalized Persons*, U.S. Department of Commerce 1976.
g. Source: National Master Facility Inventory, U.S. National Center for Health Statistics 1976.
h. Source: Rudney & Weitzman 1983.
i. Full- and part-time employment.
j. Source: U.S. Department of Commerce 1981, 1977 data.
k. Source: Bendick 1979.
l. Including vocational.
m. Source: U.S. Department of Commerce 1981, 1977 data.
n. Source: Coelen, Glantz, & Calore 1979; data are from 1976–77 and exclude small day-care centers serving less than thirteen children each.
o. Source: Clarkson 1979.
p. Source: U.S. National Science Foundation 1981. Data are 1982 estimates, by performance sector. Government includes only the federal government.
q. Source: U.S. Department of Health, Education, and Welfare 1978.
r. Source: Hirschoff, forthcoming. Public/private breakdown is by enrollment; for-profit/nonprofit breakdown is by number of schools.

**TABLE 7.2 NONPROFIT FOUR-FIRM CONCENTRATION RATIOS, BY INDUSTRY**

| | Fiscal Year | | |
|---|---|---|---|
| Industry | 1974 | 1975 | 1976 |
| Museums, zoos, etc. | 86.2 | 89.6 | 86.7 |
| Hospitals | 41.8 | 41.0 | 40.3 |
| Health clinics | 83.9 | 81.9 | 83.2 |
| Aid to handicapped | 57.8 | 53.8 | 49.5 |
| Medical research | 65.8 | 65.2 | 62.9 |
| Country clubs | 36.0 | 35.6 | 34.9 |
| Defense of rights | 81.0 | 81.4 | 77.0 |
| Aid to poor | 91.2 | 88.8 | 83.5 |

*Source:* Feigenbaum 1980b. Largest four firms' combined share of total market revenues, simple average concentration ratio across seven SMSAs, nonprofit firms only.

## FIRM STRUCTURES

For-profit firms raise initial capital through various debt instruments and obtain continuing resources through sales of goods and services. On the surface, this is a very different structure than the one employed by nonprofit firms. Initial resources are obtained through grants and bequests, and continuing resources are obtained through gifts, grants, contributions, dues, and fees as well as sales. Yet, as I shall show, the formal internal structures are not as different as they appear.

Table 7.3 summarizes the sources and uses of funds in five broadly defined nonprofit industries. Some firms rely almost exclusively on sales (Hansmann's "commercial nonprofits" [1980]), whereas others rely heavily on donations (Hansmann's "donative nonprofits"). Weisbrod's "collectiveness index" (1980; and see table 7.4) measures the share of revenues derived from gifts, grants, and donations and indexes the extent to which nonprofits are devoted to public needs. The idea behind this index is that member needs are met through payment of dues and client needs are met through purchases. Thus, donations primarily meet public needs (but see below).

### Sales and Advertising versus Donations and Solicitation

Although sales of goods and services and donations appear to be different structures for obtaining resources, they possess strong similarities. Buyers make explicit trades, obtaining goods or services in return for money. Donors often make implicit trades, obtaining direct benefits (a front-row seat at the opera, public recognition as a good citizen, job advancement), indirect benefits (the gratification of helping to eliminate poverty, a lower crime rate), and Kantian benefits (enjoyment of the act of giving). Clearly, if direct benefits motivate giving, a donation is not different from a purchase. Amos (1982) discusses ways in which indirect and Kantian motives may be empirically distinguished from direct motives (though his method is not free from problems [see Steinberg 1984]).

**TABLE 7.3 INCOME AND WEALTH STATEMENTS FOR NONPROFIT ORGANIZATIONS[a]**

| | Welfare n = 199 | Health n = 93 | Education n = 167 | Arts n = 30 | Research n = 30 |
|---|---|---|---|---|---|
| Source of Funds | | | | | |
| Sales | 166 (45%) | 4545 (91%) | 3534 (84%) | 1418 (92%) | 9474 (78%) |
| Dues and fees | 30 (8%) | 13 (0%) | 7 (0%) | 5 (0%) | 37 (0%) |
| Contributions and grants | 174 (47%) | 431 (9%) | 664 (16%) | 116 (8%) | 2686 (22%) |
| Uses of Funds | | | | | |
| Cost of goods sold | 30 (8%) | 391 (8%) | 108 (3%) | 35 (3%) | 143 (1%) |
| Fund-raising | 56 (15%) | 147 (3%) | 157 (4%) | 16 (1%) | 110 (1%) |
| Administration | 88 (24%) | 3474 (70%) | 395 (9%) | 132 (9%) | 4186 (34%) |
| Program | 168 (45%) | 627 (13%) | 3218 (77%) | 126 (8%) | 6734 (55%) |
| Retained earnings[b] | 28 (8%) | 350 (7%) | 326 (8%) | 1229 (80%) | 1022 (8%) |
| Wealth Measures | | | | | |
| Assets | 620 | 5955 | 8351 | 1170 | 16141 |
| Liabilities | 170 | 2216 | 1117 | 150 | 4789 |
| Net worth | 450 | 3739 | 7234 | 1019 | 11352 |

a. Sample consists of tax Forms 990 filed in 1975 in four metropolitan areas—Philadelphia, Minneapolis/St. Paul, Houston/Galveston, and Los Angeles. Accounting procedures are not always uniform across sectors. For a complete description of the sample selection criteria and method of classification by sector, see Steinberg (1983a, 173–78). Figures are organizational means, in 000s of 1975 dollars. Shares are in parentheses.

b. Retained earnings are calculated as the difference between total sources of funds and all other listed uses of funds.

**TABLE 7.4 INDEX OF COLLECTIVENESS, 1973–75**

| Type of Organization | Collectiveness Index (C) | Sample Size |
|---|---|---|
| Cultural | 90 | 28 |
| Religious | 71 | 32 |
| Public affairs | 47 | 29 |
| Social welfare | 41 | 40 |
| Agricultural | 41 | 50 |
| Educational | 34 | 33 |
| Legal, public administration and military | 20 | 50 |
| Veteran, hereditary, and patriotic | 12 | 45 |
| Athletic and sports | 11 | 28 |
| Honor societies | 9 | 51 |
| Scientific, engineering, and technical | 6 | 51 |
| Ethnic | 3 | 37 |
| Labor associations and federations | 3 | 70 |
| Trade, business, and commercial | 2 | 58 |
| Health | 2 | 35 |
| Hobby and avocational | 1 | 20 |
| Chambers of commerce | 0 | 27 |
| All Types | 20 | 684 |

*Source:* Weisbrod 1980. Derived from IRS tax Form 990 data. Accounting procedures are not always uniform across types of organizations.

Even when nonprofit organizations do not provide obvious services in exchange for donative resources, the method of obtaining resources is similar to that of sales in for-profit firms. Fund-raising programs are expenditures by the nonprofit firm to produce donative payments in the same sense that expenditures on marketing result in sales in for-profit firms. Thus, criteria for maximizing the surplus generated by a fund-raising program are identical to criteria for maximizing the profits generated by production and marketing (Weinberg 1980; Steinberg 1983b). Except for minor technical qualifications, net returns are maximal when an additional dollar of fund-raising expenditure adds exactly one dollar to donations—that is, when the "marginal donative product of fund-raising" (MDPF) equals 1.[5] If MDPF exceeds 1, additional fund-raising will generate more in additional contributions than in additional costs, so firms whose MDPF exceeds 1 are doing too little fund-raising.[6] Eventually, additional fund-raising yields diminishing returns; when MDPF falls to 1, no further net gains are available from further expenditures.

Although donations can thus be modeled as a trade in which nonprofit firms provide literature soliciting funds in return for donations, the exact nature of the good received by donors is subject to question. Tullock (1966) posited the rather extreme example of a nonprofit firm that provided no charitable service but sent donors handsome literature alleging (falsely) that donations were helping the starving millions. The donor would get a feeling of satisfaction and pride, the firm would get donations, and so both are "better off"; yet society gets no charitable output.

At the other extreme, when fund-raising literature is truthful, information is traded for donations, and social allocations are likely to be improved. Ehrlich and Fisher's model of advertising (1982) can be applied to fund-raising (Steinberg 1983a). In this model, donors are uncertain which nonprofit firms have the most desirable characteristics in terms of the type of service provided, the quality of service, or the efficiency with which donations are converted into service. Donors could obtain the relevant information on their own, but this is so costly that few would bother. As a result, total donations are low, as donors are not certain they can obtain desirable results from donating. Fund-raising literature is provided free by nonprofit firms. If it is regarded as reasonably truthful (say, because claims are monitored by legal authorities), the donor's cost of information is drastically reduced, and total donations will rise.

### Fund-raising and Contract Failure

The fund-raising/donative trade appears to differ from most other trades for contract failure reasons (see chapter 2 in this volume). With most goods and services, buyers can be reasonably certain the quantity purchased is the quantity they contracted for, as they receive the merchandise. When donors "purchase" services for others, they do not usually observe the quantity received by nonprofit clients; thus they seek institutional guarantees that their donation will be fully applied. Hansmann (1980) argues that contributions are not made to for-profit firms because donors cannot be certain whether their donations will be used to increase stockholder dividends or to provide incremental charitable service. He argues further that the nondistribution constraint that defines the nonprofit sector provides assurance that donations will not be diverted to stockholders.

Hansmann does not analyze a different source of potential contract failure—the potential leak of donations to fund-raising. If half of each donation is used to increase fund-raising expenditure, then the donor's "price" of a dollar of charitable service expenditure appears to be two dollars. If donors find it difficult to obtain information on the diversion of contributions toward fund-raising, they will be uncertain about the price and reluctant to donate.

Steinberg (1986) argues that this source of potential contract failure is not likely to prove bothersome when the price is properly calculated. He considers a wide range of possible objectives underlying nonprofit firm behavior (including service maximization and budget maximization as special cases), and (with minor technical exceptions) demonstrates that the price of charitable service is exactly one dollar regardless of the share of fund-raising in the overall budget.

5. There are, however, additional complications when a nonprofit firm has revenue from sales as well as from donations (Weinberg 1980). For a precise statement of the technical qualifications on this optimizing rule and a discussion of the various ways MDPF has been statistically estimated, see Steinberg (1985a).

6. In this case, too little fund-raising is taking place from the perspective of the nonprofit firm, but fund-raising may still be excessive from a social standpoint. See Steinberg (1985a) for a further discussion of this point.

The basic reason is that the optimal level of fund-raising does not change when a (small) additional donation is made, so that 100 percent of additional contributions is available for charitable service provision. This implies that (small) donors do not need to monitor fund-raising levels to be certain of the quantity of charitable expenditure resulting from their donation. Thus contract failure that is due to fund-raising does not arise.

**Dues and Fees**

Another way in which nonprofit firms obtain resources is through dues and other membership and affiliation fees. There seems to be no clear analogue in the for-profit sector, but the recent spate of take-back contracts negotiated in the steel, airline, and automobile industries has some of the same flavor—member/employees are contributing for the survival of the organization. Affiliation fees are clearly analogous to franchising fees, and the local-national structure of many nonprofit firms (such as United Way of America and the National Cancer Society) serves many of the same functions as the franchise structure (such as that of McDonald's). The national parent organization obtains economies of scale in purchasing and enforces uniform quality standards on locals to protect the reputation of the organization as a whole. In this way, donors are further assured that their contributions will be well spent.

Very little has been written about the economic role of membership fees. The economic literature on clubs (Buchanan 1965; Sandler & Tschirhart 1980) and two-part pricing rules (Oi 1971) suggests some of the elements of an adequate theory of membership fees. Downing and Brady (1981) modeled the behavior of a citizens' interest group (CIG) that acts to maximize the present value of member net benefits. In their model, the behavior of the CIG determines which individuals will choose to become members. One determinant of the probability of membership is the cost to the individual of joining, largely consisting of dues but also including the value of the member's time outside the organization and other factors. Although their model is one of the very few to take dues into account, there is room for a great deal more analysis than they conducted, for in their model the only way to contribute is through membership. A model of the donor choice between nonmember donations and membership dues is clearly called for.

**Access to Capital**

Another difference between nonprofit and for-profit organizations is in their ability to obtain financial capital. Hansmann (1981c) notes that equity capital is not available to nonprofit organizations because of the nondistribution constraint. Although debt financing is available to some extent, Hansmann argues that the costs become prohibitive beyond some point well short of 100 percent debt financing. Donations are an uncertain and inadequate source of capital in many cases, leaving retained earnings as a necessary source of growth capital. Hansmann argues that nonprofit exemption from corporate income tax permits faster growth by allowing firms to retain more earnings. Thus, both external constraints on borrowing and internal subsidization through tax exemption bias the nonprofit capital structure toward retained earnings.

Though regular banks are reluctant to lend initial capital to nonprofit organizations, nonprofits obtain analogous services in the form of foundation grants. These grants often provide long-term capital rather than operating funds and are frequently designed to provide seed money for new organizations and new programs at existing nonprofit firms (Kramer 1981).

Foundations have the potential to assist service-providing nonprofit firms to reallocate resources over the business cycle. Steinberg and Perlman (1982) note that in times of recession nonprofit firms have greater needs for funds, and yet donations are likely to fall. A policy of retaining more earnings (building endowment) during economic booms and running down the endowment during recessions can improve the allocation of service provision over time; but there are limits to the ability of firms to compensate for the business cycle with internal financial policy. Foundations can function countercyclically, however, providing more grants in times of recession and rebuilding their assets in times of boom.

**Labor Utilization**

For-profit and nonprofit firms appear to differ substantially in the utilization of labor. For one thing, volunteers provide some of the labor for nonprofit organizations, a rare phenomenon in for-profit firms. For another, even when labor is paid for in both sectors, the rate of compensation appears to differ for comparable jobs. Finally, there is reason to believe that labor unions have different effects in for-profit and nonprofit firms.

On the first issue, it is not obvious that volunteer workers are uncompensated and cost the firm nothing. Mueller (1975) details four potential personal benefits to volunteers: pleasure from the act of giving, prestige, influence over the composition and allocation of charitable output, and development (or signaling) of skills that will help them in future (paid) employment. Mueller analyzes the last two sources of gain, and finds statistical support for their influence on volunteer time among professional women. Schiff (1984) considers an additional benefit—donors can gather information on the quality and efficiency of competing nonprofit firms by working as volunteers at the respective organizations before allocating their monetary donations. Havrilesky, Schweitzer, and Wright (1973) note one more benefit—volunteers may serve as role models who encourage other individuals to contribute time and money to services valued by the volunteer. They contend that this benefit explains why many community leaders are early volunteers in and early dropouts from public good causes.

Unpaid workers thus appear to be compensated, but not

by direct payments from the firm. Does this imply that volunteer labor is a free resource to the nonprofit firm? I know of no empirical analysis of this issue, but the answer is almost surely no. Volunteers may get in the way of full-time paid workers, reducing their productivity. Volunteers require the firm to obtain more supplies and perhaps purchase more insurance. But most important, they must be attracted to the firm, trained for their positions, and encouraged to stay, all of which cost money and staff time (Weinberg 1980; Lovelock & Weinberg 1984; Schiff 1984). Although nonprofit firms may not pay salaries to their volunteer labor force, they must be attentive to turnover costs.

Thus, there is some question from the perspectives of both firm and worker regarding the extent to which volunteer labor differs from compensated labor. Yet, if there is a real difference, it remains a puzzle why nonprofit firms attract volunteers and for-profit firms do not.[7] Is a volunteer worker at a for-profit hospital less likely to obtain Mueller's four benefits? How does the nondistribution constraint affect the potential benefits of volunteering? A way to get at this question empirically would be to obtain data on volunteer labor at hospitals that converted from nonprofit to for-profit status or vice versa. I know of no work being done along this line.

The only relevant literature I have found discusses the general question of why people donate to nonprofit firms—combining donations of time (volunteer labor) and money in one explanatory model. General models of donor motivation are reviewed elsewhere in this volume (see chapters 2 and 18). But such models do not explain volunteer labor, for Schiff (1984) shows that when the nondistribution constraint is the sole reason donors prefer nonprofits, donations would come (almost) exclusively in the form of money. With minor exceptions, donors could provide more charitable service if they spent their time earning money (and contributed incremental earnings) than if they volunteered.

Though it is not clear why volunteer labor is directed exclusively to the nonprofit sector, several researchers have modeled the donor's choice between gifts of time and money (Long 1977; Menchik & Weisbrod 1981; Schiff 1984). Morgan, Dye, and Hybels (1977) note the simple correlation between the two and speculate that "anything that reduced dollar giving by 10% might reduce time given by as much as 4%" (p. 175). More sophisticated statistical analyses by Dye (1980), Menchik and Weisbrod (1981), and Schiff (1984) obtained results that were generally consistent with Morgan, Dye, and Hybel's.

Even when all workers are paid, nonprofit firms seem to differ from for-profit firms and governments in their utilization of labor. Coelho (1976) analyzed the institution of tenure in nonprofit organizations as a means of encouraging reliable information flows between workers and the board of directors (a similar point is made in Weisbrod and Schlesinger 1986). Freeman (1975) concluded that in general, nonprofit firms are likely to be more sensitive to wages and output in their hiring decisions than their for-profit counterparts. However, universities should be less sensitive to these fluctuations because of the institution of tenure and the goal of many universities to reward comparable faculty similarly regardless of nonacademic opportunities. Finally, he concluded that changes in external circumstances will affect the quality of faculty more than the quantity.

Borjas, Frech, and Ginsburg (1983) found that nonprofit nursing homes (especially those with religious affiliation) pay substantially lower wages to comparably skilled workers than for-profits, and government-operated homes pay substantially higher wages. A more sophisticated paper by Weisbrod (1983) disentangles the influences on the wage structures in for-profit law firms and nonprofit public interest law firms. He found that comparably skilled lawyers are paid substantially less in public interest law firms, that they know this, that the financial sacrifice is permanent, and that they are willing to sacrifice income because of their strong preference for public interest work. This confirms that the type of sorting/screening mechanism discussed by Young (chapter 10 in this volume) in the case of entrepreneurs also applies to workers at nonprofit firms.

A reanalysis of Weisbrod's data by Goddeeris (1984) confirmed that public interest lawyers are systematically different from other lawyers but does not confirm that they accept lower salaries in the nonprofit sector because of these differences in preferences. Rather, he found that apparently comparably skilled lawyers in the two sectors (on the basis of measured characteristics) do not have the same earnings potential in the for-profit world and that salary differences are due to the unmeasured factors that cause this earnings potential to differ. Thus, while nonprofits appear to obtain labor at a bargain price, it may be that these workers are of lower quality and do not impart competitive advantage on the sector.

A natural question arises as to whether unions have differing effects on labor utilization in the two sectors. Faine (1972) argues that in a nonprofit arts organization, such as a museum or an opera company, a strike is often welcomed by management as a means of reducing the deficit. For-profit firms, on the other hand, resist strikes, as they reduce profits. Where profits are available, unions have something to strive for, but this is not the case in nonprofits.

A deeper analysis of this question is probably warranted. It is true that nonprofit arts groups rarely cover costs through sales (Hansmann [1981b] argues that this represents a desire for voluntary price discrimination in order to cover the fixed costs of production), but they receive donative income which unions may strive to capture by striking. When donations serve only to increase union wages, however, donations may cease. The relationships among strikes, sales revenue, and donations need more careful analysis.

7. For-profit firms in particular industries attract volunteers, but to a much smaller extent than nonprofit firms. For example, figures presented in Coelen, Glantz, and Calore (1979) indicate that 17.2 percent of for-profit and 49.6 percent of nonprofit day-care firms utilized unpaid staff. These figures overstate the use of volunteers, for they include staff paid by outside agencies (such as CETA) as well as volunteers. The occasional use of volunteers by for-profits further complicates the puzzles cited in the text.

**Foundations**

So far I have concentrated on the structure of nonprofit service-providing agencies, including donative and commercial nonprofits, operated for the benefit of members or for clients. There are at least two other types of nonprofit organizations with different internal structures—foundations (private, public, community, and operating foundations) and united fund-raising organizations (such as the United Ways). (Ben-Ner in chapter 24 considers additional structures such as producer cooperatives.)

Very little has been written on the internal structure and functioning of foundations. Boulding (1972) advanced a few tentative hypotheses on the "pure theory" of foundations, but these are little more than a rehash of why people make donations of any sort. Steuerle (1977) and Steinberg and Perlman (1982) have analyzed the effect of the distribution requirements of the Tax Reform Act of 1969. Steinberg and Perlman note that the law as currently structured limits the ability of foundations to act as nonprofit banks—making large grants to service-providing organizations in times of recession and rebuilding assets at other times—since, in the case of private nonoperating foundations, grants must exceed a specified percentage of assets in each year. They propose an amendment that would positively encourage countercyclical grant making. But the lack of an adequate theory of foundation behavior hampers their analysis. The financial objectives of the foundation are unknown, as are the forces explaining the birth and death of foundations. Thus, analysis of policy impacts are incomplete and speculative.[8]

**United Fund-Raising Organizations**

The best analysis of the structure of united fund-raising organizations to date is by Rose-Ackerman (1980). She notes that membership in a united fund is determined by mutual advantages of current members and potential entrants. Current members enjoy greater contributions than they could obtain on their own for several reasons. First, since competitive fund-raising expenditure (fund-raising that seeks to divert donor dollars from one charity to another) is reduced, donors may believe their donations are more efficiently spent and thus may give more. Second, since united funds assess needs and audit performances of member agencies, donors may be convinced that their contributions will be better spent. In any case, donors need not devote as much time and effort to deciding which charities are meritorious and efficient, and this reduction in required donor effort encourages giving. Third, when donors disagree about which organizations are meritorious, tying donations into one package may help all donors. Though any one donor will find that some of his donations to the united fund are allocated to less preferred organizations, he is compensated by the fact that other donors provide funds for his favorite organization (Fisher 1977; Rose-Ackerman 1980). Finally, united funds often have local monopolies on access to payroll deduction plans.

A potential entrant, when deciding whether to seek membership, compares the advantages of membership (fund-raising costs are lower, while contributions received may be higher) with the disadvantages (loss of independence, united fund auditing requirements, restrictions on independent fund-raising that conflicts with the united fund campaign). Existing members compare the advantages of admitting a new entrant (one less fund-raising competitor, possible improvement in the fund's overall attractiveness to donors) with the disadvantages (a controversial or badly managed firm may reduce the fund's overall attractiveness to donors). Once membership is determined, the allocation process is constrained—if an organization is slighted in its allocation of the funds raised it may quit, often to the disadvantage of continuing members. In some cases, powerful members may negotiate special status within the united fund in return for their continued membership. Thus, for example, the American Cancer Society has negotiated special partnership agreements with United Ways in six states ("UW, Cancer Society . . ." 1979).

Some writers (such as Wenocur et al. 1984) have criticized the united funds for supporting only older, middle-of-the-road philanthropies. Given the determinants of membership structure discussed above, this allocation pattern is not surprising—an organization that supported a controversial cause would endanger the total donations received, and existing members would find it in their interest to oppose its entry.

Controversial causes can obtain some of the advantages of United Way fund-raising without threatening total donations through the recently emerging donor-option plans. Under these plans, donors can leave their donations undesignated (in which case they are distributed to United Way member organizations) or designate that their contribution go to any tax-exempt human service organization (eligibility requirements vary across the plans). Nonmember organizations obtain access to payroll-deduction plans, but they do not receive the other advantages of a united fund. Thus, a number of alternative funds (with central monitoring and restrictions on independent fund-raising) have arisen—more than fifty by 1983 (Wenocur et al. 1984). They serve large clusters of donors with related preferences that are too controversial for United Ways.

These new institutions certainly complicate analysis of united fund-raising organizations. Some United Way organizations are concerned that their overall campaigns will suffer if they adopt donor-option plans, but no data are available that support this fear (Cook et al. 1981). Donor-option plans reduce the antipathy of some donors to United Way giving and thus may benefit member organizations. However, with

8. There have been several studies of patterns of giving by foundations. Rhode (1975) examined the effect of asset levels, stock market prices, and bond prices on foundation support of health research and development. Wheatley (1978) analyzed patterns of giving in Chicago; Wolpert, Reiner, and Starrett (1980) analyzed giving in Philadelphia; and Steinberg and Perlman (1982) looked at grant making in four major metropolitan areas. But, without an understanding of the underlying determinants of foundation behavior, it is difficult to project how these patterns would change in response to governmental policies.

donor-option plans in place, the incentive for nonprofit firms to become members of the United Way (and thus reduce competitive fund-raising) is reduced. Local United Way organizations are confused as to whether a donor-option program is in their interest, and sometimes they administer the program in a fashion that supports the suspicion that their real aim is to stifle competition for workplace contributions rather than provide open access (Wenocur et al. 1984). Nonetheless, the Board of Governors of the United Way of America has endorsed the donor-option concept and has urged local United Way organizations to implement the plans (United Way . . . 1982). Under a court order, the Combined Federal Campaign has also adopted a donor-option plan.

## EFFECTS OF MARKET STRUCTURE ON PERFORMANCE

A common approach in the economics literature is to model the behaviors of for-profit, nonprofit, and government providers of service separately. Typically, analysts assume that for-profit firms wish to maximize profits and that their behavior can be derived and evaluated from this assumption. A different objective is postulated for nonprofit firms, such as enrollment maximization, medical-demand maximization, budget maximization, service maximization, quality/ quantity maximization, or expense-preference maximization (these models are reviewed in chapter 2 in this volume).[9] Predictions about nonprofit firms' behavior are derived under these alternative assumptions and contrasted with predictions about the behavior of for-profit firms.

I share the view in much of the existing literature that this approach is flawed for two reasons. First, nonprofit, for-profit, and government providers of service coexist in many markets. Except when there are explicit structures protecting nonprofit firms from competition, competition from these other sectors would eliminate many of the postulated nonprofit objective functions. A nonprofit firm that sought to maximize, say, managerial expense-preference objectives would be driven out of business by a for-profit firm acting to maximize its profits. Second, it is not clear that for-profit firms that compete in the same market as nonprofits would actually seek to maximize profits. "For-profit" is a legal designation, not a description of objectives, and economists have detailed a number of situations where for-profit firms would not seek maximal profits. Thus, predictions about differences in behavior between legally designated for-profit and nonprofit firms should not be predicated on the profit motive. The motives and behavior of both types of firms should be derived and analyzed in a framework incorporating the market structure.

### A Simple Market Competition Model

To emphasize the impact of market structure on nonprofit firm behavior, let us start with a simple and unrealistic competitive model, draw some conclusions, and then consider the impact of real-world complications. We shall assume that nonprofit and for-profit firms coexist in a market and that for-profit firms seek an output/quality mix and production technique that will maximize their profits. We shall assume nothing about the goal of nonprofit firms, for our argument does not depend on which theory of nonprofit behavior is relevant. Nonprofits have no special tax or regulatory advantages and receive no donations or dues. Costs of production and consumer demand for outputs are identical across sectors. Indeed, the only structural distinction allowed in this model between a nonprofit and a for-profit firm is the legal nondistribution constraint. Finally, potential entrepreneurs can enter the market as either nonprofit or for-profit firms without competitive disadvantage—there is no special cost advantage or name-brand recognition advantage possessed by preexisting firms. (Newhouse [1970], Pauly & Redisch [1973], and Rose-Ackerman [1982b] discuss alternative models of entry by nonprofit firms.)

In such a world, for-profit and nonprofit firm behavior must be identical (Manning 1973; White 1979). If any particular firm, profit-seeking or nonprofit, tried to charge a higher price (quality fixed) or sell a lower quality product (price fixed) than the prevailing market levels, that firm would lose all its business and would not survive. If a firm tried to charge a lower price (quality fixed) or sell goods of a higher quality (price fixed), its competitors would be forced to match this action or go out of business. There would still be diversity in quality levels, but an increase in product quality must be exactly (marginally) counterbalanced in the minds of consumers by an increase in product price. This is the theory of compensating differentials. The sorting out of firms by quality level is essentially arbitrary, and there is no reason to think that quality would systematically differ between the two types of firms.

All firms would have zero economic profits (economic profits are essentially equal to the difference between accounting profits and a "normal rate of return"). If any price/quality combination represented in the marketplace allowed a firm to make economic profits, a new profit-seeking firm would enter with a lower price/higher quality package that would be profitable and drive the first firm out of business. A nonprofit firm might also enter the market (depending on the unspecified objective of nonprofit entrepreneurs), but this is not essential.

All the optimality properties of perfectly competitive idealized economies typically taught in introductory economics classes apply to this hybrid model. Consumer needs are well met by total production levels and quality spectra, and production responds appropriately to changes in consumer preferences.

9. Enrollment maximization was proposed by Krizay and Wilson (1974); medical-demand maximization by Pauly and Redisch (1973); budget maximization by Tullock (1966) and Niskanen (1971); service maximization by Weinberg (1980) and Steinberg (1983a); quality/quantity maximization by Newhouse (1970), Carlson, Robinson, and Ryan (1971), Lee (1971), and Hansmann (1981b); and expense/preference maximization by Clarkson (1972), Keating and Keating (1975), Feigenbaum (1980b), Borjas, Frech, and Ginsberg (1983), and James (1983).

**Nonprofit Competitive Advantages and the Theory of Property Rights**

Let us make the model more realistic by introducing grants and donations. As Hansmann has argued, donations are given only to nonprofit firms because of contract failure. Thus, donations relate specifically to the nondistribution constraint we have retained in this simplified model.

Donations allow nonprofit firms to behave differently and survive competition from for-profits. A nonprofit firm can now, if it chooses, produce an unprofitable price/quality package, with losses subsidized by donations (James 1983). Indeed, every nonprofit firm can behave differently, and all will survive the competition of the market when donors are willing to subsidize the losses caused by these disparities.

It is in this framework that the property-rights literature (Alchian & Demsetz 1972) becomes relevant. Proponents of this approach argue that nonprofits are likely to behave inefficiently (by wasting resources or producing the "wrong" output/quality mixture) because of the nondistribution constraint. If any firm produces efficient price/quality combinations (desired by the public), it is rewarded by profits. In for-profit firms, the owners get to keep these profits, either directly in the form of dividends or indirectly through capital gains when they divest their stock. Thus, owners have a financial incentive to ensure that production is efficient as this would maximize their claim on the firm's residual. When owners do a poor job of ensuring efficiency, the firm becomes ripe for a takeover bid, which would restore efficiency, or is driven out of business by other profit-maximizing firms.

At nonprofit firms, ownership is attenuated. Although there is a board of directors with the legal authority to control the firm's actions, board members are legally prohibited from obtaining the residual. Furthermore, this same nondistribution constraint drastically reduces the incentive for others to mount a takeover bid (Frech 1980). This attenuation of property rights reduces the board's incentive to ensure efficient production.

In our initial model, property rights have little relevance, for inefficient firms are driven out of business and survivors are efficient. Donations allow nonprofit firms to behave as property-rights theorists predict and still survive. Such theorists argue that the donative advantage will be spent on managerial emoluments (or slack)—those aspects of the job environment that managers want at a zero price but would not want at their actual cost in terms of the residual. These emoluments include pleasant coworkers (who may be overpaid to ensure they will remain pleasant), discriminatory hiring practices, long lunch hours, magnificent offices, and larger, more prestigious market shares. In a (profit-maximizing) for-profit firm, such emoluments are valued by owners at actual cost, and managers and coworkers are given perks only when necessary to retain a worker who is significantly more valuable than available replacements. In a nonprofit firm, no one owns the residual, so no one has a financial incentive to restrict emoluments. Property-rights theorists are skeptical about the power of nonfinancial incentives (board preferences for efficiency per se) to constrain emoluments.

Legislators and citizens have expressed outrage over reported incidents of self-dealing, where board members of nonprofit firms covertly obtain shares of the firm's residuals for their personal use. According to property-rights theorists, this concern is misguided, for self-dealing restores the incentive for the firm to produce efficiently and market the price/quality combination most desired by consumers.[10]

**Residual Claimants and Monitoring**

The inefficiency conclusions are weakened when self-dealing (directly or indirectly) is practiced or when external agents have the ability to monitor and affect nonprofit performance through regulation or indirect incentives. Thus, many of the empirical studies to be cited below examine the extent to which medical societies dominate Blue Cross/Blue Shield. They argue that medical societies have an interest in minimizing administrative costs and managerial emoluments in order to maximize the demand for medical care and increase doctor income. This is a form of indirect self-dealing. One of the studies (Frech & Ginsburg 1981) argues that the quality of insurance will be higher than optimal in doctor-controlled Blues (in the sense that resources devoted to quality increments are better devoted to alternative uses), though most view medical-society control as efficiency improving. Medical societies retain imperfect control in most Blues, and a political compromise is struck between those desiring emoluments and those desiring administrative efficiency. Thus, the authors expect a negative correlation between measures of medical-society control of Blues and administrative costs and a positive correlation between control and doctor income.

Eisenstadt and Kennedy (1981) find that medical-society control of Blue Shield has no impact on administrative costs in states where Blues lack tax advantages (and are therefore constrained by competition with for-profit health care insurers) but has a significant negative impact on costs in other states. Empirical studies by Kass and Pautler (1979), Sloan (1981), Arnould and Eisenstadt (1981), and Arnould and Debrock (1982) found that physician control of Blue Shield caused higher physician prices, whereas Lynk (1981) found the opposite.

A number of other forces reduce inefficiency in certain cases. Political pressures have increasingly caused consumers to be selected for seats on the board of directors. Ben-Ner (1986) argues that only a few consumers or donors have to be involved in controlling the firm when it provides public goods. In many charities (especially medical research foundations), board members are intensely devoted to the chari-

10. See the discussions of residual claimants in Frech and Ginsberg (1978, 1981), Kass and Pautler (1979), Arnould and Eisenstadt (1981), Eisenstadt and Kennedy (1981), Sloan (1981), Lynk (1981), Arnould and Debrock (1982), and Hay and Leahy (1984).

ty's mission, often because family members would benefit from the resulting discoveries. A charity that desired the fund-raising advantages of membership in a United Way would have to submit to United Way oversight procedures and government attempts to monitor and regulate nonprofit performance more generally. Rose-Ackerman (1983) cites evidence that both United Way and government monitoring are minimal, however, and Boyle and Jacobs (1979) found that measures of state enforcement stringency had no effect on fund-raising costs as a share of funds raised. (Rose-Ackerman's paper [1982b] on the constraining influence of competitive entry on fund-raising behavior perhaps explains the irrelevance of regulation here.) The Better Business Bureau publishes ratings of various charities, but it is doubtful that these ratings are a major constraining influence. Donors can better monitor performance if they volunteer their labor rather than money (Mueller 1975). Grant-making agencies (governments and foundations) may require certain disclosures and/or management practices as a precondition for aid.

In many cases, the quality (price given) of a service product (education, day care, mental health care, and so on) can be evaluated by consumers only after some experience. Some clients are subsidized publicly or by some other nonprofit firm, and the subsidizer may have trouble discerning whether any particular firm is providing an efficient price/quality package. In such cases, the observed behavior of paying customers reveals firm efficiency, and subsidizers can structure their reimbursement policies to ensure efficiency by requiring that each firm serve at least one paying customer and reimburse the care of other clients at the same rate charged paying customers. Efficiency through "proxy shopping" was first proposed for the day-care industry by Nelson and Krashinsky (1973), and more generally and carefully by Rose-Ackerman (1983).

**Critique of the Property-Rights Theory**

At least five major criticisms can be made about received property-rights theory. First, for-profit firms are socially inefficient when contract failure applies. As Thompson noted (1980, 134), reduced efficiency owing to attenuated property rights "is often overshadowed by the increased efficiency in satisfying the customers that their contributions are being put to good use."

Second, the discretion afforded nonprofit managers allows nonprofits to act efficiently in an important class of situations wherein for-profit firms act inefficiently. The for-profit efficiency argument assumes that the (marginal) social benefit of an output mix can be captured by a firm in the form of (marginal) sales revenue. Weisbrod (1975) notes that many of the outputs sold by nonprofit firms provide external benefits (or are public goods, a special kind of externality). In such a case, it is well known that for-profit firms either leave the market or produce less than the efficient quantity (Atkinson & Stiglitz 1980, 505–07). If the nonprofit firm's decision maker values the provision of such goods, then it would count as an emolument that helps society as well as the manager. Managerial discretion, allowed by contributions and the nondistribution constraint, can be an efficient mechanism for the provision of goods with external benefits. This argument hinges on the "correctness" of preferences of the nonprofit decision maker, and so the entrepreneurial sorting and screening mechanisms discussed by Young in chapter 10 become relevant.

When sorting and screening mechanisms fail to ensure that nonprofit managers have the "right" preferences, nonprofit firms may nonetheless improve market provision of goods possessing external benefits. Preston (1984) has argued that nonprofit managers seeking to maximize the residual (in order, say, to raise their salary) would be forced to consider external benefits. This is because donations, she argues, depend on the social content of the goods provided. She shows that the overall market product mix is improved when such nonprofit firms are allowed to compete with for-profits.

In cases where service demand fluctuates (such as medical care), capacity is a public good, for excess capacity reduces the risk that any individual will be denied use of facilities in times of excess need (epidemics, major accidents, and so on). Holtman (1983) argues that for-profit firms provide too little capacity, so that once again nonprofit firms may improve social welfare. However, this result may depend on his assumptions that nonprofit managers value only the output level of the organization and that they are constrained to have zero profits in each period, assumptions not derived from the nondistribution constraint.

Third, the property-rights theory is incomplete. Nonprofit firms need not use all the discretion afforded by contributions to increase emoluments. Some of the slack could be used to produce a lower price/higher quality product and eliminate all competition from for-profit firms (although other nonprofits might still compete). The circumstances in which nonprofits would act to eliminate for-profit competition have not, to my knowledge, been discussed in the literature, but the lack of for-profit competition in products sold by many donative nonprofits suggests that this phenomenon may be commonplace (though of course there are a number of alternative explanations of this phenomenon).

Fourth, when there are informational asymmetries (where sellers are aware of the quality of their products but buyers are not), for-profit managers are more likely to exploit consumers. Weisbrod and Schlesinger (1986) discuss the case of nursing homes, where it is difficult to ascertain quality in advance and costly to move if the consumer (or his or her relatives) discovers upon use that the actual quality is different from the anticipated quality. In this situation, the for-profit manager could maximize the firm's residual by misleading potential consumers about the subjective aspects of quality. Further, managers who valued honesty as well as their income would tend to segregate themselves into the nonprofit sector.[11] Thus, Weisbrod and Schlesinger (1986)

11. In some cases, sorting would work the other way. If it were

conclude, "The resulting failure to maximize profit could be socially efficient; the social inefficiency resulting from the profit distribution constraint on nonprofits could offset the inefficiency resulting from the proprietary firms' taking advantage of their informational superiority over their customers." Their statistical analysis of Wisconsin nursing homes supports this conclusion. Controlling for a variety of factors, they find that the number of client complaints to regulatory authorities is significantly lower in all categories of nonprofit than in for-profit nursing homes.

Finally, the advantages of the for-profit legal form are exaggerated, for there are several important situations wherein nominally for-profit firms do not act to maximize their profits. Indeed, managerial discretion–emoluments models were originally developed and applied to for-profits. The owners of the modern for-profit corporation (stockholders) do not directly manage the firm. It is costly for the owners to engage in the kind of detailed monitoring necessary to ensure that managers maximize profits, and a certain level of inefficiency is expected. Increasingly elaborate models of this phenomenon have appeared in the literature (Berle & Means 1932; Simon 1959; Williamson 1964; Leibenstein 1966; Marris & Mueller 1980; De Alessi 1983). Moreover, many industries in which nonprofits and for-profits coexist are regulated, and Alchian and Kessel (1962) argue that regulated for-profits are likely to suffer from the same managerial discretion inefficiencies predicted for nonprofits.

Since the nominally for-profit firms that compete with nonprofits may not seek to maximize their profits, models that assume profit maximization are flawed. It would seem to be preferable to derive the objectives of each type of firm explicitly from the legal constraints defining each sector and the market structure. Some tentative progress in this direction has been achieved by Clarkson (1980), but other technical problems must be resolved before firm and meaningful conclusions are derived from this approach.

### Tests of Property-Rights Theories

Many nonprofit firms receive few or no donations. Property-rights theorists extend their models to commercial nonprofits that receive tax and/or regulatory advantages. The industry most frequently analyzed by such theorists is the health insurance market.

Three types of firms compete in health insurance: the Blues (Blue Cross/Blue Shield, organized as commercial nonprofits), mutual firms (consumer cooperatives that distribute the residual to policyholders in the form of dividend checks), and for-profit firms. Property rights are most attenuated in the Blues and least attenuated in for-profits. Blues had regional monopolies during all the periods studied, and for-profit and mutual health insurance markets were reasonably competitive, with easy entry (Frech & Ginsburg 1981).

impossible to inhibit self-dealing by nonprofit managers, dishonest managers might prefer to work in the nonprofit sector in order to obtain a share of the tax and other subsidies granted this sector (Clark 1980).

The property-rights model implies that Blues would purchase more managerial emoluments, which can be approximately measured by reported expenditures on administration (per claim processed, per enrollee, per dollar of claims paid, or as a share of premiums paid, depending on the study). Differences in administrative costs survive competition because Blues are typically granted a 2 percent lower tax rate on premiums. Frech and Ginsburg (1981) calculate that when Blue Cross administrative costs are 30 percent higher than a competitor's, overall costs are typically only 2 percent higher, so the Blues' tax advantage allows up to 30 percent administrative inefficiency. However, the tax advantage enjoyed by Blues varies from state to state. Property-rights theorists predict that Blues will have higher average administration costs and that larger tax differentials will be positively correlated with higher Blue costs.

These predictions have been statistically tested by a number of authors[12] using multiple-regression analysis (which attempts to find out how much of the variation in administrative costs is due to tax differentials or property-rights differences and how much to other factors, such as level of coverage, local cost of living, and so on). Not surprisingly, results were mixed, and each study developed its own flaws. Most of the studies confirm property-rights hypotheses, but Blair, Jackson, and Vogel (1975) and Kass and Pautler (1981) suggested contrary conclusions. Overall, I find the evidence in support of administrative inefficiency to be more persuasive.

Property-rights hypotheses have also been tested with data on nursing homes and hospitals. Borjas, Frech, and Ginsburg (1983) tested M. Feldstein's (1971, 68) philanthropic wage conjecture—that the "rents of nonprofit organizations are partly 'spent' in overpaying workers as a philanthropic or charitable act"—using data from the nursing home industry. They obtained mixed results: church-related nursing homes pay significantly lower wages and other nonprofit nursing homes pay insignificantly higher wages than for-profit homes. Schlenker and Shaughnessy (1984) analyzed overall costs and nursing costs in Colorado nursing homes. They found that nonprofit nursing homes had significantly higher costs even after controlling for differences in case mix and quality of care.

Other studies have compared costs at for-profit and nonprofit hospitals,[13] attempting to uncover the portion of the cost difference that is due to nonprofit status per se, but many of these studies failed to control for case-mix differences that were due to cream-skimming by for-profit hospitals. Bays (1979) controlled for case-mix differences and concluded

12. See Blair, Ginsburg, and Vogel (1975), Blair, Jackson, and Vogel (1975), Frech (1976, 1980), Vogel and Blair (1976), Vogel (1977), Frech and Ginsberg (1978, 1981), Berman (1978), Kass and Pautler (1979, 1981), and Eisenstadt and Kennedy (1981).

13. See Cohen (1963, 1970), Berry (1967), Carr and Feldstein (1967), Ingbar and Taylor (1968), Francisco (1970), Clarkson (1972), Ruchlin, Pointer, and Cannedy (1973), Rafferty and Schweitzer (1974), Lewin (1978), Vignola (1979), and the discussion in Clark (1980, 1460–62).

that for-profits are, in general, no less costly than nonprofits, but that chain for-profits are significantly less costly. This finding supports the contention that not all for-profits are efficient and is consistent with the Steinwald and Neuhauser (1970) argument that hospitals managed by physician-owners (a typical arrangement for nonchain for-profits) are less efficient than a typical for-profit because the physicians must divide their time between medical practice and management. Bays (1979) also speculates that the cost difference may be due to economies of scale in management that are attainable only by a chain of hospitals.

A different approach is taken in Wilson and Jadlow (1982). To minimize the impact of case-mix differences, they examined the provision of nuclear medicine services by hospitals. These services are generally offered by a self-contained unit within the hospital, and there appear to be no systematic differences among for-profit, nonprofit, and government nuclear medicine units in caseload or types of services offered. Using a variety of statistical techniques, they found that the legal status of the hospital explained 19 to 22 percent of the variation in hospital efficiency, and for-profits were significantly more efficient than nonprofits. It should be noted that their definition of efficiency is a narrow one: they examined whether outputs were maximal given the chosen input combinations but did not examine whether the input and output proportions were the correct ones (in economic jargon, they looked at technical efficiency, ignoring productive and allocative efficiency).

#### Competition among Nonprofit Firms

Very little attention has been devoted to analyzing the effect of competition among nonprofits in an industry containing only nonprofit firms. Rose-Ackerman's analysis (1982b) of competition among nonprofit firms that receive all their revenue from donations is illuminating. In her model, new nonprofit firms enter the market whenever the potential net revenues from a fund-raising campaign are positive, an assumption she admits is extreme for certain types of analysis. In the long run, entry eliminates all net returns from fund-raising; thus firms wasting resources on managerial emoluments are driven out of business (the article does not discuss slack, but this implication seems clear). A certain type of inefficiency is thereby eliminated, though a different sort replaces it: fund-raising continues in the long run (a firm that eliminated fund-raising would go out of business) even though the net return from fund-raising is zero.

The only empirical study of the effect of competition among nonprofits seems to be the analysis of the medical research charity market provided by Feigenbaum (1983). She argues that donors are unable to monitor the efficiency of their donations (in terms of the quantity and quality of output resulting from their donation), and governmental and umbrella group monitoring is imperfect, allowing managers to divert some resources toward emoluments. Competition among nonprofits does not reduce this inefficiency directly (owing to the monitoring problem) but indirectly reduces emoluments through effects on fund-raising activities. In a highly competitive market, firms must devote a greater share of their slack resources to fund-raising and reduce spending on emoluments.

This prediction was confirmed by regression analysis, which revealed that charities in highly competitive markets spent on average over 20 percent less revenue on administration than charities in less competitive areas, and fund-raising costs were 10 percent higher in competitive markets. Research expenditures constitute a greater share of revenues for larger firms, which are presumably monitored more closely by donors and the IRS. However, one prediction of the model was not borne out. Competition should affect only the allocation of slack between fund-raising and administrative expenditures, not the shares of revenues devoted to slack and to research expenditures; yet Feigenbaum found that competition significantly increases research share. If this result can be explained and replicated, it would seem to imply that efforts at merging charities to avoid "needless" overlap and duplication are misguided (see also Rose-Ackerman 1983).

#### Competition with Government

Although Rose-Ackerman (1981) has analyzed the effects of government grants on nonprofit firm performance, I am unaware of any work that discusses the effects of direct government competition in service provision. Property-rights and public-choice theorists are fond of arguing that governments are inefficient providers of service. Indeed, Niskanen (1971) modeled the behavior of government bureaus in the same fashion that he modeled the behavior of nonprofit firms. Borjas, Frech, and Ginsburg (1983) found that government-owned nursing homes paid employees 6.6 percent more than for-profits (about 10 percent more than church-related nonprofits and 5 percent more than other nonprofits), and Wilson and Jadlow (1982) found that nuclear medicine units in government hospitals produced significantly lower outputs at each level of inputs than nonprofits. Thus, it seems unlikely that governmental competition provides the same spur to efficiency that for-profit competition does.

### DETERMINANTS OF SECTORAL SHARES

Many factors have been adduced to explain the shares of output produced by for-profit, nonprofit, and governmental organizations. The few that have been tested empirically include the nature of the good or service provided and differences in the cost of provision, state regulation, and community characteristics. These factors can explain whether coexistence is expected as well as the shares provided by each sector.

Theories of the relationship between the nature of the good provided (public or private, quality observable prior to sale or only through use) and the sectoral shares are discussed by Hansmann in chapter 2 and will be dealt with only briefly here. Theories of the detailed determinants of personal and corporate donations and of foundation and government grants (which indirectly determine output shares) are reviewed in chapters 6, 18, and 19 in this volume. The effect of government provision on charitable donations, however, will be considered here, as this is a more direct intersectoral determinant. Space does not permit a general review of the determinants of government spending (Atkinson & Stiglitz [1980, chap. 10] provide an excellent introduction to the subject), though I will note the explicit considerations of voters when choosing between governmental provision and personal donations.

**Government and Nonprofit Shares**

Quite a few analysts have attempted to explain the coexistence of the third sector and government.[14] Most of this literature ignores for-profits (but see Holtman 1983), typically by restricting attention to industries in which for-profits could not compete profitably (such as welfare services, whose beneficiaries can hardly be expected to compensate a firm for services provided, or public goods industries more generally) or by assuming that for-profits are unaffected by the factors determining nonprofit and government shares. Some models examine the response of donations to changes in government expenditure on related services, but the resulting empirical analyses are subject to endogeneity bias. If, for example, a $1 million increase in government spending is correlated with a $500,000 increase in charitable donations, these models do not enable us to discern whether the government spending increase *caused* the donative increase or whether both were caused by, say, a change in tastes in favor of the service provided. At least three of the models (Seaman 1979; Roberts 1984; Steinberg 1985b) enable one, in principle, to sort out the causal from the spurious correlations by analyzing the simultaneous determination of donations and government spending.

Steinberg (1985b) suggests that the effects can be sorted out by adding local government spending to the model. When federal nonmatching aid to a community goes up, causality is much more likely to run from federal aid to local donations and local government spending than the reverse, as taste factors that might affect local community expenditures almost certainly do not cause federal aid to the community to change. In addition, this model is particularly suited for analyzing the predictions of Reagonomics that local government and charitable donations will pick up the slack when federal expenditures on social services are cut.

In Steinberg's model, both the act of giving and the total provision of the good provide utility to the donor, and these two sources of utility are imperfect substitutes for each other. That is, if you contribute a dollar to my favorite charity, I will be made happier, but my joy is not the same as when I contribute a dollar. In response to your increased contribution, my joy from my own contribution would be reduced somewhat, but not to zero.

Thus, each donor responds to the total donations of other donors and to total government spending. When government spending goes up, I would be tempted to lower my own contribution (the crowd-out phenomenon) but it would be difficult to figure out by how much since I would expect other donors to adjust as well.

Local voters would do well if they considered the effective price of local government spending relative to the effective price of donating. The effective price indicates out-of-pocket expenses necessary to provide a dollar's worth of additional service output. Both prices are reduced by federal income tax deductibility, but this does not alter the relative attractiveness of the two service-financing options. Differential efficiency affects the relative prices: if the leak of resources to managerial emoluments is greater in governments than in nonprofit firms, then nonprofits become better buys.

Two factors are somewhat more subtle. When government spending increases, private donations respond. If crowd-out is 100 percent, an increase in taxes and local government spending accomplishes nothing in the way of increased service output (the effective price is infinite). If crowd-out is negative (matching behavior), the price of output becomes quite low. Thus, all else being equal, we would expect communities with higher crowd-out parameters to rely more heavily on nonprofits.[15] This conclusion has not yet been subjected to empirical testing.

The final factor determining the effective price is the leverage effect of public provision. If I as donor devote a dollar to service provision, then total provision goes up by only a dollar. If I as politician or as decisive voter raise taxes and spending by a dollar per person, then total provision goes up by many dollars, and it costs me only a dollar. This leverage lowers the relative price of government.

When federal grants to a community go down, voters and donors face a very complicated decision process. The change in federal grants may affect the price of local government relative to nonprofit provision. There may be direct federal crowd-out (raising donations) and indirect crowd-out effects (as donors respond to induced changes in local government spending). Using the concept of Nash equilibrium to calculate long-run results, Steinberg demonstrates that any of four reactions of total spending (federal plus local plus donative) to federal spending cuts is theoretically possible—partial crowd-out (total spending falls by less than a dollar when federal spending falls by a dollar), total crowd-out (total spending is unaffected by federal spending), super crowd-out (total spending rises following federal cuts), or negative crowd-out (total spending falls by more than federal spending). The reaction is determined by the distribution of preferences in the community, and partial crowd-out seems most likely in most industries.

14. See Ireland and Johnson (1970), Hochman and Rodgers (1973), Wolpert (1977), Abrams and Schmitz (1978), YoungDay (1978), Seaman (1979), Kushman (1979), Rose-Ackerman (1981), Weiss (1981), Sugden (1982), Steinberg (1983a, 1985b), Jones (1983), Paqué (1983), Holtman (1983), Schiff (1984), and Roberts (1984).

15. Some technical qualifications to this conclusion are pointed out in Steinberg (1983a).

In Steinberg's model (1985b), nonprofit organizations are passive recipients of donations. Although this simplification allows for the derivation of certain results, Rose-Ackerman (1981) obtained results by simplifying the political model while complicating the nonprofit model. She found that, despite a general presumption that federal grants to a nonprofit firm would reduce donations, there are many circumstances where the reverse is true. Grants may be made on a matching basis, reducing the price of donation. Donors may regard grant reception as a sign that those with greater ability to monitor performance have approved the efficiency of the nonprofit firm and thus may increase their own donation. Finally, grants may encourage the organization to take a less extreme ideological position, increasing the popularity of the firm among donors.

### Empirical Studies of Government's Effect on Nonprofit Share

Steinberg (1983a) estimated his model for two industries—hospitals and recreation. A number of statistical and data problems contaminated his results, but they remain suggestive. He found that a one-dollar increase in federal grants targeted to recreation caused local government spending to fall by about 65 cents and local donations by about 2 cents. Thus, total spending increased by only 33 cents. An increase in nontargeted federal aid led to small increases in both categories of recreation spending. Results were mixed for the hospital sector, with crowd-out appearing small or negative. A reanalysis of the same data (Steinberg 1985b), which incorporated governmental user fees, found super-crowd-out in the recreation sector.

Preliminary estimates provided by Hansmann (1982) suggest that governmental competition raises the share of private nursing home output provided by nonprofit firms. He obtained a similar result for vocational schools but found that governmental competition lowers the nonprofit share of the private hospital industry. Kushman (1979) found that differing types of federal aid have differing effects on the provision of day care by local governments, nonprofits, and for-profits. The Appalachian Regional Program of federal-state aid substantially increased nonprofit care in eligible counties, at the expense of for-profit centers. However, AFDC uniformly increased day-care provision by all three sectors.

Abrams and Schmitz (1978) explained the variations over time and income class in aggregate donations with three measures of government spending on related goods. They found partial crowd-out: a one-dollar increase in government transfers per person caused a 28 cent decrease in donations. A second study by Abrams and Schmitz (1984) also found partial crowd-out when they analyzed the variation in average itemized donations across states. Donations were found to be responsive both to the percentage of families in poverty and to governmental spending, with crowd-out estimated at 30 cents on the dollar. Reece (1979) analyzed the variation in individual donations across metropolitan areas and obtained a similar result. Although the level of statistical significance was low, his estimates suggest that a 1 percent increase in government spending would cause donations to fall by 0.08 to 0.19 percent. Amos (1982) explained state variation in itemized donations with measures of state transfer payments and found that a 1 percent increase in state spending caused a 0.0005 to 0.6 percent decrease in donations. This translates to crowd-out of up to 46 cents on the dollar.

Wolch and Geiger (1983) found that both the number and the revenues of philanthropies in a community go up when intergovernmental grants constitute a larger portion of the local government budget. They also found significant inter-jurisdictional spillovers—resources of nonprofits are well explained by the income of neighboring communities. Seaman (1979) found that a local government decision to subsidize museums is well explained by the tax price of donation (as predicted in his model of simultaneous donor/voter choice), but the level of subsidy is not easily explained.

At least two studies have been conducted using foreign data. Paqué (1982), using aggregated tax data from the Federal Republic of Germany found that donations fell by 0.06 to 0.35 percent when state "social service expenditures" rose by 1 percent; state expenditures on "higher education and research" had no significant effect, but state expenditures on "health and recreation" and "cultural affairs" significantly increased donations. Thus, the literature contains statistical support for the negative crowd-out predicted for some industries by Steinberg (1985b) and Rose-Ackerman (1981). Jones (1983) explained temporal variation in charitable donations in the United Kingdom with governmental expenditure on social services and housing. He found that a 1 percent governmental increase caused donations to fall by 1.41 to 1.52 percent. Because aggregate donations are somewhat smaller in the United Kingdom, this large percentage change amounts to a small absolute change in donations—crowd-out is about one and one-half cents on the dollar. A reanalysis of the same data by Steinberg (1985c) found that crowd-out was a bit smaller (about half a cent on the dollar), but still statistically significant.

One study examined the effect of government spending on donations of time as well as money. Analyzing survey data from individual donors, Schiff (1984) found that the extent of crowd-out varied significantly with the type of government spending and the level of government doing the spending. For example, he found that a 1 percent increase in state government expenditures on noncash welfare increased donations of money to welfare organizations by 4.56 percent and decreased donations of volunteer labor by 4.96 percent. In contrast, a 1 percent increase in state cash assistance reduced donations of money by 2.88 percent and increased donations of time by 4.75 percent. An increase of 1 percent in local government welfare spending caused donations of money to rise by 0.47 percent and donations of time to fall by 0.27 percent.

### Tax and Regulatory Advantages

Tax, regulatory, and donative advantages enjoyed by nonprofit firms are often cited to explain the share of output provided by each sector, but a careful theoretical exposition of this relation has not yet appeared. We do not know exactly how nonprofit firms decide whether to utilize these cost and revenue advantages to increase their market share (by undercutting or out-advertising for-profits), build market size, increase emoluments, or all three (though an introductory analysis of this problem is presented in Frech and Ginsburg [1981]). In some cases, these advantages merely compensate for other disadvantages, such as lack of access to financial capital (Hansmann 1981c). Nonetheless, preliminary estimates provided in Hansmann (1982) strongly suggest that at least part of the tax advantage is devoted to share increases. He estimates that if three types of state tax advantages were eliminated (property, sales, and corporate income tax exemptions), the share of private nursing home beds provided by nonprofit firms would fall from the current level of 24 percent to a level of between 3 and 10 percent. He finds a smaller effect in the hospital industry, where the nonprofit share would fall from 91 percent to about 90.5 percent, and intermediate-sized effects in the primary/secondary education and vocational education industries.

Two studies by Frech and Ginsburg examined the extent to which premium tax advantages are split between slack and share goals in Blues. Residual claimants (in the form of physician-controlled boards) would utilize the cost margin to undercut competitors and increase market share, whereas other board members and staff would seek increased managerial emoluments. Their 1978 study found that the Blue Cross market share is sensitive to the size of the tax advantage; their 1981 study found that both share and cost increase with tax advantages. However, their 1981 study also found that tax advantages raise costs but do not raise share for Blue Shield plans. They explain the disparity by noting that Blue Cross plans were more tightly controlled by physicians than were Blue Shield plans during their sample period.

Regulatory advantages are not randomly imparted by political systems, nor are they always designed to maximize social welfare. Proponents of the economic theory of regulation assert that "as a rule regulation is acquired by the industry and is designed and operated primarily for its benefit" (Stigler 1971). Industries with an identifiable self-interest in regulation compete in a political arena for desired changes. The group with the largest potential net gain is likely to prevail, as it will lobby the hardest and provide the most campaign contributions.

This theory was tested by Wendling and Werner (1980) for the hospital industry. They found that passage of certificate-of-need laws, which regulate entry of new hospitals and expansion of existing hospitals, was well explained by the potential net hospital industry gains from the regulation. Specifically, "in states where the hospital industry faces strong competitive pressures and industry organization costs are low, the likelihood of enactment of certificate-of-need regulation increases" (p. 7). Further support for these theories is provided by historical analysis (Bays 1983), empirical studies of health planning agency decisions (May 1967; Hyman 1977), and opinion surveys (Havighurst 1982, 363–65). Thus, regulatory advantages seem to be explained by market structure as well as the reverse.

### Other Factors

Three facets of the good provided are important determinants of shares. First, nonprofit and governmental provision are more likely for public goods (consumption is nonrival), and for-profit provision is ruled out for nonexcludable public goods (where it is not feasible or economical to exclude nonpayers) (Weisbrod 1975). Welfare is one such good, for the benefits of poverty reduction accrue to everyone in the community. For-profit firms do not sell this good because potential buyers are hoping that someone else will pay for it so that they can benefit at no personal cost. Second, nonprofit provision is more likely in cases where the complex nature of the good and informational problems lead to contract failure (Hansmann 1980; Easley & O'Hara 1983; Weisbrod & Schlesinger 1986). Any time consumers wish to make donations, they prefer nonprofit firms because it is costly or impossible to determine whether a donation to a for-profit firm added to profits or to service. Nursing and day care are examples of another aspect of informational problems. Here, consumers may prefer nonprofit firms because they are more assured that the quality level contracted for is actually provided. Third, nonprofit provision is more likely if the demand for the good is variable and capacity must be precommitted (Holtman 1983). Emergency health care facilities are one such good—there is no time to build a new hospital when an epidemic or major accident hits a community. To my knowledge, none of these predictions has been carefully tested.[16]

Weisbrod's theory (1975) suggests that communities with more diverse preferences are likely to provide greater support to nonprofit firms, since greater diversity increases the extent to which higher than average demanders of a service will be dissatisfied with public provision. His theory has not been applied to industries in which all three sectors coexist. Feigenbaum (1980a) points out that donative provision will, in turn, reduce governmental provision, as voters take advantage of donors in order to cut back their tax burden. Thus, she predicts and tests the proposition that nonprofit provision is greater and governmental provision lower when a community is more heterogeneous (as measured by the coefficient of variation of a number of demographic variables). Analyzing income redistribution by government and by donors, her hypotheses are generally confirmed (though the level of statistical significance is low, a typical result when variables are badly measured, as they are here).

Another factor often thought to influence nonprofit share is the growth rate of overall demand for the service provided. For-profits are thought to be better able to respond to rapid increases in demand, for a variety of reasons. First, for-profits are likely to be efficiently managed because of the property-rights link. Second, for-profits often have less trouble (or face lower costs) securing capital to finance expan-

16. Preliminary evidence in support of the Holtman argument is found in Holtman and Ullman (1984), who concluded that nonpatient revenues of nursing homes (a proxy for donations) are highly related to the provision of extra capacity by these organizations.

sion. Third, the sense of community that overcomes donor free-riding incentives may not develop in rapidly growing communities (Steinwald & Neuhauser 1970). Preliminary estimates provided by Schlesinger (1980) and Hansmann (1982) confirmed this theory, but other studies of the hospital industry obtained mixed results (Kushman & Nuckton 1977; Bays, forthcoming). It is particularly difficult to test this factor, for nonprofit firms may respond one way to rapidly increasing demand when the increase is predicted long in advance and quite another way when the demand increase is a surprise. Further, if demand fluctuates (rather than growing steadily), Holtman (1983) has indicated that nonprofit firms will hold excess capacity, but for-profit firms will not. No study has properly accounted for these complications.

The final factor to be considered here is court-ordered desegregation. Desegregation seems to have led many students away from public elementary and secondary schools, but it is not immediately apparent whether private for-profit or nonprofit schools were the beneficiaries. If nonprofits respond slowly to sudden increases in demand, we would expect the for-profit share to rise. Hansmann's estimates (1982) seem to confirm this.

## SUMMARY AND CONCLUSION

Nonprofit organizations do differ from their for-profit counterparts, but the differences are not as pronounced as they first appear. Advertising is in many ways analogous to fundraising, foundations play the role of the stock market in providing initial equity capital, and sales of goods and services are important sources of revenue for both types of organization.

Although the lack of a profit motive allows nonprofits to provide needed social services in a trustworthy fashion, it also fosters inefficiency. But there can be no monolithic theory of nonprofit behavior, for the forces of competition and regulation are paramount—the functioning of each nonprofit organization depends on the level of competition by government, for-profit firms, and other nonprofits. Competition is often tempered by special regulatory and tax advantages conferred on each sector by the government, and these advantages in turn are major determinants of the respective sectoral shares. Thus, the market structure paradigm seems invaluable for understanding the functioning and performance of nonprofit organizations.

## REFERENCES


Abrams, Burton, and M. Schmitz. 1978. "The 'Crowding-Out' Effect of Governmental Transfers on Private Charitable Contributions." *Public Choice* 33:29–37.

———. 1984. "The 'Crowding-Out' Effect of Governmental Transfers on Private Charitable Contributions: Cross-Section Evidence." *National Tax Journal* 37:563–68.

Alchian, Armen, and Harold Demsetz. 1972. "Production, Information Costs, and Economic Organization." *American Economic Review* 62:777–95.

Alchian, Armen, and R. A. Kessel. 1962. "Competition, Monopoly and the Pursuit of Money." In *Aspects of Labor Economics,* 157–75. Princeton: Princeton University Press.

American Hospital Association. 1981. *Hospital Statistics—1980.* Chicago: American Hospital Association.

Amos, Orley M., Jr. 1982. "Empirical Analysis of Motives Underlying Individual Contribution to Charity." *Atlantic Economic Journal* 10:45–52.

"Antitrust and Nonprofit Entities." 1981. *Harvard Law Review* 94:802–20.

Arnould, R., and L. Debrock. 1982. "A Re-examination of Medical Society Control of Blue Shield Plans." Paper presented at the Eastern Economics Association Meeting, Washington, D.C.

Arnould, R., and D. M. Eisenstadt. 1981. "The Effects of Provider-Controlled Blue Shield Plans: Regulatory Options." In *A New Approach to the Economics of Health Care,* edited by M. Olson, 337–58. Washington, D.C.: American Enterprise Institute.

Atkinson, Anthony, and Joseph Stiglitz. 1980. *Lectures on Public Economics.* New York: McGraw-Hill.

Bartlett, Richard. 1982. "United Charities and the Sherman Act." *Yale Law Journal* 91:1593–1613.

Bays, Carson W. 1977. "Case-Mix Differences between Nonprofit and For-Profit Hospitals." *Inquiry* 14:17–21.

———. 1979. "Cost Comparisons of For-Profit and Nonprofit Hospitals." *Social Science and Medicine* 13(c):219–25.

———. 1983. "Why Most Private Hospitals are Nonprofit." *Journal of Policy Analysis and Management* 2:366–85.

———. Forthcoming. "Patterns of Hospital Growth: The Case of Profit Hospitals." *Medical Care.*

Bendick, M., Jr. 1979. "Essays on Education as a Three Sector Industry." In *The Voluntary Nonprofit Sector,* edited by Burton Weisbrod. Lexington, Mass.: D. C. Heath.

Ben-Ner, Avner. 1986. "Nonprofit Organizations: Why Do They Exist in Market Economies?" In *The Economics of Nonprofit Institutions: Studies in Structure and Policy,* ed. Susan Rose-Ackerman. New York: Oxford Univ. Press.

Berle, A., and G. Means. 1932. *The Modern Corporation and Private Property.* New York: Macmillan.

Berman, H. 1978. "Comment" (on Frech and Ginsberg chapter

in same book). In *Competition in the Health Care Sector: Past, Present and Future,* edited by W. Greenberg, 189–206. Germantown, Md.: Aspen Systems.

Berry, R. 1967. "Returns to Scale in the Production of Hospital Services." *Health Service Resources* 2:123.

Blair, Roger, Paul B. Ginsburg, and Ronald J. Vogel. 1975. "Blue Cross–Blue Shield Administration Costs: A Study of Non-Profit Health Insurers." *Economic Inquiry* 13:55–70.

Blair, Roger, J. R. Jackson, and Ronald Vogel. 1975. "Economies of Scale in the Administration of Health Insurance." *Review of Economics and Statistics* 57:185–89.

Borjas, George J., H. E. Frech III, and Paul B. Ginsburg. 1983. "Property Rights and Wages: The Case of Nursing Homes." *Journal of Human Resources* 17:231–46.

Boulding, Kenneth. 1972. *Towards a Pure Theory of Foundations.* New York: Nonprofit Report.

Boyle, Stanley E., and Philip Jacobs. 1979. "Fundraising Costs." *Philanthropy Monthly,* April, pp. 5–12.

Buchanan, James M. 1965. "An Economic Theory of Clubs." *Economica* 32:1–14.

Carlson, Robert, J. Robinson, and J. M. Ryan. 1971. "An Optimization Model of a Nonprofit Agency." *Western Economic Journal* 9:78–86.

Carr, W. J., and P. J. Feldstein. 1967. "The Relationship of Cost to Hospital Size." *Inquiry* 4:45.

Caulfield, Stephen. 1981. *Cross Subsidies in Hospital Reimbursement.* Washington, D.C.: Government Research Corporation.

Clark, Robert C. 1980 "Does the Nonprofit Form Fit the Hospital Industry?" *Harvard Law Review* 92:1416–89.

Clarkson, K. 1972. "Some Implications of Property Rights in Hospital Management." *Journal of Law and Economics* 15:363–85.

———. 1979. "Economics of Art Museums." Paper presented at the Conference on Institutional Choice, Madison, Wis., October 23–25.

———. 1980. "Managerial Behavior in Nonproprietary Organizations." In *The Economics of Nonproprietary Organizations,* edited by K. Clarkson and D. Martin. Greenwich, Conn.: JAI Press.

Coelen, C., F. Glantz, and D. Calore. 1979. *Day Care Centers in the U.S., Final Report of the National Day Care Study.* Vol. 3. Cambridge, Mass.: Abt Associates.

Coelho, P. 1976. "Rules, Authorities, and the Design of Not-for-Profit Firms." *Journal of Economic Issues* 10:416–28.

Cohen, H. A. 1963. "Variations in Cost among Hospitals of Different Sizes." *Southern Economics Journal* 33:355.

———. 1970. "Hospital Cost Curves with Emphasis on Measuring Patient Care Output." In *Empirical Studies in Health Economics,* edited by H. E. Klarman. Baltimore: Johns Hopkins University Press.

Cook, Richard V., Nancy L. Steketee, and Stanley Wenocur. 1981. *Study of United Way Donor Option Program.* Washington, D.C.: National Committee for Responsive Philanthropy.

Day, George S., William F. Massy, and Allan D. Shocker. 1978. "The Public Policy Context of the Relevant Market Question." In *Public Policy Issues in Marketing,* edited by John F. Cady. Cambridge, Mass.: Marketing Science Institute.

Day, George S., Allan D. Shocker, and Rajendra K. Srivastava. 1979. "Customer-Oriented Approaches to Identifying Product-Markets." *Journal of Marketing* 43:8–19.

De Alessi, L. 1983. "Property Rights, Transaction Costs and X-Efficiency." *American Economic Review* 73:64–81.

Downing, Paul B., and Gordon Brady. 1981. "The Role of Citizen Interest Groups in Environmental Policy Formation." In *Nonprofit Firms in a Three Section Economy,* edited by M. White. Washington, D.C.: Urban Institute.

Dye, Richard F. 1980. "Contributions of Volunteer Time: Some Evidence on Income Tax Effects." *National Tax Journal* 33:89–93.

Easley, David, and Maureen O'Hara. 1983. "The Economic Role of the Nonprofit Firm." *Bell Journal of Economics* 14:531–38.

Ehrlich, Isaac, and Lawrence Fisher. 1982. "The Derived Demand for Advertising: A Theoretical and Empirical Investigation." *American Economic Review* 72:366–88.

Eisenstadt, David, and Thomas Kennedy. 1981. "Control and Behavior of Nonprofit Firms: The Case of Blue Shield." *Southern Economic Journal* 47:26–36.

Ellman, Ira M. 1982. "Another Theory of Nonprofit Corporations." *Michigan Law Review* 80:999–1050.

Faine, H. R. 1972. "Unions and the Arts." *American Economic Review* 62:70–77.

Feigenbaum, Susan. 1980a. "The Case of Income Redistribution: A Theory of Government and Private Provision of Collective Goods." *Public Finance Quarterly* 8:3–22.

———. 1980b. "The Identification and Estimation of Inter-Industry Relationships within the Nonprofit Sector." Claremont Working Papers in Economics, Business and Public Policy, Claremont Colleges, Calif.

———. 1983. "Competition and Performance in the Nonprofit Sector: The Case of Medical Research Charities." Unpublished manuscript.

Feldstein, Martin. 1971. *The Rising Cost of Hospital Care.* Washington, D.C.: Information Resources Press.

Fisher, Franklin. 1977. "On Donor Sovereignty and United Charities." *American Economic Review* 67:632–38.

Francisco, E. W. 1970. "Analysis of Cost Variations among Short-Term General Hospitals." In *Empirical Studies in Health Economics,* edited by H. E. Klarman, 321–32. Baltimore: Johns Hopkins University Press.

Frech, H. E., III. 1976. "The Property Rights Theory of the Firm: Empirical Results from a Natural Experiment." *Journal of Political Economy* 84:143–52.

———. 1980. "Health Insurance: Private, Mutual, or Government." In *The Economics of Nonproprietary Organizations,* edited by K. Clarkson and D. Martin. Greenwich, Conn.: JAI Press.

Frech, H. E., and P. Ginsberg. 1978. "Competition among Insurers." In *Competition in the Health Care Sector: Past, Present and Future,* edited by W. Greenberg. Germantown, Md.: Aspen Systems.

———. 1981. "Property Rights and Competition in Health Insurance: Multiple Objectives for Nonprofit Firms." *Research in Law and Economics* 3:155–72.

Freeman, Richard B. 1975. "Demand for Labor in a Nonprofit Market: University Faculty." In *Labor in the Public and*

*Nonprofit Sectors,* edited by Daniel S. Hammermesh, 85–133. Princeton: Princeton University Press.

Giancola, Jeffrey S. 1984. *Unfair Competition by Nonprofit Organizations with Small Business: An Issue for the 1980s.* 3d ed. Washington, D.C.: Office of the Chief Counsel for Advocacy, U.S. Small Business Administration.

Goddeeris, John H. 1984. "Compensating Differentials and Self-Selection: An Application to Lawyers." Econometrics Workshop Paper no. 8405, Department of Economics, Michigan State University, East Lansing.

Hansmann, Henry. 1980. "The Role of Nonprofit Enterprise." *Yale Law Journal* 89:835–901.

———. 1981a. "Reforming Nonprofit Corporation Law." *University of Pennsylvania Law Review* 129:497–623.

———. 1981b. "Nonprofit Enterprise in the Performing Arts." *Bell Journal of Economics* 12:341–61.

———. 1981c. "The Rationale for Exempting Nonprofit Organizations from the Corporate Income Tax." *Yale Law Journal* 91:54–100.

———. 1982. "The Effect of Tax Exemption and Other Factors on Competition between Nonprofit and For-Profit Enterprise." Draft.

Harris, Jeffrey E. 1979. "Pricing Rules for Hospitals." *Bell Journal of Economics* 10:224–43.

Havighurst, Clark C. 1982. *Deregulating the Health Care Industry.* Cambridge, Mass.: Ballinger.

Havrilesky, Thomas, Robert Schweitzer, and Scheffel Wright. 1973. "The Supply of and Demand for Voluntary Labor in Behalf of Environmental Quality." *Proceedings of the Business and Economic Statistics Section of the American Statistical Association,* pp. 170–79.

Hay, Joel W., and Michael J. Leahy. 1984. "Competition among Health Plans: Some Preliminary Evidence." *Southern Economic Journal* 50:831–46.

Hirschoff, Mary-Michelle Upson. Forthcoming. "An Overview of Public Policy toward Private Schools: A Focus on Parental Choice." In *Private Education and Public Policy,* edited by Daniel Levy. New York: Oxford University Press.

Hochman, H., and J. Rodgers. 1973. "Utility Interdependence and Income Transfers through Charity." In *Transfers in an Urbanized Economy,* edited by K. Boulding, M. Pfaff, and A. Pfaff. Belmont, Calif.: Wadsworth.

Holtman, A. G. 1983. "A Theory of Non-Profit Firms." *Economica* 50:439–49.

Holtman, A. G., and Steven G. Ullman. 1984. "Non-Profit Firms and Donations: Some Empirical Evidence." Paper, University of Miami, Department of Economics.

Hyman, Herbert H. 1977. *Health Regulation: Certificate of Need and 1122.* Baltimore: Aspen Systems Corporation.

Ingbar, M. L., and L. D. Taylor. 1968. *Hospital Costs in Massachusetts.* Cambridge, Mass.: Harvard University Press.

Ireland, Thomas R., and David B. Johnson. 1970. *The Economics of Charity.* Blacksburg, Va.: Center for the Study of Public Choice.

James, Estelle. 1983. "How Nonprofits Grow: A Model." *Journal of Policy Analysis and Management* 2:350–66.

Johnson, Richard L. 1971. "Data Show For-Profit Hospitals Don't Provide Comparable Service." *Modern Hospital* 65:116–18.

Jones, P. R. 1983. "Aid to Charities." *International Journal of Social Economics* 10:3–11.

Joseph, Hyman, 1975. "On Interdepartmental Pricing of Not-for-Profit Hospitals." *Quarterly Review of Economics and Business* 12:33–44.

Kass, D., and P. Pautler. 1979. *Physician Control of Blue Shield Plans.* Staff Report to the FTC, Washington, D.C.

———. 1981. "The Administrative Costs of Non-Profit Health Insurers." *Economic Inquiry* 19:515–21.

Keating, Barry P., and Maryann O. Keating. 1975. "Nonprofit Firms, Decision Making and Regulation." *Review of Social Economy* 33:26–42.

Kramer, Donald W. 1981. "Foundations as a Source of Venture Capital." *Delaware Valley Agenda,* November 25, p. 9.

Krizay, John, and Andrew Wilson. 1974. *The Patient as Consumer: Health Care Financing in the United States.* Lexington, Mass.: D. C. Heath.

Kushman, J. E. 1979. "A Three-Sector Model of Day Care Services." *Journal of Human Resources* 14:543–62.

Kushman, J. E., and Carol F. Nuckton. 1977. "Further Evidence on the Relative Performance of Proprietary and Nonprofit Hospitals." *Medical Care* 15:55–67.

Lee, M. 1971. "A Conspicuous Production Theory of Hospital Behavior." *Southern Economics Journal* 38:48–58.

Leibenstein, Harvey. 1966. "Allocative Efficiency vs. 'X-Efficiency.'" *American Economic Review* 56:392–415.

Lewin, Larry. 1978. *Investor Owned Hospitals: An Examination of Performance.* Washington, D.C.: Lewin & Associates.

Long, Stephen H. 1977. "Income Tax Effects on Donor Choice of Money and Time Contributions." *National Tax Journal* 30:207–11.

Lovelock, Christopher H., and Charles B. Weinberg. 1984. *Marketing for Public and Nonprofit Managers.* New York: John Wiley.

Lynk, W. 1981. "Regulatory Control of the Membership for Corporate Boards of Directors: The Blue Shield Case." *Journal of Law and Economics* 24:159–74.

Manning, W. G. 1973. "Comparative Efficiency in Short-Term General Hospitals." Ph.D. diss., Stanford University.

Marris, Robin, and Dennis Mueller. 1980. "The Corporation, Competition, and the Invisible Hand." *Journal of Economic Literature* 18:32–63.

May, Joel J. 1967. "Health Planning—It's Past and Potential." Health Administration Perspectives no. A5. Chicago: Center for Health Administration Studies, University of Chicago.

Menchik, Paul, and Burton Weisbrod. 1981. "Volunteer Labor Supply in the Provision of Collective Goods." In *Nonprofit Firms in a Three-Sector Economy,* edited by Michelle White. Washington, D.C.: Urban Institute.

Morgan, J. N., R. F. Dye, and J. H. Hybels. 1977. "Results from Two National Surveys of Philanthropic Activity." In Commission on Private Philanthropy and Public Needs, *Research Papers,* vol. 1, 157–323. Washington, D.C.: U.S. Treasury Department.

Mueller, Marnie W. 1975. "Economic Determinants of Volunteer Work by Women." *SIGNS: Journal of Women and Culture in Society* 1:325–38.

Nelson, R., and M. Krashinsky. 1973. "Two Major Issues of Public Policy: Public Subsidy and the Organization of Supply." In *Public Policy for Day Care of Young Children,* edited by D. Young and R. Nelson. Lexington, Mass.: Lexington Books.

Newhouse, Joseph. 1970. "Toward a Theory of Non-profit Institutions: An Economic Model of a Hospital." *American Economic Review* 60:64–73.

Niskanen, William A., Jr. 1971. *Bureaucracy and Representative Government.* Chicago: Aldine-Atherton.

Oi, Walter Y. 1971. "A Disneyland Dilemma: Two-Part Tariffs for a Mickey Mouse Monopoly." *Quarterly Journal of Economics* 85:77–96.

Paqué, Karl-Heinz. 1982. "Do Public Transfers 'Crowd Out' Private Charitable Giving? Some Econometric Evidence for the Federal Republic of Germany." Kiel Institute of World Economics Working Paper no. 152, Kiel, Federal Republic of Germany.

———. 1983. "Public Subsidies to Private Charitable Giving: Some Arguments Revisited." Unpublished manuscript.

Pauly, Mark, and Michael Redisch. 1973. "The Not-for-Profit Hospital as a Physicians' Cooperative." *American Economic Review* 63:87–99.

Preston, Ann E. 1984. "The Non-Profit Firm: A Potential Solution to Inherent Market Failures." Wellesley College, Department of Economics, Working Paper no. 77.

Rafferty, J., and S. Schweitzer. 1974. "Comparison of For-Profit and Nonprofit Hospitals: A Re-evaluation." *Inquiry* 11:304–09.

Reece, W. S. 1979. "Charitable Contributions: New Evidence on Household Behavior." *American Economic Review* 69:142–51.

Rhode, William. 1975. *U.S. Private Foundation Support of Health Research and Development.* DHEW no. (NIH) 76–996.

Roberts, Russell D. 1984. "A Positive Model of Private Charity and Public Transfers." *Journal of Political Economy* 92:136–48.

Rose-Ackerman, S. 1980. "United Charities: An Economic Analysis." *Public Policy* 28:323–50.

———. 1981. "Do Government Grants to Charity Reduce Private Donations." In *Nonprofit Firms in a Three Sector Economy,* edited by Michelle White. Washington, D.C.: Urban Institute.

———. 1982a. "Unfair Competition and Corporate Income Taxation." *Stanford Law Review* 34:1017–39.

———. 1982b. "Charitable Giving and Excessive Fundraising." *Quarterly Journal of Economics* 97:193–212.

———. 1983. "Social Services and the Market: Paying Customers, Vouchers, and Quality Control." *Columbia Law Review* 83:1405–39.

Ruchlin, H., D. Pointer, and L. Cannedy. 1973. "A Comparison of For-Profit Investor-Owned Chain and Nonprofit Hospitals." *Inquiry* 10:13–23.

Rudney, Gabriel, and Murray Weitzman. 1983. "Significance of Employment and Earnings in the Philanthropic Sector, 1972–1982." Yale University, Program on Non-Profit Organizations Working Paper no. 77.

Rushing, William. 1974. "Differences in Profit and Nonprofit Organizations: A Study of Effectiveness and Efficiency in General Short-Stay Hospitals." *Administrative Science Quarterly* 19:474–84.

Sandler, Todd, and John Tschirhart. 1980. "The Economic Theory of Clubs: An Evaluative Survey." *Journal of Economic Literature* 18:1481–1521.

Schiff, Jerald. 1984. "Charitable Contributions of Money and Time: The Role of Government Policies." Ph.D. diss., University of Wisconsin at Madison.

Schlenker, Robert E., and Peter W. Shaughnessy. 1984. "Case Mix, Quality, and Cost Relationships in Colorado Nursing Homes." *Health Care Financing Review* 6:61–71.

Schlesinger, Harris. 1981. "A Note on the Consistency of Non-Profit-Maximizing Behavior with Perfect Competition." *Southern Economic Journal* 48:513–16.

Schlesinger, Mark. 1980. "Ownership and Dynamic Behavior." Paper submitted for Abt Associates Award.

Seaman, Bruce A. 1979. "Local Subsidization of Culture: A Public Choice Model Based on Household Utility Maximization." *Journal of Behavioral Economics* 8:93–131.

Simon, Herbert. 1959. "Theories of Decision Making in Economics and Behavioral Science." *American Economic Review* 49:253–83.

Sloan, F. 1981. "Physicians and Blue Shield: A Study of the Effects of Physician Control on Blue Shield Reimbursements." In *Issues in Physician Reimbursement,* edited by N. Greenspan. Washington, D.C.: Department of Health and Human Services, HCFA/ORDS.

Steinberg, R. 1983a. "Two Essays on the Nonprofit Sector." Ph.D. diss., University of Pennsylvania.

———. 1983b. "Economic and Empiric Analysis of Fundraising Behavior by Nonprofit Firms." Yale University, Program on Non-Profit Organizations Working Paper no. 76.

———. 1984. "A Comment on Motives Underlying Individual Contributions to Charity." *Atlantic Economic Journal* 12:61–64.

———. 1985a. "Optimal Fundraising by Nonprofit Firms." Virginia Polytechnic Institute, Department of Economics Working Paper no. E85–01–01.

———. 1985b. "Voluntary Donations and Public Expenditures." Virginia Polytechnic Institute, Department of Economics Working Paper no. E84–07–01 (revised June 1985).

———. 1985c. "Empirical Relations between Government Spending and Charitable Donations." *Journal of Voluntary Action Research* 14:54–64.

———. 1986. "Should Donors Care about Fundraising?" In *The Economics of Nonprofit Institutions: Studies in Structure and Policy,* edited by Susan Rose-Ackerman. New York: Oxford University Press.

Steinberg, R., and Scott Perlman. 1982. "A Study of Foundation Behavior and a Proposal for Regulatory Reform." University of Pennsylvania, Department of Regional Science, Metropolitan Philanthropy Project Working Paper.

Steinwald, B., and D. Neuhauser. 1970. "The Role of the Proprietary Hospital." *Law and Contemporary Problems* 35:817.

Steuerle, Eugene. 1977. "Distribution Requirements for Foundations." In *Papers and Proceedings of Annual Meeting.* Columbus, Ohio: National Tax Association–Tax Institute of America.

Stigler, George J. 1971. "The Theory of Economic Regulation." *Bell Journal of Economics and Management Science* 2:3–21.

Sugden, Robert. 1982. "On the Economics of Philanthropy." *Economic Journal* 92:341–50.

Thompson, Earl A. 1980. "Charity and Nonprofit Organizations." In *The Economics of Non-Proprietary Organizations*, edited by K. Clarkson and D. Martin, 125–38. Greenwich, Conn.: JAI Press.

Titmus, Richard. 1971. *The Gift Relationship: From Human Blood to Social Policy*. New York: Pantheon.

Tullock, Gordon. 1966. "Information without Profit." *Papers on Non-Market Decision Making* 1:141–59.

U.S. Department of Commerce, Bureau of the Census. 1976. *Survey of Institutionalized Persons*, Current Population Reports, Special Studies Series, p. 23, no. 69, Washington, D.C.: U.S. Government Printing Office.

———. 1979. *Statistical Abstract of the United States*. Washington, D.C.: U.S. Government Printing Office.

———. 1981. *1977 Census of Service Industries*, SC77–A–53, p. I. Washington, D.C.: U.S. Government Printing Office.

U.S. Department of Health, Education, and Welfare. 1978. *Health, U.S., 1978*. DHEW Publication no. PHC78–1232. Washington, D.C.: U.S. Government Printing Office.

U.S. National Center for Health Statistics. 1976. *Health Resources Statistics*. Washington, D.C.: U.S. Government Printing Office.

———. 1980. *Health Resources Statistics*. Washington, D.C.: U.S. Government Printing Office.

U.S. National Science Foundation. 1981. *National Patterns of Science and Technology Resources*.

United Way of America. 1982. *Donor Option*. Alexandria, Va.: United Way of America.

Urban, Glenn, and John Hauser. 1980. *Designing and Marketing New Products*. Englewood Cliffs, N.J.: Prentice-Hall.

"UW, Cancer Society, Have Pacts in 6 States." 1979. *New Haven Register*, February 12.

Vignola, Margo L. 1979. "An Economic Analysis of For-Profit Hospitals." Paper presented at the Western Economic Association Meeting, Las Vegas, Nevada.

Vogel, Ronald J. 1977. "The Effects of Taxation on the Differential Efficiency of Nonprofit Health Insurance." *Economic Inquiry* 15:605–09.

Vogel, Ronald J., and Roger D. Blair. 1976. *Health Insurance Administrative Costs*. Lexington, Mass.: Lexington Books.

Weinberg, Charles P. 1980. "Marketing Mix Decision Rules for Nonprofit Organizations." *Research in Marketing* 3:191–234.

Weisbrod, Burton. 1975. "Toward a Theory of the Voluntary Non-Profit Sector in a Three Sector Economy." In *Altruism, Morality, and Economic Theory*, edited by Edmund Phelps. New York: Russell Sage.

———. 1980. "Private Goods, Collective Goods: The Role of the Nonprofit Sector." In *The Economics of Nonproprietary Organizations*, edited by K. Clarkson and D. Martin, 139–70. Greenwich, Conn.: JAI Press.

———. 1983. "Wage Differentials between the Private For-Profit and Non-Profit Sectors: The Case of Lawyers." *Journal of Labor Economics* 1:246–63.

Weisbrod, Burton, and M. Schlesinger. 1986. "Public, Private, Nonprofit Ownership and the Response to Asymmetric Information: The Case of Nursing Homes." In *The Economics of Nonprofit Institutions: Studies in Structure and Policy*, ed. Susan Rose-Ackerman. N.Y.: Oxford Univ. Press.

Weiss, Jeffrey. 1981. "The Ambivalent Value of Voluntary Provision of Public Goods in a Political Economy." In *Nonprofit Firms in a Three-Sector Economy*, edited by Michelle White. Washington, D.C.: Urban Institute.

Wendling, Wayne and Jack Werner. 1980. "Nonprofit Firms and the Economic Theory of Regulation." *Quarterly Review of Economics and Business* 20:6–18.

Wenocur, Stanley, Richard V. Cook, and Nancy L. Steketee. 1984. "Fund-Raising at the Workplace." *Social Policy* 14:55–60.

Wheatley, Steven C. 1978. "Foundation Giving in Chicago—1976." Mimeographed.

White, William. 1979. "Regulating Competition in a Nonprofit Industry: The Problem of For-Profit Hospitals." *Inquiry* 16:50–61.

Williamson, Oliver E. 1964. *The Economics of Discretionary Behavior: Managerial Objectives in a Theory of the Firm*. Englewood Cliffs, N.J.: Prentice-Hall.

Wilson, George W., and Joseph M. Jadlow. 1982. "Competition, Profit Incentives, and Technical Efficiency in the Provision of Nuclear Medicine Services." *Bell Journal of Economics* 13:472–82.

Wolch, Jennifer, and Robert Geiger. 1983. "The Distribution of Urban Voluntary Resources: An Exploratory Analysis." *Environment and Planning* 15:1067–82.

Wolpert, Julian. 1977. "Social Income and the Voluntary Sector." *Papers, Regional Science Association* 39:217–29.

Wolpert, Julian, Thomas Reiner, and Lucinda Starrett. 1980. *The Metropolitan Philadelphia Philanthropy Study*. University of Pennsylvania, Department of Regional Science.

YoungDay, D. J. 1978. "Voluntary Provision of Public Goods: A Theory of Donations." Ph.D. diss., University of Wisconsin.

# Part II
# General Considerations

# [3]

# NONPROFIT ORGANIZATIONS IN THE MIXED ECONOMY
## A Demand and Supply Analysis

by

Avner BEN-NER*

*Industrial Relations Center*

*University of Minnesota*

and

Theresa VAN HOOMISSEN*

*Humphrey Institute for Public Affairs*

*University of Minnesota*

### Introduction

Nonprofit organizations occupy an important niche in many market economies. For example, in the United States the nonprofit sector employs nearly one-tenth of the workforce while the government and for-profit sectors employ approximately fifteen and seventy-five percent, respectively. Nonprofit organizations operate almost exclusively in service industries, where they often coexist with for-profit and government organizations. The weight of the nonprofit sector in services varies from predominance in museums and social services to insignificance in professional and personal services (see Table 1 for data on New York State). The geographical incidence of the nonprofit sector also varies greatly, even when controlling for industry (see Ben-Ner and Van Hoomissen, 1989 and 1990).

* We acknowledge helpful comments on earlier drafts by Dennis Ahlburg, Benedetto Gui, Henry Hansmann, Estelle James, Egon Neuberger, Richard Steinberg and anonymous referees.

These facts suggest the broad hypothesis that the relative prevalence of nonprofit organizations depends on the nature of an industry's output, industrial organization characteristics, and economic, demographic, political and other locality-specific attributes. This paper advances a theory that explains broadly the place of the nonprofit sector in the mixed economy, building on the literature on nonprofit organizations and on organizational economics. While accepting the important role researchers commonly accord to the demand for provision of services by nonprofit organizations, we suggest that conditions of organizational supply also play a critical role in the formation and existence of nonprofit organizations. Hence the confluence of demand *and* supply factors determines the incidence of nonprofit organizations relative to other organizational forms. The most important supply factor is the ability of some demand-side stakeholders (consumers, sponsors, or donors) to ensure that the nonprofit organizations of interest to them perform according to their wishes within economic feasibility constraints. Stakeholder control is key to the ability of nonprofit organizations to correct market and government failures, hence we characterize them as (demand-side) stakeholder controlled organizations. Control by stakeholders, which is typically incomplete, is supported by the prohibition on the distribution of profits and other provisions regarding organizational structure.

The paper is structured as follows. In the next section we examine the term "nonprofit organization" and develop a conceptual framework for the analysis of organizational choice in the mixed economy. In section 2 we develop a theory of demand for nonprofit provision, identifying circumstances in which some stakeholders demand a different organizational form than the for-profit or government forms. In section 3 we elaborate on the supply of nonprofit organizations, focusing on the costs of forming and operating such organizations. The concept of nonprofit ownership, the role of the nondistribution-of-profit constraint, and the open books policy of nonprofit organizations are discussed in section 4. In section 5 we discuss the confluence of demand and supply for nonprofit organizations. Factors affecting the incidence of nonprofit organizations are analyzed in section 6, focusing on the interaction between product characteristics, attributes of stakeholders, and market size. A summary and conclusions are offered in the last section.

## 1 Theoretical Issues and Preambles

Nonprofit organizations have been characterized in various ways. For example, Hall (1987), writing from an historical perspective, defines nonprofit organizations as "a body of individuals who associate for any of three purposes: (1) to perform public tasks that have been delegated to them by the state; (2) to perform public tasks for which there is a demand that neither the state nor for-profit organizations are willing to fulfill; or (3) to influence the direction of policy in the state, the for-profit sector, or other nonprofit organizations". Economists posit that nonprofit organizations perform activities that the for-profit and/or the government sectors do not do well, and, accordingly, view nonprofit organizations as correctives to certain market and government failures[1]. Hansmann (1980) focuses additionally on the legal form of incorporation, noting that all nonprofits assume a nondistribution-of-profit constraint: all profit earned must be used to enhance production or reduce prices and cannot be distributed to administrators, employees or owners.

We expand on these views by adding supply considerations, and arrive at a different characterization of nonprofit organizations. We regard such organizations, *at their inception,* as coalitions of individuals who associate to provide themselves and others with goods or services that are not adequately supplied by either for-profit or government organizations. When inadequate provision stems not from economic infeasibility but from market or government failures, nonprofit organizations may correct these failures at their roots. They do so not (necessarily or primarily) through the benevolence of nonprofit entrepreneurs or managers, but through demand-side stakeholder (consumer, donor, or sponsor) control. Stakeholder control in nonprofit organizations eliminates, in principle, any problems of asymmetric information between two parties to a transaction, and stakeholders may safely reveal their demands and make contributions without fear of exploitation. However, stakeholder control can materialize only if certain conditions are met, and if the organization is structured in a way which facilitates exercise of such control. Thus the demand for nonprofit provision by stakeholders can be met only if some stakeholders engage also in nonprofit supply.

---

1 See Nelson and Krashinsky (1973), Weisbrod (1975 and 1988), Hansmann (1980), Ben-Ner (1986), Gui (1987), Preston (1988), and reviews by James and Rose-Ackerman (1986), Hansmann (1987), and Holtmann (1988).

Our investigation of the problem of the existence of nonprofit organizations in the mixed economy is guided by ideas in organizational economics on the choice of organizational forms[2]. The basic paradigm can be summarized in four propositions. First, every economic transaction generates both a unity and a conflict of interest between various organizational stakeholders[3]. Second, control over a transaction affords controllers a direct way to advance their interests. Third, the benefits from control and the cost of exercising it depend on characteristics of individuals and goods. Fourth, if it can be freely exchanged, control will be acquired by those for whom its net value is greatest.

The theory laid out in the remainder of the paper is based on the paradigm described above. First, there is a conflict of interest between demand- and supply-side stakeholders. Second, the nonprofit form is a potential means of control by demand-side stakeholders. Third, a nonprofit organization will be formed if some demand-side stakeholders find that the benefits of control outweigh its costs and if this net benefit is greater than the net benefit achieved by purchasing elsewhere. Fourth, nonprofits will be established by those demand-side stakeholders for whom the net value of control is largest.

We use the term "demand" in the remainder of the paper to include *all* willingness and ability to pay, even when it is purely altruistic. Thus, individuals might demand housing for the homeless and education for the handicapped even if no one in their household is either homeless or handicapped. Rather than truly expand the economic definition of demand to include such interdependent preferences – which would entail recasting key concepts in the literature on market failure – we simply append altruistic demand to traditional demand and add a potential market failure: insufficient provision of *charitable* goods. We define charitable goods as goods which do not

2 See, for example, Williamson (1985), Hansmann (1988), Grossman and Hart (1986), Ben-Ner (1991), Hart and Moore (1990), and Van Hoomissen (1991).

3 Organizational stakeholders may be classified according to their position in the supply-of-resources—demand-for-output dichotomy, and the specific supply or demand role they fulfill. Supply-side stakeholders supply resources; they may be workers, managers, providers of equity or debt, banks, parent organizations, the state, or suppliers. Demand-side stakeholders use or have an interest in the organizational output; they may be clients, customers, donors, the state or sponsors. (Hybrid stakeholders provide more than one type of input or are on both the demand and supply sides).

benefit the payer (or his/her household) directly but rather benefit a third party. Charitable goods, like public goods, have benefits which are nonexcludable and nonrival to individuals with similar preferences (housing for the homeless, for example, directly benefits anyone who is concerned about homelessness).

Demand-side stakeholders include individuals, organizations, or public bodies that either 1) pay for and consume a good (traditional consumers), or 2) sponsor the consumption of a good by someone else. Thus, demand-side stakeholders include, in addition to traditional consumers, the parents of children in day care, family members of nursing home residents, donors to charitable or public causes, local governments that contract out the provision of certain services, theater-goers, corporate foundations that make grants to local arts groups, and so forth. They do not include, however, those individuals or organizations that are only the beneficiaries of a good made available to them by others . This distinction is based on the *potential for action,* which is an important determinant in the choice of organizational form. Note that organizations – ranging from IBM to local sanitation departments to the United States Department of Housing and Urban Development to Lions Clubs to churches – are at times demand-side stakeholders. For presentational ease, the term stakeholders (without qualifier) will henceforth refer to demand-side stakeholders only.

Our theory of organizational choice is summarized schematically in Figure 1[4]. A convenient conceptual starting point (the *status quo)* is a market economy in which the for-profit sector is the key provider of goods and services, and the government and the nonprofit sectors react to failures originating in that sector. In the presence of market failure (due, for example, to public goods, externalities and asymmetric information) some stakeholders cannot get in the for-profit sector the quantity or quality they are willing and able to buy. Such stakeholders must choose among three alternatives: 1) do nothing (which results in no change in the level or nature of provision of the good or service); 2) form a coalition to lobby the government to correct the market failure via regulation, direct provision, or contracting out; or 3) form a coalition to arrange for the provision of the good to

4 Van Hoomissen (1991) analyzes in detail the issue of organizational choice. Many branches down the government trunk in Figure 1 – including government regulation, tax incentives, and the contracting-out decision – are discussed more completely there.

**Figure 1: The Choice of Organizational Form**

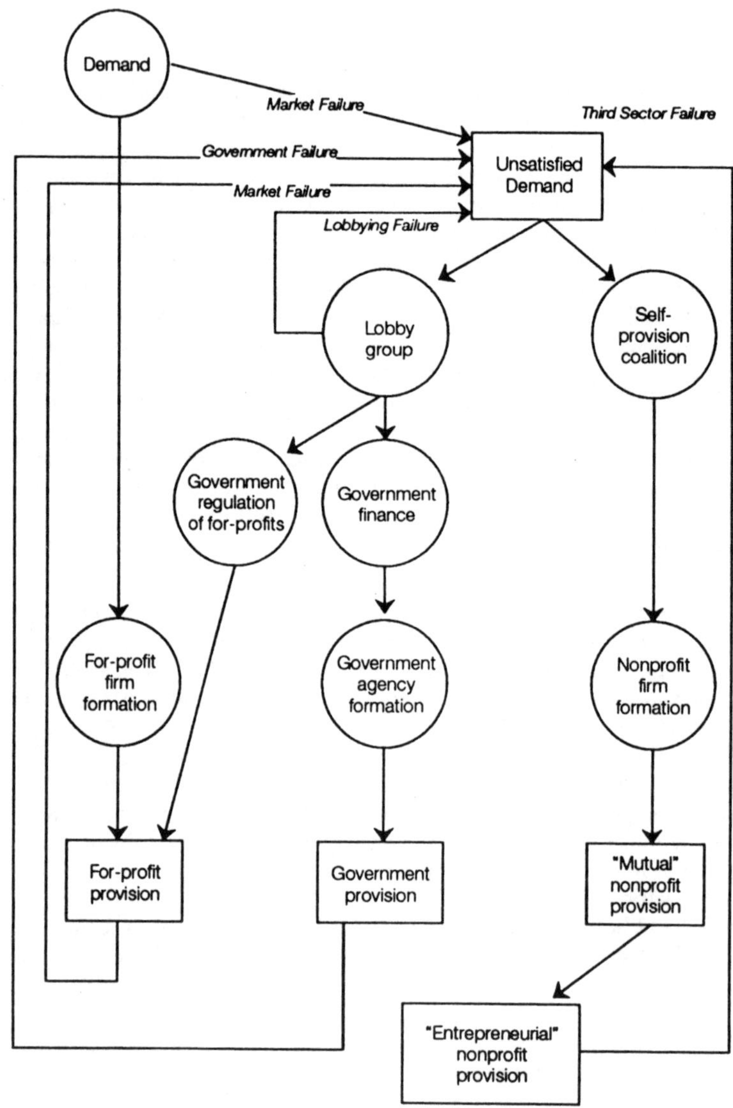

themselves. This paper examines situations in which the third option is chosen and the resulting organization adopts a nondistribution constraint. This option represents the nonprofit solution.

## 2 The Demand for Nonprofit Organizations

There is an inherent conflict of interest between demand- and supply-side stakeholders: demand-side stakeholders want more quality and quantity for a lower price while supply-side stakeholders want the opposite. Market failure exacerbates this conflict, generating a demand for alternative organizational forms. A combination of three major sources of market failure is particularly relevant to nonprofit demand: the existence of public goods and charitable goods, which we examine in terms of the underlying issues of rivalry and excludability in consumption, and asymmetric information. In many cases, government responds imperfectly to market failure, an inadequacy which is sometimes termed "government failure".

Most goods can be described according to the degree to which they are rival and excludable. The degree of excludability depends mainly on the cost of excluding nonpayers, and the degree of rivalry depends primarily on the extent to which crowding affects the quality of provision. Pure private goods are excludable and rival, pure public goods are nonexcludable and nonrival, club goods, commonly referred to as a subset of public goods, are excludable but nonrival, whereas other goods, such as air, also regarded as public goods, are nonexcludable but rival. Some goods, like a research paper, are "mixed": they are excludable but have some consumption aspects which are entirely rival (the paper copy) and some which are nonrival (the research results).

Both nonrivalry and nonexcludability play a role in the failure of markets to adequately supply public and charitable goods. For-profit firms do not adequately provide nonexcludable goods because they cannot force payment from those who wish to "free ride". Nonrival goods must be provided until marginal cost equals vertically summed marginal benefits in order for maximum net social benefit to be achieved, whereas unhindered markets will only provide a good until marginal cost equals horizontally summed marginal benefits. Optimal provision of nonrival goods, in fact, requires perfect price discrimination: each consumer must pay the value of his/her own marginal benefit at the quantity provided.

Asymmetric information may favor either stakeholders or sellers. In both cases, however, the market fails to provide goods at the same (optimal) level that they would be provided if there were no asymmetric information or, alternatively, if the conflict of interest between the parties did not exist.

There are three major situations in which asymmetric information arises to the disadvantage of stakeholders (Nelson and Krashinsky, 1973, Hansmann, 1980): (a) when there is a lag between the time of purchase and the time when the good can be evaluated, (b) when the stakeholder (payer) and the consumer (beneficiary) of the good are different entities (individuals or organizations), and (c) when the good is complex and its precise characteristics are difficult to evaluate by stakeholders. With several important exceptions, stakeholders in these situations fear that their lack of information about quality or quantity will be exploited by for-profit firms in order to enhance profit[5].

In the case of reverse asymmetric information, stakeholders fear revealing their demand schedules because the information could be used to their detriment by a for-profit firm.

Next we focus on the nature of goods to characterize the circumstances under which demand for nonprofit organizations will arise[6]. We demonstrate that two categories of goods[7], "trust" and

5 One important exception arises when firms stand to gain by establishing a reputation. A second important exception occurs when vigilant government supervision prevents firms from taking advantage of stakeholder ignorance. See Van Hoomissen (1988) for a discussion of strategies of profit-seeking firms facing imperfectly informed consumers.

6 Excludability, rivalry, and asymmetric information are not strictly intrinsic attributes of goods, but are affected by the variable circumstances under which they are transacted. One could reasonably define day care for young children provided under conditions of complete and asymmetric information as two different goods. While recognizing this, for the sake of simplicity we will mostly refer to excludability and rivalry as if they were attributes of goods, while treating asymmetric information as an attribute of both goods and transactions.

7 We are using Weisbrod's (1988) terminology, although our definitions do, in some ways, differ. For example, in Weisbrod's definition, trust goods include all goods with an asymmetric information problem for consumers, while we require also significant nonrivalry aspects.

"collective" goods, can potentially be provided more advantageously by demand-side stakeholders themselves. Asymmetric information and nonrivalry are common to both categories; asymmetric information drives stakeholders to search for a different organizational form, whereas nonrivalry makes the nonprofit form acceptable.

### 2.1 Trust Goods

We define trust goods as club goods and mixed goods for which there is an asymmetric information problem to the disadvantage of stakeholders. As noted above, in the presence of asymmetric information to their disadvantage, stakeholders suspect that for-profit firms will deceive them about quantity or quality in order to enhance profit. Thus, for trust goods, demand exists for a different organizational form, one in which profit is not the dominant motive, because it is the profit motive which gives the firm incentive to deceive.

Stakeholders of trust goods might look more favorably on an organization which is not-for-profit (i.e., adopts a nondistribution constraint), but some suspicion regarding the organization's incentives would undoubtedly remain. The not-for-profit status indicates only that the organization does not directly distribute profit, and stakeholders recognize that the incentive to deceive can arise out of other motivations as well. The organization's managers may, for example, seek to expand their salaries, perquisites, status, or power, may want to hold onto their jobs, or may wish to pursue their own preferences regarding the product of the organization.

One type of organization that will arouse more interest is one controlled by stakeholders. Because trust goods have nonrival aspects, noncontrolling stakeholders consume the same unit(s) simultaneously with controlling stakeholders; the latter can deceive others only if they are willing to "punish" themselves as well[8]. If the good were rival, controlling stakeholders could exploit others by providing them a different, relatively inferior quality-quantity-price combination, much as a for-profit firm could. Thus, stakeholder control signals trustworthiness for nonrival goods but not for rival goods[9]. We thus

8 See Olson's (1971) discussion of the closely related concept of "jointness in supply".

9 Nonrivalry can, to a certain extent, be intentionally produced. For example, an agricultural purchasing cooperative which sells fertilizer to its stakeholders members may dispense from a single and observable storage facility, from which both members and nonmembers (noncontrolling

conclude that in the case of trust goods, a demand for stakeholder-controlled organizations exists.

To illustrate some of the points made above, consider as an example a couple seeking day care for their young child[10]. They have difficulty evaluating the care provided at different centers and think it is possible that for-profit firms claim to provide higher quality care than they actually provide. They seek such indirect signals as reputation and the effectiveness of government supervision but, in their area, these signals are weak. They choose a parent-controlled nonprofit day care over others because the people on the managing committee are similar to themselves, and have also enrolled their own children. The nonprofit status of the organization further indicates lack of financial interests that may come at the expense of quality of care. An alternative scenario, considered in section 3, would have the parents join with others in similar circumstances to start a new center that then appeals to outsiders because of the parent-control. In either case, controlling parents need not be very vigil about the actions of their associates because of the nonrival nature of day care).[11]

The market for automobile repair provides a useful counter example. Stakeholders (automobile owners) often have difficulty evaluating the quality of repairs provided by repair shops and know

---

stakeholders) partake. This purposefully induced nonrivalry generates trust for noncontrollers since they are assured that the organization does not treat them differently from members and therefore does not take advantage of them. Heflebower (1980) suggests that fertilizer purchasing cooperatives came into existence because of the uncertainty regarding the quality of fertilizers sold by for-profit firms. Similarly, the famous Rochdale cooperative was founded by the local community to combat the phenomenon of adulterated flour sold by for-profit merchants. The opportunities for producing nonrivalry in rival goods seem, however, limited.

10 We use this example because it has been frequently used in the literature on nonprofit organizations to illustrate the kind of asymmetric information discussed here; see, for example, Nelson and Krashinsky (1973), Hansmann (1980), and Rose-Ackerman (1986). Day care for children also possesses important collective good attributes, discussed later.

11 See Nelson and Krashinsky (1973) for a detailed examination of the day care industry and a similar view concerning both the important role of parents and the secondary role of the nondistribution-of-profit constraint. For a view that attributes trustworthiness entirely to the nondistribution-of-profit constraint, see Hansmann (1980).

that some for-profit shops claim to provide services that they do not actually provide. In this case, however, a consumer-controlled nonprofit shop will not signal trustworthiness because the service is not nonrival: controlling stakeholders could provide quality care for their own cars and still cheat other customers. A nondistribution constraint will not imbue trust because controlling stakeholders can use amplified revenues and reduced costs to provide themselves with cheaper repair services. Thus, despite the significant asymmetric information problem, nonprofit automobile repair shops will not form, ultimately, because car repair is rival. Stakeholders must therefore either depend on reputation or participate actively in the control of a repair shop. For most stakeholders, the control option is probably costlier than the expected losses from patronizing a for-profit shop.

## 2.2 Collective Goods

We define collective goods to include pure public goods, charitable goods, and mixed goods with a large and expensive-to-produce nonrival component. These goods have in common not only nonrivalry, but also the necessity of voluntary price discrimination (donations) if they are to be provided by nongovernmental entities. Pure public and charitable goods must be paid for by way of donation because they are nonexcludable. Mixed goods with a large and expensive-to produce nonrival component require donations by high-demand stakeholders because nondiscriminating for-profit provision leaves them undersatisfied (quantity rationed)[12]. A for-profit firm that knew the demand of individual stakeholders or was otherwise able to price-discriminate (i.e., charge a higher price to high-demanders) would not ration by quantity[13].

---

12 Hansmann (1980) was first to recognize a potential role for nonprofits in this situation.

13 The intuition behind the necessity of donations for mixed goods with a large and expensive-to-produce nonrival component can be illustrated with a simple example. Opera is a mixed good because it is entirely excludable but has consumption aspects which are entirely rival (e.g., the seat at a performance) and others which are entirely nonrival (e.g., the mounting of a "production", including the nonrival directing, acting, costume and scenery). Each opera production is also very expensive to produce. Suppose there is a community with L low-demand stakeholders and H high-demand stakeholders of opera and a single for-profit provider. It is easy to show that the profit-maximizing price and quantity will leave high-demanders with excess demand if H is small enough relative to L and if the cost C of a production is high enough. Suppose the firm chooses a price P and production

The state of being quantity rationed signals high-demand stakeholders that their welfare could be increased by identifying themselves to the firm, voluntarily revealing their willingness to pay, and submitting to price discrimination. Stakeholders of pure public and charitable goods, who are also undersatisfied by for-profit provision, could do the same. The for-profit firm, however, has incentive to take advantage of the revealed information, charge inflated prices, and extract most of the consumer surplus. Thus, unless the firm consents to reveal its private cost information (accounts or audits) and make monitorable and enforceable contractual agreements on the basis of both demand *and* cost information, stakeholders will not reveal their preferences to a for-profit firm (Ben-Ner and Van Hoomissen, 1991b)[14].

In the absence of such arrangements, stakeholders of collective goods may seek an organization to which they can safely reveal demand information. A stakeholder controlled organization meets this requirement to a considerable extent. Since collective goods are nonrival, stakeholder control also indicates to noncontrolling stakeholders that the firm is operated so as to meet the unsatisfied demand of like-minded people. We thus conclude that there exists a demand for stakeholder-controlled organizations that provide collective goods.

Stakeholder controlled organizations are an instance of vertical integration between demand- and supply-side stakeholders, serving

---

quantity Q such that high-demanders want more productions but low-demanders are satisfied. (This implies that the price-quantity point is in the inelastic region on the demand curve of a typical low-demander so that increasing the price to low-demanders reduces total revenue; this is an outcome of profit-maximizing behavior. See Ben-Ner and Van Hoomissen [1991b] for details.) Consider now the circumstances in which it will not be profitable for the firm to change P or Q to satisfy high-demanders. First, note that increasing Q by one unit (staging an additional production) without increasing price will increase revenue by only H*P since low-demanders do not want more at price P. Thus, if H is small enough and C is high enough, this move will reduce profit. Second, note that increasing P (without changing Q) reduces revenue from the L low-demanders and increases revenue from the H high-demanders. Again, this will reduce profit if H is small relative to L. In sum, it will be profit-maximizing for the firm to quantity-ration high-demanders when H is small relative to L and C is high.

14 Such demand revelation may occur if one of the stakeholders is very large (e.g., the federal government or a large corporation).

as a low-cost substitute for information verification and judicial enforcement of contracts between stakeholders and sellers. High-demand stakeholders that patronize such an organization receive a superior quality-quantity-price package, although they may (voluntarily) pay more than others. This higher price may be paid through donations or through contractually specified payments, as in the case of local governments contracting out social services[15]. Only a few stakeholders-a subset of those with higher demand-need to participate in control[16].

### 2.3 Government Failure

Since governments often provide goods in an attempt to correct some market failure in the provision of public goods, their services are frequently nonrival. While government agencies determine service levels according to different criteria than for-profit firms, the outcome may resemble that which occurs in for-profit provision. Just as for-profit providers of nonrival goods may find it profitable to target the demand of 'average' stakeholders, government bodies may find it politically expedient to respond to the median voter's demand and set tax rates and service levels which leave some residents undersatisfied (Weisbrod, 1975). High-demand stakeholders may seek an alternative source to supply their unsatisfied demand. Since some market failure prevented provision by for-profit firms in the first place, the unsatisfied demand translates into a demand for nonprofit organizations when the goods in question belong to the trust or collective goods categories.

15 Like other stakeholders, government decision-makers may be in a difficult position to judge the quality or quantity provided by a private for-profit contractor or may be a high-demand buyer of a nonrival good or service that is underprovided by for-profit firms (e.g., social services). For this reason, government agencies are also a source of demand for the nonprofit form. In some cases, an agency may choose to act as a controlling stakeholder of a nonprofit organization rather than provide the service itself or interact on the market with for-profit firms.

16 This view, which applies equally to trust goods, is related to the 'voice' interpretation of nonprofit organizations (versus 'exit' in for-profit firms) by Nelson and Krashinsky (1973) and Friedman (1984, chapter 15), as well as to Williamson's (1985) interpretation of upstream vertical integration.

### 2.4 Summary of Demand Considerations

We have shown that demand for an alternative to for-profit and government provision exists for trust and collective goods, and that an organization which is stakeholder controlled may satisfy that demand. We call such firms "nonprofit organizations", although discussion of the nondistribution-of-profit constraint is postponed until section 4.

Most *goods* (in the narrow sense of the term) are rival; *services*, however, range from almost purely rival to almost purely nonrival. Services such as automobile repair and financial and legal services are essentially rival, hospital care is only somewhat rival, and day care and theater are primarily nonrival. Many nonrival services are afflicted by asymmetric information problems, suggesting a trust aspect, and many are additionally designed such that multiple consumers use the same high-cost facilities and enjoy the same quality of service, suggesting a collective aspect. Such "composite goods" include, for example, day care for children. Day care is significantly nonrival because the same physical facility and quality of service are provided to all children. And, because the nonrival aspect is produced at a relatively high cost, some parents may be willing to pay more for better day care (i.e., in accord with their preferences) than they could find on the for-profit market. This service also has trust aspects derived from the inability of parents to observe the exact care provided to their children.

## 3 The Supply of Nonprofit Organizations

The existence of demand for nonprofit organizations is insufficient to explain their existence. In the for-profit sector, entrepreneurs form new firms and satisfy existing demand because they hope to make a profit. Potential profit obviously cannot entice anyone to form a nonprofit organization. A nonprofit organization will be formed only if there is a group of stakeholders who value the expected flow of net benefits from a self-run organization more than the benefits they can derive from alternative sources and who choose not to free-ride on each other's demand revelation, contributions and control activities. The supply of nonprofit organizations is thus affected by the costs involved in their formation and operation. These entail:

- identifying and assembling a group of stakeholders willing to participate in forming and controlling an organization without receiving any direct monetary gain for that activity;

- determining that there is sufficient demand to allow for the provision of the good[17] at a price and quantity that makes the operation of the organization worthwhile to the founding body;
- assembling inputs to produce the good;
- developing and maintaining a control mechanism to ensure that stakeholder interests are pursued by the organization;
- recruiting managers whose values and personal objectives are expected to cause only limited agency problems;
- identifying and convincing high-demanders (of collective goods) that it is to their benefit to reveal their demands and provide financial support; and
- designing mechanisms to discourage some stakeholders from free-riding on the control activities of others.

Stakeholders may start the process of formation of a nonprofit organization directly by seeking out and establishing a "seed" group, indirectly through the representatives of other organizations, or with the assistance of a "nonprofit entrepreneur" who helps facilitate the establishment of a seed group. Thus, the initiative for the formation of a nonprofit organization may come from stakeholders aware of their own demand for the nonprofit form or from input providers who seek to market their inputs to a potential nonprofit organization, but in both cases demand-side stakeholders must play an active role in order for nonprofit supply to emerge.

Direct stakeholder action is the most transparent process of creation of nonprofit supply: a group of stakeholders with unsatisfied demand establish first an organizing body and then a supply organization. For example, parents of young children in a neighborhood that are unsatisfied with existing child care (or its absence) may seek each other out and consider forming a day care center, or one household may raise the issue at a meeting of their local church, community center, or cultural association. After preliminary discussions on the likely success of such an organization, a management board will be formed from among interested parents and representatives of any organization which has chosen to facilitate the parents' activities. The

17 We now again use the term "good" in the broad sense that includes services.

board will then consider the organization's feasibility in more detail, assessing interest among additional parents and perhaps hiring a consultant to provide expertise in setting up the organization and finding an administrator. The administrator will work under the direction of the board to complete the key entrepreneurial functions. Capital funds may come from interested parents, an organization whose members are interested in the services of the day care center, or a local government body committed to supporting activities that involve externalities. Once the center is in operation, the role of the board will be to determine organizational standards, policies, and long term goals, and to oversee paid administrators charged with day-to-day management. As in the for-profit sector, hired administrators may seek to free themselves from control by the board and/or affect the board's composition. Often administrators become more powerful as the organization ages and members of the founding body move on, especially if an adequate mechanism for passing on the baton has not been developed. By definition, the founding body will consist of people who have chosen not to free-ride on the control activities of others, and if a group of like-minded people does not exist among the organization's stakeholders, a control gap will develop which is often filled, by default, by hired administrators.

Often the initiative for the formation of a nonprofit organization comes from the leadership of an organization with which stakeholders are associated. Organizations such as community centers, cultural associations, churches, fraternal or political clubs, and support groups often seek to enable beneficial collective action on behalf of their members, and can assume an entrepreneurial role when demand by their members is noted. When the problem of free ridership is particularly grave, such organizations may be the primary nonprofit supply mechanism. Although direct government provision of public goods is a solution to the problem of free ridership (through compulsory taxation), political constraints and other considerations noted earlier sometimes prevent the use of this tool. In such cases, a government unit may seek to facilitate nongovernmental provision by supplying some of the entrepreneurial input and providing some financial assistance to form a new stakeholder-controlled organization, often appointing government representatives to the board of directors on behalf of the public (the free-riding stakeholders).

Another source of nonprofit initiative comes from such input suppliers as professional administrators and staff people. Because of their day-to-day immersion in a trust or collective goods industry, these professionals may be aware of the existence of unsatisfied demand (i.e., nonprofit demand) and see some potential gain to themselves from facilitating the formation of a coalition of interested parties. With this in mind, they may approach interested individuals or organizations, suggesting actions which would ultimately lead to the formation of a nonprofit organization. The motivation of such individuals may be employment, the desire to work in a particular field, and/or a purely altruistic desire to promote a valued cause (making them demand-side stakeholders). Because of the market failure associated with trust and collective goods industries, these individuals could not, even if they wanted, establish a for-profit firm.

When stakeholders are geographically dispersed, nonprofit entrepreneurs – as facilitators of the confluence of demand and supply – may be indispensable. Many national organizations (such as Mothers Against Drunk Driving and the Sierra Club) were formed by future administrators who surmised that there was enough demand to sustain these organizations. These nonprofit entrepreneurs were themselves stakeholders (had a demand for action on the issues the organization subsequently pursued), but additionally saw the potential organization as a source of desirable employment. Given the potential rewards, they proceeded to find and bring together a group of stakeholders to establish an organization, taking the risk that the organization would not succeed and their time and resources would be wasted. Once such a group was established, the remainder of the process of formation and operation was similar to the scenario developed for the parent-initiated day care center[18].

18 The Guthrie Theater in Minneapolis is yet another example of a nonprofit organization established at the initiation of input suppliers. In the early 1960s, the stage director and playwright Sir Tyrone Guthrie toured the United States in search of a community to support his theater. In the Twin Cities of Minneapolis and Saint Paul he found an "hospitable" environment: its residents were cultured, there was little professional theater, the community was relatively close knit with a strong civic spirit, and there were individuals and companies willing to support the local arts. Given this, he approached various community leaders, garnering interest and support for his theater, eventually establishing the nonprofit Guthrie Theater. In our framework, we view Tyrone Guthrie as a professional seeking desirable employment (as well as, of course, being a stakeholder of his type of theater). His search for an hospitable environment was in fact a search for unsatisfied high demanders in a community capable of exerting pressure to reduce free-ridership in the revelation of demand and the payment of donations. The

## 4 Ownership Shares, the Nondistribution-of-Profit Constraint, and Open Books

Nonprofit organizations are distinguished from both for-profit and government organizations by a unique combination of characteristics. We have discussed thus far two of these characteristics, stakeholder control and the type of goods nonprofit organizations provide (trust and collective). This section considers three additional characteristics: the lack of ownership shares, the nondistribution-of-profit constraint, and the "open books" policy.

### 4.1 Ownership Shares

Ownership of an organization can be defined as the possession of two rights: the right to control – i.e., to determine organizational objectives – and the right to returns – i.e., to dispose of any financial or physical returns resulting from the organization's activities. In the for-profit sector, these rights are divided into ownership shares, representing proportional rights to control and, returns. Sometimes these shares can be purchased and sold on an open market but if founders wish they can write into the organization's bylaws restrictions designed to keep ownership in certain hands.

Despite appearances to the contrary, nonprofit organizations are also "owned": they have objectives that are somehow fashioned and their financial and physical returns are disposed of. Instead of being embedded in shares, these rights are typically associated with one's voluntary status as a stakeholder. The absence of shares (in particular, transferable ones) in many nonprofit organizations, we posit, is primarily *a device adopted by founders to ensure the maintenance of stakeholder-control by preventing the concentration of control and return rights.* That is, founders write into the organization's bylaws (extreme) restrictions on the transferability of shares in order to keep ownership in the hands of stakeholders as a group, because they recognize that otherwise the organization may cease to be a solution

---

Twin Cities fit this description in many ways. Many other nonprofit arts organizations were formed under similar circumstances (for a recent example, compare the role of Harry Parker in the Dallas Museum of Arts with that of Tyrone Guthrie), yet many others were initiated by high-demand stakeholders (for example, New York's Metropolitan Opera and the Goodspeed Theater in Connecticut).

to the market or government failure that generated it[19]. Thus, in nonprofit organizations, the rights to control and returns are vested permanently in demand-side stakeholders generally via the absence of ownership shares. Control responsibilities are, nonetheless *delegated* (not turned over) to a minority subset of these stakeholders, either explicitly or implicitly.

4.2 The Nondistribution-of-Profit Constraint

The nondistribution-of-profit constraint (NDPC) adopted by many nonprofit organizations goes hand in hand with invisible, nontransferable ownership shares: given that demand-side stakeholders as a group are the organization's owners, the NDPC serves mainly as a distribution rule, assuring that organizational returns are not distributed to the controlling subset only[20]. Again, the organization's founders adopt this rule to ensure the organization's continued existence[21].

An organization that wishes to signal trustworthiness to its customers (in order to enhance sales and, thereby, viability) will

19 See also Ben-Ner (1986). Ellman (1982, p. 1036) states that "[e]asily negotiable, dividend-issuing equity shares, therefore, would be inappropriate [in nonprofit organizations] since they would have no purpose but to facilitate ownership by the very class of persons the organization was formed to avoid".

20 See also Gui (1990). The implied net revenue of the nonprofit organization often is not distributed equally among controlling and noncontrolling stakeholders. As we show in Ben-Ner and Van Hoomissen (1991b), the objectives of the organization, determined by controlling stakeholders, will generally tilt the distribution of net revenue in their favor.

21 The arguments regarding ownership shares and the nondistribution constraint here are essentially supply-side: founders adopt them in order to ensure the organization's continued existence. Still, this is only a supply-side concern because nonprofit demand depends on stakeholder control, and thus, as before, demand- and supply-side concerns are not entirely separable because the organization is supply oriented but controlled by demanders. Fama and Jensen (1983) argue similarly that the absence of transferable shares is a tool to prevent the development of an agency problem between donors and managers. Although they do not take the argument to its conclusion, the presumption must be that "donors" are the principals in the organization's actions (and so the organization is "donor-controlled") and the absence of transferable shares is a tool they devise to keep control in their own hands. The idea that founders impose an organizational structure that restricts future changes in the nature of the organization is also advanced by Moe (1990) in the context of government agencies.

sometimes adopt an NDPC because it suggests to buyers that the organization uses all its revenues to either improve service or reduce prices rather than pad the owner's bank account (Nelson and Krashinsky, 1973 and Hansmann, 1980). As a signal of trustworthiness, however, the NDPC is weak and imperfect because non-controlling stakeholders suspect that it can be circumvented and that managers have enough room within the constraint to pursue their own preferences. Hence an NDPC can play only a limited demand-side role, one that cannot substitute for stakeholder control.

An NDPC can also serve to discipline hired managers. In the for-profit sector, the market for the shares limits the extent that managers can pursue nonprofit goals because such behavior invites takeover by outsiders who will replace "bad" managers with better ones. Additionally, managers of for-profit firms often have a stake in the organization (through share ownership or profit-sharing schemes) which serves to align their interests with those of owners. In the nonprofit sector it is difficult to design incentive schemes that align managerial and stakeholder interests, especially because stakeholder interests are multidimensional and complex. In the presence of this agency problem, controlling stakeholders may employ the nondistribution constraint to limit self-aggrandizement by managers (Fama and Jensen, 1983, and Easley and O'Hara, 1983). Controlling stakeholders may also seek compliance with their goals by hiring "believers", managers who support the goals of the organization (Young, 1986).

A government certified and enforced NDPC can serve several additional purposes. It can indicate reduced incentive for firm misbehavior to potential buyers, and reduces monitoring costs associated with hired managers. Adoption of the NDPC, along with a charitable, public benefit or educational mission, also confers a number of tax and related financial advantages in the United States, giving stakeholder-controlled organizations yet another incentive to adopt it. These advantages include income tax exemption, unemployment insurance exemption, lower postal rates, and exemption from local property taxes in many states[22]. These benefits could not encourage for-profit owners – whose goal is to maximize shareholder returns – to adopt the NDPC.

22 See Simon (1987) for a comprehensive discussion of public policy towards the nonprofit sector.

These two government policies – subsidization via tax exemption and enforcement of the NDPC – deserve a brief comment. Policy makers, while recognizing the existence of market failure and wishing to promote the provision of undersupplied goods, who look favorably on solutions that do not require government provision, designing policies to encourage nonprofit formation, provision, and longevity[23]. Tax and other subsidies help overcome the problems of collective action by reducing startup and operation costs. Tax exemption is probably the politically most expedient method for the government to subsidize nonprofit organizations.

As time passes after the inception of a nonprofit organization, members of the founding body often move away, and control over hired administrators diminishes. As this happens, the internal agency problem intensifies and the trust noncontrolling stakeholders have in the organization – conditional on stakeholder control – weakens. For this reason the nondistribution constraint, as a support to stakeholder control and discipliner of hired managers, takes on more importance as time passes[24].

The nondistribution-of-profit constraint has negative qualities as well. Importantly, it imposes an inflexibility on the organization, forcing stakeholders to adjust prices, quantities and qualities to absorb any profit, although they may prefer to distribute it for uses outside the organization. Stakeholders will not adopt the NDPC if its net effect is to reduce stakeholder welfare. Consumer and agricultural purchasing cooperatives, for example, are essentially nonprofit organizations that do not adopt the NDPC.

### 4.3 Open Books

Another important feature found in most nonprofit organizations is their policy of making financial and managerial information public. This policy, like the NDPC, is directly related to the "invisible" ownership shares that are a hallmark of the nonprofit form. Since access to information is a prerogative of ownership (being a prerequisite for control) and since stakeholders are *de facto* owners in nonprofit organizations, an open books policy is a simple device to give owners access to internal information. Because the stakeholder

---

23 Hall (1987) suggests that in the United States, policy toward nonprofits grew out of philosophical opposition to big government combined with a desire to promote a private-sector alternative to socialism.

24 For a related analysis, see Ben-Ner (1987).

population may be unstable over time, and because direct stakeholder control can weaken as the organization ages, an open books policy which is enshrined in an organization's statutes ensures that stakeholders will always have the ability to audit the organization's activities. Thus this policy is yet another means of supporting stakeholder control. Additionally, this policy strengthens demand-side trust in the organization because it makes it more difficult for managers to employ asymmetric information in their own interest and against the interests of stakeholders[25].

## 5 The Confluence of Nonprofit Demand and Supply

The critical difference between nonprofit organizations and for-profit firms is that there must be a confluence between the demand for the organizational form and the ability to provide it in order for a nonprofit organization to be formed. Nonprofit organizations, as described here, are an instance of vertical integration by demand-side stakeholders. Although the process of nonprofit formation can be facilitated by individuals other than stakeholders, demand-side stakeholders must play an active role in forming and operating a nonprofit organization, because demand will not materialize unless the organization is stakeholder controlled. Nonprofit organizations will thus come into existence only if there are stakeholders who value the expected flow of net benefits from a self-run organization more than the benefits they can derive from alternative sources.

Stakeholders have varying demand incentives to be involved in the control and operation of an organization, and bear different costs in carrying out such activities. As a result, not all stakeholders will be actively involved in control and in the extreme, there may not be enough controlling stakeholders for a nonprofit organization to exist. In other cases, only a small minority of stakeholders will participate in control.

---

25 In their analysis of day care centers, Nelson and Krashinsky (1973:63) write: "However, while the not-for-profit legal form seems helpful in assuring trustworthy day care centers, it certainly is not foolproof. (In fact, directors of nonprofit centers can be as selfish and neglectful of children in their pursuit of power and status as their profit-seeking counterparts.) Neither is the not-for-profit organizational form absolutely necessary. What *is* most important is that day care centers be open to detailed observation by both parents and citizen groups. Day care centers must operate in a *fish bowl,* which private enterprise generally has been reluctant to do".

Stakeholders with relatively large demand have more to lose from control contrary to their preferences and so have more incentive to be involved in controlling and auditing hired managers. Even if such stakeholders are very few, other, trust seeking, stakeholders may benefit from the organization's operation relative to a for-profit firm. Some stakeholders that are neither quantity rationed nor trust seeking may benefit from a quantity-quality-price combination not available elsewhere. The fact that the ratio of controlling to noncontrolling stakeholders is low does not change the fundamental nature of the nonprofit as a stakeholder-controlled organization: the organization still exists because of a nonrivalry and/or asymmetric information problem which is solved, partly, by stakeholder control. The delegation of important decision making power to salaried managers also does not change the nature of the firm.

## 6 Determinants of the Incidence of Nonprofits

Having established that demand for nonprofit organizations exists only for trust and collective goods, we now extend the analysis to examine the major demand and supply factors that affect the existence of nonprofit organizations in particular industries and geographical areas. These factors can be classified into three interdependent categories: market size, stakeholder characteristics, and product attributes.

### 6.1 Market Size

Market size has opposite effects on the demand for nonprofits in trust and collective services. The larger a market – i.e., the larger is market demand relative to the minimum efficient scale of production – the more likely it is that diverse tastes can be satisfied in the for-profit sector because larger markets can bear more firms and thus more variants of a good. Consequently, the larger the market for a collective good, the fewer quantity-rationed high-demand stakeholders there will be and the lower will be the demand for the nonprofit form of organization.

For trust goods, a larger market size compounds the asymmetric information problem. With more firms, stakeholders must gather more information in order to be informed and firms must work harder to build a reputation. Stakeholders of this type of service must spend considerable effort to determine which firms are trustworthy, and a large market enables firms to exploit the rational choice some stakeholders make to search less than exhaustively. This will induce demand for more trustworthy stakeholder controlled nonprofit organizations.

6.2 Stakeholder Characteristics

Four characteristics of the population from amongst which stakeholders emerge play an important role in determining the incidence of the nonprofit sector: income and its distribution, education, demand heterogeneity, and social cohesion.

High income and better educated stakeholders are more capable of choosing a reliable for-profit provider of trust services because they have access to more reliable references and information sources. Poorer and less educated stakeholders are therefore more likely to rely on the nonprofit form for the provision of trust goods. For collective goods, income has a reverse effect. For many goods, high income coincides with high demand, and high demand stakeholders are the primary source of demand for nonprofit organizations in collective goods. Hence for collective goods demand for the nonprofit form is likely to be positively associated with income. In terms of ability to supply nonprofit organizations, better education and higher income are likely to reduce the costs associated with forming and controlling a nonprofit organization. Hence demand and supply considerations suggest that income and education will be positively associated with nonprofit provision of collective goods, and inconclusively and weakly with that of trust goods.

Demand heterogeneity affects the price and quantity combination set by for-profit firms and the tax and service package provided by governments in the market for collective services. The more homogeneous stakeholders are in their willingness-to-pay, the less likely it is that there will be dissatisfaction with for-profit or government provision of collective goods. Conversely, demand heterogeneity enhances demand for nonprofit provision of collective goods. As for trust goods, there appears to be no connection between demand heterogeneity and nonprofit demand. Demand heterogeneity depends on the distribution of income, and on social, cultural and religious differences that generate preference heterogeneity. Hence income inequality and social and cultural diversity in a particular geographic area are likely to enhance the demand for nonprofit organizations in collective services[26].

26 Weisbrod (1975) points out that taste heterogeneity is positively correlated with nonprofit provision. James (1987a and b) also emphasizes the role of taste heterogeneity in the provision of nonprofit education.

Social cohesion depends positively on the degree of shared economic, religious, cultural, ethnic and educational background, and negatively on the degree of geographic dispersion among stakeholders for a given market size. Related stakeholders have more opportunity to meet each other and identify common demand, can more easily exercise social pressure to prevent free ridership in the revelation of demand and payment for services, and can control an organization more cheaply. Stakeholders that belong to a common organization (e.g., a church, community center, or social club) may also find it cheaper to employ that organization to form or manage another nonprofit organization. Often, the goals of the "parent" organization are unrelated to those of the nonprofit organization (see also Olson, 1971). Examples of such situations are numerous: day care centers operated by churches[27], homeless shelters established by community centers, theaters supported by large local companies, neighborhood-association sponsored food stores (cooperatives), ski clubs sponsored by workplaces, and banking institutions operated by trade unions.

In sum, the supply of nonprofit organizations is likely to be greater in communities where diverse but internally cohesive groups exist[28]. This supply-side effect is strengthened by the demand-side finding that demand heterogeneity, which is greater in communities where diverse groups exist, also stimulates nonprofit provision.

### 6.3 Product Attributes

We established earlier that the demand for nonprofit provision is restricted to trust and collective goods, which are characterized by various degrees of nonexcludability, nonrivalry and asymmetric information. The greater these degrees, the greater is the probability that a good will be provided by a nonprofit organization. For example, among health services, facility-intensive care has stronger collective attributes than care that can be administered in the office of a family practitioner. Thus while demand for nonprofit provision may exist for both types of care, the demand is likely to be stronger for facility-intensive care. Similarly, all things equal, day care for children, which has both trust and collective attributes, is a more likely candidate for nonprofit provision than elementary or higher education,

27 But not all church-operated day care centers fall within this category, as some may be directed, for example, at spreading religion.

28 See Galaskiewicz (1985) and James (1987a and b) for discussions of the relationship between community networks and nonprofit provision.

which have weak trust aspects[29].

Demand for the nonprofit form depends not only on the strength of a good's trust or collective attributes, but also on the total utility that the good provides to stakeholders. For a given cost of participating in the formation and control of a nonprofit organization, high utility goods are more likely to be candidates for nonprofit provision than other goods. Utility may be measured in terms of expense relative to total budget, which indicates potential utility gain, or in terms of the size of the loss if provision is unsatisfactory.

## 7 Conclusions

The theory presented in this paper synthesizes and expands on extant theories, especially those of Weisbrod (1975) and Hansmann (1980). In terms of Figure 1, Hansmann's theory can be summarized by arrows from 'Demand' to 'Unsatisfied Demand' (via market failure), and from there directly to 'Nonprofit Provision'. The Weisbrod theory can be summarized by arrows from 'Demand' to 'Unsatisfied Demand' (via market failure), from there directly to 'Government Provision', back to 'Unsatisfied Demand' (via government failure), and then to 'Nonprofit Provision'. While these analyses provide important insights into the role of the nonprofit sector, neither provides a complete motivation for the formation of nonprofit organizations, and both ignore the steps between unsatisfied demand and nonprofit provision. However, these steps are crucial, as no organization comes into existence just because of the existence of demand. Moreover, the conditions of the supply of the nonprofit form of organization differ from those of both for-profit and government organizations. A nonprofit organization will be formed only if a group of interested stakeholders (individuals or organizations) has the ability to exercise control over the organization. Stakeholder control is a *sine qua non* for the existence of nonprofit organizations, because it avails the trust required for patronizing the organization, revealing demand to it, and making donations to it. These are key elements in the demand for nonprofit organizations, and must be satisfied for these organizations to exist. Nonprofit organizations are thus a case in which demanders must generate their own supply.

29 For further discussion of differences in the degree of trust and collective attributes of goods in different industries, see Ben-Ner and Van Hoomissen (1990).

However, only those stakeholders who anticipate that the benefits of control outweigh its costs will participate in the formation and control of a nonprofit organization. This net benefit must also be greater than the net benefit achieved by purchasing elsewhere. Noncontrolling stakeholders will also purchase from the nonprofit organization, trusting it because of the nonrivalry of its services (which suggests that they cannot be exploited by controlling stakeholders who partake in the consumption of the same units), or simply preferring its price-quantity-quality package over that of other organizations.

Direct control by stakeholders is never complete, and the residual agency problem may deter stakeholders from patronizing it. In order to enhance stakeholder control, founders of nonprofit organizations impose an organizational structure aimed at guarding their present and future group interests. Three prominent features of this structure include (a) the absence of ownership shares, (b) the nondistribution-of-profits constraint, and (c) the open books policy. Respectively, these (a) prevent concentration of control in the hands of a few stakeholders-owners, (b) enhance control over hired managers, serve as a distribution of economic surplus rule, and signal the reinvestment of the surplus in the organization, and (c) ensure free access to information required for the exercise of control. In addition, the statutes of nonprofit organizations vest formal control in boards of directors representing stakeholders.

Clearly, not all stakeholders will have equal demand for nonprofit organizations, nor will they all have similar abilities to control them. Factors such as stakeholders' education, income, social cohesion, and demand heterogeneity affect both the degree to which they suffer from market and government failures and therefore their demand for nonprofit provision, as well as their ability to provide the requisite conditions for nonprofit supply, primarily the ability to exercise control. Thus the geographical prevalence of nonprofit organizations will depend on characteristics of stakeholders in different communities[30].

The industrial incidence of nonprofit organizations depends on attributes of different goods and services. The primary attributes that are relevant to nonprofit provision are the degrees of excludability, rivalry and informational asymmetries that are associated with dif-

30 We explore these issues empirically in Ben-Ner and Van Hoomissen (1991a), providing support for the main hypotheses presented in this paper.

ferent goods. On this basis we concluded that services rather than consumer goods are the most likely candidates for nonprofit provision. Table 1, which presents the industrial distribution in New York State, confirms this hypothesis. Furthermore, among services, industries with stronger rivalry, nonexcludability, and asymmetric information attributes, such as health and social services, are heavily populated by nonprofit organizations, whereas services with strong private good attributes (essentially nonrival and excludable), such as personal and financial services, are provided mainly by the for-profit sector. These hypotheses are broadly confirmed by the industrial distribution figures presented Table 1.

**Table 1: For-Profit, Nonprofit and Government Employment Shares In New York State, by Industry Group 1987, In percent**

| | For-profit | Nonprofit | Government |
|---|---|---|---|
| ALL SERVICES | 51 | 21 | 28 |
| Financial Services | 95 | 1 | 3 |
| Personal and Business Services | 99 | 1 | 0 |
| Amusement & Recreation | 79 | 8 | 12 |
| Health Services | 31 | 47 | 22 |
| Legal Services | 97 | 3 | 0 |
| Education & Libraries | 3 | 32 | 65 |
| Social Services | 9 | 87 | 4 |
| Museums, Bot. & Zoo. Gardens | 1 | 92 | 6 |
| Membership Organizations | 39 | 61 | 0 |
| Other Services (prof'l, etc.) | 98 | 0 | 1 |
| Government | 0 | 0 | 100 |
| ALL NON-SERVICES | 92 | 1 | 7 |
| Agriculture | 99 | 1 | 0 |
| Mining | 100 | 0 | 0 |
| Construction | 100 | 0 | 0 |
| Manufacturing | 100 | 0 | 0 |
| Transportation | 78 | 0 | 22 |
| US Postal Service | 0 | 0 | 100 |
| Communications | 99 | 1 | 0 |
| ALL OTHER INDUSTRIES | 98 | 0 | 2 |
| Commerce | 99 | 1 | 0 |
| Printing & Publishing | 76 | 0 | 24 |
| Electricity, Gas & Sanitation | 99 | 0 | 1 |
| ALL INDUSTRIES | 73 | 11 | 17 |

(1)Reproduced from Ben-Ner and Van Hoomissen (1990), where sources for the data are given.
(2)Totals may not add up to 100 due to rounding.
(3)The nonprofit sector here comprises organizations covered by section 501(c)(3) of the United States Internal Revenue Code. Other nonprofits (mostly in membership organizations) are included as for-profit organizations. The 501(c)(3) segment employs about 92% of the nonprofit sector workforce (Rudney, 1987).

## REFERENCES

BEN-NER A., 1986, "Nonprofit Organizations: Why Do They Exist in Market Economies?" in *The Economics of Nonprofit Institutions: Studies in Structure and Policy,* ed. Susan Rose-Ackerman, 94-113, Oxford, Oxford University Press.

——, 1987, "Birth, Change and Bureaucratization in Nonprofit Organizations: An Economic Analysis", in *Politics, Public Policy and the Voluntary Sector,* ed. Robert Herman, 119-137, Proceedings of the Fifteenth Annual Meeting of the Association of Voluntary Action Scholars.

——, 1991, "Cooperation. Conflict, and Control in Organizations", Forthcoming in Samuel Bowles, Herbert Gintis and Bo Gustafsson (eds.), *Democracy and Markets: Participation, Accountability and Efficiency,* Cambridge, Cambridge University.

BEN-NER A. and VAN HOOMISSEN T., 1989, *A Study of the Nonprofit Sector in New York State; Its Size, Nature, and Economic Impact,* Albany, NY, The Nelson A. Rockefeller Institute of Government.

——, 1990, "The Nonprofit Sector's Growth in the 1980s : Facts and Causes", in *Nonprofit Management and Leadership* 1(2): 99-116.

——, 1991a, "An Empirical Investigation of the Joint Determination of the Size of the For-Profit, Nonprofit and Government Sectors", University of Minnesota, Mimeo.

——, 1991b, "The Provision of Mixed Goods: Markets, Contracts, and Consumer Control", University of Minnesota, Mimeo.

BERGSTROM T. and GOODMAN R., 1973, "Private Demand for Public Goods", in *American Economic Review* 63: 280-96.

DUBIN J. and NAVARRO P., 1988, "How Markets for Impure Public Goods Organize: The Case of Household Refuse Collection", in *Journal of Law, Economics, and Organization* 4(2): 217-41.

EASLEY D. and O'HARA M., 1983, 'The Economic Role of Nonprofit Firms", in *Bell Journal of Economics* 14:531-38.

ELLMAN I., 1982, "Another Theory of Nonprofit Corporations", in *Michigan Law Review* 80: 999-1050.

FAMA E. and JENSEN M., 1983, "Separation of Ownership and Control", in *Journal of Law and Economics* 26: 301-25.

FRIEDMAN L., 1984, *Microeconomic Policy Analysis,* Mc Graw-Hill.

GALASKIEWICZ J., 1985, *Social Organization of an Urban Grants Economy: A Study of Business Philanthropy and Nonprofit Organizations,* Orlando, Academic Press.

GROSSMAN S., and HART O., 1986, "The Costs and Benefits of Ownership: A Theory of Vertical and Lateral Integration", in *Journal of Political Economy*, 94 (August): 691-719

GUI B., 1987, "Productive Private Nonprofit Organizations: A Conceptual Framework", in *Annals of Public and Cooperative Economics* 58(4): 415-35.

——, 1990, "The 'Non-Distribution Constraint' in Economic Organizations", in *Ricerche Economiche*, XLIV(1): 115-30.

HALL, DOBKIN P., 1987, "A Historical Overview of the Private Nonprofit Sector", in *The Nonprofit Sector: A Research Handbook,* ed. Walter W. Powell, 3-26, New Haven, Yale University Press.

HANSMANN H., 1980, "The Role of Nonprofit Enterprise", in *Yale Law Journal*, 89: 835-98.

——, 1987, "Economic Theories of Nonprofit Organization", in *The Nonprofit Sector: A Research handbook,* ed. Walter W. Powell, 27-42, New Haven, Yale University Press.

——, 1988, "The Ownership of the Firm", in *Journal of Law, Economics, and Organization* 4:267-304.

HART O. and MOORE J., 1990, "Property Rights and the Nature of the Firm", in *Journal of Politicial Economy,* 98 (December), 1119-58.

HEFLEBOWER R.B., 1980, *Cooperatives and Mutuals in the Market System,* Madison, WI, University of Wisconsin Press.

HOLTMANN A., 1988, "Theories of Nonprofit Organizations", in *Journal of Economic Surveys,* 2.

JAMES E., 1987a, "The Political Economy of Private Education in Developed and Developing Countries", in *World Bank Discussion Paper* EDT 81.1987.

——, 1987b, "The Public/Private Division of Responsibility for Education: An International Comparison" in *Economics of Education Reciew*.

JAMES E. and ROSE-ACKERMAN S., 1986, "The Nonprofit Enterprise in Market Economies", in *Fundamentals of Pure and Applied Economics,* eds. Jacques Lesourne and Hugo Sonnenschein, New York, Harwood Academic Publishers.

MOE T. M, 1990, «The Politics of Structural Choice: Toward a Theory of Public Bureaucracy", in *Organization Theory: From Chester Barnard to the Present and Beyond,* ed. Oliver E. Williamson, Oxford, Oxford University Press.

NELSON R.R. and KRASHINSKY M., 1973, "Two Major Issues of Public Policy : Public Subsidy and the Organization of Supply", in *Public Subsidy for Day Care of Young Children,* eds. Richard Nelson and Dennis Young, Lexington, MA, D.C. Heath.

OLSON M., 1971, *The Logic of Collective Action,* Cambridge, MA: Harvard University Press.

PRESTON A., 1988, "The Nonprofit Firm: A Potential Solution to Inherent Market Failures", in *Economic Inquiry* 26: 493-506.

ROSE-ACKERMAN S., 1986, "Altruistic Nonprofit Firms in Competitive Markets: The Case of Day-Care Centers in the United States", *Journal of Consumer Policy,* 9: 291-310.

RUDNEY G., 1987, "The Scope and Dimensions of Nonprofit Activity», in *The Nonprofit Sector: A Research Handbook,* ed. Walter W. Powell, 55-64, New Haven, Yale University Press.

SIMON J. G., 1987, "The Tax Treatment of Nonprofit Organizations: A Review of Federal and State Policies", in *The Nonprofit Sector: A Research Handbook,* ed. Walter W. Powell, 67-98, New Haven, Yale University Press.

VAN HOOMISSEN T., 1988, "Price Dispersion and Inflation: Evidence from Israel", in *Journal of Political Economy,* 96 (December): 1303-14.

——, 1991, "On the Choice of Organizational Form", University of Minnesota, Mimeo.

WEISBROD, B. A., 1975, "Toward a Theory of the Voluntary Nonprofit Sector in a Three-Sector Economy", in *Altruism, Morality and Economic Theory,* ed. Edmund Phelps, 171-95, New York: Russell Sage Foundation.

——, 1988, *The Nonprofit Economy,* Cambridge, MA, Harvard University Press.

WILLIAMSON O., 1985, *The Economic Institutions of Capitalism: Firms, Markets, Relational Contracting,* New York and London, The Free Press and Collier Macmillan Publishers.

YOUNG D. R., 1986, "Entrepreneurship and the Behavior of Nonprofit Organizations: Elements of a Theory", in *The Economics of Nonprofit Institutions: Studies in Structure and Policy,* ed. Susan Rose-Ackerman, 161-184, Oxford and New York, Oxford University Press.

# [4]

# Public Policy and the Performance of Nonprofit Organizations: A General Framework

*Richard Steinberg*

*This article discusses various attempts by economists to model the behavior and performance of nonprofit organizations, and it provides four desiderata of a model suitable for policy analysis: the legal definitions of nonprofit status must be incorporated into the model; the objective function must emerge from the regulatory and competitive environment; the emergence of competitors (for-profit, nonprofit, and governmental) must be endogenous; and the information structure must be fully specified and self-consistent. The article discusses how to incorporate each of these desiderata into a model.*

Economists have been attempting to model the performance of nonprofit organizations for at least twenty-five years (seminal works include Tullock, 1966; Newhouse, 1970; Pauly and Redisch, 1973), yet we still cannot confidently answer the central policy questions. How should we regulate, tax, and subsidize nonprofits when, to borrow Young's (1983) book title, the question If not for profit, for what? remains unanswered. Should we abolish the privileged tax and regulatory status of nonprofit organizations when they fail to provide sufficient special social benefits? Alternatively, does any failure to provide special social benefits result from inadequate subsidies, so that the privileged position of nonprofit organizations needs to be enhanced?

All of the early work, and much of the current work, on the subject is unsatisfying, ad hoc, or incomplete. Researchers start by asserting some

*Note:* This research was supported by a grant from the Center on Philanthropy at Indiana University, and through facilities provided by the Center for Urban Affairs and Policy Research at Northwestern University, for which I am grateful. I appreciate the helpful remarks from Avner Ben-Ner, Catherine Eckel, Lewis Segal, and anonymous reviewers.

plausible organizational goal (objective function), then they derive the implications when this objective is maximized in a given market and regulatory setting. While this is a helpful beginning, the models have conflicting policy implications and there is no completely satisfactory method for selecting a particular model to analyze a particular policy problem.

For two reasons, real progress will be made only when economists can successfully implement a unified policy framework. First, a unified framework allows us to formulate public policies with a comprehensive view to the interrelatedness of performance. Sometimes, the best way to solve one regulatory problem is to refine regulations in an entirely different area. For example, in Steinberg (1991a), I argue that the best way to curb fund-raising abuses is to better enforce and refine those restrictions that are designed to keep insiders from profiting from the financial success of the organization. If I had focused too narrowly on the fund-raising problem, I would have missed this superior solution; because a unified and mathematically complete framework for policy analysis is not yet available, I could not demonstrate my conclusion with the sort of rigor that economists find most persuasive.

Second, a unified framework achieves logical consistency. The same nonprofit organization decides whether to engage in unrelated commercial activities and how to conduct its fund-raising campaign, respond to government reimbursement policies, respond to competition, and respond to tax incentives. Despite this essential unity, approaches that separately analyze these behaviors make mutually inconsistent assumptions about the objectives of the organization and the constraints under which it operates.

My goal in this article is to advocate a unified framework, discuss four essential elements of such an approach, and discuss the literature to see how close others have come to implementing these elements either separately or together. The four standards of logical rigor and completeness discussed here, which I think a satisfactory model must meet, are not the first attempt in the literature to discuss the requirements for a satisfactory theory of nonprofit organizations (see, for example, Steinberg, 1987; Gassler, 1989; Zietlow, 1992), but they represent the first attempt that focuses on the requirements for a theory that is designed to guide public policy reforms. In formulating these standards, I focus on what should be the primitive assumptions or underlying axioms of behavior and what should be a result emerging from those assumptions. Primitive assumptions, which are not explained within the model, are referred to as "exogenous"; results that emerge as logical corollaries or theorems derived from these assumptions are referred to as "endogenous."

The four minimal requirements for an adequate policy framework are as follows: First, the model must properly incorporate the legal constraints that define an organization as nonprofit. Second, the postulated objective function should emerge endogenously from the regulatory environment or, at a minimum, should be consistent with the regulatory environment. Third, the relevant competing organizations (for-profit, nonprofit, and governmental) should emerge endogenously. Fourth, the model must carefully and consistently specify the information structure under which agents operate. Each is considered here in turn.

The proposed framework is more complete than existing theories, but of course it leaves something out. First, I leave out the role of nonprofits in establishing the environmental and systemic preconditions for an economy (Gassler, 1990). To some extent, nonprofit organizations are established in order to change individuals' preferences, as universities mold new scholars or religiously affiliated charities seek converts (Weisbrod, 1988; James, 1989); they also have played roles in the initial allocation of property rights. Indeed, I suspect that the mere act of labeling one as a pastor, trustee, or provost in what is labeled as a nonprofit enterprise can transform a person. Second, I leave out those political and ethical considerations that do not easily fit into the neoclassical economics paradigm. Specifically, I omit consideration of the legitimacy of the power structure and of the inherent value of pluralism, although these factors create, in my mind, a strong presumption in favor of policies that affirm the nonprofit sector.

As long as one is endogenizing everything else, one might be tempted to endogenize the tax and regulatory policies (that is, to explain why the policies inevitably result from political and economic forces). There are certainly political factors at work explaining why certain nonprofit organizations get tax or regulatory breaks that are denied to other nonprofits (see, for example, Wendling and Werner, 1980), and empirical analyses should incorporate these factors (to avoid "endogeneity bias"). However, one cannot endogenize that which one seeks to improve. Any model suitable for policy analysis must presume that the analysts' work has the potential to alter policies, or else the exercise is a waste of time.

## Incorporating the Legal Definition of the Sector

Although not without controversy, most economists define nonprofit organizations as those that obey the nondistribution constraint (NDC) (Hansmann, 1980). Under the NDC, nonprofits can earn "profits" (what else are endowments but retained earnings?) but cannot distribute those profits to those in control of the organization (the board of directors). Thus, profits must be reinvested in the organization or given to other nonprofit organizations, and they must not inure to the private benefit of any individual. The NDC is consistent with most state incorporation statutes.

Many state nonprofit incorporation statutes include additional restrictions, and most tax and regulatory advantages granted to nonprofit organizations are conditioned on more than simple adherence to the NDC. It is unclear whether these additional restrictions belong as part of the definition of "nonprofit" for modeling purposes. In particular, many state statutes enumerate a list of allowed services, although the list differs from state to state and is different still under the federal tax code. Almost all such lists include charitable services and other goods with external benefits (that is, goods that benefit other people in addition to or instead of the direct purchaser), and so Preston (1990) has chosen to incorporate a "public benefit constraint" as part of the formal definition of nonprofitness in her model. This constraint requires that a certain minimum percentage of the benefits of nonprofit services flow to nonpaying customers. I disagree with her nomenclature, though not her intent. The public benefit constraint certainly captures an important regulatory alternative, but an organization that violates this constraint should retain the nonprofit label. There are too many clearly private purposes that are permissible under statutes for me to feel that this public benefit constraint is an inherent part of the definition of the sector.

Most published models simplify by assuming that there is only one time period. The natural way to incorporate the NDC in a one-period model is as a "zero-profit" constraint, which leads to misplaced analysis. For example, Freeman (1979) asserts that the need to spend all net proceeds in each period makes nonprofit employment levels more sensitive to changes in wage rates than would be the case in for-profit firms. This does not seem to be a proper model, especially for tenured faculty at nonprofit universities.

Some of the results of Easley and O'Hara (1983) are also subject to this criticism. An additional problem with the zero-profit constraint approach is that it makes nonprofits no different from any other regulated-profit organization such as some regulated for-profit utilities. On the other hand, technical problems limit the usefulness of existing multiperiod models (only Austen-Smith and Jenkins [1985] have emphasized this approach, although Emanuele [1991], Chillemi and Gui (1990b), and Steinberg [1986] have incorporated aspects of a multiperiod model). I do not think that one must abandon single-period models to fruitfully analyze policy toward nonprofits, but one must employ them with due care.

Single-period models that emphasize the nonappropriability of profits by controlling agents but do not coerce expenditures on any ad hoc residual input or output are preferable (Chillemi and Gui, 1990a; Gassler, 1989). Thus, a sorting model such as Gui's (1990), in which different types of entrepreneurs are attracted to work in the nonprofit setting because of the zero-profit constraint, seems acceptable. In contrast, Freeman's (1979) model is inadequate, for there is no reason to suppose that nonprofits would always spend the totality of annual surplus on new hires, rather than build endowment or cross-subsidize output.

One corollary of the NDC is that salaries must be reasonable. The statutes provide little guidance on how this is to be judged, but it is clear that some forms of executive compensation could represent disguised profit distribution. Most of the legal guidance comes from the Internal Revenue Service (IRS), interpreting the NDC for purposes of determining exemption from the corporate income tax. Until recently, the IRS required that executive compensation be fixed in advance and be no higher than corresponding compensation in the for-profit sector, but now limited forms of profit sharing are permitted (Steinberg, 1990b). The general idea is that exemption can be retained if the compensation plan does not conflict with the organization's exempt purpose and is the result of arm's length bargaining between the organization and its employees (General Counsel Memorandum 39674, 1987).

Unfortunately, some of the models of nonprofit performance depend on the assumption that nonprofit compensation is strictly lower than found in for-profits (as in Gui, 1990), a requirement stronger than the law requires (especially as enforcement of the reasonable compensation constraint is spotty at best). These models are still useful for management purposes (to enlighten the board of directors on the consequences of alternative compensation packages) and describe the consequences of reforming the nonprofit corporation law, but they do not describe something that is inherent to the nonprofit form as currently interpreted.

## Endogenizing the Objective Function

One finds an abundance of suggested objective functions in the literature, such as maximizing budget (Tullock, 1966; Niskanen, 1971), maximizing quality and quantity in proportions specified by the manager (Newhouse, 1970; Hansmann, 1981), maximizing use of preferred inputs (doctors, high-technology and prestigious medical procedures, or handicapped employees; see Lee, 1971; Clarkson, 1972; Pauly and Redisch, 1973; Feigenbaum, 1987), maximizing a combination of commercial and charitable or public benefit outputs (James, 1983; Schiff and Weisbrod, 1991; Eckel and Steinberg, forthcoming), maximizing "profits" (Preston, 1988), or social welfare (a mathematical specification of the ideal attainable economic state; see Holtman, 1983). These competing objective functions are detailed in the surveys of James and Rose-Ackerman (1986), Hansmann (1987), Steinberg (1987), and Gassler (1990). However, in most of these models, the objective functions are given exogenously.

Ideally, one needs to know where the organization's objective function comes from; at a minimum, one needs to know whether the postulated objective function is consistent with the regulatory and competitive environment. It must be possible to break even with the assumed objectives under the given environment, otherwise the nonprofit organization will be forced into bankruptcy and possibly replaced by a nonprofit with a different objective. Realistically, organizations can compromise their core objectives in times of financial stringency. Thus, an adequate specification of the objective function must include details of the compromises that the organization is willing to make. For example, Rose-Ackerman's (1987) symphony conductors are forced to select overplayed popular classics when government grants are cut, picking avant-garde pieces that better fit their self-defined missions in times of financial plenty. In her model, the core objective is compromised in adverse regulatory environments, but we know exactly which trade-offs management is willing to make in order to survive because a complete objective function is specified.

Mere knowledge that the organization's postulated objective allows the firm to survive is not enough, however, for there may be other survivable objective functions with different policy implications. For example, the property rights school holds that nonprofit organizations produce at high cost because the owners do not financially benefit from cost reductions when the NDC is enforced. Schlesinger (1985) shows that this conclusion depends heavily on which objective function the organization is assumed to follow, and that there are survivable objective functions that lead to low-cost production despite the absence of financial incentives. Thus, Schlesinger highlights the importance of uncovering actual nonprofit objective functions.

It is not enough to uncover the organization's current objective function and verify that this objective remains viable following regulatory change, for the change in policies may induce an organizational transformation. In such cases, the ceteris paribus policy effect (the predicted effect if the objective function were held constant) would differ from the mutatis mutandis effect (the actual effect after induced changes in objectives) in ways that can only be predicted if we know where the objective function comes from. Eckel and Steinberg's (1991) draft illustrates that this difference can be important, as discussed below.

Young (1983) assumes that the organizational objective is defined by the founding or governing entrepreneur. Different types of entrepreneurs self-sort into nonprofit industries on the basis of differences in potential executive compensation, in the character of the services provided, the degree of control by professional organizations, the degree of economic concentration, the bureaucratic structure, the extent to which a job fosters postemployment mobility, and the social priority attached to the field. He is undoubtedly right (for a summary of supporting evidence, see Weisbrod,

1988, pp. 31–33), but he did not embed his analysis in a rigorous and complete model. Eckel and Steinberg (1991) applied Young's approach to mathematically model the effects of price regulation on nonprofit monopolies and found that different kinds of entrepreneurs are attracted to govern nonprofits when prices are regulated, causing the organization's objectives to change. It is my view that further formalization of Young's ideas remains the most promising route for researchers in this area.

A complete model will look at the sorting not only of entrepreneurs but also of board members, donors, and customers. For example, Ben-Ner (1986, 1987) stresses the role of competing groups of consumers in governing the performance of a class of nonprofit organizations. Indeed, for him, a desire for patron control is the reason that the organization is established in the first place. Whether that control is exercised for the improvement of social welfare policies depends on specified details of the market environment. Ben-Ner's analysis could be fruitfully extended to policy analysis by showing how public policy can affect those details. In a similar spirit, Downing and Brady (1981) analyzed the dynamics of an environmental lobbying group whose behavior is established by member voting, but whose membership evolves with both short-term behavior and the regulatory environment. Here, too, the extension to policy levers should prove useful.

Entrepreneurial sorting may be restricted by the articles of incorporation. In Hansmann's (1980) terminology, mutual organizations are controlled by patrons (customers and donors), whereas entrepreneurial nonprofits are controlled by self-perpetuating boards, political appointments, and so on. Clearly, mutual status is important for public policy analysis. For example, in Steinberg (1992), I argue that the legal presumption in antitrust merger cases should favor merging nonprofits if their articles of incorporation ensure that they will remain mutuals. The reason for this is that when patrons control the organization, it is more plausible that proposed mergers will serve the interests of those patrons (say, through achieving economies of scale or scope and consequent price reductions) than that they will oppose patron interests (through monopoly underproduction and consequent price increases).

Finally, an adequate theory should account for the possibility that an organization's nonprofit status is itself endogenous. For example, Winkle (1991) reports that two nonprofit waste-recycling organizations recently converted to for-profit. In one case, it was asserted that the conversion occurred because the recycling market became profitable; in the other, because nonprofit status no longer seemed relevant. Legorreta and Young (1986) report on three for-profits and two government organizations that converted to nonprofit status. Formal economic analysis has not yet, to my knowledge, addressed these sectoral conversions.

## Endogenizing the Competition

Organizational behavior is tightly constrained by the presence of actual and prospective new competing organizations. First, I discuss the general effects of competition. Next, I show that the baseline model of entry by new competitors implies that nonprofit organizations will not survive unless they essentially act like for-profit firms. The concluding two sections qualify this result and suggest alternative models of entry.

*Why Competition Matters.* The behavior of individual organizations is largely determined by the behavior and quantity of competitors—for-profit, nonprofit, and governmental. Regulatory policies typically affect both a given organization and all (or many) of its competitors, so that once again the ceteris paribus policy effects (holding constant the behavior of competitors) differ from the mutatis mutandis effects (allowing for induced reactions of competitors). Organizations must react once to the new public policy and then react strategically to the changed behavior of rivals. Thus, one must model all of the relevant players, not just the individual organization.

The number of competitors is endogenous and critical to individual performance, so that any adequate model must specify the determinants of entry by both nonprofit and for-profit organizations (and, perhaps, by government enterprises). Universally, entry makes it more difficult for individual organizations to obtain resources, whether from sales (Eckel and Steinberg, 1993) or from donations and grants (Rose-Ackerman, 1982). Not only is a count of the number of existing competitors needed but also a theory as to why that number is present. This requires a complete specification of the determinants of entry and exit. Without that specification, cause and effect can easily be confused, leading to incorrect policy pronouncements. This was the lesson from the "contestability" revolution in antitrust policy, which holds that if there is a monopoly in some market in a situation where potential competitors could costlessly enter and leave that market, then that monopoly should be allowed to continue. When markets are contestable, divestiture (forcing a monopoly to split up) would destroy, rather than enhance, the competitive process and harm social welfare.

*Effect of Free Entry.* The common assumption that economists make in the for-profit context (at least to start the analysis) is that entry is "free," which implies that a new firm enters the market whenever economic profits (essentially, accounting profits minus the normal rate of return) are positive. This drives down the price of the product and hence profits per firm. Long-run equilibrium is achieved when there is sufficient entry to drive economic profits to zero for every firm (assuming the same production-cost possibilities are available to each entrant and incumbent). Each firm produces its long-run equilibrium quantity at the lowest possible cost because high-cost production results in negative economic profits (hence exit from the market). Firms only produce goods and services that can be sold—benefits to nonpurchasers are ignored in firm decision making. Indeed, any firm that tried to provide charity care or otherwise incur costs in order to benefit nonpurchasers would be driven out of business by for-profit competitors who chose not to make those expenditures. In certain cases of asymmetric information, where the seller could profit by misleading the customer, chiseling is required for survival (these are cases where reputation, guarantees, court suits, and the like are imperfect remedies). Profit maximization and its corollary of cost minimization are not ethical decisions but rather prerequisites for survival in this setting.

These assumptions have an alarming implication for nonprofits: In order to survive the competition with for-profits, they must behave exactly like for-profits. They cannot remedy market failures or serve as private agents of redistribution, regardless of their objective function.

In order for nonprofits to function in a distinctive fashion, they must somehow be "cushioned" from competition; that is, they must be provided with a source of revenue that is not ultimately eroded away by entry of competitors. Entrepreneurial and patron sorting are irrelevant, at least in the long run, if there is no cushion. The size of the cushion determines the scope for distinctive behavior.

Cushions allow both socially beneficial and detrimental deviations from for-profit behavior. Two good deviations are possible. First, cushions might be devoted to provision of pure public goods or, more generally, goods with external benefits (that is, goods that benefit more than just the purchaser). Governments also provide goods with external benefits, but one should not expect perfection from political systems so that a role remains for nonprofits (Weisbrod, 1975). Second, cushions might allow nonprofits to become "trustworthy," that is, to avoid the temptation to take advantage of the relative ignorance of patrons.

There are two bad deviations. First, production might take place at higher than necessary cost, wasting scarce productive resources. When nonprofit production is cushioned, productive inefficiency can survive competition at the going market price, but it is also logically possible for the nonprofit to undersell the going price, driving efficient competitors out of business.

In the for-profit context, the absence of entry barriers implies that firms enter the market whenever they can do so without generating an economic loss. In the existing nonprofit literature (such as Rose-Ackerman, 1982), this sometime consequence of free entry has been taken as a definition of free entry. With this admittedly extreme definition (less extreme alternatives are discussed below), free entry of other cushioned nonprofits would drive the price down until efficient for-profits were driven from the market. Nonetheless, all surviving nonprofits would be efficient, so there would be no net economic loss.

Second, organizations might behave in a perverse and untrustworthy fashion in a market setting where for-profits would not for fear of damaging their reputations. There is no force impelling cushioned nonprofits to act this way, merely the absence of a market check and balance; once again, the extreme free-entry assumption restores the competitive force that eliminates this possibility. The literature does not mention the possibility of dishonest nonprofits. Rather, it stresses the reverse conclusion for situations where reputation is an insufficient remedy for asymmetric information, so that for-profits are compelled to act less scrupulously.

Finally, cushioned nonprofits could serve as agents of private income redistribution, allowing use of sliding-scale fees, need-based financial aid for college, and charity care (redistributions from poor to rich are also logically possible). It is unclear whether these redistributions are socially valuable or harmful (see James, 1983; Steinberg, 1992; and sources cited therein).

Free entry tends to eliminate cushions. Free entry of for-profits wipes out cushions through otherwise profitable sales of goods and services. If a tax or regulatory break is provided (unconditionally) to nonprofits, then free entry of nonprofits drives down prices until all for-profit competition is eliminated and surviving nonprofits have no cushion. If nonprofits obtain surplus from donations (that is, if gross donations exceed fund-raising expenditures), then free entry of other donative organizations wipes out that surplus as well (Rose-Ackerman, 1982).

If government or foundation (unconditional) grants are available but are distributed on the basis of competitive bids, then competition wipes out any surplus from winning bids. Finally, if labor is volunteered, aggregate volunteer time is scarce, and organizations must devote resources to recruiting, then free entry will wipe out any surplus from volunteered labor as well.

***Deviations Under Free Entry.*** Conditioned revenue sources provide a long-term cushion that is not eroded by entry but constrains the behavior of recipient organizations. For example, tax breaks may be made conditional on particular deviation behaviors, as in current proposals to make continuance of tax-exempt status by nonprofit hospitals conditional on provision of sufficient charity care (Suhrke, 1990). An entering nonprofit that did not provide sufficient charity care would have higher after-tax costs and thus could not drive the tax-exempts out of the market.

Viewed in this light, some current policies are mystifying. For example, nonprofit exemptions from local property taxes provide their largest cushions to those organizations that occupy large amounts of valuable land, making inefficient land use a survivable behavior (Clotfelter,

1988–1989). Exemptions from both the corporate and unrelated-business income taxes provide their largest cushions to those organizations providing commercial services, a task that for-profits already perform well (Hansmann, 1989). These forms of subsidization encourage bad deviations that the nonprofits would likely never have otherwise considered (although this is far from the end of the story, as I argue in Steinberg, 1991b).

Revenue-conditioning policies can only reward observable outputs (redistribution and most external benefit goods). There would be no point in trying to encourage and allow more trustworthy behavior through revenue conditioning. Indeed, if authorities could tell whether the conditions were being met, consumers could learn as well and there would be no need for revenue conditioning (see the argument in the next paragraph). The general problem, as Weisbrod (1989) observes, is one of rewarding performance that is hard to measure, and it seems that only an unconditional cushion has a chance at success (provided entrepreneurial sorting keeps this cushion from being abused, as discussed below).

Sometimes, revenue conditioning is inherent to the behavior of relevant players, requiring no policy intervention. For example, consumers are willing to pay more for nonprofit outputs if they believe that nonprofit status alone conveys trustworthiness. This willingness to pay provides a cushion that makes trustworthy behavior survivable (more on this later). Preston (1988) models another example, where donors reward organizations whose output mix provides external benefits. This provides a cushion that makes provision of public benefit goods survivable, and this cushion is not eroded by entry. (There is no "commons externality" whereby entry of another charity reduces net donations to existing charities in her model. Perhaps the cushion would erode if the model incorporated this possibility.) A third example is provided by several models (including some by Preston) surveyed in Steinberg (1990a). In these models, workers, in effect, partially donate their time by accepting lower wages when their employer's output mix provides external benefits. Lower labor costs then provide a cushion that supports provision of these goods. Finally, Schiff and Weisbrod (1991) assume that donors dislike commercial activity and reward those organizations that avoid it.

Conditioned revenue sources allow only deviations that meet the conditions (when that conditioning can be securely enforced), so that there is little scope for entrepreneurial sorting to play an active role in nonprofit behavior. Suppose, for example, that a nonprofit hospital is granted a $75,000 tax break if it provides $25,000 worth of charity care. Then, the $50,000 free cushion would be eroded by entry of other nonprofits that also provided charity care. In effect, entry would drive down the price of medical care, causing the net proceeds from sales of service to fall by $50,000. (For purposes of illustration, I neglect the many special considerations that make health care pricing different from the standard model.)

Sorting does have two roles to play, however. First, when there are several types of deviations that are consistent with the conditioning, entrepreneurial sorting may determine which behavior prevails. For example, hospital tax exemption may be conditioned on the sum of charity care and medical research expenditures meeting a specified threshold. Sorting would then determine the proportions of each permitted activity in the ultimate equilibrium output mix. Second, sorting may make it easier to enforce the conditioning. Consider again the conditioning of tax exemption on charity care. Immediately following imposition of this new requirement, managers would be tempted to play accounting tricks to make it look like they were complying well with the requirement, and the government would have to devote sufficient enforcement resources to deter this sort of behavior. In the long run, managers who personally cared about charity care would likely sort into positions of control (of course, this interpretation is speculative without a complete and formal model), and the requirement would become self-enforcing.

***Alternatives to Free Entry.*** There are five alternative modeling assumptions: two involving legal restrictions on entry, and three involving natural barriers to entry. First, for-profit organizations might be legally prohibited from engaging in specified activities, either explicitly or as an inevitable effect of other policies. For example, the state may allow monopoly education accreditation bureaus to deny accreditation to for-profit universities while immunized from legal challenge under antitrust statutes, or the state may refuse to provide grants for low-income housing to for-profits. In this setting, nonprofits would continue to enter freely.

When for-profit provision is legally prohibited, one can imagine an equilibrium in which nonprofits function uniformly and distinctly, acting in a trustworthy manner. No entering nonprofit would seek to cut costs by cheating its customers because there would be no motivation to do so (Hansmann's, 1980, original argument). The problem with this scenario is that it relies heavily on the enforceability of the NDC (Steinberg, 1991b). A kind of Gresham's law prevails when the constraint can be successfully evaded; the bad drives out the good. A few for-profits-in-disguise (FPIDs) would have the incentive (personal enrichment) and the ability to cheat customers. Customers could not distinguish FPIDs from legitimate nonprofits, so their willingness to pay for items sold by those who claim to be nonprofits would go down. This drives the price down to the point where legitimate nonprofits would have difficulty surviving unless they acted in a less trustworthy fashion, driving the price down further. Ultimately, only FPIDs may survive, although this conclusion is speculative given the dearth of appropriate formal analysis. I suspect that the ultimate conclusion depends on the schedule of incremental costs for acting in a trustworthy fashion as compared to the schedule of incremental consumer willingness to pay for scrupulous behavior, for these are the sorts of factors that matter in the related literature on the economics of "lemons" (for example, Kreps, 1990, pp. 625–629).

If, as suggested above, FPIDs wiped out all deviations from for-profit behavior, their presence could help or harm society. If legitimate nonprofits practiced bad deviations, imperfect enforcement of the NDC would help society; if deviations were good, we would want the NDC enforced.

The situation is markedly different if a survivable cushion is provided to all nonprofits (legitimate and FPIDs). Although consumers reduce their payments in proportion to the estimated share of FPIDs in the market, there is no feedback effect whereby legitimate nonprofits are forced to compromise their integrity or go out of business. Legitimate nonprofits could finance their integrity through the cushion, FPIDs get a cushion too (which cannot be helped), and the average organization claiming to be nonprofit is more trustworthy. However, the cushion would only be survivable for legitimate nonprofits if entry of FPIDs were somehow restricted. Thus, restrictions on the entry of nominal for-profits are insufficient to allow distinctive performance by nonprofits; some limits on FPID entry are probably necessary as well (again, this conclusion remains speculative without a formal model).

A second way to ensure survivability is to restrict entry by all organizations. This is quite common. Licensing restrictions can be used to ensure standards, but they more often are used to keep the number of entrants low and thus keep up prices. (Why else can residents of forty-eight states pass the bar exam but still not be allowed to practice law without a degree from an accredited law school?) Some restrictions are more blatant: Witness the certificate-of-need program designed to restrict entry of hospital facilities, which are then subject to antitrust prosecution due to this barrier to entry. (Crazy world we live in, eh?) Economists are generally suspicious of barriers to entry, but in this case barriers may make sense. Although entry restrictions permit inefficient behavior to survive, they are nearly essential if we are to have any hope of good deviations (Steinberg, 1992). New empirical studies are required to determine whether the inefficiencies or the good deviations dominate behavior.

There are two (interrelated) reasons why this extreme version of free entry does not naturally occur in specified markets. First, there may be a scarcity of entrepreneurial talent. If there are only a few visionaries who can produce more cheaply or stimulate more donations than can others, their unique talent provides a cushion. If this unique talent can perform in several settings, then a bidding war will ensure that most of this cushion is given to that prodigy. If the unique talent functions well in only one setting, the entrepreneur will be unable to capture the benefits of his or her talent in the form of financial remuneration. In this case, the resulting cushion can finance any good or bad deviation, as the board wishes. Unfortunately, bidding wars for talented fund-raisers and development officers are becoming more common, but even the superstars still generate substantial cushions for their employers.

Entrepreneurial sorting interacts with scarcity of talent here: If the prodigy is talented enough to produce any product (trustworthy or not) at a lower cost than offered by competitors, and this prodigy has a preference for honest dealings with consumers, then for-profits will be unable to bid him or her away. Nonprofits will compete by offering a package of output perquisites (trustworthy behavior) and financial remuneration that leaves room to finance that trustworthy behavior. Thus, the empirical correlation between talents and preferences is a critical determinant of nonprofit performance.

Another possibility is that there is some economy of scale or scope such that larger or more diversified organizations have an inherent advantage over smaller ones. This situation leads to a natural monopoly, whether the market is for-profit or nonprofit. Natural monopolies can obtain a cushion through limit pricing (pricing higher than costs but not so high that a high-cost firm could enter and steal market share), which can then be applied in any manner that the monopoly wants. There is one important difference between most for-profit and nonprofit natural monopolies, however. If the for-profit monopoly is publicly held, then the market for ownership restricts survivable behavior. A for-profit monopoly that sacrificed enormous financial gain in order to help the poor would find itself the subject of a successful hostile takeover bid, and its generosity could not survive. In contrast, nonprofit monopolies cannot be subject to financially motivated takeover bids because they cannot sell meaningful shares of stock when governed by the NDC. Thus, alternative nonprofit monopoly behaviors could persist.

Sorting itself implies alternatives to free entry. Tautologically, nonprofit entrepreneurs will found new organizations whenever the utility that they could expect from founding exceeds the utility that they would get in their next best alternative (their reservation utility). Sometimes, this relationship implies that entry occurs whenever potential financial surplus is positive (the traditional specification of free entry), because many entrepreneurial objectives are fostered by positive financial resources. However, entrepreneurs concerned about paying set-up costs would need a sufficiently larger-than-zero financial surplus before entry became worthwhile. Ben-Ner (1987) analyzed a variety of factors that cause set-up costs for nonprofits to differ from those for for-profits, so that entry conditions may be market-specific. Also, entrepreneurs who favor particular outputs or inputs would not enter in cases where profits could be positive if their favored input and output proportions were violated. Thus, sorting models generally imply that entry will stop somewhat short of the standard model.

It is important to recognize that if entrepreneurial preferences determine entry into the nonprofit sector, these same preferences govern for-profit entry decisions (Gassler, 1989). Some analysts have not been consistent here. For example, Folland (1990) admirably models the entry decision of nonprofit entrepreneurs (with a rich specification of the elements of managerial utility, an explicit set-up cost, and a reservation utility that varies with the level of entry by others), then he simply asserts that for-profit entrepreneurs enter whenever potential profits are positive. To be consistent, Folland needs to argue either that for-profit entry is less than free and governed by the same managerial utility function as nonprofits, or that there are two types of entrepreneurs, one who cares solely about profits and one with an elaborate specification of preferences. For the second explanation to work, a complete separating equilibrium must be consistent with the model—that is, no entrepreneur who cared solely about profits would wish to enter the nonprofit sector, and no entrepreneur who cared about other things would wish to enter the for-profit sector. This approach was asserted, although not fully developed, in Schiff and Weisbrod (1991); a draft by Gassler (1989) makes a similar attempt. Unfortunately, existence of a separating equilibrium is a strong requirement, and pooling equilibria are more commonly expected. In addition, the separating equilibrium must remain viable over the entire policy space, which need not be the case (Steinberg, 1991b).

For further progress, the multichotomous (more than two employment options are available to entrepreneurs) and multidimensional (entrepreneurs care about several distinct characteristics) aspects of screening need to be modeled. Preston (1990) addresses the first of these problems with a model in which agents choose whether to found a nonprofit firm or a for-profit firm, or simply to work as a laborer. I am unaware of any analyses of the second problem; the literature on multidimensional screening in other contexts suggests that the problem is likely to be quite serious. The conditions in which it is possible to achieve a separating equilibrium, say, to segregate those entrepreneurs with a distaste for commercial activities into the nonprofit sector, may be inconsistent with the conditions necessary to achieve separation along some other dimensions (say, to segregate those entrepreneurs who care about quality, trustworthiness, redistribution, or public good provision).

## Modeling the Information Structure

Hansmann (1980) developed the importance of "contract failure," that "nonprofits of all types typically arise in situations in which, owing either to the circumstances under which a service is purchased or consumed or to the nature of the service itself, consumers feel unable to evaluate accurately the quantity or quality of the service a firm produces for them"

(Hansmann, 1987, p. 29). He suggested that the NDC both removes the incentive for firms to cheat on the promised quantity or quality and provides a basis for entrepreneurial sorting; he thus anticipated the general framework proposed here. However, it has become clear in the various attempts to model Hansmann's arguments more formally that the details of the information structure are important.

The ultimate resolution of consumer uncertainty matters. Easley and O'Hara (1983) assume that product quality or quantity is never observed by the contractor (as in donations to multinational aid charities). In a very different model, Gui (1990) makes the same assumption. In contrast, Chillemi and Gui (1990b) assume that product quality is perfectly observed after purchase, and that any consumer's postpurchase experience with the product of a particular firm is shared with all other potential consumers. Satterthwaite (1979) and Pauly and Satterthwaite (1981) assume that quality is uncovered through postpurchase experience, but because consumers differ in tastes, any one consumer's experience provides little information to other consumers. Each of these models has different implications for the role and functioning of the nonprofit sector, and a general framework should consider the various logical possibilities separately.

Some models carefully delineate the informational constraints that make nonprofit status necessary, then they make implausible information assumptions elsewhere. For example, Chillemi and Gui (1990b) note that in a repeated-game equilibrium, only certain price and quality combinations are consistent with the firm's long-run survival. For some price and quality combinations, the firm's one-period gain from cheating is outweighed by the future loss from loss of reputation (recall that any consumer's experience informs all other consumers in this model), so that honesty is assured. There is one set of price and quantity combinations that guarantees quality among for-profits, and a different set among nonprofits even when the NDC is imperfectly enforced. However, there is no natural force to keep hit-and-run entrepreneurs from undercutting the price that makes honest behavior rational unless consumers take low price as a signal of untrustworthiness. But consumers cannot do this unless they know the utility function of the manager. Thus, their model depends on the implausible combination of assumptions that consumers cannot observe the quality of the product that they buy but can observe the underlying preferences of the entrepreneur from whom they buy.

In contrast, other models make plausible combinations of assumptions about ignorance and information. For example (although not a formal model), Weisbrod (1988) argues that the nonprofit form is adopted when it is easier to monitor compliance with an NDC than to monitor output quality. The point needs to be formally developed with imperfectly enforceable constraints.

## Conclusion

After twenty-five years of ad hoc theorizing about the nature of nonprofit performance, researchers are independently discovering the elements of a satisfactory theory for policy analysis. If these separate elements can be appropriately combined in a model with endogenous objectives and competition and a fully specified objective function, researchers will be able to provide far more persuasive answers to basic policy questions: Should nonprofit organizations be subsidized? Which combination of subsidies and regulations is optimal? What is the role of the nonprofit sector in a three-sector world?

## References

Austen-Smith, D., & Jenkins, S. (1985). A multiperiod model of nonprofit enterprise. *Scottish Journal of Political Economy, 32,* 119–134.

Ben-Ner, A. (1986). Nonprofit organizations: Why do they exist in market economies? In S. Rose-Ackerman (Ed.), *The economics of nonprofit institutions: Studies in structure and policy* (pp. 94–113). New York: Oxford University Press.

Ben-Ner, A. (1987). *Birth, change, and bureaucratization in nonprofit organizations: An economic analysis.* In R. Herman (Ed.), *Politics, public policy and the voluntary sector* (Proceedings of the 1987 AVAS conference, pp. 119–137). Kansas City: University of Missouri.

Chillemi, O., & Gui, B. (1990a). Product quality in trust type nonprofits: An expository evaluation of three economic models. In *Towards the 21st century: Challenges for the voluntary sector* (Proceedings of the 1990 AVAS conference, pp. 121–130). London: Center for Voluntary Organisation, London School of Economics.

Chillemi, O., & Gui, B. (1990b). *Uninformed customers and nonprofit organizations: Modelling "contract failure theory"* (Working Paper). Trieste, Italy: University of Trieste, Department of Economics and Statistics.

Clarkson, K. (1972). Some implications of property rights in hospital management. *Journal of Law and Economics, 15,* 363–385.

Clotfelter, C. (1988–1989). Tax-induced distortions in the voluntary sector. *Case Western Reserve Law Review, 39,* 663–694.

Downing, P., & Brady, G. (1981). The role of citizen interest groups in environmental policy formation. In M. White (Ed.), *Nonprofit firms in a three-sector economy.* Washington, DC: Urban Institute.

Easley, D., & O'Hara, M. (1983). The economic role of the nonprofit firm. *Bell Journal of Economics, 14,* 531–538.

Eckel, C., & Steinberg, R. (1991). *Cooperation meets collusion: Antitrust and the nonprofit sector* (Working Paper No. 92-10). Indianapolis: Indiana University/Purdue University, Department of Economics.

Eckel, C., & Steinberg, R. (forthcoming). Competition, performance, and public policy towards nonprofits. In D. Hammack & D. Young (Eds.), *Nonprofit organizations in a market economy.* San Francisco: Jossey-Bass.

Emanuele, R. (1991). Constrained by demand or budget? An inquiry into the revealed objective function of the nonprofit organization. In S. Wernet (Ed.), *Collaboration: The vital link across practice, research, and the disciplines* (Proceedings of the 1991 ARNOVA conference, pp. 101–110). Pullman, WA: ARNOVA.

Feigenbaum, S. (1987). Competition and performance in the nonprofit sector: The case of U.S. medical research charities. *Journal of Industrial Economics, 35*(3), 241–253.

Folland, S. (1990). *Nonprofit entry: A theory and an empirical test for the case of hospitals* (Working Paper). Rochester, MI: Oakland University, School of Business Administration.

Freeman, R. (1979). The job market for college faculty. In D. Lewis & W. Becker, Jr. (Eds.), *Academic rewards in higher education* (pp. 63–103). New York: Ballinger.

Gassler, R. S. (1989). *The economics of the nonprofit motive: A suggested formulation of objectives and constraints for firms and nonprofit enterprises* (Working Paper). Brussels, Belgium: Vrije Universiteit Brussel, Vesalius College.

Gassler, R. S. (1990). Nonprofit and voluntary sector economics: A critical survey. *Nonprofit and Voluntary Sector Quarterly, 19*(2), 137–150.

Gui, B. (1990). *Nonprofit organizations and product quality under asymmetric information* (Working Paper). Trieste, Italy: Trieste University, Department of Economics and Statistics.

Hansmann, H. (1980). The role of nonprofit enterprise. *Yale Law Journal, 89,* 835–901.

Hansmann, H. (1981). Nonprofit enterprise in the performing arts. *Bell Journal of Economics, 12,* 341–361.

Hansmann, H. (1987). Economic theories of nonprofit organization. In W. W. Powell (Ed.), *The nonprofit sector: A research handbook* (pp. 27–42). New Haven, CT: Yale University Press.

Hansmann, H. (1989). Unfair competition and the unrelated business income tax. *Virginia Law Review, 75,* 605–635.

Holtman, A. G. (1983, November). A theory of non-profit firms. *Economica, 50,* 439–449.

James, E. (1983). How nonprofits grow: A model. *Journal of Policy Analysis and Management, 2,* 350–366.

James, E. (1989). Introduction. In E. James (Ed.), *The nonprofit sector in international perspective: Studies in comparative culture and policy* (pp. 3–27). New York: Oxford University Press.

James, E., & Rose-Ackerman, S. (1986). *The nonprofit enterprise in market economies.* New York: Harwood.

Kreps, D. M. (1990). *A course in microeconomic theory.* Princeton, NJ: Princeton University Press.

Lee, M. (1971). A conspicuous consumption theory of hospital behavior. *Southern Economics Journal, 38,* 48–58.

Legoretta, J. M., & Young, D. R. (1986). Why organizations turn nonprofit: Lessons from case studies. In S. Rose-Ackerman (Ed.), *The economics of nonprofit institutions: Studies in structure and policy* (pp. 196–206). New York: Oxford University Press.

Newhouse, J. (1970). Toward a theory of nonprofit institutions: An economic model of a hospital. *American Economic Review, 60,* 64–73.

Niskanen, W. A., Jr. (1971). *Bureaucracy and representative government.* Hawthorne, NY: Aldine.

Pauly, M., & Redisch, M. (1973). The not-for-profit hospital as a physicians' cooperative. *American Economic Review, 63,* 87–99.

Pauly, M., & Satterthwaite, M. (1981). The pricing of primary care physicians' services: A test of the role of consumer information. *Bell Journal of Economics, 12,* 488–506.

Preston, A. E. (1988, July). The nonprofit firm: A potential solution to inherent market failures. *Economic Inquiry, 26,* 493–506.

Preston, A. E. (1990). *Entrepreneurial self-selection into the nonprofit sector: Effects on motivations and efficiency* (Working Paper). Stony Brook: State University of New York at Stony Book, W. Averell Harriman School for Management and Policy.

Rose-Ackerman, S. (1982). Charitable giving and "excessive" fundraising. *Quarterly Journal of Economics, 97,* 195–212.

Rose-Ackerman, S. (1987). Ideals versus dollars: Donors, charity managers, and government grants. *Journal of Political Economy, 95,* 810–823.

Satterthwaite, M. (1979). Consumer information, equilibrium industry price, and the number of sellers. *Bell Journal of Economics, 10,* 483–502.

Schiff, J., & Weisbrod, B. (1991). Competition between for-profit and nonprofit organizations in commercial activities. *Annals of Public and Cooperative Economics, 62,* 619–640.

Schlesinger, M. (1985). *Economic models of nonprofit organizations: A reappraisal of the property rights approach* (Working Paper). Cambridge, MA: Harvard University, John F. Kennedy School of Government.

Steinberg, R. (1986). Should donors care about fund-raising? In S. Rose-Ackerman (Ed.), *The economics of nonprofit institutions: Studies in structure and policy* (pp. 347–366). New York: Oxford University Press.

Steinberg, R. (1987). Nonprofit organizations and the market. In W. W. Powell (Ed.), *The nonprofit sector: A research handbook* (pp. 118–138). New Haven, CT: Yale University Press.

Steinberg, R. (1990a). Labor economics and the nonprofit sector: A literature review. *Nonprofit and Voluntary Sector Quarterly, 19*(2), 151–170.

Steinberg, R. (1990b). Profits and incentive compensation in nonprofit firms. *Nonprofit Management and Leadership, 1*(2), 137–151.

Steinberg, R. (1991a). *Regulation of charity fundraising: Unintended consequences* (Working Paper No. 92-11). Indianapolis: Indiana University/Purdue University, Department of Economics.

Steinberg, R. (1991b). "Unfair" competition by nonprofits and tax policy. *National Tax Journal, 44*(3), 351–364.

Steinberg, R. (1992). Antitrust policy: Are nonprofits different? In D. Young, V. A. Hodgkinson, R. Hollister, & Associates, *Governing, heading, and managing nonprofit organizations: New insights from research and practice.* San Francisco: Jossey-Bass.

Suhrke, H. (1990, June). Philanthropy and the poor [Editorial]. *Philanthropy Monthly,* p. 2.

Tullock, G. (1966). Information without profit. *Papers on Non-Market Decisionmaking, 1,* 141–159.

Weisbrod, B. (1975). Toward a theory of the voluntary nonprofit sector in a three-sector economy. In E. Phelps (Ed.), *Altruism, morality and economic theory* (pp. 171–195). New York: Russell Sage Foundation.

Weisbrod, B. (1988). *The nonprofit economy.* Cambridge, MA: Harvard University Press.

Weisbrod, B. (1989, May 5) Rewarding performance that is hard to measure: The private nonprofit sector. *Science, 244,* 541–546.

Wendling, W., & Werner, J. (1980). Nonprofit firms and the economic theory of regulation. *Quarterly Review of Economics and Business, 20,* 6–18.

Winkle, C. (1991). *The shifting role of the nonprofit sector in waste recycling* (Working Paper). Chicago: University of Illinois, School of Urban Planning and Policy.

Young, D. (1983). *If not for profit, for what?* Lexington, MA: Heath.

Zietlow, J. T. (1992). *Emergent microeconomic and financial theories of nonprofit organizations: Synthesis and research agenda* (Working Paper). Terre Haute: Indiana State University, School of Business.

*Richard Steinberg is associate professor of economics and adjunct professor of philanthropic studies at Indiana University/Purdue University at Indianapolis, and copresident of ARNOVA.*

# [5]

# The Distributional Consequences of Nonprofit Activities

*Charles T. Clotfelter*

As this century enters its final decade, countries in all parts of the world are rethinking the roles traditionally played by government in providing social services. In the United States this rethinking has been encouraged by Presidents Reagan and Bush, who pushed for cuts in federal domestic spending and called for private voluntary action to assume greater responsibility for meeting social needs. In fact, the collection of institutions loosely referred to as the nonprofit sector has been playing an important part in education, health, and other social services from the nation's earliest days. To a degree unparalleled elsewhere, the nonprofit sector in the United States is enshrined in constitutional law, instrumental in the delivery of many essential social services, and inextricably bound up with broad social processes of change and governance.

The sector employs some ten percent of the nation's work force. Governments at all levels in this country have placed nonprofit organizations in a special position, exempting them from most taxation and encouraging their supporters in other ways. One of the most important of these is the income tax deduction for charitable contributions, for which much of the $90 billion donated annually is eligible. The nonprofit sector also relies on direct government support for a quarter of its income. By virtue of both their size and special treatment, nonprofit organizations have become an important subject of study for those interested in the implementation of public policy in this country.

In studying other institutions that affect public policy, economists and other policy analysts find it useful to examine at least two important aspects of performance: efficiency and distributional equity. The first of these two aspects has received considerable attention in the growing literature about nonprofit organizations. Several important analyses have evaluated the effect of such organizations on the efficiency of resource allocation. These studies have focused on the role of nonprofit organizations in providing services about which consumers are poorly informed or those which governments have for some reason failed to provide sufficient quantity.[1] In addition, there have been a number of empirical studies to determine the relative cost-effectiveness of using government, nonprofit, or for-profit institutions to produce and deliver certain kinds of services, often on a contract basis.[2] However, scholars have paid less attention to the second aspect—the distributional implications of our reliance on nonprofit institutions—this despite the fact that distributional considerations have always held a prominent position in American political debate.

This is not to say that observers of the nonprofit sector have never speculated on what might be the distributional impact of the sector's institutions and the voluntary donations that support them. They have, and for the most part the tenor of scholarly commentary suggests that the redistributive impact of the sector is minimal. In an essay on philanthropy, for example, William Vickrey put forth the hypothesis that most donors direct their gifts not toward the most disadvantaged in society but rather to those only slightly below them on the income ladder, concluding that "the role of philanthropy in redistribution is relatively slight" (Vickrey 1962, 44–45). Teresa Odendahl (1989, 246) is even more emphatic in arguing that such voluntary institutions result in little in the way of redistribution of resources: "The philanthropy of elites is not a system whereby the fortunate distribute resources to the less fortunate. Instead, philanthropy is primarily a system whereby the wealthy help to finance their own interests and institutions."

Similar arguments have been made about specific subsectors of the nonprofit world. For example, one commentator has said that "arts-funding is in practice an income-transfer program for the upper-middle class" (Bethell 1978, 136). Private health clubs have accused some YMCA's of catering to the affluent (Bailey 1989, 1). Still others have noted the "elitist" character of private universities (Shils 1973, 7). One paper compiled in the 1970s for the Commission on Private Philanthropy and Public Needs, popularly known as the Filer Commission, noted that "grants made directly for social change or to assist the powerless are dwarfed by the massive philanthropic contributions made annually in support of education, the

1. See, for example, Hansmann (1980) and Weisbrod (1988).

2. For studies of the relative efficiency of nonprofit organizations, see Savas (1982) or Schlesinger (1990). Taking the somewhat broader view that efficiency encompasses how social wants are satisfied, studies of the historical roots of nonprofit institutions can also be placed in the category of empirical work related to the efficiency of nonprofit organizations.

*Charles T. Clotfelter*

arts, health services and the like" (Carey 1977, 1110). And some scholars have argued that there is very little redistributive aspect to the biggest category of charitable giving, that directed to religious organizations (for example, see Schaefer 1968, 30). Moreover, the issue of distributional impact is bound up with the concern about the ultimate goal of nonprofit institutions. In this connection, the Donee Group report to the Filer Commission urged wider citizen involvement in governing boards and ways to "democratize" charitable giving in order for philanthropy to become "an advocate for those who are most in need" (Donee Group 1977, 57).

At the center of these and other related policy discussions is the question of who benefits from the nonprofit sector and public policies affecting the sector. Although few would argue that redistribution is the most important justification for maintaining nonprofit institutions, distributional impact remains one significant consideration, as it is in most areas of public policy. Such distributional concerns are certainly involved when Congress reexamines laws that will affect the size of the voluntary sector, such as the definition and taxation of "unrelated" business income earned by nonprofit organizations, or the establishment of limitations on the deductibility of charitable contributions. These concerns also arise on the local level in connection with granting property exemptions for nonprofit organizations. Despite the importance of these issues, however, we simply do not have a good idea about the sector's distributional consequences. Our lack of knowledge regarding these consequences invites empirical research. The purpose of this volume is to offer such research, using the conventional tools of empirical social science. Although they employ definitions and techniques unfamiliar to many readers, the studies have been written so as to be accessible to a broad audience. Taken together, the findings contained in the volume show that the distributional impact of the nonprofit sector can be characterized neither by the pro-poor charity of the Salvation Army nor by the affluent-orientation of some arts groups. Distributional impact differs by subsector and must be analyzed accordingly.

Before turning to the studies themselves, it is useful to introduce the topic in a general way and to discuss some of the methodological issues confronting all of the studies. The next section presents a brief descriptive overview of the nonprofit sector, noting the special tax treatment given to nonprofit institutions. The following section discusses the general approach taken by the papers in this volume to assess the distributional impact of nonprofit institutions. In particular, it deals with the methodological issues that are common to all of the papers and discusses the assumptions on which the analyses are based. There follow a short section describing the distribution of charitable contributions by income, a summary of the findings of these empirical studies, and a brief concluding section.

## I. The Nonprofit Sector

Whether it is referred to as the "voluntary sector," the "private not-for-profit sector," or simply the nonprofit sector, there exists in this country a vast and diverse collection of religious groups, schools, hospitals, associations, and other nongovernmental organizations that fulfill a host of important functions. In size they range from the tiniest day-care center to the major research universities and established national charities. Some of them exist entirely for the benefit of their members, while others are devoted to helping others. Many of them operate quite independently of government, while others act as virtual extensions of government programs. In 1987 there were over one million separate nonprofit organizations in operation.

Probably the most important sign of recognition of the special role of nonprofit organizations in public law is the general exemption from federal income taxation; thus it is a useful approximation to equate "nonprofit" with "tax-exempt."[3] In fact, one useful way of categorizing nonprofit institutions is according to the gradations of tax treatment they receive. Table 1.1 defines three groups of tax-exempt organizations. The first two groups—including foundations and other charitable, religious, and educational organizations—constitute the so-called 501(c) (3) organizations, all of which are subject to provisions of the section of the Internal Revenue Code so numbered. The most important tax provision applying to these organizations is that contributions made to them may be deducted by donors in calculating their income tax. Institutions in the first group, foundations, are separated because they have traditionally been subject to more stringent tax provisions than other 501(c) (3) organizations. The special provisions applying to foundations are of two kinds. First, contributions to foundations have usually been subject to lower limits, as a percentage of a donor's income, and gifts of appreciated property have also been treated less favorably when given to foundations. Second,

3. Not all income generated by nonprofits is exempt from income taxation. Specifically, such an organization must pay tax on income that is deemed to be unrelated to its central charitable purpose. For a discussion of the relevant tax law and the issue of commercial activities of nonprofits, see articles in part two of Hodgkinson and Lyman (1989).

TABLE 1.1 Number of Tax-Exempt Organizations, 1987 (thousands)

| | |
|---|---|
| Foundations | 27.7 |
| Churches and other charitable, educational and scientific organizations | |
| Churches and other religious bodies | 346.1 |
| Other | 394.4 |
| Other tax-exempt organizations | 517.0 |
| Total | 1,285.2 |

SOURCE: Hodgkinson and Weitzman (1989, tables 1.2, 1.3, and 5.1; pp. 28, 29, and 121).

foundations themselves are subject to a number of rules, including a minimum payout requirement, stated as a percentage of investment assets, and regulations covering the governance and financial dealings of principal donors and their families.[4] In 1987 there were some 28,700 foundations in the United States. This number included a small number of widely recognized large private foundations such as Ford and Rockefeller, hundreds of others with assets in the millions, and a galaxy of miniatures. Further distinctions among foundations are discussed in chapter 7.

Numerically, the second and third groups of tax-exempt organizations listed in table 1.1 are much larger. The second group is composed of the organizations besides foundations eligible to receive tax-deductible contributions. Numerically most important here are the 346,000 churches and other individual religious bodies that are perhaps the most visible part of the country's nonprofit sector. This second group also includes some 394,000 other organizations, including private colleges and universities, hospitals, nursing homes, social welfare agencies, international relief agencies, museums, and other cultural institutions. The third group of organizations listed in the table, comprising over one-half million entities, is made up of organizations that generally do not receive the benefit of being able to receive tax-deductible contributions. By and large, these can be described as mutual-benefit organizations. They include groups such as civic clubs, fraternal societies, credit unions, business and labor associations, and farmers' cooperatives.[5] This book follows the practice in much of the research on the nonprofit sector by focusing entirely on the first two groups listed in table 1.1. While it is convenient to accept the distinction made in the tax law, this grouping is by no means pure. For example, organizations

4. For a description of the tax provisions applying to foundations, see Clotfelter (1985, 260–64).

5. In fact, contributions to several groups of non-501(c)(3) organizations are deductible: those to cemetery companies, veterans organizations, and corporations organized under an act of Congress (see Clotfelter 1985, table 1.1, 4–5).

in the first two groups certainly display some aspects of mutual-benefit groups, as Biddle discusses in chapter 4. By the same token, there are organizations in the excluded category that perform charitable functions. But, for the most part, the organizations that have been granted 501(c) (3) status generally have earned that special status by having certain characteristics that make them worthy of special attention.

In order to provide some descriptive background on the institutions that make up this sector, table 1.2 presents information on the sources of revenue and employment for each of six major subsectors. Overall, the charitable nonprofits summarized in this table employed some seven million workers, received volunteer services worth an additional 4.5 million worker-years, and brought in over $300 billion in revenue. Of this total revenue, fees and other private payments constituted the largest single source, followed by private donations and payments from government. Measured in terms of either total revenues or total work force, the health-related nonprofits constitute by far the largest subsector. At roughly half the size is the second largest subsector, education and research. Both the health and education subsectors are heavily dependent on fees by paying customers, with private payments accounting for at least half of total revenues in both cases. The second most important source of revenue for both of these subsectors was government, with private contributions ranking a distant third.

Religious organizations ranked third in total revenues, but they were by far the biggest recipients of charitable contributions, receiving about half of all such contributions. The religious subsector is distinctive in two other ways as well. First, like foundations and community chests, churches regularly transfer a significant portion of their income to nonprofit organizations in other subsectors. Second, the religious subsector accounts for a disproportionate share of contributed volunteer labor.

Social and legal services, comparable to what Salamon calls "human services" in chapter 5, constitute the next largest subsector. Institutions in this group are routinely used by governments, sometimes on a contract basis, to provide "public" services. It is not surprising that this is the only subsector for which government is the largest source of funds. In terms of the measures used in table 1.2, arts and culture and foundations are the smallest of the six subsectors shown, neither having gross revenues of more than $12 billion in 1987. Yet these two subsectors contain some of the most prominent nonprofit institutions in the country, and their activities have a profound effect on how the sector as a whole is perceived.

TABLE 1.2 Sources of Income and Employment in the Charitable Nonprofit Sector, 1987

| | Sources of Funds ($ billions) | | | | | | | Employment (thousands) | |
|---|---|---|---|---|---|---|---|---|---|
| | Contributions | Private Sector | Government | Investment Income | Church | Other | Total | Paid Employees | Volunteers (FTE) |
| Health Services | 10.5 | 78.3 | 54.8 | 1.7 | 8.2 | 2.8 | 156.3 | 3,367 | 817 |
| Education/Research | 8.3 | 38.7 | 12.8 | 4.0 | 4.3 | 1.9 | 70.0 | 1,666 | 516 |
| Religious Organizations | 43.6 | 3.1 | — | 0.9 | −12.9 | 3.8 | 38.4 | 650 | 2,015 |
| Social and Legal Services | 11.3 | 4.0 | 12.1 | 0.9 | 0.3 | 0.6 | 29.2 | 1,196 | 819 |
| Arts and Culture | 6.3 | 1.1 | 1.2 | 0.4 | 0.1 | 0.8 | 9.9 | 122 | 240 |
| Foundations | −5.5 | 3.8 | — | 7.7 | — | — | 6.0 | 22 | 84 |
| Total | 86.3[a] | 125.2 | 80.9 | 15.6 | 0.0 | 9.9 | 317.6 | 7,024 | 4,528[b] |

SOURCE: Hodgkinson and Weitzman (1989, tables 2.7 and 8.1, pp. 43 and 177).
[a]Includes $8.0 billion of contributions not allocated to any subsector.
[b]Includes 37,000 for international activities not allocated to any subsector.

It is worth noting the ways in which government policy affects the nonprofit sector. As has been mentioned, federal tax policy makes explicit concessions for nonprofit institutions, exempting their incomes from taxation and allowing donations to a subset of institutions to be deductible in the computation of personal and corporate income taxes and the estate tax. Similar concessions are contained in most state tax structures, and nonprofits are also typically exempted from paying state sales taxes. At the local level, nonprofits receive another important source of subsidy by being exempted from property taxation in most jurisdictions. These tax policies, along with other forms of favorable treatment, such as subsidized federal postal rates, are clear evidence of friendly public policy toward nonprofit institutions. Both the nature and the extent of these favorable policies make the performance of nonprofit institutions, including their distributional effects, a public policy issue.

## II. Issues of Methodology

There is a long tradition in economics of attention to income distribution and the distributional effects of government policy. Particularly in the area of public finance, analysts have used theory and empirical tools to examine the ways in which taxes and government expenditures affect the well-being of households in different economic situations. Although there are a number of alternative schemes by which households can be grouped for these purposes—including age, race, region, and source of income—distribution is most commonly measured in terms of income class. Adopting this common approach, the studies in this volume examine the distributional pattern of the benefits produced by nonprofit institutions and thus, by implication, the distributional impact of policies that influence the scope of those institutions. The studies focus only on the "output" side of the nonprofit sector; they generally ignore any distributional effects arising from the financing of nonprofit institutions. Although these latter effects are certainly important in any overall assessment of the sector's distributional consequences, issues of financing seem sufficiently general that they can be dealt with separately, as they are later in this chapter.

### The Basic Approach Taken in These Studies

This book is concerned with the distributional impact of our reliance on nonprofit institutions to carry out important social functions. Within the constraints imposed by data limitations, each of the empirical studies attempts to address two basic questions related to this impact. First, what are the benefits produced by the nonprofit institutions in the subsector? Second, how are these benefits distributed across households of different incomes? Although these questions sound straightforward, answering them even in the presence of abundant data is by no means simple. The first question cannot be answered without asking the more basic question of what social functions nonprofit institutions serve in the first place. Only when their output is identified is it possible to proceed to the difficult question of valuing the benefits.

The valuation of benefits is an issue familiar in the subfield known as welfare economics. In theory, the value of a good or service is equal to the amount a person would be willing to pay for it. The net benefit to a consumer can be defined as this value minus any amount actually paid, or the consumer surplus. Applying this approach is fraught with difficulties, however, as the applied work in applied welfare economics makes clear. One obvious difficulty is placing dollar values on services for which there are no comparable services that are purchased in the market. What would be the theoretical value, for example, of a special exhibit of Italian Renaissance paintings or of the services supplied by a family planning clinic? A related problem arises with benefits that may be spread widely over the population or over more than one generation. For example, how would one value a foundation grant to support an adult literacy program or a university research project in high-energy physics? Another difficulty arises when the appreciation of a service is an "acquired taste." A young person's first symphony concert may be the least appreciated over a lifetime, though it may also be the most important one as well. In practice, conceptual difficulties such as these merely add to the general problem of inadequate information. In evaluations of the distributional effects of public expenditures, the distinction between expenditures and willingness-to-pay is often ignored.[6] Similarly, in the empirical work that follows, the best that can usually be done to measure benefits is simply to calculate per capita expenditures by income class.

The second task, assessing the distributional pattern of the benefits, requires knowledge of who uses the services produced by nonprofit organizations. Although it presents data problems of its own, this is generally a much more nearly attainable objective than the first. For this reason, the authors in this volume in most cases had to be content simply to identify

6. For example, Musgrave and Musgrave (1989, 246) use total expenditures in an assessment of overall fiscal incidence although they state that consumer surplus is the correct measure of the benefits of public programs (p. 136).

the nature of the benefits and estimate the pattern of usage across the population. While this is by no means a fully satisfactory answer to the question of distributional effect, it constitutes a step forward in our knowledge of the impact of nonprofit institutions.

### Philanthropic Transfers and Production

A comprehensive assessment of the impact of the nonprofit sector on the distribution of income would certainly include more than just the benefits derived from the operations of nonprofit firms. In particular, one would want to take into account the effects of both financial contributions and volunteer services, since donors often are in different income classes from those of the beneficiaries of nonprofit services. In order to illustrate the sorts of redistribution that may occur, it is useful to consider five possible roles in which individuals may find themselves. These are shown in table 1.3 along with a description of the costs and benefits to the individual that arise directly as a result of each role. The first role shown is that of a beneficiary or client of a nonprofit organization, and it is this role that figures prominently in the present book. As noted above, each study would ideally examine the distribution of the net benefits, defined as the difference between the value of the service received and any fees paid.

The second role listed in the table, that of taxpayer, seems not to be directly relevant to the nonprofit sector. It is listed partly because government funds are an important source of revenue for nonprofits and partly because the role of taxpayer provides a useful contrast with the other roles shown in the table. To the individual in the role of taxpayer, the tax burden is a clear cost.[7] The benefits of government are many, but if they are not tied to tax payments on a quid pro quo basis, tax payments per se bring no direct benefit. In studies of tax incidence, therefore, it may be exceedingly hard to determine who bears the burden of a tax, but there is no doubt that that burden—viewed separately from the benefits of government—has a negative effect on those who bear it.

As donors and volunteers, individuals provide major sources of funding and labor for nonprofit institutions. Like the role of taxpayer, each of these roles carries a cost. In the case of financial contributions, the cost is the dollar amount of the gift less any tax savings that arise from using the

7. Taxes are said to be "shifted" if all or part of the attendant drop in potential consumption is borne by individuals other than those who actually make the tax payment. Thus the tax burden may not be equivalent to tax liability.

*Charles T. Clotfelter*

TABLE 1.3 Five Possible Roles for Individuals, with Associated Costs and Benefits of Each Role

| Role | Participant's Cost | Participant's Direct Benefit |
|---|---|---|
| Beneficiary/client of nonprofit organization | Fee, if any | Value of output received |
| Taxpayer | Tax burden | None |
| Donor | Contribution (net cost) | Unmeasurable |
| Volunteer | Value of time | Unmeasurable |
| Employee | Wages and salaries available elsewhere | Wages and salaries |

charitable tax deduction.[8] In the case of volunteering, there is a cost measured in terms of the value of the person's time.[9] Both of these roles are distinctly unlike that of the role of taxpayer in that the activities are voluntarily undertaken. As such, these activities must carry with them some form of benefit or satisfaction. It is possible, for example, that voluntary gifts of money or time may bring financial rewards, political power, or prestige. Even an act of purest altruism may be thought of as bringing its own rewards, although the amount and form of such benefit is a matter of debate.[10] It is the voluntary nature of giving that makes it difficult to apply to the problem posed in this book the standard models of fiscal incidence that are used in assessing the distributional impact of government taxes and expenditures. It is nevertheless important to keep in mind that there are probably distributional consequences that arise from the funding of nonprofit organizations as well as from their operation.

One other possible role through which nonprofit organizations might have a distributional impact is employment. For example, a foundation that paid its directors extraordinary fees would be exerting a "pro-rich" effect on the distribution of income, assuming those directors inhabited high-income classes. However, to the extent that nonprofit organizations pay their employees the market wage and the kinds of skills called for are not extremely rare in the labor force, the normal functioning of the labor

8. For a discussion of the net cost of making contributions, see, for example, Clotfelter (1985, 39–43).

9. For discussions of the valuation of time and volunteer labor supply, see Menchik and Weisbrod (1981) or Clotfelter (1985, chap. 4).

10. Sen (1977), for example, argues that to assume that the benefits of altruistic acts are always assumed to be at least as great as the costs is to assume away a form of giving that may well be important, namely sacrificial giving or acting out of commitment.

market will tend to minimize any distributional effects arising from employment. In those circumstances, those who work for nonprofit institutions will be paid about what they would be paid in comparable jobs in for-profit and government organizations.[11] For this reason, the studies in this book ignore any distributional effects that occur as a result of employment, though some of these probably are in fact at work.

## Incremental Effects

What exactly is meant by "the" distributional consequences of a large sector of the economy? "Compared to what?" is an understandable response.[12] There is an implicit counterfactual situation used for comparison when a question of effect is asked—the situation that would have obtained in the absence of the factor in question. In the present case, it would be quite impossible and not very useful to try to use as a point of comparison a United States without a nonprofit sector. This sector is and has been too important a fact of life for such a comparison to be very interesting. But it would not be too difficult to imagine a sector that is slightly smaller or slightly larger than the one we have now. In that vein, the studies in this volume should be seen as relevant to the evaluation of incremental changes in the size of the nonprofit sector or its components. The research here can then be seen as bearing on policies that might lead to the expansion or contraction of the nonprofit sector. What would be the distributional effects of such incremental changes in the extent of the sector? Who would benefit and who would be hurt? One might also explore the effects of more specific policies, such as changes in certain programs that help to fund nonprofit institutions. In practice, data limitations make it impossible to dis-

11. Of central importance here is the elasticity of supply of labor of different varieties, which in turn depends on the scarcity of the skills being demanded by nonprofit firms. An expansion of nonprofit firms that occasioned an increase in the demand for clerks, for example, would be unlikely to affect the wage level of clerks and thus would have negligible distributional effects. Similar expansions leading to increases in the demand for professors or symphony musicians, however, might affect wages, especially in the short run. For a discussion of factor market effects in the context of higher education, see Nerlove (1972, S209).

12. In one of the two analogies that he offers in his commentary, Henry Aaron compares the nonprofit sector to a water pump in a car. He argues that determining the distributional impact of the nonprofit sector is as difficult as assessing the water pump's effect on the car's horsepower. If the water pump were missing, something else would be (and certainly has been in some models) inserted to perform its function. This certainly seems to be the case of nonprofit institutions as well. However, focusing on incremental changes allows one to ask a sensible question, namely, what would be the effect of a small change in the size of the water pump, or the size of the sector?

tinguish marginal as opposed to the average beneficiaries, so the practical application of the incremental concept requires the assumption that small changes in the size of nonprofit institutions would affect beneficiaries in a way that is reflected by data on the distribution of average benefits.

### General Equilibrium Adjustments

Changes in the size of the nonprofit sector, even marginal changes, would likely be accompanied by other adjustments in the economy. For example, a reduction in the number of nonprofit day-care centers might lead to an increase in the capacity of the for-profit day-care industry. Or it might stimulate local governments to provide more day-care services. Adjustments of this sort are implicit in the notion of "crowding out" that has often appeared in the economic literature on charitable giving. If donors are interested in the total amount of a public good available, an increase in government provision of that good would be expected to result in a corresponding reduction, or crowding out, of charitable giving for that purpose.[13] There is in fact some evidence of this kind of adjustment, particularly reductions in philanthropic activity in the face of significant expansions of government services. For example, Ginzburg (1962, 74–79) reported that both the financing and functions of hospitals changed following the Depression, as the government assumed an increased responsibility for supporting the treatment of indigent patients. Whether the size of government, or the for-profit sector, would adjust in response to a change in the size of the nonprofit sector is uncertain, but it is surely a question that bears on an assessment of the distributional impact of changes in the nonprofit sector. If one assumes that increases in nonprofit services come about at the expense of government services, for example, it would be important to compare the incomes of those who use government services with the incomes of those who use services offered by nonprofits and to consider whether the characteristics of marginal clients would be the same as those of the average clients. Again, the limitations imposed by data may make it impossible to consider such factors thoroughly, but it is useful to keep the possibility in mind when assessing empirical findings.

In his commentary, Henry Aaron expresses doubt that empirical studies such as those presented here can adequately capture the distributional im-

13. For a theoretical treatment of crowding out in the case of altruistic giving, see Andreoni (1988).

pact of changes in the size of the nonprofit sector. He argues that any such changes probably would be compensated for by other sectors, just as a decline in output by General Motors would tend to be matched by increases in the output of other manufacturers. Knowing the income distribution of GM customers will not be very helpful in determining the distributional impact of a decline in GM output, owing to these likely adjustments by other suppliers. This argument seems especially apt when applied to subsectors where there exist comparable suppliers in the public or the for-profit sectors, such as health and education. Two characteristics of these subsectors increase the chance that variations in the size of the nonprofit sector will tend to be matched by countervailing variations in other sectors, with minimal impact on the distribution of benefits. First, to an extent greater than most organizations in the other subsectors, nonprofit institutions in health care and education tend to provide services that are quite similar to their government (and for-profit, in the case of health) counterparts. Second, they receive a significant share of their revenues in the form of earmarked government funds. To the extent that such funds will be spent on the same population regardless of provider, the clienteles of nonprofit providers tend to look more like those of other institutions using the same kinds of funds. This degree of similarity may exist as well in some human services institutions, but is decidedly not present in religion, the arts, and foundations. To summarize, the empirical studies in this book for the most part present evidence on the income level of current clients of nonprofit institutions. To what extent the distributional impact of changes in the nonprofit sector would parallel these existing patterns depends in part on whether there exist similar for-profit or government providers.

## III. The Distribution of Charitable Contributions

Although the studies in this volume focus on the distribution of the outputs of nonprofit firms, their findings are obviously relevant to the larger question of the distributional impact of the entire philanthropic sector, which includes charitable giving. It is useful, therefore, to include here some summary information on such giving, especially on patterns of contributions by income level. The bulk of charitable contributions are made by living individuals; these amounted to some $80.8 billion in 1987. Much smaller in size were bequests, which totaled $6.6 billion, and corporate donations, which were $4.6 billion (Hodgkinson and Weitzman 1989, 71). Table 1.4 summarizes data on individual contributions taken from household sur-

TABLE 1.4 Patterns of Charitable Giving by Income

| Income | Volunteers as % of all households 1989 | Average Contribution, 1989 | | Percentage of Contribution to Religious Organizations | |
|---|---|---|---|---|---|
| | | Total | As % of Income | 1989 | 1987 |
| Under $10,000 | 30 | $ 186 | 2.5 | 67 | 82 |
| $10,000–19,000 | 42 | 316 | 1.9 | 69 | 83 |
| $20,000–29,999 | 56 | 560 | 2.1 | 64 | 69 |
| $30,000–39,999 | 65 | 732 | 2.0 | 69 | 72 |
| $40,000–49,999 | 67 | 702 | 1.5 | 71 | 64 |
| $50,000–74,000 | 63 | 936 | 1.5 | 62 | 63 |
| $75,000–99,999 | 62 | 2,575 | 2.9 | 72 | 63 |
| $100,000 and over | 74 | 2,512 | 2.4 | 66 | 51 |

SOURCE: Hodgkinson and Weitzman (1990, table 1.17, pp. 41–42).

veys in 1987 and 1989. The first column shows the percentage of households who reported doing any volunteer work during the year; this percentage generally rises with income. The next column shows average contributions for each income group and confirms the findings of other studies that contributions generally rise with income. Giving as a percentage of income, shown in the third column, has the familiar U-shape (see, for example, Clotfelter and Steuerle 1981).

The only aspect of the 1989 figures that do not appear to correspond to other data on giving is the split between religious and other giving. The table's last two columns show the percentage of contributions by income class reportedly made to religious organizations. Whereas the 1989 figures show little variation in this percentage among the income classes, figures based on a similar survey in 1987 show this percentage declining with income. In fact, all of the previous studies touching on this question indicate that the importance of religious giving does decline with income. One of these was a national survey on philanthropy taken in 1973. Data from that survey, which are based on the four major gifts made by respondents, are summarized in table 1.5. This table suggests that the distribution of gifts of the most affluent households is quite different from those of lower- and middle-income households. At higher income, giving to colleges, universities, and cultural institutions becomes much more prominent.[14]

14. Other sources of data on the distribution of contributions by type of donee are the 1962 *Statistics of Income* and a 1978 survey done by the Gallup Organization for CONVO, survey

TABLE 1.5 Percentage Distribution of Contributions, Major Donees, by Income, 1973

| Income | Religion | Education | | Combined Appeals | Medical and Health | Culture | Other Major | Not Identified[a] | Total |
|---|---|---|---|---|---|---|---|---|---|
| | | Higher | Other | | | | | | |
| $0–9,000 | 59(%) | 1(%) | 0(%) | 2(%) | 3(%) | 0(%) | 2(%) | 33(%) | 100(%) |
| $10,000–19,999 | 67 | 1 | 0 | 3 | 3 | 0 | 4 | 22 | 100 |
| $20,000–29,999 | 59 | 2 | 1 | 5 | 4 | 0 | 10 | 19 | 100 |
| $30,000–49,999 | 42 | 5 | 7 | 6 | 3 | 3 | 6 | 28 | 100 |
| $50,000–99,999 | 16 | 9 | 1 | 10 | 11 | 4 | 19 | 30 | 100 |
| $100,000–199,999 | 10 | 14 | 5 | 9 | 10 | 5 | 6 | 41 | 100 |
| $200,000–499,999 | 8 | 27 | 6 | 10 | 11 | 6 | 8 | 24 | 100 |
| $500,000 or more | 9 | 24 | 3 | 6 | 6 | 9 | 16 | 27 | 100 |
| All | 46 | 5 | 2 | 6 | 5 | 2 | 8 | 26 | 100 |

SOURCE: Morgan et al. (1977, table 38).
[a]Information as to donee was obtained only for the four major gifts of each donor; therefore additional giving could not be allocated to donee categories.

*Charles T. Clotfelter*

In considering the distributional impact of the voluntary sector as a whole, one would ideally want to consider these flows of charitable contributions as well as the benefits produced by nonprofit organizations. As implied by the discussion of table 1.3, however, information on voluntary contributions provides evidence on only part of their distributional impact. While the dollar amount of charitable contributions generally reflects the value of the benefit to the donee (except in cases where gifts are earmarked for purposes not highly valued by the donee), it does not reveal the extent to which donors might benefit from their own contributions.[15] If, despite this conceptual roadblock, one wanted to calculate a broader measure of distributional impact than that contained in the studies in this volume, one might use some simplifying assumption regarding the net value of contributions. One possible assumption would be that donors receive no benefit and thus that contributions can be treated in the same way as taxes in studies of fiscal incidence; another would be that donors receive benefits equal to the net dollar cost of their gifts. If the first assumption were adopted, one could compare the flows of contributions and tax revenues going to support nonprofit activities with the benefits flowing out. To give a rough idea of the pattern of those two sources of funding, table 1.6 presents estimates of the percentage distribution of federal income taxes, the major source of federal revenue, and contributions by five broad income classes. The figures show that households at higher income levels provide a disproportionate share of both of these sources of funding. Therefore, if it were found that the per-capital benefits of the services of nonprofit organizations were, say, equal across the income spectrum, the net distributional effect of the nonprofit sector would be pro-poor. However, if one were to adopt the alternative assumption that donors derive benefits from their gifts, such a conclusion would not be justified.

While information on the distribution of charitable contributions and tax revenues is useful in describing the sources of funding for the nonprofit sector, it is not sufficient for judging the overall distributional consequences of the voluntary sector of the economy. For that reason, the studies

GO 7993, July 1979. The former is based on itemized returns only and showed a marked decline in the percentage of giving to religious organizations. The latter included few high-income respondents but showed that the percentage of giving to religious organizations was smallest in the highest income class for which detailed data were given, the $20,000 to $50,000 class.

15. The benefit to the donee is the actual dollar value of the gifts, whereas the cost to the donor, shown in table 1.3, is the net-of-tax cost.

TABLE 1.6 Percentage Distribution of Households, Income, Federal Income Taxes, and Contributions by Income Class, 1988

| Income Class | Households | Income | Income taxes | Contributions |
|---|---|---|---|---|
| Under $10,000 | 17 | 5 | 1 | 3 |
| $10,000 under 30,000 | 37 | 25 | 16 | 21 |
| $30,000 under 50,000 | 25 | 25 | 21 | 24 |
| $50,000 under 100,000 | 18 | 24 | 27 | 28 |
| $100,000 and over | 3 | 21 | 36 | 24 |
| Total | 100 | 100 | 100 | 100 |

SOURCE: U.S. Bureau of the Census, *Current Population Reports,* series P-60, no. 166, *Money Income and Property Status in the U.S. 1988,* table 3; Michael Strudler and Emily Ring, "Individual Income Tax Returns, Preliminary Data, 1988," *SOI Bulletin* 9 (Spring 1990): 15, 25; Hodgkinson and Weitzman (1990, 41–42).

NOTE: Calculations of contributions are based on average contributions from surveys for 1987 and 1989 reported in Hodgkinson and Weitzman by income class, except for the $100,000 and above class, for which itemized deductions in 1988 are used. Percentage distribution of income and income taxes are based on categories of adjusted gross income of taxpayers.

in this book focus on the distribution of the outputs of nonprofit organizations. Still, the studies do provide a great deal of new information about who the beneficiaries of nonprofit activities are and, thus, how the distribution of these benefits corresponds to the distribution of funding sources.

## IV. Summary of the Findings

Despite the important simplifying assumptions employed in the empirical studies in this volume, it will soon be clear to any careful reader that the findings of these studies are still by no means simple. As in so many things, the closer one gets to the object of study, the more diversity one discovers. As subsectors within the nonprofit sector differ from each other, even more so do individual institutions within the subsectors. They differ in both function and clientele. Other factors also conspire to prevent easy summary of the findings, among them the difficulty of measuring outputs and the unevenness of data on the income level of beneficiaries. Nevertheless, these studies do bring together an unprecedented amount of information on the distributional aspects of nonprofit services.

David Salkever and Richard Frank's study of the massive health subsector ably illustrates how the diversity among institutions prevents easy generalization regarding the distributional pattern of benefits. This subsector is distinguished by the coexistence of nonprofit, government, and for-profit providers. And, as noted above, the nonprofits in this subsector rely to a great extent on revenues from patient fees, third-party insurance payments, and government health programs. Salkever and Frank look separately at community hospitals, nursing homes, mental health institutions, and programs providing alcohol and drug treatment. How the nonprofit providers compare to their public and for-profit private counterparts in serving low-income patients differs across these types of institutions. The authors find that the clienteles of nonprofit and for-profit community hospitals are similar but that hospitals run by state and local governments serve a higher proportion of uninsured or poor patients. Among nursing homes, nonprofits tend to have the lowest concentration of Medicaid, signifying low-income, patients among the three types of providers. In the mental health area, nonprofits lie between public and for-profit providers in their tendency to serve the uninsured and those under Medicaid, but in outpatient care their clientele tends to be more affluent than both public and for-profit providers. Among alcohol and drug treatment providers, public facilities again tend to lead in their tendency to serve the poor, with nonprofits taking a middle position among the three types.

With the exception of proprietary vocational schools, there are few for-profit educational institutions, so Saul Schwartz and Sandra Baum's chapter on the education subsector uses public institutions as the point of comparison with nonprofits. Their study looks first at elementary and secondary schools and then at colleges and universities. Evidence on the income level of elementary and secondary school students shows that those attending private nonprofit schools are on average somewhat more affluent than students in public schools, and this is especially true of non-Catholic nonprofit schools. Schwartz and Baum go beyond this comparison of clienteles to examine evidence on the educational effects on students of attending different types of schools. In particular, they compare school outcomes of students in public schools versus those in Catholic schools. They cite evidence that Catholic schools are associated with slightly higher achievement gains than public schools, although the differences are small and clouded by difficult issues of interpretation. There is also some evidence that Catholic schools may hold a special advantage for students from low-income families.

At the college level, Schwartz and Baum show that there are clear differences between public and private institutions in the average income level of students, though there are certainly affluent students who attend public institutions, just as there are poor students at the most expensive private colleges and universities. As in the case of health care, there is no readily available measure of educational benefits, but the authors do present measures of subsidies to students, defined as the difference between average instructional costs and the out-of-pocket costs borne by students and their families. Among students attending private institutions, the average amount of these subsidies falls with family income, owing to the pro-poor nature of scholarship programs. Once the lower college enrollment rates of the poor are factored into the equation, the private college subsidy per young person increases with income, though not as sharply as it would in the absence of need-based scholarship programs. By comparison, the subsidy available from public colleges and universities, per young person, also increases with family income, in line with earlier results by Hansen and Weisbrod (1969).

In contrast to the health and education subsectors, few institutions outside of the nonprofit sector resemble religious congregations. In his study, Jeff Biddle distinguishes two kinds of services produced by religious congregations: those provided to members of the congregation and those provided to others. The first of these are "clublike" services, which include most so-called sacramental activities. Biddle estimates that these activities account for about 70 percent of congregational spending, including most of the costs of buildings, maintenance, utilities, and staff salaries. Of the remaining 30 percent, Biddle estimates that about one-fifth is directed toward expenditures that benefit the poor. There is also some redistribution that occurs within congregations, with the relatively affluent subsidizing the less well-off, though the degree of such intracongregational redistribution is probably less when members are compared on the basis of lifetime income. When these forms of redistribution are taken together, Biddle concludes that neither the rich nor the poor consume a disproportionate share of the subsector's expenditures. One other form of redistribution that came up in discussion is that from the unreligious to the religious. Because the tax code allows expenditures for religious purposes to be deducted but not other forms of nonbusiness expenditures, it has a redistributive as well as an incentive effect.

Lester Salamon's chapter deals with the variagated subsector usually referred to as social services or human services. Organizations in this subsector provide such services as child day-care, job training and vocational rehabilitation, residential care, adoption services, foster care, legal services, and advocacy. Salamon's data come from a survey of 1,474 organizations in which the agencies were asked about the composition of their clienteles. Of all the agencies surveyed, 27 percent said that most of their clients were poor, defined as below the poverty line. Those most likely to focus primarily on the poor were in the areas of employment, training and income support (53 percent), and legal rights and advocacy (43 percent). Salamon uses these survey data to test several theories about the behavior of nonprofit organizations. Among his findings, one especially strong one is the high correlation between the agency's orientation toward the poor and the source of its funding, with those receiving federal aid more likely to focus on service to the poor. Like most of the organizations in the health and education subsectors, many of those in this subsector are profoundly influenced by their reliance on government funding.

In his chapter on nonprofit institutions in arts and culture, Dick Netzer examines data from several national surveys of attendance and participation related to the arts and other cultural institutions. There is good reason, he argues, to take survey data in this area with a grain of salt, but data from them can nevertheless be useful in examining patterns of participation across income classes. As might be expected, the proportion of households who take part in arts activities such as visiting museums and attending performances rises with income. In addition, the average number of visits also rises with income; these are highly income-elastic activities. This income effect is perhaps most evident in ballet and opera. Those with incomes of $50,000, which comprised only about 16 percent of all households, accounted for approximately one-third of ballet attendance and over 40 percent of opera attendance. Yet the survey data show that there was participation at all income levels, not just at the top. And when Netzer compares these participation patterns to the distribution of contributions and taxes paid, he finds no evidence that the affluent enjoy benefits that are disproportionate to their payments. There is little doubt that the distribution of benefits in this subsector favors the affluent more than in any other area. In passing, Netzer also notes the possibility that government subsidies to the arts may produce quite sizable benefits in the form of income for some star performers.

In no other subsector is it more difficult to identify the "clients" than it is in studying foundations. The externalities, the broad and ill-defined effects that certainly apply to some other institutions seem to predominate in the case of foundations. Partly because of the difficulty of assigning benefits in this case, Robert Margo's chapter was commissioned with the intention that it would take a somewhat more historical approach than the other essays, in that way allowing a longer perspective with which to judge effects. Margo uses data on foundation assets and grants to assess comparative rates of expenditure. His findings suggest, as has some previous work, that the payout requirements contained in the 1969 tax reform act had the effect of increasing average payout rates. He also examines the geographical distribution of foundation grants but notes the difficulty in matching the grants with their ultimate beneficiaries. After examining the stated purpose of a number of foundation grants, he concludes that few grants clearly benefit low-income groups directly, although there remains the possibility that grants may have important indirect benefits not immediately evident from a short description.

## V. Answers and Questions

The purpose of these empirical studies is to examine the distributional effects of nonprofit institutions, or rather of our system of reliance on such institutions. This is not to say that redistribution is or should be the primary objective of the nonprofit sector or that its redistributive effects should be the principal criterion for judging policy toward the sector. Distributional effect is one relevant criterion, however. It is relevant to the larger question of whether we should keep or modify the rules by which we regulate, tax, and subsidize activities of the voluntary sector. These studies focus on quantifiable measures of distributional effect, largely based on identifying the clients of various nonprofit institutions. What is the usefulness of studies such as these? If one hopes to determine the ultimate effect on the income distribution of a change in the reliance on the nonprofit sector, complete with the effects that would result from the adjustments in demand and supply in the economy, the results of these studies will not be satisfactory. However, if knowing the first-round impact of marginal changes in the extent of nonprofit activities is useful in assessing current policy toward nonprofit institutions, these findings will be useful.

Three general conclusions emerge from these studies, taken together. First, there is great diversity within the nonprofit sector, and no overarching conclusions about distributional impact can be made. This said, a second finding is one stated in the negative: in no subsector is there evidence that benefits are dramatically skewed away from the poor and toward the affluent. Conversely, there is also evidence that relatively few nonprofit institutions serve the poor as a primary clientele. A third general conclusion is that an institution's source of funding appears to be important in determining the distribution of its benefits. Institutions which receive funding that is tied to certain objectives or recipients will tend to make expenditures reflecting those requirements.

*Charles T. Clotfelter*

Many questions remain, however. Most fundamentally, we have only the most rudimentary understanding of the outputs of nonprofit institutions—their forms, how broadly they are distributed, and how they should be valued. A second unanswered question relates to the general equilibrium effects that would likely accompany a change in policy toward the nonprofit sector. While theoretical models could be worked out on the order of tax incidence analysis, this approach is quite unlikely to yield satisfactory empirical answers. Another question has to do with how we treat charitable contributions in considering the distributional effects in the voluntary sector. Although contributions certainly provide an important source of funding, they are voluntarily made and thus presumably yield benefits of their own. What is the nature of these benefits, and how might they be compared to those received by the donees? Finally, the studies contained here raise the fundamental question of the nature of nonprofit organizations. For many institutions it is possible that this designation is little more than an accident of history and that tax laws and patterns of government funding have a greater impact on the organization's behavior than characteristics intrinsic to the nonprofit form. As questions such as these reveal, it is hard to study the issue of distributional effect without bumping into other basic issues about the objectives and behavior of these organizations.

# References

Andreoni, James. 1988. "Privately Provided Public Goods in a Large Economy: The Limits of Altruism." *Journal of Political Economy* 35: 57–73.

Bailey, Anne. 1989. "Private Health Clubs Assail Tax Exemptions of 'Yuppie' YMCA's with Fancy Facilities." *Chronicle of Philanthropy* (May 30).

Bethell, Tom. 1978. "Welfare Arts." *The Public Interest* 53: 134–38.

Carey, Sarah. 1977. "Philanthropy and the Powerless." In *Research Papers*, Commission on Private Philanthropy and Public Needs, Vol. 2, pp. 1109–64. Washington, D.C.: Treasury Department.

Clotfelter, Charles. 1985. *Federal Tax Policy and Charitable Giving*. Chicago: University of Chicago Press.

Clotfelter, Charles T., and C. Eugene Steuerle. 1981. "Charitable Contributions." In *How Taxes Affect Economic Behavior*, ed. Henry J. Aaron and Joseph A. Pechman, pp. 403–37, Washington, D.C.: The Brookings Institution.

Donee Group. 1977. "Private Philanthropy: Vital and Innovative or Passive and Irrelevant?" In *Research Papers*, Commission on Private Philanthropy and Public Needs, vol. 1, pp. 49–85. Washington, D.C.: Treasury Department.

Ginzburg, Eli. 1962. "Hospitals and Philanthropy." In *Philanthropy and Public Policy*, ed. Frank G. Dickinson, pp. 73–101. New York: National Bureau of Economic Research.

Hansen, W. Lee, and B. A. Weisbrod. 1969. "The Distribution of Costs and Direct Benefits of Public Higher Education: The Case of California." *Journal of Human Resources* 4: 176–91.

Hansmann, Henry B. 1980. "The Role of Nonprofit Enterprise." *Yale Law Journal* 89: 835–98.

Hodgkinson, Virginia A., and Richard W. Lyman, eds. 1989. *The Future of the Nonprofit Sector*. San Francisco: Jossey-Bass Publishers.

Hodgkinson, Virginia A., and Murray S. Weitzman. 1989. *Dimensions of the Independent Sector: A Statistical Profile*. Washington, D.C.: Independent Sector.

Menchik, Paul, and Burton A. Weisbrod. 1981. "Volunteer Labor Supply in the Provision of Collective Goods." In *Nonprofit Firms in a Three Sector Economy*, ed. Michelle J. White, pp. 163–81. Washington, D.C.: Urban Institute.

Morgan, James N., Richard F. Dye, and Judith H. Hybels. 1977. "Results from Two National Surveys of Philanthropic Activity." In *Research Papers*, Commission on Private Philanthropy and Public Needs, vol. 1, pp. 157–323. Washington, D.C.: Treasury Department.

Musgrave, Richard A., and Peggy B. Musgrave. 1989. *Public Finance in Theory and Practice*, 5th ed. New York: McGraw-Hill.

Nerlove, Marc. 1972. "On Tuition and the Costs of Higher Education: Prolegomena to a Conceptual Framework." *Journal of Political Economy* 80: pp. S178–S218.

Odendahl, Teresa. 1989. "The Culture of Elite Philanthropy in the Reagan Years." *Nonprofit and Voluntary Sector Quarterly* 18: 237–48.

Savas E. S. 1982. *Privatizing the Public Sector*. Chatham, NJ: Chatham House.

Schaefer, Jeffrey. 1968. "Philanthropic Contributions: Their Equity and Efficiency." *Quarterly Review of Economics* 8: 25–35.

Schlesinger, Mark. 1990. "Privatization and Change: Organizational Ownership and the Diffusion of Innovations in Human Services." Unpublished paper. Kennedy School of Government, Harvard University.

Sen, Amartya K. 1977. "Rational Fools: A Critique of the Behavioral Foundations of Economic Theory." *Philosophy and Public Affairs* 6: 317–44.

Shils, Edward. 1973. "The American Private University." *Minerva* 11: 6–29.

Vickrey, William. 1962. "One Economist's View of Philanthropy." In *Philanthropy and Public Policy*, ed. Frank G. Dickinson, pp. 31–56. New York: National Bureau of Economic Research.

Weisbrod, Burton. 1988. *The Nonprofit Economy*. Cambridge: Harvard University Press.

# [6]

# Ideals versus Dollars: Donors, Charity Managers, and Government Grants

Susan Rose-Ackerman

*Columbia University*

This paper demonstrates how changes in untied, lump-sum government grants or income from unrestricted endowments will affect the behavior of charities operated by managers with strong philosophical or professional commitments. An increase in such funds will reduce the charity's accountability to private donors and lower its fund-raising activities. The grant will not be spent entirely on raising the quantity of output. Instead, it will permit the charity manager to reduce his or her dependence on the costly solicitation of donors who do not completely share the manager's preferences.

In order to understand nonprofit charities one must recognize both their diversity and the independent role of their managers in furthering this diversity. We will miss much of their special character if we view them as mere conduits seeking faithfully to reify the wishes of their contributors.[1] In this paper I demonstrate how an increase or a fall in untied, lump-sum government grants or income from unrestricted endowments will affect the behavior of charities operated by managers with strong philosophical or professional commitments to some service mixes rather than others. An increase in such funds will reduce the charity's accountability to private donors and lower its fund-raising activities. The grant will not be spent entirely on raising

The paper is a revised version of one presented at the annual meeting of the American Economic Association, New York City, December 28, 1985. I am grateful for the comments of Tim Brennan, Richard Steinberg, James Strnad, and the *Journal*'s editor and referee.

[1] For work that takes this point of view, see Warr (1982) and Bergstrom, Blume, and Varian (1986).

[*Journal of Political Economy*, 1987, vol. 95, no. 4]

the quantity of output. Instead, it will permit the charity manager to reduce his or her dependence on the costly solicitation of donors who do not completely share the manager's preferences.

To make this argument I begin by outlining the kind of service variety I have in mind. I then present a hypothesis about the differences between for-profit and nonprofit entrepreneur-managers and argue that a perfect match between donors' and managers' preferences is unlikely. Given these conditions, I develop a model of a single charity that must choose both a level of fund-raising activity and the characteristics of its service mix. I consider first a world with no lump-sum resources and then a world with untied public grants or investment earnings.

The services provided by nonprofits vary along a large number of dimensions—dimensions that are observable and generally known to potential donors even if they are often intangible. Charities may be affiliated with one or another religious group. Thus in the United States, Jewish, Catholic, and Protestant groups operate schools, hospitals, nursing homes, foster care agencies, and a wide range of other charities (Young 1985). A similar pattern is found elsewhere in the world (James 1987). Nonprofit managers may also subscribe to different theories of how to help needy people. Thus private programs for the homeless might specialize in providing psychoanalytic therapy along with food and shelter, might emphasize job training, or might simply concentrate on keeping as many people as possible off the streets. Charities also differ in their method of selecting clients. Some, run by professionals, may look for "interesting" cases. Others might try to locate the most needy subjects (Rose-Ackerman 1981). Finally, either because of philosophical differences or for other reasons, managers may vary in the types and amounts of capital and labor they use (James and Rose-Ackerman 1986, pp. 39–41).[2] Some may emphasize state-of-the-art equipment, while others emphasize warm and pleasant surroundings. Some have a large professional staff; others rely on volunteers and a paid staff without graduate degrees but with a deep commitment to the organization's mission.

While private for-profit firms also produce a wide variety of goods and services, my hypothesis is that nonprofit managers are much more directly interested in the character of the services they provide

[2] In a study of a broad range of British arts organizations, Gapinski (1980, 1986) found that both artists and capital are used in inefficiently large amounts, indicating that quality is higher than the profit-maximizing level. In another effort (1984) he found that the British Royal Shakespeare Company produces more output and sets lower prices than would a profit-maximizing firm. Wilson and Jadlow (1982) found that nonprofits with nuclear medicine facilities tended to be farther from a hypothetical efficiency frontier than for-profits.

than are for-profit managers. Charity managers are trying not only to satisfy donors and clients but also to please themselves through their choice of service mix. This is not an obvious case of "shirking," that is, overusing expense accounts, sleeping on the job, or purchasing expensive office furniture. Instead, the managers wish to use the nonprofit to put into practice their own ideas about how best to help people.[3] Thus I hypothesize that a selection mechanism is at work. The people attracted to managerial positions in the nonprofit sector are those who care relatively little about financial gain and relatively highly about putting their own ideals into practice. They realize that money is necessary to pursue their goals, and institutional survival may be a necessary precondition to furthering their aims, but financial health will be traded off against their own preferences for service quality.[4] Such managers may well try to operate an efficient operation in the sense of keeping perquisites to a minimum and seeking to avoid waste, but their choice of service quality may not perfectly match the preferences of either donors or clients.

One might suppose, however, that if donors are dissatisfied with a manager's choices, then they will simply donate to more appealing charities that solicit gifts from them. While this check is important, it may not lead to a perfect match of donors with institutions. An imbalance can persist if there is a scarcity of nonprofit entrepreneurs combined with fixed costs of establishing new organizations. In fact, given the low levels of financial rewards, it does not seem implausible to assume that not all points in the ideology-service spectrum will be provided (Rose-Ackerman 1981). For example, donors to universities might prefer a practical orientation to the curriculum because they are practical people themselves. Such people, however, would never consider managing a university themselves because of the financial sacrifice required. Instead, those who choose to manage universities

[3] For other applications of this perspective, see the introduction in Rose-Ackerman (1986), pt. 5 of James and Rose-Ackerman (1986), and Rose-Ackerman (1981, 1982).

[4] For a similar perspective, see Etzioni (1975, p. 284), Weisbrod, Handler, and Komesar (1978), James (1983), Young (1983, 1985), Schlesinger et al. (1986), and Weisbrod (1986). One implication of this theory is that, ceteris paribus, within the nonprofit sector itself the incomes of managers in strongly programmatic organizations should be lower than those of managers in organizations with weaker philosophical commitments. To writers who focus on nonprofit managers, the need to reach an accommodation with donors is the "Achilles heel of donor dependency" that may lead to "goal deflection" (Kramer 1985, p. 19). The Wolfenden Committee (1978, pp. 150–51), which studied the charitable sector in England, was sensitive to this trade-off: "The voluntary sector . . . must go further than mere [financial] accountability, and accept that the funder too has rights and duties to his own constituents." Conversely, the need to raise funds can cause a charity to downgrade the interests of its clients. The committee quotes a memorandum from the Howard League for Penal Reform, which worries that "a charity which runs homes or hostels . . . may feel pressed into seeking publicity which is distasteful to the residents in them" (p. 151).

may largely consist of people who do not share these donors' interests. The managers must juggle their interest in the organization's financial health with their beliefs in its proper mission.

With this background we are ready to consider the link between service mix, private donations, and lump-sum income from government grants or investments. Before beginning the theoretical discussion, it is important to understand the relatively simple role that government grants play in this preliminary analysis. They are modeled as exogenous resources that rise and fall independently of any actions taken by managers or donors. They are unaffected by the manager's philosophy or choice of service mix. Studies cited by Kramer (1985, pp. 5–6) suggest that this is, at least, a plausible assumption for some types of government grants.[5] The model can also be interpreted as representing a charity's response to an unanticipated rise or fall in untied endowment income.[6] In short, my emphasis is on the manager's response to an unpredicted increase or fall in resources. Of course, this is a strong simplifying assumption since it is doubtful if many resources are truly unencumbered. It does, however, permit a clear focus on the link between donors and managers operating through fund-raising expenses and the choice of service mix. A more general model would consider the relationship between the strings attached to public funds and the preferences of donors (for a fuller exposition of these issues, see Rose-Ackerman [1981]).

In developing a model of a single charity, it will be impossible to capture adequately the several dimensions along which service mix and philosophical outlook can vary in nonprofit charities. Nevertheless, the basic trade-off between service mix and financial health can be represented with a much simpler formulation. Thus I assume that there is a single variable $x$ that stands for the qualitative features of the service that matter both to the manager and to donors. The variable $x$ is calibrated so that, ceteris paribus, the manager always prefers more $x$ to less up to some maximum, $x_{max}$.[7] I assume that the

[5] His own international comparisons suggest "that the impact of governmental funds in controlling voluntary organizations is much less than is commonly believed" (Kramer 1985, pp. 5–6). Other studies of New York United Way agencies (Hartogs and Weber 1978), of a broad sample of nonprofits in the United States (Salamon 1984), and of nonprofits in England (Wolfenden Committee 1978, pp. 68, 149–50; Judge 1982, pp. 405–6, 409) came to similar conclusions.

[6] Hansmann (1986, p. 25), in a study of university endowment funds, argues that a large endowment protects "a university administration and faculty from the need to cater too closely to the desires of those who ultimately provide the institution's income."

[7] This maximum can be thought of as either "technological," i.e., no better $x$'s exist, or utility based, i.e., $x_{max}$ is the manager's most preferred level of $x$. In the discussion in the text I assume that it is a technological constraint. This condition on $x$ is not needed in the model without government grants, but it is a necessary constraint when grants are introduced.

basic charity "market" is as I have outlined it above. Thus the manager is likely to find it worthwhile to solicit some donors who do not rank $x$ in exactly the same way as the manager.[8]

I begin with a world in which no lump-sum funds are available from either government or unrestricted endowments and concentrate my attention on the charity's own attempts to raise funds. The behavior of all other charities besides the one under consideration is held constant. The manager must then decide how many people to solicit and what kind of services to provide. Fund-raising is costly, and individual donations depend on donors' perceptions of the value of the charity's services. No one donates unless he or she is solicited, and donations from those who are solicited depend on $x$, the qualitative index, and on $q$, the quantity of services produced. As long as $x < x_{\max}$, the manager values both increases in $x$ and increases in total output, $q$, positively. Given his utility function $U(q, x)$, we have $U_q > 0$, $U_x > 0$, $U_{qq} < 0$, and $U_{xx} < 0$ for $x < x_{\max}$.

Donors, however, may not share the manager's priorities. Since $x$ is an index that aggregates a variety of qualitative features using the manager's weights, its value to donors may not always be increasing in $x$. For example, suppose that the donations of any individual $i$ as a function of $x$ and $q$, $D(x, q, i)$, increase up to $\hat{x}_i$, where $\hat{x}_i < x_{\max}$ for all $i$, and then fall as a function of $x$ for any given level of $q$; that is, $D_x > 0$ if $x < \hat{x}_i$ and $D_x < 0$ if $x > \hat{x}_i$. Thus $\hat{x}_i$ is the optimal level of $x$ as far as donor $i$ is concerned, and its level is independent of $q$; that is, the donor's preferences for $x$ are "single-peaked."[9] Suppose further that donors can be ranked unambiguously in terms of the level of their donations at each $x$; thus $D(x, q, i) \geqq D(x, q, j)$ for all $x$ and $q$ and $i < j$, where $0 < i, j \leqq N$ and $N$ is total population. This condition means that the ranking of donors in terms of the size of their gifts is independent of the levels of the quality and output indexes. The charity manager always knows in what order to solicit potential donors.[10] To simplify the exposition I will also assume that all donors have the same optimal $\hat{x}$, but this condition, as I demonstrate below, is not essential to the analysis.

[8] My formulation contrasts with a recent article on nonprofit objective functions by Steinberg (1986*a*), in which there is no explicit tension between donors' and managers' preferences. In his model, marginal contributions are a function only of fund-raising expenses and not of the quantity and quality of output as well. Although they are not modeled explicitly, ideological differences are assumed to be reflected in firm-specific intercepts that do not affect the marginal productivity of fund-raising (p. 510).

[9] This formulation is similar to work on markets with product variety (see, e.g., Eaton and Lipsey 1975; Salop and Stiglitz 1977; Lancaster 1979). It is also comparable to public choice models with single-peaked preferences (see, e.g., Sen 1970).

[10] Some models of public choice in a multiple government system make a similar assumption (see, e.g., Westhoff 1977; Rose-Ackerman 1979).

Next consider the way donations depend on the level of services provided, for example, the number of people served. Two effects work in opposite directions. The first is a substitution effect. A donor may give less the higher the level of services because he or she believes that the marginal value of a gift is lower. Conversely, for donations to an individual charity, a "buying-in" effect may dominate. Here the donor gives more the larger the charity because he or she benefits more from giving to a larger charity than to a smaller one, since any given quality level is spread over a larger number of units of output (Rose-Ackerman 1982). In short, $D_q \gtreqless 0$.

Suppose that no one donates unless solicited and that the cost of soliciting a donor is fixed. Then for any $x$, if $z$ is the cost of soliciting one person and if we let $i$ be a continuous variable, then when $n/N$ of the population is solicited, total revenue is total donations from those solicited minus the cost of solicitation, or

$$R(n, q, x) = \int_{i=0}^{n} D(x, q, i)di - zn. \tag{1}$$

The final element of the problem is the cost of producing various levels of $x$ and $q$, $C(x, q)$. Obviously the marginal cost of an extra unit of output is positive, $C_q > 0$. However, $x$ is an index of quality using the manager's weights. Thus higher levels of $x$ are not necessarily more costly than lower levels. Think of $x$ as an index recording the color a product is painted or measuring the ethical or religious orientation of a charity. Therefore, with little loss in generality I will set $C_x = 0$ and write $C(x, q)$ in the simple form $cq$, where $c$ is a constant.[11] The cost to the manager of increasing $x$ is reflected not in production costs but in the possibly lower productivity of fund-raising activity. The manager maximizes $U(q, x)$ subject to the break-even condition $R \geqq cq$ by choosing the utility-maximizing levels of $x$, $q$, and $n$.

For each $x$ and $q$ there is an optimal number of people to solicit, $\bar{n}(x, q)$. The optimal level occurs where marginal cost of soliciting equals marginal revenue, that is, where $D(x, q, \bar{n}) = z$ for $\bar{n} < N$.[12] Thus at the optimal $\bar{n}$ the cost of soliciting an extra person just equals the marginal donation. The proportion of the population solicited is highest at the donors' preferred level of $x$, $\hat{x}$, because fund-raising is most productive at that service quality. In contrast, there are very low and very high levels of $x$, both of which are unattractive to donors, where the biggest giver contributes just enough to cover the cost of sending him or her a brochure.

[11] Clearly $x$ could involve a fixed cost that is independent of the particular $x$ chosen without changing the analysis.

[12] If $D(x, q, N) > z$, then $\bar{n} = N$. In the subsequent discussion I will assume that some people are such low givers that $\bar{n} < N$ for all $x$ and $q$.

The maximization problem now is

$$\max U(q, x)$$

$$\text{subject to } x \leqq x_{\max} \text{ and } TD(x, q) - z\tilde{n}(x, q) = cq,$$

where $TD(x, q) = \int_{i=0}^{\tilde{n}(x,q)} D(x, q, i)di$. Let $D_x^* = \int_0^{\tilde{n}} D_x di$ and $D_q^* = \int_0^{\tilde{n}} D_q di$. Then $U$ is maximized at[13]

$$\frac{U_x}{U_q} = \frac{-D_x^*}{c - D_q^*} \qquad (2)$$

as long as the $x$ that satisfies (2) is less than or equal to $x_{\max}$. This is a variant of the familiar result in economics that utility is maximized when the marginal utilities per dollar of each argument in the utility function are equal. This is so because $-D_x^*$ is the implicit price of an extra unit of $x$ and $c - D_q^*$ is the implicit price of a unit of $q$. This unit "costs" $c$ minus any change in donations that results. For this condition to be a utility maximum, both $D_x^* < 0$ and $c > D_q^*$ must hold.[14] Therefore, $x > \hat{x}$ since $D_x^*$ is negative only when $x$ exceeds the donors' most preferred level, $\hat{x}$. Given $x$ and $q$, $\tilde{n}(x, q) < \tilde{n}(\hat{x}, q)$ can be found. The level of $x$ is not the one most preferred by donors, and some people are not solicited who would be worth approaching if $x = \hat{x}$. Furthermore, since $c > D_q^*$, $D_q^*$ may be greater than, less than, or equal to zero, but it cannot be too large and positive. Thus the buying-in effect cannot be very strong at the equilibrium. For example, when output is low, the buying-in effect may be dominant so that gifts increase as $q$ increases, but eventually, as $q$ increases, the substitution effect takes over. I will suppose in the subsequent discussion that (2) can be satisfied; that is, an equilibrium exists.

The equilibrium can be illustrated graphically as follows. Figure 1 graphs donations net of fund-raising costs ($R$) against output ($q$) for different levels of $x$. Let $\hat{q}$ be the point at which the substitution effect

[13] The function $U$ is maximized at

$$U_q \frac{dq}{dx} + U_x = 0,$$

where

$$\frac{dq}{dx} \cdot c = [D(q, x, \tilde{n}) - z]\left(\frac{\partial \tilde{n}}{\partial q} \cdot \frac{dq}{dx} + \frac{\partial \tilde{n}}{\partial x}\right) + \int_{i=0}^{\tilde{n}} \left(\frac{\partial D}{\partial q} \cdot \frac{dq}{dx} + \frac{\partial D}{\partial x}\right) di.$$

The first term in brackets equals zero in equilibrium when marginal solicitation cost equals marginal benefit. Thus this term drops out, so

$$\frac{dq}{dx} = \frac{D_x^*}{c - D_q^*} \text{ and } \frac{U_x}{U_q} = \frac{-D_x^*}{c - D_q^*}.$$

[14] If the signs were reversed, the result would not be a maximum. Then even though the marginal condition holds, it would clearly be worthwhile for the manager to increase *both* $x$ and $q$ since they have negative prices.

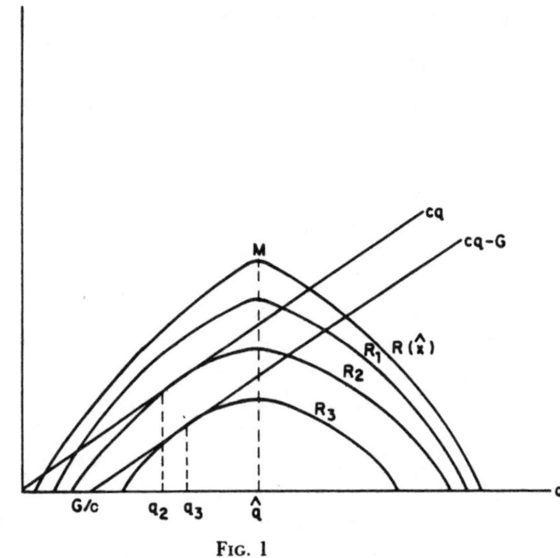


Fig. 1

begins to dominate the buying-in effect and assume, to simplify the graph, that it is independent of $x$. Then, with $x$ held fixed, net donations increase for $q < \hat{q}$ and fall for $q \geqq \hat{q}$. For any $q$, the highest level of donations occurs along $R(\hat{x})$, where $x = \hat{x}$. The curves labeled $R_1$, $R_2$, and $R_3$ each correspond to two quality levels, one greater than $\hat{x}$ and the other less than $\hat{x}$, which are equivalent as far as donors are concerned. The charity's break-even points are found by drawing the total cost relationship $c(q, x) = cq$ and finding the points of intersection with the net donation curves. Notice that $M$, the point of maximum donations, is not a break-even point. The charity would earn a surplus at $M$. In figure 2 the intersection points between $cq$ and $R$ have been translated into quantity-quality, $q$, $x$, space to form the closed curve labeled $F$. All points on or inside $F$ are feasible. The manager then maximizes his or her utility at $Y$, where the highest utility surface touches the locus of opportunities. Point $M$, although producing higher revenues, is less desirable to the manager than $Y$ where $x$ is higher.[15]

Now we can consider the impact of lump-sum government grants, endowment earnings, or other untied resources. Grants affect both the opportunity set of the managers and the choices of donors. They have an income effect for managers that, ceteris paribus, will lead to

[15] Although in fig. 2 the equilibrium $q$ exceeds $\hat{q}$, in general, it may be greater than, equal to, or less than $\hat{q}$.

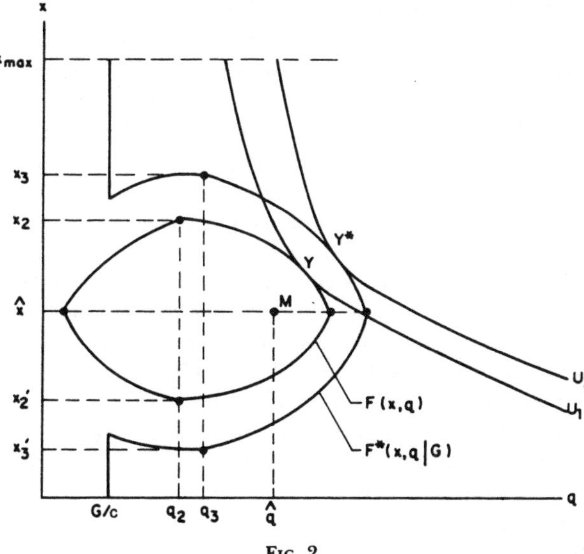


FIG. 2

an increase in both $q$ and $x$ since both are normal goods. But managers must also take into account the impact of their choices on private donations. An increase in $x$ harms donors since $x > \hat{x}$ at equilibrium without grants. The increase in $q$ benefits donors but may reduce individual donations if the substitution effect dominates the buying-in effect. Thus the manager must recalculate the optimal level of fund-raising, and revenues net of fund-raising costs increase by less or more than the level of grants depending on which effect dominates. To see this, consider figures 1 and 2 again. Subtract the grant, $G$, from $cq$ in figure 1 to produce a new locus of break-even points in figure 2, labeled $F^*$, that is everywhere outside the old locus. At point $Y^*$ condition (2) holds. However, for $q \leqq G/c$, the manager can choose any level of $x$ since he does not need to raise funds from private donors. Thus to ensure an interior maximum at $Y^*$, let $U(G/c, x_{\max}) < U(x^*, q^*)$, where $x^*$ and $q^*$ are the quality and quantity levels that hold at $Y^*$.

The equilibrium increase in $q$ is less than the maximum possible, or $G/c$, because the manager moves to a level of $x$ that is more preferred by him and less preferred by donors. Since the substitution effect is dominant in equilibrium, the charity solicits fewer people at $Y^*$. Thus government grants reduce private gifts because individual donors will give less *if* solicited, and, therefore, fewer potential contributors are worth soliciting. Of course, the converse result also holds. When government grants fall, the manager reduces $q$ and chooses a level of $x$ closer to that preferred by donors. He or she also increases fund-raising expenses when $G$ falls because fund-raising is more productive when $G$ is low.[16]

Although these results may seem quite straightforward, it is important to recognize that they depend critically on the assumptions of the model. If, instead, managers share donors' tastes so both believe that $\hat{x}$ is the best level of $x$, then the equilibrium with no grants is at $\hat{x}$. While output, $q$, will fall as grants fall, the level of $x$ will be unaffected by the level of grants and the level of fund-raising expenses will depend only on the impact of $q$ on giving. Fund-raising will still increase when $G$ falls but only insofar as reductions in the level of $q$ do not adversely affect donations. We would not observe charities making a special effort to satisfy donors' preferences for service mix. The conventional wisdom that cuts in public support induce a closer attention to donors' wishes is consistent with my model and inconsistent with one in which no underlying conflict exists in the first place.

The results here thus depend on some mismatch between donor and manager preferences and on an imperfectly competitive environment that permits those differences to persist. Clearly, if entry occurred whenever there were monetary gains to be made, an entrepreneur would establish a charity that produced at $\hat{x}$ and obtain all the donations. Instead of this free-entry assumption, one can generalize the analysis above by assuming that donors have different preferred levels of $x$, $\hat{x}_i$. Then any charity, $k$, will find that, for some subset of the population, $|\hat{x}_i - x_k|$ is less than $|\hat{x}_i - x_j|$ for all the other $j$ charities that these donors know about. Donors examine the $q$, $x$ choices of the charities that solicit them and choose the one they prefer the most. When entry is costly, many donors will give to charities that do not perfectly match their preferences for service mix. Then as long as managers with a personal stake in their charity's service quality are willing to accept lower financial returns than profit maximizers, they will dominate the sector and cuts in grants will move charities closer to the preferences of those who are prepared to donate generously. In the general case the direction of movement will depend on the way both donors and charities are distributed across the ideological spectrum.[17]

[16] Young's (1985, pp. 153–69) case study of the Florida Sheriffs Youth Fund illustrates the behavior of a charity that receives no government support and as a consequence engages in sophisticated fund-raising and an attempt to match its program to the preferences of donors. Several of Young's other case studies illustrate more complex relations between public and private support and managerial preferences.

[17] An analogous model can be developed for the case in which managers and paying customers have divergent tastes, and it can be extended to include the three-cornered relationship among donors, managers, and customers. For example, donors may want

In the current environment of cutbacks in government support for nonprofits, my analysis can help explain the interest among nonprofit managers in "making up" for the loss in government support. First of all, it is important to recognize that if net revenue or output maximization were the organization's only goal, it would always be looking for new ways to raise funds. A cutback in public support would not spur any extra effort unless it raised the marginal productivity of fund-raising. (In fact, if public money were awarded in the form of matching grants, the marginal productivity of fund-raising could well fall when grants are cut.) Second, if managers care directly about service quality, they will not necessarily maximize revenue or output if this would require some sacrifice of managers' interest in quality. Third, if private donations are more constraining than government money, then in times of stable or growing government support the nonprofit may concentrate on providing "high-quality" charitable output as defined by the manager and will not worry about pushing for the last dollar available from donors. However, if government grants fall, managers and trustees may become more interested in increasing revenue from other sources and may, as a consequence, seek to be more accountable to donors. My perspective can, then, explain why the current interest in expanding the revenue base of nonprofit organizations coincides with a drop in their public support, and it also suggests that a corresponding shift in service mix will occur.

But what has, in fact, happened in recent years as government support for nonprofits has fallen? While the basic trade-offs seem to be well understood by both scholars and nonprofit managers (see, e.g., Baumol and Bowen 1966; Gapinski 1980, 1984, 1986; Young 1983, 1985; Kramer 1985; Netzer 1986; Salamon 1987), data on the nonprofit sector, unfortunately, provide little direct evidence either on donors' perceptions or on the underlying goals of nonprofit managers and entrepreneurs and the strategies that they actually follow in the face of declines in public support. There are no systematic data on changes in fund-raising practices or service quality.[18] Broad-based

a college to contain a broad-based mixture of students from all classes and races while some paying customers may prefer a more socially elite institution. University administrators and faculty may want to expand the liberal arts while students prefer courses that will help them get into professional graduate schools. Donors may support experimental projects by symphony orchestras and ballet companies while most customers prefer the classics (see Baumol and Bowen 1966, pp. 253–57; Gapinski 1986).

[18] The Urban Institute Survey (Salamon, Musselwhite, and DeVita 1986, table 9) found that 56 percent of organizations devoted more resources to fund-raising and that 17 percent eliminated specific programs or services, 12 percent reduced the number of clients served, 10 percent tightened eligibility requirements, and 10 percent reduced service levels. Unfortunately, their data provide no further detail.

information from the Urban Institute records only the overall dollar changes and does not record the portion of revenues used to provide charitable services (Salamon 1984). Yet an accurate view of the health of the sector requires one to subtract fund-raising costs from donations. Since the available evidence does suggest that both fund-raising and promotion are costly (Paton 1986; Weisbrod and Dominquez 1986), only a portion of the loss in services from government cutbacks might be made up even if revenues hold constant.[19]

The inadequacies of the data thus suggest areas for further empirical and theoretical research. As a first step, scholars should attempt to measure the marginal fund-raising cost of obtaining increased donations on a sector-by-sector basis.[20] Next, they ought to try to find out if nonprofit organizations do change their service mix in response to cutbacks in public funding and explore the consequences of these shifts for those who use the charity's services.[21]

### References

Baumol, William J., and Bowen, William G. *Performing Arts: The Economic Dilemma.* New York: Twentieth Century Fund, 1966.

Bergstrom, Theodore; Blume, Lawrence; and Varian, Hal. "On the Private Provision of Public Goods." *J. Public Econ.* 29 (February 1986): 25–50.

Eaton, B. Curtis, and Lipsey, Richard G. "The Principle of Minimum Differ-

[19] The Urban Institute's estimates for 1981–82 indicate that total nonprofit revenue did, in fact, hold constant (Salamon 1984) but that the increase in gifts and sales by no means made up for the economywide fall in government social service spending. A cross-section study by Schiff and Weisbrod (1986) for the mid-1970s suggests that in the social welfare area increases in gifts and sales will make up for only 12 percent of the fall in total direct government spending on these services and that low levels of direct subsidies to these organizations will reduce the number but not the average size of the organizations.

[20] Existing data from the Internal Revenue Service (IRS) measure only the average level of fund-raising per dollar of contributions (see Steinberg 1986*a*, 1986*b*; Weisbrod and Dominquez 1986). Weisbrod and Dominquez found that donors respond to the net "price" of donations, a variable that takes into account both marginal tax rates and the share of fund-raising in total revenues. Thus donors are hypothesized to act as if the marginal productivity of fund-raising equals the average productivity. In contrast, Steinberg (1986*b*), using the same data source but a different functional form, found that the implicit price of giving is not generally related to the average fund-raising share. He hypothesized that this result shows that donors perceive the difference between the average fund-raising share and the impact of a marginal dollar on the nonprofit's fund-raising budget.

[21] On a more comprehensive agenda of research topics would be a study of nonprofits' increased use of fees and subsidiary profit-making activities. According to Independent Sector's tabulation of IRS 990 data (Hodgkinson and Weitzman 1986, p. 139, table 4.19), service revenue (including government vendor payments) was 63.4 percent of the revenue of nonprofit charitable organizations and net income from sales was 5 percent of the total. The Urban Institute survey (Salamon et al. 1986, table 7) shows that fees increased by 6.6 percent when government support fell by 6.3 percent in 1981–82 but provides no breakdown by type of service within organizations.

entiation Reconsidered: Some New Developments in the Theory of Spatial Competition." *Rev. Econ. Studies* 42 (January 1975): 27–49.

Etzioni, Amitai. "Alternative Conceptions of Accountability: The Example of Health Administrations." *Public Admin. Rev.* 35 (May/June 1975): 279–86.

Gapinski, James H. "The Production of Culture." *Rev. Econ. and Statis.* 62 (November 1980): 578–86.

———. "The Economics of Performing Shakespeare." *A.E.R.* 74 (June 1984): 458–66.

———. "The Lively Arts as Substitutes for the Lively Arts." *A.E.R. Papers and Proc.* 76 (May 1986): 20–25.

Hansmann, Henry. "Why Do Universities Have Endowments?" Working Paper no. 109. New Haven, Conn.: Yale Univ., Program Non-Profit Organizations, Inst. Soc. and Policy Studies, January 1986.

Hartogs, Nelly, and Weber, Joseph. *The Impact of Government Funding on the Management of Voluntary Agencies.* New York: Greater New York Fund, United Way, 1978.

Hodgkinson, Virginia Ann, and Weitzman, Murray S. *Dimensions of the Independent Sector: A Statistical Profile.* 2d ed. Washington: Independent Sector, 1986.

James, Estelle. "How Non-Profits Grow: A Model." *J. Policy Analysis and Management* 2 (Spring 1983) 350–65. Reprinted in Rose-Ackerman (1986).

———. "The Nonprofit Sector in Comparative Perspective." In *The Nonprofit Sector: A Research Handbook,* edited by W. Powell. New Haven, Conn.: Yale Univ. Press, 1987.

James, Estelle, and Rose-Ackerman, Susan. *The Nonprofit Enterprise in Market Economies.* Fundamentals of Pure and Applied Economics, no. 9. Chur, Switzerland: Harwood, 1986.

Judge, Ken. "The Public Purchase of Social Care: British Confirmation of the American Experience." *Policy and Politics* 10 (October 1982): 397–416.

Kramer, Ralph M. "The Voluntary Agency in a Mixed Economy: Dilemmas of Entrepreneurialism and Vendorism." Working Paper no. 85. New Haven, Conn.: Yale Univ., Program Non-Profit Organizations, Inst. Soc. and Policy Studies, January 1985.

Lancaster, Kelvin. *Variety, Equity, and Efficiency: Product Variety in an Industrial Society.* Cambridge: Cambridge Univ. Press, 1979.

Netzer, Dick. "Dance in New York: Market and Subsidy Changes." *A.E.R. Papers and Proc.* 76 (May 1986): 15–19.

Paton, G. Jeffry. "Microeconomic Perspectives Applied to Development Planning and Management." In *Enhancing the Management of Fund Raising,* edited by John A. Dunn. San Francisco: Jossey-Bass, 1986.

Rose-Ackerman, Susan. "Market Models of Local Government: Exit, Voting, and the Land Market." *J. Urban Econ.* 6 (July 1979): 319–37.

———. "Do Government Grants to Charity Reduce Private Donations?" In *Nonprofit Firms in a Three Sector Economy,* edited by Michelle J. White. Washington: Urban Inst., 1981. Reprinted in Rose-Ackerman (1986).

———. "Charitable Giving and 'Excessive' Fundraising." *Q.J.E.* 97 (May 1982): 193–212. Reprinted in Rose-Ackerman (1986).

———, ed. *The Economics of Nonprofit Institutions: Studies in Structure and Policy.* New York: Oxford Univ. Press, 1986.

Salamon, Lester M. "Nonprofit Organizations." In *The Reagan Record: An Assessment of America's Changing Domestic Priorities,* edited by John L. Palmer and Isabel V. Sawhill. Cambridge, Mass.: Ballinger, 1984.

———. "Partners in Public Service: Toward a Theory of Government-Nonprofit Relations." In *The Nonprofit Sector: A Research Handbook,* edited by W. Powell. New Haven, Conn.: Yale Univ. Press, 1987.

Salamon, Lester M.; Musselwhite, James, Jr.; and DeVita, Carol. "Partners in Public Service: Government and the Nonprofit Sector in the American Welfare State." Paper delivered at Independent Sector Research Forum, New York, March 1986.

Salop, Steven, and Stiglitz, Joseph E. "Bargains and Ripoffs: A Model of Monopolistically Competitive Price Dispersion." *Rev. Econ. Studies* 44 (October 1977): 493–510.

Schiff, Jerald, and Weisbrod, Burton. "Government Social Welfare Spending and the Private Nonprofit Sector: Crowding Out, and More." Mimeographed. Madison: Univ. Wisconsin, November 1986.

Schlesinger, Mark; Benkover, Judy; Blumenthal, David; Musacchio, Robert; and Willer, Janet. "The Privatization of Health Care and Physicians' Perspectives of Access to Hospital Services: Profits, Competition and Multi-Hospital Corporations." *Milbank Q.* (Winter 1987), in press.

Sen, Amartya. *Collective Choice and Social Welfare.* San Francisco: Holden-Day, 1970.

Steinberg, Richard. "The Revealed Objective Functions of Nonprofit Firms." *Rand J. Econ.* 17 (Winter 1986): 508–26. (*a*)

———. "Should Donors Care about Fund-raising?" In *The Economics of Nonprofit Institutions: Studies in Structure and Policy,* edited by Susan Rose-Ackerman. New York: Oxford Univ. Press, 1986. (*b*)

Warr, Peter G. "Pareto Optimal Redistribution and Private Charity." *J. Public Econ.* 19 (October 1982): 131–38.

Weisbrod, Burton A. "Nonprofit and For-Profit Organizational Behavior: Is There a Difference?" Mimeographed. Madison: Univ. Wisconsin, December 1986.

Weisbrod, Burton A., and Dominquez, Nestor. "Demand for Collective Goods in Private Nonprofit Markets: Can Fundraising Expenditures Help Overcome Free-Rider Behavior?" *J. Public Econ.* 30 (February 1986): 83–95.

Weisbrod, Burton A.; Handler, Joel F.; and Komesar, Neil K. *Public Interest Law: An Economic and Institutional Analysis.* Berkeley: Univ. California Press, 1978.

Westhoff, Frank. "Existence of Equilibria in Economies with a Local Public Good." *J. Econ. Theory* 14 (February 1977): 84–112.

Wilson, George W., and Jadlow, Joseph M. "Competition, Profit Incentives, and Technical Efficiency in the Provision of Nuclear Medicine Services." *Bell J. Econ.* 13 (Autumn 1982): 472–82.

Wolfenden Committee. *The Future of Voluntary Organisations.* London: Croom Helm, 1978.

Young, Dennis R. *If Not for Profit, for What? A Behavioral Theory of the Nonprofit Sector Based on Entrepreneurship.* Lexington, Mass.: Lexington, 1983.

———. *Casebook of Management for Non-Profit Organizations: Entrepreneurship and Organizational Change in the Human Services.* New York: Haworth, 1985.

# Part III
# Nonprofits as Providers of Public Goods

# [7]

# Rational Nonprofit Entrepreneurship

Marc Bilodeau

*Indiana University–Purdue University at Indianapolis*
*Indianapolis, IN*
*and*
*Université de Sherbrooke*
*Sherbrooke, Quebec, Canada, J1K 2R1*
*mbilodea@iupui.edu*

Al Slivinski

*University of Western Ontario*
*London, Ontario, Canada N6A 5C2*
*aslivins@julian.uwo.ca*

*This paper derives the decision to found a nonprofit firm as the equilibrium outcome of a multistage game among individuals who would like a public good to be provided. The model predicts that if individuals will voluntarily contribute towards provision of the public good, then it is in the self-interest of the entrepreneur to impose a nondistribution constraint on herself by founding a nonprofit firm.*

## I. Introduction

Why do entrepreneurs found *nonprofit* enterprises[1]? More specifically, how could it be rational for an individual who invests her time and money to found and manage an enterprise, to publicly renounce any claim to her firm's profits? Nonprofit firms are founded every day. For example, in the US, from 1987 to 1989, 110,000 new charita-

The authors have benefited from comments on previous drafts by Robin Cowan, Jim Davies, Ig Horstmann, Bart Lipman, Glenn MacDonald, Motty Perry, and Rich Steinberg. An anonymous coeditor and two anonymous referees also provided comments that helped to improve the paper. The authors thank the Social Sciences and Humanities Research Council of Canada for financial support.

1. A nonprofit enterprise is a firm that has no residual claimants. It can be profit-making in the sense that it can earn and accumulate any level of surplus from its activities, but is subject to a legally enforced nondistribution constraint (NDC) on its net cash flows. Throughout this paper, we will use the word "profit" to refer to any difference between the firm's revenues and expenditures, even if the revenues are constituted entirely of voluntary donations received by the firm.


Journal of Economics & Management Strategy, Volume 7, Number 4, Winter 1998, 551–571

ble organizations were founded,[2] and in 1990, nonprofit firms accounted for 6.8% of total national income and 4.2% of all firms.[3]

Nonprofit firms operate in a wide variety of industries, offering services ranging from family planning to Little League sports, and include soup kitchens, universities, theatrical and musical companies, nursing homes, and cemeteries. No single model could account for the diversity of possible motivations in founding such a list of organizations. In this paper, we focus on one particular type of nonprofit firm: those providing a public good and receiving a substantial part of their revenues in the form of donations.[4] Charities of all kinds, medical research institutions, political parties and environmental defense funds are all obvious examples.

It is not by coincidence that almost all the firms receiving donations and providing a public good are nonprofit. Fama and Jensen (1983) argue that general donations pose a particular agency problem for proprietary firms. Individuals may want to give a firm money to finance the production of a public good, but if the firm is proprietary, they have no assurance that their contributions will be used for this purpose, because they do not receive an immediate *quid pro quo* for their gifts. By comparison, when the firm is nonprofit, the NDC provides assurance to donors that their contributions will not be appropriated by the firm's residual claimants. So nonprofit firms have a *raison d'être* in situations in which a public good is to be provided privately through voluntary contributions.[5]

However, the fact that a nonprofit firm may fulfill a socially desirable economic role does not explain why an individual would find it in her private interest to found such a firm, especially if there are time and money costs to being a nonprofit entrepreneur. To understand nonprofit-firm formation, we need models in which a

2. Source: Hodgkinson et al. (1992, p. 12).

3. Source: Hodgkinson et al. (1992, p. 4).

4. There is a large economic literature on voluntary contributions to public goods, e.g., Bernheim (1986), Bergstrom et al. (1986), Andreoni (1988, 1989), Sugden (1982), and Varian (1994).

5. An explanation for nonprofit firms' receiving donations to provide public goods is due to Weisbrod (1975). He argues that when preferences are heterogeneous, individuals who are dissatisfied with the levels of provision of public goods will supplement government provision by contributing to nonprofits. Other roles for nonprofit firms have been proposed in the literature. For example, Hansmann (1980) suggests that when the quality of a firm's output is hard to observe, a nonprofit firm may be more trustworthy because the inability to claim profits removes an incentive to defraud customers. Formalizing this idea, Easley and O'Hara (1983) show that a nonprofit firm can be the solution to an optimal social contracting problem with asymmetric information. The thrust of papers written in this vein has been to show that nonprofits perform a socially desirable role and/or that there is a demand for their existence. James and Rose-Ackerman (1986), Gassler (1990), and Steinberg (1993) provide surveys of the economic literature on nonprofit firms.

rational self-interested entrepreneur founds a nonprofit firm, not because this is socially optimal in some sense, but because it is in her best interest to do so.

An obvious but simplistic possibility is to assume that there are rewards to being a nonprofit entrepreneur that do not accrue to the founder of a proprietary firm. For example, the entrepreneur's motivations could include the desire for status or recognition, or feelings of "warm glow," which she would not receive if she founded a proprietary enterprise. Without denying that these factors could influence the choice of whether to found a nonprofit rather than a proprietary enterprise, we wish to ask whether an ordinary individual who only cares about her consumption of a public and a private good would rationally choose to found a nonprofit firm. If not, these private rewards would be a necessary component of any theory of nonprofit entrepreneurship. Our model provides a simpler, more fundamental explanation for nonprofit entrepreneurship, which does not rely on the existence of purely private rewards.

A second possibility is that the preferential tax treatment enjoyed by nonprofits in many countries may induce entrepreneurs to choose the nonprofit organizational form. Without denying that the extent of adoption of the nonprofit form may be influenced by the tax code, there is much evidence to suggest that tax privileges are neither necessary nor sufficient to generate a nonprofit sector. For example, in the United States donations to qualifying nonprofit organizations are deductible from the donor's taxable income. But donations to political organizations like the Republican Party are not deductible from taxable income, and yet such organizations provide a public good, rely almost wholly on donations to survive, and still manage to thrive. Some nonprofit organizations are also exempted from paying corporate income tax. However, as Hansmann (1980, p. 882) notes, "...by the time the corporate income tax first appeared in the late nineteenth century, nonprofit organizations were already well established in many of the areas in which they are found today." The exemption of many nonprofit organizations from state and local real property taxes is probably the most financially significant aspect of the tax treatment of nonprofits in the US. However, this exemption has not, for example, been sufficient to allow nonprofit hospitals or nursing homes to dominate the markets in which they operate. Indeed, Chang and Tuckman (1990) found that the magnitude of the property tax rates from which nonprofit hospitals are exempted had no significant effect on their market share, suggesting that the exemption is not an overriding factor in the choice of organizational form. Thus, it seems worthwhile to inquire into the existence of a rationale for founding a nonprofit firm that operates even in the absence of preferential tax treatment.

A final possibility would be to assume that the NDC either is not perfectly enforceable or only restricts the form rather than the amount of profit distribution, so that a nonprofit manager could at least partially circumvent it by using some of the firm's net revenues for perks or an inflated salary. Using this approach, Eckel and Steinberg (1993) show that a manager who is skilled at cheating or who prefers perks to cash might be better off seeking employment in —or founding—a nonprofit rather than a proprietary enterprise. While there is surely some truth to the hypothesis that the NDC is not always perfectly enforced or only restricts the form of profit distribution, this begs the question as to why anyone would voluntarily impose such a constraint in the first place. After all, the founder of a proprietary firm can also pay inflated salaries and provide perks to herself and her managers, and can do so legally. To understand nonprofit-firm formation, we need models in which it is in the entrepreneur's own interest to impose this constraint on herself. Of course, *ex post*, once donations have been collected or profits realized, it may never be in the entrepreneur's interest to obey the NDC, but at least it should be in her interest *ex ante* to impose it. Would anyone found a nonprofit enterprise even if they knew that the NDC disallowed all forms of surplus distribution and would be strictly enforced?

To answer this question, we build a model in which an entrepreneur can choose to found either a nonprofit or a proprietary firm to produce a public good. It predicts that in situations in which the entrepreneur would herself contribute toward the public good's provision and in which the firm would also receive voluntary contributions from others, it will be in the entrepreneur's own interest to found a nonprofit rather than a proprietary enterprise because the NDC induces greater contributions from the public. We thus establish a formal connection between privately provided public goods and nonprofit firms: the institutional form preferred by an entrepreneur relying on donations to provide a public good will always be a nonprofit firm. This testable prediction of the model is confirmed by the commonplace observation that virtually all firms receiving donations are nonprofit.

## 2. Model

### 2.1 The Institutional Context

Consider a group of individuals who have preferences over commodity bundles consisting of their own private consumption and a nonexcludable public good.[6] Suppose, however, that initially there is no institution engaged in producing the public good. In particular, government expenditures on the public good are assumed to be zero.[7] Then even if individuals wanted to contribute voluntarily toward its provision, there is no one to collect their contributions and use them to produce the public good. If any of the public good is to be provided, someone must *organize* its production.

We assume that doing this requires someone—an entrepreneur—to set up a firm. By assumption, the entrepreneur's only motivation is to maximize the utility she derives from her consumption of private and public goods, just like everyone else. It is only her role as owner/manager of the firm that distinguishes her from other individuals in the population. A decision that must be made by the entrepreneur at the outset is whether to incorporate her firm as *nonprofit* or as *proprietary*. Since part of our purpose is to determine whether it can be in an entrepreneur's self-interest to impose a NDC on herself, we assume that this NDC would be perfectly enforced.

Once a firm has been set up, the next phase in the provision process is to gather funds to cover the costs of producing the public good. The simplest way to model voluntary provision of a public good is to assume that all individuals contribute simultaneously. However, such a simple model does not allow for the fact that the entrepreneur *controls* the fund-raising process. She collects the money others give her, and this gives her certain prerogatives not available to others, perhaps including the option of keeping some of it for herself. These prerogatives cannot be captured in a model in which the entrepreneur is only one individual contributing simultaneously with all others.

As founder of the firm, an entrepreneur always has the option to contribute some of her own private funds to the firm before

6. If the good in question is, for example, the building of a new hospital wing or the founding of a theater company, then some or all of the goods and services such a facility ultimately provides may be excludable. However, so long as individuals anticipate future receipt of surplus from the *existence* of such a facility (even if its services will be charged for), the facility itself has a nonexcludable public-good aspect, and individuals might want to contribute voluntarily to ensure it is made available. Weisbrod (1964) refers to this as the "option demand" motivation for contributing to a facility that will ultimately be used to provide private goods. Those who see no value in the existence of the facility will of course not voluntarily contribute funds for its establishment.

7. The politically determined government provision of some public goods does not generally eliminate completely the demand for private supplementation when individuals have heterogeneous preferences. See Weisbrod (1975). To simplify the analysis, we assume that the government does not provide any of this public good.

appealing to the public for donations.[8] We model this by allowing the entrepreneur to contribute before everyone else if she so chooses. Some part of this initial contribution may very well be nonmonetary, as the entrepreneur may have to devote substantial amounts of labor and entrepreneurial talent to getting the project off the ground and to organizing a first successful fund-raising drive. Further, as the person controlling when and how the money collected will be used, she also has the option of contributing again after the fund-raising campaign is over, if she feels that a higher level of provision is preferable. What is important for our model is that she has no means to commit to *not* contributing more after observing what others have donated.

Another prerogative of the entrepreneur is choosing the production technology and the quantity of the public good to be produced by her firm. To abstract from issues of output quality, X efficiency, and agency problems within the firm,[9] we assume that there is only one production process for the public good and that output quality and costs of production are certain and immediately observable by everyone. This means that once everyone has contributed, the only decision left to the entrepreneur is how much of the public good to provide with the money collected by the firm. In particular, if her firm is proprietary, she could choose to produce less of the public good than would be possible with the funds collected, and appropriate the residual to increase her private consumption. We model this by allowing the entrepreneur to contribute again, after everyone else, and we allow this later contribution to be negative only if the firm is proprietary.

This model captures the essence of what entrepreneurs actually do: whether proprietary or nonprofit, entrepreneurs are individuals who found new enterprises and decide how they operate. The entrepreneur in our model can be viewed in much the same way as the entrepreneur who appears in the theory of profit-taking firms. The entrepreneur's roles of seeing a demand for some public good and of founding and then managing a firm that provides it may in reality be shared among several individuals. Nonetheless, it is not hard to find examples of nonprofit organizations whose origins accord quite closely with the particulars of our model. The great philanthropic foundations such as the Carnegie, Mellon, and Ford Foundations were founded by single individuals with an initial (and large) finan-

8. For simplicity, we assume that the entrepreneur does not raise funds in the capital market, and does not receive government grants.

9. Slivinski (1997) analyzes the effects of moral hazard among a nonprofit's employees on the organization's costs and the way it compensates employees.

cial donation. Similarly, the Lincoln Center in New York City was founded in 1959 by John D. Rockefeller and now operates as a nonprofit organization, which continues to collect donations towards its mission of providing a wide array of cultural events. There are countless smaller organizations that originated as assumed in our model. The Reverend Bruce Ritter's founding of Covenant House, a nonprofit agency that provides services to children and teens from broken families, is another example.[10] As we noted previously, in many instances the initial donation of the entrepreneur may include labor and human capital in addition to or instead of dollars. That was true in all of the examples just cited, although nonmonetary donations probably formed the bulk of the entrepreneurial contribution in only the last case. We will return to this possibility as we develop the model below.

The principal result of what follows is the demonstration that in this extremely stark setting (the nondistribution constraint is perfectly enforced, and there are no nonpecuniary rewards to nonprofit entrepreneurship, no issues of asymmetric information between the firm and others, no scope for influencing the characteristics of the output, and no tax advantages to nonprofits) it is in a rational entrepreneur's self-interest to found a nonprofit firm to produce the public good.

### 2.2 FORMALIZATION

Consider a community of $n+1$ individuals, labeled $i = 0, 1, \ldots, n$. Let $w_i > 0$ denote $i$'s wealth, $x_i$ be $i$'s private consumption, and $Z$ be the level of provision of some public good. Assume that preferences can be represented by continuous, strictly quasiconcave utility functions $U_i(x_i, Z)$ for all $i$ and that both goods are normal. Let $d_i$ be $i$'s contribution to the public-good-producing firm, $D = \Sigma_{i \in N} d_i$ be the sum of all contributions, and $D_{-i} = D - d_i$ be the total contributions by everyone except $i$. Henceforth, we will let individual 0 be the entrepreneur. Let $F(Z)$ be the level of donations required to produce $Z$ units of the public good, and assume that the cost function $F(\cdot)$ is continuous, strictly increasing, and convex. Without loss of generality, we will from now on write individual utility functions as $u_i(x_i, D) = U_i(x_i, F^{-1}(D))$. The convexity of $F(\cdot)$ guarantees that the functions $u_i(\cdot)$ are quasiconcave in $x_i$ and $D$.

10. Young (1983) presents many examples of nonprofit entrepreneurship, although not all involve organizations that collect donations from the public.

We postulate the following sequence of actions:

1. Individuals choose simultaneously whether or not to organize the production of the public good. The individual who so volunteers is called the *entrepreneur*. If no one volunteers, no public good is provided. If more than one volunteers, the role of entrepreneur is assigned randomly.
2. The entrepreneur elects to found either a nonprofit or a proprietary enterprise to produce the public good.
3. The entrepreneur may invest some of her private wealth[11] in the firm she has founded before soliciting voluntary contributions from the general public.
4. After observing the entrepreneur's actions, other members of the community can contribute simultaneously to the public-good-producing enterprise.
5. The entrepreneur may make a final contribution (possibly negative if the firm is proprietary), and then produces the public good using all the funds received by her firm.

This sequence of decisions defines a multistage game with observed actions in which the strategy sets include the choices {*volunteer, do not volunteer*} and {*proprietary, nonprofit*} in stages 1 and 2, respectively. In stage 3, the entrepreneur chooses an initial contribution $d_0 \in [0, w_0]$. In stage 4, everyone else simultaneously chooses a contribution level $d_i$, knowing $d_0$ and knowing whether the firm is proprietary or nonprofit. Finally, in stage 5, the entrepreneur chooses whether to add (or subtract, if the firm is proprietary) an additional amount $e$, knowing what has been contributed already and whether she is subject to a nondistribution constraint.

## 3. Equilibrium Strategies

A useful benchmark for our analysis is provided by a restatement of the results for a game in which all donors simultaneously determine their private contributions to the provision of the public good. We follow the formulation of Bergstrom et al. (1986), to which the reader

11. Since we have assumed that everyone's income is fixed, the model encompasses both contributions of labor and contributions of cash. In fact, $w_0$ can be interpreted as the market value of the entrepreneur's time endowment plus all other wealth. Monetary donations as well as reductions in her full income due to time spent by the entrepreneur in initially founding and running the firm will both then appear as part of $d_0$.

is referred for additional details. Let

$$h_i(y) = \arg\max_D \{u_i(y - D, D)\}$$

be $i$'s preferred level of expenditures on the public good out of any sum of money, $y$. Geometrically, $h_i(\cdot)$ is $i$'s Engel curve. Normality of both goods ensures that its derivative is strictly between zero and one. For convenience, we assume that the entrepreneur's Engel curve, $h_0(\cdot)$, is concave.

The equilibrium contribution levels in the simultaneous contribution game will then be $d^s = (d_0^s, d_1^s, \ldots, d_n^s)$, where

$$d_i^s = \max\{0, h_i(w_i + D_{-i}^s) - D_{-i}^s\}, \qquad i = 0, 1, \ldots, n. \tag{1}$$

When both $x_i$ and $Z$ are normal for all $i$, Bergstrom et al. (1986) show that $d^s$ is unique.[12]

While it is not essential to our analysis, for simplicity we assume that $d_i^s > 0$ for all $i$. Figure 1 illustrates this equilibrium when there are only two individuals. The equilibrium of a simultaneous-contributions game would be at $S$, where the two reaction functions given by (1) intersect, so that contributions are $d_0^s$ and $d_1^s$ respectively, and total provision is $D^s$. We restate this result only because the level of contribution $d_i^s$ will be referred to later, and to introduce some of the notation that will be used in the analysis. In particular, we do not imply by this that the entrepreneur could choose to set up a simultaneous-contributions game instead of a multistage game.

### 3.1 The Entrepreneur Has the Final Word

To determine the subgame perfect equilibria of this game, we begin by analyzing the behavior of the entrepreneur[13] in the last stage.

12. Bergstrom et al. (1986) also show that individuals who contribute a positive amount behave as though they had private wealth equal to $w_i + D_{-i}$, which implies that their private demand for $D$ is $h_i(w_i + D_{-i})$. They then donate the difference between this demand and the value of $D_{-i}$. Nondonors are those individuals for whom $h_i(w_i + D_{-i}) \leq D_{-i}$.

13. To avoid unnecessary complexity, only the analysis of the subgames in which only one entrepreneur has volunteered is presented here. It is shown below that in any subgame perfect equilibrium, one and only one individual will found a firm.

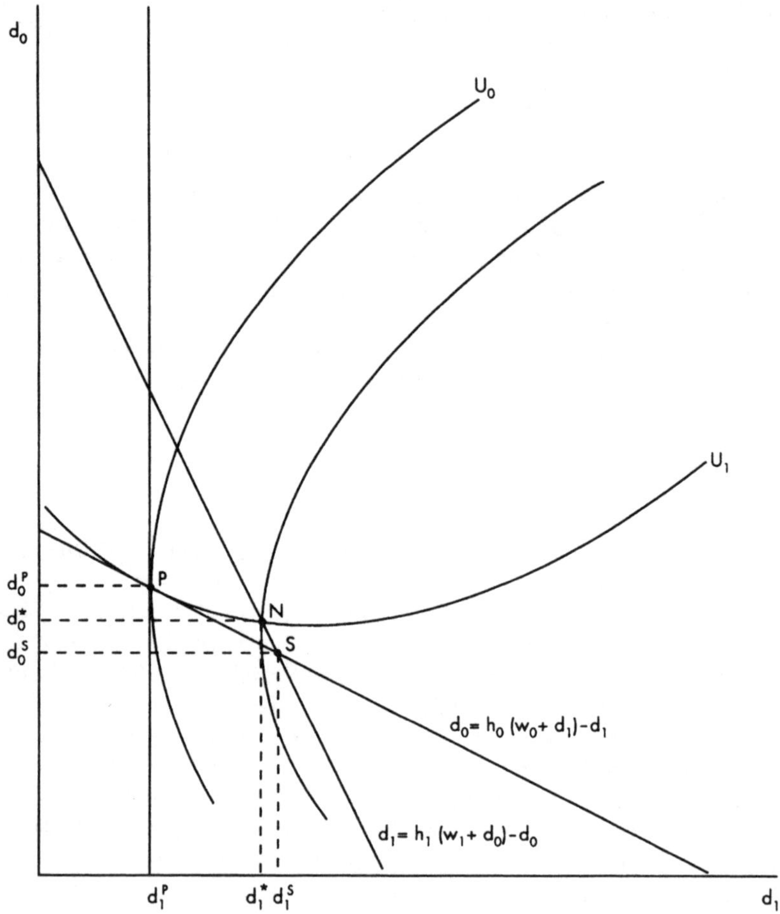


FIGURE 1.

Upon reaching this stage, the entrepreneur has already contributed $d_0 \geq 0$, and the public has contributed $D_{-0} = \Sigma_{j=1}^{n} d_j$.

If the enterprise is proprietary, the entrepreneur's only equilibrium strategy is to contribute

$$e^p(d_0, D_{-0}) = \max\{-(D_{-0} + d_0), h_0(w_0 + D_{-0}) - (D_{-0} + d_0)\}. \tag{2}$$

That is, she contributes the difference between the level of expenditures she considers optimal, $h_0(w_0 + D_{-0})$, and what she and the public have already contributed. The entrepreneur is in a situation similar to that of a follower in a Stackelberg game, the only difference being that she may already have contributed some amount $d_0$ earlier. In Figure 1, for any level of contribution by the other, she would choose $e^p(\cdot)$ such that the final level of provision is $h_0(w_0 + d_1)$ on her reaction function. Note that $e^p(\cdot)$ may be negative if $h_0(w_0 + D_{-0}) < D$, in which case the entrepreneur would choose to appropriate for her personal consumption some or all of the donations made by others to the enterprise.

If instead the firm is nonprofit, her unique equilibrium strategy is to contribute

$$e^n(d_0, D_{-0}) = \max\{0, h_0(w_0 + D_{-0}) - (D_{-0} + d_0)\}. \tag{3}$$

The NDC prevents the entrepreneur from appropriating the donations of others and from reneging on her own initial contribution. This means that in Figure 1, the entrepreneur will bring the final level of provision up to $h_0(w_0 + d_1)$ if vector $(d_0, d_1)$ is below her reaction function, but she cannot bring it down if it is above this function. She will in this latter instance choose $e^n(\cdot) = 0$, and all the funds collected so far will be used to provide the public good. Note that at this stage, for any given values of $D_{-0}, d_0$, the entrepreneur cannot be better off by virtue of being subjected to the NDC.

Equation (2) illustrates the agency problem outlined by Fama and Jensen (1983) that general donations pose to a proprietary firm. Individuals may want to give it money to finance the production of a public good, but if the firm is proprietary, they have no assurance that their contributions will be used for this purpose. By comparison, when the firm is nonprofit, the NDC assures individuals that each dollar they contribute will increase the expenditures earmarked for the public good's production by a dollar, provided of course that the NDC is binding on the entrepreneur.

### 3.2 The Public Knows What She's Up To

In stage 4 the $n$ other community members contribute simultaneously, knowing whether the firm is proprietary or nonprofit, and knowing the entrepreneur's initial contribution, $d_0$. In a subgame perfect equilibrium, everyone also anticipates that the entrepreneur will contribute optimally in the last stage.

Suppose first that the entrepreneur has chosen to found a proprietary firm, and made an initial contribution of $d_0$. Contributors then realize that total contributions of $D_{-0}$ at this stage will result in total expenditures of

$$d_0 + D_{-0} + e^p(d_0, D_{-0}) = h_0(w_0 + D_{-0})$$

towards production of the public good. Since $h_0(\cdot)$ increases at a rate less than one, then a dollar contributed by the public will result in a less than one dollar increase in expenditures to produce the public good.

Letting $D_{-0i} = D_{-0} - d_i$, then individual contributions will be

$$d_i^p = \arg \max_{d_i \in [0, w_i]} \{u_i(w_i - d_i, h_0(w_0 + D^p_{-0i} + d_i))\}, \quad i = 1, 2, \ldots, n, \tag{4}$$

in a subgame perfect equilibrium. Note that $d_0$ does not appear in (4). Since the entrepreneur remains free to take back any amount she previously contributed to her enterprise, this money is not committed to be spent on the production of the public good, and other potential donors ignore it. Their equilibrium actions at this stage are therefore independent of the entrepreneur's initial contribution. In the two-individual case illustrated in Figure 1, individual 1 is in the position of a Stackelberg leader. In determining his optimal contribution to the proprietary firm, he anticipates that the entrepreneur will bring the final level of provision to $h_0(w_0 + d_1)$ and therefore contributes $d_1^p$, leaving her to adjust her final contribution so as to obtain the vector $P$ where his indifference curve is tangent to her reaction function.[14]

If instead the entrepreneur had founded a nonprofit firm, public contributors could calculate that total donations of $D_{-0}$ would result in equilibrium expenditures of

$$d_0 + D_{-0} + e^n(d_0, D_{-0}) = \max\{d_0 + D_{-0}, h_0(w_0 + D_{-0})\}$$

toward production of the public good. Individual contributions at this stage would then be

$$\delta_i(d_0) = \arg \max_{d_i \in [0, w_i]} \left\{ u_i\left( w_i - d_i, d_0 + d_i + \sum_{j \neq i} \delta_j(d_0) + e^n\left( d_0, d_i + \sum_{j \neq i} \delta_j(d_0) \right) \right) \right\} \tag{5}$$

in a subgame perfect equilibrium.

14. Varian (1994) presents a complete analysis of such a Stackelberg model.

The level of individual contributions will depend on whether individual contributors anticipate that the NDC will be binding on the entrepreneur or not. If $d_0 + D_{-0} < h_0(w_0 + D_{-0})$, the NDC is not binding, so that $i$ expects the entrepreneur to contribute again. In this case, individual contributors are in the position of a Stackelberg leader and anticipate that each additional dollar contributed to the firm will induce the entrepreneur to reduce her final contribution by a fraction of a dollar. Individual equilibrium contributions are then identical to (4). The imposition of the NDC cannot have any impact on equilibrium behavior if it is not binding. When the NDC is binding on the entrepreneur, then $e^n(d_0, d_i + \Sigma_{j \neq i}\delta_j(d_0)) = 0$ and individual contributors are in the position of a Stackelberg follower. An additional dollar contributed to the firm then increases the expenditures dedicated to the public good's production by a dollar.

When the firm is nonprofit, equilibrium contributions generally depend on $d_0$, because a larger $d_0$ increases the funds earmarked for the public good's production and decreases the entrepreneur's available wealth. This, in turn, reduces the level of public donations that is necessary to cause the NDC to bind. For any value of $d_0$ there is a level of contributions, $\overline{D}(d_0)$, that makes the NDC just binding on the entrepreneur.[15] Note that $\overline{D}(d_0)$ is decreasing in $d_0$, because the more money the entrepreneur commits to the enterprise initially, the less wealth she has left at the last stage, and hence the smaller the level of total contributions required to induce her to contribute no further.

In the two-individual case, the typical decision problem facing individual 1 is illustrated in Figure 2. Contributing any $d_1$ such that $d_1 + d_0 < \overline{D}(d_0)$ leaves the entrepreneur wanting to contribute again and therefore reducing her contribution at the rate implicit in $h_0(\cdot)$ for each dollar he contributes. On the other hand, a contribution greater than this makes the NDC binding on the entrepreneur, so that each dollar contributed increases $D$ by one dollar. For any $d_0$, his choice set is bounded by the outermost of the two curves, $D = h_0(w_0 + w_1 - x_1)$ and $D = d_0 + w_1 - x_1$, and this second curve depends on $d_0$. For example, if the entrepreneur's initial contribution is $d_0^a$ in Figure 2, then individual 1 chooses $d_1^p$ such that $d_0^a + d_1^p < \overline{D}(d_0^a)$, and the entrepreneur contributes again in the last stage so that $D^p$ is provided in total. On the other hand, an initial contribution of $d_0^b > d_0^a$ induces him to contribute $d_1^b > d_1^p$. Interestingly, by increasing her initial contribution sufficiently, the entrepreneur can induce the other

15. Formally, $\overline{D}(d_0) = \max\{D \mid h_0(w_0 + D - d_0) \geq D\}$, so that $h_0(w_0 - d_0 + \overline{D}(d_0)) \equiv \overline{D}(d_0)$.

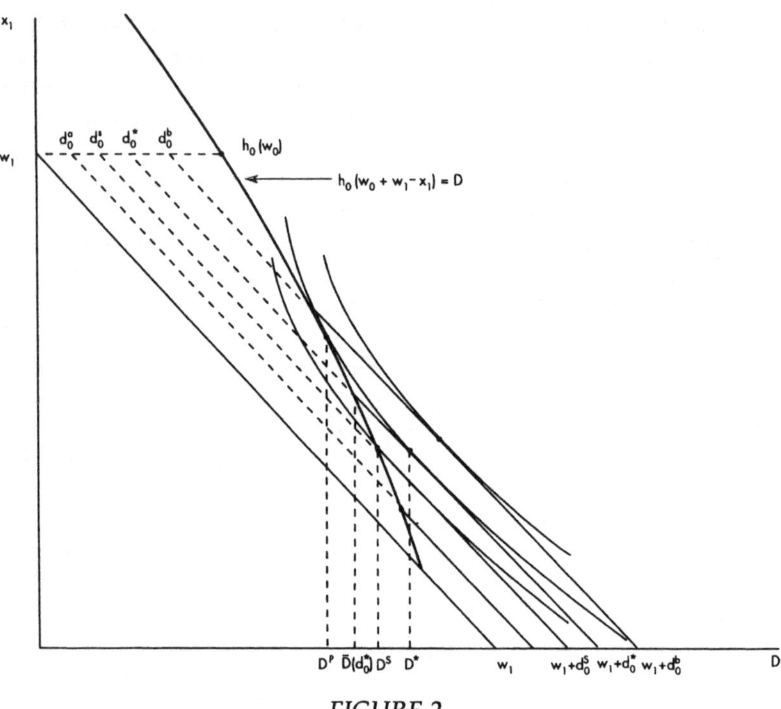


*FIGURE 2.*

to contribute more. This happens because when the enterise is non-profit, a bigger initial contribution decreases the threshold at which the NDC becomes binding. This makes it easier for the entrepreneur to convince the public that she does not intend to contribute again and forces the public to take responsibility for the final level of provision.

The essential point here is that the only effect a variation in $d_0$ has on the continuation of the game is that it changes the location of the kink in the other individual's choice set. Note also that the segment of individual 1's choice set given by $D = h_0(w_0 + w_1 - x_1)$ is a subset of the one he faces in the proprietary subgame, so a small enough initial contribution by the entrepreneur would be followed by $d_1^p$. It follows that there is a unique $d_0^*$ that, if contributed by the entrepreneur initially, leaves the other individual indifferent between contributing $d_1^p$ and contributing a larger amount $d_1^*$ that is just sufficient to make the NDC exactly binding on the entrepreneur.

In Figure 1, if the firm is nonprofit, individual 1's reaction function is made up of two segments. If $d_0 \leq d_0^*$, he cannot do better than contributing $d_1^p$, in which case the NDC would not be binding, and the equilibrium continuation again would yield an outcome at $P$, with individual 1 on indifference curve $u_1$, just as if the firm had been proprietary. But if $d_0 \geq d_0^*$, then individual 1's best response is to choose his own contribution along the locus $d_1 = h_1(w_1 + d_0) - d_0$, since the NDC would then be binding. If the entrepreneur contributes exactly $d_0^*$ initially, the other individual will be indifferent between contributing $d_1^p$ (and letting the entrepreneur contribute again to obtain the outcome at $P$) and contributing $d_1^*$ (and obtaining the outcome at $N$).

### 3.3 Contributing Once is Optimal

In stage 3, the entrepreneur chooses an initial contribution level. The logic underlying her equilibrium choice is not transparent when there are many other contributors, so here we only discuss the $n = 1$ case. The analysis of the case of $n > 1$ identical contributors is presented in detail in Bilodeau and Slivinski (1997b), and we outline it briefly below.

In Figure 1, if the entrepreneur has chosen to found a proprietary firm, then she cannot avoid being in the position of a Stackelberg follower, and the final outcome will be at point $P$. Individual 1 anticipates that the entrepreneur will adjust her final contribution so that, for any initial $d_0$ and any contribution by him of $d_1$, total donations satisfy $d_0 + e = h_0(w_0 + d_1) - d_1$, and so individual 1 chooses $d_1^p$. If $h_0(\cdot)$ is increasing and concave as assumed, then $d_1^p$ is unique. So in the unique equilibrium outcome, the entrepreneur contributes any $d_0$ initially, the other individual contributes $d_1^p$, and the entrepreneur makes up the difference (positively or negatively) in the last stage to attain a level $D^p$ of total donations. Therefore $d_1^p$ is independent of $d_0$, and the entrepreneur always contributes $d_0^p$ in total.

Note that if the entrepreneur derived no utility from the public good, so that $h_0(\cdot) \equiv 0$, individual contributors would expect her to appropriate for her own private consumption every dollar they contribute [see (2) above], and so would contribute nothing. Individuals may be willing to contribute voluntarily even to a proprietary firm ($d_1^p > 0$), provided its founder/manager cares enough about the public good aspect of what the firm provides to allocate part of any donations received to it. In such a case, they effectively face a price for the public good that is inversely related to the entrepreneur's income elasticity of demand for the public good.

If the enterprise is nonprofit, the unique subgame perfect equilibrium is at N in Figure 1, where the entrepreneur contributes $d_0^*$ initially and the other responds by contributing $d_1^*$. The entrepreneur gives no less than $d_0^*$, because giving less would result in a discontinuous decrease in the contribution of the other individual to $d_1^p$, which would force her to contribute again, up to $d_0^p$ in total. The outcome would be at $P$, and she would be on the indifference curve $u_0 < u_1$. Thus any $d_0 < d_0^*$ would result in a larger outlay by the entrepreneur, but less total contributions than if she contributes $d_0^*$. On the other hand, any larger $d_0$ causes $d_1$ to fall in response at a less than one-for-one rate and yields an outcome on 1's reaction function to the northwest of point $N$, and this is also strictly worse for her. In equilibrium then, the entrepreneur makes an initial donation just large enough that she will not want to contribute again after the other has contributed optimally in response. As for individual 1, even though he is indifferent between contributing $d_1^p$ and $d_1^*$, only $d_1^*$ is an equilibrium response to $d_0^*$, because if he contributed $d_1^p$, the entrepreneur would be better off contributing $d_0^* + \varepsilon$ initially.

When $n > 1$ the analysis is substantially more complex, because contributors are then playing a game with each other as well as with the entrepreneur. The analysis of the subgame that follows from the entrepreneur choosing to found a proprietary firm is unchanged, however, and results in a choice of $d_0^p > d_0^s$ by the entrepreneur, and total donations of $D^p < D^s$. The nonprofit subgame may have a continuum of equilibrium continuations, but all pure-strategy equilibrium continuations are qualitatively similar to the case of $n = 1$: Total donations are greater than they are in the profit-taking subgame ($D^n > D^p$), and the entrepreneur contributes less than if the firm had been for profit ($d_0^n < d_0^p$). Thus, the entrepreneur still finds it in her own interest to choose to found a nonprofit firm. The interested reader is referred to Bilodeau and Slivinski (1997b) for a detailed analysis, as well as a proof that equilibria exist and display the above features in a game with many donors under specific assumptions about preferences.[16]

16. Specifically, we show that if the preferences of individuals are identical and affinely homothetic, there is always an interval $I$ of values of $d_0$, which lies between $d_0^s$ and $d_0^p$, such that if the entrepreneur chooses a $d_0 \in I$, then one equilibrium continuation has the $n$ donors contributing amounts such that she contributes nothing more. The subgame perfect equilibria thus all have the entrepreneur choosing to found a nonprofit organization and then donating an amount in the interval $I$. Without the preference restriction it is possible that for some choices of $d_0$ in stage 3 there is no equilibrium continuation in pure strategies. We do not characterize the mixed-strategy continuations in that case; hence we do not know what these equilibria look like.

### 3.4 To Profit or Not to Profit?

So far we have found that if the firm is nonprofit, the equilibrium will be at point $N$ in Figure 1, where the entrepreneur contributes $d_0^*$ and total contributions are $D^*$, while if the firm is proprietary, the equilibrium will be at point $P$, where she contributes $d_0^p$ and total contributions are $D^p$. Which will she prefer? The answer is immediate from Figure 1: $d_0^* < d_0^p$ while $D^* > D^p$.[17] The entrepreneur gets to consume *more* public good while contributing *less* to its provision when the firm is nonprofit.

So an entrepreneur who wants to produce a public good will always find it in her interest to found a nonprofit firm.[18] The NDC, when enforced by the government, provides the entrepreneur with a means of committing to not appropriate funds that others wish to assign to the provision of the public good, and so it induces higher donations by the public. Imposing a perfectly enforced NDC on herself is in the entrepreneur's interest because it allows her to contribute less and consume more of the public good than if she were not subject to this constraint.

When there are just two individuals contributing positively, the public donor is indifferent as to whether the public-good-producing firm is proprietary or nonprofit. However, since the entrepreneur is strictly better off with a nonprofit firm, nonprofit institutions Pareto-dominate proprietary firms when it comes to producing public goods. This rare opportunity to make possible actual Pareto improvements could explain why governments have enacted legislation allowing the incorporation of nonprofit organizations and provided the institutional mechanisms for the enforcement of the nondistribution constraint on the net cash flows of nonprofit enterprises.[19] However, possible welfare gains need not be relevant to the *entrepreneur's*

17. The total level of contributions at $N$ and $P$ can be seen by drawing a line with slope $-1$ from these points to either axis. These lines have been omitted to avoid cluttering the diagram.

18. A sufficient condition for this result to hold is that $d_0^s > 0$ and $d_i^s > 0$ for at least one $i \neq 0$, as we have assumed. The entrepreneur and at least one other individual must get sufficient utility from the firm's output and have sufficient income that they would contribute positively toward its provision. If this is not the case, she may contribute nothing or collect no voluntary contributions from others whether the firm is proprietary or not, and so would have no reason to prefer a nonprofit firm.

19. This is not, however, a rationale for tax exemption of nonprofit organizations, nor for the tax deductibility of contributions made to them. See Hall (1987) for a historical overview of the evolution of legislation governing the nonprofit sector in the US. Note also that the equilibrium outcome still falls short of Pareto efficiency, so nonprofit enterprises are not a solution to the free-rider problem. The NDC is only a means of overcoming the particular agency problem arising when donors cannot receive an immediate *quid pro quo* for their gifts.

decision. If she would be a positive contributor herself and expects any contributions from the public, a rational self-interested entrepreneur will always choose to incorporate her public-good-producing organization under nonprofit regulations, not because this is socially optimal in some sense, but because it is in her best interest to do so.

### 3.5 Why Me?

So far, we have found that in any subgame perfect equilibrium, the entrepreneur will found a nonprofit firm. She will also invest sufficiently in it that the NDC will be binding on her. The last question that remains to be answered is whether it can be in anyone's interest to be a nonprofit entrepreneur.

An important factor affecting individuals' decisions to volunteer or not for this task is the fact that not only will the entrepreneur not profit from this venture, but there is a cost to being the entrepreneur. To see this, consider Figure 1 again. In equilibrium, the entrepreneur contributes $d_0^* > d_0^s$ while the other individual contributes $d_1^* < d_1^s$. But if the roles were reversed, it is individual 0 who would contribute less than $d_0^s$ while individual 1 as entrepreneur would contribute more than $d_1^s$. The individual who volunteers must therefore always contribute more than she would if someone else organized the public good's production. Everyone would therefore prefer to let someone else be the provider of nonprofit entrepreneurial services.

While it is true that each would prefer to let the other volunteer nonprofit entrepreneurial services, this does not mean that no one will do so. On the contrary, the outcome that would result if no one volunteered is that the public good would not be provided at all. Any individual who does volunteer to be the entrepreneur must be better off with her resulting consumption bundle than with $(w_i, 0)$, because as the entrepreneur she has available the strategy of choosing $d_i = e_i = 0$. So if no one else volunteers, $i$ would rather incur the cost of entrepreneurship than consume no public good at all. If we also assume that if two or more individuals volunteer simultaneously, one of them is chosen at random to be the entrepreneur, then the game at the first stage is simply a *game of chicken*. In any pure-strategy equilibrium, one and only one individual will volunteer nonprofit entrepreneurial services. Therefore, even though there is a cost to doing so, it is consistent with an individual's self-interest to volunteer nonprofit entrepreneurial services. Of course, as in any game of chicken, there are equilibria in which any one individual is the volunteer. Deriving predictions regarding the traits of those individuals in a heterogeneous population who will volunteer nonprofit entrepreneurial services is beyond the scope of this paper, but such a derivation is undertaken in Bilodeau and Slivinski (1996b).[20]

## 4. Conclusions

The model developed in this paper provides a simple explanation for the existence of nonprofit firms: Whenever the provision of a public good is financed by voluntary contributions, it is in the private interest of an entrepreneur that the firm collecting donations be subject to a nondistribution constraint. An empirically testable prediction of this model is that firms receiving donations to provide a single public good will be nonprofit. This explanation is not based on welfare or efficiency considerations, or on public demand for the existence of such firms, but on the self-interest of the entrepreneur who founds the firm.

It may prove useful to reiterate the significance of the game-theoretic structure of our model. Specifically, we allow the entrepreneur to contribute both before and after everyone else, to reflect the fact that the entrepreneur *controls* the fund-raising process and has opportunities to add money to or subtract money from the firm's cash flow at any time. The last stage is essential, because this is the point at which the agency problem posed by general donations arises: the entrepreneur has collected a pot of money, and must decide what to do with it. In the absence of a NDC, it may be privately optimal for her to appropriate some of the money previously donated to the firm. Founding a nonprofit firm, which subjects her to a NDC, allows the entrepreneur to commit to not making a *negative* donation at this stage.

The initial donation stage plays a different role. Since the entrepreneur controls the fund raising process, she may be viewed by others as the donor of last resort. Everyone can anticipate that it would be optimal for her to contribute again if she feels that public donations are too low, and relying on her to do so induces them to make smaller contributions. To mitigate the effect of this expectation by donors and thereby generate more public donations, the entrepreneur needs a means to commit to not making a *positive* donation in the last stage. She can do this by making a sufficiently large

20. Other relevant papers on this topic are Bliss and Nalebuff (1984), Bilodeau and Slivinski (1996a), and Eckel and Steinberg (1993). In the simple model presented here, only one individual founds a nonprofit firm, so the possibility of competing charities does not arise. A model of rival charities competing for donations is presented in Bilodeau and Slivinski (1997a).

*initial* donation. In many of the examples one can think of, the founder does make a large initial donation of time or money. Of course, the entrepreneur is allowed to donate nothing in the initial stage, and that may indeed be what happens in some cases. If so, it is still true that if she founds a nonprofit firm she will be barred from appropriating others' donations, whereas she could do so if the firm were proprietary. Thus, the motivation to choose the nonprofit form remains. On the other hand, our model suggests that founding entrepreneurs who do make initial donations have an incentive to give a *larger* donation than they would as a member of the contributing public, although it need not be large in absolute terms. It may even happen that someone who would donate nothing as a member of the public actually donates a positive amount when it is she who is founding the firm. This model is therefore consistent with the observation that founders of nonprofit organizations sometimes seed them with a personal donation—as happened with philanthropic foundations like Carnegie and Ford. Andreoni (1997) analyzes this same phenomenon in a model in which public-good provision is subject to a *threshold effect* due to a discontinuity in the cost function of the public good. Our model generates the same behavior without this debatable technological assumption.

Finally, the model presented here is rooted in a very standard economic notion—preferences over public goods. This suggests an extension of the model with further interesting implications. Many nonprofit firms provide a range of different public goods with the funds they receive, and one would expect that preferences over such bundles of public goods differ across individuals. This suggests that donors may have preference-based reasons for donating to one nonprofit firm rather than another, since entrepreneurs will vary in the way they use donations. This provides the basis for a model of competition via "product differentiation" among charities in Bilodeau and Slivinski (1997a). There it is shown that specialized charities that provide only one service have a competitive advantage in attracting donations.

## References


Andreoni, J., 1988, "Privately Provided Goods in a Large Economy: The Limits of Altruism," *Journal of Public Economics*, 35, 57–73.

——, 1989, "Giving with Impure Altruism: Applications to Charity and Ricardian Equivalence," *Journal of Political Economy*, 97, 1447–1457.

——, 1997, "Toward a Theory of Charitable Fundraising," SSRI Working Paper 9712, University of Wisconsin, Madison.

Bergstrom, T., L. Blume, and H. Varian, 1986. "On the Private Provision of Public Goods," *Journal of Public Economics*, 29, 25–50.

Bernheim, D., 1986, "On the Voluntary and Involuntary Provision of Public Goods," *American Economic Review*, 75, 789–793.

Bilodeau, M., and A. Slivinski, 1996a, "Toilet Cleaning and Department Chairing: Volunteering a Public Service," *Journal of Public Economics*, 59, 299–308.

—— and ——, 1996b, "Volunteering Nonprofit Entrepreneurial Services," *Journal of Economic Behavior and Organization*, 31, 117–127.

—— and ——, 1997a, "Rival Charities," *Journal of Public Economics*, 66, 449–67.

—— and ——, 1997b, "Rational Nonprofit Entrepreneurship," Working paper 9709, University of Western Ontario.

Bliss, C. and B. Nalebuff, 1984, "Dragon-Slaying and Ballroom Dancing: The Private Supply of a Public Good," *Journal of Public Economics*, 25, 1–12.

Chang, C. and H. Tuckman, 1990, "Do Higher Property Tax Rates Increase the Market Share of Nonprofit Hospitals?" *National Tax Journal*, 43, 175–188.

Easley, D. and M. O Hara, 1983, "The Economic Role of Non-profit Firms," *Bell Journal of Economics*, 14, 531–538.

Eckel, C. and R. Steinberg, 1993, "Tax Policy and the Objectives of Nonprofit Organizations," *ARNOVA 1993 Conference Proceedings*, 92–97.

Fama, E. and M. Jensen, 1983, "Agency Problems and Residual Claims," *Journal of Law and Economics*, 26, 327–350.

Gassler, R., 1990, "Nonprofit and Voluntary Economics: A Critical Survey," *Nonprofit and Voluntary Sector Quarterly*, 19, 137–150.

Hall, P., 1987, "A Historical Overview of the Private Nonprofit Sector," in W. Powell, ed., *The Nonprofit Sector: A Research Handbook*, Yale University Press.

Hansmann, H., 1980, "The role of nonprofit enterprise," *The Yale Law Journal*, 89, 835–898.

Hodgkinson, V. and associates, 1992, *Nonprofit Almanac 1992–1993, Dimensions of the Independent Sector*, Jossey-Bass.

Slivinski, A. 1997, "Moral Hazard in Nonprofit Teams," Mimeo, University of Western Ontario.

Steinberg, R., 1993, "Public Policy and the Performance of Nonprofit Organizations: A General Framework," *Nonprofit and Voluntary Sector Quarterly*, 22(1), 13–31.

Sugden, R., 1982, "On the Economics of Philanthropy," *The Economic Journal*, 92, 341–350.

Varian, H., 1994, "Sequential Provision of Public Goods," *Journal of Public Economics*, 53, 165–186.

Weisbrod, B., 1964, "Collective-consumption services, of individual-consumption goods," *Quarterly Journal of Economics*, 78, 471–477.

——, 1975, "Towards a Theory of the Voluntary Nonprofit Sector in a Three-Sector Economy," in E. Phelps, ed., *Altruism, Morality and Economic Theory*, Russell Sage Foundation, 171–195.

Young, D., 1983, *If Not for Profit, for What?*, Lexington, MA: Heath.

# [8]

ELSEVIER

Journal of Public Economics 66 (1997) 449–467

# Rival charities

Marc Bilodeau[a,*], Al Slivinski[b]

[a]*Département d'Économique, Université de Sherbrooke, and Department of Economics, IUPUI, Cavanaugh Hall 517, Indianapolis, IN 46202-5140, USA*

[b]*Department of Economics, University of Western Ontario, London, Ontario, Canada*

Received 1 June 1996; received in revised form 1 February 1997; accepted 8 April 1997

**Abstract**

The paper develops a model in which a number of charities (or other nonprofit firms) provide various bundles of public goods or services through private donations. The motivation for individuals to found and operate such firms is that it allows them to influence the mix of public goods. It is their decisions regarding the allocation of donations across uses that matter in the end. Donors to these firms take into account the allocation decisions that will be made by the organizations to which they contribute. We find a propensity for such organizations to specialize in the provision of services, and further find that diversification by such firms diminishes the equilibrium level of contributions they will collect. We demonstrate the possibility that a commitment by a monopoly charity to an allocation rule that is, ex-post, privately sub-optimal can eliminate this effect, and may therefore be advantageous, ex-ante. The allocation rule which accomplishes this involves honouring donor designations of their contributions to specific uses. This is a policy that is frequently adopted by local chapters of the United Way. © 1997 Elsevier Science S.A.

*Keywords:* Nonprofit enterprises; Public goods; Voluntary contributions; Spatial competition

*JEL classification:* H41; L31

## 1. Introduction

This paper is an attempt to understand rivalry among "donative" nonprofit firms, which we define as firms that provide public goods using voluntary

*Corresponding author. E-mail: mbilodea@ivpvi.edu



*PII* S0047-2727(97)00046-7

donations. While "commercial" proprietary and nonprofit firms producing private goods compete for paying customers, these nonprofit firms compete for donations toward the provision of the particular public goods they supply.

The type of competition we focus on occurs when firms can attempt to differentiate themselves by offering to provide public goods that have particular characteristics. For example, communities often include several nonprofit organizations that provide a variety of in-kind assistance to the indigent, shelters for battered spouses or runaway teenagers, or support alternative kinds of medical research. Private post-secondary educational institutions in the U.S. differ considerably in the nature of the education they provide, and are partly funded through private contributions. The towns of London, Ontario and Sherbrooke, Quebec are each home to a number of youth hockey leagues, each of them offering different programs and each soliciting private contributions to aid their operations.

In this paper we present a simple model in which the following decisions are analyzed: At the first, *entry* stage, individuals decide whether or not to found a nonprofit firm. Doing so is costly, but entitles one to collect voluntary donations from others, which may then be used to provide some mix of public goods. Next, at the *contributions* stage, all individuals choose whether and how much to contribute to the various nonprofit firms that are operating. Finally, at the *allocation* stage, the entrepreneurs determine how they will allocate the funds collected to the provision of various public goods. To keep the analysis tractable, we analyze a model in which there are only two public goods.

The model predicts an inherent propensity for donative nonprofit organizations to specialize. This explains why, for example, it is more common to see several separate organizations raising funds for medical research into particular diseases, rather than a single organization raising funds for research into a whole range of diseases. Specialization is useful to donors because they can then control how their contributions are used. The fact that a diversified charity may allocate donations differently than would the donors themselves affects the amounts that they are willing to contribute. The model predicts that, in a well-defined sense, the level of provision of both public goods will be higher if there are two rival specialized firms rather than a single diversified firm.

An institution like the United Way can be regarded as a diversified nonprofit firm. Bilodeau (1992) shows that donations to a 'united charity' like the United Way can be rationalized without reference to any informational or fund-raising advantages, but the model in that paper does not incorporate the incentives of those who operate the organization. We show below that a diversified charity like the United Way can arise as an equilibrium outcome in the richer model presented here even though it may end up providing less of both goods than would two specialized organizations.

It has become increasingly common for local United Way chapters to allow donors to designate how their contributions are to be used. To consider the implications of this, we allow the firm to commit to honour such donor designations. We show that such a policy benefits donors, and may also be in the best interests of the organization. Allowing donor designations is a way to reintroduce the benefits of inter-firm competition in situations in which there is a monopoly charity. However, such a policy may be ineffective if a significant fraction of contributors fail to earmark their contributions. This is because a pool of undesignated donations gives the organization a means to offset the effects of any donor designations, and doing so is in the organizations interest once it has been given the donations. This result is a mirror-image of Becker's (Becker, 1974) Rotten Kid Theorem, in which an altruistic household head guarantees an efficient outcome by reallocating income among household members. We go on to show, however, that by also committing to allocate undesignated funds according to a fixed rule, the monopoly charity can overcome this problem, and regain the mutual benefits that arise from donor designation or specialization by firms.

## 2. The model

Consider a population of $n$ individuals, with individual $i$ having private wealth $w^i$ which can be used to buy private consumption, $x^i$, or to provide the public goods $Z_1$ and $Z_2$. Assume that individual preferences can be represented by utility functions $u^i(x^i,Z_1,Z_2)$.[1] We assume utility functions are increasing in each good, strictly quasi-concave, and that all goods are normal. We further assume that preferences over the public good bundle $(Z_1,Z_2)$ are separable from $x^i$, and are homothetic. Utility functions can therefore be written as $u^i(x^i,g^i(Z_1,Z_2)$ with $g^i$ homogeneous of degree one. Homotheticity is not necessary for any of the results below, but allows us to characterize each individual $i$ by the constant share of expenditures $s^i = Z_2/(Z_1 + Z_2)$ which $i$ would like to see allocated to good 2, and thus simplifies the exposition.[2] We assume finally that the public goods can be produced at a constant cost of 1 per unit, and that there are no economies of joint production. The environment is one of complete information and the only providers of public goods are nonprofit firms. The model used is a three-stage game with observed actions.

[1] The different $Z_i$ can be thought of as different characteristics that can be embodied in a public good (e.g., abortion and/or religious counselling at a shelter for pregnant teenagers), or simply as different public goods (e.g., a shelter for pregnant teenagers and a shelter for runaway kids). We also abstract from the fact that some public facilities may confer private benefits to the direct recipients of the services. The specification used here implies that individuals care only about the total quantity of each public good or characteristic. In particular, they are indifferent about whether a given total quantity of a public good is provided by one or many firms, and about whether any firm provides more than one public good.

[2] It is sufficient that the income-expansion paths of different individuals in $(Z_1,Z_2)$ space not intersect, so that individuals can still be characterized by their desired relative level of expenditure on the two public goods.

The first, *entry* stage, produces a set of nonprofit firms. Each firm is operated by some *nonprofit entrepreneur* who is also a member of the community. The entry of any individual into nonprofit entrepreneurship entails a cost, $c$, which is the cost of founding a firm to collect donations from the rest of the population.[3]

At the *contributions* stage, all individuals (including those who chose previously to become entrepreneurs) *simultaneously* make non-negative contributions of their private wealth to the $k$ firms founded at Stage I.[4] We let $d^i = (d_1^i, \ldots, d_k^i)$ be individual $i$'s vector of contributions to these firms, where $d_h^i$ is his contribution to the firm founded by entrepreneur $h$. Then $D^i = \Sigma_{h=1}^k d_h^i$ is the amount contributed by $i$, and $D = \Sigma_{i=1}^n D^i$ is the total contributed by everyone. $b_h = \Sigma_{i=1}^n d_h^i$ is the total (i.e., the *budget*) received by firm $h$ and $b = (b_1, \ldots, b_k)$ is the vector of donations received by the $k$ firms. It will also be useful to denote $b_h^{-i} = \Sigma_{j \neq i} d_h^j$ as the amount received by firm $h$ from all donors other than $i$, and $b^{-i} = (b_1^{-i}, \ldots, b_k^{-i})$ as the amounts collected by each firm from donors other than $i$.

At the final *allocation* stage, all entrepreneurs simultaneously allocate the contributions they have received at Stage II (i.e., the amounts $b_h$) to the various public goods. That is, entrepreneur $h$ chooses a vector $z^h = (z_1^h, z_2^h)$ such that $z_1^h + z_2^h = b_h$. The fact that these are nonprofit firms implies that a non-distribution constraint (NDC) exists, and thus it cannot be that $z_1^h + z_2^h < b_h$. None of the donations received by firm $h$, including any contribution the entrepreneur may have made from her own wealth, can be used to augment her private consumption, $x^h$. In our model this is the important sense in which these are nonprofit firms, since if this constraint were not present, entrepreneurs could choose to devote *less* than $b_h$ to the provision of public goods.

$Z_j = \Sigma_{h=1}^k z_j^h$ will denote the total quantity of public good $j$ provided and $Z_j^{-h} = \Sigma_{i \neq h} z_j^i$ will be the quantity of good $j$ provided by all firms except $h$.

To reiterate, the order of play in this one-shot game is as follows:

*Stage I*: Individuals simultaneously choose whether or not to become entrepreneurs.

*Stage II*: Individuals simultaneously make private donations to the firms that arose in Stage I.

*Stage III*: Entrepreneurs simultaneously choose allocations of the donations

[3] See Bilodeau and Slivinski (1994) and Bilodeau and Slivinski (1996) for models in which an individual rationally founds a nonprofit firm despite the fact that it is privately costly for her to do so.

[4] One could have the entrepreneurs make any personal contributions before the general public, as in Varian (1994), or both before and after, as in Bilodeau and Slivinski (1994). The specification used here is simpler, and allows us to focus on the effect of the entrepreneurs' ability to allocate donations received across various uses.

received in Stage II to the two public goods. These allocations must satisfy the NDC.

The game then ends, and individuals receive their payoffs. The payoff function of individual $i$ is $u^i(w^i - D^i - E^i c, g^i(Z_1, Z_2))$, where $E^i$ is 1 if $i$ chooses to become an entrepreneur, and is 0 if not, and the $Z_j$ are derived from the choices of $d^i_h$, $z^h_j$ as defined above.

## 3. The allocation stage

We seek to characterize the subgame perfect equilibria of this game and therefore we start by deriving equilibrium behaviour at the last stage, when $k$ entrepreneurs have already founded nonprofit firms, and have received donations in the amounts $(b_1, b_2, \ldots, b_k)$. Without loss of generality we label them according to the share, $s^h$, of funds they would prefer to devote to good 2, so that $s^h < s^{h+1}$. Given $b^h$, then, and any allocation of funds $Z^{-h} = (Z_1^{-h}, Z_2^{-h})$ by the other firms, entrepreneur $h$ chooses $z^h = (z_1^h, z_2^h)$ to maximize $g^h(z_1^h + Z_1^{-h}, z_2^h + Z_2^{-h})$ subject to $z_1^h + z_2^h = b_h$.[5] The form of this best-response is most easily understood via a diagram like Fig. 1. The curve $z^h(\cdot)$ emanating from the origin is entrepreneur $h$'s income expansion path, defined as $z^h(D) = z^{h*}(D,0)$. That is, $z^h(\cdot)$ expresses how individual $h$ would allocate total donations $D$ across the two public goods, were he the only one with funds to allocate, (i.e., if $Z^{-h}$ were 0).[6] The allocations of all other firms determine point $Z^{-h}$. Entrepreneur $h$ can then allocate the funds $b_h$ to obtain an allocation anywhere on the line segment labelled $\alpha\beta$.[7]

If $z^h(D)$ does not intersect $F^h(b_h, Z^{-h})$, the entrepreneur's best-response will be to allocate nothing to the good which she feels is already relatively overprovided by other firms. This is the case for good 2 in Fig. 1. Firms that provide only one public good will be said to be specialized.

The only situation in which an entrepreneur would allocate positive amounts to the provision of both goods is when $z^h(D) > Z^{-h}$. Then entrepreneur $h$ would, if alone, allocate total donations $D$ to provide more of both public goods than are being provided by her rivals' current allocations. In this case $z^h(D)$ intersects

[5]The separability assumption implies that the entrepreneur's view of the optimal allocation of $b_h$ is independent of his private consumption, and hence does not depend on his wealth, or on the amount he may have donated on his own.

[6]The homotheticity assumption implies that $z^h(D) = ((1-s^h)D, s^h D)$ for some $s^h$ between 0 and 1. Fig. 1 is drawn for an entrepreneur with non-homothetic preferences, as none of the analysis of this stage depends on this assumption.

[7]This is formally defined as the set

$$F^h(b_h, Z^{-h}) = \left\{ (Z_1, Z_2) \middle| \sum_{j=1}^{2} Z_j = \sum_{j=1}^{2} Z_j^{-h} + b_h, Z_j \geq Z_j^{-h}, j = 1,2 \right\}.$$

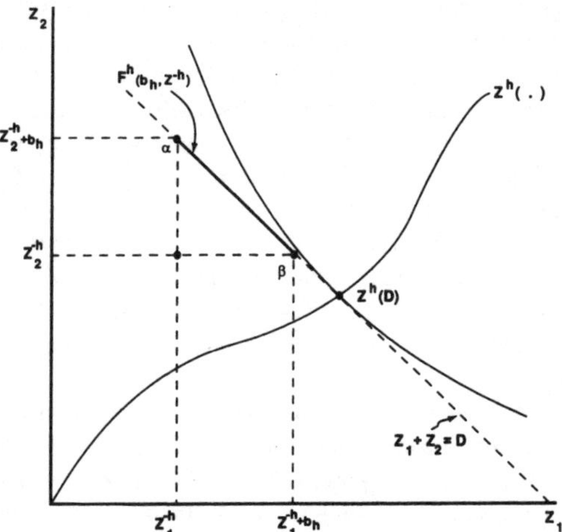


Fig. 1. A specialized firm.

$F^h(b_h,Z^{-h})$, as in Fig. 2 and entrepreneur $h$'s allocation will be $z^{h*}(b_h,Z^{-h}) = z^h(D) - Z^{-h}$.

If in equilibrium there is a firm $h$ such that $z^h(D) > Z^{-h}$, this firm will be called a dominant firm, because the resulting quantities of the two public goods will be as

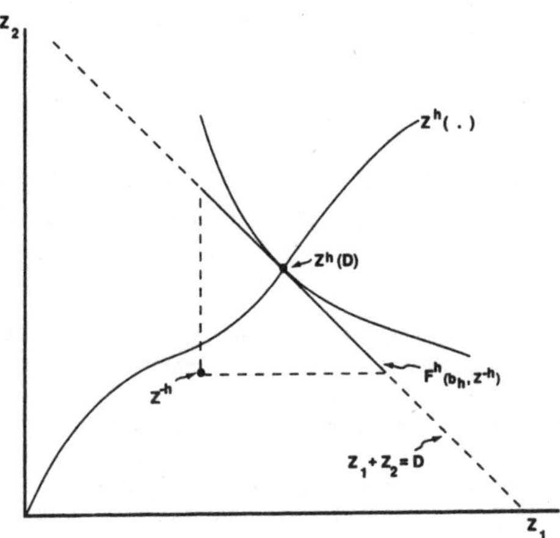


Fig. 2. A diversified firm.

if that firm were a monopoly allocating the entire $D$ on it's own.[8] Further, any reallocation of funds by other firms that leaves each $Z_j^{-h}$ less than $z_j^h(D)$ can and will be offset by firm $h$ so as to maintain the outcome $Z = z^h(D)$. A firm is *more likely* to be dominant the more donations it has collected, because then $F^h(b_h, Z^{-h})$ spans a larger fraction of the line $Z_1 + Z_2 = D$. However, what is *required* for firm $h$ to be dominant is that, given total donations of $D$, $z_j^h(D) > Z_j^{-h}$ for $j = 1,2$.

For any set of entrepreneurs, and any non-negative amounts $b_h$ collected by them, the allocation stage has a unique Nash equilibrium outcome in pure strategies.[9] We denote the resulting public goods bundle as $Z^*(b)$, and denote the equilibrium share of good 2 as $\rho(b) = Z_2^*(b)/(Z_1^*(b) + Z_2^*(b))$. To lighten the notation, the dependence of these variables on $b$ will be suppressed when it will result in no confusion.

Given any set of entrepreneurs with distinct $s^h$, in equilibrium at most one of them can be dominant, and the equilibrium share of total donations allocated to good 2 will then be the one preferred by that entrepreneur. Further, in *any* equilibrium, all entrepreneurs whose $s^h$ is less than $\rho$ will provide only good 1, while only good 2 is provided by all entrepreneurs whose $s^h$ is greater than $\rho$.

The equilibrium allocations for any set of $k$ entrepreneurs and any contributions $b = \{b_1, \ldots, b_k\}$ by the public, have the following properties:

- There will be at most one dominant firm. That is, $\rho(b) = s^h$ for at most one entrepreneur $h$, and this entrepreneur will allocate his funds so that $z^{h*}(b_h, Z^{-h}) = z^h(D) - Z^{-h}$, so $Z^*(b) = z^{h*}(D,0)$.
- If there is no dominant firm, then there must be entrepreneurs $i$, $j$ such that $s^i < \rho(b) < s^j$.
- In any equilibrium, $s^1 \leq \rho(b) \leq s^k$.
- Any entrepreneur $h$ for whom $s^h < \rho(b)$ provides $z_1^h = b_h$ (specializes in providing good 1), and any for whom $s^h > \rho(b)$ provides $z_2^h = b_h$ (specializes in providing good 2).

A noteworthy aspect of this allocation stage is the tendency for the nonprofit firms to specialize, even when entrepreneurs value the provision of both public

[8] Note that the definition of a dominant firm does *not* require that the firm has collected more than half the total donations. Both $z^h(D)$ and $Z^{-h}$ are *vectors* of provision of the two goods, not scalar sums of money. $z^h(D)$ is the bundle that entrepreneur $h$ would provide in the hypothetical situation in which his firm was a monopoly and had collected total amount $D$, while $Z^{-h}$ is the bundle actually provided by all other firms in equilibrium.

[9] This last stage game has a finite set of players choosing allocations $z^h$ from a compact and convex set, and payoff functions $g^h(\Sigma_{h=1}^k z_1^h, \Sigma_{h=1}^k z_2^h)$ which are continuous and strictly concave in all $z_j^h$, so that a Nash Equilibrium in pure strategies exists (see Fan (1952) or Debreu (1952)). The proof of uniqueness in the two goods case is identical to that found in Bilodeau (1994) p. 55.

goods. This result from this two-good model is an extreme manifestation of a tendency that would still be present with $m$ goods, as it follows from each entrepreneur's desire to modify the overall package of public goods to be closer to that which she most prefers. To summarize:

- If there is a dominant firm, then the equilibrium outcome is the same as if this firm was a monopoly, regardless of how many competitors it has. This is true in the sense that the final allocation of donations across goods would be no different if the dominant firm received all the donations. All other firms will specialize in providing only one public good.
- If there is no dominant firm, then all firms specialize in producing only one public good and at least one firm specializes in each good.

## 4. The contributions stage

At this stage, $k$ entrepreneurs have entered and founded nonprofit firms. Each individual $i$ chooses a vector of contributions $d^i=(d^i_1,\dots,d^i_k)$ to the $k$ firms in existence, and it may be that many individuals contribute nothing to some or all firms.

This stage differs from the allocation stage in two basic ways. First, the total amount donated is chosen by each individual at this stage, while at the following stage the NDC implied that the total amount to be allocated by each firm was fixed. Entrepreneurs could not allocate less to public good provision than they had received, and had no desire to allocate more. Second, individual donors do not contribute directly to the provision of particular goods, but must contribute to firms whose entrepreneurs then allocate their contributions as they wish. Thus, donors are responding to the contributions of others while also taking into account the way in which firms will later allocate the donations they receive. Therefore, individual $i$'s best-response to any $b^{-i}$ will depend on the equilibrium outcome of the last stage, $Z^*(b^{-i}+d^i)$, because his equilibrium payoff is $u^i(w^i-D^i-E^ic, g^i[Z^*_1(b^{-i}+d^i), Z^*_2(b^{-i}+d^i)])$. In what follows, we simplify notation by writing $Z^*(b^{-i})=Z^{-i}$ for the mix of public goods that would be provided in equilibrium from the donations of all contributors other than $i$.

A donor's best-response to any $Z^{-i}$ will depend on the set of firms that have entered. However for any entry configuration, if firms behave optimally at the next stage, a donor at this stage faces one of only two qualitatively different possibilities: either there is a dominant firm or not.

Suppose first that a single firm has entered. Then trivially this firm is dominant and individuals have a simple choice: to contribute to it or not at all. If they contribute, their donations buy a composite public good in which the two goods are present in the ratio chosen by the firm. Thus, if the entrepreneur prefers the public good mix $s^h \in ]0,1[$, an individual contributor with $s^i \neq s^h$ would prefer that donations be allocated in a different ratio. However, so long as he values at least one of the $Z_j$ he will place some value on the provision of the two goods in the ratio $Z_2/Z_1 = s^h/(1-s^h)$ chosen by the firm and may, therefore, be willing to contribute to this firm. The outcome is then essentially the same as a game where individuals contribute simultaneously to a single public good, as in Bergstrom et al. (1986).

If two or more firms have entered, then two possibilities can arise: either all firms are specialized, or one of them is dominant. If one firm is dominant, it does not matter how many firms have entered, as the outcome must be as if this firm is a monopoly. If some firm $m$ is dominant, the other firms will allocate all their funds to one good, with firms 1 through $m-1$ providing only good 1 and firms $m+1$ through $k$ providing only good 2. It may seem that this implies that every donor for whom $s^i < s^m$ also contributes only to the first $m-1$ firms, in an effort to increase the provision of good 1. However, it does not matter at the margin to which firm any donor contributes. While any dollar contributed to firm $m+1$, say, will be allocated by that firm solely to the provision of good 2, this will also result in Firm $m$ altering it's own allocation in the next stage so as to keep the proportion of good 2 at $s^m$. Thus, at the margin, all donations to *any* firm will result in an increase in provision of a composite public good which contains goods 1 and 2 in the proportions $1-s^m$ and $s^m$, respectively. It follows that the targeting of donations to firms by individuals is not unique if in equilibrium one firm is dominant.

Note then that a dominant firm, if one exists, plays a role much like the benevolent head of the household in the "Rotten Kid Theorem" in Becker (1974). There, a household head who has sufficient income of his own and cares about the consumption of all family members will neutralize actions of other family members which would otherwise alter the distribution of consumption within the family from that which the head views as optimal.[10]

The other possibility is that all firms are specialized. Then the equilibrium mix of public goods, $\rho$, must differ from the $s^h$ of *all* entrepreneurs, otherwise one of them would be dominant. If $s^1 < \rho < s^2$, for example, then firms $2, \ldots, k$ allocate all their funds to good 2, while Firm 1 allocates everything to good 1. All donors for whom $s^i < \rho$ contribute only to firm 1, and all those with $s^i > \rho$ contribute only to firms $2, \ldots, k$ (the division of any given amount between these firms being

[10] The economic literature contains other models of similar flavour, in which some players are essentially rendered impotent by other players' ability to completely offset anything they do. In Barro (1974)'s model of government debt with altruistic bequests, the bequestors can completely offset changes in government debt, rendering changes in government policy meaningless. Warr (1983) and Bernheim (1986)'s neutrality results in an economy with a privately provided public good are also in the same vein: if the government is limited to small enough income redistributions, its efforts to alter the income distribution would be completely offset by changes in donations.

a matter of unanimous indifference). Only an individual with $s^i = \rho$ (if any such individuals exist) might contribute to Firm 1 *and* to one or more of the others. In such an equilibrium firms are acting as perfect agents for donors in that they can be relied on to use all donations in a particular way-providing *one* of the public goods. In equilibrium, each donor is then trying to move the equilibrium mix closer to the one he prefers by contributing to a specialized firm whose entrepreneur feels the same way.

To summarize this discussion, for any entry configuration, only two types of equilibrium continuations are possible:

- All firms specialize and individuals contribute to the firm(s) which provide the one good they feel is relatively underprovided by other firms. We will refer to this outcome as a 'specialized firms outcome'.
- One firm is dominant and it does not matter at the margin to which firm anyone contributes. This outcome will be referred to as a "dominant firm outcome".

Both of these outcomes could arise as equilibria for a given entry configuration, and in general there could be more than one equilibrium outcome of each type. Proposition 1 in the appendix shows that if preferences are additively separable then there can be at most one equilibrium outcome of the first type (in which all firms specialize). On the other hand, given any set of entering firms, there may be an outcome in which *any one* of those firms is dominant.[11]

It is possible to compare the behaviour of individual donors when all firms are specialized (which gives them the choice to contribute to the good they like the most) to their behaviour when there is a dominant firm (which constrains them to contribute toward a composite good). In general, the response of each individual will differ, some contributing more, others less, depending on the proportions favoured by the dominant firm. Also, since the proportions of both goods may not be the same in each case, a dominant firm might provide more of one good but less of the other. To establish a benchmark for comparison, suppose that with specialized firms the unique equilibrium bundle is $Z^b$ and that the share of funds devoted to good 2 is $s^b$. For such an equilibrium to exist, no individual $i$ for whom $s^i = s^b$, if any exist, can have founded a firm. Now suppose that such an individual does exist and has founded a firm. At the equilibrium where his firm is dominant, the share of good 2 would also be $s^b$. Let $Z^m$ be the bundle provided in this case. The following proposition, stated formally and proved in the appendix, shows that,

[11]Conditions for the existence of a dominant firm are established in Bilodeau (1992). For any firm $h$. if everyone contributes only to $h$, then unless some contributor is willing and able to deviate by contributing more to one of the other specialized firms than firm $h$ is allocating to the same good, this is an equilibrium. Any firm whose $s^h$ is not too close to 0 or 1 (i.e., whose preferences are not too extreme) can therefore be dominant.

under a mild preference assumption, more of both goods are provided in the specialized equilibrium.

**Proposition.** *If all individuals view the two public goods as substitutes, then* $Z_j^b > Z_j^m$, *for* $j = 1,2$.

An easy way to see the intuition behind this is to suppose that all those individuals for whom $s^i < s^b$ in fact get no utility from $Z_2$, and those for whom $s^i > s^b$ get none from $Z_1$. Call these groups 1 and 2, respectively. Then a dominant firm essentially "taxes" their contributions by devoting a fraction of every dollar they contribute to a good they care nothing about, which raises the unit price of contributing a dollar to the provision of their favourite good. The firm also cross-subsidizes the good they care about by allocating to it a fraction of the contributions of the individuals who do not care about it. In equilibrium, this leads each group of individuals to reduce their own contributions below what they would be when two specialized firms are present. As for individuals for whom $s^i = s^b$, they see no difference in the two situations, except that the other groups contribute less to the dominant firm. Although they respond by increasing their own contributions, they do so by less than a dollar for each dollar reduction in the group 1 and 2 donations. In the general case where individuals care about both goods things are not so simple, but the assumption that individuals view the two public goods as substitutes is sufficient to maintain the result.

If the dominant firm prefers a proportion other than $s^b$, it is generally ambiguous whether total contributions to it will be higher or lower than when there are two specialized firms. In Fig. 3, for the values of $s$ defined by each point on the curve labelled $\omega(s)$, the corresponding vector $Z = \omega(s)$ indicates the public good bundle that would emerge from the existence of a monopoly firm whose founder preferred that particular value of $s$. From the above proposition, we know that $\omega(s^b) < Z^b$. It is immediate that $\omega(.)$ is continuous, however, so that, as Fig. 3 illustrates, more of both goods will be provided by specialized firms than by a dominant firm whose $s^h$ is anywhere between $s'$ and $s''$. Since there will generally be underprovision of the public goods even in the specialized equilibrium, it follows that (neglecting the entry cost to the entrepreneurs) specialization represents a Pareto-improvement over any of the monopoly equilibria involving entrepreneurs with $s^h$ in this range.

## 5. Entry decisions

Many different equilibrium continuations can arise in any subgame following the entry of more than one firm, and this significantly complicates the analysis of entry decisions. Virtually any entry configuration can be sustained as an equilibrium, including configurations in which there are redundant firms collecting no

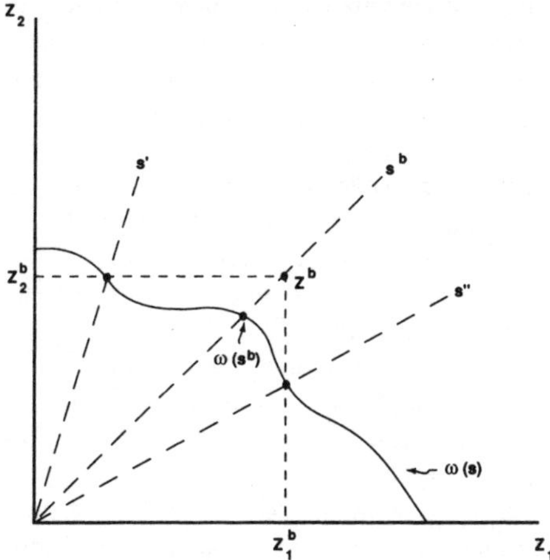


Fig. 3. Specialization vs. diversified monopoly.

money. However, all of the equilibrium *outcome* possibilities can be summarized in two cases:

1. Diversified "monopoly". Whenever one firm is dominant, the outcome is as if that firm were in fact a monopoly.
2. Rival specialized firms. There can be more than one firm specializing in each good, but the outcome is invariant to the number of firms (again neglecting the entry costs).

Given this, we do not attempt to characterize equilibrium entry decisions in greater detail. We merely note that adding more firms to the specialized outcome requires the payment of additional entry costs, without affecting the outcome, unless one of the entrants becomes dominant. If that happens, however, there is no reason for the other firms to remain, and if it does not, there is no reason to enter. Similarly, there is no reason for other firms to remain active if some firm is dominant, and no reason to enter against a dominant firm unless the result is specialization.

## 6. Commitments

In subgame perfect equilibria, the entrepreneurs must, in the last stage, allocate received donations in accordance with their own preferences. In this section we analyze the possibility that entrepreneurs are able to commit to rules for utilizing donations – even if it is not optimal for the entrepreneur to adhere to the rule *after* donations have been made. If a commitment to some allocation rule results in an entrepreneur's firm receiving greater donations, then such a commitment may pay even if the rule implies a less desirable allocation of those donations.

There are an infinity of possible rules an entrepreneur might commit to, and attempting to determine an optimal commitment is beyond the scope of this paper. We restrict ourselves to a particular strategy that corresponds to observed behaviour in some nonprofit organizations: a commitment to honour donor instructions regarding the allocation of their donations.

We saw above that when there is a diversified monopoly, donors contribute less than they would to rival specialized firms, if the allocation of donations is sufficiently similar in both cases. If a monopoly can find a way to present donors with the same choice opportunities that they would have when faced with specialized firms, more of both public goods can then be provided.

One policy to consider involves donors having the option of designating to which uses their contributions should be allocated, together with a commitment to honour these designations. If enough donors[12] take advantage of this option, the outcome will be just as if two rival specialized firms were operating. However, if enough donations are *not* earmarked, the designation option becomes meaningless because the monopoly will be able to allocate these undesignated funds so as to offset the effect of any designations. So if the monopoly retains discretionary use of undesignated funds, either of these outcomes could obtain in equilibrium even when the monopoly commits to honouring donor designations. Nonprofit managers then must face the fact that the *failure* to earmark by a significant set of donors can render the designation option meaningless, and prevent the firm from achieving an outcome which everyone may prefer.

We noted above the apparent similarity between the dominant-firm equilibrium and Becker's "Rotten Kid Theorem". However, the result of the household head's ability to reallocate income within the household is the attainment of an efficient outcome while here the presence of a dominant firm with sufficient non-earmarked funds to allocate can result in a Pareto-inferior allocation of resources to public goods. This is because Becker's patriarch is altruistic, in that his utility depends positively on the utilities of all household members, while our dominant firm entrepreneur's utility depends only on her own consumption and the mix of public goods.

The difficulty caused by non-designated donations can be circumvented by a further commitment to a fixed rule for allocating those contributions. That is, the organization can specify the proportion of its undesignated revenues that will be

[12] An exact formulation of what "large enough" means is given in Bilodeau (1992). Essentially, individuals must earmark more money in aggregate to each good than the monopoly would from the undesignated funds it has.

allocated to each good. Almost any such commitment will cause everyone to earmark because it prevents the firm from using undesignated funds to offset individual designations, while also implying an allocation of those funds that individuals do not find optimal. A commitment to honour donor designations, coupled with a commitment to allocate non-designated funds according to a fixed rule would therefore always yield a preferred outcome if the entrepreneur's $s^m$ is close to the $s^b$ that results from specialization.

In practice, perhaps due to decision-making costs (like the cost of gathering information about each member charity of a United Way organization) it is likely that some individuals will fail to earmark. The monopoly may also receive undesignated funds from government grants, fees for service, sales, or investment income. If so, the rule the monopoly commits to for using undesignated funds will then affect the outcome. By choosing the rule appropriately, the entrepreneur can influence the final allocation for the better. This is illustrated in Fig. 4. The monopolist prefers that the fraction $s^m$ of each dollar be allocated to good 2 and has $D^u$ in undesignated revenues. Designated donations are $\bar{Z}_1$ and $\bar{Z}_2$. If she does not commit to a rule, fewer contributions will be received and the outcome will be $Z^m$. By committing to allocate the fraction $s^c$ of all undesignated donations to good 2, the firm receives more donations, and achieves outcome $Z^b$ which she prefers. What is crucial is that undesignated funds are committed to being spent in a particular way *before* individuals start contributing, and not allocated after they have done so.

It has recently become more common for local United Way Chapters, which can surely be viewed as diversified charities, to allow this sort of donor designation.

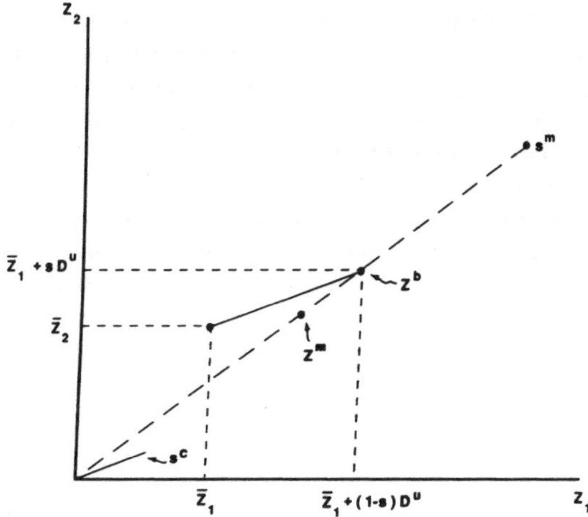


Fig. 4. Donor designations.

However, those chapters which do allow donors to designate vary in the way they treat these designations, and in the way they allocate undesignated funds. In practice, when United Way chapters do allow for donor designation of contributions (and not all do so) they do it in one of two ways. One is to count the designated funds as part of the "regular allocation" of funds to that use. That is, the United Way chapter lays out an ex-ante allocation policy, and any funds designated to a particular use are simply subtracted from the amount of non-earmarked funds that will go to it. In effect this leaves the United Way in a position to use the undesignated funds to offset individual designations at the margin and therefore is not useful. Unless enough individuals designate their contributions that more is designated to each particular use than the United Way would allocate to it otherwise, all designations are meaningless. The other method used is to have a separate allocation policy that applies only to non-designated funds. If this policy specifies a particular fraction of non-designated funds going to each use, this is a commitment to a particular $s$ for non-designated funds *only*. Since these policies are typically set by "citizen review boards", this can be seen as a means of committing to some $s$. This second method should, according to our model, yield higher amounts of total contributions. This suggests that data on the way in which various chapters deal with designations, and the amount of designated donations they receive, could allow for an empirical test of this prediction.

## 7. Conclusion

The model developed in this paper generates a number of results regarding the behaviour of nonprofit firms competing for voluntary contributions. We showed that in the presence of competitors, firms will tend to differentiate themselves by specializing, rather than imitating their competitors. Competition between nonprofit firms may also be desirable in the sense that if public goods are underprovided, competing nonprofit firms will elicit larger voluntary contributions from the public than will a monopoly firm. We also showed that commitments to allocation rules may be in the nonprofit entrepreneur's interest. A monopoly firm may wish to commit to honour donor designation about how their contribution should be spent in order to increase the level of total contributions. For such a commitment to be successful however, the firm must also commit to a fixed rule for allocating any undesignated funds.

## 8. Appendix

**Proposition 1.** *Consider a voluntary provision game in which $n$ individuals simultaneously contribute voluntarily to the provision of 2 public goods. If* *individual preferences can be represented by additively separable utility functions which are strictly concave in each of $x_i$, $Z_1$ and $Z_2$, then this game has a unique equilibrium outcome.*

**Proof.** The separability assumption implies that utility functions have the form $u^i = f_i(x_i) + g_i(Z_1) + h_i(Z_2)$.

Suppose there is an equilibrium in which the outcome is $(Z_1, Z_2)$, and the sets of contributors to each good are $C_1$ and $C_2$. For all $i$ in $C_1$ we have $g_i'(Z_1) = f_i'(x_i) \geq h_i'(Z_2)$, and for all $i$ in $C_2$ we have $g_i'(Z_1) \leq f_i'(x_i) = h_i'(Z_2)$.

Suppose by way of contradiction that there is another equilibrium in which the outcome is $(\hat{Z}_1, \hat{Z}_2)$, and assume without loss of generality that $\hat{Z}_1 > Z_1$. Then $\hat{Z}_1 > Z_1 \Rightarrow g_i'(\hat{Z}_1) < g_i'(Z_1)$ by strict concavity.

$\forall i \notin C_2$, $g_i'(Z_1) \leq f_i'(x_i)$, so $g_i'(\hat{Z}_1) < f_i'(x_i)$. If any such $i$ contributed to good 1 in the second equilibrium, he would choose $\hat{x}_i$ such that $g_i'(\hat{Z}_1) = f_i'(\hat{x}_i)$. So $f_i'(\hat{x}_i) < f_i'(x_i)$ and hence $\hat{x}_i > x_i$. And if he were to contribute nothing to good 1, he would also choose $\hat{x}_i \geq x_i$. Therefore $\hat{x}_i \geq x_i$ $\forall i \notin C_2$ and since $x_i + d_1^i = w^i$ then they must all be contributing no more to good 1 in the second equilibrium. Since $\hat{Z}_1 > Z_1$ by assumption, it must then be that some $i \in C_2$ contributes more to good 1 in the second equilibrium. Therefore the set $C_2 \cap \hat{C}_1$ is not empty.

However, $\forall i \in C_2 \cap \hat{C}_1$, $g_i'(Z_1) \leq f_i'(x_i) = h_i'(Z_2)$, and $f_i'(\hat{x}_i) = g_i'(\hat{Z}_1) \geq h_i'(\hat{Z}_2)$. But since $\hat{Z}_1 > Z_1$, then $g_i'(\hat{Z}_1) < g_i'(Z_1)$. So

$$f_i'(x_i) = h_i'(Z_2) \geq g_i'(Z_1) > g_i'(\hat{Z}_1) = f_i'(\hat{x}_i) \geq h_i'(\hat{Z}_2).$$

This implies that $\hat{Z}_2 > Z_2$ and $\hat{x}_i > x_i$ $\forall i \in C_2 \cap \hat{C}_1$.

Now consider all $i \in C_2 \backslash \hat{C}_1$. If any are in $\hat{C}_2$ then $f_i'(\hat{x}_i) = h_i'(\hat{Z}_2)$ and since $\hat{Z}_2 > Z_2$ then $h_i'(\hat{Z}_2) < h_i'(Z_2)$. So for any such $i$, $f_i'(\hat{x}_i) = h_i'(\hat{Z}_2) < h_i'(Z_2) = f_i'(x_i)$. Therefore it must be that $\hat{x}_i > x_i$. And if some are not in $\hat{C}_2$ then they are not contributing at all and for them also $\hat{x}_i = w_i > x_i$.

But we cannot have $\hat{x}_i \geq x_i$ $\forall i$ at the same time as $\hat{Z}_1 > Z_1$ and $\hat{Z}_2 > Z_2$ without violating the budget constraints.

**Proposition 2.** *Let* $x_1^i(Z_1^{-i}, t, Z_2) = \text{argmax}_{x^i}\{u^i(x^i, Z_1^{-i} + t(w^i - x^i), Z_2)$, *and* $h_1^i(Z_1^{-i}, t, Z_2) = Z_1^{-i} + t(w^i - x^i)$. *Define* $x_2^i(Z_2^{-i}, t, Z_1)$ *and* $h_2^i(Z_2^{-i}, t, Z_1)$ *symmetrically. If* $\partial h_{-j}^i / \partial Z_j \leq 0$ *for all i, then* $Z_j^b > Z_j^m$, *for* $j = 1, 2$.

**Proof.** Since the two goods are provided in the same ratio $s^b$ in both $Z^m$ and $Z^b$, the only other possibility is that $Z^b < Z^m$ so suppose by way of contradiction that this is the case. Let $T_1$ be the set of individuals $i$ for whom $s^i < s^b$, let $T_2$ be the set of all $i$ for whom $s^i > s^b$, and let $T_0$ be the set of those for whom $s^i = s^b$.

If any $i \in T_1$ chooses $d_i^m = 0$, then $d_i^m \leq d_i^b$ trivially. Suppose that $d_i^m > 0$ for some $i \in T_1$. Dropping the $i$ superscripts for the remainder of the proof, define $x_1(Y_1,t,Z_2)$ and $h_1(Y_1,t,Z_2)$ as above[13], letting $Y_1 = Z_1^{-i}$.

Now, define $G(x,t,Z_2) = h_1(x_1^{-1}(x|t,Z_2),t,Z_2)$, where $x_1^{-1}(\cdot|t,Z_2)$ is the inverse of the $x_1$ function in $Y_1$. $G(x,t,Z_2) = Z_1$ is then just the function that describes the income expansion path showing the combination of $x^i$ and $Z_1$ that $i$ will choose as his "income" varies, when the price of $Z_1$ is $t$, and the level of public good 2 is fixed at $Z_2$. Normality implies that the income expansion path is upward sloping so $G(.)$ is increasing in $x$, and so long as $w > x$, $G$ is also increasing in $t$.

Let $f \equiv x_1^{-1}$ to ease the notation, and noting that $f(x_1(A,t,Z_2)|t,Z_2) \equiv A$, it follows that $\frac{\partial f}{\partial x}\frac{\partial x_1}{\partial Z_2} + \frac{\partial f}{\partial Z_2} \equiv 0$, so that $\frac{\partial f}{\partial Z_2} = -\frac{\partial f}{\partial x}\frac{\partial x_1}{\partial Z_2}$.

From the definition of $G$ it follows that $\frac{\partial G}{\partial Z_2} = \frac{\partial h_1}{\partial Z_2} + \frac{\partial h_1}{\partial A}\frac{\partial f}{\partial Z_2} = \frac{\partial h_1}{\partial Z_2} - (\frac{\partial h_1}{\partial A} / \frac{\partial x_1}{\partial A})\frac{\partial x_1}{\partial Z_2}$, where the last equality also uses the fact that $\frac{\partial f}{\partial x} = 1/\frac{\partial x_1}{\partial A}$.

Since $\frac{\partial h_1}{\partial Z_2}$ and $\frac{\partial x_1}{\partial Z_2}$ cannot have the same sign, it follows that $\frac{\partial G}{\partial Z_2} \le 0 \Leftrightarrow \frac{\partial h_1}{\partial Z_2} \le 0$, and thus the assumption in the Proposition implies that $\frac{\partial G}{\partial Z_2} \le 0$.

Now, in the specialized equilibrium, an individual from $T_1$ donates only to $Z_1$, and therefore his private consumption, $x^b$, and $Z_1^b$ satisfy $Z_1^b = G(x^b,1,Z_2^b)$.

For the same individual, in the dominant firm equilibrium his private consumption, $x^m$ must be the solution to $\max_x\{u(x, (1-s)(w-x)+Y_1, s(w-x)+Y_2)\}$, and so $x^m$ must satisfy:

$$u_x(x_m,Z_m) = (1-s)u_{Z_1}(x_m,Z_m) + su_{Z_2}(x_m,Z_m)$$

with the subscripts on $u$ denoting partial derivatives, and $Z_1^m = (1-s)(w-x^m)+Y_1$, and $Z_2^m = s(w-x^m)+Y_2$. Further, since he is in $T_1$, it must be that $u_{Z_1}^m > u_{Z_2}^m$ where these are the derivatives evaluated at $(x^m,Z^m)$.

However, if we now let $t^m \equiv (1-s)+su_{Z_2}^m/u_{Z_1}^m < 1$, and $y^m \equiv Z_1^m - t^m(w-x^m)$, then it can be shown that if he faces the problem: $\max_x\{u(x,y^m + t^m(w-x),Z_2^m)\}$, then the solution is in fact $x^m$.

It follows that $x^m = x_1(y^m,t^m,Z_2^m)$ and $Z_1^m = h_1(y^m,t^m,Z_2^m)$, so that if the hypothesis is true, then $G(x^m,t^m,Z_2^m) = Z_1^m > Z_1^b = G(x^b,1,Z_2^b)$.

Then $t^m < 1$ and $Z_2^m > Z_2^b$, together with the above results on the derivatives of $G$ imply that $x^m > x^b$ if $x^m < w$, and thus no individual in $T_1$ donates more in the dominant firm equilibrium. A symmetric result holds for all those in $T_2$.

Now all $i \in T_0$ can be viewed as consumers of two goods $x_i$ and $v_i = g^i(Z_1,Z_2)$. In the dominant firm case, $Z = (1-s_b,s_b)D$ so letting $\rho^i = g^i(1-s_b,s_b)$, we can write

$$u_i(x_i,g^i(Z_1,Z_2)) = u_i(w_i - d_i,(D_{-i} + d_i)\rho^i).$$

[13] These are just individual $i$'s demands for private consumption and one public good, given that the provision of the other public good is fixed at some level, donations by others to the one public good are some $Z_j^{-i}$, and the "price" of the one public good is $1/t$. Note further that for each $i$, then, a change in $Z_1$, say, cannot move $x_2^i$ and $h_2^i$ in the same direction.

Therefore it must be that if $d_i^m > 0$, then

$$D_m = \text{argmax}_D\{u_i(w_i - (D - D_{-i}^m), D\rho^i)\} \equiv H_i(\rho^i, D_{-i}^m)$$

Therefore $d_i^m \geq H_i(\rho^i, D_{-i}^m) - D_{-i}^m$ (with equality if $d_i^m > 0$).

Let $\alpha_1(Z^{-i}) = (Z_2^{-i}/s_b) - (Z_1^{-i} + Z_2^{-i})$ and $\alpha_2(Z^{-i}) = s_b(Z_1^{-i} + Z_2^{-i}) + Z_2^{-i}$. Note that $\alpha_1(Z^{-i}) = \alpha_2(Z^{-i}) = 0$ if $Z_2^{-i}/(Z_1^{-i} + Z_2^{-i}) = s_b$ and that at most one of $\alpha_1(.)$ or $\alpha_2(.)$ can be positive. Define $\gamma(Z^{-i}, d_i) = (\gamma_1(Z^{-i}, d_i), \gamma_2(Z^{-i}, d_i))$ as follows:

$$\begin{aligned}
\gamma(Z^{-i}, d_i) &= (Z_1^{-i} + d_i, Z_2^{-i}) && \textit{if } 0 \leq d_i \leq \alpha_1(Z^{-i}) \\
&= (Z_1^{-i}, Z_2^{-i} + d_i) && \textit{if } 0 \leq d_i \leq \alpha_2(Z^{-i}) \\
&= (Z_1^{-i} + Z_2^{-i} + d_i)(1 - s_b, s_b) && \text{otherwise}
\end{aligned}$$

If there are two specialized firms then the payoff to any $i \in T_0$ is $u_i(w_i - d_i, g^i(\gamma(Z^{-i}, d_i)))$ if he allocates any total $d_i$ optimally for any $Z^{-i}$. Further,

$$g^i(\gamma(Z^{-i}, d_i)) \leq (Z_1^{-i} + Z_2^{-i} + d_i)\rho_i$$

(with equality iff $d_i \geq \max\{\alpha_1(Z^{-i}), \alpha_2(Z^{-i})\}$). In particular, in equilibrium

$$g^i(\gamma(Z^{-ib}, d_i^b)) = (Z_1^{-ib} + Z_2^{-ib} + d_i^b)\rho^i$$

also. So $D^b = H_i(\rho^i, D_{-i}^b)$. But $D^m > D^b$ by assumption, so if $d_i^m > 0$, we have

$$D^m = H_i(\rho^i, D_{-i}^m) > D^b \geq H_i(\rho^i, D_{-i}^b)$$

and therefore

$$d_i^m = H_i(\rho^i, D_{-i}^m) - D_{-i}^m < H_i(\rho_i, D_{-i}^b) - D_{-i}^b \leq d_i^b$$

and if $d_i^m = 0$ then $d_i^m \leq d_i^b$ trivially. So $d_i^m \leq d_i^b$ for all $i \in T_0$, also.

Therefore if $Z^m \geq Z^b$ it must be that $d_i^m \leq d_i^b$ for all $i$, which is a contradiction.

**Acknowledgements**

We thank David Austen-Smith, Rich Steinberg, Pete Streufert and an anomymous referee for helpful suggestions, and gratefully acknowledge financial support from the Aspen Institute's Nonprofit Sector Research Fund and the Social Sciences and Humanities Research Council of Canada. Part of the work on this paper was done while the authors were visitors at the Indiana University Centre on Philanthropy. We thank the Centre and the IUPUI Department of Economics for their financial and other support during these visits.

## References

Barro, R.J., 1974. Are government bonds net wealth?. Journal of Political Economy 82, 1095–1117.

Becker, G.S., 1974. A theory of social interactions. Journal of Political Economy 82 (6), 1063–1093.

Bergstrom, T., Blume, L., Varian, H., 1986. On the private provision of public goods. Journal of Public Economics 29, 25–49.

Bernheim, D., 1986. On the voluntary and involuntary provision of public goods. American Economic Review 75, 789–793.

Bilodeau, M., 1992. Voluntary contributions to united charities. Journal of Public Economics 48, 119–133.

Bilodeau, M., 1994. Tax-earmarking and separate school financing. Journal of Public Economics 54, 51–63.

Bilodeau, M., Slivinski, A., 1994. Rational nonprofit entrepreneurship. Working Paper 93-2, Université de Sherbrooke.

Bilodeau, M., Slivinski, A., 1996. Volunteering nonprofit entrepreneurial services. Journal of Economic Behavior and Organization 31, 117–127.

Debreu, G., 1952. A social equilibrium existence theorem. In: Proceedings of the National Academy of Sciences, USA, pp. 386–393.

Fan, K., 1952. Some properties of convex sets related to fixed-point theorems. Math. Ann. pp. 519–537.

Varian, H., 1994. Sequential provision of public goods. Journal of Public Economics 53, 165–186.

Warr, P.G., 1983. The private provision of a public good is independent of the distribution of income. Economics Letters 13, 207–211.

# [9]

# THE NONPROFIT FIRM: A POTENTIAL SOLUTION TO INHERENT MARKET FAILURES

ANNE E. PRESTON*

*This article analyzes the differences in products offered by nonprofit and for-profit firms in a monopolistically competitive industry where goods are differentiated both by product attributes and by the degree to which benefits are public. Because nonprofit firms receive donations, they provide a Pareto improvement of the equilibrium product set: nonprofit firms will be less biased against goods with a high social good component than will their for-profit counterparts. In addition, the optimal donations function which equates the nonprofit equilibrium product set to the set which maximizes societal welfare is derived.*

## I. INTRODUCTION

Monopolistic competition in industries which generate both public and private benefits guarantees a nonoptimal product set. Specific goods whose contribution to social welfare is positive yet whose benefits are largely public will not be offered. While the public finance literature has generated a variety of imaginative solutions to the general public goods problem, there is also a small but growing literature on a corrective mechanism which has naturally emerged in these inherently flawed markets—the nonprofit firm. This paper seeks to bridge the two sets of literature by analyzing the effect of nonprofit production on product selection in industries where benefits are both private and public. These findings are particularly important given the current environment of reductions in government financing of services with a large public good component.

Much of the literature on nonprofit firms has focused on the emergence of nonprofit firms as private suppliers of public goods in economies where there exists excess demand for public goods. While this work implies that the emergence of nonprofit firms has caused a Pareto improvement in the product mix, this implication has never been formally proved.[1] In addition much of the theoretical literature on nonprofit firms analyzes the firm in isolation or in a monopolistic setting (see Hansmann [1980] and Ben-ner [1986]). However,

* Assistant Professor, W. Averell Harriman College and Department of Economics, State University of New York at Stony Brook. I would like to thank two anonymous referees who made useful comments on the paper.

1. Weisbrod [1986] implies that public services will be higher with the existence of nonprofits and that Pareto superior allocations will result. Weiss [1986] uses cooperative game theory to show that this implication may not always be the case in three-person games where there are two low demanders of the public good and one high demander of the public good. This paper uses an alternative approach to determine whether a Pareto superior outcome occurs; here, the approach is to look at firm behavior in monopolistically competitive markets where there are profits to be made from providing a good with both public and private benefits.



Economic Inquiry
Vol. XXVI, July 1988, 493–506

most nonprofit activity occurs in oligopolistic or monopolistically competitive markets and many of these markets include for-profit competitors.[2] Rose-Ackerman [1986a, 1986b] analyzes the nonprofit firm in a monopolistically competitive setting where the behavior of managers is governed by the desire to promote a certain ideology. However, she addresses the effect of competition on the levels of charitable service provision in markets with and without entry barriers rather than the effect of competition on the varieties of services provided by nonprofit and for-profit firms.[3]

This paper presents a partial equilibrium analysis of how the emergence of nonprofit firms in an industry which also includes for-profit firms will alter that industry's equilibrium product set. Following Spence's [1976] framework for analyzing product selection, the focus is on firm behavior in a monopolistically competitive market. Here, however, goods are not only differentiated according to product attributes but also according to the degree to which benefits are public.[4] In the model social benefits are defined as social externalities, benefits enjoyed by parties external to the transaction, or more specifically by society as a whole.[5] The arts industry is one example of an industry which houses both for-profit and nonprofit firms that are in part differentiated by the degree to which services generate public benefits. First-run movies have primarily private benefits; however, museums have a much larger social benefit component under this definition of social externality. Specifically, while a private transaction with private benefits occurs when an individual pays admission to a museum, the provision of the exhibits to the public increases the education level and the cultural awareness of the society as a whole.

The model generates three principal results: (1) the presence of nonprofit firms in industries which produce both public and private benefits results in a Pareto improvement of the product set as long as income donated to the nonprofit firm is positively related to social benefits; (2) the extent to which the nonprofit equilibrium approximates the optimum depends on the form of the donations function; and (3) a well-defined donations function exists which ensures that the optimum product set is offered.

The remainder of the paper is divided into three sections. Section II compares the product biases of nonprofit and for-profit firms under a specific form of

2. According to Rudney and Weitzman [1983], in 1982 nonprofit firms were located in thirty three-digit Standard Industrial Code (SIC) industries. Of those thirty industries, only twelve did not include private for-profit firms, and only seven did not include both private for-profit firms and government firms.

3. Without giving formal analysis, Rose-Ackerman [1983] does observe differences in the types of services provided by nonprofit and for-profit day care centers. Nonprofit day care centers provide high quality services and generally cater to disadvantaged and minority children, while for-profit centers provide a more standard service and cater to a wealthier clientele. These observations are consistent with the predictions in section I of this paper.

4. In many instances the methodology used here is identical to that used by Spence [1976].

5. Weisbrod [1986] uses a similar definition of social benefits to characterize nonprofit organizations.

the donations function. Section III describes the long run characteristics of both the optimum and the nonprofit equilibrium, and compares the ultimate nonprofit product set to that set which maximizes social welfare. This section also derives the optimal donations function. Section IV discusses testable hypotheses and potential policy applications that follow from the results of the model.

## II. THE EFFECT OF DONATIONS ON MARKET BIASES OF NONPROFIT FIRMS

As in Spence's model, the monopolistically competitive industry consists of $n$ varieties of goods where $x_i$ represents the quantity of the $i$th variety. However, one or more of the $n$ varieties may generate social externalities. Social externalities are defined as benefits to society generated by private market transactions. The total benefits function for each of the $n$ varieties is the sum of private benefits and social benefits:

$$TB_i(x_i) = PB_i(x_i) + SB_i(x_i). \tag{1}$$

Similarly, the total benefits generated by industry production can be represented by the following:

$$TB(\mathrm{x}) = PB(\mathrm{x}) + SB(\mathrm{x}) \tag{2}$$

*where* $\mathbf{x}$ is $(x_1, \ldots, x_n)$—the total supply of goods produced in the industry.

Assume that social benefits are linearly related to private benefits by a coefficient $S_i$ whose value can vary across the different goods.

$$SB(x_i) = S_i PB(x_i) \tag{3}$$

$$TB(x_i) = (1 + S_i)PB(x_i) \tag{4}$$

The particular concern here is whether nonprofit and for-profit firms have different biases towards goods with different social benefit components; thus the behavior of the nonprofit firm becomes an important issue. A common hypothesis in the literature on nonprofit firms is that managers of nonprofit firms derive utility from generating social benefits. Since these managers are not disciplined by the profit maximizing motive, they are free to exercise their discretion over firm behavior, and a high level of social benefit provision results.[6] This assumption is not sensible in the situation where nonprofit and for-profit firms coexist in a monopolistically competitive industry. Here, the limiting case in which the nonprofit firm maximizes profits in a fashion similar to its for-profit competitors is more realistic. While any positive profits accruing to nonprofit firms in the short run may be used to increase managerial utility, there presumably will be no supranormal profits in the long run. New brands

6. See Hansmann [1980], Weisbrod [1983], Young [1986] and Preston [1987] for discussions of alternative motivations of nonprofit managers. While all these authors do not discuss social benefits per se, they do hypothesize that profits may not be the sole motivating force behind behavior of nonprofit managers.

will be offered by both for-profit and nonprofit firms which will crowd the marketplace and decrease the demand faced by profitable firms.[7]

Each of the $n$ products is produced by at most one firm. Costs to the firm, whether for-profit or nonprofit, are represented by $c_i(x_i) + F_i$. However, an important differentiating characteristic between for-profit and nonprofit firms is that nonprofit firms receive donations. Actually, for-profit firms may also receive donative income, but tax laws make it less expensive for a donor to give money to a nonprofit firm than to a for-profit firm.[8] If the value of for-profit donations are normalized to zero, then the preceding assumption is realistic.[9] While donations may be tied to firm behavior in a number of ways, one assumption is that donations are allocated among firms so that a firm whose product generates higher social benefits will receive more donations. To ensure tractability, assume further that donations are linearly related to social benefits by the constant $D$:[10]

$$D_i = DS_iPB_i(x_i), \qquad D > 0. \tag{5}$$

In addition the summation of donations need not equal the sum of social benefits; therefore $D$ can range from zero to one.

As in Spence's [1976] analysis, specify benefits and costs by the following functions:

$$PB_i(x_i) = a_i x_i^{\beta_i} - 2 \sum_j A_{ij} x_i x_j, \tag{6}$$

$$c_i(x_i) = c_i x_i. \tag{7}$$

7. Even in the case of profit-maximizing behavior, one expects that in equilibrium nonprofit managers will achieve their own personal goals by providing that product type which most closely fits their ideological preferences. While economic viability may prevent the manager from producing his most preferred product, he will provide that viable product closest to his first choice along ideological grounds. Rose-Ackerman [1986a] develops this view of managers who array themselves according to their tastes in ideology space.

8. In a monopolistically competitive market, the different treatment of nonprofit and for-profit firms under the tax law is sufficient to generate a difference in donations received by nonprofit and for-profit firms. In other market situations where nonprofit managers can follow strategies other than profit maximization, differences in the objectives of the two types of organizations may lead to further differences in the levels of donations.

9. Preston [1983] finds that, on average, nonprofit day care centers receive monthly donations equal to $161.00 while for-profit day care centers receive monthly donations equal to $11.00. This difference is significant at the .01 level.

10. This particular allocation of donations would be generated by a set of consumers whose utility of giving is given by the following Cobb-Douglas function:

$$U(\text{giving}) = \Pi\, DON_i^{SB_i/TSB}$$

where

$$DON_i = \text{donations given to firm i,}$$
$$SB_i = \text{social benefits of firm i,}$$
$$TSB = \text{total social benefits of all firms.}$$

Here, each individual might determine that amount of giving, $DON$, which will maximize his utility and then allocate $DON$ across firms such that $\Sigma\, DON_i = DON$.

Further define

$$e_i = 2 \sum_j A_{ij}x_j . \quad (8)$$

Here $e_i$ defines the effects of the substitutability between $x_i$ and other products in the industry on the demand for $x_i$. Because this expression is linear with respect to product substitutes, increases in the levels of other products within the industry will shift the inverse demand curve of $x_i$ downward by a constant vertical amount.

This form of the benefit function, $PB_i(x_i)$, is especially useful because the change in surplus resulting from the introduction of a product is given by the total benefits function of the product less costs. In addition the differences between the optimum and the market equilibrium are a function of the parameter $\beta$. $\beta$ equals the ratio of revenue accruing from sales at the profit-maximizing level of output to surplus contribution (gross of costs) at the surplus-maximizing level of output. $\beta$ is bounded between zero and one if there are no negative externalities associated with the product. Spence shows that $\beta$, which is a measure of the revenue-producing potential of the good, is an important determinant of product selection. Subsequent results in this paper also depend on the value of $\beta$ and its relation to the donations sensitivity coefficient, $D$.

The net surplus generated by $x_i$ can then be represented:

$$\Delta TS_i = (1 + S_i)(a_i x_i^{\beta i} - e_i x_i) - c_i x_i - F_i . \quad (9)$$

Profits of the nonprofit and for-profit firms can be represented in a similar manner.

$$\text{for-profit: } \pi_i^P = a_i \beta_i x_i^{\beta i} - e_i x_i - c_i x_i - F_i \quad (10)$$

$$\text{nonprofit: } \pi_i^{NP} = a_i \beta_i x_i^{\beta i} - e_i x_i - c_i x_i - F_i + DS_i(a_i x_i^{\beta i} - e_i x_i) \quad (11)$$

Generating first order conditions for surplus maximization and profit maximization for the two types of firms allows development of expressions for maximized profits of the nonprofit firm and the for-profit firm as functions of maximized surplus. Using these expressions, the effect of higher social benefit coefficients on profits is calculated for the two types of firms (see Appendix).

Because industry goods are substitutes, each firm maximizes its profits subject to the output of its competitors. Ultimately a Nash solution establishes an equilibrium output vector, $(x_1, \ldots, x_n)$. In an equilibrium of for-profit firms, because each firm faces a downward sloping demand curve for its product and because each product generates social benefits not recognized by producing firms, the contribution to surplus is much greater than the contribution to firm revenue. Goods which generate high net benefits may not generate enough revenue to cover costs; thus they may not be produced by for-profit firms. More specific to the analysis, $\partial \pi_i / \partial S_i$ will be negative; for-profit firms will be biased against producing goods with high social benefit components.

Because the nonprofit firm has often been regarded as a partial correction to this type of market failure, the goal of the current analysis is to estimate the effect of the social benefit coefficient, $S_i$, on profits of the nonprofit firm. The calculation of $\partial\pi_i/\partial S_i$ for nonprofit firms is complex, therefore I focus on two situations: $D = 1$, or the donations received by a firm are equal to the social benefits generated; and $D < 1$, or donations received are less than social benefits.

In the limiting case where $D$ is equal to one, because social benefits generate donative revenue, nonprofit firms will be biased toward producing those varieties with a high social good component. However, if $D$ is less than one, the conclusion is not so simple, and the direction of the bias depends on the sign of the expression $D - \beta$. As long as the ratio of donations to social benefits exceeds the ratio of revenue originating from sales to surplus contributions ($D > \beta$), nonprofit firms will be biased toward producing goods with a high social benefit component. On the other hand, if the ratio of donations to social benefits is small relative to the ratio of sales revenue to surplus contributions ($D < \beta$), firms may continue to be biased against goods which generate social externalities.

These results support the hypothesis that nonprofit production will result in an alternative set of varieties produced. Spence uses a similar analysis to show that goods with a low $\beta$, or more intuitively specialty goods with a steep inverse demand curve, may not generate the revenue necessary to justify private production. However, if donations are sensitive to social benefits, nonprofit firms will find that goods with a low $\beta$ and a high $S$ may generate enough donative income to cover costs of production. The combined set of results presents an intuitively appealing picture. Products with a high ratio of revenue to consumer benefits will be privately consumed goods. They may be produced by either for-profit or nonprofit firms.[11] On the other hand, goods with a low ratio of revenue to private benefits, goods which can loosely be defined as speciality goods, can only be maintained in the market place if they have a large public benefit component. These types of products will be produced by nonprofit firms, and a majority of their funding will come from donative income.

One industry which can be used to illustrate the results of this model is the day care industry. A large portion of day care centers care for healthy children of working mothers. The clientele is broad-based, and private revenue sources are sufficient to support most operations. However, some day care services cater to mentally retarded, developmentally disabled, or poverty stricken children. One can think of this type of service as a specialty service where private revenue sources will not be sufficient to cover the costs of the operation. In

11. In practice, because nonprofit managers may have motivations different than income maximization, they may be less inclined to produce the products with a large revenue producing potential. They may locate in product space on ideological rather than on income producing grounds.

addition the care of the sick and incompetent has large social externalities associated with it. These types of centers are heavily financed by donations.[12]

These theoretical predictions may be helpful for policy analysis. As the price of giving is reduced, more donations will be allocated across firms and $D$ will move closer to one. Therefore existing government policy which allows charitable expenses to be deducted from income creates a Pareto improvement of the product set since nonprofit firms that receive sufficient donations can produce goods with a sizeable social benefit component. However, new tax laws which decrease marginal tax rates will increase the price of giving and decrease $D$. The viable product set will be reduced: those goods with large social benefits which were marginally viable under the previous tax laws will not survive. Once one generalizes to situations where individuals have heterogeneous preferences over social benefits, existing government policy which creates differences in the price of giving according to income tax brackets will have important effects on the types of products which are produced. Specifically, if preferences for types of social benefits differ according to income,[13] goods whose social benefits are favored by the working class will be less likely to be produced than those with social benefits favored by the rich, all else equal. Here, $D$ is lower for those goods whose social benefits are favored by the working class than for other goods whose social benefits are favored by the wealthy. In addition, the goods which do survive and which receive donative income from the working class are less likely to be specialty goods (goods for which $\beta$ is high) but more likely to be goods with broad appeal, such as churches or community recreation organizations. However, goods supported by the donative income of the wealthy may be very specialized, such as the America's Cup challenges and modern dance companies.

## III. MARKET ORDERING AND THE OPTIMAL DONATIONS FUNCTION

The preceding section establishes that the availability of donations which are in some way related to social benefits affects the product mix offered by nonprofit firms. Generally, nonprofit production in an industry previously dominated by for-profit firms will result in a Pareto improvement of the product set. Nonprofit firms will increase the number of varieties offered, and each added product will have a high social benefit component, a characteristic against which for-profit firms are strongly biased. However, there is no reference to the form which donations must take to ensure that the optimal product set is offered. The two algorithms applied here were introduced by Spence [1976]; they order products according to their profit-generating and their social welfare-generating potentials. This ordering provides the basis for

12. Preston [1983] finds a positive correlation between the donations received by a day care center and the percentage of children who are physically, developmentally or economically disabled.

13. The heterogeneity of preferences by income for different types of social benefits has been considered and analyzed by Simon [1986] and by Strnad [1986].

comparing the set of products in the market to the set which maximizes social welfare.[14] Therefore, the market equilibrium and the social optimum can be compared. The donations function which equates the two sets of products is the optimal donations function.

To ensure the calculation of an industry equilibrium, let the private benefits function of **x**, the vector of products offered by the industry, be a generalized CES utility function.

$$PB(\mathbf{x}) = G\left[\int_i \phi_i(x_i)\, d_i\right] \tag{12}$$

where $G$ and $\phi_i$ are concave functions.

$$p_i = PB_i = G'(m)\phi_i'(x_i) \tag{13}$$

where

$$m = \int_j \phi_j(x_j)\, d_j, \tag{14}$$

and $m$ is an index of product congestion. As $m$ increases, $G'(m)$ decreases, because $G(m)$ is a concave function. The more products in the market, the smaller the demand for any specific product.[15]

Because the object is the derivation of the donation function which ensures optimal ordering of products, the function itself is not specified beyond the fact that it is a function of $S_i$ and $x_i$. Therefore, each nonprofit firm's profits are represented by

$$\pi_i^{NP} = G'(m)\phi_i'(x_i)x_i - [c_i(x_i) + F_i] + D(S_i, x_i). \tag{15}$$

Each firm's ability to survive increased congestion of the industry depends on the ratio of costs less donations to revenue. Assuming that each firm produces a level of output which minimizes this ratio, a survival coefficient can be represented:

$$sc_i = \min_{x_i} [c_i(x_i) + F_i - D(s_i, x_i)]/x_i\phi_i'(x_i). \tag{16}$$

Positive profits exist when $sc_i$ is less than $G'(m)$.

To characterize the nonprofit equilibrium, firms can be ranked from those most likely to succeed (i.e., firms with the lowest survival coefficients, $sc_1$) to those least likely to succeed (firms with the highest survival coefficient, $sc_n$). Let product introduction follow this ranking. As entry occurs and the number of varieties increases, product congestion also increases. $G'(m)$ falls. In equi-

14. A complete mathematical treatment is available from the author.

15. For a more complete discussion of the characteristics of the benefits function and the congestion index, $m$, see Spence [1976, 227]. It is important to recognize that the CES functional form implies that the ratio of revenues to the contribution of surplus is not affected by entry of new firms. There are no drastic shifts in demand elasticities as new firms enter. In addition, the analysis continues with the implicit assumption that the $i$th firm does not acknowledge the effect which changes in $x_i$ have on $G'(m)$.

librium, each firm maximizes profits, the last firm to enter breaks even, and no technically feasible product exists for which potential revenue is greater than costs of production. Therefore in an industry equilibrium with $k$ varieties produced,

$$G'(m) = sc_k \text{ and } G'(m) \geq sc_j \text{ for any } j < k.$$

The optimal ordering and introduction of products is slightly different. The total surplus generated by industry production can be represented by

$$TS = G(m)(1 + S_\Sigma) - \int_{i \in \Sigma} (c_i + F_i) \tag{17}$$

where $\Sigma$ is the set of products actually produced, and $S_\Sigma$ is the social benefit coefficient of industry production.

Each firm's contribution to surplus in the face of increased product congestion depends on the ratio of costs to total (public and private) consumer benefits. Therefore, products can be rated according to a new set of surplus contribution coefficients:

$$\rho_i = \min_{x_i} (c_i + F_i)/[(1 + S_i)\phi_i(x_i)]. \tag{18}$$

Goods with a lower $\rho_i$ contribute a greater amount to total surplus. Let products be introduced according to this alternative ranking. Only those goods for which $\rho_i \leq 1$ are introduced; products with a $\rho_i > 1$ would cause the total surplus to decrease.

The total surplus is maximized when each firm maximizes net surplus generated, the marginal firm is one for which costs equal total benefits, and no technically feasible product exists for which the net surplus contribution is nonnegative. At the optimum,

$$G'(m) = \rho_n \text{ and } G'(m) \geq \rho_i \text{ for all } i \leq n.$$

One can compare the ordering and the final product set of the optimum and the market equilibrium. Fixing $m$ at some arbitrary level, $m$, the nonprofit firms order goods according to $sc_i^{NP}$ and produce goods for which $G'(m) \geq sc_i^{NP}$. At the optimum goods are ordered according to $\rho_i$ and only goods for which $G'(m) \geq \rho_i$ are produced. Comparing the social optimum coefficients with the market equilibrium coefficients, the survival coefficients for both the for-profit and the nonprofit firms can be represented as a function of the coefficients for optimal ordering.

$$\text{nonprofit: } sc_i^{NP} = [(1 + S_i)/\beta_i] [\![\rho_i - \{D(S_i, x_i)/[(1 + S_i)\phi_i(x_i)]\}]\!] \tag{19}$$

$$\text{for-profit: } sc_i^{P} = [(1 + S_i)/\beta_i] (\rho_i) \tag{20}$$

where for-profit firm donations are normalized to zero. As long as donations to the nonprofit firm are greater than zero, $sc_i^P > sc_i^{NP} \geq \rho_i$. Because $\beta_i < 1$ and $S_i \geq 0$, the for-profit firm undervalues socially beneficial products. All else equal, goods with a higher $S_i$ are more severely undervalued. As long as donations are positive, the nonprofit firm improves the market ordering. Because the difference between the nonprofit and for-profit coefficients is $D(S_i, x_i)/\beta_i\phi_i(x_i)$, those goods with a high social good component are most drastically revalued by the nonprofit firm.

The donations function which equates the nonprofit survival coefficient with $\rho_i$ ensures a socially optimal ordering of varieties by nonprofit firms. This equilibrium exists when

$$D(s_i, x_i) = [c_i(x_i) + F_i]\{1 - [\phi_i'(x_i)x_i/(1 + S_i)\phi_i(x_i)]\} \qquad (21)$$

| Total Donations | = | Total Costs of Production | × | Ratio of Total Benefits Less Revenue to Total Benefits |
|---|---|---|---|---|

Donations are allocated optimally when the total value of donations received by each firm equals a percentage of total costs equal to the percentage of total societal benefits not paid for by sales revenue. Contrary to expectations, the donations received by each firm need not be exactly equal to the social benefits which it generates. However, the notion that donations must cover a specified share of the costs of production has strong intuitive appeal. Socially worthwhile products are not produced in the market if private revenue cannot cover costs. At a nonprofit optimum, donative income covers the losses. In addition the share of those costs which must be covered is related to the percentage of total benefits not accounted for by sales revenue.

It is important to note that marginal products are those whose societal benefits are equal to costs of production. The donative income necessary to ensure production of these goods is $s_i\phi_i(x_i) + \phi_i(x_i) - x_i\phi_i'(x_i)$, a value greater than the external benefits generated. In fact this value is equal to the total consumer (private and public) surplus. Hence, the optimal donations function can exist only if donors are responsive to the private consumer surplus as well as the social surplus or if donors are consumers as well.

While there is no reason to expect that the optimal allocation of donations will necessarily approximate the actual allocation of donations in the economy, some types of charitable giving may resemble optimal behavior to some extent. For example, in the arts industries, donors tend to be consumers; thus donations may be tied to consumer surplus.[16] The existing product set may be more similar to the optimal product set in this industry than in the welfare and relief industries where donor and customer are entirely separated. This latter type of industry may need further government subsidization through a direct grant system to improve the allocation of donations and generate large Pareto improvements in the product set.

16. Hansmann [1980, 1981] describes how in the performing arts industry, donative income helps explain why an organization might want to price tickets below the price which maximizes total ticket sales receipts. While some of his arguments differ from the ones presented here, the important relations between donations and sales revenue and between customer and donor are maintained.

## IV. CONCLUDING REMARKS

The first section of the paper shows that nonprofit firms have different product biases in a monopolistically competitive industry than for-profit firms. In particular, even if the goals of both types of organizations are profit maximization, the existence of donations which are sensitive to social externalities will reduce, and in some instances reverse, market biases against goods whose benefits are largely public. If donations are a linear function of the social benefits generated by the firm, the nonprofit firm, when faced with decisions concerning the introduction of goods with poor revenue-producing powers, will be biased towards goods whose benefits are largely public.

The paper also examines the ordering of goods introduced by the nonprofit firm. Nonprofit production leads to a Pareto improvement of the for-profit ordering. Goods that would be produced in a for-profit market will remain unless the alternative nonprofit substitutes drastically reduce demand, and new socially worthwhile goods will be introduced. The new products will be biased towards a high social externality component. Ideally, donations would equal the portion of total societal benefits not covered by sales revenue.

The specific results of the paper can be extended to more general predictions concerning economy-wide production. Clearly, the results help describe the characteristics of a market equilibrium in a mixed industry in which both nonprofits and for-profits compete. However, one may first question why mixed industries exist at all, if the two types of firms differ only by the amount of donations they receive. A manager must operate under specific legal constraints if he organizes his firm under a nonprofit status. Any profits made by the nonprofit firm can not be distributed to those in control. As a result the entrepreneur in a mixed industry must incorporate his organization as a for-profit firm. In addition, managers whose production is driven by ideological beliefs may seek to organize as a nonprofit firm in order to have the opportunity to solicit donations from individuals with similar ideological beliefs. These observations strengthen the result of this study that the goods produced by nonprofit firms and for-profit firms in the same industry are markedly different. For-profit firms produce goods which generate large sums of private revenue. Nonprofits, on the other hand, may introduce products with a lower private revenue-producing potential but greater social benefits.[17]

Observations about industries in which both nonprofit and for-profit firms operate support these hypotheses. Public television and radio stations rarely produce commercially successful programs. However, their programs often have an educational or a cultural focus which, while appealing only to a limited set of viewers, may signal a large public good component. Similar statements

17. This point has been a recurring theme in the literature on nonprofit organizations. Holtman [1983] notes that "... when demand is stochastic this objective function, which gives consumers' benefits and producers' benefits equal weight, will determine an optimal price for the service that covers operating costs but not optimal costs." Similarly, Hansmann [1981] notes that nonprofit managers in the performing arts charge lower prices, causing private revenue to fall short of costs, in order to attract higher donations.

can be made about the arts where commercially successful art forms such as first run movies and Broadway plays are produced by for-profit firms. The more experimental art forms, intent on extending the creative frontier, are offered by nonprofit companies.[18] In industries where the public good component does not vary quite as widely, the differences between nonprofit and for-profit production will be less obvious, but will still remain. In the day care industry, for example, nonprofit day care centers cater to a less privileged clientele, provide a greater number of auxiliary services, and operate with a higher staff-to-child ratio than do their for-profit counterparts.[19] Day care by either for-profit or nonprofit centers will generally have a social benefit component, since care and education of the young and labor productivity of working mothers benefit society.[20] However, increasing the quality level and extending services to underprivileged children may result in an increase in the value of these associated social externalities. Although such observations support the theoretical predictions of this study, more sophisticated empirical analysis and measurement of the types of benefits provided by these industries must be performed to determine the dimensions on which nonprofit and for-profit firms differ.

Donations are a little-understood exception to the free rider problem. However, without increased knowledge of the actual mechanism by which donations are allocated to firms, the nonprofit firm will never reach its ultimate potential as a public goods provider. This paper reveals that the current government policy towards nonprofit organizations which allows the deductions of charitable giving from taxable income will result in Pareto improvements of the existing product set. However, because tax policy creates differences in the price of giving by income groups, these improvements will be most evident in the charities favored by the wealthy. The theoretical results further predict that the actual allocation of donations may be closest to the optimal allocation in instances where donors are also customers. Clearly the optimal donations function helps define a standard for developing policy recommendations for government support of nonprofit organizations. While this paper gives the general form of the donations function which ensures optimal product selection, there is an obvious need for empirical research which can compare the actual with these theoretical predictions.

18. Again in these examples, donors may also be customers, a condition which would help ensure a donations function closer to the optimal function.

19. In a case study of the day care industry, Preston [1983] shows that the quality level of nonprofit centers is significantly higher than the quality level of for-profit centers. Nonprofit centers are more likely to offer physical and psychological tests to children and parental assisting and counseling. In addition the nonprofit clientele includes a significantly higher percentage of racial minorities and single-parent children. Finally staff-to-child ratios are significantly higher in nonprofit firms.

20. A complete discussion of the social benefits accruing to day care services is made by Richard Nelson and Dennis Young in chapter 1 of *Public Policy for Day Care of Young Children*.

## APPENDIX

### THE EFFECTS OF SOCIAL BENEFITS ON PROFITS

Differentiating the expression of $\Delta TS_i$ (equation 9) with respect to output level allows one to solve for the optimal $\Delta TS_i$:

$$\Delta TS_i^* = [(1 - \beta_i)/\beta_i]\{1/[e_i(1 + S_i) + c_i]\}^{\beta_i/(1-\beta_i)} \cdot[(1 + S_i)\beta_i a_i]^{1/(1-\beta_i)} - F_i. \tag{1a}$$

Differentiating the profits equations of each type of firm (equations 10 and 11) with respect to $x_i$ allows one to solve for maximum profits for the nonprofit and for-profit firm:

$$\pi_i^{P*} = [(1 - \beta_i)/\beta_i][1/(e_i + c_i)]^{\beta_i/(1-\beta_i)}(\beta_i^2 a_i)^{1/(1-\beta_i)} - F_i, \tag{2a}$$

$$\pi_i^{NP*} = [(1 - \beta_i)/\beta_i]\{1/[e_i(1 + DS_i) + c_i]\}^{\beta_i/(1-\beta_i)} \cdot[\beta_i a_i(\beta_i + DS_i)]^{1/(1-\beta_i)} - F_i. \tag{3a}$$

A relationship between profits and surplus can be established by first isolating $\Delta TS_i^* + F_i$ in equation (1a) and $(\pi_i^* + F_i)$ in equations (2a) and (3a). Then the ratio of $\Delta TS_i^* + F_i$ and $(\pi_i^* + F_i)$ can be used to solve for $\pi_i^*$.

$$\pi_i^{P*} = [1 + (e_i S_i)/(c_i + e_i)]^{\beta_i/(1-\beta_i)}\,[\beta_i/(1 + S_i)]^{1/(1-\beta_i)} \cdot(\Delta TS_i^* + F_i) - F_i \tag{4a}$$

$$\pi_i^{NP*} = \{[e_i(1 + S_i) + c_i]/[e_i(1 + DS_i) + c_i]\}^{\beta_i/(1-\beta_i)} \cdot[(\beta_i + DS_i)/(1 + S_i)]^{1/(1-\beta_i)}(\Delta TS_i^* + F_i) - F_i \tag{5a}$$

The effect of social benefits on profits is determined by the sign of $\partial\pi_i/\partial S_i$. This expression will always be negative in for-profit firms. In the case of nonprofit firms, if $D = 1$,

$$\partial\pi_i^{NP}/\partial S_i = [1/(1 + S_i)^2][(\beta_i + S_i)/(1 + S_i)]^{\beta_i/(1-\beta_i)}(\Delta TS_i + F_i) > 0. \tag{6a}$$

If $D < 1$,

$$\partial\pi_i^{NP}/\partial S_i = \{[1/(1 - \beta_i)][(\pi_i^{NP} + F_i)/(\Delta TS_i + F_i)]\}\cdot([\beta_i e_i(e_i + c_i)(1 - D)]/\{[e_i(1 + S_i) + c_i]\,[e_i(1 + DS_i) + c_i]\}] + \{(D - \beta_i)/[(\beta_i + DS_i)\,(DS_i)]\})\cdot(\Delta TS_i + F_i) \gtrless 0. \tag{7a}$$

The sign of the expression, $([[\beta_i e_i(e_i + c_i)(1 - D)]/\{[e_i(1 + S_i) + c_i][e_i(1 + DS_i) + c_i]\}] + \{(D - \beta_i)/[(\beta_i + DS_i)(DS_i)]\})$ determines the sign of $\partial\pi_i^{NP}/\partial S_i$. The first term in this expression, $[[\beta_i e_i(e_i + c_i)(1 - D)]/\{[e_i(1 + S_i) + c_i][e_i(1 + DS_i) + c_i]\}]$, is always positive since by assumption $D < 1$. However, the sign of the second term, $\{(D - \beta_i)/[(\beta_i + DS_i)(DS_i)]\}$, depends on the sign of $D - \beta$.

## REFERENCES

Ben-ner, Avner. "Nonprofit Organizations: Why Do They Exist in Market Economies?" in *The Economics of Nonprofit Institutions,* edited by Susan Rose-Ackerman. New York: Oxford University Press, 1986.

Hansmann, Henry. "Nonprofit Enterprise in the Performing Arts." *Bell Journal of Economics,* Autumn 1981, 341–61.

———. "The Role of the Nonprofit Enterprise." *The Yale Law Review Journal,* April 1980, 835–98.

Holtman, A. G. "A Theory of Nonprofit Firms." *Economica,* November 1983, 439–49.

Nelson, Richard R. and Dennis R. Young. *Public Policy for Day Care of Young Children.* Lexington, MA: Lexington Books, 1973.

Preston, Anne E. *The Nonprofit Firm in a For-Profit World: A Comparative Study of Labor Market and Product Market Outcomes in the Nonprofit and For-Profit Sectors.* Ph.D. dissertation, Harvard University, 1983.

———. "The Nonprofit Worker in a For-Profit World." Working paper, State University of New York at Stony Brook, 1987.

Rose-Ackerman, Susan. "Charitable Giving and Excessive Fundraising," in *The Economics of Nonprofit Institutions,* edited by Susan Rose-Ackerman. New York: Oxford University Press, 1986a.

———. "Do Government Grants to Charity Reduce Private Donations?" in *The Economics of Nonprofit Institutions,* edited by Susan Rose-Ackerman. New York: Oxford University Press, 1986b.

———. "Unintended Consequences: Regulating the Quality of Subsidized Day Care." *Journal of Policy and Management,* Fall 1983, 14–30.

Rudney, Gabriel and Murray Weitzman. "Significance of Employment and Earnings in the Philanthropic Sector, 1972–1982." Program on Nonprofit Organizations Working Paper No. 77, Yale University, 1983.

Simon, John. "Charity and Dynasty Under the Federal Tax System," in *The Economics of Nonprofit Institutions,* edited by Susan Rose-Ackerman. New York: Oxford University Press, 1986.

Spence, Michael. "Product Selection, Fixed Costs and Monopolistic Competition." *Review of Economic Studies,* June 1976, 217–35.

Strnad, Jeff. "The Charitable Contribution Deduction: A Politico-Economic Analysis," in *The Economics of Nonprofit Institutions,* edited by Susan Rose-Ackerman. New York: Oxford University Press, 1986.

Weisbrod, Burton A. "Nonprofit and Proprietary Sector Behavior: Wage Differentials Among Lawyers." *Journal of Labor Economics,* July 1983, 246–63.

———. "Toward a Theory of the Voluntary Nonprofit Sector in a Three-Sector Economy," in *The Economics of Nonprofit Institutions,* edited by Susan Rose-Ackerman. New York: Oxford University Press, 1986.

Weiss, Jeffrey. "Donors: Can They Reduce a Donor's Welfare?" in *The Economics of Nonprofit Institutions,* edited by Susan Rose-Ackerman. New York: Oxford University Press, 1986.

Young, Dennis. "Entrepreneurship and the Behavior of Nonprofit Organizations: Elements of a Theory," in *The Economics of Nonprofit Institutions,* edited by Susan Rose-Ackerman. New York: Oxford University Press, 1986.

# [10]

# Nonprofit enterprise in the performing arts

**Henry Hansmann***

*This article explores the reasons for the current dominance of the nonprofit form in the high-culture performing arts, and concludes that this development is a response to the need for price discrimination in that sector. The article develops a model of a nonprofit performing arts organization based on this analysis, and employs the model to explore, first, the consequences to be expected if such an organization adopts any of various plausible objective functions, and second, the circumstances in which subsidies to such an organization are justified and the way in which such subsidies should be structured.*

## 1. Introduction

■ The live performing arts—including orchestral music, opera, theater, and ballet—are today in large part the product of nonprofit institutions. At the same time, there remain some segments of the performing arts, such as Broadway theater, that are vigorously for-profit (and profitable—see Moore, 1968, p. 12). Moreover, in the past profit-seeking institutions were apparently the rule rather than the exception in the performing arts; not only serious theater but even symphony orchestras were commonly proprietary. The dominance of nonprofit institutions in this industry is largely the product of recent decades, and is still far from complete.[1]

The existing literature offers no satisfying analysis of the factors that have caused this industry to become so heavily nonprofit, nor does it offer much in the way of a positive or normative perspective on the behavior of the nonprofit firms involved. Perhaps as a consequence, there also exists no well-articulated rationale for public subsidies to the performing arts, much less a coherent set of criteria by which to determine the appropriate amount and structure of such subsidies. This article addresses each of these issues.

## 2. Why are the performing arts nonprofit?

■ **Donative financing.** Nearly all nonprofit performing arts groups depend upon donations for a substantial fraction—commonly between one-third and one-

* University of Pennsylvania.

I am particularly indebted to Alvin Klevorick, Richard Nelson, Oliver Williamson, Sidney Winter, and the referees for helpful comments. Preparation of this paper was supported by a grant from the Program on Non-Profit Organizations at the Institution for Social and Policy Studies, Yale University.

[1] Among theaters, nonprofits are most commonly to be found in local and regional stock and repertory companies and off-Broadway, and are primarily a development of the period since World War II (Moore, 1968, pp. 16–20, 100; Baumol and Bowen, 1968, pp. 57–60). On the institutional history of symphony orchestras, see Mayernik (1976, p. 19).

half—of their income (Baumol and Bowen, 1968, pp. 147–157). Because, for reasons that I shall return to below, an organization that is dependent upon donations must generally be organized as a nonprofit, this pattern of financing provides a preliminary explanation for the predominance of the nonprofit form in this industry. But why are the performing arts so heavily financed by donations?

In other sectors such donative financing for nonprofits sometimes serves as a means for supporting the private production of public goods (Hansmann, 1980, pp. 848–854; Weisbrod, 1975). Consistent with this notion, it has frequently been argued that the performing arts exhibit substantial beneficial externalities, and that this in turn provides a rationale for both public and private subsidies (Baumol and Bowen, 1968, chapter 16; Netzer, 1978, chapter 2). For example, prominent cultural institutions bring prestige and tourism to both the city and the nation. Likewise, such institutions may, through indirect processes of cultural stimulus and transmission, ultimately contribute to the cultural experience even of people who do not attend their performances. But the ratio of such external benefits to the private benefits (that is, those enjoyed by members of the audience) for any performance is doubtless rather small—much smaller than the ratio of contributions to ticket receipts for the organizations involved.[2] In any case, it does not appear that such external benefits are a major stimulus for the donations received by performing arts groups. Indeed, the evidence is strongly to the contrary, for it appears that the great bulk of the donations received by performing arts groups comes from people who actually attend the groups' performances, and not from the other members of the public who partake only of the prestige and other external benefits that the performances confer upon them.[3]

Another explanation commonly encountered is that donations are a private subsidy that enables ticket prices to be kept down to levels at which they can be purchased by people who could not otherwise afford them. Undoubtedly this is part of the motivation of at least some who contribute. Yet the vast majority of people who attend the performing arts are quite well-heeled (Baumol and Bowen, 1968, chapter 4). Surely it is doubtful that the performing arts are organized on a nonprofit basis primarily to provide a vehicle whereby the rich can subsidize the merely prosperous.

The situation, then, is at first appearance rather paradoxical. Here we have a service, essentially private in character, financed partly by donations and partly by revenue from ticket sales. Yet the people who donate are also the people who attend the performances—that is, who buy tickets. Moreover, it appears that performing arts organizations commonly price their tickets so low that they operate well within the inelastic portion of their demand curve, thus failing to maximize receipts from ticket sales (Baumol and Bowen, 1968, pp.

---

[2] Moore (1968, chapter 8) and Peacock (1976) are also skeptical about the magnitude of the public benefits involved.

As noted below, however, a performing arts production is to an important extent a public good *for those individuals who are among the audience*. Thus, if someone who has already purchased a subscription to the Metropolitan Opera makes a donation to that organization, the improvement in the quality of the performances that the donation permits will be enjoyed as a public good by all others who also hold subscriptions.

[3] Direct data on the proportion of donations coming from audience members are apparently unavailable. Some indication is provided, however, by the evidence, discussed below, indicating that a substantial percentage of those who attend also contribute.

272–278). Why do these organizations seek to extract part of their revenues from the audience through donations, rather than simply by raising their ticket prices?

☐ **Price discrimination.** These phenomena all become understandable if we simply recognize contributions in the performing arts as a form of voluntary price discrimination.[4]

The considerable costs of organizing, directing, rehearsing, and providing scenery and costumes for a performing arts production are essentially fixed costs, unrelated to audience size. Marginal costs are correspondingly low: once one performance has been staged, the cost of an additional performance is relatively small, and, as long as the theater is unfilled, the cost of admitting another individual to a given performance is close to zero. At the same time, the potential audience for high-culture live entertainment is limited even in large cities; consequently, for any given production there are typically only a few performances over which to spread the fixed costs—often three or fewer for an orchestral program and only several times that for opera, ballet, and many theatrical productions. Thus, fixed costs represent a large fraction of total costs for each production.[5]

The result is that if ticket prices are set close to marginal cost, admissions receipts will fail to cover total costs. Indeed, it appears likely that for most productions staged by nonprofit performing arts groups the demand curve lies below the average cost curve at all points, so that there exists *no* ticket price at which total admission receipts will cover total costs.

If the organizations involved could engage in price discrimination, they might be able to capture enough of the potential consumer surplus to enable them to cover their costs.[6] In the performing arts, however, the effectiveness of discriminatory ticket pricing is limited by the difficulty of identifying individuals or groups with unusually inelastic demand, and by the difficulty of making admission tickets nontransferable. To be sure, a degree of price discrimination can be, and often is, affected by charging higher prices for more desirable seats: if those patrons whose demand for a given performance is most inelastic also have the strongest relative preference for good seats over bad seats, then it may well be possible to establish a price schedule that will channel those with inelastic demand into the good seats at high prices,

[4] Moore (1968, pp. 120–121) also alludes briefly to contributions as a means of price discrimination, though he does not pursue the issue.

[5] It is difficult to obtain useful data comparing fixed costs with variable costs for productions by performing arts groups. Existing studies of economies of scale in the nonprofit performing arts (Baumol and Bowen, 1968, chapter 8; Globerman and Book, 1974) simply correlate cost per performance with the total number of performances per year for different organizations (e.g., symphony orchestras or theater groups) without taking into account the number of different productions represented by those performances. Data on Broadway theater assembled by Moore (1968, chapter 3) are, however, suggestive; they show that, for the 1960–1961 season, weekly operating cost—i.e., the (variable) cost of a week's performances—for a show was, on average, less than a fifth as large as the (fixed) cost of producing the show.

[6] Here and in what follows I assume that nonprofit performing arts firms have some degree of monopoly power, and thus face downward-sloping demand curves. This is in keeping with the observation that demand is limited and fixed costs are high, thus presumably making competition unworkable. It is also in keeping with the very limited competition that in fact prevails among the nonprofit performing arts; even New York City supports only one major symphony orchestra, two substantial opera companies, and a handful of (highly differentiated) dance groups.

and those with more elastic demand into the inferior seats at lower prices.[7] This device is limited, however, by the strength of the preference for good seats over bad that is exhibited by patrons whose demand for performing arts productions is relatively inelastic.[8]

Yet, even if it is difficult to establish effective price discrimination via ticket pricing, it is still possible to ask individuals simply to *volunteer* to pay an additional amount if the value they place upon attendance exceeds the price charged for admission. And this, in effect, is the approach taken by nonprofit organizations in the performing arts.

Of course, the services paid for by a voluntary contribution to a performing arts group are public goods for all individuals who attend the group's performances,[9] and there is a clear incentive to be a free rider. As a consequence, many people contribute nothing, and presumably most of those who do contribute give something less than their full potential consumer surplus. Nevertheless, many individuals *do* contribute when confronted with solicitations pointing out that, in the absence of contributions, the organizations on which they depend for entertainment may disappear. Indeed, it appears that roughly 40% of those who attend the live performing arts contribute at least occasionally (Baumol and Bowen, 1968, pp. 307–308).

The fact that contributions to nonprofit performing arts groups are deductible under the federal income tax is undoubtedly important in reducing the incentive to be a free rider (see Section 4). Donors' committees and other organizational strategies are also presumably important in creating incentives and social pressure to help overcome free-rider behavior[10]—though here, as in the case of many other private nonprofits providing public goods (such as those devoted to political causes, environmental protection, and medical research), a surprisingly large number of individuals seem willing to respond even to impersonal solicitations received by mail.

Those areas of the performing arts that are organized on a profit-seeking basis typically differ from the areas that are nonprofit in having a much larger audience over which to spread the fixed costs of a production, so that the ratio of fixed to variable costs is relatively small, and there is consequently little difference between marginal and average cost. Broadway shows, for example, typically run for several hundred performances (Moore, 1968, chapter 1 and Table A-6). Similarly, although the cost of producing a movie commonly runs into many millions of dollars, the audience over which that cost can be spread is enormous; consequently, only about 15% of movie theater receipts is devoted to covering production costs (Gordon, 1976). Therefore, substantial price dis-

---

[7] See Winter's (1968) analysis of essentially the same issue in a different context. It also follows from Winter's analysis that, when constructing a new theater, there may well be gains to be had from creating a high ratio of bad seats to good seats, even if it would be as cheap or cheaper to construct a larger proportion of good seats for the same total capacity.

[8] Likewise, the performing arts are not well situated to take advantage of the type of two-part tariffs described by Oi (1971), since many people wish to attend only one performance by a given organization and since it is difficult to make tickets nontransferable.

[9] See note 2.

[10] To some extent, contributions undoubtedly represent an effort to buy recognition and status. Many organizations in the performing arts exploit this motivation quite consciously by publicizing the names of donors and by arranging special social events for them. But the development of the performing arts as a locus for such conspicuous giving seems most probably a consequence rather than a cause of their nonprofit donatively-financed status.

crimination—and, in particular, voluntary price discrimination—is not necessary for survival, and thus the nonprofit form loses its special comparative advantage. Since, in the absence of such a comparative advantage, nonprofit firms seem, for a number of reasons, to be less efficient producers than for-profit firms (Hansmann, 1980, pp. 877–879), it is to be expected that competition should favor for-profit firms in these areas.

Note that this analysis also suggests an explanation for the observed tendency, noted above, of nonprofit performing arts organizations to price their tickets below the level that maximizes total admissions receipts—much less the level that maximizes receipts in excess of variable costs. It seems likely that an increase in ticket prices will generally lead to a decrease in donations, since the total reservoir of consumer surplus from which those donations derive will decrease.[11] Consequently, total revenue—which includes both ticket sales receipts and donations—will be maximized at a lower ticket price than that which maximizes admissions receipts alone.

☐ **Some historical evidence.** The analysis offered here may also help to explain why nonprofit organizations have become increasingly prominent in the performing arts through the years. Because productivity in the live performing arts has not grown at the same pace as in the economy at large, the cost of performing arts productions has increased disproportionately to that of most other goods (Baumol and Bowen, 1968, chapters 8, 9). As a consequence—and also, undoubtedly, because of competition from new entertainment media such as movies, radio, and television—demand for the live performing arts has remained small, and even, by some measures, declined (Baumol and Bowen, 1968, chapter 3). Beyond this, however, it appears that fixed costs have consistently risen at a faster rate than have variable costs, and thus have come to represent an increasingly large share of total costs.[12] These developments have presumably given nonprofit organizations, with their access to the form of price discrimination described above, an increasing advantage over their profit-seeking counterparts, which are dependent upon ticket sales alone to cover both fixed and variable costs.

☐ **The nonprofit form.** Thus far I have been assuming that even if an individual is willing to donate money to a performing arts group above and beyond the amount he must pay for a ticket, he will do so only if the organization involved is nonprofit, and not if it is profit-seeking. That is, only nonprofits will have access to the form of voluntary price discrimination I have been describing. Although the reason that this is so may seem obvious, it is perhaps worth

[11] Baumol and Bowen (1968, p. 277) report that their interviews with managerial personnel in fact revealed a fear that increased ticket prices would lead to reduced contributions. Although Baumol and Bowen devote little attention to this relationship between contributions and ticket prices, they offer no alternative explanation for the tendency to set prices at a level where demand is inelastic, other than the possibility that management feels that by keeping prices low they are fulfilling a social obligation to make the performing arts available to as much of the populace as possible. The behavior of a firm that has the latter objective, yet is dependent upon donative financing, is explored in Sections 3 and 4 below.

[12] In terms of constant dollars, average production costs for Broadway theater increased by 236% between 1927 and 1961, while weekly operating costs increased by only 80%. This relative increase in production costs was evidently responsible for the fact that the length of run required for a Broadway show to make a profit roughly tripled over this period (Moore, 1968, pp. 11–12, 34).

being somewhat more explicit. A more detailed discussion appears in my earlier article (1980) on nonprofit enterprise.

When a contributor gives money to, say, an opera company, he is actually trying to "buy" something—namely more and better opera. Such contributions differ from ordinary prices paid for goods and services in that the latter are clearly and directly conditioned upon specific, identifiable activity on the part of the person to whom the price is paid, such as delivering certain goods to the purchaser or permitting him to occupy a given seat at a given performance in a given theater. That is, when one pays what we usually term a "price," one commonly knows whether the services offered in exchange were performed satisfactorily and can seek redress if they were not. But with those payments that we term "donations," things are more difficult.

Suppose that an opera company solicits donations and asserts that it will devote all funds received to the production of opera. And suppose that an individual, in reliance on that representation, contributes. How does he know that his money was in fact devoted to opera productions? His only meaningful assurance lies in the opera company's nonprofit form of organization. For a nonprofit organization is in essence an organization that is barred by law from distributing net earnings—that is, anything beyond reasonable remuneration—to persons who exercise control over it, such as its directors, officers, or members. Consequently, one can make contributions to such an organization with some assurance that they will be devoted to production of the organization's services. With a profit-seeking organization it is difficult to obtain such assurance where, as with the performing arts, the connection between an individual contribution and increased production of services is not directly observable.

□ **Summary.** In sum, it appears that nonprofit firms in the performing arts, like their for-profit counterparts, serve primarily to sell entertainment to an audience. The difference between the two types of firms lies simply in the way in which payment is received. But the difference has significant consequences. The nonprofit firm, through its access to voluntary price discrimination, is viable in segments of the performing arts market where for-profit firms cannot survive.[13]

## 3. The economic behavior of performing arts organizations

■ **The firm's objectives.** Presumably profit maximization is excluded as an objective for any legitimate nonprofit; consequently, the organization must select other goals. This choice of goals may be in the hands of any one or more of several individuals or groups, including performers, directors, producers, professional managers, substantial donors, and donors' committees.

---

[13] There are areas other than the performing arts in which similar factors seem to be at work. For example, one of the most interesting and most obvious examples of the type of voluntary price discrimination described here is provided by New York's Metropolitan Museum of Art, which requires that every visitor pay some amount to gain admission, but leaves each visitor entirely free to determine how much to pay. In this connection it should be noted that museums are seemingly characterized by an even higher ratio of fixed costs to marginal costs than are the performing arts, yet, like performing arts groups, are in a relatively poor position to implement nonvoluntary price discrimination.

One likely possibility—particularly if control over the organization lies with professionals who have devoted their careers to a particular art form—is that the organization will place special emphasis upon the quality of its performances. Such a pursuit of quality might take either of two forms. First, the organization could seek to make its production of any given work as impressive as possible, for example by hiring exceptionally skilled performers, constructing lavish stage sets, and so forth. Second, the organization could choose to produce works that appeal only to the most refined tastes, avoiding the more popular items in the repertoire.

Alternatively, a performing arts group might feel a mission to spread culture to as broad a segment of the populace as possible, and consequently seek to maximize attendance for any given production. Or, as yet another possibility, control might lie in the hands of managers who are organizational empire-builders, and who seek simply to maximize the total budget they administer.

In what follows I shall develop a simple model of a performing arts organization, based on the analysis in Section 2, that permits exploration of the consequences of pursuing each of the alternative objectives just described. The exercise is of interest not just as a matter of positive theory but for normative purposes as well. At present there is considerable debate concerning the way in which the management of performing arts organizations should exercise the substantial degree of discretion they enjoy. A recurrent theme in this debate is the choice between quality of production and refinement of taste on the one hand, and outreach to broader audiences—via lower prices and appeal to more popular tastes—on the other (Brustein, 1978).

In the discussion of the model the term "quality" will generally be used in the first of the two senses described here (lavishness of production). As noted below, however, the model can be interpreted in terms of the second form of quality (appeal to refined tastes) as well.

□ **The basic model of the firm.** The size of the audience that the organization attracts for all performances of a given production (or, alternatively, for all of its productions combined) will be denoted by $n$,[14] while $q$ represents the quality of the work(s) performed. The ticket price $P$ charged for admission to a performance is expressed by the inverse demand function $P = P(n, q)$, $P_n < 0$, $P_q > 0$. Total donations received by the firm are taken to be inversely related to $P$ and directly related to $q$, $D = D(P, q)$, $D_p < 0$, $D_q > 0$. Expressed in terms of $n$ and $q$, $D = D[P(n, q), q] = D(n, q)$, $D_n > 0$, $D_q \gtreqless 0$. A special case is

$$D = \delta\left\{\int_0^n P(v, q)dv - nP(n, q)\right\}. \tag{1}$$

This is the donation function that would result if all donations were to come from individuals who attend performances, and if such individuals were to

[14] In Broadway theater each production is usually organized as a separate "firm" (Baumol and Bowen, 1968, p. 20). Most nonprofit performing arts organizations, in contrast, are relatively permanent and produce a large number of productions. (This difference in structure is presumably explainable at least in part by the need for nonprofit groups to develop strong and stable reputations that will provide assurance to potential donors.) Since I shall not be concerned with the effect that one production has upon demand for another, the number of productions that a given organization undertakes will not be important here.

donate, on average, a given fraction, $\delta$, of the consumer surplus that they would otherwise enjoy at price $P$ and quality $q$.[15]

Total costs are given by $C = C(n, q)$, $C_n > 0$, $C_q > 0$. Since the firm is nonprofit, net revenue, $NR$, is constrained to be zero:

$$NR \equiv nP(n, q) + D(n, q) - C(n, q) = 0. \tag{2}$$

The firm's objective function is given by $U = U(n, q)$, $U_n \geq 0$, $U_q \geq 0$, $U_{nn} \leq 0$, $U_{qq} \leq 0$. For the pure quality maximizer $U(n, q) = q$; for the pure audience maximizer $U(n, q) = n$; and for the budget maximizer $U(n, q) = C(n, q)$.

The firm maximizes $U(n, q)$ subject to (2).[16] The Lagrangian is

$$\phi = U(n, q) + \lambda[nP(n, q) + D(n, q) - C(n, q)]. \tag{3}$$

Assuming an interior solution,[17] the first-order conditions are (2) and

$$NR_q \equiv nP_q + D_q - C_q = -\frac{U_q}{\lambda} \tag{4}$$

$$NR_n \equiv P + nP_n + D_n - C_n = -\frac{U_n}{\lambda}, \tag{5}$$

where $NR_q \equiv \partial NR/\partial q$, etc., and $\lambda$ is the Lagrange multiplier.

The slope of the nonprofit constraint (2) at the point at which the firm operates is, from (4) and (5):

$$\left.\frac{dq}{dn}\right|_{NR=0} = -\frac{NR_n}{NR_q} = -\frac{U_n}{U_q}. \tag{6}$$

For the quality maximizer, for which $U_n = 0$ and $U_q = 1$, this slope is zero; for the audience maximizer, for which $U_n = 1$ and $U_q = 0$, the slope is $-\infty$. These points are shown, respectively, as $a$ and $b$ in Figure 1. If the firm values both quality and audience size, so that $U_n > 0$ and $U_q > 0$, then the firm will operate at a point such as point $c$ on the arc between points $a$ and $b$.

Consumer surplus, which I shall denote by $S$, and which I shall use as a measure of welfare (see Willig, 1976), is given by[18]

$$S = \int_0^n P(v, q)dv - C(n, q). \tag{7}$$

This expression is at a maximum with respect to $q$ and $n$ when

$$S_n = P - C_n = 0 \tag{8}$$

$$S_q = \int_0^n P_q(v, q)dv - C_q = 0. \tag{9}$$

[15] An important issue that will be avoided here is the degree to which an organization can and will use some of its income to solicit further donations.

[16] See Newhouse (1970) and Feldstein (1971) for other models of nonprofit firms (in particular, hospitals) with similar objective functions.

[17] The second-order condition, both here and for the altered models of the firm below, is

$$\lambda[2NR_nNR_qNR_{nq} - NR_n^2NR_{qq} - NR_q^2NR_{nn}] + 2NR_nNR_qU_{nq} - NR_n^2U_{qq} - NR_q^2U_{nn} > 0.$$

[18] Note that, by virtue of the nonprofit constraint (2), (monetary) producer surplus is necessarily zero here. For simplicity I ignore, in computing $S$, changes in the mangers' utility $U(n, q)$.

FIGURE 1

FIRM BEHAVIOR AND WELFARE OPTIMIZATION

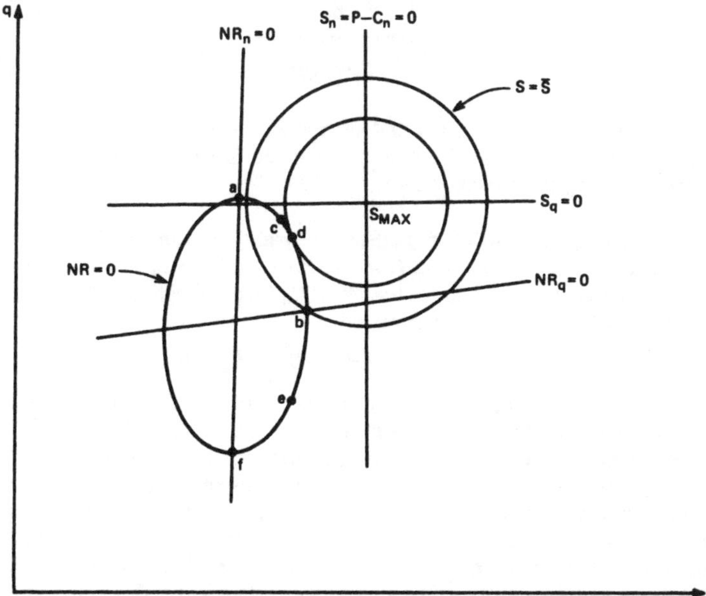


Condition (8) says simply that price should be set equal to marginal cost. Condition (9) says that quality should be at a level at which the marginal cost of greater quality just equals the marginal valuation put upon quality by the audience as a whole. There is no reason to believe, however, that these marginal conditions are consistent with the financial constraints under which the nonprofit firm must operate. Thus, for example, price can be set as low as marginal cost only if donations are sufficiently large to cover fixed costs.

More relevant to evaluating the performance of the nonprofit firm is the constrained social optimum determined by maximizing (7) subject to the nonprofit constraint (2). The resulting Lagrangian is $\theta = S + yNR$, where $y$ is a Lagrange multiplier. The first-order conditions are

$$\frac{\partial \theta}{\partial n} = S_n + yNR_n = P - C_n + yNR_n = 0 \tag{10}$$

$$\frac{\partial \theta}{\partial q} = S_q + yNR_q = \int_0^n P_q(v, q)dv - C_q + yNR_q = 0. \tag{11}$$

The slope of the constraint, $NR = 0$, at the constrained social optimum, shown as $d$ in Figure 1, is therefore

$$\frac{NR_n}{NR_q} = -\frac{P - C_n}{\int_0^n P_q(v, q)dv - C_q}. \tag{12}$$

The nonprofit firm will be operating at the social optimum, given its financing constraints, only if the slope given in (12) is equal to that in (6), i.e., only if, at the $(n, q)$ combination chosen by the firm,

$$\frac{U_n}{U_q} = \frac{P - C_n}{\int_0^n P_q(v, q)dv - C_q}. \tag{13}$$

Whether or not this condition is satisfied will depend upon the firm's objective function as well as upon the cost and demand functions that the firm faces, as the following discussion shows.

☐ **The quality-maximizing firm.** For the quality-maximizing firm, for which $U_q = 1$ and $U_n = 0$, condition (13) will hold, and the firm will be operating at the constrained optimum, only if $P = C_n$. From condition (5), however, it follows that for the quality maximizer

$$NR_n \equiv P + nP_n + D_n - C_n = 0. \tag{14}$$

That is, for any given quality level, $q$, the quality maximizer will choose the audience size, $n$, that maximizes its net revenue, which it can in turn use to purchase more quality. This is consistent with the condition that $P = C_n$ only if $D_n = -nP_n$, which is to say that, at the margin, when audience size increases (because of a decrease in ticket price) members of the audience increase their donations by precisely as much as their ticket prices decrease.[19] In terms of the donation function (1), for example, this will be the case only if $\delta = 1$—that is, only if audience members donate 100% of their consumer surplus to the firm. In the face of less generous—but more plausible—contribution levels, the firm will sacrifice audience size too heavily for the sake of quality.

☐ **The audience-maximizing firm.** For the audience maximizer $U_q = 0$; it therefore follows from (4) that

$$NR_q = nP_q + D_q - C_q = 0. \tag{15}$$

That is, for any given audience size, the audience maximizer will choose that level of quality that maximizes net revenues, since those revenues can be used to reduce ticket prices, which will in turn attract a larger audience.

From (13), we see that the audience maximizer will operate at the constrained optimum only if $S_q = 0$ so that condition (9) holds. For (9) to obtain when the firm is an audience maximizer—and hence (15) holds—we must have:

$$\frac{1}{n}\int_0^n P_q(v, q)dv - P_q = \frac{D_q}{n}. \tag{16}$$

If $D_q = 0$, then (16) is equivalent to the condition shown by Spence (1975) and Sheshinski (1976) to be necessary for a profit-maximizing monopolist

[19] This is a necessary but not a sufficient condition for the quality maximizer to operate at the constrained social optimum. If, for example, the locus $S_q = 0$ lies below the locus $NR_q = 0$—the conditions for which are explored below—it is possible that the constrained social optimum will be at the quality-*minimizing* point $f$ rather than the quality-*maximizing* point $a$ in Figure 1 when donative behavior is such that $D_n = -nP_n$.

A similar qualification applies to the discussion of the audience maximizer below.

to select the socially optimal level of quality for its product: the valuation put upon increases in quality by the average member of the audience must equal the valuation put upon such increases by marginal members of the audience.

The interesting fact established by (16), however, is that the responsiveness of donations to changes in quality, $D_q$, can serve to reduce the incentive for the firm to choose a nonoptimal level of $q$ in those cases where the average and marginal audience members value quality differently, because donations presumably reflect primarily the preferences of inframarginal—and hence more typical—audience members. This point appears clearly if we rewrite condition (16) using the donation function (1):

$$(1 - \delta)\left[\frac{1}{n}\int_0^n P_q(v, q)dv - P_q\right] = 0. \tag{17}$$

Here we see that the firm's choice of quality moves closer to the optimum, not only as marginal and average consumer valuations of quality converge, but also as $\delta \rightarrow 1$.

If donations respond as in (1), and if $\delta < 1$, it is easy to show that, as with the profit-maximizing monopolists considered by Spence and Sheshinski, when marginal consumers value quality increases less than does the average consumer—i.e., when $P_{qn} < 0$—the audience maximizer will choose a level of $q$ below that which represents the constrained social optimum, while the reverse is true if $P_{qn} > 0$. (In diagrammatic terms, if $P_{qn} < 0$, the locus $S_q = 0$ lies above the locus $NR_q = 0$, as in Figure 1, while the reverse is true if $P_{qn} > 0$, as in Figure 2 in Section 5; the two loci coincide if $P_{qn} = 0$.)

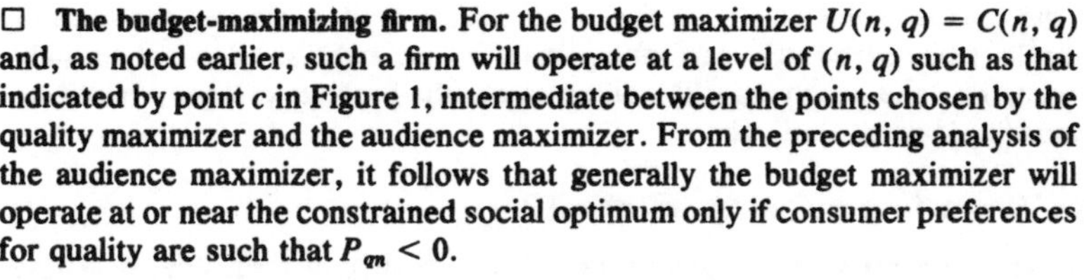

□ **The budget-maximizing firm.** For the budget maximizer $U(n, q) = C(n, q)$ and, as noted earlier, such a firm will operate at a level of $(n, q)$ such as that indicated by point $c$ in Figure 1, intermediate between the points chosen by the quality maximizer and the audience maximizer. From the preceding analysis of the audience maximizer, it follows that generally the budget maximizer will operate at or near the constrained social optimum only if consumer preferences for quality are such that $P_{qn} < 0$.

□ **Some comparisons.** Of the three types of firms analyzed above, which is likely to perform most in accord with maximal social welfare? There is, interestingly, no simple response—the answer evidently depends heavily upon the nature of consumer demand and donative behavior.

If $P_{qn} \geq 0$, the audience maximizer will unambiguously turn in the best performance—at least if donations respond as modeled in (1). In the intuitively more plausible case where $P_{qn} < 0$, however, the budget maximizer or the quality maximizer might perform better; their higher emphasis on quality compensates for the atypically low taste for quality that characterizes the marginal consumer, whose tastes dictate the prices at which tickets can be sold.

□ **Quality as refinement of taste.** The discussion so far has proceeded largely on the assumption that the variable $q$ represents the first type of quality discussed earlier, namely the lavishness with which any given work is produced. The model as developed above can, however, alternatively be interpreted with

$q$ representing the degree to which the firm's productions appeal to highly refined tastes. Viewing the model in these terms, one might assume that the amount to be spent on performers, sets, costumes, the director's fee, etc., are fixed, leaving the firm free to choose only among works that can be staged with these given resources. A quality-maximizing firm would then be one that chooses works that appeal to a highly cultured, but also small, audience.[20] In terms of the model, this means that $C_q = 0$ and, beyond a certain minimal level of $q$, $P_q < 0$.[21]

The preceding analysis and conclusions remain valid for this alternative interpretation of $q$ and the accompanying change of values for $C_q$ and $P_q$. Note, however, that with $C_q = 0$ the budget maximizer and the audience maximizer are identical.

## 4. The rationale for subsidies

■ If the analysis of Section 2 is correct, then the most compelling rationale for providing subsidies to performing arts organizations is not that they produce external benefits or serve as a vehicle for redistribution of income—which are the rationales that have been the primary focus of discussion to date (see Baumol and Bowen, 1968, chapter 16; Netzer, 1978, chapter 2)—but rather that the high fixed costs that such firms face will, in the absence of a subsidy, force them to set prices too high to satisfy marginal criteria for efficiency, and may well make them unviable.[22]

As in the case of all such subsidies, there is a substantial conflict between equity and efficiency. Although the subsidy may help establish efficient pricing, the individuals who consume the services financed by the subsidies are likely to constitute only a small fraction of the people who pay for them—at least if the source of the subsidy is the public fisc. Indeed, given that the class of people who attend the performing arts is not only small but unusually prosperous and geographically concentrated, the problem of equity raised by subsidies is particularly acute.

## 5. When is a subsidy efficient?

■ If a performing arts organization, in the absence of a subsidy, is setting its ticket prices well above marginal cost to cover the fixed costs associated

[20] See Baumol and Bowen (1968, pp. 253–257) for a discussion of the desire of performing arts groups to perform contemporary works, and the adverse consequences this has for demand.

[21] The level of $q$ at which $P_q(n, q)$ reaches zero should presumably depend on $n$. For very low values of $n$, at which point one is dealing only with true enthusiasts, $P_q$ might even remain positive for all values of $q$.

[22] Moore (1968, pp. 120–121, 122) also makes a brief, though puzzlingly dismissive, reference to "price discrimination" as a possible rationale for performing arts subsidies, by which he evidently means something like the declining-average-cost rationale suggested here.

I should emphasize that I am speaking here only of subsidies for the performance of existing works. Subsidies to authors and composers for the creation of new works are an entirely different matter. It is often extremely difficult for an artist to capture for himself even a small fraction of the benefits society derives from his work, and thus there is much to be said for subsidizing them. Since public acceptance of new works often lags considerably behind their creation, and since it is probably helpful to the artist to see his work performed when he produces it, this may also lead to some justification for subsidies to performing arts groups that are specifically earmarked for performance of new works. (The Ford Foundation, for example, has sometimes pursued this course; see Ford Foundation (1974, Vol. 1., p. 42).)

with its productions, then it is possible that a subsidy will lead to more efficient levels for price and output. But this need not be the case. As the following discussion shows, a subsidy can in some cases lead to even greater inefficiency, quite apart from its likely adverse distributional consequences.

☐ **The general model.** For the moment I shall confine the analysis to a lump-sum subsidy. Similar results for other kinds of subsidies follow directly from the analysis in later sections.

Consider the same firm modeled above, except that its revenue now includes a lump-sum subsidy, $L$. Thus the firm now seeks to maximize $U(n, q)$ subject to

$$NR = nP(n, q) + D(n, q) + L - C(n, q) = 0. \quad (18)$$

Assuming an interior solution, the first-order conditions for a constrained maximum with respect to $n$ and $q$ are unchanged from (4) and (5) above; the constraint (18) becomes the third condition. In diagrammatic terms, the consequence of increasing the subsidy, $L$, is to enlarge the closed curve representing the nonprofit constraint, as shown in Figure 2. The loci $NR_n = 0$ and $NR_q = 0$ remain unchanged. The quality maximizer, which operated at point $a$ without the subsidy, will operate with the subsidy at point $\hat{a}$, while the audience maximizer will shift from $b$ to $\hat{b}$.

To determine whether such shifts will lead to an increase in social welfare, we can differentiate (7) with respect to $L$,

$$\frac{dS}{dL} = S_q \frac{dq}{dL} + S_n \frac{dn}{dL} = \left[\int_0^n P_q(v, q)dv - C_q\right]\frac{dq}{dL} + [P - C_n]\frac{dn}{dL}, \quad (19)$$

FIGURE 2

THE EFFECT OF A LUMP-SUM SUBSIDY

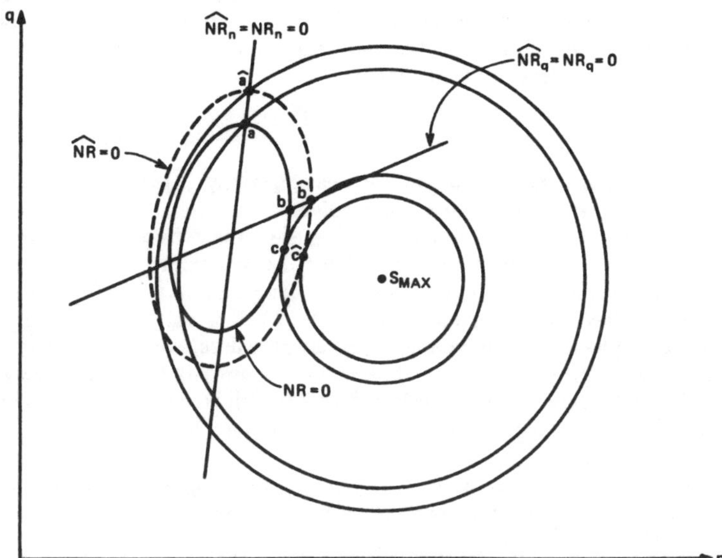

and then evaluate (19) by using simple comparative statics to determine $dq/dL$ and $dn/dL$ for the firm.

For simplicity, I shall confine the analysis to the polar cases of the audience-maximizing firm and the quality-maximizing firm.

□ **The quality maximizer.** Consider first the quality maximizer. Setting $U_q = 1$ and $U_n = 0$ in (4) and (5), and totally differentiating (4), (5), and (18) with respect to $L$ yield:

$$\frac{dn}{dL} = \frac{NR_{qn}}{NR_q NR_{nn}} \tag{20}$$

$$\frac{dq}{dL} = \frac{-1}{NR_q} . \tag{21}$$

Since the quality maximizer operates where $NR_q < 0$, it follows from (21) that $dq/dL > 0$: increasing the subsidy, $L$, will, as expected, cause the quality maximizer to raise its quality level.

Whether an increase in the subsidy will also generally lead to an increase in the size $n$ of the audience that sees a given production is less certain. Since $NR_q < 0$, and since, if the second-order condition holds, $NR_{nn} < 0$, the sign of $dn/dL$ is the same as that of $NR_{qn}$, which equals $P_q - C_{qn} + (1 - \delta)nP_{qn}$ when the donation function is given by (1). Given that $P_q > 0$, $C_{qn} > 0$ (if we are again speaking of quality in the first of the two senses defined in Section 3[23]), and $P_{qn} \lesseqgtr 0$, it follows that $NR_{qn}$, and thus $dn/dL$, are indeterminate in sign. Conditions favorable to an audience increase are: (1) a low value of $C_{qn}$ (increasing the audience does not much increase the cost of quality), and (2) $P_{qn} > 0$ (the new (marginal) audience members admitted have an unusually strong taste for quality).

Turning to the welfare implications of such behavior, we have $S_n = P - C_n$, and as discussed in Section 3 this will always be nonnegative for the quality maximizer. Thus, increases in audience size are unambiguously desirable for the quality maximizer. On the other hand, the desirability of an increase in quality is less clear; using (1), we have:

$$S_q = \int_0^n P_q(v, q)dv - C_q = (1 - \delta)\left[\int_0^n P_q(v, q)dv - nP_q\right] - \frac{1}{\lambda} . \tag{22}$$

Since $\lambda > 0$, this expression will be unambiguously negative whenever $P_{qn} > 0$. Only where $P_{qn} < 0$ can $S_q$ be positive.

The overall effect on welfare of increasing the subsidy, $L$, is therefore indeterminate. The condition required for the first term in (19), $S_q[dq/dL]$, to be positive, $P_{qn} < 0$, is simultaneously conducive to a low, and possibly negative, value for the second term, $S_n[dn/dL]$. It is easy, however, to construct examples in which increasing $L$ decreases welfare, even though the quality maximizer's ticket price in the absence of a subsidy is well above marginal cost.[24] Such a case is illustrated in Figure 2 (which is drawn so that $P_{qn} > 0$), where $\hat{a}$ lies on a lower iso-social-welfare curve than does $a$.

---

[23] As in Section 3, the results here and below can be reinterpreted for the case in which $q$ represents quality of the second type by assuming, instead, that $C_q = 0$ and that, beyond some level of $q$, $P_q < 0$.

[24] As an example, consider a quality-maximizing firm that faces a demand function

□ **The audience maximizer.** Turning to the audience maximizer we have

$$\frac{dn}{dL} = \frac{-1}{NR_n} \tag{23}$$

$$\frac{dq}{dL} = \frac{NR_{qn}}{NR_n NR_{qq}} . \tag{24}$$

By logic parallel to that employed in analyzing the quality maximizer, it follows that $dn/dL > 0$, while the sign of $dq/dL$ is the same as that of $NR_{qn}$, and therefore ambiguous.

From (19), an increase in $n$ will be desirable as long as $P > C_n$. Using (1), the $S_q$ term in (19) becomes

$$S_q = (1 - \delta)\left[\int_0^n P_q(v, q)dv - nP_q\right] . \tag{25}$$

Thus $\operatorname{sgn} S_q = -\operatorname{sgn} P_{qn}$. If follows that $S_q[dq/dL]$, and hence (19), are ambiguous in sign: it is possible that a lump-sum grant to an audience-maximizing firm, as to a quality maximizer, can lead to a reduction in welfare, even when, in the absence of a subsidy, the firm is operating where $P > C_n$.[25] (Figure 2 illustrates a case where $dS/dL > 0$.)

## 6. Donation subsidies

■ In fact, subsidies to the performing arts are frequently not lump-sum in nature, but rather take the form of matching grants for donations—that is, $\mu$ dollars of subsidy are given for every dollar in individual donations received by the organization. This is true, for example, of a substantial portion of the performing arts grants provided by the National Endowment for the Arts, and of some foundation and corporate grants as well. It is also the approach that characterizes what is by far the largest public performing arts subsidy program of all, namely, the deductibility of contributions under the federal personal income tax.[26] Are such donation subsidies superior to lump-sum subsidies?

□ **The general model.** In making the comparison I shall assume, as seems empirically the case (Feldstein, 1975a and b; Feldstein and Clotfelter, 1976), that donations respond positively, if at all, to a matching subsidy. Thus, if

---

$n = \sqrt{q}[A - P]$ or equivalently the inverse demand function $P = A - n/\sqrt{q}$, so that $P_{qn} > 0$. Assume also that the firm's cost function takes the simple form $C = q + n$ and that the subsidy level $L$ is initially zero. Solving the first-order conditions for $q$ and $n$ and substituting these values into (19) gives $dS/dL = -1/(2 - \delta)$. Thus here $dS/dL < 0$ for all values of $\delta$ between 0 and 1. (In this example $dq/dL = 2 > 0$, $dn/dL = 2/(A - 1) > 0$.)

Note that here $P - C_n = (A - 1)[(1 - \delta)/(2 - \delta)]$, and therefore $P > C_n$ so long as $A > 1$, $0 \leq \delta < 1$.

[25] For example, assume that an audience maximizer faces the demand and cost functions in the preceding footnote, and assume that initially $L = 0$. Then $dS/dL = (2 - 5\delta)/3(2 - \delta)$, so that $dS/dL < 0$ for $\delta > 2/5$. Here $P - C_n = (A - 1)(2 - 3\delta)/3(2 - \delta)$, so $P > C_n$ whenever $\delta < 2/3$ and $A > 1$. In this case (assuming $A > 1$), $dn/dL = 3/(A - 1) > 0$, $dq/dL = 4/3 > 0$, $S_n = (A - 1)(2 - 3\delta)/3(2 - \delta) > 0$ for $\delta < 2/3$ and $S_n < 0$ for $1 \geq \delta > 2/3$, $S_q = -(1 - \delta)/(2 - \delta) < 0$ for $0 \leq \delta < 1$.

[26] Netzer (1978, pp. 44, 95) estimates the cost to the federal government of the deduction for gifts to arts organizations as $400 million or more, while he estimates total direct public support of the arts at all governmental levels as just under $300 million for 1975.

$\mu$ is the rate at which donations are matched, then $D = D(n, q, \mu)$, $\partial D/\partial\mu > 0$. In particular, I shall sometimes assume (as a special case of (1)) that

$$D(n, q, \mu) = \delta(\mu)\left[\int_0^n P(v, q)dv - nP(n, q)\right], \tag{26}$$

where $\delta'(\mu) > 0$.

With a donation subsidy at a rate $\mu$, the firm's nonprofit constraint becomes

$$NR = nP(n, q) + (1 + \mu)D(n, q, \mu) - C(n, q) = 0. \tag{27}$$

If the firm maximizes $U(n, q)$ subject to this constraint, the first-order conditions are, in addition to (27),

$$P + nP_n + (1 + \mu)D_n - C_n = -\frac{U_n}{\lambda} \tag{28}$$

$$nP_q + (1 + \mu)D_q - C_q = -\frac{U_q}{\lambda}, \tag{29}$$

where $\lambda$ is a Lagrange multiplier.

Proceeding as in the case of the lump-sum subsidy, we can evaluate the effect of an increase in the subsidy rate $\mu$ on $n$, $q$, and $S$ by differentiating (27)–(29) with respect to $\mu$, solving for $dn/d\mu$ and $dq/d\mu$, and then determining $dS/d\mu$ by means of

$$\frac{dS}{d\mu} = S_q\frac{dq}{d\mu} + S_n\frac{dn}{d\mu} = \left[\int_0^n P_q(v, q)dv - C_q\right]\frac{dq}{d\mu} + [P - C_n]\frac{dn}{d\mu}. \tag{30}$$

☐ **The quality maximizer.** For the quality maximizer we have

$$\frac{dq}{d\mu} = \frac{dq}{dL}[D + \mu D_\mu] + \frac{dq}{dL}D_\mu \tag{31}$$

$$\frac{dn}{d\mu} = \frac{dn}{dL}[D + \mu D_\mu] + \frac{dn}{dL}D_\mu - \frac{1}{NR_{nn}}[D_n + (1 + \mu)D_{n\mu}] \tag{32}$$

$$\frac{dS}{d\mu} = \frac{dS}{dL}[D + \mu D_\mu] + \frac{dS}{dL}D_\mu - \frac{(P - C_n)}{NR_{nn}}[D_n + (1 + \mu)D_{n\mu}], \tag{33}$$

where $dq/dL$, $dn/dL$, and $dS/dL$ are the effects upon $q$, $n$, and $S$ of a one-dollar lump-sum subsidy as given above by (21), (20), and (19), respectively.

Here $D_\mu \equiv \partial D/\partial\mu > 0$ reflects the increase in private donations induced by the increase in the matching rate $\mu$. (In the case of (26), $D_\mu = (\delta'/\delta)D$.) The expression $D + \mu D_\mu$ gives the dollar increase in expenditure on the subsidy associated with a unit increase in $\mu$. The first term on the right-hand side of (31)–(33) reflects the direct effect of the increase $D + \mu D_\mu$ in expenditure on the subsidy; this effect has the same sign and magnitude as would an equivalent expenditure on a lump-sum subsidy, as analyzed above. The second term on the right-hand side of (31)–(33) reflects the additional effect resulting from the increase in private donations induced by increasing $\mu$.

Turning to the third term on the right-hand side of (32), we have, using the donation function (26),

$$D_n + (1 + \mu)D_{n\mu} = -[\delta + (1 + \mu)\delta']nP_n. \tag{34}$$

This expression is positive, and thus, since $NR_{nn} < 0$ by virtue of the second-order condition, the final term in (32) is positive. This term reflects the incentive to increase $n$ (and lower $P$) given to the firm by virtue of the fact that, with a higher $\mu$, the firm will effectively be able to capture a larger fraction of the increase in consumer surplus created by such a move. The final term in (33) derives from the increase in $n$ reflected in the final term in (32), and will be positive whenever $P > C_n$.

It follows from (33) that, in terms of our welfare measure $S$, a donation subsidy will always be superior to an equivalent expenditure on a lump-sum subsidy in any case in which a lump-sum subsidy would itself be justifiable (i.e., where $dS/dL > 0$). The extent by which the donation subsidy dominates an equivalent lump-sum subsidy is given by the second and third terms on the right-hand side of (33), reflecting, respectively, the increase in private donations and the increase in the donation matching rate $\mu$.

☐ **The audience maximizer.** For the audience maximizer we have

$$\frac{dq}{d\mu} = \frac{dq}{dL}[D + \mu D_\mu] + \frac{dq}{dL} D_\mu - \frac{NR_{q\mu}}{NR_{qq}} \tag{35}$$

$$\frac{dn}{d\mu} = \frac{dn}{dL}[D + \mu D_\mu] + \frac{dn}{dL} D_\mu \tag{36}$$

$$\frac{dS}{d\mu} = \frac{dS}{dL}[D + \mu D_\mu] + \frac{dS}{dL} D_\mu + \left[\int_0^n P_q(v, q)dv - nP_q\right]\frac{-NR_{q\mu}}{NR_{qq}}, \tag{37}$$

where $dq/dL$, $dn/dL$, and $dS/dL$ are the effects of a unit increase in the lump-sum subsidy as given by (24), (23), and (19).

The interpretation of the first two terms on the right-hand side of (35)–(37) parallels that given for (31)–(33) above. Using the donation function (26), the final term in (35) becomes

$$\frac{-NR_{q\mu}}{NR_{qq}} = \frac{-[\delta + (1 + \mu)\delta']\left[\int_0^n P_q(v, q)dv - nP_q\right]}{NR_{qq}}, \tag{38}$$

which has the same sign as $P_{qn}$ (since $NR_{qq} < 0$ by virtue of the second-order condition). This term reflects the increased incentive to adjust quality to conform to the tastes of inframarginal donors that the firm faces owing to the larger fraction of consumer surplus that it can (in effect) capture with a higher value of $\mu$. The final term in (37) reflects the same phenomenon. Using (26), that term becomes

$$\left[\int_0^n P_q(v, q)dv - nP_q\right]\frac{-NR_{q\mu}}{NR_{qq}} = -\frac{[\delta + (1 + \mu)\delta']\left[\int_0^n P_q(v, q)dv - nP_q\right]}{NR_{qq}}. \tag{39}$$

This term will always be nonnegative, reflecting the fact that bringing quality more into line with average, as opposed to marginal, audience members will always enhance consumer welfare as measured by $S$.

It follows from (37), then, that whenever $dS/dL \geq 0$, a lump-sum subsidy is dominated by a donation subsidy of equivalent amount—or, in other words, for the audience maximizer as for the quality maximizer, a donation subsidy is to be preferred to a lump-sum subsidy whenever a subsidy of either type is justifiable at all.

□ **Summary.** The advantages of the donation subsidy here are two-fold. First, by inducing further donations it yields to the firm a larger increase in revenue per dollar of subsidy than does the lump-sum subsidy. Note, in this connection, that since part of the increased revenues due to a donation subsidy come from donors who benefit from—and value highly—the performances involved, donation subsidies also have stronger equitable appeal than do lump-sum subsidies, at least where public funds are the source of the subsidy.[27]

Second, a subsidy geared to donations gives the firm an additional incentive to attract donations. Since we have been assuming that donations are proportional to consumer surplus, this means that with a donation subsidy the firm has an incentive to adjust its quality and price (or, equivalently here, audience size) closer to the levels that maximize consumer welfare.

## 7. Ticket subsidies and taxes

■ Admissions subsidies for the performing arts might also seem attractive (Netzer, 1978, pp. 32–33). Such subsidies might take either of two forms. First, the subsidy can be offered on the basis of a fixed amount per admission, regardless of the price charged for admission. Second, the subsidy can be designed to match total admissions (ticket) receipts on a fixed percentage basis, similar to the donation subsidy discussed above. In both cases incentives will be created for the organization that are absent in the case of a lump-sum subsidy.

At present neither of these types of admission subsidies is common. However, a negative subsidy applied to total ticket receipts, in the form of a sales tax on theater tickets, has commonly been applied to commercial performing arts groups and sometimes to nonprofit organizations as well. Since the effects of such a tax are precisely the reverse of those resulting from a subsidy of the same type, analysis of the subsidy also yields an analysis of the tax.

□ **The model.** I shall confine myself here to analysis of a per-receipts subsidy. Rather similar results follow from an analysis of a subsidy of a fixed amount per admission.

Let $\sigma$ represent the rate at which ticket receipts are matched by the ticket receipts subsidy, so that the total amount expended through this subsidy is $\sigma nP$. The firm's nonprofit constraint becomes

$$(1 + \sigma)nP + D - C = 0. \tag{40}$$

□ **The quality maximizer.** Proceeding as in the analysis of the donation sub-

[27] The donation subsidy modeled here has a matching rate $\mu$ that does not vary from one donor to another—as would be the case with a uniform tax credit, and as is typically the case with NEA grants. The subsidies channeled through the charitable deduction under the personal income tax, in contrast, involve a matching rate that ranges from 0% to 70% depending upon the donor's tax bracket. Such a deduction may well be dominated, in terms of both equity and efficiency, by a tax credit of equivalent amount. See Hochman and Rodgers (1977).

sidy, the effects of increasing the ticket subsidy rate for the quality maximizer are:

$$\frac{dq}{d\sigma} = \frac{dq}{dL} nP \tag{41}$$

$$\frac{dn}{d\sigma} = \frac{dn}{dL} nP - \frac{P + nP_n}{NR_{nn}} \tag{42}$$

$$\frac{dS}{d\sigma} = \frac{dS}{dL} nP - (P - C_n) \frac{P + nP_n}{NR_{nn}} . \tag{43}$$

The expression $nP$ here represents the dollar increase in expenditure on the ticket subsidy associated with a unit increase in $\sigma$. The first term on the right-hand side in (41)–(43) gives the direct effect of the increase $nP$ in the amount of the subsidy; it is the same as the effect of an equivalent expenditure on a lump-sum subsidy. The final term in (42) will be positive if the firm is operating where demand is elastic ($nP_n/P > -1$), and negative otherwise, reflecting the fact that the net-revenue-maximizing value of $n$ (which is the value of $n$ chosen by the quality maximizer) changes with $\sigma$. It follows from (42) that a ticket subsidy will actually lead to a *smaller* increase in audience size (and thus, from (43), a smaller increase in welfare) than would an equivalent lump-sum subsidy if (as is possible) the quality maximizer is operating in the inelastic portion of the demand curve.[28]

☐ **The audience maximizer.** For the audience maximizer we have

$$\frac{dq}{d\sigma} = \frac{dq}{dL} nP - \frac{nP_q}{NR_{qq}} \tag{44}$$

$$\frac{dn}{d\sigma} = \frac{dn}{dL} nP \tag{45}$$

$$\frac{dS}{d\sigma} = \frac{dS}{dL} nP - \left[ \int_0^n P_q(v, q) dv - nP_q \right] \frac{nP_q}{NR_{qq}} . \tag{46}$$

Since $nP_q/NR_{qq} < 0$, it follows from (44) that a ticket subsidy will lead to a larger increase in quality than will an equivalent expenditure on a lump-sum subsidy. The reason for this is that increasing $\sigma$ increases $P_q$, and hence raises the level of $q$ that maximizes net revenue. As the final term in (46) indicates, this (additional) increase in $q$ will raise, rather than lower, welfare only if $P_{qn} < 0$.

☐ **Summary.** Interestingly, for the audience-maximizing firm a ticket subsidy has no greater effect on audience size than does a lump-sum subsidy, while for the quality maximizer a ticket subsidy may actually lead to a smaller audience than would a lump-sum subsidy. For both the audience maximizer and the quality maximizer, there is a range of cases in which a ticket subsidy is dominated by a lump-sum subsidy in terms of our welfare measure $S$. From the results in Section 6 we can in turn conclude that there is a much larger class of cases in which a ticket subsidy is dominated by a donation subsidy—

[28] In the model developed here, the quality maximizer will operate where $nP_n/P < -1$ when marginal cost ($C_n$) is low and the increase in donations ($D_n$) in response to lower ticket prices is relatively large (see (5)).

though there may be instances in which a ticket subsidy is superior to both donation and lump-sum subsidies.

## 8. Conclusion

■ The live performing arts are commonly characterized by fixed costs that are high relative to marginal costs, and by overall demand that is relatively small. As a consequence, performing arts groups often must engage in price discrimination if they are to survive without subsidy. The opportunities for effective discrimination through ticket pricing are limited, however. Therefore, nonprofit firms, which can, in effect, employ a system of voluntary price discrimination, can often survive in areas of the performing arts where for-profit firms cannot.

In many cases, free-rider incentives presumably keep donations below the level necessary for efficient production. In such cases, public subsidies can be justified on efficiency grounds, although such subsidies clearly present problems of equity.

As it is, the arts in the United States, including the performing arts, receive public subsidies that compare favorably in amount with those provided in other industrialized democracies (Netzer, 1978, pp. 50–52). The United States is unique, however, in providing most of its public subsidies in the form of matching grants for private donations. This policy has a great deal to recommend it. Donation subsidies not only serve to increase the level of private contributions, but may also cause performing arts groups to pay greater attention to the desires of inframarginal consumers.

### References

BAUMOL, W.J. AND BOWEN, W.G. *Performing Arts: The Economic Dilemma*. Cambridge: Harvard University Press, 1968.

BRUSTEIN, R. "The Metropolitan Opera—The High Price of Being Best." *New York Times* (February 12, 1978, Section 2, cols. 1 and 6).

FELDSTEIN, M. "Hospital Price Inflation: A Study of Nonprofit Price Dynamics." *American Economic Review*, Vol. 61, No. 5 (December 1971), pp. 853–872.

———. "The Income Tax and Charitable Contributions: Part I—Aggregate and Distributional Effects." *National Tax Journal*, Vol. 28 (1975), pp. 81–99.

———. "The Income Tax and Charitable Contributions: Part II—The Impact on Religious, Educational, and Other Organizations." *National Tax Journal*, Vol. 28 (1975), pp. 209–226.

——— AND CLOTFELTER, C. "Tax Incentives and Charitable Contributions in the United States." *Journal of Public Economics*, Vol. 5 (1976), pp. 1–26.

FORD FOUNDATION. *The Finances of the Performing Arts*. New York: 1974.

GLOBERMAN, S. AND BOOK, S.H. "Statistical Cost Functions for Performing Arts Organizations." *Southern Economic Journal*, Vol. 40 (April 1974), pp. 668–671.

GORDON, D. "Why the Movie Majors are Major" in T. Balio, ed., *The American Film Industry*, Madison: University of Wisconsin Press, 1976.

HANSMANN, H. "The Role of Nonprofit Enterprise." *Yale Law Journal*, Vol. 89 (April 1980), pp. 835–901.

HOCHMAN, H. AND RODGERS, J. "The Optimal Tax Treatment of Charitable Contributions." *National Tax Journal*, Vol. 30 (March 1977), pp. 1–18.

MAYERNIK, M. "Rhapsody in Red: The Economic Future of the Philadelphia Orchestra." Unpublished manuscript, Department of Economics, University of Pennsylvania, Spring 1976.

MOORE, T.G. *The Economics of the American Theater*. Durham: University of North Carolina Press, 1968.

NATIONAL ENDOWMENT FOR THE ARTS. *Annual Report*. 1978.

NETZER, R. *The Subsidized Muse*. Cambridge: Cambridge University Press, 1978.

NEWHOUSE, J. "Toward a Theory of Nonprofit Institutions: An Economic Model of a Hospital." *American Economic Review*, Vol. 60, No. 1 (March 1970), pp. 64–74.

OI, W. "A Disneyland Dilemma: Two-Part Tariffs for a Mickey Mouse Monopoly." *Quarterly Journal of Economics*, Vol. 85 (February 1971), pp. 77–96.

PEACOCK, A.T. "Welfare Economics and Public Subsidies to the Arts" in M. Blaug, ed., *The Economics of the Arts*, London: Westview, 1976.

ROCKEFELLER BROTHERS FUND. *The Performing Arts: Problems and Prospects*. New York, 1965.

SHESHINSKI, E. "Price, Quality and Quantity Regulation in Monopoly Situations." *Economica*, Vol. 43 (May 1976), pp. 127–137.

SPENCE, A.M. "Monopoly, Quality, and Regulation." *Bell Journal of Economics*, Vol. 6, No. 2 (Autumn 1975), pp. 417–429.

WEISBROD, B.A. "Toward a Theory of the Voluntary Nonprofit Sector in a Three-Sector Economy" in E. Phelps, ed., *Altruism, Morality, and Economic Theory*, New York, 1975.

WINTER, S. "A Problem." Unpublished manuscript, May 1968.

# [11]

# Why Do Different Countries Choose a Different Public-Private Mix of Educational Services?

**Estelle James**

ABSTRACT

*We observe a wide range across countries in the percentage of total enrollments that attend private rather than public schools. This paper seeks to explain 1) the systematically higher proportion of private enrollments (%PVT) in developing as compared with developed countries at the secondary level, and 2) the seemingly random variation across countries within a given level of education and stage of development. I argue that the latter is due to differentiated demand and nonprofit supply, both of which stem from cultural heterogeneity, especially religious heterogeneity. In contrast, the large %PVT at the secondary level in developing countries is hypothesized to stem from limited public spending, which creates an "excess demand" from people who would prefer to use the public schools but are involuntarily excluded and pushed into the private sector. The limited public spending on secondary education, in turn, is modelled as a collective decision which is strongly influenced by the many families who opt for quantity over quality of children, in developing countries. The results of regressions that determine private sector size recursively and simultaneously with public educational spending are consistent with these hypotheses.*

*Estelle James is a senior economist at the World Bank, and a professor of economics at the State University of New York, Stony Brook.* *She wishes to thank the numerous people in the United States and abroad who helped with the study that has been partially summarized in this paper. She especially appreciates the typing and related work carried out by Suzanne Lane and the data analysis carried out by Renqui Xiao, H.K. Lee, Amy Salsbury, and Johan van der Sluis. Financial support received from the Spencer Foundation, the Exxon Foundation, the Agency for International Development, and the Program on Nonprofit Organizations at Yale University is gratefully acknowledged. Anonymous referees also made very helpful comments in connections with earlier versions. The data used in this article can be obtained beginning in December 1993 through December 1996 from the author at the World Bank, 1818 H Street, NW, Washington, DC 20433.*
[Submitted July 1990; accepted June 1992]

## I. Introduction

Impure public goods such as education yield both public and private benefits and hence can be financed through the public or private sectors. Even when government funding predominates, production can be carried out through public or private management. Thus, different combinations of public and private provision (funding and management) are feasible and are, in fact, observed in different countries. For example, the percentage of enrollments that are private at the primary and secondary levels covers the entire spectrum from 1 percent to 100 percent, as shown in Table 1. At higher educational levels the dispersion is also substantial.

What demand and supply factors account for these differences across societies? How does the process of economic development affect the role of the private sector in education? To what degree can government policies influence the out-

**Table 1**
*Relative Role of the Private Sector in Education*

| | % Private Primary (1) | % Private Secondary (2) |
|---|---|---|
| 12 Advanced Industrial Societies | | |
| Australia | 20 | 26 |
| Belgium | 51 | 62 |
| Denmark | 7 | 6 |
| England & Wales* | 22 | 16 |
| France | 15 | 21 |
| Germany | 2 | 9 |
| Italy | 8 | 7 |
| Japan** | 1 | 15 |
| Netherlands | 69 | 72 |
| New Zealand | 10 | 12 |
| Sweden | 1 | 2 |
| United States | 10 | 9 |
| Median | 10 | 13.5 |
| Mean | 18.0 | 21.4 |
| 38 Developing Countries | | |
| Kenya | 1 | 49 |
| Lesotho | 100 | 89 |
| Sudan | 2 | 13 |
| Cameroon | 43 | 57 |
| Chad | 10 | 6 |
| Liberia | 35 | 43 |
| Niger | 5 | 14 |

continued over

**Table 1** (*continued*)

| | % Private Primary (1) | % Private Secondary (2) |
|---|---|---|
| Nigeria | 26 | 41 |
| Togo | 29 | 16 |
| Upper Volta | 7 | 43 |
| Algeria | 1 | 1 |
| Iran | 8 | 17 |
| Jordan | 30 | 7 |
| Morocco | 5 | 8 |
| Saudi Arabia | 3 | 2 |
| Syria | 5 | 6 |
| Argentina | 17 | 45 |
| Bolivia | 9 | 24 |
| Brazil | 13 | 25 |
| Chile | 18 | 23 |
| Colombia | 15 | 38 |
| Costa Rica | 4 | 6 |
| Ecuador | 17 | 30 |
| El Salvador | 6 | 47 |
| Guatemala | 14 | 43 |
| Haiti | 42 | 76 |
| Honduras | 5 | 51 |
| Jamaica | 5 | 76 |
| Mexico | 6 | 25 |
| Panama | 5 | 14 |
| Paraguay | 13 | 37 |
| Peru | 13 | 37 |
| Venezuela | 13 | 17 |
| India | 25 | 52 |
| Indonesia | 13 | 60 |
| Philippines | 5 | 38 |
| Singapore | 35 | 1 |
| Thailand | 11 | 32 |
| Median | 11 | 27.5 |
| Mean | 16.1 | 31.3 |

* These numbers include both the independent and voluntary aided sectors in the U.K.

** Data include upper and lower secondary. Figure for upper secondary is 28 percent.

Mean *%PVT* = 22.7 percent (Mean *%PVTPRI* = 16.5 percent; *%PVTSEC* = 28.9 percent).

Source: See Appendix 1.

come? This paper investigates these closely related questions. The answers are important since private schools may differ from public schools with respect to cost and quality, and a system that is largely private may provide a different educational service and distribution from one that is largely public.

More specifically, I seek to explain (1) the systematically higher proportion of secondary school private enrollments (*%PVT*) in developing as compared with developed countries (mean = 31.3 percent for developing versus 21.4 percent for developed countries in my sample); and (2) the seemingly random variation across countries within a given level of education and stage of development.

I hypothesize that the large *%PVT* at the secondary level in developing countries is due to limited public spending, which creates an "excess demand" from people who would prefer to use the public schools but are unable to find a place. The low public spending on secondary education is modelled as a collective decision which is strongly influenced by a coalition of high income, high tax families and low income families who have opted for quantity over quality of children, in developing countries. This "excess demand" explanation helps resolve a seeming anomaly: why the private sector has grown relatively large in some developing countries where, paradoxically, the public sector is considered superior, and vice versa.

In contrast, I argue that the seemingly random variation across countries within a given educational level and stage of development is due to differentiated demand and nonprofit supply, stemming mainly from cultural heterogeneity, especially religious heterogeneity. On the demand side, differentiated tastes about ideology lead people voluntarily to opt out of the public system even when space is available, to secure the kind of education they prefer. On the supply side, private schools are a convenient institution for diverse non-profit-maximizing religious organizations to use in their competition for a larger market share of "souls."

Part II develops the conceptual framework for analyzing private sector size and public spending on education. Part III presents the empirical results, using both a recursive model in which public spending is regarded as predetermined and a simultaneous model in which size of the private sector and educational spending in the public sector are jointly determined. The recursive and simultaneous models lead to similar conclusions. Based on this sample of 50 developed and developing countries (all the countries for which data are available on private enrollments plus the most important explanatory variables), it appears that, if one knows the answers to a few key questions about a society, one can make a reasonably good prediction about the size of its private versus public educational sectors. Moreover, the predictive model is the same for developed and developing countries, despite the large differences in their private sector size.

But first, a caveat: the definition of "private" is by no means clear-cut in a situation where many "private" schools are heavily funded and regulated by the state. In most developing countries private schools depend mainly on private funding, but in many developed countries subsidies cover a large proportion of total expenses, and government control over hiring and firing of teachers, salaries, and student admissions criteria accompany these subsidies. "Source of funding" and "decision-making authority" then yield different public-private categories and many mixed rather than polar cases. In this paper private schools are defined as those which had private founders and continue to have private management, although varying amounts of public funding may be present.[1]

## II. Conceptual Framework

### *A. Basic Model*

This section sets forth a theory in which the relative size of the private educational sector in a country (*%PVT*) depends on its excess demand and differentiated demand for education, its supply of nonprofit entrepreneurship, and government policies that influence public and private supply.

#### *1. Demand*

Consider a family utility function in which:

(1) $U_i = U_i(QPUB_i, QPVT_i, EXTQ_i, Y_i - T_i - PQPVT_i)$

That is, family welfare depends on its own public and private education ($QPUB_i$ and $QPVT_i$), other peoples' consumption of education ($EXTQ_i$), and its disposable income to purchase other goods after paying taxes and private school tuition ($Y_i - T_i - PQPVT_i$). We assume here that public education is financed out of taxes and uses nonprice rationing, while private education finances and rations, at least partially, on the basis of price. We are examining the choice, aggregated over all families, of $QPUB_i$ versus $QPVT_i$, for a given $Y_i$, $T_i$ and $P$, as well as the collective choice of public educational spending which influences $T_i$.

As a first step, the family formulates its optimal consumption of public and private education, $QPUB_i^*$ and $QPVT_i^*$. If public and private schools are perfect substitutes and $P > 0$, $QPVT_i^* = 0$. The supply of public places may be less than demand, however, so some people are excluded, in other words, actual $QPUB_i < QPUB_i^*$ for some $i$. Then, if the private benefits from education perceived by family $i$ are high enough to cover the price of private education (for examples, because family $i$'s income is high), they will seek places in the private sector as a second-best solution. I call this demand, stemming from families who would have preferred to enter the free or low-price public system, the *excess demand* motive for private education. (See Weisbrod 1975, 1977, for one of the earliest formulations of the excess demand hypothesis). Excess demand existed in many Western countries in the nineteenth century, before public systems became open access. I argue that it also exists in many developing countries today, and constitutes the major reason for large private sectors at the secondary and higher levels.[2] The greater the total effective demand for education and the smaller the

1. See James (1991b), for a more detailed discussion of these mixed cases, and the relationship between subsidies and regulations.

2. Examples are Kenya, where the majority of secondary school enrollments were privately founded, Brazil and the Philippines where 80 percent of college enrollments are private. Among industrialized countries currently, Japan best fits the "excess demand" model at both the secondary and higher levels; over one-quarter of all high school (upper secondary) students and three-quarters of higher education

capacity of the public sector, the larger will be the excess demand for private education, ceteris paribus.

Now suppose that public and private schools are imperfect substitutes, because people have diverse tastes about the kind of education to be consumed, but the public system is constrained to be relatively uniform. If family $i$ prefers to enter the private sector, $QPUB_i^* = 0$. I call this demand, stemming from people who prefer the product variety offered in the private sector, the *differentiated demand* for private education. Preliminary evidence from many countries indicates that much of this taste differentiation stems from religious, linguistic and nationality differences that concern group identification.[3] The greater the cultural heterogeneity of the population and the more uniform the public educational system, the larger will be the differentiated demand for private education, both in developed and developing countries.

Differential preferences about quality can also lead to the development of private schools. In particular, a low quality public system may stimulate the growth of a high quality private sector, meeting the demand of those willing and able to pay the price. If we assume that educational quality has a high income elasticity of demand and if the public sector provides a quality level that just satisfies the median family, greater income diversity within the population implies greater dissatisfaction among upper income people, who will seek superior education in the private market.[4]

### 2. *Private supply*

Of course, the ability of people who are dissatisfied with the amount or type of public provision to find private alternatives depends on the supply behavior of private schools. This paper does not seek to fully explain this behavior but does analyze one important determinant—the role played by the *nonprofit sector in education*. Private schools are often established as nonprofit organizations, in other words, as organizations that cannot distribute dividends or stock that can be sold for capital gains. Indeed, nonprofit status is legally required for educational

students attend private institutions, mainly because of limited space in the preferred public schools and universities. See James (1986a and 1991a); James and Benjamin (1988). Also see West (1967 and 1970) for data on the United States and the United Kingdom in the nineteenth century.

3. The many private schools and colleges that accommodate religious or linguistic minorities (for example, schools for Muslims, Parsees, Sikhs in India, Chinese and Indians in Malaysia) are examples of private sector response to differentiated demand. Among Western countries, the best example of the cultural heterogeneity model is the Netherlands, where two-thirds of all students attend privately managed schools, a response to the pervasive religious cleavage which dominated that country at the turn of the century. For other examples of the importance of cultural heterogeneity see James (1984, 1986b, and 1987).

4. Two examples are Brazil and the Philippines, at the secondary level, where 25 and 38 percent of enrollments, respectively, are in private schools, which are generally considered to be better than public secondary schools. But if greater income diversity means that upper income groups also control the government, they may use this power to choose a public system that is high in quality, low in quantity and rationed to them. In that case, a large excess demand may develop, as at the higher education level in Brazil and the Philippines. Thus income dispersion is predicted to lead to a large private sector, but we cannot be sure a priori whether this will be due to excess demand for quantity or differentiated demand for quality.

institutions in many countries, in part because nonprofits are considered more "trustworthy" (see James and Rose-Ackerman, 1986). This characteristic greatly influences the supply of private schools. For example, private schools may not spring up even though a potential profit exists, because there is no pecuniary return on equity and non-profit-motivated capital and entrepreneurship are not available. On the other hand, nonprofit schools may spring up in situations where for-profits could not break even, because of their nonpecuniary goals and lower monetary cost functions due to donated capital, volunteer labor and tax advantages. We must therefore ask: what are the motives of people who start nonprofit schools and what factors determine their availability?

I argue that most founders of private nonprofit schools are ideological organizations, especially religious organizations. (See James and Rose-Ackerman, 1986, for a fuller development of this point.) Proselytizing religions such as Christianity have historically used schools as a mechanism for shaping values, socializing old members and attracting new ones; the Catholic Church has traditionally run its own school system around the world with these objectives. And competing ideologies have often been forced to start their own schools, as a defensive strategy.[5] The nonprofit form is used because these founders are interested in maximizing membership or faith rather than pecuniary profits. Therefore, for reasons of nonprofit supply as well as differentiated demand, I would expect the private educational sector to be larger in countries with many strong independent religious organizations competing for members and member loyalty, through their schools.

### 3. Government Policies

Finally, it should be clear that many government policies influence the demand for and supply of private schools. For example, governments can and have prohibited private schools or have imposed costly requirements that have a similar effect (for example, Catholic schools were strongly restricted in England and Holland during the eighteenth century, private schools were outlawed in Tanzania and Pakistan during the 1970s, and extensive regulations deterred private school entrepreneurship in Sweden until very recently). Governments have required nonprofit status of private schools or given tax privileges to nonprofit schools (the United States and Japan are two examples). Some governments (for example, the United States and Switzerland) allow local control over public schools, which should increase diversity within the public sector, hence diminish the differentiated demand for private schools.

It is very difficult to secure data on all these policies for the entire sample of countries. However, the effects of two important public policies, for which data could be secured, are analyzed in this paper: (1) the provision of subsidies to

5. For example, the caste groups in Southern India and the independence movements in India and Kenya before independence started their own schools, with the expressed intention of inculcating their own values and keeping their members out of the Western-dominated Christian schools. Other examples of the ideological/religious origin of private nonprofit schools are sectarian schools in the United States and the United Kingdom, schools run by Catholic orders in France and Latin America, Calvinist schools in Holland, orthodox Jewish schools in Israel, educational services provided by Muslim waqfs (religious trusts) in the Middle East and by missionaries in many developing countries.

private schools, which increases the supply of private education; and (2) government spending on public schools, which increases their quantity and/or quality and decreases disposable income, hence decreases the demand for private education.

In sum, these demand and supply forces are hypothesized to stem from per capita income (*PCI*), stage of development (*DV* and *ADV*), cultural heterogeneity (*CULT HET*), income diversity (*INC DIV*), public educational spending (*EDSP*), and public subsidies to private education (*SUB*). The reduced form equation is:

(2) $\%PVT = f[PCI, DV, ADV, CULT\ HET, INC\ DIV, EDSP, SUB]$

*4. Public Educational Spending*

An immediate problem concerns the endogeneity of *EDSP*, which may be determined by *%PVT* or by unobserved forces that also influence *%PVT*. For example, people who intend to opt out to the private sector may push for a low spending public sector, so the effect of *EDSP* on *%PVT* may be biased in a negative direction by OLS. Conversely, an unobserved taste for education may lead both to a large public and private sector, in which case the public spending effect on *%PVT* would be biased in a positive direction. To deal with these problems in the estimation of *%PVT*, I also develop a model determining *EDSP* and compare the predictions of the recursive and simultaneous models.

More specifically, I assume:

(3) $EDSP = g(SEC, DV, PCI, AG0\text{-}14, TOT, GOVSP, \%PVT)$

where *AG0-14* = proportion of the population aged 0–14, *TOT* = an index of totalitarian control, *GOVSP* = noneducational public spending as a proportion of *GDP*, and *%PVT* is included in the simultaneous model. The next two sections describe the key variables in the private sector Equation (2) and provide the rationale for the collective choice about public spending in Equation (3). (See Appendix A for definition of variables and data sources).

***B. Key Variables in the Private Sector Equation***

*1. Per capita income and stage of development*

*DV* and *ADV* are used to represent developing and advanced industrial societies, respectively, and per capita income (*PCI*) picks up smaller income differences within each stage of development. These enter into Equations (2) and (3) as indicators of the gross demand for education and the effective demand for differentiated education. If *EDSP* does not change in the course of economic growth, *PCI* would have a positive effect, *DV* a negative effect on *%PVT* and the interactions of heterogeneity with *ADV* would be positive in Equation 2. However, if *EDSP* increases with economic growth in Equation 3, this would have the opposite effect, so the net impact of growth on *%PVT* is ambiguous a priori and the regression results may vary depending on whether or not *EDSP* is controlled. One object of this paper is to examine this process, as it throws light on the relatively greater role of the private sector at the secondary level in developing countries.

*2. Cultural heterogeneity*

Cultural heterogeneity enters into Equation 2 as the major determinant of differentiated demand for and nonprofit supply of private education. To measure this, I secured the religious and linguistic breakdown of the populations of all the countries in my sample; indeed, the need for this information was the major factor that limited the sample size.

I started with a measure of religious heterogeneity which weights all religions equally: $RELIG = \Sigma R_i \ln 1/R_i$, where $R_i$ = proportion of the population constituted by religion *i*. As the number of religions grow, so too does *RELIG*; the index is highest where the population is equally divided among a large number of religions.[6]

However, some religions are much more active proselytizers than others. As noted above, Christianity in general and Catholicism in particular have done so historically, using schools as a major competitive weapon, so I wanted to weight these groups more heavily in my "religious competition" index. I consequently constructed a "Christian" weight, $WT_{CH} = R_{CH}$ or $(1 - R_{CH})$, whichever is smaller, and similarly, a Catholic weight, $WT_{CA} = R_{CA}$ or $(1 - R_{CA})$, whichever is smaller. These weights increase as $R_{CH}$ (or $R_{CA}$) increase until $R = 0.5$ is reached, after which they decrease; the weights are maximized when Christians (and Catholics) are a large minority or a small majority, the situation where their need to use schools as a competitive instrument is maximized. Therefore my index of religious heterogeneity and religious competition is $REL = WT_{CH} WT_{CA} \Sigma R_i \ln 1/R_i$. Both for demand and supply side reasons it is predicted to have a positive effect on *%PVT*.

Linguistic heterogeneity, *LANG*, was measured parallel to *RELIG*, as $\Sigma L_i \ln 1/L_i$, where $L_i$ = proportion of the population speaking language *i*. Language may also serve as a proxy for more general cultural heterogeneity (for example, based on nationality or ethnicity) and as such its effect is expected to be positive.

*3. Income Distribution*

Comparable data on income distribution over large sets of countries are exceedingly difficult to find. I used the "Gini coefficient of sectoral inequality" (*GINI*) which is based on product per worker across economic sectors. This index takes on larger values if product proportions are smaller than labor proportions for some sectors, indicating inter-sectoral inequality. Since it is calculated on the basis of large economic sectors rather than individuals or households it under-

6. For a discussion of the properties of this index see Theill (1972) and Allison (1978). For its use in an international comparative study of homicide see Hansmann and Quigley (1982). Obviously, this index is sensitive to the fineness with which one disaggregates various religions. I used all the subcategories found in my data sources which constituted more than 0.1 percent of the population, including "Other Religions" as a separate category.

states total inequality and, more importantly, distorts the relative inequality positions of different countries. As an alternative, I also used the proportion of national income received by the bottom 20 percent of households (*DISTRIB*), which is inversely related to individual inequality; however, such measures are known to be unreliable. Although inequality is predicted to have a positive sign on theoretical grounds given above, it is not clear whether these indices will be capable of detecting that effect.

#### *4. Subsidies*

Most countries subsidize their private schools in some way but detailed data are generally not available and the existence of implicit tax subsidies further complicates the situation. Given this paucity of data, a dummy variable, *SUB*, is included for those countries (mostly advanced industrial societies) that cover more than 70 percent of the costs of their private schools out of public funds.

#### *5. Public Educational Spending*

Many developing countries restrict access to their public systems at the secondary and higher levels, using nonprice mechanisms to ration the limited number of places among the excess demanders, and this capacity constraint can clearly be relaxed by additional spending (*EDSP*). *EDSP* may also proxy public school quality (in which case a low *EDSP* leads to a differentiated demand for private school quality) but this relationship is ambiguous (see Hanushek 1986). In this paper *EDSP* is expressed as a proportion of *GDP* and measures differences across societies in their share of *GDP* devoted to public educational finance. It is measured separately for the primary and secondary levels and is expected to have a negative effect on *%PVT*.[7] Public educational spending is treated as predetermined in Equations (1–3), while its determination is simultaneously modelled in Equation (4), Tables 2 and 3.

### *C. Collective Choice About EDSP*

To fix ideas about the *EDSP* choice, let us suppose that only two alternatives are available—low public spending ($EDSP^{LO}$), which will provide a public school system large enough to accommodate only a minority of the age cohort and high public spending ($EDSP^{HI}$), which will accommodate a majority. I assume that *EDSP* is financed by taxes, $T^{LO}$ or $T^{HI}$, in which everyone knows his share in advance, and is determined by a collective choice process in which:

7. The only source giving education financial information for large sets of countries is the UNESCO *Statistical Yearbook*. There are many practical problems with these data. They often give planned rather than actual expenditures, they sometimes exclude local government spending, the allocation between primary and secondary levels is admittedly imprecise, and in many cases they include government spending in public schools as well as subsidies to private schools. The number of years contained in the primary versus the secondary cycle varies among countries. To eliminate the bias this introduces into spending data in cross-national analyses, I calculated an "expenditure per year" for each country and multiplied this by a standard six-year duration at each level.

1. If public provision is the only option (in other words, *QPVT* is required to be 0), families will be willing to expand *EDSP* so long as their marginal (private and external) benefits exceed their marginal (tax) costs; and

2. Given a private alternative (in other words, *QPVT* can be = or > 0), families will additionally compare the net benefits to them of high public spending ($EDSP^{HI}$) versus low public spending ($EDSP^{LO}$) plus optimal *QPVT* at $EDSP^{LO}$, and will choose to expand public educational spending if and only if they derive a greater "consumer surplus" from the former.[8]

Referring back to Equation (1), it is clear that families favoring $EDSP^{HI}$ (who I call Group *HI*) are those who will thereby receive a positive redistribution because their probable benefits are greater and/or their costs are lower than under $EDSP^{LO}$ due to a combination of the following factors:

1. Their tax share is low, possibly because their taxable income is low;

2. Their desired consumption of public schooling is high because they have school-age children who want to attend, they perceive a high return to education, and they do not have a strong preference (on quality or ideological grounds) for private schooling;

3. Their probability of being admitted to the marginal public school places is high;

4. The external benefit they will derive from the educational consumption of others is high and is more easily achieved through the public sector where their tax share is matched by the tax share of others; in some cases this externality may depend on public control over detailed school decisions such as the beliefs and values that are imparted by schools.[9]

On the other hand, families favoring $EDSP^{LO}$ (Group *LO*) are those who will be "redistributed away from" by $EDSP^{HI}$ for the opposite reasons. In this paper I do not specify the collective decision process (for example, I do not assume a majority voting scheme) but I do assume that as the relative size and political power of Group *HI* increases, the likelihood of $EDSP^{HI}$ also increases, and vice versa.[10] Therefore, the key variables hypothesized to determine *EDSP* in the recursive model are *PCI*, *DV*, the proportion of the population aged 0–14

8. It can easily be shown that the availability of a private alternative reduces the probability that families will favor $EDSP^{HI}$. This is, of course, particularly true for families that have strong ideological or quality preferences for private education.

9. For example, external benefits may stem only from schools that instill a common language or that inculcate values such as nationalism or support for the existing political regime. The historical literature on the development of American public education focuses on the desire of the old-timers to control the language, ideology, and values of the newcomers to the "melting pot" as one of the major motivating forces behind increased public funding and management of schools in the nineteenth century, particularly in the Northeastern part of the country. Control over the language of instruction has also been an important object of public educational spending in several African and Asian countries, and control over political ideology has been an impetus to public spending in Communist countries. Of course, people who have minority beliefs may oppose high *EDSP* and may make contributions to private schools for the same reason.

10. One would expect public spending to be highest in societies where political power is concentrated in Group *HI*, which uses *EDSP* as a mechanism for achieving a redistribution of real income from Group *LO*. For example, in Malaysia the politically dominant Malays are redistributing real income from the wealthy Chinese and Tamil communities, via their control over and preferred access to the public education institutions, especially at the higher educational level.

(*AG*0-14), an index of totalitarian control (TOT), and noneducational government spending (*GOVSP*); in the simultaneous model, *%PVT* is added.

*AG*0-14 is a proxy for effective demand, which is expected to raise desired public school expenditures at the primary level (particularly for large families whose tax share is below the private school price for multiple children), but which may not raise desired *EDSP* at the secondary level, because of the family's quantity-quality trade-off. *TOT* is a "totalitarian index," evidence of dictatorial power that may have a positive or negative effect on *EDSP* depending on whether the dictator is trying to maximize the utility of Group *HI* or Group *LO* (in other words, is a populist or elitist dictator) and whether he wishes to use schools as an instrument for tightening his control.[11] *GOVSP* captures the fact that some countries use public rather than private spending to finance other services; if the same group will benefit from public educational spending, this indicates they probably have the motivation and political power to enforce a high *EDSP*. *%PVT* is expected to have a negative effect if people who anticipate that they will attend the private system are in Group *LO*, ceteris paribus. *%PVT* is obviously endogenous so *2SLS* is used in the equations where it is included.

## III. Empirical Results

### A. Methodology

The analysis was conducted by pooling data from the primary and secondary levels in 12 developed and 38 developing countries, 100 observations altogether—the largest number for which I could get data on *%PVT* and the most essential independent variables. My unit of analysis was the country, by educational level. Although the sample was not random it also was not biased in any obvious way and includes a wide variation in all variables as well as substantial representation from all geographic areas. To ensure that influential outliers were not strongly influencing my results in this small sample, I also reran my regressions omitting the observations with the six highest and six lowest *%PVT*. While their omission affected the magnitude of the coefficients, it did not change their signs or the pattern of significant results.

In estimating *%PVT* a linear probability model and logit analysis were both used, and yielded very similar conclusions. The former has the advantage that the coefficients are easier to interpret but it has the disadvantage that the predicted value of *%PVT* may turn out to be >one or <zero for some countries; however, this was not a big problem since it only occurred in two or three cases in all my regressions, and by very small amounts. Logit has the potentially greater

11. *TOT* is an index of political and civil rights as coded by Gastil, published by Freedom House and reprinted in Taylor and Jodice (1983). I used, alternatively, the 1975 score and the mean score for 1972–78. There is very little difference between the two and the latter are given in Table 3. The range in this index is from two (highest political liberty and civil rights) to 14 (highest totalitarian control). See Appendix 1 on data sources for more details.

disadvantage that the estimated parameters are sensitive to small measurement errors if *%PVT* is close to zero or one, which holds for several countries in this study, and it assumes a smaller marginal effect at extreme values of *%PVT* than in the middle range, which may be a misspecification. Since both methods yielded very similar conclusions, the linear probability results are presented in this paper and the logit results are available upon request.

### *B. Determination of %PVT in a Recursive Model*

Table 2 presents the OLS and *2SLS* results for *%PVT*; the first three columns assume a recursive model in which *EDSP* influences *%PVT* and not vice versa; the last column uses a simultaneous model and is discussed in a later section.

Column (1) sets forth a simple model, based on the most clearly exogenous variables, in which *%PVT* depends on stage of development (*DV*, *SECDV*), per capita income (*PCI*), level of education (*SEC*), and heterogeneity (*REL*, *LANG*, *GINI*, separately and interacted with *ADV*). This equation was designed to test whether heterogeneity is as important as expected on theoretical grounds (it is), to ascertain whether it has different effects in advanced (*ADV*) and developing countries (it doesn't), and to capture the systematically larger private sector at the secondary level in developing countries—as in the coefficient of 11.8 on *SECDV* (the secondary-developing interaction term).

I hypothesized above that the latter difference stems mainly from an excess demand for quantity in developing countries, and this depends on public policies, particularly public educational spending. Therefore, Column (2) adds *EDSP* (and *SUB*) to the model. As expected, *SUB* has a positive and *EDSP* a strong negative effect. More important, the inclusion of *EDSP* causes the positive *SECDV* coefficient virtually to disappear (and the negative *PCI* coefficient becomes insignificant).

Column (3) presents a more parsimonious version of this model, eliminating the stage of development variables which have become redundant and focusing on the heterogeneity and policy variables which, both on a priori and ex post grounds, are most important.

Several conclusions can be drawn from these simple recursive equations:

1. On the basis of a few variables, which proxy excess demand, differentiated demand, nonprofit entrepreneurship and relevant public policies, we are able to explain over half the variation in percentage of enrollments that are private.

2. The most important explanatory factor is cultural heterogeneity, particularly religious heterogeneity. *REL* is always significant at the .1 percent level; if *REL* increases by one standard deviation, *%PVT* increases by 11 percentage points. This effect holds both for developing countries and advanced industrial societies, equally at the primary and secondary levels,[12] evidence of the importance of religious entrepreneurship in private education. *LANG*, too, has a positive effect, although somewhat weaker.

12. I tested whether heterogeneity had different effects at the primary and secondary levels by interacting *REL*, *LANG*, and *GINI* with *SEC*. The interaction terms were always small and insignificant and their inclusion did not affect the other variables.

**Table 2**
*Dependent Variable: Proportion of Enrollments that are Private (%PVT)*

| | OLS (1) | OLS (2) | OLS (3) | 2SLS (4) | Variable Means (Standard Deviation) (5) |
|---|---|---|---|---|---|
| $R^2$ | 0.46 | 0.56 | 0.52 | 0.52 | — |
| *C* | 27.2 | 38.4 | 19.9 | 21.6 | — |
| | (2.07)**** | (2.15)** | (3.37)**** | (2.69)*** | |
| *SEC* | 3.4 | 8.4 | 9.7 | 9.2 | — |
| | (0.56) | (1.48) | (2.78)*** | (2.44)** | |
| *SEC*DV* | 11.8 | 1.4 | — | — | — |
| | (1.66)* | (0.19) | — | — | |
| *DV* | −15.4 | −16.1 | — | — | — |
| | (1.13) | (0.97) | — | — | |
| *PCI* | −2.8 | −1.5 | −0.4 | −0.3 | 2.0 |
| | (1.96)** | (1.01) | (0.45) | (0.28) | (2.4) |
| *REL* | 3.9 | 3.8 | 4.0 | 4.1 | 1.8 |
| | (3.81)**** | (4.99)**** | (6.27)**** | (6.41)**** | (2.8) |
| *LANG* | 5.2 | 4.3 | 6.3 | 6.4 | 0.6 |
| | (1.51) | (1.4) | (2.04)** | (2.05)** | (.5) |
| *GINI* | −1.1 | −0.3 | −0.8 | −0.8 | 2.6 |
| | (0.8) | (0.27) | (0.75) | (0.7) | (1.6) |
| *REL*ADV* | 0.5 | 0.4 | — | — | — |
| | (0.25) | (0.27) | — | — | |
| *LANG*ADV* | 13.1 | 16.1 | — | — | — |
| | (0.72) | (1.18) | — | — | |
| *GINI*ADV* | −7.0 | −14.1 | — | — | — |
| | (1.18) | (1.6) | — | — | |
| *SUB* | — | 8.4 | 10.2 | 10.1 | 0.2 |
| | — | (1.78)* | (2.24)** | (2.24)** | (0.4) |
| *EDSP* | — | −9.1 | −8.1 | −9.6 | 1.4 |
| | — | (3.03)*** | (2.42)** | (1.72)* | (0.6) |

Notes: Mean *%PVT* = 22.7 (mean *%PVTPRI* = 16.5, *%PVTSEC* = 28.9). *t*-statistics are corrected for heteroscedasticity using White's method. *EDSPZ* was also included in all equations to denote countries where the primary/secondary division of *EDSP* was missing and was imputed.
**** Significant at 0.1 percent level.
*** Significant at 1 percent level.
** Significant at 5 percent level.
* Significant at 10 percent level.

3. Income diversity (GINI), on the other hand, has an insignificant effect—possibly because of the data problems discussed above. When I measured income diversity by *DISTRIB* instead of *GINI* it also had an insignificant effect. Nevertheless, if we remove the heterogeneity variables as a group from Column (3), the $R^2$ falls from 52 percent to 27 percent, evidence of their key role.

4. Although basic cultural factors thus matter a great deal, public policies are also important. For example, *SUB* increases *%PVT* ten percentage points, despite its crudeness as a variable. This effect is particularly important in developed countries, where mean *SUB* is higher.

5. More important, once public educational spending enters in Column (2), the large difference between developed and developing countries in *%PVT* at the secondary level disappears. The *F* test shows that the stage of development variables (including their interaction terms) become insignificant, both individually and jointly [$F(6,86) = 1.15$]. That is, the same explanatory factors work for developed and developing countries; the large difference in private sector size at the secondary level is due almost completely to the large difference in public secondary education spending.

On average, both sets of countries in my sample spend about 1.6 percent of their *GDP* on public education at the primary level. The advanced industrial societies spend more than that—2 percent—at the secondary level, where the technological cost requirements are higher. But the developing countries spend only 0.9 percent of their *GDP* on public secondary education, thereby creating an excess demand for quantity (and/or a differentiated demand for quality). If secondary *EDSP* in developing countries were increased by 1.1 percentage points (in other words, to the developing country mean), Columns (2) and (3) tell us that *%PVT* would fall 9–10 percent, roughly to parity with *%PVT* in advanced industrial societies.

### *C. Determination of Public Educational Spending*

However, these results may be biased, if *EDSP* is really endogenous. Therefore, this section deals with the estimation of *EDSP* and the following section explores the simultaneous determination of *EDSP* and *%PVT*.

Column (1), Table 3, presents a simple OLS version of Equation 3 designed to capture some of the most important variables influencing *EDSP* and, in particular, to reproduce the low level of educational spending at the secondary level in developing countries. To be consistent with the recursive model in Columns (1)–(3), Table 2, *%PVT* is omitted from this equation. As expected, *SEC*, *PCI*, *AG0-14*, and *GOVSP* have positive effects. *TOT* has a negative effect, consistent with a model of elitist dictatorial control.[13] Stage of development has virtually no effect at the primary level but *SECDV* has a significant coefficient of $-1$, thereby almost fully accounting for the fact that the mean *EDSP* at the secondary level in

13. The negative coefficient suggests that many totalitarian regimes spend less on public education, because they are more immune to popular pressures. In this respect, my results are contrary to those of Lott (1990), possibly because of a different sample and a different variant of the dependent variable.

**Table 3**
*Dependent Variable: Public Educational Spending as a Proportion of GDP (EDSP)*

| | OLS (1) | OLS (2) | OLS (3) | 2SLS (4) | Variable Means (Standard Deviation) (5) |
|---|---|---|---|---|---|
| $R^2$ | 0.43 | 0.44 | 0.44 | 0.41 | — |
| *C* | −0.17 | −0.66 | −0.77 | −1.01 | — |
| | (0.28) | (0.97) | (1.24) | (1.46) | |
| *SEC* | 0.38 | 1.36 | 1.54 | 1.58 | — |
| | (1.86)* | (2.01)** | (3.55)**** | (3.68)**** | |
| *SEC*DV* | −1.0 | −0.21 | — | — | — |
| | (4.23)**** | (0.36) | — | — | |
| *DV* | 0.23 | −0.16 | — | — | — |
| | (0.58) | (0.35) | — | — | |
| *PCI* | 0.05 | 0.05 | 0.06 | 0.08 | 2.0 |
| | (0.79) | (0.78) | (1.15) | (1.36) | (2.4) |
| *GOVSP* | 0.02 | 0.02 | 0.02 | 0.02 | 18.9 |
| | (2.98)*** | (3.03)*** | (3.25)*** | (3.83)**** | (9.8) |
| *TOT* | −0.03 | −0.03 | −0.04 | −0.03 | 7.7 |
| | (1.48) | (1.5) | (1.84)* | (1.67)* | (3.9) |
| *AGO-14* | 0.03 | 0.05 | 0.05 | 0.05 | 39.1 |
| | (2.19)** | (2.65)*** | (3.73)**** | (3.83)**** | (9.2) |
| *AGO-14*SEC* | — | −0.04 | −0.05 | −0.05 | — |
| | — | (1.52) | (4.53)**** | (4.66)**** | |
| *%PVT* | — | — | — | 0.003 | 22.7 |
| | — | — | — | (0.74) | (21.5) |

Notes: Mean *EDSP* = 1.4 (mean *EDSPPRI* = 1.6, *EDSPSEC* = 1.2). *EDSPZ* was also included in all equations to denote countries where the primary/secondary division of *EDSP* was missing and was imputed.
**** Significant at 0.1 percent level.
*** Significant at 1 percent level.
** Significant at 5 percent level.
* Significant at 10 percent level.

developing countries is 1.1 percent of *GDP* lower in developed than in developing countries.

Column (2) seeks to explain where this large *SECDV* effect on *EDSP* is coming from. I conjectured above that a high proportion of school-age children (*AG0-14*) might have different effects at the primary and secondary levels, since it involves a quantity-quality trade-off. Large families, especially those with low incomes, might have a high desired consumption of public education at the primary level to make their children literate, but a low desired consumption at the secondary level because of a limited willingness to invest in each child and because their demand for other goods is more pressing.[14] Moreover, high income, high taxpaying families might be willing to subsidize the primary education of children from large poor families because they perceive externalities from having a literate citizenry with the "right" values and habits, but their external benefits and willingness to subsidize secondary education might be much lower, since that would facilitate labor market competition with their own children. Thus, while the high *AG*0-14 in developing countries increases the size of Group *HI* and *EDSP* at the primary level, it may not have this effect at the secondary level. To test whether this is the case, Column (2) adds an *AG*0-14**Secondary* interaction term. As expected, this has a negative effect and almost completely dissipates the separate effect of *SECDV*.

Finally, Column (3) presents a more parsimonious version of this model, omitting *SECDV* and *DV*, which are now redundant and, with no loss of explanatory power, focuses on the remaining important variables—*SEC*, *PCI*, *GOVSP*, *TOT*, and *AG*0-14. In all, 44 percent of the variance of *EDSP* is explained by these variables.

### *D. Simultaneous Versus Recursive Determination of* EDSP *and* %PVT

Column (4) in Tables 2 and 3 present the *2SLS* version of this simultaneous model, based on the equations in Column (3), with *%PVT* added to the *EDSP* equation. The equations are identified by the exclusion of the heterogeneity variables and *SUB* from the *EDSP* equation, *AG*0-14, *GOVSP*, and *TOT* from the *%PVT* equation. Our results are virtually unchanged. Cultural heterogeneity remains the main determinant of *%PVT* for all educational levels and country groups, and *EDSP* is the second most important variable in Table 2, while *AG*0-14 and *AG*0-14**SEC* play a key role in Table 3.

*%PVT* is never close to significance as a determinant of *EDSP*. The reason may be that when high cultural heterogeneity leads to a high *%PVT*, this diminishes the private benefit of public educational spending among the minorities but increases the external benefit among the dominant group, who want to use the public schools as a means of inculcating a common language and values (see endnote 9). The net effect on the relative size of Groups *HI* and *LO* and the equilibrium *EDSP* is therefore negligible. Thus it appears that *EDSP* influences *%PVT* but not vice versa; and the recursive OLS model of *%PVT* discussed earlier does not lead one astray.

To recapitulate how this model works let us compare the derivation of *EDSP* and *%PVT* for an "average" developing country at the primary and secondary levels, respectively. Its low per capita income and government spending combined with its high totalitarian index, lead it to choose a low *EDSP*; this is offset at the primary but not the secondary level by its high proportion of school-age children. Thus this country ends up with high public educational spending at the

14. Many such families cannot afford the opportunity cost of secondary school. Often their children have dropped out of primary school, hence are not even candidates for secondary school. They may believe their children are unlikely to be admitted to a public secondary school. For empirical evidence on the quantity-quality trade-off and the negative relationship between family size and secondary school attendance in developing countries see Knodel (1990).

primary level, much like that in developed countries, but relatively low public spending, hence a small public sector, at the secondary level.

At the same time, many people who are excluded from the small public secondary sector perceive benefits from education that exceed its private price. This includes (1) high income, high tax share families from Group *LO* who prefer private education for their children; (2) high tax share families from Group *LO* who want a small public sector but would be willing to use it if admitted; and (3) some low income families from Group *HI* (in other words, those who chose quality over quantity of children) who want a large public sector but, having lost the collective choice battle, now exercise their personal choice in the private market. Table 2 shows that the low level of public secondary spending in developing countries greatly increases the excluded students from the latter two categories and hence their excess demand for private education, as a second choice.

### *E. The Political Economy of Public-Private Choices*

At this point one might ask: Why are people not willing to spend publicly, if they are willing to spend privately, in excess-demand-drive private sectors? If the real cost of a private school place equals that of a public school place and if private enrollments are, on average, 31 percent of the total at the secondary level in developing countries, it follows that private spending augments public spending by 45 percent. If people are not willing to spend more in the public sector, why are they willing to spend so much in the private sector?

Part of the answer is that costs per student are generally lower in the private sector. (See James 1991a, James and Benjamin 1988, Levy 1986, and Jimenez, Lockheed, Luna, and Paqueo 1991). If low costs lead to low price in a private competitive market, this increases the number of families who will favor low public spending, even though they value education.

But the more basic reason is that the distributional consequences of public and private spending differ when taxes are not based on benefits. To see this, suppose that a country has chosen $EDSP^{LO}$, $T^{LO}$ (in other words, Group *LO* has prevailed) and consider a low-tax share, high-benefit member of Group *HI* who is excluded from the public schools. That family will purchase education in the private market. We know (by its membership in Group *HI*) that this family would have preferred $EDSP^{HI}$, $T^{HI}$, where its total costs would have been lower and/or its benefits higher (in other words, it would have received a positive redistribution). But it was outvoted by families in Group *LO*, whose marginal tax costs would have exceeded their marginal benefits if the public system expanded (in other words, they would have received a negative redistribution). Group *LO* apparently could not raise Group *HI*'s tax share to match its benefits, but it could successfully impose a low *EDSP*, thereby forcing Group *HI* to spend more via fees in the private sector. (Of course, some members of Group *HI* will not spend more and will not acquire education, as they might have in a larger public system).[15]

15. A similar explanation is likely to hold for excess-demand-driven higher education sectors. For a closely related analysis of the limited public spending on secondary and higher education in Japan see James (1986a), James and Benjamin (1988).

Thus, if an equivalent amount of public spending replaced private spending, the distribution of costs and benefits would be quite different. Consequently, different groups will favor public versus private spending. I have tried to show why the size of Group *HI* versus Group *LO* changes over the course of economic development due to demographic change, thereby shifting the political equilibrium at the secondary level from $EDSP^{LO}$, $T^{LO}$ to $EDSP^{HI}$, $T^{HI}$ and eliminating the excess demand motive for private education. This explains why the private sector at the secondary level is systematically larger, even though it may be considered inferior, in developing countries; while developed countries are characterized by a larger public sector and a correspondingly smaller private sector, based on differentiated demand rather than excess demand.

## IV. Conclusion

In summary, I have asked why different societies have made different choices about their reliance on public versus private provision of education. The relative size of the private sector was modeled as depending on excess demand, differentiated demand, the supply of nonprofit entrepreneurship, and government policies. I hypothesized that excess demand stemming from low public spending is the major explanation for the systematically larger size of the private sector at the secondary level in developing countries, while differentiated demand and nonprofit supply, both stemming from cultural heterogeneity, are the major explanations for variations in private sector size within a given stage of development and educational level.

Regression analyses conducted across a pooled primary-secondary sample of 50 countries (100 observations) produced results that were consistent with these hypotheses. Religious competition and entrepreneurship have highly significant positive effects in all cases. Linguistic heterogeneity plays a positive (but somewhat lesser) role. These findings have important implications for the behavior of private schools. For example, they suggest that private schools may segment the population along religious, linguistic, nationality or ideological lines, because of the motivations of their nonprofit producers and consumers.

While basic cultural forces thus play a large role, public policies can also influence the size and nature of the private sector. In particular, public educational spending, which increases the capacity (and possibly quality) of the public system, has a negative effect on *%PVT*. Since public educational spending is particularly low at the secondary level in developing countries, this result is consistent with the excess demand explanation for the large private sector there. Once public educational spending is taken into account, the same predictive model works for developed and developing countries, despite the large differences in their private sector size.

I also modeled the collective decision process that determines public educational spending. The coalition favoring higher public spending at the secondary level is predicted to increase with development, due to income and demographic changes, especially the decline in family size. As the public sector expands, people who have been involuntarily excluded can now find places, so excess-demand-driven private schools are crowded out. According to our estimates, this process ultimately reduces *%PVT* to the level found in developed countries, which is explained mainly by cultural heterogeneity. While large excess-demand-driven private sectors can flourish in countries with limited public systems even if they are considered inferior, the differentiated-demand-driven private schools that survive in countries with open access public systems are likely to be considered superior (academically or ideologically), by the revealed preference of their consumers.

## Appendix 1

### *Symbols and Data Sources*

*PCI* = per capita income, 1975 in thousands of U.S. dollars, World Tables (Washington, D.C.: World Bank, 1988–89). Foreign exchange converted to U.S. dollars according to the World Bank Atlas method, to smooth the impact of temporary under or over-evaluation. (Purchasing power parity figures not available for most countries in sample).

*REL* = an index of religious heterogeneity = $100(WT_{CA}\, WT_{CH} \Sigma R_i \ln 1/R_i)$ where $R_i$ = proportion of population constituted by religion $i$. Calculated from data in Taylor and Hudson (1971) and Coxill and Grubb (1968). See text for discussion.

*LANG* = an index of linguistic heterogeneity = $\Sigma L_i \ln 1/L_i$ where $L_i$ = proportion of population whose main language is $i$. Calculated from data in Taylor and Hudson (1970).

*GINI* = Sectoral *GINI*, based on comparison between proportion of product coming from and proportion of labor engaged in each sector of the economy. Data for selected years in 1970s from Taylor and Jodice (1983).

*SUB* = Dummy variable of 1 for countries that subsidized more than 70 percent of the total cost of their private sectors in 1975.

*TOT* = Index of political and civil rights as coded by Raymond D. Gastil and published by Freedom House. This index is based on criteria such as the existence of elections, more than one political party, local governments, an independent judiciary and free media (press, radio & TV). The 1975 data are from *Freedom at Issue,* Freedom House, 1976, 11–20. Mean scores for 1972–78 from Taylor and Jodice (1983), Range is from 2 (highest political liberty and civil rights) to 14 (highest totalitarian control).

*GOVSP* = Current general (central and local) government spending minus educational spending, as percent of *GDP*, 1973. Taylor and Jodice (1983).

*EDSP* = Current educational spending on primary and secondary levels, respectively, 1975. To control for the fact that different countries have different years' duration for the primary and secondary cycles, I adjusted all to a standard six-year duration. Division between primary and secondary imputed for Denmark, Australia, U.S.A., and New Zealand. *Unesco Statistical Yearbook*, 1980–85.

*AG0-14* = Percentage of population age 0–14, 1975. *World Tables* (1983).
*SEC* = Dummy taking the value of 1 for secondary education.
*DV* = Dummy taking the value of 1 for developing countries.
*ADV* = Dummy taking the value of 1 for advanced industrial societies.
*%PVT* = Percentage of total enrollments that were in private schools, selected years between 1975 and 1981, calculated separately for primary and secondary levels.

Sources: *Sweden (1978):* Marklund, S. (1979). *Educational Administration and Educational Development.* Stockholm: University of Stockholm, Institute of International Education. *Denmark (1981):* Communications with Ministry of Education, Copenhagen. *Rest of Europe (1980):* Neave, G. (1985). "The non-state sector in education in Europe: A conceptual and historical analysis," *European Journal of Education, 20,* 321–37; and Mason, P. (1983). *Private education in the EEC.* London: Independent Schools Information Service. *Australia (1980): Australian School Statistics.* Canberra: Commonwealth Schools Commission, 1984. *Japan (1980): Mombusho.* Tokyo: Ministry of Education, 1981. *New Zealand (1978): Educational Statistics of New Zealand.* Wellington: Department of Education, 1978. *U.S.A. (1980): Digest of Educational Statistics.* Washington, D.C.: National Center for Educational Statistics, U.S. Department of Education, 1982. *India (1978): Fourth All-India Educational Survey.* New Delhi: National Council of Educational Research and Training, 1978. *Other Developing Countries (1975). Financing Education in Developing Countries.* Washington, D.C.: World Bank, 1986.

## References


Allison, Paul D. 1978. "Measures of Inequality." *American Sociological Review* 43(6):865–80.

Coxill, H. W., and K. Grubb. 1968. *World Christian Handbook.* Nashville, N.Y.: Abingden Press.

Hansmann, Henry, and John Quigley. 1982. "Population Heterogeneity and the Sociogenesis of Homicide." *Social Forces* 61(1):206–24.

Hanushek, Eric 1986. "The Economics of Schooling: Production and Efficiency in Public Schools." *Journal of Economic Literature* 24(2):1141–77.

James, Estelle 1984. "Benefits and Costs of Privatized Public Services: Lessons from the Dutch Educational System." *Comparative Education Review* 28(4):255–76.

———. 1986a. The Private Nonprofit Provision of Education: A Theoretical Model and Application to Japan." *Journal of Comparative Economics* 10(1):255–76.

———. 1986b. "The Private Provision of Public Services: A Comparison of Sweden and Holland." In *The Nonprofit Sector in International Perspective,* ed. E. James, 61–83. New York: Oxford University Press.

———. 1987. "The Public-Private Division of Responsibility for Education: An International Comparison." *Economics of Education Review* 6(1):1–14.

———. 1991a. "Private Higher Education: the Philippines as a Prototype." *Higher Education* 21(2):189–206.

———. 1991b. "Public Policies Toward Private Education." *International Journal of Educational Research* 15(5):359–76.

James, Estelle, and Gail Benjamin. 1988. *Public Policy and Private Education in Japan.* London: Macmillan.

James, Estelle, and Susan Rose-Ackerman. 1986. *The Nonprofit Enterprise in Market Economics*. New York: Harwood Academic Publishers.

Jimenez, Emmanuel, Marlene Lockheed, E. Luna, and Vic Paqueo. 1991. "School Effects and Costs for Private and Public Schools in the Dominican Republic." *International Journal of Educational Research* 15(5):393–410.

Knodel, J., N. Havanon, and W. Sittitra. 1990. "Family Size and the Education of Children in the Context of Rapid Fertility Decline." *Population and Development Review* 16(1):31–62.

Levy, Daniel. 1986. *Higher Education and the State in Latin America*. Chicago: University of Chicago Press.

Lott, John. 1990. "An Explanation for Public Provision of Schooling: The Importance of Indoctrination." *Journal of Law and Economics* 33(1):199–231.

Taylor, Charles L., and Michael C. Hudson. 1970. "Raw Data File: Fractionalization and Concentration Measure and Inequality Indices." In *World Handbook of Political and Social Indicators II*, Section V. Ann Arbor: University of Michigan.

———. 1971. *Cross-National Aggregate Data for World Handbook of Political and Social Indicators*. MRDF. Ann Arbor: Center for Political Studies, University of Michigan, ICPSR.

Taylor, Charles L., and David A. Jodice. 1983. *World Handbook of Political and Social Indicators*, 3rd ed. New Haven: Yale University Press.

Theill, Henri. 1972. *Statistical Decomposition Analysis*. Amsterdam: North Holland.

Weisbrod, Burton. 1975. "Toward a Theory of the Voluntary Nonprofit Sector in a Three-Sector Economy." In *Altruism, Morality, and Economic Theory*, ed. E. Phelps, 171–91. New York: Russell Sage Foundation.

———. 1977. *The Voluntary Nonprofit Sector*. Lexington, Mass.: D.C. Heath.

West, E. G. 1967. "The Political Economy of American Public School Legislation." *Journal of Law and Economics* 10(1):101–28.

———. 1970. *Education and the State*. London: The Institute of Economic Affairs.

White, H. 1978. "A Heteroscedasticity Consistent Covariance Matrix and a Direct Text for Heteroscedasticity." *American Economic Review* 48(4):817–38.

*World Tables*, Vol. II. 1983. Washington, D.C.: World Bank and Johns Hopkins Press.

# Part IV
# Nonprofits and Asymmetric Information

# [12]

# The Economic Role of Commercial Nonprofits: The Evolution of the U.S. Savings Bank Industry*

*Henry Hansmann*

## 1. Introduction

In previous work, I and others have argued that nonprofit firms in general tend to arise as a response to problems of asymmetric information facing consumers – or, as I termed it in my earlier work, "contract failure" (Hansmann 1980). The notion, simply put, is that individuals prefer to deal with nonprofit firms rather than for-profit firms when they have difficulty policing the quality or quantity of the goods or services that the firm offers or provides. Under such circumstances, nonprofit firms – which operate under a "non-distribution constraint" that prohibits the distribution of the firm's net earnings to anyone who exercises control over it (such as its directors, officers, or members) – hold the promise of behaving less opportunistically than would for-profit firms toward the individuals who patronize them, since those who control the firms cannot profit directly from opportunism and thus have less incentive to engage in it.

This theory is persuasive, and indeed seems to be widely accepted, for donative nonprofits – that is, nonprofits that rely upon gifts or grants for a significant portion of their income. Here the "customers" who have a contract failure problem are the organization's donors, and the nonprofit form is undoubtedly employed in large part to provide them with a degree of fiduciary protection. The theory is more controversial, however, in the case of those nonprofits that I have elsewhere termed "commercial" nonprofits (Hansmann 1980). These are nonprofit organizations that receive little or no income from donations, but rather derive all or nearly all of their income from prices they charge for the goods and services they produce and sell. Such commercial nonprofits are becoming increasingly common in the United States today. For example, they account for most of the nation's hospital care, and also have large shares of other important service industries such as nursing care for the elderly, day care for children, and primary medical

* I wish to thank Eric Rasmusen for helpful comments on an earlier draft.

care.[1] It is not obvious that, in industries such as these, consumers are at such an informational disadvantage that the crude protection from opportunism afforded by the non-distribution constraint could be very important. As a result, many analysts, myself included, have wondered whether we should look elsewhere for an explanation of the development of commercial nonprofits (Hansmann 1987a).

One alternative theory is that commercial nonprofits are just historical anachronisms. This seems like a persuasive theory where hospitals are concerned, for example. Nonprofit firms first came to dominate the hospital industry in the United States when it was entirely charitable and all the nonprofit firms in it were donatively supported. Health technology and financing techniques have since changed, however, in ways that have now rendered donative funding of hospitals largely unnecessary. Yet the nonprofit firm has survived in this industry, perhaps just through institutional inertia; hospitals that were formerly donatively supported institutions have simply evolved into commercial nonprofits.

Another theory is that commercial nonprofits are often just a response to tax exemption and other implicit and explicit subsidies that give them artifical cost advantages over their for-profit competitors: take away the subsidies, and eventually the commercial nonprofits would largely disappear.

There have been some efforts by economists in recent years to test these different theories empirically. For example, in an effort to provide a direct test of the asymmetric information theory, Burton Weisbrod and his students have sought to determine whether there are discernible differences in the quality of services provided by nonprofit and for-profit firms in service industries containing both types of firms (e. g. Weisbrod and Schlesinger 1986). Similarly, there have been efforts to determine empirically the extent to which commercial nonprofits in particular industries are simply a response to tax exemption (Hansmann 1987b). But, in general, this work has not yet provided us with a clear answer as to whether, and to what degree, the asymmetric information theory helps explain the role of commercial nonprofits in many, or even any, industries.

I now believe, however, that we can discern at least one industry in the United States in which commercial nonprofits clearly arose, from the beginning, primarily as a response to contract failure. And that is the savings bank industry. I shall explore the evolution of that industry in some detail

[1] In primary medical care, nonprofits appear in the form of firms of doctors organized as group practices – commonly termed health maintenance organizations – that sell their services on a prepaid basis. Such firms are also often organized on a for-profit basis.

here, both as an illustrative case study in the role of nonprofit enterprise and in an effort to explain in otherwise puzzling diversity of organizations that populate the banking industry today.[2]

## 2. The Origins of the Savings Bank Industry

Nonprofit firms appear in the banking industry in the United States in the form of so-called mutual savings banks. Although the term "mutual" suggests that these banks are consumer cooperatives that are owned by their depositors, this is not the case. The depositors in a mutual savings bank have no voting rights or other means of exercising direct control over the organization, and thus are not members or owners in any proper sense. Instead, control over mutual savings banks lies in the hands of a self-perpetuating board of directors that holds the bank's assets in trust for its depositors. "The term 'mutual' only indicates that all distributed earnings must be shared by the depositors" (Teck 1968: 13). (In addition, depositors in mutual savings banks arguably have the right, upon dissolution of the organization, to share among themselves the organization's accumulated surplus.[3]) Thus, mutual savings banks are appropriately classified as true nonprofit organizations rather than as cooperatives.[4] In this respect, they should not be confused with mutual savings and loan associations, which are also common in American banking and – as discussed further below – are (at least formally) true consumer cooperatives that are owned by their depositors collectively.

Mutual savings banks arose in the United States early in the nineteenth century, following earlier English models. The first mutual savings bank was chartered in Massachusetts in 1816; by 1849, 87 mutual savings banks were

[2] After writing an earlier draft of this paper I discovered a paper by Eric Rasmusen, since published (1988), that makes much the same argument about the historical role of mutual savings banks.

[3] See Teck (1968: 13–14). The term "arguably" is used here, because depositors' rights to the distribution of surplus upon dissolution are a bit unclear; see *In re Dissolution of Cleveland Savings Society*, Ohio Ct. Com. Pls. (1961); *Morristown Institute for Savings v. Roberts*, 42 N.J. Eq. 496, 8 A. 315 (1887).

[4] In classifying nonprofits, I have elsewhere (Hansmann 1980) distinguished between "mutual" nonprofits, in which control of the organization is in the hands of the class of patrons for which the organization is a fiduciary, and "entrepreneurial" nonprofits, in which control is vested in a board of directors that is self-perpetuating or appointed by third parties. Within this scheme, mutual savings banks, despite their name, are appropriately classified as entrepreneurial rather than mutual nonprofits.

in operation, primarily in urban centers in the northeastern and mid-atlantic states (Teck 1968: 8, 16). They were typically founded as philanthropic institutions, with their initial capital donated by wealthy businessmen. The founders' motivation, it is said, was to help prevent pauperism, and relieve the burden on public charity, by encouraging thrift among the working class (Welfling 1968: 17).

Given this early history, one might conclude that mutual savings banks were established simply as a vehicle whereby the rich could provide charitable services to the poor, in the form of subsidized interest on the latter's savings. Indeed, this is the conventional view. These banks would then have assumed the nonprofit form, rather than being established as proprietary organizations, for the same reasons of contract failure that lead donative institutions in general to be formed almost universally as nonprofits: in order to provide some degree of fiduciary protection for the organization's donors, who otherwise would have little assurance that their contributions were being used for the purposes they intended rather than simply going into the pockets of the organization's proprietors.

Yet this theory seems unsatisfying for several reasons. To begin with, although hard data seem to be lacking, the amounts of capital contributed by the founders were probably inadequate to yield more than a trifling subsidy per individual depositor. Thus, it seems implausible that mutual savings banks were established merely as charitable intermediaries through which the rich could redistribute some of their income to the poor, or even to the frugal poor. Likewise, the subsidy per investor must surely have been too small to provide any important incentive in itself for saving, and thus to encourage noticeable changes in the savings behavior of the working classes.

Further, and more important, commercial banks at the time did not serve as places where individuals could deposit their savings. Although commercial banks were numerous in the early nineteenth century – there were over 300 in the United States in 1820 (Polakoff 1970: 68) –, they did not accept small deposits from individuals (Gup 1980: 137). Rather, they generally dealt only with businesses. They served primarily a monetary function, creating money in the form of bank notes, which were then the principal circulating currency (Polakoff 1970: 17). These bank notes were issued in exchange for notes from merchants, which the bank purchased at a discount.

"... neither the merchant, nor the saver, [of the early nineteenth century] thought of banks in connection with deposits. A bank ... meant primarily a place of discount for his notes. He owed bills ... [but] [h]is own note would not suffice to pay those bills, even though his credit were excellent, because it would not pass acceptably from hand to hand. But if he exchanged it for the note of some bank, paying for the privilege, through a discount, he would obtain something which would pass acceptably" (Bennett 1924: 20–21).

Commercial banks obtained their working capital not through deposits, but through sale of stock in the banks. And the savings that went to purchase this stock were, presumably, large sums accumulated by wealthy merchants, not the meager weekly savings of the working class.

In the early nineteenth century, then, there was no convenient vehicle through which persons of modest income could invest. Thus, the mutual savings banks were not founded simply to provide a place where the working poor could get a more attractive rate of return on their savings; they were founded as the *only* place where such people could deposit their savings at all. To understand the role of the early mutual savings banks, therefore, we have to understand why it was that there were no commercial savings banks until well into the nineteenth century. That is, why did the commercial banks not take deposits from individuals, and consequently obviate the need for the mutual savings banks?

The principal reason, it seems, is that commercial banks were too untrustworthy to serve as a repository for the savings of persons of modest means. That is, the problem was probably not on the supply side but on the demand side. If individuals had been willing to entrust their savings to commercial banks, the latter might well have taken them; but willing depositors were probably too few to make the activity worthwhile.

The reason that commercial banks were so untrustworthy in the early nineteenth century is that they were then largely unregulated; they did not have to maintain minimum levels of reserves, and there were no restrictions on the ways in which they could invest their assets. Commercial banks therefore had both the incentive and the opportunity to behave opportunistically toward their depositors. In particular, they had an incentive to invest depositors' savings in highly speculative ventures that would pay off handsomely if successful, but that ran a substantial risk of not paying off at all. If the bank was lucky in such investments, it would earn a large profit. And if it was unlucky, it would go bankrupt, leaving its depositors to bear most of the losses. Further, commercial banks had an incentive to maintain only very small reserves. That way, if the bank's investments went sour, only a minimum of the owners' assets would be exposed; most of the losses would fall on the depositors.[5]

Depositors would, of course, have had an incentive to try to bind banks by contract to maintain adequate reserves and not to undertake excessively speculative investments with their savings (and banks, in turn, would have

[5] Similar incentive problems are now well recognized as a limitation on the feasible debt/equity ratios for business corporations (Jensen and Meckling 1976). And they also go far toward explaining why mutual firms dominated the life insurance business in its early days in the first half of the nineteenth century (Hansmann 1985).

had an incentive to bind themselves in this way in order to attract more business). But, under the circumstances, it was probably impossible to draft a contract of this type that was both effective and enforceable.

In short, consumer deposit banking was characterized by a high degree of asymmetric information (contract failure) in its early years: depositors could not know, or control, what commercial banks were doing with their funds.

Indeed, the early commercial banks often engaged in speculation, and not infrequently behaved opportunistically toward holders of their notes (for example, by making it difficult for them to be redeemed in specie) (Scoggs 1924). And they were, in fact, highly risky ventures: nearly 50% of all commercial banks formed between 1810 and 1820 closed by 1825, and the same proportion of banks formed between 1830 and 1840 failed before 1845 (Trescott 1963: 19). For these reasons, commercial banks were popularly viewed with distrust during the first half of the nineteenth century (Clain-Stefanelli 1975: 51). Individuals would, with reason, have been very hesitant to permit such institutions to hold their life savings for any length of time. Thus the commercial banks confined themselves to short-term transactional services, such as discounting notes, that exposed their customers to only limited losses in case the bank failed.

There was, consequently, a demand for savings banks that would provide a higher degree of fiduciary protection for depositors than commercial banks could offer. This demand grew particularly strong in the early nineteenth century, when for the first time there was a large class of urban industrial workers who received their income in the form of wages rather than in kind, and who lacked the traditional supports of the farm communities to tide them through periods of unemployment (Welfling 1968: 5). The mutual savings banks met this need. They obtained their seed capital – a problem for nonprofits in general, since they cannot obtain equity capital – from wealthy philanthropists. The mutual (nonprofit) form thus served the useful purpose of providing a degree of fiduciary protection both to the depositors and to the donors.[6] But, unlike other types of donative nonprofits (such as

[6] Although commercial banks did not take consumer savings deposits until the middle of the nineteenth century, there did exist before then a number of commercial trust companies that administered private and charitable trusts. Why did these commercial trust companies develop and survive in this period, while commercial savings banks did not? The answer presumably lies in the size of the individual trusts and the method of remuneration devised for trust managers. The trust companies, then as now, took a percentage of the total assets as their form of compensation. This reduced their incentive to behave opportunistically; indeed, it essentially made each individual trust into a small nonprofit firm. The trust managers could not keep any fraction of the gains from speculating irresponsibly with the trust assets, so they had little incentive to engage in such activity. In a savings

traditional redistributive charities), mutual savings banks were evidently not established as nonprofit rather than proprietary firms primarily to protect donors. Rather, the mutual savings banks sought donative financing *because* they were nonprofit, and they were nonprofit to protect their "commercial" customers, the depositors. Confirming this, donative financing seems to have been largely confined to the initial formation of mutual savings banks; once established, they tended to become purely commercial nonprofits.

## 3. The Development of Commercial Savings Banks

The mutual savings banks grew rapidly throughout the nineteenth century, reaching their peak in number of banks around 1900, when there were 652 such banks with a total of $ 2.1 billion in deposits (Teck 1968: 13). By the turn of the century, however, commercial banks had begun actively entering the savings field. In 1900, commercial banks held only $ 600 million in savings deposits; by 1915, this had increased to $ 3 billion (Welfling 1968: 58 – 59). By 1983, total deposits at commercial banks were roughly ten times those at mutual savings banks (FDIC 1983: Table 1).

Why did the commercial banks begin entering the savings account business late in the nineteenth century? A likely explanation is that the advent of

account, the depositor receives a fixed rate of return on his savings, and the bank keeps all profits (or absorbs all losses) that result from its investment of these funds. Thus the incentive for the bank to behave opportunistically is much higher than in the case of a trust account.

Of course, the banks could have arranged a method of remuneration for savings accounts that looked more like that of trusts. An individual savings account is generally too small to permit a bank to segregate and account separately for the investments it makes with the amounts deposited in the account; the funds from a number of such accounts must be pooled for efficient administration. Nevertheless, a bank could simply have confined itself to a fixed rate of compensation for the entire pool of savings, such as a percentage of the total assets. All earnings beyond this would be returned pro rata to the depositors as interest on their accounts. Yet this approach would essentially turn the bank into a nonprofit entity. Such a method of compensation makes the bank a trustee of the depositors' funds. The pool of assets administered by the bank would be held by it in trust for the beneficial owners, who are the depositors. In effect, this is the type of contractual relationship that was established between the managers of the mutual savings banks and their depositors. (Alternatively, the pooled assets could be owned by the depositors as a group not just beneficially, but directly; acting as a group, they would then simply hire the bank's management. This is the arrangement employed in the mutual savings and loan associations.)

state and federal banking regulation did what private contractual mechanisms could not – namely, make commercial banks a relatively safe place for members of the general public to deposit their savings. Prior to 1860, there was relatively little regulation of banks in general, and the regulation that existed was directed almost exclusively at protecting holders of the banks' notes rather than depositors. A number of states passed legislation during this period that required banks to maintain reserves of some kind.

Massachusetts was evidently the first to act, in 1829, and the movement toward such legislation accelerated rapidly after the banking crisis of 1837 (Dewey 1915: 155; Sharp 1970). Typically, this legislation limited note issues by a bank to some stated multiple of the amount of specie or other reserves held by the bank. Absent from most of this legislation, however, was any provision for a reserve requirement against deposits, whether demand deposits or time deposits. Louisiana was the first state to enact a reserve requirement against deposits as well as notes, in 1842. Prior to 1860, it was followed in this only by Massachusetts, which enacted a reserve requirement covering both deposits and notes in 1858 (Sharp 1970: 112–113).

In 1863 and 1864, however, the federal government, in response to the financial pressures created by the Civil War, passed legislation providing for federally chartered banks. This legislation required that banks chartered under it maintain a specie reserve of 25% against both notes and deposits. Many states copied this chartering system after the Civil War, and thus laws requiring reserves against deposits as well as notes became common (Rodkey 1934). This legislation, by limiting the ability of banks to act opportunistically toward their depositors, was probably a critical precondition for the increasingly strong role that the commercial banks played in savings banking in the latter part of the nineteenth century. On the other hand, such legislation still provided something less than complete protection to depositors. The reserve requirements were often rather lax; most states, for example, permitted banks to keep a substantial portion of their reserves in the form of demand deposits at other banks (Rodkey 1934: 393). Thus it is not surprising that the mutual savings banks continued to grow during this period, and at the end of the century still held in aggregate far more savings deposits than did commercial banks.[7]

A further decisive step in banking regulation took place in 1933, however, when the federal government passed legislation establishing federal deposit insurance that provided complete insurance for savings deposits at commercial banks (and mutual savings banks as well). This insurance essentially

[7] It should be noted, however, that other factors, such as governmental regulation of the types of investments that could be made by commercial banks and mutual savings banks, respectively, probably also contributed to the relative shares of the savings deposit business held by these two types of institutions.

eliminated the problem of contract failure between depositors and commercial banks; mutual savings banks could, therefore, no longer offer a higher degree of protection for savings deposits than could commercial banks. Thus, mutual savings banks quite suddenly lost whatever remaining efficiency advantage they had over commercial banks.

Yet the mutual savings banks did not disappear after 1933. Although virtually no new mutual savings banks have been established since then, many of the preexisting ones have remained in business. This presumably reflects the fact that there has been, at least until recently, no easy way for capital to leave the mutual savings bank industry. The managers and directors of the savings banks, having no claim on the banks' net assets, have little incentive to liquidate the banks – a step that could threaten their jobs. Yet nobody else has any control. Thus, so long as the mutual savings banks are not so inefficient relative to commercial banks as to waste away their capital, they tend to remain in business even though they are anachronistic. Only recently have large numbers of mutual banks begun to convert to the stock form (i. e. to commercial banks) through transactions that are brokered and promoted by investment banks (which take substantial remuneration from the transaction) and that secure the approval of the existing management through a bit of self-dealing in which they acquire some of the stock in the newly formed commercial bank at a bargain price (and perhaps keep their jobs in the bargain).

## 4. Mutual Savings and Loan Associations

Mutual savings banks have a close cousin in the form of mutual savings and loan associations (MSLAs), which have also played an important role in savings banking. Unlike the mutual savings banks, however, MSLAs are not nonprofits, subject to a strict non-distribution constraint, but rather are true cooperatives: their depositors have formal voting control over the organization as well as the sole claim to residual earnings. Although space precludes extensive discussion of these institutions here, a few words about their role may be appropriate, for purposes of comparison with mutual savings banks.

MSLAs first began to be formed in the United States in the 1830s. They originally arose as institutions in which small groups of working people would pool their savings, and from which they would then take loans, by turns, with which to finance the construction or purchase of a house. In the early stages of their development, an MSLA would be dissolved once all of its original members had acquired a house; subsequently, they became perpetual organizations with fluid membership (see generally Teck 1968). Evidently the impetus for the formation of MSLAs was in large part the same as that described above for the formation of mutual savings banks: asymmetric information in the management of consumer deposits by commercial banks. Mutual ownership, like the nonprofit form of the mutual savings banks, mitigated the hazards of opportunistic conduct.

Part of the impetus for the formation of the MSLAs, however, evidently came as well from the fact that, at the time, commercial banks commonly refused to make loans for the purchase or construction of a house (Teck 1968: 18, 21). The advantage that the MSLAs had over the commercial banks here was presumably that they were better at dealing with adverse selection and moral hazard on the part of the borrowers. A group of workingmen undoubtedly had better information with which to determine which of their friends and fellow workers would be good risks, and thus should be permitted to join the mutual, than a commercial bank would have had. Further, when times are hard, a borrower is likely to be less inclined to default when he knows that his friends and neighbors will bear the loss than when he knows that the owners of a commercial bank will bear it.

Thus mutual savings and loan associations had the potential of solving two different problems, where the mutual savings banks only solved one. Whether for this or other reasons, mutual savings banks never took root in those sections of the country where MSLAs developed – which were essentially those parts of the country (the South and West) where development occurred primarily after the 1830s.[8]

## 5. Conclusion

Commercial nonprofits are the great puzzle of the nonprofit sector today. The historical experience with mutual savings banks throws some important light on the possible roles that commercial nonprofits can play, and on the patterns of evolution that characterize them.

To begin with, the experience with mutual savings banks shows that nonprofit firms can play an important role in the early stages of purely commercial industries that are characterized by severe problems of asymmetric information. In effect, they offer a form of consumer protection. But that experience also indicates that public regulation is likely, in the long run,

[8] For further discussion of the role of cooperative enterprise, and of the way in which it compares and contrasts with the role of nonprofit enterprise, see Hansmann (1988).

to be more effective than the nonprofit form as a means of dealing with problems of asymmetric information in commercial enterprise. Regulation can make for-profit firms viable; and for-profit firms, with better access to capital than nonprofit firms, and better incentives for customer responsiveness and cost efficiency as well, are then likely to begin to take over the industry. Yet, nonprofit firms, once established, tend to become embedded and do not quickly leave an industry, even after the conditions to which they initially responded have long disappeared. And thus we see that mutual savings banks have survived for more than half a century after they became anachronistic.

Nursing care and day care are arguably two other industries that have evolved along paths similar to that followed by mutual savings banks. When, several decades ago, these industries were new, consumers might reasonably have been wary of trusting commercial firms to provide the sensitive services involved, and therefore preferred nonprofit providers. Yet, as public regulation of these industries became tighter, as consumers became more knowledgeable, and as for-profit firms developed stronger reputations, the need, and hence the special demand, for the nonprofit form of organization presumably diminished. Nevertheless, the already established nonprofits still occupy a substantial market share in these industries, and may continue to for some time to come.

## References

Bennett, Frank P. (1924): *The Story of Mutual Savings Banks*, Boston: Frank P. Bennett & Co.

Clain-Stefanelli, Elvira and Vladimir (1975): *Chartered for Progress: Two Centuries of American Banking*, Washington, D.C.: Acropolis Books.

Dewey, Davis Rich (1915): *Financial History of the United States*, New York: Longmans Green & Co.

Federal Deposit Insurance Corporation, Division of Accounting and Corporate Services, Bank Statistics Branch (1983): *Banks and Branches Data Book: Summary of Accounts and Deposits in all Commercial and Mutual Savings Banks and Domestic Branches of Foreign Banks, 1983*, Washington, D.C.: FDIC.

Gup, Benton E. (1980): *Financial Intermediaries: An Introduction*, Boston: Houghton Mifflin Co.

Hansmann, Henry (1980): "The Role of Nonprofit Enterprise," *Yale Law Journal* 89, 835–901.

Hansmann, Henry (1985): "The Organization of Insurance Companies: Mutual Versus Stock," *Journal of Law, Economics, and Organization* 1, 125–153.

Hansmann, Henry (1987a): "Economic Theories of Nonprofit Organization," in *The Nonprofit Sector: A Research Handbook*, Walter Powell (Ed.), New Haven: Yale University Press.

Hansmann, Henry (1987b): "The Effect of Tax Exemption and Other Factors on the Market Share of Nonprofit Versus For-Profit Firms," *National Tax Journal* 40, 71–82.

Hansmann, Henry (1988): "Ownership of the Firm," *Journal of Law, Economics, and Organization* 4, 267–304.

Jensen, Michael and William Meckling (1976): "Theory of the Firm: Managerial Behavior, Agency Costs, and Capital Structure," *Journal of Financial Economics* 3, 305–360.

Polakoff, Murray E. (1970): *Financial Institutions and Markets*, Boston: Houghton Mifflin Co.

Rasmusen, Eric (1988): "Mutual Banks and Stock Banks," *Journal of Law and Economics* 31, 395–422.

Rodkey, Robert (1934): *Legal Reserves in American History*, Ann Arbor: University of Michigan Press.

Scoggs, William D. (1924): *A Century of Banking Progress*, Garden City, N.Y.: Doubleday.

Sharp, James Roger (1970): *The Jacksonians Versus the Banks*, New York: Columbia University Press.

Teck, Alan (1968): *Mutual Savings Banks and Savings and Loan Associations: Aspects of Growth*, New York: Columbia University Press.

Trescott, Paul B. (1963): *Financing American Enterprise: The Story of Commercial Banking*, New York: Harper & Row.

Weisbrod, Burton and Mark Schlesinger (1986): "Ownership Form and Behavior in Regulated Markets with Asymmetric Information," in *The Economics of Nonprofit Institutions: Studies in Structure and Policy*, Susan Rose-Ackerman (Ed.), Oxford: Oxford University Press.

Welfling, Weldon (1968): *Mutual Savings Banks*, Cleveland, Oh.: Case Western Reserve University Press.

# [13]

Economics Letters 35 (1991) 5–8
North-Holland 

# Uninformed customers and nonprofit organization *

## Modelling 'contract failure' theory

Ottorino Chillemi
*University of Padova, 35100 Padova, Italy*

Benedetto Gui
*University of Trieste, 34127 Trieste, Italy*

Received 11 April 1990
Accepted 21 June 1990

When product quality is unobservable before purchase, the equilibrium price may be inefficiently high in order to signal high quality. We present a reputation model where under reasonable assumption nonprofit organizations can credibly charge lower prices than for-profit organizations.

### 1. Introduction

The starting point of the economic literature on nonprofit organizations (NPOs) is credited to Kenneth Arrow, who suggests in a passage that a reason why so many U.S. hospitals are nonprofit is asymmetric information (1963, p. 950). After being developed by Nelson and Krashinsky (1973) with reference to the day care industry, this idea provides the basis for Hansmann's (1980, 1987) 'contract failure' theory of NPOs.

The constraint not to distribute profits that characterizes NPOs – Hansmann argues – protects customers in circumstances where normal contractual arrangements fail, since it reduces the incentive for those controlling the organization to supply less quantity or quality than agreed.

Despite the popularity of this theory, the only attempt to formalize its claims we know of is Easley and O'Hara's (1983, sect. 4; 1988, sect. 5). The authors consider a situation where a customer entrusts a manager with the provision of a service, but he can observe neither the output nor effort above a minimum level. While an unconstrained manager would pocket the price without supplying anything, the nonprofit manager is forced to spend in costs of production the revenue exceeding his salary. Therefore 'nonprofit' contracts may dominate 'profit' contracts. This model applies to situations such as donations for needy.

* Financial support from Consiglio Nazionale delle Ricerche and Ministero della Pubblica Istruzione is gratefully acknowledged.

In this paper we formalize the 'contract failure' theory with reference to a situation where a competitive market is conceivable, such as the purchase of medical or nursing services. Following Klein and Leffler (1981) and Allen (1984), we assume that customers cannot observe quality before purchase, but the experience of only one consumer reveals quality to the whole market. So in later periods nobody purchases from producers with a bad reputation.

We characterize NPOs with respect to for-profit organizations by the fact that in the former the entrepreneur is allowed to appropriate a smaller share of profits than in the latter.

## 2. The model

Consider a competitive market for a good whose quality, $q$, can be either high, $q_{\mathrm{H}}$, or low, $q_{\mathrm{L}}$. The supply side is constituted by a continuum of identical firms, each producing in a period a quantity $x$ at a cost $C(x, q)$, with $C(x', q_{\mathrm{H}}) > C(x', q_{\mathrm{L}})$ for all $x^* > 0$, $C_x > 0$, $C_{xx} < 0$. Costs include a salary $w$ accruing to the entrepreneur for providing managerial services. His per period utility function is $U(R)$, with $U' > 0$, where $R = w + a\pi$ is income, $\pi = p(x)x - C(x, q)$ is profit, and $1 > a > 0$ is the profit appropriation parameter. The supply of entrepreneurs is unlimited provided the lyfe cycle utility level is not less than $U(w)/r > 0$, where $r > 0$ is the per period rate of interest. All functions are twice continously differentiable. We also denote $R_J$ and $\pi_J$ the entrepreneur's income and profit when quality is $J = \mathrm{H}, \mathrm{L}$.

The demand side is constituted by a continuum of identical consumers. Each consumer is unwilling to pay any positive price for low quality, while he is willing to buy one unit of the high quality good if its price is not greater than $p^m$.

Consumers and firms play an infinitely repeated game of asymmetric information. Only Nash stationary equilibria are considered. The consumers' strategy is to boycott firms that previously produced low quality, and buy at random from the remaining firms offering the lowest price, provided:

(a) $p \leq p^m$ and

(b) $p$ and $x$ satisfy the following credibility condition:

$$U(w + a\pi_{\mathrm{H}})/r \geq U(w + a\pi_{\mathrm{L}})/(1 + r). \tag{1}$$

The LHS of (1) is the payoff of the honest strategy, whereas RHS is the payoff of the dishonest strategy. In writing (1) we have normalized to zero the utility stream that the dishonest entrepreneur obtains after his firm closes down. This formalizes the fact that the loss of reputation is costly. Given this strategy of consumers, a firm which previously produced low quality goes out of business. The optimal strategy of other firms is obtained by solving the following program

$$\max_{p,x} = U(w + a\pi_H),$$

s.t.

$$x = 0 \quad \text{when} \quad \begin{cases} U(w + a\pi_{\mathrm{H}})/r < U(w + a\pi_{\mathrm{L}})/(1 + r), \\ p > p^m, \\ p > p^*, \end{cases}$$

$$x \leq \sigma \quad \text{when} \quad p = p^* \leq p^m,$$

$$x \leq \infty \quad \text{when} \quad p < p^* \quad \text{and} \quad p \leq = p^m,$$

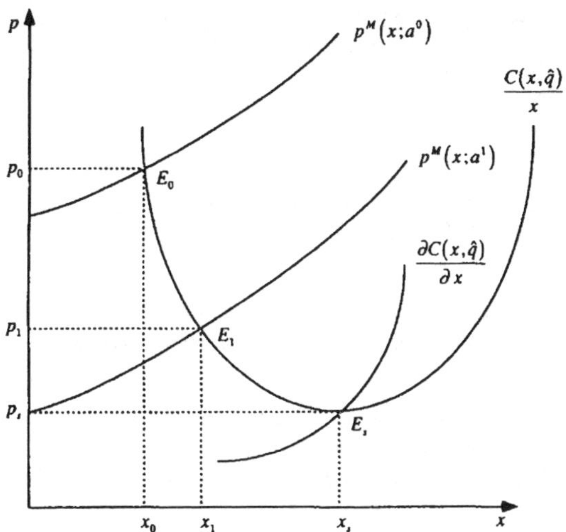


Fig. 1. The credibility constraint $p^M(x, a^0)$ – or $p^M(x, a^1)$ – prevents the first best equilibrium $E_s$ from being reached. The smaller the appropriation parameter $a(a^1 < a^0)$, the lower the equilibrium price.

where $p^*$ is the price other firms are charging [1] and $\sigma$ is the ratio between the exogenous number of consumers and the endogenous number of operating firms (both real numbers). Given this firm strategy, the consumer strategy outlined above is an optimal response.

In equilibrium no entry occurs. Therefore the entrepreneur's utility stream is at the reservation level, which implies that profit is zero. We are interested in those long run equilibria where the price is prevented from falling to the minimum average cost because the corresponding price/output couple is not credible. [2] We examine sufficient conditions for a decrease in the appropriation parameter a to lead the industry to a more efficient long run equilibrium.

First we state a preliminary result.

*Proposition 1. There exists a non-empty set of utility functions which includes linear ones, such that* (i) $\partial p^M x;\, a)/\partial a > 0$, *for all* $x > 0$, *where* $p^M$ *is implicitly defined by* (1) *considered as an equality. So, when the parameter a decreases, the locus of minimum-credible-price/quantity couples* $(x, p^M)$ *shifts downward in the* $x$, $p$ *space.*

*Proof.* By differentiating (1) as an equation with respect to $p^M$ and $a$ we have

$$\frac{\mathrm{d}p^M}{\mathrm{d}a} = \frac{\pi_H U'(R_H) - \pi_L U'(R_L) r/(1+r)}{ax(U'(R_H) - U'(R_L) r/(1+r))}. \tag{2}$$

With concave utility functions the denominator in (2) is always positive. The sign of numerator is negative – and thus (2) is positive – if marginal utility does not fall too much when the per period

[1] Assuming that all other firms charge the same price $p^*$ is not restrictive since, as Allen shows, this is the case in equilibrium.

[2] The existence conditions of these equilibria can easily be obtained by adapting Allen (1984, pp. 318–319).

revenue of the entreprenuer increases from $R_H$ to $R_L$. (see fig. 1, where $a^1 < a^0$). It can be shown this is the case with utility functions with constant relative risk-aversion, $U(x) = x^{1-c}$, $0 \leq c < 1$ (linear utility functions are obtained when $c = 0$). □

Proposition 1 tell us that there are cases in which a decrease in the appropriation parameter, $a$, enlarges the set of feasible equilibrium prices. Now we are ready to state our main result.

*Proposition 2. Assume that for $a = a^*$ in long run equilibrium* (1) *is binding. Then if the utility function is such that condition (i) in Proposition 1 holds, following a small decrease in a the new long run equilibrium is Pareto superior.*

*Proof.* In equilibrium utility is independent of the value of a and therefore entrepreneurs are unaffected. If (i) in Proposition 1 holds, however, a decrease in a allows long run equilibrium price to decrease. Therefore consumers' utility increases. □

Proposition 2 shows that NPOs may increase social welfare. Notice that condition (i) in Proposition 1 is unnecessarily demanding in order to obtain such a result. It would be sufficient that, when (1) is binding for $a = a^*$, the condition $\partial p^M(x, a)/\partial a > 0$ holds in a neighborhood of the equilibrium production level.

## 3. Concluding remarks

The results presented in section 2 confirm Hansmann's claim that NPOs may indeed represents a correct institutional response to a weakness of customers' information. The reason is that reducing the extent to which profits can be appropriated may increase the 'trustworthiness' of the firms, which exerts a beneficial effect on social welfare. Of course, this effect will have to be weighted against other effects, such as a possible reduction in $X$-efficiency.

Among the situations characterized by asymmetric information ex-ante, the one we have examined is the least favorable to NPOs' superiority. In fact, the more quality is known ex-post, the smaller the value of the specific protection NPOs guarantee their customers. Therefore, our argument should hold 'a fortiori' in more realistic situations found between Easley and O'Hara's and ours, as in Rogerson (1983) and in Shapiro (1983).

## References

Allen, F., 1984, Reputation and product quality, Rand Journal of Economics 15, no 3, 311–327.

Arrow, K.J., 1963, Uncertainty and the welfare economics of medical care, American Economic Review 53, 941–973.

Easley, D. and M. O'Hara, 1983, The economic role of the nonprofit firm, Bell Journal Of Economics 14, 531–538.

Easley, D. and M. O'Hara, 1988, Contracts and asymmetric information in the theory of the firm, Journal of Economic Behavior and Organization 9, 229–246.

Hansmann, H, 1980, the role of nonprofit enterprise, Yale Law Journal 89, 835–901.

Hansmann, H., 1987, Economic theories of nonprofit organizations, in: W.W. Powell, ed., The nonprofit sector (Yale University Press, New Haven, CT) 27–42.

James, E. and S. Rose-Ackerman, 1986, The nonprofit enterprice in market economies (Harwood Academic Publishers, Chur).

Klein, B. and K.B. Leffler, 1981, The role of market forces in assuring contractual performance, Journal of Political Economy 89, 615–641.

Nelson, R. and M. Krashinsky, 1973, Two major issues in public policy, in: R. Nelson and D. Young, eds., Public subsidy for day care of young children, (Lexington, Heath, MA).

Rogerson, W.P., 1983, Reputation and product quality, Bell Journal of Economics 14, 508–516.

Shapiro, C., 1983, Optimal pricing of experience good, Bell Journal of Economics 14, 497, 507.

# [14]

ELSEVIER Journal of Health Economics 18 (1999) 219–240

# Consumer information and competition between nonprofit and for-profit nursing homes

Richard A. Hirth *

*Department of Health Management and Policy, Department of Economics, Department of Internal Medicine, University of Michigan, School of Public Health, 109 S. Observatory, Ann Arbor, MI 48109-2029 USA*

Received 1 January 1997; revised 1 March 1998; accepted 21 April 1998

**Abstract**

This paper develops implications of Arrow's hypothesis that nonprofit organizations are prevalent in health care because of quality uncertainty. The model analyzes the ability of nonprofits to mitigate market failures created by asymmetric information in an environment characterized by potential competition from both explicitly for-profit firms and for-profits in disguise (profit-motivated firms who obtain nonprofit status in order to exploit the perceived trustworthiness of the nonprofit sector). Under certain conditions, it is shown that nonprofit status can serve as a credible signal of quality and that nonprofits can decrease the underprovision of quality both by providing high quality services and indirectly via a spillover effect on quality in the for-profit sector. Applicability to long-term care and implications for empirical research and policy towards nonprofits in health care are discussed. 

*Keywords:* Consumer information; Competition; Nonprofit nursing homes

## 1. Introduction

The relative desirability of for-profit and nonprofit ownership of health care facilities is widely debated [e.g., Relman and Reinhardt, 1986; Gray, 1993; Frank and Salkever, 1994; Schlesinger et al., 1996; Ad Hoc Committee to Defend Health Care, 1997]. However, little theoretical work has addressed issues related to

* Tel.: +1-734-936-1306; Fax: +1-734-764-4338; E-mail: rhirth@umich.edu

0167-6296/99/$ - see front matter 
PII: S0167-6296(98)00035-6

competition between for-profit and nonprofit firms. Most models treat for-profit and nonprofit firms as if they each existed in isolation, analyzing a representative firm of each type facing an exogenous demand curve. Thus, these models have little to say about conditions under which nonprofits can achieve social goals despite competition from for-profits or the welfare implications of the coexistence of multiple types of ownership in the same industry. In response, Weisbrod (1991) has called attention to the need for theory on intersectoral competition.

Given this lack of theory, empirical work has also focused on the ownership of individual firms without controlling for the ownership of competitors. If competition from one type of firm influences performance of the other type, this omission can bias inferences about the relationship between ownership and outcomes such as quality or cost of care. The models developed here show why this may occur and imply that empirical research should take account of competitors' ownership.

The next section provides background on nonprofit organizations (NPOs) and long-term care, a prototypical industry to which the model may apply. Section 3 develops a model incorporating the Arrow/Hansmann hypothesis that NPOs are prevalent in markets for complex personal services because they have less incentive than for-profits to underprovide quality to poorly informed consumers. This model demonstrates conditions under which nonprofits can mitigate market failures created by asymmetric information despite potential competition from both explicitly for-profit firms and for-profits in disguise (profit-motivated firms who obtain nonprofit status in order to exploit the nonprofit sector's reputation for trustworthiness). The role of the nondistribution constraint (NDC) in regulating intersectoral competition is also explored. Section 4 sketches an alternative model that motivates the ownership/quality relationship without appealing to asymmetric information. Section 5 discusses implications for empirical research and policy towards nonprofits in health care.

## 2. Background

### 2.1. *The nonprofit sector and the 'Arrow / Hansmann hypothesis'*

The idea that quality uncertainty explains NPOs' prevalence in health care originates in Arrow (1963), who claims that NPOs are considered more trustworthy because the concept of profit contradicts the trust relationships required to encourage the provision of high quality. Hansmann (1980) classifies most nonprofit health facilities as 'commercial' NPOs. These firms produce private goods for which some dimensions of quality are difficult to observe, and obtain most of their revenue by selling services rather than from voluntary contributions.

Economic theory implies that for-profits produce the socially efficient product array when consumers can easily evaluate products before purchase, contract over delivery terms, monitor contractual compliance and obtain redress for violations. When these conditions are not satisfied, difficulty in contracting over some product attributes leaves an element of discretion to producers (Hansmann, 1980). The nondistribution constraint (NDC) imposed on NPOs, which prohibits payment of profits to owners or employees, may diminish incentives to misrepresent quality to poorly informed consumers. Thus, NPOs may represent an appropriate response to contracting failures arising from quality uncertainty. A natural implication is that clients who cannot easily judge quality may prefer dealing with NPOs, using non-profit ownership as a signal of honesty.

### *2.2. Applicability to long-term care*

One industry to which the model developed here may apply is long-term care, where concern about quality has remained high for several decades. Books on the industry have borne such suggestive titles as *Tender Loving Greed* (Mendleson, 1974) and *Unloving Care: The Nursing Home Tragedy* (Vladeck, 1980). Many nursing home residents are vulnerable to opportunistic behavior due to impaired physical and cognitive capabilities and the often urgent nature of care decisions (e.g., following a hospital discharge). Ownership can provide a low cost signal that the promised quality will be delivered if nonprofit homes, often affiliated with religious or charitable organizations, are less willing to compromise care for the sake of profit.

Numerous studies have attempted to identify quality differences by ownership. However, even reviews of this literature have drawn different conclusions. O'Brien et al. (1983) claim that quality is similar across sectors. Hawes and Phillips (1986, p. 521) disagree, concluding that studies are "fairly uniform in finding nonprofit facilities superior in quality to for-profit nursing homes." Davis (1991) argues that the evidence is inconclusive, making it 'premature' to conclude that nonprofits provide higher quality. Finally, more recent work in the economics literature has continued to find mixed evidence on this issue (e.g., Gertler, 1992; Holtmann and Idson, 1993; Cohen and Spector, 1996).

However, existing studies generally fail to control for ownership of a firm's competitors. Empirical studies of the ownership/quality relationship implicitly assume that finding (not finding) quality differences between sectors constitutes *prima facie* evidence for (against) the desirability of nonprofit enterprise. It will be demonstrated that either implication can be false. Under asymmetric information, competition from NPOs can improve the for-profit sector's performance. Thus, nonprofits may enhance welfare even if they do not appear very 'different' in equilibrium. Alternatively, if consumers are well-informed, ownership may be unrelated to welfare despite quality differences that can exist if the sectors occupy different market niches. Thus, relying on the ad hoc reasoning that NPOs must appear 'different' to justify public support can yield errant policy implications.

### *2.3. Applicability of existing industrial organization theory*

Mixed ownership industries have not been extensively investigated by industrial organization theory and other work in the literature has limited applicability. In models with some informed consumers, high price signals high quality to uninformed consumers because informed consumers will pay a premium and the loss of their business can make it unprofitable for a low quality firm to charge a price consistent with high quality (e.g., Wolinsky, 1983). However, these models are generally derived in a monopoly context to ensure the sustainability of a price premium for high quality. If competition for sales to informed consumers drives the high quality price close enough to average cost, low quality firms would find it profitable to mimic the high quality price, preventing price from serving as a credible signal of quality to uninformed consumers. Since markets for complex personal services are seldom monopolized, application of these models seems dubious.

In models with repeat purchases, high quality firms signal their type via low introductory prices, recouping losses by subsequently charging higher prices to their satisfied clientele. This requires mobile consumers who quickly learn quality and purchase frequently. For example, Klein and Leffler (1981) rely on infinite repetition, immediate post-purchase learning and costless communication between consumers. Even with these strong assumptions, the outcome is less efficient than the full information equilibrium. Further, these conditions do not even approximate the long-term care environment. Monitoring is difficult and the learning period is non-trivial relative to the duration of care. The service recipient (e.g., ill parent) is often neither the decision-maker nor able to easily evaluate care. Non-monetary switching costs are high, including 'transfer trauma' or 'transplantation shock' that occur because residents often suffer disorientation, anxiety and functional decline if they move. Thus, long-term care has the character of a once-and-for-all purchase. Vogel (1985, p. 586) concludes that those at risk of institutionalization ''hardly [have] the characteristics of the well-informed, rational, and mobile consumer that economic theory would have making choices.''

Cooper and Ross (1984) present one of the few quality models that relies on neither repeated purchases nor market power. The model developed here extends their framework, under which opportunistic behavior arises naturally: if uninformed consumers use prices as quality signals, low quality firms charging high quality prices can distort the ability of prices to convey information.

## 3. Asymmetric information model of intersectoral competition

Despite the well-known conjecture that nonprofit organizations play an important role in health care markets by providing quality assurance to poorly informed consumers (the 'Arrow/Hansmann hypothesis'), there have been few attempts to formally model this proposition. In order to explore the implications of this hypothesis, a premise of the model is that a subset of firms have objectives consistent with becoming the trustworthy providers envisioned by Arrow and Hansmann. However, if nonprofit status is to serve as a credible signal of quality, not only must these 'honest' entrepreneurs be able to remain viable, but entrepreneurs motivated solely by profit must not find it profitable to disguise themselves as nonprofits in order to exploit consumers' trust of the nonprofit sector.

Steinberg (1993) calls for theories of nonprofit behavior to endogenize the self-selection of consumers and entrepreneurs into sectors and to ensure that the posited NPO objective function can survive in the competitive environment. These criteria are satisfied here by modeling the relationship between consumers' information and choice of sector, allowing for the possibility that some profit-motivated firms find it advantageous to obtain nonprofit status, determining the effect of competition from nonprofits on the observed performance of the for-profit sector, and exploring how the nondistribution constraint (even if imperfectly enforced) regulates competition between for-profit and nonprofit firms.

Competition between for- and nonprofit firms is modeled in a simplified fashion, omitting some important industry-specific details. For example, regulated capacity and low public reimbursement rates lead nursing homes to compete primarily for private pay patients (Scanlon, 1980; Cutler and Sheiner, 1993). Thus, for long-term care, the model pertains primarily to the private segment of the market, where consumers are most likely to have a meaningful choice of providers even in states with strict capacity constraints. [1]

### 3.1. Assumptions and notation

#### 3.1.1. Firms

F1. AC(Q,s) represents the average cost of producing $Q$ units of the good with quality $s$. Raising quality is costly $[s_1 > s_2 \Leftrightarrow \mathrm{AC}(Q,s_1) > \mathrm{AC}(Q,s_2)]$. For any quality, average costs are U-shaped with respect to quantity. [2]

As shown below, there is no loss of generality in restricting attention to two quality levels represented by $s \in \{L,H\}$ with $H > L$ (i.e., only these qualities are offered in equilibrium). These qualities can be produced at minimum average costs of $c_H > 0$ and $c_L \in (0,c_H)$. $Q_{\mathrm{EH}}$ is the scale that minimizes high quality average cost and $Q_{\mathrm{min}}$ denotes the smallest output at which low quality firms can break even if they charge $p = c_H$ (see Fig. 1). Among for-profits claiming to provide high quality, $\lambda = N_H/(N_H + N_L)$ is the fraction actually delivering high quality, where $N_H$ and $N_L$ are the numbers of high and low quality for-profits, respectively.

[1] Some evidence suggests that capacity constraints are not binding in many states (Harrington et al., 1992) and are weakening over time (Nyman, 1993).

[2] Proposition 2 in Cooper and Ross (1984) shows that equilibrium does not exist under constant returns to scale. Hirth (1993) proves that this result continues to hold when a non-profit sector is added to the model. U-shaped average costs appear reasonable in long-term care based on cost studies and the moderate average facility size of 85 beds (National Center for Health Statistics, 1987).

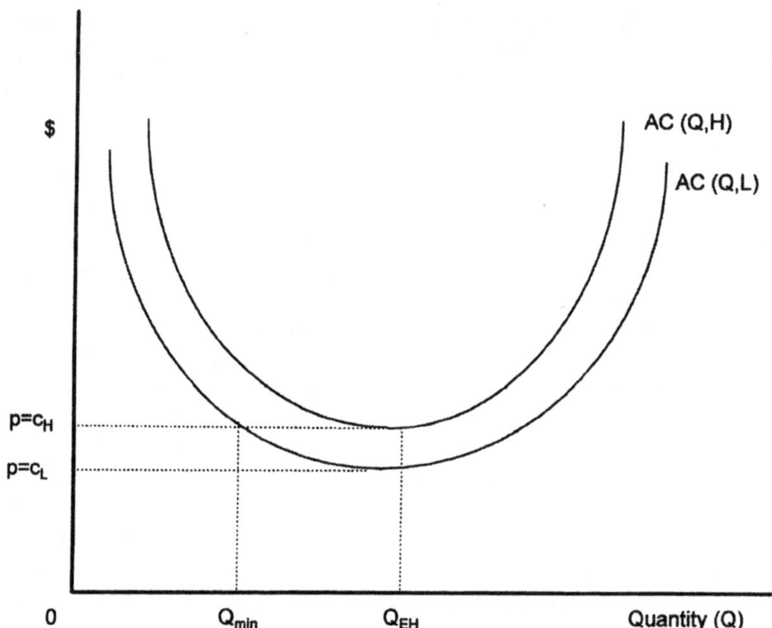


Fig. 1. Average costs of high and low quality firms.

F2. The industry is competitive.

F3. Enforcement of the nondistribution constraint is imperfect. Stricter enforcement raises the minimum price that a firm attempting to circumvent the NDC must be able to charge (when selling the equilibrium quantity) in order to appropriate a competitive return for personal gain. Define this threshold price as $p_{\mathrm{FPID}}$.[3]

By treating NPOs as facing a binding break-even constraint, most models of nonprofit behavior implicitly assume perfect enforcement of the NDC. The approach taken here relaxes this assumption. Legal restraints and the risk of detection and punishment make removal of profits from an NPO more difficult, but not impossible. The NDC, even if imperfectly enforced, makes obtaining nonprofit status less attractive to a firm motivated solely by profit because it effectively requires the firm to earn supercompetitive profits in order to be able to

[3] In the extreme case of perfect enforcement of the NDC, private appropriation of surplus is impossible and there exists no finite price at which firms interested only in profit will find it attractive to obtain nonprofit status. Thus, perfect enforcement corresponds to $p_{\mathrm{FPID}} = \infty$. Conversely, a completely unenforced NDC (free appropriability of profit) implies that a firm interested only in profit can appropriate at least a competitive return at any price that covers average costs. For low quality, this corresponds to $p_{\mathrm{FPID}} = c_L$.

appropriate at least a competitive return for personal gain. For example, suppose enforcement is sufficient to prevent profits from being removed from the firm as cash. To circumvent the NDC, the firm's owners can only appropriate profits as in-kind benefits (e.g., plush offices). If they value these in-kind benefits at 50% of their cash value, the firm must earn twice the competitive profit level to generate enough in-kind benefits to justify their investment in the firm.

F4. There are two types of firms. 'Honest' firms voluntarily comply with the nondistribution constraint (NDC) and deliver the promised quality provided they can break even. 'Honest' firms are assumed to organize as nonprofits. [4] The second type of firm is motivated only by profit and will take on whichever organizational form allows it to appropriate the greatest return. A profit-motivated firm can either avoid the NDC by organizing as a for-profit or it can obtain nonprofit status, subjecting itself to the NDC. Any profit-motivated firm that obtains nonprofit status is called a 'for-profit in disguise' (FPID).

F5. Honest NPOs' aggregate supply curve is upward sloping. $\gamma(p_n)$ denotes honest nonprofits' aggregate supply as a function of the nonprofit price. Enough capital is available to profit-motivated firms to exploit all profit opportunities that exist in either sector.

The assumption that honest NPOs have an upward sloping supply curve can be motivated by free-riding in the private provision of public goods or limited access to capital. Market failures created by asymmetric information encourage the provision of philanthropic capital if altruists care about quality or about not exploiting vulnerable clients. However, those who value nonprofit activities may free-ride on the provision of others. [5] Since higher prices would help honest NPOs overcome the restricted access to credit and equity markets that accompanies nonprofit status, it is expected that supply is upward sloping. However, the results also hold if honest NPOs' supply does not respond to price.

The assumption that all profit opportunities will be exploited in either sector implies that some profit-motivated entrepreneur will provide the needed capital even if some traditional sources of credit or equity are unavailable to a firm that has obtained nonprofit status. Since for-profits in disguise care only about profit and not about any public goods such as quality assurance to uninformed consumers, there is also no free-rider problem to limit their supply. This assumption is

[4] Honest entrepreneurs may enter the non-profit sector because the NDC imposes a lower utility cost on owners/managers with goals other than financial gain. Their underlying utility function may contain a 'fixed cost' in terms of utility lost by a small deviation from honesty. In a different context, Erard and Feinstein (1994) show that a model in which some taxpayers report honestly despite incentives to cheat fits the US data better than one in which all taxpayers are presumed to report strategically.

[5] This process, a standard private provision of public goods problem, is not explicitly modeled here. Private provision of public goods in Nash equilibrium is generally suboptimal. Thus, supply by honest NPOs is expected to be insufficient to serve all uninformed consumers.

essentially a worst case scenario for honest nonprofits. If FPIDs also faced constraints on their growth (or if there simply were no scenarios under which profit-motivated firms would be willing to take on nonprofit status), it would be easier for honest nonprofits to maintain a high enough price to cover their costs without facing the prospect of competition from profit-motivated firms that obtain nonprofit status to exploit uninformed consumers' trust of the nonprofit sector.

### 3.1.2. Consumers

C1. If consumers purchase the good, they have unit demands.

C2. Consumers have identical preferences [6] over quality and price given by $U(s,p) = \theta s - p$ where $H$ and $L$ satisfy $\theta H - c_H > 0$ and $\theta H - c_H > \theta L - c_L$. [7] Therefore, efficiency requires that all consumers receive high quality. Not purchasing yields the reservation utility of zero. Further assume that $\theta L - c_L < 0$, which implies that a consumer would not purchase care they know to be of low quality even if the price equalled the minimum average cost of production. [8]

C3. A consumer is informed with probability $0 < \alpha < 1$. [9] Informed consumers know prices and qualities of all firms. Since uninformed consumers observe only prices and ownership status, they form beliefs over quality given these attributes. [10]

C4. The population, which is normalized to one, is large relative to the number of firms.

## 3.2. Outline of the model

(1) Honest nonprofits produce high quality and choose a price, $p_n$.

(2) Each profit-motivated firm chooses its ownership status (for-profit or nonprofit), quality, and price to maximize its profits. In equilibrium, a firm hoping to attract informed consumers must offer high quality. A firm trying to exploit its

[6] The homogeneous preference assumption focuses on the market failure (underprovision of quality). Quality differences arising from heterogeneous preferences do not imply inefficiency. 'High' quality could be interpreted as *the promised quality* and 'low' quality as *below the promised quality*. The homogeneous preference assumption could be relaxed to allow submarkets for different levels of quality without changing the intuition of the results.

[7] Cooper and Ross (1984) use a standard utility function to derive a similar 'partially indirect' utility function.

[8] Relaxing the assumption that $\theta L - c_L < 0$ implies that there are scenarios in which some low quality firms 'self-reveal' their quality by charging a low price. Proofs allowing for this case are available from the author.

[9] Information acquisition is endogenized in Hirth (1993). After observing prices, suppose consumers can learn quality at some cost. All consumers becoming informed ($\alpha = 1$) cannot be an equilibrium since price would then reveal quality, giving any individual an incentive to avoid costly information collection.

[10] Heterogeneity of consumer information in the long-term care market arises from variations in the ability to obtain and process information. Endowments of cognitive, physical, economic and social/familial resources vary widely across individuals at risk of institutionalization.

informational advantage relative to uninformed consumers by delivering low quality has two alternatives. It can organize as a for-profit and mimic the price charged by high quality for-profits or it can obtain nonprofit status and mimic the price charged by honest nonprofits. Nonprofit status is a perfect signal of quality only if no profit-motivated firms choose the latter strategy.

(3) Informed consumers observe the prices and qualities of all firms and choose randomly from the set of firms offering their preferred price/quality bundle. Since informed consumers observe quality, ownership status is irrelevant to their decision. Uninformed consumers observe only ownership status and prices. They form beliefs about the probability of receiving high quality at each price/ownership combination and choose randomly from the set of firms that offers the price/ownership combination that maximizes their expected utility.

### *3.3. Benchmark cases with only a for-profit sector*

Full information ($\alpha = 1$) and asymmetric information ($\alpha < 1$) cases with only a for-profit sector will serve as benchmarks to which the results with a nonprofit sector can be compared. Equilibrium in the full information case is characterized in Rosen (1974) and is Pareto optimal. Only goods of quality $H$ are sold and price equals the minimum average cost of delivering quality $H$, where $H$ is the quality such that $(H,c_H)$ is the zero profit quality/price combination that maximizes consumers' utility.

With asymmetric information, some consumers observe only prices and must form expectations about quality conditional upon price. Producers take these expectations as given. Informed consumers receive the first-best pair $(H,c_H)$ because they do not suffer an information disadvantage and the industry is competitive. Thus, the uninformed can reasonably conjecture that any firm charging a price other than $c_H$ produces quality $L$. In a rational expectations equilibrium, beliefs must be consistent with actual qualities provided and an equilibrium is a set of beliefs such that markets clear and firms maximize profits but earn zero economic profits.

Lemma 1 characterizes price and quality decisions of firms trying to exploit their information advantage.

**Lemma 1**: All firms not providing the optimal quality/price pair $(H,c_H)$ produce the lowest quality $(L)$ that uninformed consumers cannot distinguish from the optimal quality.

**Proof**: See Cooper and Ross (1984).

Lemma 1 demonstrates that firms trying to exploit asymmetric information provide as little quality as possible, confirming that there is no loss of generality in focusing on two quality levels. It also implies that low quality firms do not cause a reduction in the price of care claimed to be high quality. This is because high quality firms cannot cut prices without becoming unprofitable and firms exploiting asymmetric information must mimic the high quality price to avoid revealing their low level of quality to uninformed consumers.

Before introducing a nonprofit sector, it will be useful to characterize equilibrium in a market in which all firms are organized as for-profits and are motivated solely by profit. This is an extension of the Cooper and Ross model.

**Proposition 1**: Under the stated assumptions and conjectures on beliefs, an equilibrium exists if among firms claiming to provide high quality, the proportion actually delivering high quality ($\lambda$) exceeds the proportion at which uninformed consumers are indifferent between buying or accepting their reservation utility of zero [$\lambda'$ such that $\text{EU}(\lambda', c_H) = 0$]. The following conditions characterize equilibrium:

(i) At most, two types of firms operate in equilibrium:

(a) Firms providing the optimal quality/price bundle, $(H, c_H)$.

(b) Firms mimicking the price charged by high quality producers but actually delivering low quality. These firms offer the quality/price bundle $(L, c_H)$.

(ii) The number and types of firms operating in equilibrium depends on the proportion of consumers that are informed with respect to quality.

(a) If $\alpha \geq (Q_{\text{EH}} - Q_{\min})/Q_{\text{EH}}$, then only firms providing the optimal quality/price bundle can survive. The equilibrium number of firms is $N_H = 1/Q_{\text{EH}}$.

(b) If $\alpha < (Q_{\text{EH}} - Q_{\min})/Q_{\text{EH}}$, the equilibrium numbers of high quality firms and low quality firms mimicking the high quality price, respectively, are:

$$N_H = \frac{\alpha}{Q_{\text{EH}} - Q_{\min}} \quad \text{and} \quad N_L = \frac{1-\alpha}{Q_{\min}} - \frac{\alpha}{Q_{\text{EH}} - Q_{\min}}.$$

**Proof**: See Appendix A.

To illustrate, suppose 40% of consumers are informed ($\alpha = 0.4$), uninformed consumers purchase as long as they expect at least half of the firms actually deliver high quality ($\lambda' = 0.5$), the cost-minimizing output level for a high quality firm is $Q_{\text{EH}} = 0.02$, and the smallest output at which a low quality firm could break even when mimicking the high quality price is $Q_{\min} = 0.01$. High quality firms make sales to both informed and uninformed consumers and additional high quality firms are profitable until their sales per firm fall to $Q_{\text{EH}}$ and price falls to $c_H$. Low quality firms charging the high quality price make sales only to uninformed consumers and additional low quality firms are profitable until their sales per firm fall to $Q_{\min}$. Using the characterization of equilibrium in Proposition 1, $N_H = 40$ and $N_L = 20$, yielding $\lambda = 0.667$.

Proposition 1 provides several insights. The ability to attract informed consumers helps some high quality for-profits remain viable. Since the relative prevalence of high quality firms ($\lambda$) rises with the proportion of consumers who are well informed ($\alpha$), informed consumers create a beneficial externality for uninformed consumers. Nonetheless, an exclusively for-profit market fails to deliver the optimal quality/price combination to all consumers unless there are too few uninformed consumers for the strategy of charging the high quality price while providing low quality to be profitable.

### *3.4. Adding the nonprofit sector to the model*

Since the for-profit sector does not deliver the first best outcome unless nearly all consumers are informed, there exists an opportunity for nonprofit status to serve as a signal of quality. For honest nonprofits to be able to alleviate the market failure created by asymmetric information, they must charge a price that satisfies three criteria. First, the price must be high enough to allow them to remain economically viable. Second, it must make the nonprofit sector attractive primarily to uninformed consumers to prevent nonprofits from serving a clientele that would have received the optimal quality even in an exclusively for-profit market. Third, the price must not be so high that it induces profit-motivated firms to obtain nonprofit status, which would prevent nonprofit status from serving as a credible signal of quality. Since the precise objective function of honest nonprofit is unknown, no attempt is made to predict the exact price that will prevail in the nonprofit sector. However, as described below, these three factors bound the range of feasible nonprofit prices.

The break even constraint places a lower bound on nonprofit prices. Beginning with the case in which nonprofits receive no external subsidies and, hence, must break even on the basis of operating revenues alone, an honest nonprofit delivering the promised 'high' level of quality must be able to charge at least $c_H$ to remain viable. At any such price, informed consumers can locate a for-profit facility offering the same quality at a price as low or lower than the nonprofit price. [11]

Uninformed consumers' willingness to pay places an upper bound on nonprofit pricing. Uninformed consumers' utility in the nonprofit sector is $\theta H - p_n$ if they are certain to receive high quality (i.e., when enforcement of the NDC is sufficient to make the for-profit in disguise strategy unprofitable). For any probability of receiving high quality in the for-profit sector ($\lambda \leq 1$), there exists a unique price $p_{n^*} \geq c_H$ at which uninformed consumers are indifferent between sectors. This

[11] Based on the author's calculations from the 1985 National Nursing Home Survey, the price charged to private pay patients by nonprofit homes is substantially higher than the price charged by for-profits.

price defines uninformed consumers' maximum willingness to pay for certain high quality given the probability of obtaining high quality in the for-profit sector.

The price charged by honest NPOs is also limited by the threat of entry by for-profits in disguise. Like low quality firms had to mimic the high quality price in the for-profit sector, for-profits in disguise must mimic the price of honest NPOs in order to fool uninformed consumers. If honest NPOs charge a high enough price, some profit-motivated firms will find obtaining nonprofit status and mimicking this price while delivering low quality care to be a profitable strategy. Recall that $p_{\mathrm{FPID}}$ is the minimum price at which for-profits in disguise could appropriate a competitive return for personal gain and that increasing strictness of the nondistribution constraint raises $p_{\mathrm{FPID}}$ by making it more difficult to convert operating profits for personal benefit. If enforcement of the NDC is sufficient to ensure that $p_{\mathrm{FPID}} > c_H$, there exists a range of prices at which honest non-profits can remain viable but FPIDs seeking to mimic them cannot.

To summarize, the nonprofit price must lie in the range $[c_H, \min(p_{\mathrm{n}^*}, p_{\mathrm{FPID}})]$. If enforcement of the nondistribution constraint is sufficient that $p_{\mathrm{FPID}} > p_{\mathrm{n}^*}$, then uninformed consumers' maximum willingness to pay for certain high quality care is the effective upper bound on the nonprofit price. That is, even if honest nonprofits charge the highest price consistent with the demand for quality assurance, nonprofit ownership remains a credible signal of quality since profit-motivated firms will not obtain nonprofit status. Alternatively, if the nondistribution constraint is so weak that $p_{\mathrm{FPID}} < p_{\mathrm{n}^*}$, the price at which for-profits in disguise could appropriate a competitive return is the effective upper bound on the nonprofit price. If honest nonprofits were to charge more than $p_{\mathrm{FPID}}$, some profit-motivated firms will obtain nonprofit status, debasing the credibility of ownership as a signal of quality and threatening the viability of honest nonprofits in the market (unlike high quality for-profits, honest nonprofits do not have sales to informed consumers to help them remain viable).

Three regimes are possible depending on how strictly the nondistribution constraint is enforced.

### 3.4.1. Regime 1: Strict nondistribution constraint

Suppose the NDC is enforced strictly enough that $c_H < p_{\mathrm{n}^*} < p_{\mathrm{FPID}}$. This implies that the feasible range for the nonprofit price lies between $c_H$ and $p_{\mathrm{n}^*}$. At any price in this range, (1) informed consumers will not patronize the nonprofit sector because they can find a less expensive, high quality firm in the for-profit sector, (2) uninformed consumers prefer the nonprofit sector, (3) honest NPOs can cover the costs of providing high quality, and (4) profit-motivated firms cannot appropriate a competitive return at the nonprofit price and hence do not obtain nonprofit status. Since only honest NPOs are viable in the nonprofit sector, uninformed consumers' use of nonprofit ownership as a quality signal is validated.

Since informed consumers remain in the for-profit sector when $p_{\mathrm{n}} > c_H$, the fraction of consumers in the for-profit sector that is informed with respect to quality is $\alpha/(1-\gamma)$, where $\gamma \leq 1-\alpha$ denotes the size of the nonprofit sector. That is, since NPOs disproportionately attract uninformed consumers, consumers remaining in the for-profit sector are better informed than a random draw from the patient population. This decreases the opportunities to exploit poorly informed consumers in the for-profit sector, resulting in a positive spillover effect from nonprofit market share to for-profit performance. Comparative statics describing these intersectoral spillovers are stated as Proposition 2.

**Proposition 2**: If $c_H < p_n < p_{FPID}$, the equilibrium fraction of high quality firms in the for-profit sector, $\lambda$, rises with nonprofit market share. Only honest NPOs are viable in the nonprofit sector and these honest NPOs displace low quality for-profits from the market.

**Proof**: See Appendix A.

Competition from the nonprofit sector improves the performance of the for-profit sector. This can be characterized as an 'Inverse Gresham's Law' as honest NPOs drive out low quality for-profits charging high quality prices. As the nonprofit sector becomes dominant, for-profits become more like NPOs in their likelihood of delivering the promised care. By raising average for-profit quality, NPOs even increase the welfare of poorly informed consumers who remain in the proprietary sector.

If honest NPOs charge $p_{n^*}$, the nonprofit sector faces no excess demand because, in equilibrium, uninformed consumers are distributed across sectors such that they are indifferent between paying the nonprofit 'premium' to assure high quality or taking their chances in the for-profit sector. [12] That is, once enough uninformed consumers buy from NPOs, quality in the for-profit sector improves sufficiently that the remaining uninformed consumers are unwilling to pay the higher price. However, uninformed consumers are better off *in either sector* than they would be if the nonprofit sector did not exist.

As shown in Proposition 1, no low quality for-profits are viable if a sufficient fraction of consumers is informed. Therefore, with a large enough nonprofit sector, intersectoral quality differences can even disappear. Combined with consumer self-selection into sectors, a welfare implication is stated as Proposition 3.

**Proposition 3**: The nonprofit sector does not have to be large enough to serve all uninformed consumers in order to ensure that only high quality is provided in the market.

[12] The objectives of honest NPOs determine what price they will choose within the feasible range. If they are very concerned with expanding output, they are likely to price at or near the indifference price $p_{n^*}$. Alternatively, if they are mainly interested in the well-being of their existing clientele, they would be expected to charge a price closer to the lower end of the feasible range ($c_H$) even though they would face excess demand at such a price due to honest nonprofits' limited aggregate supply.

**Proof**: See Appendix A.

Proposition 3 indicates that coexistence of for-profits and nonprofits can lead to the efficient outcome. If enough uninformed consumers are served by the non-profit sector, the fraction of consumers in the for-profit sector who are well-informed rises sufficiently that only high quality for-profits remain viable. This makes further expansion of the nonprofit sector unnecessary to alleviate the market's failure to provide optimal quality. There would be no observable quality difference between for-profit and nonprofit firms. Further, as the prevalence of low quality for-profits goes to zero, $p_{\mathrm{n}}$ must converge to $c_H$ because uninformed consumers' willingness to pay a price premium for quality assurance approaches zero. Thus, with a large enough nonprofit sector and sufficient enforcement of the NDC to prevent profit-motivated firms from obtaining nonprofit status, the Pareto efficient outcome characterized by Rosen (1974) in the full information case can be attained.

*3.4.2. Regime 2: Moderately enforced nondistribution constraint*

If the NDC is enforced less vigorously, the lowest price at which FPIDs could break even price may fall below uninformed consumers' maximum willingness to pay for high quality but remain the minimum average cost of high quality ($c_H < p_{\mathrm{FPID}} \leq p_{\mathrm{n}^*}$). That is, at the price at which uninformed consumers are indifferent between certain high quality and taking their chances in the for-profit sector, profit-motivated firms could appropriate a competitive return by mimicking honest nonprofits. Thus, at any $p_{\mathrm{n}} \geq p_{\mathrm{FPID}}$, FPIDs pool with honest NPOs making such a price unsustainable by destroying the credibility of nonprofit status as a signal of quality. Honest NPOs can prevent profit-motivated firms from obtaining nonprofit status by keeping their prices below $p_{\mathrm{FPID}}$. However, since $p_{\mathrm{n}} < p_{\mathrm{FPID}} \leq p_{\mathrm{n}^*}$, all uninformed consumers prefer nonprofits and excess demand will exist in the nonprofit sector.

This provides a new and novel explanation for observations of rationing by the nonprofit sector. [13] With imperfect enforcement of the nondistribution constraint, nonprofit pricing is constrained by the threat of entry by FPIDs. Effectively, if acting like a nonprofit is profitable, the nonprofit sector would attract for-profits in disguise, but NPOs can prevent this by 'limit pricing' (charging $< p_{\mathrm{FPID}}$). Thus, potential competition from FPIDs due to imperfect enforcement of the NDC forces

[13] Author's calculations from the 1986 Inventory of Long-Term Care Places indicate that NPOs are more likely to have very high occupancy rates and Weisbrod (1988) finds that NPOs are more likely to have waiting lists.

honest nonprofits to keep their prices below $p_{n^*}$. The positive spillover effect of nonprofit market share on for-profit quality identified in Propositions 2 and 3 continue to hold in this regime.

#### *3.4.3. Regime 3: Weak nondistribution constraint*

If enforcement of the NDC is so weak that FPIDs' break even price is below the minimum average cost of high quality care ($p_{\text{FPID}} \leq c_H$), the difficulty of converting operating surpluses for private gain is insufficient to offset the low quality cost advantage enjoyed by for-profits in disguise. This makes the for-profit in disguise strategy profitable at any price high enough for honest NPOs to break even without subsidies. To prevent nonprofit status from being debased as a signal of quality, honest NPOs must have better access than FPIDs to subsidies such as donations, volunteer labor, or other inputs provided for less than their full economic cost. Subsidies available on an equal basis to all nonprofits, such as tax exemptions, will not give honest NPOs a substantial comparative advantage because these subsidies are almost as good as cash to FPIDs when the NDC is weak. There are three subcases depending on the amount of subsidies available to honest nonprofits but not to FPIDs.

(a) If honest NPOs receive sufficient subsidies that they can break even at a price $p_n < p_{\text{FPID}}$, they can engage in a limit pricing strategy analogous to that in Regime 2. Since no FPIDs would be viable at $p_n < p_{\text{FPID}}$, the credibility of nonprofit status as a signal of quality is preserved. However, since the price would necessarily be less than $c_H$, informed consumers will also patronize the nonprofit sector. Thus, the quality signal conferred by nonprofit status is used inefficiently because the segmentation of the market by consumer information is not maintained. An increase in supply by honest NPOs would raise quality *in the market as a whole*. However, since all consumers prefer the lower priced nonprofit sector, the fraction of consumers in the for-profit sector who are informed would not rise. Thus, the spillover effect on for-profit sector quality characterized in Propositions 2 and 3 would not occur.

(b) If honest nonprofits do not have sufficient access to subsidies to break even at a price unattractive to FPIDs, they may still be able to remain viable by using whatever subsidies they have to support a price below the minimum average cost of high quality care ($p_{\text{FPID}} < p_n < c_H$). At such a price, informed consumers prefer the nonprofit sector and their business helps honest NPOs remain viable in the same way that sales to informed consumers allow high quality for-profits to break even. However, some FPIDs can also remain viable, just like low quality firms could be viable in the for-profit sector. This is the only case in which honest NPOs and FPIDs coexist.

(c) If honest NPOs have little or no access to subsidies that are unavailable to for-profits in disguise, honest NPOs cannot break even and nonprofit status cannot serve as a credible signal of quality. Uninformed consumers' trust of the nonprofit sector will not be validated as only for-profits in disguise could remain viable.

## 4. Sketch of an alternative, full information model

In the model developed in the previous section, consumers were assumed to have identical preferences. Thus, any variations in quality result from asymmetric information and constitute a failure of the market to provide optimal quality to all consumers.

As an alternative, consider a model with full information and heterogeneous quality preferences. For-profits are treated as profit-maximizers, nonprofits are assumed to maximize a utility function with quality as one of its arguments, and the industry is again assumed to be competitive. Managerial preferences might lead nonprofits to stake out the high quality market niche (for example, managers of NPOs may value their community image as high quality caregivers), leaving the lower quality niche to the for-profit sector. However, if nonprofits were eliminated, high quality for-profits could profitably replace them because higher quality commands a higher price when consumers are well-informed, making the ownership structure of the industry irrelevant to consumer welfare despite observable intersectoral quality differences. The optimal quality spectrum would be provided even by an exclusively for-profit industry.

The welfare implications of quality differences across sectors would be quite different in the two models. With full information and heterogeneous preferences, the market provides the mix of qualities demanded by consumers regardless of the relative prevalence of for- and nonprofit firms. Any observed relationship between ownership and quality would result from differences in managerial preferences but would not have any welfare implications to consumers. Conversely, in the asymmetric information model with homogeneous preferences, the existence of multiple quality levels implies a market failure and nonprofits reduce the extent of this market failure even if there appears to be little or no quality difference across sectors. Thus, presence or absence of observable quality differences between for- and nonprofits does not provide *prima facie* evidence that the nonprofit sector is either socially useful or superfluous.

## 5. Implications for empirical research and policy

The model developed here yields two primary empirical implications. First, a natural implication of the Arrow/Hansmann hypothesis that NPOs enjoy a comparative advantage in trustworthiness is that NPOs should disproportionately attract poorly informed consumers. Using data from the 1985 National Nursing Home Survey, Hirth (1993) found evidence that residents of nonprofit nursing homes were more likely to have certain characteristics that indicated high information acquisition costs (e.g., no living spouse or children to help with decision-making). Holtmann and Ullmann (1991) also report evidence consistent with self-selection of more poorly informed consumers into nonprofit nursing homes, and Schlesinger et al. (1996) report similar findings for utilization review organizations.

Second, a result of this sorting of uninformed consumers into the nonprofit sector is a competitive spillover: the larger the nonprofit market share, the higher the likelihood that for-profits deliver the promised quality (the 'Inverse Gresham's Law'). Thus, areas with higher nonprofit market shares are expected to have higher quality both at market level and in the for-profit sector unless the nondistribution constraint is very weak. Previous studies of the relationship between ownership and quality use categorical variables for type of ownership to capture the direct effects of ownership, but omit any measure of the prevalence of nonprofit firms in the market. Omitting such a measure, which could capture the spillover effect, can bias the coefficient on the ownership variables. If beneficial spillovers occur, the coefficient on an ownership variable will be biased towards zero because the performance of for- and nonprofit firms will tend to converge in areas with high nonprofit shares. Any observed differences would represent only a lower bound on the effect of the nonprofit sector on quality. Since nonprofit enterprise is more likely to be welfare-enhancing when beneficial spillovers occur, this bias raises the likelihood of errant policy prescriptions. Conversely, if provision of high quality or social goods by NPOs crowds out provision by the for-profit sector (as would occur in the full information model sketched in Section 4), the coefficient on an ownership variable will be biased away from zero.

The influence of competition from the nonprofit sector on the performance of the for-profit sector depends on nonprofit market share which varies by industry, time, and location. Since nonprofit market share may be endogenous, exogenous determinants of nonprofit market share can be used as instrumental variables. Estimates by Hansmann (1987) of the determinants of nonprofit market share in several industries suggest several plausible instruments such as proxies for demand growth (areas in which demand is growing rapidly are likely to have higher for-profit market shares since the capital market constraints faced by NPOs make rapid expansion difficult) and state tax rates (NPOs have a greater competitive advantage in areas with higher corporate income or property tax rates).

Since very little empirical research has focused on competition between firms of different ownership types, there is insufficient evidence on how ownership affects socially important dimensions of performance at the market level.[14]

[14] See Hirth (1997) for a review of the evidence on competition, ownership, and provision of socially desired services in the hospital industry. One particularly interesting study by Frank and Salkever (1991) examined how an increase in the provision of charity care by one nonprofit hospital affects charity care provision by its nonprofit competitors. They find that competitors raised their level of charity care, presumably to maintain their goodwill or social prestige. Extending their approach to competition between nonprofit and for-profit facilities would be useful.

Further, most discussions of mixed ownership industries emphasize a negative aspect of competition: for-profits might force NPOs to focus on activities and behaviors rewarded by the market, eroding their ability to mitigate market failures. Such an outcome is certainly possible, particularly if the nondistribution constraint is weak. However, this paper demonstrates beneficial spillovers of intersectoral competition that have previously gone unrecognized.

Weisbrod (1988, p. 163) states two goals for public policy towards nonprofit organizations. First, policy should "insulate nonprofits from pressures to deviate from [their] social role..." Second, policy should help achieve "a better balance of institutional responsibilities" between for- and nonprofits. With these goals in mind, this paper provides insights as to how public and private actions can increase the likelihood that NPOs engage in socially beneficial activities.

If the nondistribution constraint is poorly enforced (Regime 3), subsidies contingent only upon nonprofit status, such as tax exemptions, are almost as good as cash to for-profits in disguise. Expanding such subsidies invites their abuse unless the expansion is accompanied by greater enforcement of the NDC. Thus, benefits available to all nonprofits unlikely to help the nonprofit sector achieve its social goals unless they are accompanied by a meaningful nondistribution constraint. In this sense, nontargetted subsidies and enforcement of the NDC are complements in promoting the economic viability of honest nonprofits. [15]

Conversely, tax deductions for donations can substitute for enforcement of the nondistribution constraint. If some potential donors can identify high quality facilities, honest NPOs will have a comparative advantage in access to contributions. Thus, policies to encourage donations can help honest NPOs remain viable even when enforcement of the NDC is insufficient, by itself, to make the for-profit in disguise strategy unprofitable. This may be relevant in the nursing home industry where most nonprofits are run by religious or fraternal societies and many donations are in the form of volunteer labor and gifts from patients' families or board members. Such donors are likely to be well-positioned to ensure that their contributions accrue to worthy homes.

These considerations provide qualified support for proprietary firms' complaints of 'unfair competition' from the nonprofit sector. Since exemptions and other general subsidies may primarily benefit NPOs that are actually profit-seekers in disguise, grievances against these publicly provided competitive advantages appear justified if the nondistribution constraint is weak. However, with lax

[15] The US Internal Revenue Service's ability to enforce the NDC has received considerable attention (Gray, 1993; US House of Representatives Committee on Ways and Means, 1993). Recent legislation expanded the set of sanctions available to the IRS to use against organizations violating the NDC (Johnsson, 1996).

enforcement, honest NPOs have an equally valid claim about unfair competition from for-profits in disguise.

**Acknowledgements**

This work has benefited from comments by Mark Pauly, Bob Inman, Paul Taubman, Mike Chernew, Elizabeth Powers, Edward Norton, Adel Varghese, and two anonymous reviewers. I am also grateful for the financial support of the Agency for Health Care Policy and Research (HS 06934-01), a National Institute on Aging training grant and a Boettner Institute for Financial Gerontology dissertation grant. I retain exclusive property rights to all errors.

**Appendix A**

**Proof of Proposition 1**: Recall that $\lambda'$ is the proportion of high quality firms at which uninformed consumers are indifferent between purchasing and leaving the market. If mimicking becomes an unprofitable strategy before uninformed consumers leave the market (i.e., while $\lambda \geq \lambda'$), equilibrium exists: there is no entry or exit incentive for firms and consumers maximize expected utility and have no incentive to change their purchasing decisions. However, if $\lambda < \lambda'$, equilibrium fails to exist once $\lambda$ falls below $\lambda'$ because the market will 'cycle.' Uninformed consumers' expected utility from purchasing becomes negative, causing them to drop out of the market (receiving their reservation utility of zero). However, once uninformed consumers drop out of the market, only informed consumers remain and, hence, only high quality firms can break even and uninformed consumer will want to re-enter the market. Once they re-enter, low quality firms will also want to enter and entry will be profitable until $\lambda < \lambda'$, again causing uninformed consumers to leave the market.

(i)(a) The results of Rosen (1974) carry over. Some firms can break even providing the first best bundle to informed consumers and the 'lucky' uninformed. With free entry, undercutting prices above $c_H$ is a profitable strategy while prices below $c_H$ are not remunerative. Entry continues until each firm produces at the average cost minimizing level because any other scale fails to break even.

(i)(b) From Lemma 1, uninformed consumers believe that any firm offering $p \neq c_H$ provides the lowest quality level, $L$. Thus, low quality firms attract no customers unless they charge $c_H$. Since raising quality is costly $[\partial c(Q,s)/\partial s > 0]$ and does not alter beliefs, higher quality does not increase sales. Entry proceeds as long as profit opportunities exist. Since low quality firms are price takers at $p = c_H$, sales per firm must decline to $Q_{\min}$ before profits fall to zero.

(ii) These are simply the numbers of firms such that (i)(a) and (b) hold. Due to the free entry assumption, this amounts to solving the zero profit conditions for each type of firm active in the market.

(a) and (b) The zero profit condition for high quality firms is:

$$\frac{1-\alpha}{N_H+N_L}+\frac{\alpha}{N_H}=Q_{\mathrm{EH}}. \tag{A.1}$$

This condition requires that total demand faced by the firm equals the efficient scale of production. The first left-hand side term represents per firm demand from the uninformed while the second term reflects demand from informed consumers.

The low quality zero profit condition is:

$$\frac{1-\alpha}{N_H+N_L}=Q_{\min} \tag{A.2}$$

Eq. (A.2) equates low quality firms' demand from the uninformed to the break-even level of output. Solving Eqs. (A.1) and (A.2) for $N_H$ and $N_L$:

$$N_H=\frac{\alpha}{Q_{\mathrm{EH}}-Q_{\min}} \tag{A.3}$$

and

$$N_L=\frac{1-\alpha}{Q_{\min}}-\frac{\alpha}{Q_{\mathrm{EH}}-Q_{\min}}. \tag{A.4}$$

To see that only high quality firms are viable if a sufficient factions of consumers is informed, suppose $\alpha=(Q_{\mathrm{EH}}-Q_{\min})/Q_{\mathrm{EH}}$. Substituting into Eq. (A.1) yields $N_H=1/Q_{\mathrm{EH}}$. Thus, the number of uninformed consumers per firm is $(1-\alpha)/N_H=(1-\alpha)Q_{\mathrm{EH}}$. Substituting the expression for $\alpha$ and simplifying, implies that the number of uninformed consumers per firms is $(1-\alpha)Q_{\mathrm{EH}}=Q_{\min}$. Therefore, if a low quality firm joins the market, the number of uninformed consumers per firm would fall below $Q_{\min}$, which is the minimum scale at which a low quality firm could break even when mimicking the high quality price.

**Proof of Proposition 2**: As discussed in the text, only uninformed consumers purchase from NPOs and only honest NPOs are viable if $c_H<p_n<p_{\mathrm{FPID}}$. For any fraction of informed consumers ($\alpha$) such that some low quality firms are viable in the for-profit sector ($\lambda<1$), the zero profit conditions that must hold for high and low quality for-profits, respectively, are:

$$\frac{1-\alpha-\gamma}{N_H+N_L}+\frac{\alpha}{N_H}=Q_{\mathrm{EH}} \tag{A.5}$$

and

$$\frac{1-\alpha-\gamma}{N_H+N_L}=Q_{\min}. \tag{A.6}$$

From Eq. (A.6), the number of for-profits in equilibrium is $N_H+N_L=(1-\alpha-\gamma)/Q_{\min}$, which declines in $\gamma$. Substituting Eq. (A.6) into Eq. (A.5) and solving for $N_H$ yields $N_H=\alpha/(Q_{\mathrm{EH}}-Q_{\min})$, the same number of high quality firms as in Proposition 1. Since $N_H$ is independent of $\gamma$, a smaller number of low quality firms accounts for the entire decrease in the total number of firms and equilibrium $\lambda$ increases in $\gamma$. Once $\lambda=1$ is attained, the zero profit condition for *Hs* becomes:

$$\frac{\alpha}{N_H}+\frac{1-\alpha-\gamma}{N_H}=Q_{\mathrm{EH}} \tag{A.7}$$

which implies $N_H=(1-\gamma)/Q_{\mathrm{EH}}$.

**Proof of Proposition 3**: Suppose the size of the nonprofit sector is $1-\alpha$. Proposition 1 implies that no low quality for-profits operate if the number of uninformed consumers purchasing from for-profits is below $Q_{\min}N_H$. Thus, reducing the size of the nonprofit sector to $1-\alpha-Q_{\min}N_H$ still leaves the first low quality for-profit with demand below its minimum profitable scale. Thus, all consumers continue to receive high quality and firms still earn zero profits.

## References


Ad Hoc Committee to Defend Health Care, 1997. For our patients, not for profits. Journal of the American Medical Association 278, 1733–1734.

Arrow, K.J., 1963. Uncertainty and the welfare economics of medical care. American Economic Review 53, 941–973.

Cohen, J.W., Spector, W.D., 1996. The effect of medicaid reimbursement on quality of care in nursing homes. Journal of Health Economics 15, 23–48.

Cooper, R., Ross, T.W., 1984. Prices, product qualities and asymmetric information: the competitive case. Review of Economic Studies 51, 197–207.

Cutler, D., Sheiner, L., 1993. Policy options for long-term care, NBER working paper No. 4302.

Davis, M.A., 1991. On nursing home quality: a review and analysis. Medical Care Review, pp. 129–166.

Erard, B., Feinstein, J.S., 1994. Honesty and evasion in the tax compliance game. RAND Journal of Economics 25, 1–19.

Frank, R.G., Salkever, D.S., 1991. The supply of charity services by nonprofit hospitals: motives and market structures. RAND Journal of Economics 22, 430–445.

Frank, R.G., Salkever, D.S., 1994. Nonprofit organizations in the health sector. Journal of Economic Perspectives 8, 129–144.

Gertler, P.J., 1992. Medicaid and the cost of improving access to nursing home care. Review of Economics and Statistics 74, 338–345.

Gray, B.H., 1993. Ownership matters: Health reform and the future of nonprofit health care. Inquiry 30, 352–361.

Hansmann, H., 1980. The role of nonprofit enterprise. Yale Law Journal 89, 835–901.
Hansmann, H., 1987. The effect of tax exemption and other factors on the market share of nonprofit vs. for-profit firms. National Tax Journal 40, 71–82.
Harrington, C., Preston, S., Grant, L., Swan, J.H., 1992. Revised trends in states' nursing home capacity. Health Affairs 11, 170–180.
Hawes, C., Phillips, C.D., 1986. The changing structure of the nursing home industry and the impact of ownership on quality, cost, and access. In: Gray, B.H. (Ed.), For-profit enterprise in health care. Washington, DC: National Academy Press, Washington, DC, pp. 492–541.
Hirth, R.A., 1993, Consumer information and ownership in the nursing home industry. Unpublished Ph.D. dissertation, University of Pennsylvania.
Hirth, R.A., 1997. Competition between for-profit and nonprofit health care providers: Can it help achieve social goals?. Medical Care Research Review 54, 414–438.
Holtmann, A.G., Idson, T.L., 1993. Wage determination of registered nurses in proprietary and nonprofit nursing homes. Journal of Human Resources 28, 55–79.
Holtmann, A.G., Ullmann, S.G., 1991. Transactions costs, uncertainty, and not-for-profit organizations. Annals of Public and Cooperative Economy 62, 641–653.
Johnsson, J. 1996. New IRS tax penalties target doctors in deals with hospitals. American Medical News 39, September 9, 1,41.
Klein, B., Leffler, K., 1981. The role of market forces in assuring contractual performance. Journal of Political Economy 89, 615–641.
Mendleson, M.A., 1974. Tender Loving Greed. Alfred A. Knopf, New York.
National Center for Health Statistics, 1987. Advance data, no. 131, March 27.
Nyman, J.A., 1993. Testing for excess demand in nursing home care markets. Medical Care 31, 680–693.
O'Brien, J., Saxberg, B.O., Smith, H.L., 1983. For-profit or not-for-profit nursing homes: Does it matter?. Gerontologist 23, 341–348.
Relman, A.S., Reinhardt, U.E., 1986. Debating for-profit health care and the ethics of physicians. Health Affairs 5, 5–31.
Rosen, S., 1974. Hedonic prices and implicit markets: Product differentiation in pure competition. Journal of Political Economy 82, 34–55.
Scanlon, W.J., 1980. Nursing home utilization patterns: implications for policy. Journal of Health Politics, Policy and Law 4, 619–641.
Schlesinger, M., Gray, B., Bradford, E., 1996. Charity and compassion: the role of nonprofit ownership in a managed health care system. Journal of Health Politics, Policy and Law 21, 697–751.
Steinberg, R., 1993. Public policy and the performance of nonprofit organizations. Nonprofit and Voluntary Sector Quarterly 22, 13–32.
US House of Representatives Committee on Ways and Means, 1993. Federal Tax Laws Applicable to the Activities of Tax-Exempt Charitable Organizations. US Government Printing Office, Washington, DC.
Vladeck, B.C., 1980. Unloving care: The nursing home tragedy. Basic Books, New York.
Vogel, R.J., 1985. The industrial organization of the nursing home industry. In: Vogel R.J., Palmer, H.C., (Eds.), Long-term Care: Perspectives from Research and Demonstrations. Aspen, Rockville, MD.
Weisbrod, B.A., 1988. The nonprofit economy. Harvard Univ. Press, Cambridge, MA.
Weisbrod, B.A., 1991. The health care quadrilemma: An essay on technological change, insurance, quality of care, and cost containment. Journal of Economic Literature 29, 523–552.
Wolinsky, A., 1983. Prices as signals of product quality. Review of Economic Studies 50, 647–658.

# [15]

JOURNAL OF COMPARATIVE ECONOMICS **26**, 246–261 (1998)
ARTICLE NO. JE981520

# The Wage Differential between Nonprofit Institutions and Corporations: Getting More by Paying Less?[1]

Femida Handy

*Faculty of Environmental Studies, York University, Toronto, Ontario, Canada M3J 1P3*

and

Eliakim Katz*

*Department of Economics, Faculty of Arts, York University, Toronto, Ontario, Canada M3J 1P3*

Received August 14, 1997; revised November 21, 1997

**Handy, Femida, and Katz, Eliakim**—The Wage Differential between Nonprofit Institutions and Corporations: Getting More by Paying Less?

In this paper, we suggest that lower wages in nonprofits may reflect a successful policy of generating trust by causing positive self selection in managerial employees of nonprofits. In this way, nonprofits resolve a major principal-agent problem. Our paper ties in three aspects of nonprofit institutions. First, nonprofits often emerge in markets which are characterized by asymmetric information and the need for consumer trust. Second, nonprofits tend to pay their employees, and especially managers, a lower wage than for-profits. Third, managers of nonprofits have very different characteristics from their counterparts in the for-profit sector. *J. Comp. Econom.*, June 1998, **26**(2), pp. 246–261. Faculty of Environmental Studies, York University, Toronto, Ontario, Canada M3J 1P3; and Department of Economics, Faculty of Arts, York University, Toronto, Ontario, Canada M3J 1P3. © 1998 Academic Press

*Key Words:* nonprofits; self-selection; wage differentials.

*Journal of Economic Literature* Classification Numbers: L31, J31.

## 1. INTRODUCTION

In terms of economics research nonprofit institutions[2] have traditionally been the poor relatives of their counterparts in the for-profit and government

* Corresponding author.

[1] We thank Burton Weisbrod, Robert Frank, two anonymous referees, and John Bonin, the editor of this Journal, for extensive comments and suggestions. All remaining errors are ours. We also thank the Faculty of Environmental Studies and the Faculty of Arts at York University for partial financial support.

[2] The term "nonprofit institution" refers to nongovernment organizations that are legally subject to a "nondistribution constraint," which implies that residual earnings cannot be distrib-

0147-5967/98 $25.00

sectors.[3] In recent years this has changed and now the nonprofit sector attracts considerable attention in the economics literature. This increased interest in nonprofits reflects their significant and growing role in modern economies: In 1966, 3.3% of gross national product in the United States originated in the nonprofit sector. By 1985, this sector generated 4.4% of gross national product, and a recent estimate suggests that nonprofits in the United States now account for 6% of gross national product. Indeed, a recent survey of current business (Bureau of Economic Analysis, 1997) estimates that the gross domestic product produced by the nonprofit sector is equal to almost 20% of the gross product produced by the for-profit sector, and exceeds the output of the Federal Government.[4]

In particular, the nonprofit sector is a major player in the labor market. Its share of service-sector employment was 14% in 1982 (Rudney, 1987) and, more recently (Zagorin, 1993), has been estimated at over 7 million people. Moreover, the above figures are likely to represent a lower bound since they often exclude items such as volunteer time and non receipted donations of money and goods.

In this paper, we focus on a labor market issue relating to nonprofits. Specifically, we explain why nonprofits tend to pay their managers[5] a lower wage than for-profits and link this to two other major differences between nonprofits and for-profits. First, nonprofits are relatively more prevalent in markets that are characterized by asymmetric information and in which, therefore, consumer trust is an issue. Second, managers of nonprofits have been found to have personality traits that are significantly different from their counterparts in the for-profit sector.

The emergence of nonprofits in addition to, or instead of, for-profits in a particular sector of the economy, has often been explained in the literature in terms of trust.[6] Nonprofit institutions may dominate for-profit institutions

---

uted to individuals who control the organization, such as officers, members, or directors (see Hansmann, 1987). This definition encompasses, for example, most universities, hospitals, and charities. However, it excludes organizational arrangements like labor cooperatives, in which members do have a claim to earning residuals.

[3] The seminal works in this field include Weisbrod (1977, 1988), Hansmann (1980), and Young (1983). There are also several journals that are devoted to this sector including the *Non-Profit and Voluntary Sector Quarterly* and the *Annals of Public and Cooperative Economics.*

[4] Considering contributions and assets, an equally impressive picture emerges. In 1985, nonprofits received contributions of over $75 billion, representing 2.4% of gross national product, from private sources (Weisbrod, 1988) and, in the early 1990s, this figure reached $124.3 billion (Zagorin, 1993). The value of the assets of the U.S. tax-exempt nonprofits was in the neighborhood of $670 billion as of 1988 (Renz, 1991).

[5] For the rest of this paper, the term "manager" is used to refer to an individual who is employed in a decision-making capacity. This includes executives and is likely to include certain professionals as well.

[6] A parallel discussion examining nonprofits versus *government* institutions has tended to focus on electoral considerations. For example, the supply of certain goods and services by nonprofits

in markets that exhibit a principal-agent problem between consumers and producers. Implicit in this claim is the assumption that nonprofits have a comparative advantage over for-profits in generating consumer, and donor, trust (Hansmann, 1980 and Weisbrod, 1988).

However, the mere absence of a profit motive is a weak basis for trust. The exploitation of the consumer in the name of profit maximization can easily be replaced by reduction in managerial or employee effort and the increase of perquisites (Liston, 1977; Zagorin, 1993). In order to fulfil their role effectively, nonprofit will have to convince the public that such abuses are unlikely to occur. Therefore, they will actively pursue policies aimed at enhancing public trust.

In a recent paper, Handy (1995) considers the issue of trust afforded to a nonprofit by the public. She argues that the board of trustees secures public trust for the nonprofit by offering its reputation as collateral. The public infers correctly that its own risk has been reduced from the fact that the board of trustees has exposed itself to a correlate of this risk. The board of trustees will wish to minimize its own, and therefore the public's, risks. This policy increases the *external* trust afforded to the nonprofit.

In general, however, trustees are not involved in the day to day running of nonprofits, and they have to rely on the management of the nonprofit to ensure quality and efficiency. Hence, in addition to the consumer/producer agency problem, nonprofits have to deal with an incentive issue regarding trustees and management. To safeguard their reputational collateral, trustees must be able to trust the management of the nonprofit to do its job honestly and conscientiously. There is, therefore a need for *internal* trust within the nonprofit.

Certainly, the board of directors of a for-profit institution faces a similar agency problem. However, there are relatively straightforward measures of managerial performance in a for-profit, e.g. profit, that are not, in general, available to a nonprofit. Hence, the agency problem between the trustees of a nonprofit and its management is potentially more severe in a nonprofit than in a for-profit. Moreover, problems of external trust are likely to be correlated with problems of internal trust.[7] Hence, nonprofits will tend to face more incentive problems than for-profits.

One way in which nonprofits may reduce the internal trust problem is to

rather than by the public has been explained in terms of satisfying the public-good needs of groups that do not straddle the median voter (Weisbrod, 1988; Handy, 1997).

[7] The dearth of performance measures required by the public (external trust) will often imply a dearth in the type of measures required by the trustees (internal trust). The issue is one of quantifiable measures. For example, relatives of a resident at an old age home cannot measure certain aspects of the treatment, e.g., the tenderness and respect accorded the patient, and it seems likely that trustees will not be able to measure it either.

attract committed[8] individuals to managerial positions in these institutions. There is a general consensus in the literature that nonprofit managers are significantly different in this regard from their counterparts in the for-profit sector (see Young, 1983; Weisbrod, 1983; Mirvis and Hackett, 1983). Nonprofits appear to have managed to attract individuals who have a strong commitment to the philosophy of the nonprofit and a subordinate interest in monetary gains. In other words, the internal agency problem within nonprofits seems to be at least partially resolved through self-selection of managerial personnel.[9]

This paper suggests that nonprofits attract committed individuals by offering them compensation packages that promote self-selection among potential employees. We suggest that such compensation packages may well involve lower money wages and, possibly, a larger component of institution-specific fringe benefits compared with those offered in others sectors of the economy. Our approach interprets the lower monetary wages of management in the nonprofit sector as reflecting a supply side compensating differential combined with demand side implications for the product of the employee. Committed individuals like working for nonprofits and are, therefore, prepared to work for less while also doing a better job than uncommitted managers.[10]

Our interpretation of the fact of lower managerial incomes in nonprofits compared with for-profits may initially appear counter-intuitive. The efficiency wage hypothesis proposes that difficulties in the monitoring of managers may be partially resolved by an *excessive* wage, because a high wage implies that a greater penalty is imposed on shirkers who are caught and fired. Hence, to the extent that the monitoring of nonprofit managers is more difficult than the monitoring of for-profit managers, their wages in the nonprofit sector might have been expected to be *higher* than in other sectors (Ito and Domian, 1987). However, managerial wages in the nonprofit sector are persistently lower than in other sectors.

It has been suggested that the paying of lower wages in nonprofits "may be a false economy," since "by overpaying, the firm may obtain a more than

[8] A committed individual may be defined as one whose preferences are such that, given the same parameters (prices, wage rate, etc.), he will provide the nonprofit with greater output than a uncommitted individual with the same abilities.

[9] To the extent that the public recognizes that the internal trust problem has been resolved, the external trust problem is also reduced.

[10] Eckel and Steinberg (1994) assume that nonprofit managers have utility functions that include "perks, public goods, and income." They argue that, because potential managers differ in their marginal rate of substitution between perks and public goods, policies to encourage the selection of managers with preference for public goods over perks and income would result in better-managed nonprofits. Our model complements Eckel and Steinberg's model, in that we describe a particular policy that will achieve the effects suggested by them. See also Preston (1990), Gassler (1989), and Schiff and Weisbrod (1991) for related discussions.

corresponding increase in productivity'' (Steinberg, 1990, p. 161). Alternatively, and this is the contention of this paper, adverse selection issues, i.e. the attempt to screen out uncommitted managers, may dominate moral hazard issues, i.e. the need to ensure that such employees do not shirk. For a related discussion, see Steinberg (1990). Indeed, in the case of nonprofits, the effect of self-selection reduces the need both for monitoring and for the payment of an efficiency wage.

Before proceeding, a word regarding our focus on management rather than other employees. The principal-agent problem between trustees and management is especially acute in nonprofits; the absence of a measure of managerial success implies that managers may have a considerable amount of freedom in determining the way in which things are done in a nonprofit. Thus, the commitment of the manager of a nonprofit to the goals of the trustees is crucial. In contrast, nonmanagers tend to have less discretion in their jobs, so that the importance of commitment by such employees will not significantly differ between nonprofits and for-profits. In analyzing self-selection mechanisms aimed at enhancing commitment, we restrict our attention to management.[11]

In Section 2, we examine the evidence on managerial compensation in the nonprofit sector, as well as the differences between the personal characteristics of nonprofit and for-profit managers. In Section 3, we present a formal model showing how nonprofits may induce managerial self-selection through a policy of lower wages. We analyze the factors that affect the costs and benefits of such a policy. In Section 4, we examine the potential role of fringe benefits in promoting self selection. Section 5 summarizes our findings.

## 2. EMPLOYEE COMPENSATION AND CHARACTERISTICS IN NONPROFIT INSTITUTIONS

Nonprofits appear to pay managers and professionals lower wages than for-profits or than public-sector firms. In contrast, there is little difference between the wages paid by nonprofits and for-profits to other employees. Using data from a 1979 census survey and a 1980 survey of job characteristics, Preston (1989) analyzes the wage differentials for employees in the for-profit and nonprofit sectors in the United States. Controlling for human capital, demographic structure, occupation, flexibility and rigidity of work schedules, she finds a negative wage differential of 20% for managers and professionals

[11] In addition to the smaller role that commitment plays in the productivity of nonmanagerial workers, its supply-side considerations will also be smaller. Nonmanagerial workers will be less willing to give up income in order to work for a nonprofit because their jobs are less likely to influence the cause and direction of the nonprofit. Furthermore, nonmanagers will tend to be in lower income categories and the demand for a fulfilling job is likely to be a normal good.

but no significant difference among clerical employees. The differential is especially robust for nonprofits that supply economic public goods.

The negative wage differential for professionals is confirmed in several further studies that compare earnings for lawyers working in public interest, i.e. nonprofit firms[12] and in for-profit law firms. Weisbrod's (1983) findings indicate that for-profit law firms pay almost 20% more than do nonprofit law firms for graduates with similar qualifications.[13] Other studies find that average starting salaries for lawyers in nonprofit law firms are almost 40% lower than in private practice. Indeed, in the late eighties, the starting salary for a New York City lawyer working in large and highly visible nonprofits was 66% less than in large for-profits (Linden, Pencil, and Studley, 1989; Studley, 1989).

In a similar vein, Frank (1996) reports on an employment survey done at Cornell University that indicates that Cornell graduates employed in the for-profit sector earned 59% more on average than those employed in the nonprofit sector, after controlling for employee variations based on gender, choice of curriculum, and academic performance.[14] In view of this and other evidence,[15] lower managerial and professional wages in nonprofits appear to be a stylized fact that this paper aims to explain.

Managers and professionals working for nonprofits and for for-profits differ significantly in characteristics that are suggestive of commitment or devotion to the organization and its cause. Young (1983) suggests that the managers of nonprofits have strong commitment to the philosophy of the nonprofit and primarily view the nonprofit organization as fulfiling a social need rather than as a business.

Rawls, Ulrich, and Nelson (1975) report on a study of students at Vanderbilt University that notes very different characteristics in those individuals who had subsequently entered the nonprofit sector compared with and those who worked in the for-profit sector. This study finds major differences in ''person-

[12] Such firms represent the poor and lobby for social causes. They do not rely on fees but are subsidized by endowments and donations.

[13] Goddeeris (1988) raises doubts about the results obtained by Weisbrod (1983) regarding the observed wage differentials. He reworks the data to show that a selection bias may have resulted in the findings as noted by Weisbrod.

[14] While there appears to be no information on the specific jobs in which these graduates were employed, it seems likely, given that that they had obtained a university degree from a top school, that they were employed in managerial or professional capacity on the whole.

[15] Several other studies also indicate that lower wages are paid for certain managerial occupations in the nonprofit sector as compared with those in the for-profit sector. (See Mirvis and Hackett, 1983; Shackett and Trapani, 1987; Preston, 1988; Ball, 1991; Roomkin and Weisbrod, 1994; Emanuele, 1995). Leete's (1994) findings replicate Preston's findings. However, on using a larger set of control variables, she does not find negative wage differentials for the sector as a whole, although she continues to find evidence of lower nonprofit wages in some industries.

ality, values, and behavior'' but no significant differences in problem solving ability, intelligence, or creativity. Those choosing employment in the nonprofit sector gave higher ranking to being cheerful, forgiving, and helpful, while those who chose the for-profit sector attached a high priority to financial prosperity, ambition, neatness, and obedience.

Mirvis and Hackett (1983) assert that an important difference between for-profit and nonprofit managers is their attitude towards the goals of the nonprofit, since ''the latter bring to their jobs a greater commitment and nonmonetary orientation'' (Mirvis and Hackett, 1983, p. 10). Self-sorting is suggested by Hansmann who writes that nonprofits attract ''managers from that class of individuals whose preferences are most in consonance with the fiduciary role that the organization is designed to serve'' (Hansmann, 1980, p. 852).

At the same time, Weisbrod (1988) and Frank (1996) suggest that there are no significant differences between individuals accepting employment in the for-profit and nonprofit sectors, in terms of these individuals' educational attributes. Sorting by difficult to measure characteristics is not correlated with other, measurable attributes; nonprofits do not attract less capable managers. Indeed, according to Preston (1989), the wage differentials between nonprofits and for-profits do not reflect differences in productivity. These studies therefore support the notion that nonprofits have been successful in attracting individuals who have characteristics desirable by the nonprofits without incurring the cost of attracting the rejects of the for-profits sector.

## 3. WAGE STRATEGIES TO PROMOTE SELF-SELECTION

Consider a nonprofit firm that wishes to hire a single manager and that draws on an infinitely large[16] pool of potential managers who can be classified in two ways, namely high or low ability (*H* or *L*) and devoted or indifferent (*D* or *I*). The devotion characteristic is specific to the nonprofit and all managers are indifferent in a for-profit. The output of high-ability and devoted managers is denoted by $X_{hd}$ and the output of a high-ability and indifferent manager is $X_{hi}$. The output of a low-ability manager, regardless of devotion or indifference,[17] is $X_l$. We assume that $X_{hd} > X_{hi} > X_l$ in a nonprofit firm, but that $X_{hd} = X_{hi} > X_l$ in a for-profit firm.

The reservation wages of *H* and *L* managers in a for-profit are $W_h$ and $W_l$, respectively, such that $W_h > W_l$. The reservation wage of an *HI* manager in the nonprofit firm is similarly $W_h$. To reflect the psychic benefits that committed

[16] This obviates the need to consider supply constraints. Within the context of our model the firm employs a single worker so that the assumption of an infinite pool of potential managers is not restrictive.

[17] The assumption that the output of a low-ability manager is not affected by his devotion considerably simplifies the analysis without sacrificing the essential results.

managers derive from working for a nonprofit, the reservation wages of an *HD* manager within a non-profit, $W_{hd}$, is, however, assumed to be lower than $W_h$. To simplify the analysis and without affecting the essential results, we assume that the reservation wage of low-ability managers is unaffected by their employer or by their level of devotion; the reservation wage for all *L* managers is $W_l$,[18] such that $W_h > W_{hd} > W_l$.[19]

The proportions of high ability and devoted managers in the population are $a$ and $b$, respectively, and these proportions are independent of one another. The nonprofit firm knows the values of all the above parameters.[20]

The nonprofit is not able to screen for devotion but a costless test for ability levels is available,[21] although this test may not be completely accurate. Denote the event that a manager is tested as having high ability as $H^s$. The nonnegative probability that an *L* manager tests as high ability, $P(H^s | L)$, is $\alpha$. The probability that a high ability manager tests as high ability, $P(H^s | H)$, is $1 - \beta$ and $1 > \beta \geq 0$. The firm requires one manager and, while it discovers the manager's correct classification once he is hired, it must employ the manager for the given period. The firm's aim is to maximize the expected surplus; we examine and compare two alternative wage strategies.[22] The sequence of decision making under both strategies is as follows:

1. Nature determines both the ability and devotion of each manager. This information is known to the manager but not to the firm.
2. The firm announces its strategy.

[18] This parallels the assumption made above, that the output of a low-ability manager is constant across type of employer and commitment.

[19] Whether $W_{hd}$ is greater or smaller than $W_l$ depends on the balance of the preferences of *HD* individuals. However, in this section we focus on the case, where $W_h > W_{hd} > W_l$, since, as will become clear, the alternative assumption, $W_h > W_l > W_{hd}$, yields the trivial result that only devoted workers are employed by the firm. Later in the paper, we show briefly that, because the output of an *HD* worker exceeds that of an *HI* worker in a nonprofit, the results derived here are compatible with $W_{hd} > W_h$.

[20] Of these, the assumption that the firm knows the reservation wages of the different types of workers, is, probably, the most difficult to justify. However, this assumption is no stronger and very possibly weaker than assumptions typically made in the labor economics literature, e.g. those that require employers to know such parameters as workers' risk aversion, or workers' rate of substitution between income and leisure. Presumably, in all these cases, firms learn by experience. We return to this issue in a later footnote.

[21] Given the generally low costs of tests, at least for potential employers, this seems a reasonable assumption. If the costs of the test are substantial, however, strategies aimed at self-selection by committed managers are less likely to be optimal.

[22] In confining our discussion to just two policies we are not suggesting that these are the only possible strategies. Rather, we are providing a flavor of the distinction between policies aimed at inducing self-selection by commitment, and policies aimed at maximizing the pool of high-ability applicants.

3. Given the strategy announced by the firm, all interested managers apply for the job.

4. A manager is chosen at random from the pool of applicants and tested for ability. If he tests as high ability he is given the job and the game ends. If he tests as low ability, the firm selects another manager at random, and this step is repeated until the job is filled.

We begin by considering a strategy aimed at inducing self-selection of devoted managers and denote it as Strategy *I*. In this strategy, the firm offers to pay a wage $W_h^* = W_{hd}$ to a manager who tests high and rejects a manager who tests low. When using Strategy *I*, the firm does not attract any *HI* managers but may end up employing an *L* manager who tested as high. Hence, the downside of this strategy is that because *HI* managers are absent, the probability that a low ability manager who tests as high gets the job is greater. Clearly, the likelihood that this occurs is lower for a smaller number of low ability managers, i.e. a lower $a$ or a more accurate ability test, i.e. a smaller $\alpha$. Indeed, if $\alpha = 0$, this strategy is always optimal, since it ensures that the firm ends up employing an *HD* manager.

In this case, since $W_h^* < W_h$, the applicant pool does not contain any *HI* managers. Hence, the expected output is

$$X_I = P(HD \mid H^s)X_{hd} + P(L \mid H^s)X_l. \tag{1}$$

We have

$$P(HD \mid H^s) = \frac{P(HD \cap H^s)}{P_I(H^s)} = \frac{P(H^s \mid HD)P(HD)}{P_I(H^s)} = \frac{(1-\beta)ab}{P(H^s)} \tag{2}$$

and

$$P(L \mid H^s) = \frac{P(L \cap H^s)}{P_I(H^s)} = \frac{P(H^s \mid L)P(L)}{P_I(H^s)} = \frac{(1-a)\alpha}{P_I(H^s)}, \tag{3}$$

where

$$P_I(H^s) = ab(1-\beta) + \alpha(1-a) \tag{4}$$

is the probability that Strategy *I* will generate an applicant who will test as high ability.

Hence,

$$X_I = \frac{ab(1-\beta)X_{hd} + \alpha(1-a)X_l}{ab(1-\beta) + \alpha(1-a)}. \tag{5}$$

Consider now a strategy aimed at inducing high ability managers to apply. In this strategy, which we call Strategy *II*, the firm offers to pay a wage $W_h^* = W_h$ to a manager who tests high and rejects a manager who tests low. In adopting strategy *II*, the firm attracts all managers and is therefore less likely to employ either an *HD* or an *L* manager. Hence, the costs associated with the higher wage paid out and the lower probability that an *HD* manager will be employed must be offset by the benefits associated with the increased probability that an *HI* rather than an *L* manager will be employed.[23]

In this case the expected output is

$$X_{II} = P(HD|H^s)\cdot X_{hd} + P(HI|H^s)\cdot X_{hi} + P(L|H^s)X_l.$$

We have

$$P(HD|H^s) = \frac{P(HD \cap H^s)}{P_{II}(H^s)} = \frac{P(H^s|HD)P(HD)}{P_{II}(H^s)} = \frac{(1-\beta)ab}{P_{II}(H^s)}, \tag{6}$$

$$P(HI|H^s) = \frac{P(HI \cap H^s)}{P_{II}(H^s)} = \frac{P(H^s|HI)P(HI)}{P_{II}(H^s)} = \frac{(1-\beta)a(1-b)}{P_{II}(H^s)}, \tag{7}$$

and

$$P(L|H^s) = \frac{P(L \cap H^s)}{P_{II}(H^s)} = \frac{P(H^s|L)P(L)}{P_{II}(H^s)} = \frac{(1-a)\alpha}{P_{II}(H^s)}, \tag{8}$$

where

$$P_{II}(H^s) = (1-\beta)ab + (1-a)\alpha + a(1-\beta)(1-b) \tag{9}$$

is the probability that Strategy *II* will generate an applicant who will test as high ability.

Hence

$$X_{II} = \frac{ab(1-\beta)X_{hd} + a(1-\beta)(1-b)X_{hi} + \alpha(1-a)X_l}{ab(1-\beta) + \alpha(1-a) + a(1-\beta)(1-b)}. \tag{10}$$

We now compare output under Strategy *I* with output under Strategy *II*. Defining $\Phi \equiv X_I - X_{II}$, we can write $\Phi$ as

$$\Phi = \frac{(1-b)a(1-\beta)}{P_I(H^s)}\cdot\frac{V}{P_{II}(H^s)} = \mu V, \tag{11}$$

where

[23] As mentioned above, this formulation requires that the firm knows the reservation wages of the different types of workers. Even if it does not, however, it might be able to determine them by experimentation. For example, if the firm underestimates $W_{hd}$, it will find that it is recruiting no HD workers. If it greatly exceeds $W_{hd}$ it will attract both *HI* and *HD* workers. It is true that if it offers a wage which is between $W_{hd}$ and $W_h$, its output will be no different than if it offers $W_{hd}$. However, given a long run horizon, the firm may be expected to experiment to determine $W_{hd}$. This experimentation is not modelled in this paper.

$$V = ab(1 - \beta)(X_{hd} - X_{hi}) - \alpha(1 - a)(X_{hi} - X_l) \quad (12)$$

and

$$\mu = \frac{(1 - b)a(1 - \beta)}{((1 - \beta)ab + (1 - a)\alpha))((1 - \beta)ab + (1 - a)\alpha + (1 - \beta)a(1 - b))} > 0. \quad (13)$$

Thus, a positive V implies that output under Strategy *I* exceeds output under Strategy *II*.

When Strategy *I* replaces Strategy *II*, the firm may gain output because an *HD* manager replaces an *HI* manager or it may lose output because an *L* manager replaces an *HI* manager. These changes can only occur if an HI manager was employed under Strategy *II*. The first term in (11) is the probability that an *HI* manager is employed divided by, or conditional on, the probability that a manager is tested as high ability under Strategy *II* or, equivalently, the probability that an *HI* manager is employed under Strategy *II*.

The first term in (12) is the gain in output when an *HD* manager replaces an *HI* manager, i.e. $X_{hd} - X_{hi}$ times the probability that this occurs, i.e. $ab(1 - \beta)$. The second term in (11) is the loss in output that occurs when the *HI* manager is replaced by an *L* manager, i.e. $X_{hi} - X_l$ times the probability that this occurs, i.e. $(1 - a)\alpha$. The relevant probabilities are divided by, or are conditional on, a manager being tested as high ability under Strategy *I*. Hence, $V$ is divided by $P(H^s|\,Strategy\ I)$.

Clearly, the sign of $V$ determines whether or not output under Strategy *I* is greater, equal to, or smaller than output under Strategy *II* and $\mu$ then acts as a scaling factor. To investigate the conditions under which output rises with the introduction of Strategy *I*, note that $V > 0$ can be expressed as $X_{hd} > X^c_{hd}$, where

$$X^c_{hd} = X_{hi} + \frac{\alpha(1 - a)(X_{hi} - X_l)}{ab(1 - \beta)}. \quad (14)$$

Intuitively, this condition states that output will be higher under Strategy *I*, which accentuates *HD* managers, if the output of an *HD* manager exceeds the output of an *HI* manager by at least the expected gain in output due to the replacement of an *L* manager by an *HI* manager, i.e. the second term in (14). The condition that Strategy *I* is superior depends on the various parameters of the model, $a$, $b$, $\alpha$, $\beta$, $X_{hi}$, and $X_l$.

We now examine the comparative statics of the model by considering the sensitivity of $X^c_{hd}$ to these parameters. The following results obtain:

$$\frac{\partial X^c_{hd}}{\partial a} = -\frac{\alpha(X_{hi} - X_l)}{a^2b(1 - \beta)} < 0, \quad (15)$$

$$\frac{\partial X^c_{hd}}{\partial b} = -\frac{\alpha(1-a)(X_{hi}-X_l)}{ab^2(1-\beta)} < 0, \tag{16}$$

$$\frac{\partial X^c_{hd}}{\partial \alpha} = \frac{(1-a)(X_{hi}-X_l)}{ab(1-\beta)} > 0, \tag{17}$$

$$\frac{\partial X^c_{hd}}{\partial \beta} = \frac{\alpha(1-a)(X_{hi}-X_l)}{ab(1-\beta)^2} > 0, \tag{18}$$

$$\frac{\partial X^c_{hd}}{\partial X_{hi}} = 1 + \frac{\alpha(1-a)}{ab(1-\beta)} > 0 \quad \text{and} \quad \frac{\partial X^c_{hd}}{\partial X_l} = -\frac{\alpha(1-a)}{ab(1-\beta)} < 0. \tag{19}$$

A high $a$ indicates that the likelihood of recruiting low ability managers is low. This reduces the critical level of *HD* output, $X^c_{hd}$ for which output will be higher under Strategy *I*. A high $b$ implies that a greater proportion of those who screen as high ability will be devoted. This increases the probability that an *HD* manager will be attracted to the firm when Strategy *I* is adopted and reduces the critical level of *HD* output, $X^c_{hd}$.

A large $\alpha$ implies that testing for ability involves a high probability of incorrectly identifying low ability managers as having high ability. Hence, the applicant pool under Strategy *I* will have a smaller proportion of high-ability individuals. To compensate for this, the minimum level of *HD* output must rise. Also note that if $\alpha$ is sufficiently small, then, given that $X_{hd} > X_{hi}$, the net output effect of Strategy *I* will be positive. Indeed, as $\alpha$ tends to zero, Strategy *I* always dominates since $X^c_{hd}$ tends to $X_{hi}$.

A large $\beta$ means that a high proportion of high ability managers will be mistakenly identified as having low ability. Everything else being equal, this implies that the probability that a low-ability manager will get the job is higher. To compensate for this, the minimum value of the output of an *HD* manager, $X^c_{hd}$, must rise.

Finally a large $X_{hi}$ makes the condition that output rises more stringent. And a large $X_l$ makes this condition less stringent.[24]

[24] We focus on output rather than surplus because this represents a more stringent condition for the superiority of Strategy *I*. The firm's net benefit from adopting Strategy *I* rather than Strategy *II* is $\mu V + W_h - W_{hd}$. Let the pivotal level of output $X^{cc}_{hd}$ be defined as the output for which the two strategies yield the firm equal benefits. Then,

$$X^{cc}_{hd} = X_{hi} + \frac{\alpha(1-a)(X_{hi}-X_l)}{ab(1-\beta)} + \frac{W_{hd}-W_h}{\mu ab(1-\beta)}$$

so that, if $X_{hd} > X^{cc}_{hd}$, Strategy *I* will dominate. The wage saving is added to (14) to get a new critical value. Since $W_{hd} < W_h$ by assumption, $X^{cc}_{hd} < X^c_{hd}$. Hence, the condition that Strategy *I* dominates is less stringent than the condition for output to be higher. Because it saves on wages, the firm may do better by using Strategy *I* even if this results in less output.

## 4. FRINGE BENEFITS

As shown above, output can increase as a result of self-sorting by managers. Thus, even if we relax our earlier assumption that devoted managers cost less, self-sorting strategies may increase the surplus of the firm. If devoted managers cost more than indifferent managers, the firm may be prepared to incur this higher cost, provided self-sorting is maintained. Such self-sorting might be promoted by emphasizing institution-specific fringe benefits (Katz and Ziderman, 1986).

Let a devoted manager be characterized by valuing a particular fringe benefit more highly than an indifferent manager. For example, it seems likely that research-oriented professors will value research funding more than professors without such interest. Hence, offering an academic wage package consisting of less cash but more research funding and facilities, increases the likelihood that research-minded professors will self-select. This strategy can work even if a devoted manager values a dollar of fringe benefit at less than a dollar in cash.[25]

A simple example illustrates the point. Let the firm pay a manager who screens as high-ability a compensation package consisting of $W$ dollars and $Y$ dollars worth of a fringe benefit. The cost of the manager to the firm is therefore $W + Y$ dollars. Also, let a devoted manager value a unit of fringe benefits at $k$ dollars where $0 < k < 1$ and an indifferent manager value it at $h$ dollars where $0 < h < k < 1$. Managers are prepared to accept a compensation package valued at no less than their reservation wages. Hence, an *HD* manager will be prepared to work for a package consisting of $W$ dollars and $Y$ units of fringe benefit, where $W + kY \geq W_{hd}$. Similarly an *HI* manager will be prepared to work for $W$ dollars and $Y$ units of fringe benefit, where $W + hY \geq W_h$.

If $W_h > W_{hd}$ it is possible to screen out all *HI* managers by paying a compensation package consisting of $W_{hd}$ in cash and no fringe benefits. However, even in this case the firm might benefit from a compensation package with some positive fringe benefits. This occurs if the policy deters indifferent *L* managers and consequently raises the ratio of *HD* to *L* managers attracted by the firm.[26] Therefore, the sorting may be more efficient.

[25] We suspect that most professors would rather have a dollar in income than a dollar in research funds and be allowed to translate their sabbatical into its cash value. Hence, given that a reasonable test for ability is in place, the presence of fringe benefits that will attract professors with a stronger preference for research may be expected to generate a higher research output.

[26] For this to occur it is necessary that $W + kY \geq W_{hd} > W_l > W + hY$ which requires that $Y > (W_{hd} - W_l)/(k - h)$. Hence, since the maximum value of $Y$ is defined by the inequality $hY \leq W_l$, paying strictly positive fringe benefits when $W_h > W_{hd}$ may be optimal if $kW_l \geq hW_{hd}$.

Even if $W_h \leq W_{hd}$, a self-sorting policy is possible providing fringe benefits are used. While a compensation package that consists solely of cash and attracts *HD* managers will also attract *HI* managers, the firm can ensure that no *HI* managers apply if $W_h > W + hY$. Of course, since $k < 1$, $W + kY$ will have to exceed $W_{hd}$, but such a policy may still be beneficial to the firm if output and surplus are increased. Hence, the relative emphasis on fringe benefits, when combined with lower monetary compensation, may act as a powerful tool in enhancing the quality of management in nonprofits.[27]

## 5. CONCLUDING COMMENTS

This paper puts forward a theory and formalizes a model that explains why nonprofit institutions tend to pay their managers a monetary wage that is lower than the one paid to similarly qualified managers in for-profits. We suggest that this lower monetary wage, which may be compensated for partially by a higher component of fringe benefits, is adopted by nonprofits to generate positive self-selection among its managerial staff. The need for such self-selection is particularly important in nonprofits because they are not subject to the usual checks and balances imposed by shareholders on for-profits.

Lower wages will attract managers that are more committed to the cause of the nonprofit. This will be made easier for such managers by the fact that a low managerial income earned in a nonprofit is less detrimental to social status than a low managerial income earned in a for-profit. They will also attract less able managers who are unable to command a higher income in for-profits. Hence, the payment of lower monetary wages in nonprofits is less likely to be effective if it is difficult to distinguish between the high ability and low ability individuals. The data currently available does not permit us to conclusively determine whether or not this difficulty has been overcome. Nonetheless, nonprofits appear to be able to attract managers with an output that is not lower than that of managers in the for-profit sector. They do so by paying less.

## REFERENCES

Ball, Chris, "Remuneration Policies and Employment Practices: Some Dilemmas in the Voluntary Sector." In Julian Batsleer, Chris Cornforth, and Rob Paton, Eds., *Issues in Voluntary and Nonprofit Management: A Reader,* pp. 69–82. Wokingham, UK: Addison–Wesley, 1992.

[27] Such benefits may include the supply of public goods in the workplace. For example, the availability of support systems or emphasis on the quality of output may be conducive to self-selection, but these will not be captured in typical measures of compensation.

Bureau of Economic Analysis, "Survey of Current Business." U.S. Department of Commerce-Economics and Statistics Administration, pp. 0–3, 1997.

Eckel, Catherine, and Steinberg, Richard, "Tax Policy and the Objectives of Nonprofit Organizations in a Mixed-Sector Duopoly." Indianapolis, IN: Indiana University Working paper 95–16, 1994.

Emanuele, Rosemarie, "Total Cost Differential in the Nonprofit Sector: Some New Evidence from Michigan." *Nonprofit and Voluntary Sector Quart.* **26,** 1:56–64, March 1997.

Frank, Robert, H., "What Price the Moral High Ground?" *South. Econ. J.* **63,** 1:1–17, July 1996.

Gassler, Robert Scott, "The Economics of the Nonprofit Motive: A Suggested Formulation of Objectives and Constraints for Firms and Nonprofit Enterprises." Paper presented at the Atlantic Economic Society Conference, Montreal, Canada, Oct. 1989.

Goddeeris, John H., "Compensating Differentials and Self Selection: An Application to Lawyers." *J. Polit. Econ.* **96,** 2:411–428, April 1988.

Handy, Femida, "Reputation as Collateral: An Economic Analysis of the Role of Trustees of Nonprofits." *Nonprofit and Voluntary Sector Quart.* **24,** 4:293–305, Winter 1995.

Handy, Femida, "Coexistence of Nonprofit, For-Profits, and Public Sector Institutions." *Ann. Pub. Coop. Econ.* **68,** 2:201–223, June 1997.

Hansmann, Henry, "The Role of the Nonprofit Enterprise." *Yale Law J.* **89,** 5:835–901, Apr. 1980.

Hansmann, Henry, "Economic Theories of Nonprofit Institutions." In Walter W. Powell, Ed., *The Nonprofit Sector: A Research Handbook.* pp. 27–42. New Haven, CT: Yale Univ. Press, 1987.

Ito, Takatoshi, and Domian, Dale, "A Musical Note on the Efficiency Wage Hypothesis—Programmings, Wages, and Budgets of American Symphony Orchestras." *Econ. Lett.* **25,** 1:95–99, January 1987.

Katz, Eliakim, and Ziderman, Adrian, "Incomplete Information, Non-Wage Benefits and Desirable Worker Self Selection." *Aust. Econ. Papers* **25,** 47:252–256, Dec. 1986.

Leete, Laura, "The Nonprofit Wage Differential in the US: New Estimates from the 1990 Census." Discussion paper, Mandel Center for Nonprofit Organizations, Case Western University, October 1994.

Linden, Paula S., Pencil, Gail G., and Studley, Jamienne S., "What Happened to the Class of '87." *Natl. Law J.* **11:** March 27, 1989.

Liston, Robert A., *The Charity Racket.* New York: Nelson, 1977.

Mirvis, Philip H., and Hackett, Edward J., "Work and Workforce Characteristics in the Nonprofit Sector." *Mon. Lab. Rev.* **106,** 4:3–12, Apr. 1983.

Preston, Anne E., "The Effects of Property Rights on Labor Costs of Nonprofit Firms: Application to the Day Care Industry." *J. Indus. Econ.* **36,** 3:337–350, Mar. 1988.

Preston, Anne E., "The Nonprofit Worker in a For-Profit World." *J. Lab. Econ.* **7,** 4:438–463, Oct. 1989.

Preston, Anne E., "Entrepreneurial Self-selection Into the Nonprofit Sector: Effects on Motivations and Efficiency." Working paper, Dept. of Economics, SUNY at Stony Brook, April 1990.

Rawls, James R., Ulrich, Robert A., and Nelson Jr., Oscar T., "Comparison of Managers Reentering the Profit and Nonprofit Sectors." *Acad. Manage. J.* **18,** 3:616–623, September 1975.

Renz, Loren, *Foundation Giving.* New York: Foundation Centre, 1991.

Roomkin, Myron J., and Weisbrod, Burton, A., "Managerial Compensation in the For-profit and Nonprofit Hospitals: Is there a Difference?" Unpublished manuscript, Northwestern University, December 1994.

Rudney, Gabriel, "The Scope and Dimensions of Nonprofit Activity." In Walter W. Powell,

Ed., *The Nonprofit Sector: A Research Handbook,* pp. 55–66. New Haven, CT: Yale Univ. Press, 1987.

Schiff, Jerald, and Weisbrod, Burton, ''Competition Between For-Profits and Nonprofit Organizations in Commercial Markets.'' *Ann. Pub. Coop. Econ.* **62,** 4:619–639, Oct.–Dec. 1991.

Shackett, Joyce, and Trapani, John M., ''Earnings Differentials and Market Structure.'' *J. Human Resources* **22,** 4:518–531, Fall 1987.

Steinberg, Richard, ''Labor Economics and the Nonprofit Sector: A Literature Review.'' *Nonprofit and Voluntary Sector Quart.* **19,** 2:151–169, Summer 1990.

Studley, Jamienne S., ''Financial Sacrifice Outside the Private Sector.'' *Natl. Law J.* **11:** March 27, 1989.

Weisbrod, Burton A., *The Voluntary Nonprofit Sector: An Economic Analysis.* Lexington, MA: Heath, 1978.

Weisbrod, Burton, A., ''Private Goods, Collective Goods: The Role of the Nonprofit Sector.'' In Kenneth Clarkson and Donald Martin, Eds., *The Economics of Nonproprietary Organizations.* CT: JAI Press, 1980.

Weisbrod, Burton A., ''Nonprofit and Proprietary Sector Behavior: Wage Differentials Among Lawyers.'' *J. Labor Econ.* **1,** 3:246–263, July 1983.

Weisbrod, Burton A., *The Nonprofit Economy.* Cambridge, MA: Harvard, 1988.

Young, Dennis, R., *If Not for Profit, For What?.* Lexington, MA: Lexington Books, 1983.

Zagorin, Adam, ''Remember the Greedy.'' *Time* **142:**36–38, August 16, 1993.

# [16]

ELSEVIER Journal of Public Economics 81 (2001) 99–115
www.elsevier.nl/locate/econbase

## Not-for-profit entrepreneurs

Edward L. Glaeser, Andrei Shleifer*

*Department of Economics, Littauer Center, Harvard University, Cambridge, MA 02138, USA*

Received 31 May 1999; accepted 31 July 2000

**Abstract**

Entrepreneurs who start new firms may choose not-for-profit status as a means of committing to soft incentives. Such incentives protect donors, volunteers, consumers and employees from ex post expropriation of profits by the entrepreneur. We derive conditions under which completely self-interested entrepreneurs opt for not-for-profit status, despite the fact that this status limits their ability to enjoy the profits of their enterprises. We also show that even in the absence of tax advantages, unrestricted donations would flow to non-profits rather than for-profit firms because donations have more significant influence on the decisions of the non-profits. 

*Keywords:* Soft incentives; Non-profit; Entrepreneur; Donations

### 1. Introduction

Many, if not most, not-for-profit firms are started by entrepreneurs. In 1864, Jean-Henri Dunant, after witnessing the bloody battle of Solferino, founded the Red Cross. Dunant co-founded another significant non-profit, the World's Young Men's Christian Association, and (after spending most of his life in poverty and obscurity having neglected his business affairs) won the first Nobel Peace Prize in 1901. In 1892, the American John Muir founded the non-profit Sierra Club. In recent years, Michael Brown and Alan Khazei founded City Year, a program dedicated to promoting national service among young people, and Wendy Kopp

*Corresponding author. Tel.: +1-617-495-5046; fax: +1-617-496-1708.
*E-mail address:* ashleifer@harvard.edu (A. Shleifer).

0047-2727/01/$ – see front matter 
PII: S0047-2727(00)00130-4

founded Teach for America, a non-profit service organization attracting recent college graduates to teaching disadvantaged students.

In this paper, we ask a simple question: why would an entrepreneur wish to start a not-for-profit rather than a for-profit firm? We present an answer motivated by the work of Hansmann (1980, 1996) and Weisbrod (1988).[1] Our theory uses the assumption of Hansmann (1996) that 'the critical characteristic of a nonprofit firm is that it is barred from distributing any profits it earns to persons who exercise control over the firm.' Instead, a nonprofit firm can distribute its profits only through improvements in the working environment of the entrepreneur and the employees, which may include lower effort levels, free meals, shorter workdays, longer vacations, better offices, more generous benefits, or even improvements in the quality of the product.[2] In general, such 'perquisites' are not as valuable to an entrepreneur as income, and so it is not obvious why a rational entrepreneur would constrain himself by choosing a non-profit status. Our key point is that such status weakens his incentives to maximize profits. This commitment to weaker incentives is valuable in markets where entrepreneurs might be able to take advantage of their customers, employees, or donors, since it reduces their interest in profiting from such opportunities. When customers, employees, or donors feel protected by the non-profit status of the firm, the entrepreneur has a competitive advantage in the marketplace.

We present a model that attempts to capture this idea using the elements of an incomplete contracts framework of Klein et al. (1978), Holmstrom (1999), Grout (1984), Grossman and Hart (1986), Hart (1995) and Holmstrom and Milgrom (1991, 1994). In some situations, particularly strong incentives lead to inefficient behavior and cannot be controlled by explicit contracts. In our context, high powered incentives resulting from profit maximization encourage shirking on quality. Commitment to non-profit status softens these incentives, and thus reassures the customers that quality will be higher.[3] When quality cannot be part of a contract, such a commitment can benefit both the entrepreneur and consumers.

There are several theoretical ways to make this point. Hansmann (1980), whose views we largely follow, uses the general label of 'contractual failure' to explain the benefits of the not-for-profit status, but does not present a formal model. Hansmann (1996) and Easley and O'Hara (1983) stress more specifically asymmetric information between consumers and entrepreneurs, and the latter paper presents a formal model. We choose instead an ex-post expropriation framework that does not rely on asymmetric information between the entrepreneur and

[1]Earlier work on non-profit firms includes Arrow (1963) and Nelson and Krashinsky (1973).

[2]Non-profit firms can also retain their profits for long periods of time. Duggan (2000) shows that Californian non-profit hospitals have saved rather than spent their windfalls from increased transfers from the government. Universities, of course, have retained their income for centuries.

[3]Similar issues come up in the discussions of government ownership, see Hart et al. (1997) and Shleifer (1998).

consumers. One way, though not the only way, to interpret the incomplete contracts framework that we rely on is asymmetric information between the trading parties and the contract-enforcing judge. Our paper adds to the literature not so much with the novelty of its ideas as with an especially simple way to model them.

Many recent discussions of non-profits have focused substantially on their tax advantaged status (Weisbrod, 1988, Lakdawalla and Philipson, 1998). Our model does not rely on any tax benefits of non-profit firms to explain their existence. While the non-profit status brings significant tax benefits in the United States both for the firms and for the donors, it does not seem to be the essential characteristic of the non-profit firms. First, non-profits such as the Sierra Club were created long before the introduction of the income tax in the United States, and hence are unlikely to be a byproduct of income taxation. Second, and along the same lines, the majority of donors to non-profit firms in the United States do not derive significant tax benefits from their contributions. In 1994, while 50 percent of charitable dollars came from households with incomes over $100,000, 55 percent of the actual contributors came from households with incomes below $40,000 (Schervish and Havens, 2001). Third, noncharitable non-profits cannot receive tax-deductible contributions but still exist. Fourth, perhaps the greatest contributions to the non-profits come from the millions of volunteers, who donate non-deductible time rather than the possibly deductible money, and who account for nearly 40 percent of the non-profits' labor input. The tax story thus does not appear to be at the heart of the matter.

Some recent literature (Hart and Moore, 1997; Kremer, 1997) focuses on cooperatives and the consequences of collective decision making. In contrast, we focus on firms — for profit or not-for-profit — started by entrepreneurs, which do not face this particular problem.

Our basic model examines a firm that sells a commodity to a single consumer. The quality of this commodity is non-verifiable, and is chosen by the entrepreneur after the sale. The entrepreneur bears some non-cash costs from choosing a lower non-contractible quality. The source of these costs might be a lower reputation not immediately translated into profits, or a genuine preference from providing goods of higher quality derived from altruism for the consumers. Consumers are willing to pay higher initial prices if they expect a higher quality good. As a mechanism of such a commitment to higher quality, non-profit status ensures higher prices. Entrepreneurs choose the non-profit status if the benefits of committing to higher quality outweigh the costs of having to take their net revenues in the form of perquisites rather than cash.

Customers may not be the only ones to prefer dealing with non-profit firms. Employees may invest more in specific human capital at not-for-profit firms because these firms have less financial incentive to cut wages or perquisites ex post. Donors, who almost never have clear contracts specifying their wishes, are better protected against expropriation when they give to non-profits. When customers, employees and donors prefer to contract with not-for-profit entrepreneurs, the latter can get higher utility by committing to not-for-profit status ex ante. This status commits the entrepreneur to softer incentives and higher quality and consequently, in equilibrium, enables him to charge more or get more donations.

The model predicts a larger role for non-profit firms in sectors with more opportunities for ex post expropriation of consumers, employers, or donors. Sectors dominated by non-profit firms, such as child care, long term care for the aged, the performing arts, hospitals and schools, indeed face such expropriation problems. With child care or schools, parents who pay up front worry that these institutions may hire cheaper but less competent teachers. With the repertory theatres, performers invest in the company, and worry about being underpaid or fired. Donors to universities worry that the money be used for the purposes they intend. Weisbrod (1988) discusses the case of long term care for the aged, where for-profit nursing homes evidently used more sedatives (a cheap way to keep patients calm) than the non-profits — a dramatic example of a cost-reducing strategy adversely affecting non-contractible quality. Hansmann (1996) applies the same idea to saving and loan mutuals in the United States. When these firms were founded, the risk of misuse and appropriation of savings of middle-class consumers was significant, and the mutual status was used in part as a commitment to softer incentives.[4]

Our basic results are driven by the effect of the non-profit status on incentives, and do not depend on entrepreneurial altruism, since the non-cash cost of inferior quality to the entrepreneur can come from a reputational loss. Still, most founders of non-profits — such as Dunant or Muir — appear to have a strong altruistic interest in their causes (Drucker, 1990; Rose-Ackerman, 1996). If we interpret the entrepreneur's cost of delivering low quality as a reflection of altruism, our model shows that more altruistic entrepreneurs would opt for non-profit status.

Finally, we examine general (non-targeted) donations from charitable donors who wish to improve product quality. Donations to for-profit firms do not to a first approximation change the marginal conditions for production of quality. However, donations to non-profit firms lower the marginal utility of revenues and soften incentives. Through this channel, unverifiable quality in non-profits may improve. For similar reasons, governing boards of non-profit firms are often structured to have very low benefits of perquisites, and also staffed by donors.

In the next section, we present a simple model in which firms sell a product to consumers and later choose non-contractible quality. This model gives formal

[4]Not-for-profit status is only one of many solutions to expropriation problems; reputation-building, certification, and competition are others. Sherwin Rosen asked why the sellers of diamonds do not use not-for-profit status. The quality of diamonds can be, and often is, certified by the Gemological Institute of America. Interestingly, GIA is a non-profit, presumably in part to assure diamond buyers that its incentives to be corrupted by the sellers are weak.

conditions under which non-profit firms dominate a market. Section 3 discusses the role of non-profits when potential donors seek to increase the quality of products with their donations. Section 4 concludes.

## 2. The basic model

We consider an entrepreneur's decision of whether or not to obtain non-profit status for his firm. All firms face the same technological opportunities. Non-profit status only limits the ability of the entrepreneur to distribute profits to himself.

At time zero, the entrepreneur decides on non-profit or for-profit status. At time one, the entrepreneur sells exactly one unit of a good to a competitive market of consumers. At the time of sale, the entrepreneur collects the price P and agrees to deliver at time two a product of non-verifiable quality $q$.[5] At time two, the firm produces the good of non-verifiable quality $q$ and delivers it to consumers. The key assumption is that consumers cannot go to a court and complain that the firm has produced shoddy quality, because the court cannot verify it.[6] We assume that consumers are willing to pay $P = z - m(q^* - \hat{q})$ for the good, where $z$, $m$, and $q^*$ are constants, and $\hat{q}$ is the consumers' expectation of the non-contractible quality. We assume that $z$ is sufficiently high that firms earn a positive profit when they set $q = q^*$.

The total cash profits of the firm are $P - c(q)$. If the firm is for-profit, these profits are realized as income to the entrepreneur. If the firm is not-for-profit, the entrepreneur is forced to spend these revenues on perquisites, denoted by $Z$. We further assume that each entrepreneur, regardless of his firm's status, bears a non-cash cost of $b(q^* - q)$ of shirking on quality. This non-cash cost can come from a reputational loss from low quality, or from the entrepreneur's own altruistic preferences of providing higher quality. Entrepreneurs maximize a quasi-linear utility function:

$$\text{Income} + V(\text{Perquisites}) - B + bq = I + V(Z) - b(q^* - q) \qquad (1)$$

In this section, we further assume that $V(Z) = d \cdot Z$, with $d < 1$. The entrepreneur would rather have cash than perquisites at the going price for perquisites. Since the entrepreneur could buy many of the perquisites in the open market, compensation in this form is worse than receiving cash.

When the entrepreneur chooses $q$, he has already collected the price $P$. Total utility of a for-profit entrepreneur is $P - c(q) - b(q^* - q)$. His optimal quality

[5] The model can be easily extended to also incorporate a verifiable component of quality.

[6] An alternative way to specify this model is by relying on asymmetric information about quality, in the spirit of Hansmann (1996), but it seems to us that in many examples, such as substitution of inferior teachers in schools or use of sedatives in nursing homes, the issue is not customer ignorance but rather contractual incompleteness.

choice is given by $c'(q) = b$. Define $q_f$ as the effort level that satisfies this first order condition.

The not-for-profit firm cannot distribute profits. This constraint defines spending on perquisites: $Z = P - c(q)$. In this case, the entrepreneur chooses the level of effort to maximize $d \cdot [P - c(q)] - b(q^* - q)$, and first order condition is $d \cdot c'(q) = b$. We let $q_n$ denote the quality level that solves this equation. Comparing $q_n$ and $q_f$, and using the fact that $c(\cdot)$ is concave, yields:

**Proposition 1.** *Non-verifiable quality of the non-profit firm exceeds that of the for-profit firm.*[7]

When consumers contract with the firm, they agree to pay an initial price $P$ that correctly anticipates the quality level $q$. The price charged by non-profit entrepreneurs is therefore higher.[8]

The non-profit status serves as a valuable commitment to higher quality only if the entrepreneur cannot pocket the profits by converting the firm to a for-profit status after collecting the revenues. Such conversions do occur in the United States, particularly in the hospital industry, but they restrict the use of profits by the for-profit firm. If effective, this device eliminates incentive to convert in order to distribute the profits, although some abuses do occur. As the law stands, then, non-profit status is a pretty credible commitment to non-collection of profits by the entrepreneur.

At time zero, the entrepreneur chooses not-for-profit status if:

$$\begin{aligned} &d(z - m(q^* - q_n) - c(q_n)) - b(q^* - q_n) \\ &> z - m(q^* - q_f) - c(q_f) - b(q^* - q_f) \end{aligned} \tag{2}$$

or,

$$(b + m)(q_n - q_f) - (c(q_n) - c(q_f)) > (1 - d)(z - m(q^* - q_n) - c(q_n)) \tag{3}$$

The left hand side of (3) represents the benefits that a for-profit firm would obtain by committing to the non-profit firm's higher level of quality. The right hand side represents the loss imposed on a non-profit firm by the restriction that profits can only be enjoyed as perquisites. This comparison represents the fundamental

[7] All the proofs are contained in Appendix A.

[8] Our basic model is set up in terms of the choice of quality and price by a selfish entrepreneur facing consumers. Some entrepreneurs might choose to have lower prices because they are altruists, or because they want to attract donations from donors who are altruists. In this case, non-profit firms would receive donations and ration their products, rather than charge higher prices. Thus Harvard and other top universities ration the slots in their entering classes, as do some of the non-profit long term care facilities. An alternative view is that low prices make administration easier, since there is less need for advertising and management (since there is always a queue of customers) and that non-profits set lower prices to avoid effort.

tradeoff between non-profit and for-profit status. The following proposition describes conditions determining the entrepreneur's choice of status:

**Proposition 2.**

(*A*) *There is a unique value of m (denoted $m^*$) given by:*

$$m^* = \frac{(1-d)z + b(q_f - q_n) - c(q_f) - dc(q_n)}{(1-d)\,q^* - q_f + dq_n}$$

*below which all entrepreneurs choose non-profit status and above which all entrepreneurs choose for-profit status.*
(*B*) *If $c(q) = \underline{c}r\tilde{c}$ (8), then as profits rise because either z rises or as $\underline{c}$ falls, $m^*$ falls and non-profit status becomes less attractive.*
(*C*) *If for-profit firms produce positive utility levels for entrepreneurs, then for low enough levels of d, for-profit status strictly dominates non-profit status.*
(*D*) *If $c''(q)^2 > mc'''$ (8), then $m^*$ is increasing with b, and non-profit status becomes more attractive. If there is a distribution of b's in the population, then entrepreneurs with higher level of b will choose non-profit status.*

Part (A) illustrates a crucial point. Markets for goods whose non-contractible quality is not valued by consumers would be dominated by for-profit firms, but markets where consumers do value such quality — by the non-profits. When consumers care deeply about non-verifiable quality, entrepreneurs prefer non-profit status because it softens incentives and brings higher prices ex ante. The more valuable such quality, the more valuable is the ability to commit.

According to part (B), when net revenues are high, entrepreneurs prefer for-profit status because spending these revenues on perquisites is too unattractive. With heterogeneity in costs among producers, the lower cost ones choose for-profit and the higher cost the non-profit status. One implication of parts (B) and (C) together is that a very profitable firm, for which the marginal benefit of perquisites to an entrepreneur is trivial, is unlikely to be a non-profit.

According to part (D), quality-altruists prefer non-profit status because non-profit firms produce higher quality products. This, however, is not true in all cases, because there is a countervailing effect. Entrepreneurs with a greater taste for quality, which is known to all, may be able to earn greater revenues, which makes the for-profit status more appealing. The technical assumption rules out this possibility. Presumably, Mother Theresa could have assured everyone of her commitment to quality of care for the indigent even if she ran a for-profit firm.

In many situations, consumers do not directly observe the producers' commitment to quality. Non-profit status may then signal that the entrepreneur cares more about quality relative to pecuniary rewards. Examples of this inference exist both in the health and the schooling industries, where consumers may be suspicious of for-profit firms because such firms may be more willing to cut services to raise profits. While we do not present a model in which non-profit status serves as a signal of altruism, such a model is straightforward to construct (the single-crossing property holds here). This point suggests that non-profit status is even more important in situations where individuals' altruism is not readily recognized.

The critical assumptions of our model are that ex post expropriation (1) hurts the buyer (or employee or donor), (2) yields financial returns, and (3) has non-financial costs such as reputation. Since non-profit status reduces the financial returns, but not the non-financial costs, it softens incentives and cuts ex post expropriation in any setting that has these three features.

### 2.1. Market equilibrium

When consumer tastes and the producer technology are homogeneous, inequality (3) either holds or fails for all possible entrepreneurs. As a consequence, all firms in an industry choose the same status. Indeed for-profit firms almost completely dominate some industries (automobile manufacture), while non-profits dominate others (child care). In other industries, such as healthcare and theatres, for-profit and non-profit firms coexist. One possible reason for such coexistence is heterogeneity of consumer tastes. Assume, as an illustration, that (3) holds for most consumers and most firms choose non-profit status. If a small fraction of consumers receive no utility from non-contractible product quality, then for-profit firms would enter and supply just these consumers. Two types of firms then coexist in equilibrium: for-profits and non-profits, with the latter catering to consumers who demand high quality.

Co-existence of the two types of firms in equilibrium can also arise because of heterogeneity of employment relationships. For example, repertory theaters might need the non-profit status to commit to good treatment of actors who make large investments in their jobs, whereas more conventional theatres do not rely on such investments, and hence can be for-profit.

Hospitals to a significant extent cater to the interests of the doctors who treat patients there (Pauly and Redisch, 1973; Herzlinger and Krasker, 1987). If hospitals are organized as for-profit institutions, doctors may be concerned that the profits would be expropriated by the owners, whereas the non-profit status may serve as a commitment to spend the profits on wages and perquisities for doctors, including research.[9] This argument would suggest that doctors who care the most about perquisites would gravitate toward non-profit hospitals. This argument also suggests that, as profitability and hence the perquisite potential of hospitals declines, the attractiveness of the non-profit status declines as well. Consistent

[9]In recent work, Hassett and Hubbard (2000), following the approach outlined here, find that not-for-profit hospitals with a relatively high share of revenues devoted to wages are less likely to convert to for-profit status.

with this view, a significant number of non-profit hospitals have recently converted to a for-profit status under revenue pressure from managed care providers (Cutler and Horwitz, 2000). A more general message here is that the doctors' perspective on hospital quality may be as important as that of the patients.[10]

One potentially interesting dimension of heterogeneity among consumers is the difference in the ability to monitor suppliers. Consumers who are bad at monitoring would then select non-profit firms to deal with. If governments are particularly weak at monitoring contracts (because of their own incentive problems), they will specialize in dealing with non-profit firms.

### *2.2. Examples and discussion*

Not-for-profit status is not the only means of softening incentives. Other institutional arrangements may supplement (or replace) it. For example, entrepreneurs with a known taste for perquisites that is low, or whose consumption of perquisites can be restricted by a higher authority, might make particularly effective operators of non-profit firms. This may be the reason why so many non-profits such as schools and hospitals are operated by or affiliated with particular religions that restrict consumption.

Another device that serves the same purpose is a governing board consisting of people who are unable to consume perquisites, uninterested in the consumption of perquisites, or, perhaps ideally, are donors to the institution and therefore have an interest in restricting the consumption of perquisites. In fact, not-for-profit institutions typically have such governing boards. The benefits of the not-for-profit status for quality, then, can be amplified through additional devices reducing the value of perquisites to the decision-makers.

Two further mechanisms that can help guarantee quality in either for- or not-for-profit firms are reputations and ex post competition. Our model already incorporates the possibility that low quality providers pay a non-cash reputational cost, but bad quality also reduces prices and profits in the future (entails cash costs). If a firm can establish a reputation for producing high quality, it may charge high prices regardless of its status. American universities, for example, try hard to maintain reputations for quality, as do the for-profit luxury car-makers.

Competition may further the same goal as well. Consider the ex post

[10]Even when markets are divided between for-profit and non-profit firms, it will be difficult to distinguish empirically between the quality of their output. The reason is that both types of firms may well produce output of the same contractible quality, but non-profit firms would choose higher non-contractible quality. To the extent that non-contractible quality is hard to put in a contract and verify in court, it may also be difficult for an econometrician to measure. This may explain why some comparative studies of quality across for-profit and non-profit firms such as hospitals had trouble identifying any differences in observable quality (Norton and Staiger, 1994) A further problem is that these studies focus on quality from the perspective of patients, whereas the relevant perspective might be that of the doctors.

appropriation problem that results from worker investment in specific human capital (as in Rotemberg and Saloner, 1990). A firm can protect the worker by locating in an area where a large number of other employers also demand this particular form of human capital. When competition reduces risks of ex post appropriation, competition among for-profit firms may again render non-profit status unnecessary. In the absence of such competition, however, the non-profit status becomes all the more essential. For example, universities in the US have traditionally served local markets (Hoxby, 1998) and only one university of a particular quality level often still serves a given metropolitan area. There is then little local competition for the services of professors who invest heavily in university-specific human capital. If universities were able to expropriate the rents from such investments, professors would refuse to invest. Non-profit status protects professors against this problem.

These examples raise the obvious question: what are the markets in which reputation and/or competition suffice for quality assurance by for-profit firms, and what are the markets where the not-for-profit status is necessary? Non-profit status is usually only necessary when the potential expropriation problem — and the disutility to consumers or donors from reduced quality — are very large. In the case of donations in particular, where the donor cannot take the money back or switch, the non-profit status might be essential. This logic might explain why we see non-profit hospitals (they deal with life and death and rely on donations) but not non-profit doctors (it is easier to switch or get a second opinion, and there are no donations). This logic might also explain why universities are non-profit (rely on donations) while vocational schools are not (no donations). Finally, this logic might explain why, for most goods where quality matters, market mechanisms are good enough for assuring quality production by for-profit firms.

## 3. Donors

In many situations, nonprofit firms provide charitable services for which they charge below cost, if anything. As a consequence, not-for-profit firms often rely on outside donations for part of their revenues.[11] Many individuals, with the help of the tax exemption for charitable donations, are willing to donate funds. Many donations can be understood as attempts to fund a particular project or interest of the donor or to gain social standing through displays of wealth and altruism. Such donors are best thought of as customers of the non-profit, and thus fit nicely into the model described above. The non-profit is supplying the donor with prestige or a very particular service (e.g. a full time researcher at a distinguished university dedicated to Gender Studies). The firm has the opportunity to either comply with

[11]Weisbrod (1998) reports that private contributions as percentage of all nonprofit operating expenditures in the United States were 53.5% in 1964, falling steadily to 23.6% in 1993.

the wishes of the donor (glorify her name or fulfill the implicit agreement) or to renege and use the money for other purposes. While any institution has its reputation at stake in such a situation, a non-profit has less of an incentive to completely renege because of the limits placed on its use of new funds (Rose-Ackerman, 1996). Non-profits have an advantage with donors, not only because of their tax status, but also because the inability to personally profit makes the people who run them more trustworthy.

A large number of donations are general funds given to an institution, not funds given for a particular purpose. In fact, donations sometimes lose their tax advantages when an explicit contract describing the terms of the arrangement is written. Moreover, in many non-profit institutions, funds are substantially fungible, and even specifically targeted gifts can be used for general purposes. To understand the role of general gifts to a non-profit institution, we must return to the previous model and explicitly incorporate an altruistic donor. Furthermore, we now assume that $V(Z)$ is not linear, but an increasing, strictly concave function.

The timing of the model must be adjusted to include a donor. In period zero, the entrepreneur decides on the not-for-profit or the for-profit status. In period one, a donor decides on a level of general donations, denoted by $D$. The donor correctly anticipates the effect of his donation on the future price and the non-contractible quality level. In period two, the entrepreneur sells the good to the consumer at a price $P$. In period three, the entrepreneur chooses the non-contractible quality level q and delivers the good to the consumer.

We assume that a donor wishes to improve q, but can only do so through general donations and cannot in any sense contract to directly induce the firm to deliver a higher quality product. The donor chooses the level of general donations, denoted by $D$, to maximize $(1-t)(Y-D)+F(q)$, where $Y$ is the donor's taxable income, $t$ is the tax rate and $F(q)$ is an increasing, twice differentiable concave function. The function $F(q)$ is meant to capture the idea that the donor just wants to see good health, good universities or good theater. We assume that there is no competition, so a single entrepreneur is maximizing the utility function specified previously. If there is an interior solution for $D$, the donor sets its level so that $\mathrm{d}q/\mathrm{d}D \cdot F'(q)=1-t$. To ensure that this first order condition is a maximum, we assume that second order conditions hold.

In a for-profit firm, quality is set so that $c'(q)=b$. Increases in the firm's income do not change this first order condition, and donations have no effect on quality. This conclusion is too strong if the entrepreneur has diminishing marginal utility of income because of satiation. However, satiation with consumption as a whole is likely to set in much slower than satiation with perquisites, and hence for the comparison of non-profit and for-profit firms, we can assume constant marginal utility of income.

In a non-profit firm, in contrast, donations influence the marginal utility of perquisites and thereby affect quality. To solve the model, we proceed recursively and first solve for effort. The first order condition for quality is $c'(q)\cdot V'(Y)=b$, where we use $Y$ to denote net income of the firm: $Y = P + D - c(q)$. We can then use the equilibrium relationship $P = z - m(q^* - q)$ to find the relationship between $q$ and $D$ that incorporates the idea that donations affect the price.

If $\hat{q}$ reflects consumers expectations about the quality of the good, then conventional stability arguments require that:

$$\frac{\partial q}{\partial \hat{q}} = \frac{-mc'(q)V''(Y)}{c''(q)V'(Y) - c'(q)V''(Y)} < 1$$

which we assume. If this condition does not hold, then the problem is inherently unstable. A slight increase in expected quality will raise actual quality by an even greater amount. We then have:

**Proposition 3.** *Quality rises with the level of donations.*

**Proposition 4.** *Donations rise with the tax rate and decline one-for-one as the firm obtains alternative sources of income.*

Proposition 4 suggests that tax deductible donations will be higher among donors who face a higher marginal tax rate and that, as the firm acquires alternative sources of revenue, donations dry up. When firms are already rich, donors expect their donations to have less of a marginal impact on quality-related incentives and contribute less. Segal and Weisbrod (1998) find some evidence that donations and sales revenues are indeed substitutes for non-profit firms.

This result may explain why state-supported institutions receive few donations. In our model, state funding reduces private donations because private donors do not expect to have much of an impact on quality.[12] In practice, there does appear to be a strong substitution between private charity and state funding. City Year, the national service organization founded by Brown and Khazei (discussed in the Introduction), originally faced tremendous difficulties finding private donors to fund its programs, evidently because it already received sizable public funds. State universities in the United States have traditionally been less successful in fundraising than private schools. Indeed, both Yale and Harvard received most of their funding from state governments until the first quarter of the 19th century. The two schools only focused on private donations after the states cut them off for refusing to cater to the prevailing religious winds (Hansmann, 1990). More recently, state universities in California also turned to private donors after state funding became scarcer. In European countries, which have a long tradition of government funding of artistic, educational and medical institutions, there is much less of a tradition of private giving to such firms (until government funds dry up,

[12] In addition, donors may fear the ratchet effect whereby their gifts reduce future state funding.

as they did for British universities in the 1980s and Finnish musical institutions in the 1990s). Since the government has already created soft incentives for state-supported firms, private donors are not needed to further soften their incentives.

Our results are related to a large literature in public economics on whether government funding of public goods crowds out private contributions to the provision of these goods. Warr (1983), Bergstrom et al. (1986), and Bernheim (1986) ask how much contributors reduce donations when the government taxes them to pay for the public goods directly. Under some circumstances, government spending crowds out private contributions 100 percent. The empirical evidence on this issue from the United States is extensive, and generally does find significant crowding out (e.g. Kingma, 1989; Payne, 1998), although not 100 percent. Our analysis is consistent with this literature but the economic mechanism we focus on is different: the donors in our model are concerned with the incentives of the producer to shirk on quality rather than with the ultimate quantity of the public good produced.

Proposition 3 also suggests that institutions will put themselves in situations where donations have a real effect on their incentives. For example, they may overcommit their resources so as to become cash poor. Alternatively, non-profits may have rules such as 'spend only 5% of the endowment every year regardless of market returns' or 'every tub on its own bottom,' which means that every new project must find its own financing. Our analysis explains why some non-profits with lush endowments work hard to stay poor on the cash flow basis.

## 4. Conclusion

Not-for-profit firms are often controlled by entrepreneurs, and not by their employees or customers. The decision of entrepreneurs to establish such firms can be understood as an attempt to commit themselves to softer incentives. Soft incentives protect customers, volunteers, donors, and employees of the firm against ex post expropriation. Donors in particular would favor non-profits with unrestricted donations even if such donations had no tax advantages because the risk of diversion of funds is much smaller. While sufficient reputation or competition may substitute for the non-profit status, in many cases we still expect entrepreneurs to seek the non-profit status, even if they are completely self-interested.

This basic framework yields several empirical predictions about non-profit firms. According to the theory, we expect to find non-profit firms in activities where:

1. There exist substantial opportunities for reductions of the quality of the good after it is purchased, or for other forms of expropriation of consumers;
2. The activity is not too profitable, or — more importantly — relies on charitable donations;

3. Altruism or public spiritedness are important motivators of entrepreneurs;
4. It is costly for consumers or employees to change firms they deal with.

The need for donations to assure the survival of a business is probably the most important determinant of the preference for non-profit status, because it is difficult to imagine a market mechanism that would support donations to for-profit firms.

Furthermore, in the activities where for-profit and non-profit firms coexist, we expect the latter to deliver higher quality to consumers. Finally, we expect to find higher levels of perquisites in non-profit firms, which may show up as better working conditions, wages, and benefits for the employees. Many of these implications appear to be consistent with the available evidence, while others are at least potentially testable.

**Acknowledgements**

We are grateful to Gary Becker, David Cutler, Mark Duggan, John Dunlop, Xavier Gabaix, Claudia Goldin, Henry Hansmann, Oliver Hart, Bengt Holmstrom, Larry Katz, Tomas Philipson, James Poterba, Sherwin Rosen, David Scharfstein, Fiona Scott-Morton, Burton Weisbrod, Daniel Wolfenzon, and two anonymous referees for comments. Financial support was provided by the NSF and the Sloan Foundation.

## Appendix A. Proofs of Propositions

**Proposition 1.** The first order conditions for maximization yield $c'(q_n) = b/d > b = c'(q_f)$. As $c(\cdot)$ is convex $c'(q_n) > c'(q_f)$ implies that $q_n > q_f$.

**Proposition 2.** Part A: Define $w$ as the returns non-profit status relative to for-profit status:

$$w = m((1-d)\,q^* - q_f + dq_n) - (1-d)\,z - (bq_f - c(q_f) + bq_n - dc(q_n)) \tag{A1}$$

We define the value of $m$ at which $w=0$ as $m^*$. Since $q^* > q_f$ the denominator of $m^*$ is positive. As $bx - c(x)$ is maximized at $x = q_f$, $bq_f - c(q_f) > bq_n - c(q_n)$. Since firms earn positive profits if $q = q^*$, we have $z > c(q^*) > c(q_n)$. Thus, the numerator is also positive and $m^*$ is positive. As $\partial w/\partial m = (1-d)\,q^* - q_f + dq_n > 0$, $w$ is less than zero for $m < m^*$ and greater than zero for $m > m^*$.

Part B: Differentiation of $m^*$ yields that:

$$\frac{\partial m^*}{\partial z} = \frac{(1-d)}{(1-d)\,q^* - q_f + dq_n} > 0$$

Letting $c(q) = \underline{c} + \tilde{c}(q)$, differentiation produces:

$$\frac{\partial m^*}{\partial \underline{c}} = \frac{-(1-d)}{(1-d)\,q^* - q_f + dq_n} < 0$$

Hence increases in $z$ raise $m^*$ and make non-profits less attractive. Increase in $\underline{c}$ lower $m^*$ and make non-profits more attractive.

Part C: When $d=0$, $w = -[z - m(q^* - q_f) - c(q_f) - b(q^* - q_f)] - b(q^* - q_n)$. The first term equals $-1$ times the utility from being a for-profit firm (which we have assumed is positive) and the second term is negative because $q^* > q_n$. Thus, the expression is negative and at $d=0$, for profit status dominates non-profit status. Since the relative returns to for-profit status are continuous in $d$, there must be some interval around $d=0$, where $w<0$.

Part D: Differentiating (A1) yields:

$$\frac{\partial m^*}{\partial b} = \frac{\left(q_f - \frac{m^*}{c''(q_f)}\right) - \left(q_n - \frac{m^*}{c''(q_n)}\right)}{(1-d)\,q^* - q_f + dq_n}$$

If $c''(q)^2 > mc'''(q)$, then $x - m^*/c''(x)$ is strictly increasing in $x$ and, as $q_n > q_f$, it follows that $q_n - (m^*/c''(q_n)) > q_f - (m^*/c''(q_f))$, and hence $\partial m^*/\partial b < 0$.

Differentiating $w(\cdot)$ with respect to $b$ yields: $q_n - (m/c''(q_n)) - q_f + (m/c''(q_n))$, which is positive because $c''(q)^2 > mc'''(q)$. Hence, entrepreneurs with higher levels of $b$ will gain more from non-profit status.

**Proposition 3.** Firm's first order condition is: $c'(q)V'(D + z - m(q^* - q) - c(q)) = b$. Differentiation with respect to $D$ yields:

$$\frac{\partial q}{\partial D} = \frac{-c'(q)\,V''(Y)}{c''(q)\,V'(Y) + (m - c'(q))\,V''(q)\,c'(q)}$$

As $V(\cdot)$ is concave, and $c(\cdot)$ is increasing, the numerator is positive. By assumption, $1 > (-mc'(q)\,V''(Y))/(c''(q)\,V'(Y) - c'(q)\,V''(Y))$ or $c''(q)\,V'(Y) + (m - c'(q))\,V''(Y) > 0$, which means that the denominator is positive as well, and quality rises with donations.

**Proposition 4.** Part A: The donor's first order condition is $1 - t = F'(q)(\partial q/\partial D)$. Second order conditions require that:

$$\frac{d}{dD}\left[F'(q)\frac{\partial q}{\partial D}\right] < 0$$

Differentiating the first order condition yields that:

$$\frac{\partial D}{\partial t} = -1 \Big/ \frac{\mathrm{d}}{\mathrm{d}D}\left[F'(q)\frac{\partial q}{\partial D}\right] > 0$$

Part B: Consider the effect of an exogenous increase in $z$, which will increase profits for the firm. The terms $z$ and $D$ only enter together into the firm's decision, so we can write the donor's decision as:

$$1 - t = \frac{F'(q(z+D))}{\dfrac{c''(q(z+D))\,V'(z+D-m(q^*-q(z+D))-c(z+D))}{c'(q(z+D))\,V''(z+D-m(q^*-q(z+D))-c(z+D))} + m - c'(q(z+D))} \tag{A3}$$

where $q(\cdot)$ is an increasing function of $z + D$. The stability condition ensures that there is a unique level of $z + D$ that solves this equation. Thus, if $z$ rises, $D$ must fall one-for-one.

## References


Arrow, K., 1963. Uncertainty and the welfare economics of medical care. American Economic Review 53, 941–973.

Bergstrom, T., Blume, L., Varian, H., 1986. On the private provision of public goods. Journal of Public Economics 29, 25–50.

Bernheim, D., 1986. On the voluntary and involuntary provision of public goods. American Economic Review 76, 789–793.

Cutler, D., Horwitz, J., 2000. Converting hospitals from nonprofit to for profit status: why and what effects. In: Cutler, D. (Ed.), The Changing Hospital Industry. University of Chicago Press for the NBER, Chicago.

Duggan, M., 2000. Effects of ownership structure on hospital behavior. Quarterly Journal of Economics 115, 1343–1374.

Drucker, P., 1990. Managing the Non-profit Organization: Practices and Principles. Harper Collins, New York.

Easley, D., O'Hara, M., 1983. The economic role of the nonprofit firm. Rand Journal of Economics 14, 531–538.

Grossman, S.J., Hart, O., 1986. The costs and benefits of ownership: a theory of vertical and lateral integration. Journal of Political Economy 94, 691–719.

Grout, P., 1984. Investment and wages in the absence of binding contracts: a Nash equilibrium approach. Econometrica 52, 449–460.

Hansmann, H., 1980. The role of the nonprofit enterprise. Yale Law Journal 89, 835–901.

Hansmann, H., 1990. Why do universities have endowments? Journal of Legal Studies 19, 3–42.

Hansmann, H., 1996. The Ownership of Enterprise. Harvard University Press, Cambridge, MA.

Hart, O., 1995. Firms, Contracts, and Financial Structure. Oxford University Press, Oxford.

Hart, O., Moore, J., 1997. Cooperatives versus outside ownership. Harvard University, Mimeo.

Hart, O., Shleifer, A., Vishny, R., 1997. The proper scope of government: theory and an application to prisons. Quarterly Journal of Economics 112, 1127–1162.

Hassett, K., Hubbard, G., 2000. Noncontractible quality and organizational form in the US hospital industry. Columbia University, Mimeo.

Herzlinger, R., Krasker, W., 1987. Who profits from nonprofits. Harvard Business Review January–February, 93–106.

Holmstrom, B., 1999. Managerial incentive problems: a dynamic perspective. Review of Economic Studies 66, 169–182.

Holmstrom, B., Milgrom, P., 1991. Multi-task principal–agent analyses: incentive contracts, asset ownership and job design. Journal of Law, Economics and Organization 7, 24–52.

Holmstrom, B., Milgrom, P., 1994. The firm as an incentive system. American Economic Review 84, 972–991.

Hoxby, C., 1998. How the changing market structure of US higher education explains college tuition. Harvard University, Mimeo.

Kingma, B.R., 1989. An accurate measurement if the crowd-out effect, income effect, and price effect for charitable contributions. Journal of Public Economics 97, 1197–1207.

Klein, B., Crawford, R., Alchian, A., 1978. Vertical integration, affordable rents and the competitive contracting process. Journal of Law and Economics 21, 297–326.

Kremer, M., 1997. Why are worker cooperatives so rare. MIT, Mimeo.

Lakdawalla, D., Philipson, T., 1998. Nonprofit production, competition, and long-term care. University of Chicago, Mimeo.

Nelson, R., Krashinsky, M., 1973. Two major issues of public policy: public policy and the organization of supply. In: Nelson, R., Young, D. (Eds.), Public Subsidy for Day Care of Young Children. D.C. Heath, Lexington, MA.

Norton, E., Staiger, D., 1994. How hospital ownership affects access to care for the uninsured. Rand Journal of Economics 25, 171–185.

Pauly, M., Redisch, M., 1973. The not-for-profit hospital as a physicians' cooperative. American Economic Review 63, 87–99.

Payne, A., 1998. Does the government crowd-out private donations? New evidence from a sample of non-profit firms. Journal of Public Economics 69, 323–345.

Rose-Ackerman, S., 1996. Altruism, non-profits, and economic theory. Journal of Economic Literature 34, 701–728.

Rotemberg, J., Saloner, G., 1990. Competition and human capital accumulation: a theory of interregional specialization and trade. MIT, Mimeo.

Schervish, P., Havens, J., 2001. Wealth and the commonwealth new findings on wherewithal and philanthropy. Nonprofit and Voluntary Sector Quarterly, forthcoming.

Segal, L., Weisbrod, B., 1998. Interdependence of commercial and donative revenues. In: Weisbrod, B. (Ed.), The Nonprofit Economy. Harvard University Press, Cambridge, MA, pp. 105–127.

Shleifer, A., 1998. State versus private ownership. Journal of Economic Perspectives 12, 133–150.

Warr, P., 1983. The private provision of a public good is independent of the distribution of income. Economic Letters 13, 207–211.

Weisbrod, B., 1988. The Nonprofit Economy. Harvard University Press, Cambridge, MA.

Weisbrod, B., 1998. To Profit or Not to Profit. The Commercial Transformation of the Nonprofit Sector. Cambridge University Press, Cambridge, UK.

# [17]

*Annals of Public and Cooperative Economics 68:2 1997* *pp. 201–223*

# COEXISTENCE OF NONPROFIT, FOR-PROFIT AND PUBLIC SECTOR INSTITUTIONS

by

Femida HANDY*

*Faculty of Environmental Studies, York University (Canada)*

Received July 1996; final revision accepted January 1997

**ABSTRACT****: *If nonprofit organizations are superior institutions in resolving informational asymmetry and resulting contract failure, why do nonprofit (NPs), for-profit (FPs) and government/public institutions (GPs) survive in the same industry? This article explicitly models the nonconvex budget set for the consumer that arises through the juxtaposition of the inefficiencies and contract failures that occur in the three sectors. Because the consumer is willing to trade quality for efficiency and price, varying market shares for NPs, FPs and GPs can exist in the same industry. The theory offered complements the functionalist explanation of the existence of nonprofits advanced by Weisbrod and Hansmann using a micro-analysis.*

## 1 Introduction

There are two major explanations for the existence of nonprofit organizations (NPs): the 'contract failure' rationale, which is based on the ability of NPs to engender consumer trust (Hansmann 1980); and the government failure explanation, which focuses on the ability of NPs to straddle the median voter and cater to a heterogeneous and minority demand (Weisbrod 1977). If NPs are more successful than

* I am grateful to Eli Katz and Burton Weisbrod, who offered their comments on an earlier version of this work. The anonymous referees provided important counsel and insights that have been most helpful. The shortcomings, however, remain my own. This research was supported by a grant from the Faculty of Environmental Studies at York University.

** *Résumé en fin d'article; Zusammenfassung am Ende des Artikels; resúmen al fin del artículo.*

others at resolving the contract and government failures, it is necessary to explain why they coexist with for-profit organizations (FPs) and government or public sector institutions (GPs) in the same industry.[1]

The argument presented in this article complements work by other authors who have been intrigued by this coexistence. Weisbrod and Schlesinger (1986) posit that such coexistence is temporary and due to the delayed flow of information regarding the quality of the service, or in some cases the slowness of NPs' response to the excess demand for services. They also suggest that coexistence may be permanent if some consumers are better at detecting cheating than others. Schiff and Weisbrod (1991) provide an explanation why NPs and FPs sometimes engage in similar commercial activities. They suggest that despite 'the negative utility provided to the [nonprofit] managers by producing commercial output' (p. 636), NPs are willing to engage in limited profit-maximizing commercial activities simply in order to cross-subsidize their preferred nonprofit activities, leaving any excess demand to be met by FPs.[2]

In this paper, I explore this issue by examining the behaviour of individuals who must choose the type of institution to patronize when purchasing similar goods and services provided by NPs, FPs and GPs. I model consumer behaviour in response to the inefficiencies and contract failures that occur in the three sectors and I demonstrate that because the consumer is willing to trade quality for efficiency and price, varying market shares for NPs, FPs and GPs can exist in the same industry. The model is presented in intuitive and diagrammatic terms to demonstrate the relevant ideas.

In Section 2, I first set out a version of the asymmetric information problem, and discuss a particular feature of informational symmetry which causes a market failure. But such informational asymmetries between producers and consumers may be bridged by a variety of institutional arrangements of which NPs is but one. I therefore examine, in Section 2, which products will elicit supply by FPs and which will provide a major role for NPs. In Section 3, I briefly look at some of the factors which are likely to enhance trust in NPs. I introduce the GPs in Section 4, and consider the potential coexistence

1 See Steinberg (1993) for a review of the literature that uses the contract failure rationale as a *raison d'ètre* of NPs.

2 Chillemi and Gui (1991) argue that FPs charging higher prices and behaving honestly (to protect their reputations) could coexist with NPs. Gassler (1986) addresses coexistence from the motivational standpoint of the NPs entrepreneur.

of NPs, FPs and GPs within the same industry.[3] In Section 5, the market shares between FPs, NPs are delineated and Section 6 discusses the role of GPs in an industry and where FPs and NPs exist and models this discussion. Concluding remarks are offered in Section 7.

## 2 The problem: asymmetric information and contract failure

The asymmetric information problem is illustrated by reference to a home for elderly people. Consumers, who are the aged, or their families contract for full-time care from the home. Care, the service purchased from the homes in general comprises several components. These components may be viewed as intermediary inputs into the final good purchased by the consumer.[4]

These intermediary inputs may be divided into two types: inputs that are easily observed, evaluated and measured by the consumer, which I denote by $X_1$; and inputs that the consumer finds it difficult or costly to observe, evaluate or measure, which I denote by $X_2$. For example, $X_1$ may include professional expertise, use of appropriate medical technology and physical amenities, while $X_2$ may comprise tender and compassionate care. While $X_1$ and $X_2$ may obviously be vectors, I shall treat them as scalars for expositional simplicity.

The benefit, $B$, derived by consumers from the care supplied by a home for the elderly is therefore a function of $X_1$ and $X_2$, $B = B(X_1, X_2)$. Assuming the usual shape for such a benefit (utility) function, it is possible to draw an indifference curves map relating benefits to $X_1$ and $X_2$. Such a map, drawn for a given type of consumer, is shown in Figure 1, where indifference curves are denoted by $B_i$ such that the higher the value of i the greater is the level of consumer benefits. The technology of caring for the old is such that there can be many types of homes, each catering to a different type of consumer. Consumers are therefore able to choose the home that provides combinations of $X_1$ and $X_2$ which

3 Bennett and Dilorenzo (1988), Cleary et al. (1991), Hansmann (1987), Pauly (1987), Preston (1988), Rose-Ackerman (1986), Weisbrod and Schlesinger (1986), and White (1992) all provide various examples of such coexistence.

4 Weisbrod (1988) makes the point of goods and services having different kinds of attributes whereby consumer decisions are made. He refers to Type I (easy to assess) and Type II (costly to assess) attributes. In an example on care in a nursing home, the Type I attribute is the size of a nursing home and the Type II attribute referred to "tender loving care" (p. 147). My definitions follow this closely.

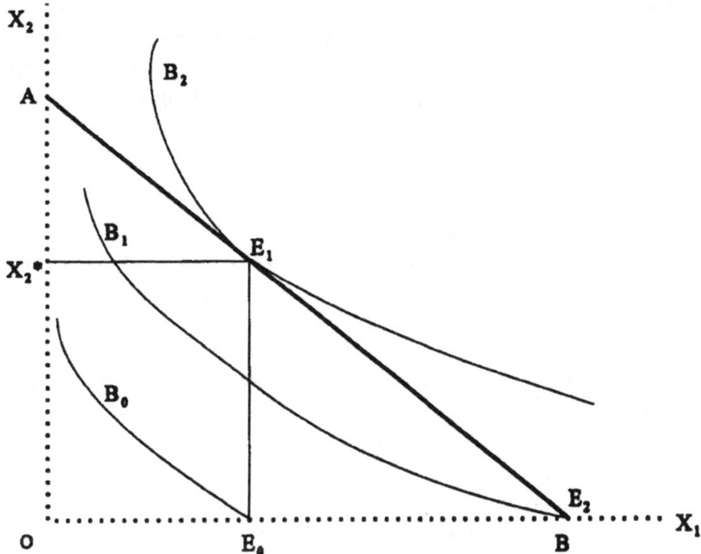


**Figure 1—Market failure: FPs and NPs**

yields them the greatest benefit, given their budget constraint. Assume homothetic indifference curves[5] and let the prices of $X_1$ and $X_2$ be constant and independent of one another. Let the budget of the consumer be S (yielding a budget constraint such as AB in Figure 1). If the consumer is able to observe both $X_1$ and $X_2$, then, as seen in Figure 1, she/he will choose a home that supplies the combination of $X_1$ and $X_2$ given by $E_1$, which yields a benefit level equal to $B_2$.

As mentioned above, some inputs into care, such as tenderness and compassion ($X_2$), are not easily observable by the consumer or purchaser. And, especially in the context of a home for the elderly, consumers may be unable to tell with any degree of certainty what level of $B$ is being provided. The purchaser of the service is often a relative rather than the elderly person, whose reports are often judged unreliable by members of the family, especially if he/she is ill or mentally handicapped. In such cases, the elderly person's condition may make a meaningful report of the value of $X_2$ (or $B$) impossible.

A market failure may ensue because this informational asymmetry enables unethical FPs to increase profits by supplying less than the level

5 These indifference curves have the property that their slopes are constant along any ray through the origin.

of $X_2$ requested and paid for by the consumer. Though the consumer pays for a quantity $X_2$* of compassionate care, she/he may, in the limit, receive only receive $X_1$ and no $X_2$. If consumers are completely unable to observe $X_2$, and are unaware that they will be cheated, an unethical profit-maximizing home will set $X_2 = 0$, leading to the point $E_0$ in Figure 1, and a benefit level of $B_0$.

Moreover, ethical FP homes may be driven out of the market, because supplying compassionate care is costly. FPs that do supply the amount of compassionate care contracted for by the consumer will have to charge higher prices than unethical FPs, which do not. And, since consumers may be unable to distinguish between ethical and unethical FPs, they will shun the higher-priced institutions. This will make the ethical FP homes nonviable. Furthermore, consumers will be aware that (in equilibrium) FP homes will not supply the amount of compassionate care contracted for. Hence, consumers will neither demand, nor be prepared to pay for, any compassionate care.[6] Thus, an equilibrium will be established at $E_2$, where the FP homes supply only $X_1$, and consumers attain a benefit level $B_1$ rather than $B_2$. Hence, the inability of consumers to observe the amount of $X_2$ supplied will cause the market in care for the elderly to be inefficient.

Before proceeding to analyse the role of NPs, note that an inability to observe $X_2$ might not be sufficient to render the market inefficient. What is also required is an inability to observe the level of benefits, $B$. For if $B$ is observable, then $X_2$ may be deduced. I therefore begin by considering when benefits might not be observable, or when the observability of $B$ will not enable consumers to deduce input levels.

A primary explanation for this might be that the benefit function may contain random components, so that the relation between $X_2$ and $B$ is partially masked. If $B=B(X_1, X_2, \theta)$ where $\theta$ is a random variable, a particular level of $B$ need not imply a given level of $X_2$, even if $X_1$ is known. An actual realization of $B$ does not contain sufficient information to determine $X_2$. This is especially likely in certain medical situations where patients respond idiosyncratically to different treatments and approaches. In this case, the benefit-indifference curves may be viewed as reflecting 'expected' benefits.

6 This lemons-type equilibria may not always lead to the elimination of ethical FPs. It will depend on consumer willingness to pay (given a probability of being dealt with ethically) versus costs.

Also, and especially in the context of homes for the elderly, as mentioned above, purchasers may be unable to tell with any degree of certainty what level of $B$ is being provided even if consumers can.

In yet other cases, there exists a long lag between the service received and the realization of $B$, so that by the time the true values of $X_2$ and $B$ are determined, it is irrelevant to the welfare of the consumer. In many cases, the long delay in determining $B$ is equivalent to never being able to observe $X_2$. Time introduces many considerations, all of which neutralize the ability of consumers to deduce $X_2$ from $B$. Even if $X_2$ can be eventually verified from B it is not evident that all components of $X_2$ can be reliably determined, such as kindness, or treatment with love and respect. Court suits could impose penalties (sufficient to cover the transaction costs of suing) which would provide a sufficient deterrent from opportunistic behaviour in instances such as gross negligence, over-use of drugs or lack of timely medical attention. However, there are many components of $B$, including certain random components, which would make it difficult for courts to enforce implicit contracts that dealt with respect, kindness and so on. Such factors can be verified only by consumer experience[7] and cannot provide persuasive evidence in courts, and therefore have limited impact on the firm's reputation and behaviour.

The demand for privacy is likely to make the problem more difficult still. If a consumer shared information regarding $B$ with others, a true 'average' of $X_2$ supplied in relation to the 'average' promised $X_2$ might be deduced. Where consumers have a strong wish for privacy, or such privacy is supported by law or social norm (as they frequently do in relation to medical matters), the inability of consumers to determine $X_2$ directly or indirectly becomes more pronounced. The asymmetric information problem therefore requires that $X_2$ cannot be observed directly and that it cannot be deduced from $B$. In the next section, I examine and compare some potential solutions to this market failure.

## 3 Nonprofit and for-profit organizations and regulations

From the above it follows that the efficiency problem in the market for care may be resolved by increasing the ability of consumers to

7 Since consumers differ in their tastes, any one consumer's experience provides little information for others. For a further exposition into this and how reputation can affect from behaviour see Pauly and Satterthwaite (1981).

monitor the amount of compassionate care ($X_2$) being provided or by increasing consumers' trust in the supplying institutions. Monitoring information has certain elements of a public good. Also, the information has to be trusted. Hence, the reduced-cost monitoring solution will usually be undertaken by GPs or NPs.[8] Trust may be elicited by FPs within a framework of repeated interactions or reputation. Alternatively, for reasons which will discussed later, consumers may place trust in NPs or in GPs. In his 1980 paper, Hansmann states that NPs are better positioned to supply services whenever the consumer cannot evaluate 'accurately the quantity or quality of the service' that was being purchased. This could occur either because of the nature of the service itself or the circumstances of its provision. Several other authors have modelled this information asymmetry between producer and consumer to explain the economic role of NPs. Easley and O'Hara's (1983) model formalizes Hansmann's argument of asymmetric information to explain the role of the NPs. The nondistribution constraint alters the incentive structure of the institution and NPs may be the preferred option when asymmetric information exists. They suggest that if the asymmetry can be resolved with a cost that the consumer finds acceptable, it is likely that FPs will be the institutional choice for the consumer. Their approach varies the cost of reducing the asymmetry to explain the coexistence of NPs and FPs.

Easley and O'Hara (1988) continue to examine the optimal nature of institutions that arise in an economy producing a multitude of goods and services that are characterized by asymmetrical information. The optimal contract (used to define the institutions) will depend on the type of asymmetry present. The nature of the firm will be on a continuum ranging from FPs at one extreme to NPs at the other, with various forms of constrained-profits institutions between. The Easley and O'Hara models assume that the surplus of NPs is observable, and that it is knowledge of this which facilitates the economic role of NPs. While clearly appropriate for charities, this may be less relevant for institutions that produce essentially private goods. Moreover, their models do not explain why different institutional forms exist for the same type of asymmetry which this paper does.

8 NPs supplying information on other institutions constitute a case of NPs whose *raison d'ětre* is the need for trust and whose output is not of interest to the median voter. The Toronto Kashrut Commission, a NP providing the Jewish community with free information on the conformity of food products and restaurants to Jewish dietary laws, is a perfect example of this.

In reviewing the day-care industry in the US, Rose-Ackerman (1986) explains the long-term stable coexistence of FPs and NPs: although NPs may be the consumer's preferred option, FPs will enter the market in response to a lack of sufficient supply by NPs. Furthermore, FPs and NPs differentiate their product sufficiently to provide different varieties of care and appeal to different groups in the population. In reviewing NP hospitals, Pauly (1987) argues that ownership differences in NP and FP hospital are not important with 'free entry and markets that adjust' (p. 261). He advances asymmetric information to explain the existence of NPs and introduces the idea of discriminating consumers to explain the *raison d'être* of FP hospitals.

Another interesting interpretation of the coexistence of NPs and FPs in the day-care industry is made by Mauser (1993), who posits that consumers' choice of NPs or FPs reflects a variation in their levels of information. The need to trust a seller is dependent on how much information is available to the consumer. The best-informed consumer may choose to espouse the latter and the less-informed consumer may choose the former. Hence, the level of information available to the consumer will dictate the choice of NPs versus FPs. Holtzman and Ullman (1991) examine data on FP and NP nursing homes and confirm their hypothesis that they coexist because the demand for nursing care by patients differs by their need for a 'guarantee of quality' and the transaction costs involved in monitoring quality. Gulley and Santerre (1993) examine the effect of a variety of tax rates on the market shares of NP, FP and GP hospitals, and find that valuable exemptions from taxes have positive impacts on the market share of NPs.

I want to add to the above discussion by focusing on the *type* of goods and services wherein NPs tend to exist. After all, there are very many goods and services for which there exist information asymmetries between consumer and seller or producer, and NPs do not appear to have an economic role. And with technological advances, such informational asymmetries will become more prevalent. Indeed, whether it is the purchase of day care, health services, or education, or used cars, computers, pharmaceuticals, banking and legal services, the consumers possess considerably less information than the seller. And yet very few car dealers or banks are NPs.

One solution to the problem of asymmetric information is repeated interaction and/or reputation. The role of repetition and reputation is enhanced by a low discount factor, a high cost to loss in reputation and high future payoffs. Chillemi and Gui (1991) formalize one such reputation model, and show that NPs and FPs can coexist in equilibrium. But this model does not seem adequate to explain why NPs play no role in many 'lemon' problems.

Moreover, for certain goods or services, the consumer may be protected by governments through regulation and licensing. For example, a consumer can buy a drug without worrying whether the drug sold will be the drug promised, even if she/he does not have sufficient knowledge to verify this. Consumers know that they are protected by existing regulation, which will thwart the manufacturer from benefiting from the consumer's ignorance. Thus, governments can and do intervene to safeguard consumers, which may obviate the need for NPs. Weisbrod (1988) does suggest that the NP institutional form may be a superior solution to the asymmetric information problem when it is easier to monitor the NPs' compliance with the nondistribution of profits than it is to monitor the quality/quantity of the product.

I consider three different scenarios wherein NPs will play a major role in an industry, in other words, situations where repetition or monitoring by government regulation may be insufficient to allow FPs to become the typical seller in the industry. These scenarios may, but need not, overlap.

(i) *The quality of the service is not objectively well defined, so that subjective judgements are integral to evaluating it.* One possibility is that quality is fluid and has unmeasurable characteristics and is, at least partially, in the 'eye of the beholder'. (How do you define or measure 'compassionate care'? How do you judge whether a student has received sufficient training in critical skills at a university?) Or quality is multidimensional, and, at least partially, depends on the subjective judgement by the seller.

With a one-shot purchase of the type of service described above, 'contract failure' cannot be satisfactorily remedied by regulations, licensing and monitoring, though these may be used to prevent gross abuse. Consumers will try to remedy this failure by purchasing such services from sellers whom they trust, thus lowering the probability of being exploited. Even for repeated interactions, the difficulty of monitoring will reduce the ability of consumers to verify the occurrence of 'cheating'.

(ii) *If the costs of changing supplier are large (in financial or utility terms), then once consumers have selected a supplier, they will be relatively captive.* Hence, they are likely to demand long-term contracts from the supplier (Weisbrod and Schlesinger 1986). But contracts cannot be written for all eventualities. And, the longer the time horizon of the contracts, the greater will be the likelihood that exogenous changes will occur, which will render the contracts inefficient. This means that consumers will end up consuming inefficiently and possibly paying excessive prices. The possibility of 'opportunistic' behaviour by sellers is often viewed as a reason for vertical integration within industry, since vertical integration obviates the need of firms to rely on the goodwill of long-term partners (Ben-Ner 1986). Patronizing NPs for such long-term services may be viewed as a form of vertical integration by consumers and communities. If the risk is internalized, NPs can be trusted (Ben-Ner and Van Hoomissen 1991).

FPs with a good reputation may resolve the problem, if the privacy and information issue is not too serious. But as is well known, reputations are hard to build, especially in the presence of other institutions that already sell the same service or good. Hence, if NPs exist in a given market, FPs will find it hard to make inroads into that market. The point of origin *will* matter, and NPs will dominate.

Moreover, FPs alter their behaviour in the face of economic changes outside the control of the consumer. For example, an increase in the probability that a FP will stop operating (because of adverse economic conditions, say) will reduce its supply of the unobservable input to decrease costs.[9] But such probabilities are not, in general, public knowledge. Given the importance of the service in question, consumers who are risk averse and/or have a strong preference for the unobservable input will prefer NPs even if FPs have a good reputation and are more efficient than NPs, providing that FPs – due to changing market conditions – are known to act opportunistically.[10] Such risk aversion will be magnified if the service in question involves the consumer in actual and/or potential costs of considerable magnitude, or in certain irreversibilities.

(iii) *In certain services the relation between the buyer and the seller (or agent of the seller) may affect the quality of the service and institutional arrangements may cause self-selection among sellers and/*

9 FPs, it has been argued by Chillemi and Gui (1991), remain trustworthy only when the price remains high enough for it to sustain its reputation and thus cannot adequately respond to changing market conditions. This is not the case for NPs.

10 FPs, to be privately efficient, will not only be cost minimizers, but may act opportunistically. To survive, other FPs will also have to act opportunistically. This may occur in the provision of the unobservable input ($X_2$). Such behaviour will cause a divergence in private and social efficiency, as FPs may be privately efficient but not socially efficient.

*or their agents.*[11] If consumers prefer the service to be provided by people who prefer to work for NPs, then there is a clear role for NPs. An example will clarify. Assume that you want your children to learn to be kind, and that kindness can be effectively taught by only kind people. Then, if the nondistribution constraint causes kind people to prefer to work for NPs, say, you will, *ceteris paribus*, enrol them in a NP school, rather than in a FP school (Hansmann 1980).

## 4 Trust in nonprofit organizations and public sector institutions

If consumers believe that NPs will supply the amount of compassionate care actually promised, the asymmetric information/moral hazard problem may be partially or fully resolved, and the risk that compassionate care will be undermined is partly controlled. If, because they lack a profit-maximizing incentive to cheat, NPs are trusted, then utility level $B_2$ will be once again attainable by consumers with budget $S$. Efficiency will increase. But why would consumers trust NPs to supply the promised amount of $X_2$ (compassionate care)?

It is increasingly recognized that the legal constraint of 'nondistribution' of profits is too 'passive' to imply that NPs will be trusted. Managers who cannot have access to profits may choose to distribute profits via increased perquisites. This can provide NPs management with an incentive to increase profits at the expense of the customer. And, of course, the management of a NP can always ensure that no profits are generated by combining the exploitation of consumer ignorance (or positional weakness) with a low level of work-related effort.

While there are several potential solutions to this issue, I prefer to focus on what I believe to be the correct, though relatively obvious and

11 In many ways, the institutional form, itself, may signal the quality of the service to under-informed consumers. Two differences are being suggested here: first, consumers differ in their marginal rates of substitution of $X_1$ and $X_2$ (i.e., their preferences) and have equal information and make the choice of institutional form based on their preferences; and second, consumers may have similar preferences (equal marginal rates of substitution) but differ in the levels of information that they may have regarding the service. It is the first difference that I use to model the coexistence problem, but either one or both differences can explain the coexistence of the institutional form.

less elegant, explanation: the managers of NPs are chosen because they possess particular values and ethics which suggest that they are less likely to 'cheat' consumers (Young 1983, Weisbrod 1988). This may work in two ways. First, the NPs may be affiliated with a particular religion. Profit maximization is not, in general, the principal aim of most religious organizations.[12] And, honesty, altruism and equity are high on the agenda of most religions. Hence, in the minds of consumers, a religious affiliation may reduce potential consumer exploitation. The religious affiliation of so many NPs can clearly be seen against this background.

Secular NPs do not have this automatic (and recognizable) stamp of being 'good'. They must therefore convince consumers that they can be trusted. And, their ability to gain consumer confidence must be greater (more efficient) that the ability of FPs to obtain the trust of consumers. The board of trustees of a NP is selected to provide this legitimacy. By offering their reputations as collateral, trustees make a commitment to the integrity of the NPs in question (Handy 1995). In turn, in order to safeguard this collateral board members will select management that has the appropriate attributes and actively monitor the NP.

The implications of this are that NPs will tend to be managed by people with value systems that make them considerably less likely to exploit consumers. But such value systems are likely to encompass more than just honesty. The managers of NPs, religious or secular, will bring with them other values, which will affect other aspects of services provided by NPs that they manage, and thereby consumer attitudes to them.

Since the need for trust makes FPs dubious suppliers of certain goods, it is natural to consider the potential role of the government in resolving the resultant market failure. It is necessary to understand why GPs do not dominate such markets. And, depending on the answer, why they have any role at all in such markets.

GPs may engender more trust than FPs, inasmuch as, like FPs, profits are not their goal. And yet, as in NPs, the nonprofits constraint may be too passive to warrant a great deal of trust. On the other hand, government bureaucracies do (in a diluted way) respond to public

12 The vow of penury is, of course, a personal form of the nonprofit constraint. See James (1986), who argues that NPs are often formed by religious entrepreneurs and are trusted because they are backed by trusted religious orders.

pressure. This suggests that they will supply some $X_2$, if only to achieve a minimum level of satisfaction. Insofar as this happens, GPs may be viewed as commanding more trust than FPs, but less trust than NPs. Moreover, they are likely to be less efficient than FPs (and, perhaps, also less efficient than NPs).

Nonetheless, GPs may have a role to play in markets requiring trust. And this role relates to the value systems brought to bear upon NPs by their management. NPs affiliated with a religion may adopt rules and practices that reflect their beliefs, and those rules will be offensive to some consumers. Some residents of homes for the elderly may object to crosses over their beds, to being tended by nuns, or to the very fact that they are patronizing a religious institution. Children and their parents may be unhappy in trustworthy and caring schools, because they object to prayers and the teaching of religious beliefs. Similarly, the management and board of directors of secular NPs may believe in and enforce greater equity among consumers, or impose certain a regime which many consumers object to.

Such disaffected consumers may want to trade some of the trust they have in NPs for other attributes, yet not give up $X_2$ altogether. They may therefore purchase the service in question from GPs and avoid being subjected to codes of rules and beliefs (religious or secular) that they do not welcome. Alternatively, and in addition, GPs may indeed enter the market, but only so as to satisfy the majority vote (Weisbrod 1977, 1988). In such cases, NPs would emerge to provide service for consumers whose preferences differ from those of the median voter.

## 5 Market shares between for-profit and nonprofit organizations

Since they are subject to the checks and balances of the market, it is reasonable to assume that FPs are more efficient than NPs. Hence, while FPs supply no $X_2$, they supply more units of $X_1$ per consumer dollar than NPs. This implies that the budget constraint facing a consumer with a budget S is as illustrated by $ABC$ in Figure 2. The segment $AB$ relates to NPs and the segment $BC$ relates to FPs. If a consumer is prepared to forego $X_2$ altogether, she/he will purchase the service from a FP, obtaining an additional amount of $X_1$ equal to BC.

Consumers with different preferences for $X_1$ and $X_2$ are shown in Figure 2. Define a consumer whose indifference curve touches the AB segment budget line at $E_1$ and intersects the $X_1$ axis at $C$ as Type 'i'. This

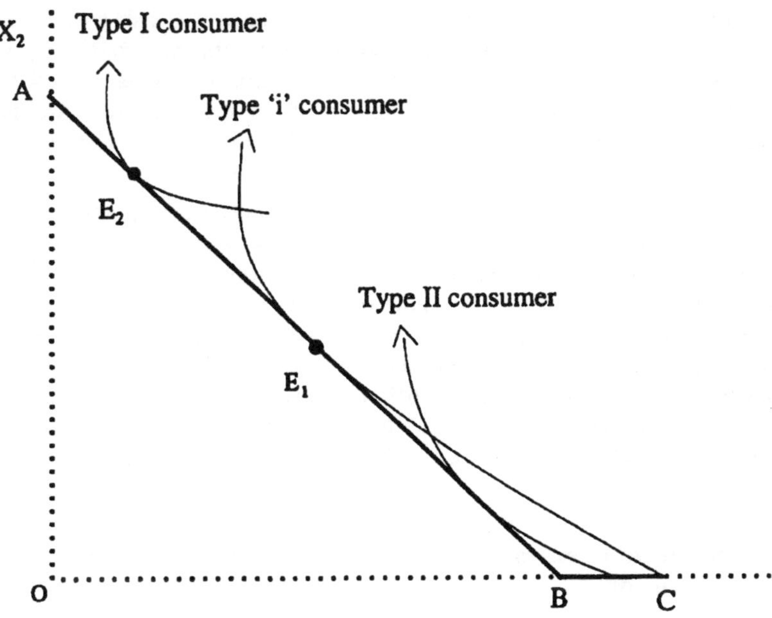


**Figure 2—Consumer preference: NPs or FPs?**

consumer is indifferent between FPs and NPs as sources of care, since he receives equal benefits at $E_1$ or $C$. This suggests that those consumers with indifference curves that are steeper than those of the consumer of Type 'i' at $C$ (i.e., whose indifference curve would intersect the $X_1$ axis any point between $B$ and $C$) would be better off purchasing care from FPs along the $BC$ segment[13] of the constraint line at $C$. Those consumers with relatively greater preference for $X_1$ will buy care from the FPs at $C$ for maximum benefits.

Different consumers will prefer different combinations of $X_1$ and $X_2$ given their budget constraints. Some will prefer, say, a home that has more state-of-the-art technology and modern amenities ($X_1$), whereas others may prefer a more informal atmosphere with greater emphasis on compassionate care and a sympathetic staff ($X_2$).

However, those consumers (Type I) who have a relative preference for $X_2$ (indicated by indifference curves which are flatter than those of Type 'i' consumer at $C$) will purchase care from the NPs for maximum

13 *C* being the only relevant point.

benefit at $E_2$. The Type II consumer, who purchases at $C$, will prefer FPs to NPs. Hence, if we assume that there exists heterogeneity of preferences among consumers purchasing care, as characterized by their differing preferences for the intermediary inputs $X_1$ and $X_2$, the above analysis explains the emergence and continued coexistence of NPs and FPs in the market for the care of the aged.

This then explains why we see the continued presence of NPs and FPs in certain areas. One testable prediction of this theory is that the technologies utilized by the alternative institutional forms will differ. Evidence of this nature is available in some recent empirical work on nursing homes and facilities for the mentally handicapped (Weisbrod 1994). In this study the differences in input utilization and output measures were compared for different institutional forms. Overall differences between the FPs and NPs were found and, furthermore, NPs were found to provide more of the $X_2$-type inputs/outputs than FPs.

## 6 For-profit or nonprofit organizations or public sector institutions?

Governments are likely to be involved in the production of these services for two reasons: to correct for a general market failure and for contract failure. For certain services such as national defence, education and health there exist positive externalities associated in their consumption.[14] The classical public finance economics argument is that if there exist externalities (positive or negative externalities) for certain goods and services, the market (FPs) will not provide the optimal amount. This is generally recognized as 'market failure' and the role of governments is to correct this failure by providing such goods and services. Some forms of contract failure can be resolved by regulation and licensing by governments. However, when this is difficult to do, and there exists a large demand for such services, it is likely that the government may wish to resolve the contract failure not by regulation, but by producing those goods and services itself.

For services that require 'trust', FPs may not provide optimal amounts, as argued earlier. However, if GPs (which, like NPs, are also subject to the nondistributional constraint) enjoy the trust that NPs

14 Externalities are generally defined as consequences of production and consumption of goods or services that are not factored into the usual (private) cost–benefit calculations made by the producer or consumer.

enjoy and are not subject to the vagaries of donations for financing, the question arises: why do we not see the demise of NPs and their replacement by government-run institutions (GPs)?

To be sure, the advantages GPs have versus NPs is substantial (financing, legislating tax exemptions and subsidies, erecting barriers to entry, etc.). Yet, they are constrained in a fundamental way. They must respond to the majority needs. They cannot provide services that do not appeal to the majority, nor partisan services differentiated on the basis of religion or ethnicity. Weisbrod (1988) has argued that the fundamental reason for the existence of NPs is to satisfy a demand for services that was unfulfilled by GPs. If consumers are heterogeneous and are not satisfied with the services provided by GPs, they will form NPs to satisfy their differing demands.[15]

Reconsider the home for the elderly previously discussed. Let us assume that the for-profit sector continues to be more efficient than the public sector or the nonprofit sector in producing $X_1$. The budget constraint for a NP consumer is AE. Consumer's trust of GPs and NPs differ and one such consequence may be that GPs will offer less of $X_2$ than NPs. Thus, the public sector (due to its internal structure, political mandate and the use of tax revenues) offers different combinations of $X_1$ and $X_2$ at different prices than the NPs. In Figure 3, FC is an example of a budget constraint facing a GPs consumer.

FPs, as discussed earlier, will produce $X_1$ and for a given budget will produce at D. Thus, the effective budget constraint facing the consumer who is free to choose from alternative forms of production will be *ABCD* (as seen in Figure 3). Clearly, when the consumer is on the *AB* section of the budget constraint she/he purchases from the NPs and when on the *BC* section of the budget constraint she/he is a GPs consumer. The consumer on the *CD* portion of the budget line purchases from the FPs. Consider the three kinds of consumers whose relative preferences for $X_1$ and $X_2$ give rise to the indifference curves

15 Gassler (1986, p. 101) asks why we see the establishment of NPs, FPs and GPs in an economy. He analyses this question from a motivational standpoint. Why would an economy with neoclassically selfish rational individuals create FPs, GPs and NPs? His answer uses the self-interested motives for the establishment of FPs and GPs, but relies on 'partly nonselfish' motives of an altruistic entrepreneur to explain the NPs. While I acccept this argument at the motivational level for the establishment of NPs, I seek to explain further why in a world of self-interested individuals, such organizations continue to coexist *and persist* from a consumer perspective.

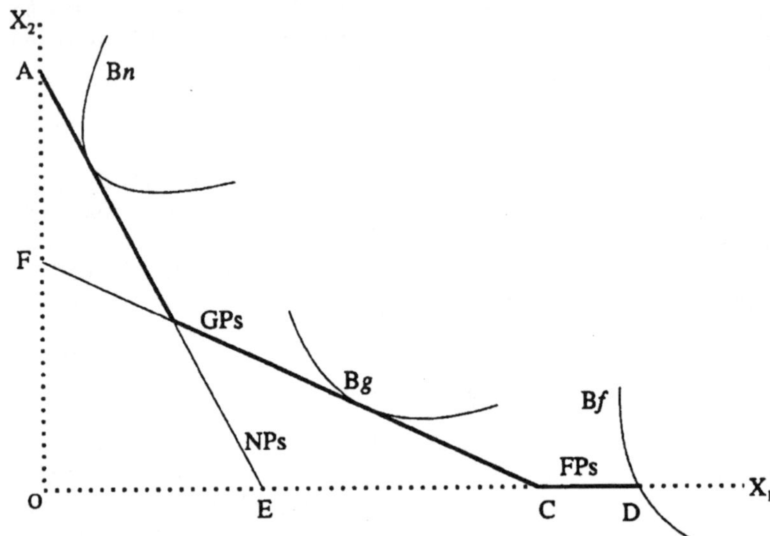


**Figure 3—The heterogeneity of consumers and the coexistence: NPs, FPs, and GPs**

(*Bn*, *Bg*, *Bf*), as illustrated in Figure 3. These consumers will prefer to purchase from NPs, GPs and FPs, respectively.

Thus, given a heterogeneity of discriminating consumers, there will be a set of consumers who will maximize their benefits from purchasing from FPs, GPs or NPs.

Now consider the case where GPs enjoy relatively greater advantages in producing care. This may be because of their advantage in raising money through taxes to provide the service. It is possible that they will offer the service at a lower price than FPs or NPs. However, because they are bound by the constraint of offering only that mix of $X_1$ and $X_2$ desired by the majority of the voters, they are restricted to a single kind of output. Thus, it is entirely possible that the relevant GPs budget constraint consists of only one point.[16] This is shown in Figure 4 by the point *B*. Thus the effective budget set are all points on the line *ACD* plus *B*.

16 For expositional simplicity I use a single point related to one particular service offered to satisfy the majority vote. It is likely that a limited spectrum of services would be offered by the government owing to log rolling; however, this does not affect the conclusions drawn from the model.

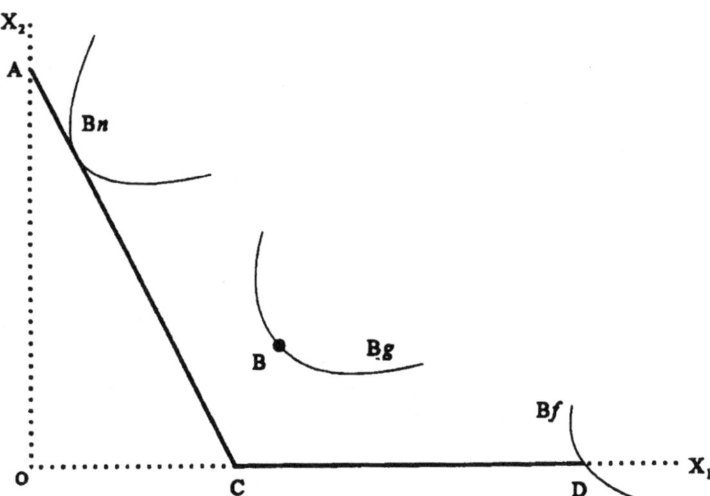


**Figure 4—Coexistence of NPs, FPs and GPs with a single output B supplied by GPs**

Although GPs may also be active in the market for care, and enjoy a subsidy to produce care cheaply, the majority-vote constraint which limits their combinations of $X_1$ and $X_2$ in the production of care ensures a market share for FPs and NPs.

However, changing these mixes will simply result in different market shares. Furthermore, NPs may also be restricted in the kind of care they provide. As NPs are generally founded on a religious or ideological basis, they may be restricted to the types of output they provide. A similar analysis can demonstrate differing market shares for NPs, FPs and GPs. It follows from the above that changes in trust, efficiency and relative prices of the inputs, will alter the distribution between GPs, FPs, and NPs.[17]

17 Hansmann (1987) found that tax subsidies (which lower the costs to NPs) increase the market share of NPs to FPs in the US. Other examples of changes in market shares due to change in relative price and/or efficiency are seen in the health-care industry (Pauly 1987, Cleary et al. 1991), the recycling industry (White 1992), the software and audio visual industry (Bennett and Dilorenzo 1988), the performing arts (Hansmann 1981); education and health services (Hansmann 1987); and the day-care industry (Rose-Ackerman 1986, Preston 1988).

## 7 Conclusion

While care of the aged is used as an example in the above analysis, the results may be used to explain the emergence and coexistence of NPs and FPs whenever the output being sold incorporates a mix of observable and unobservable components by decision-making clients. Furthermore, as supply by the NPs is idiosyncratic, based on an religious or ideological basis, governments will enter the market to provide the care demanded by a majority of voters.

Various types of NPs exist that are bound by the legal nondistribution of profits constraint. Religious or church-affiliated NPs may coexist at the same time as NPs formed by secular groups. If religious NPs command greater trust on the part of some consumers than other NPs, it is likely that they would attract those consumers who have the greatest preference for $X_2$ type of outputs. On the other end of the spectrum, GPs could also provide the service to satisfy demand. If GPs enjoy less consumer trust than secular NPs but enjoy greater trust than FPs (though some may argue that this is not likely), we may have a continuum of institutional forms, with varying degrees of consumer trust and efficiency they elicit.

Furthermore, even if GPs price their services at zero, they are not exclusive, nor do they dominate the market share (for example, in secondary schools). NPs continue to thrive despite charging high fees. In services where governments cannot respond to a heterogeneous demand for various kinds of education, such as religious instruction, sports instruction, various kinds of extracurricular education, small class size, elitism, and so on, consumers will be willing to pay higher prices to obtain differing kinds of quality via trusted institutions such as NPs, but not from FPs (Weisbrod 1988).

The model recognizes that NPs, FPs and GPs are subject to their own internal constraints: nondistribution of profits and in some cases religious or ideological constraints for NPs; profit maximizing and market discipline for FPs; majority voting for GPs. These constraints limit the type or quantity of output that is produced in each of the sectors. I add to this the discriminating consumer, who is willing to trade quality for efficiency and price and vice versa and I am able to demonstrate varying market shares for NPs, FPs and GPs. I conclude that the coexistence in the market of NPs, FPs, and GPs is efficient and plays and important role in satisfying heterogeneous demand for services where there exists some degree of informational asymmetry resulting in contract failure.

## REFERENCES

BEN-NER A., 1986, 'Nonprofit organisations: why do they exist in market economics?', in S. Rose Ackerman, ed., *The Economics of Nonprofit Institutions: Studies in Structure and Policy*, Oxford University Press, New York, pp. 94–113.

— and VAN HOOMISSEN T., 1991, 'Nonprofit organizations in the mixed economy: a demand and supply analysis', *Annals of Public and Cooperative Economics*, 62(4), 519–49.

BENNETT J. T. and DILORENZO T. J., 1988, 'The profits of nonprofits: unfair competition in the computer software and audiovisual industries', *Journal of Small Business Management*, 26(2), 17–24.

CHILLEMI O. and GUI B., 1991, 'Uninformed customers and nonprofit organisation: modelling contract failure theory', *Economics Letters*, 35, 5–8.

CLEARY P. D., SCHLESINGER M., and BLUMENTHAL, D., 1991, 'Factors affecting the availability and use of haemodialysis facilities', *Health Care Financing Review*, 13(2), 49–55.

EASLEY D. and O'HARA M., 1983, 'The economic role of the nonprofit firm', *Bell Journal of Economics*, 14, 531–8.

— and —, 1988, 'Contracts and asymmetric information in the theory of the firm', *Journal of Economic Behaviour and Organisation*, 9(3), 229–46.

GASSLER R. S., 1986, *The Economics of Nonprofit Enterprise*, United Press of America, Madison, CT.

GULLEY O.D. and SANTERRE R. E., 1993, 'The effect of tax exemption on the market share of nonprofit hospitals', *National Tax Journal*, 46(4), 477–86.

HANDY F., 1995, "Reputation as collateral: An economic analysis of the role of trustees of nonprofits", *Nonprofit and Voluntary Sector Quarterly*, 24(4), 293–305.

HANSMANN H., 1980, 'The role of the nonprofit enterprise', *Yale Law Review*, 89, 835–99.

—, 1981, "Nonprofit Enterprise in Performing Arts", *Bell Journal of Economics*, Autumn, 341–61.

—, 1987, 'Economic theories of nonprofit organisations', in Walter W. Powell, ed., *The Nonprofit Sector: A Research Handbook*, Yale University Press, New Haven, CT.

HOLTMAN A. G. and ULLMAN S. G., 1991, 'Transaction costs, uncertainty, and not-for-profit organisations: the case of nursing homes', *Annals of Public and Cooperative Economics*, 62, 641–54.

JAMES E., 1986, 'Comment', in S. Rose-Ackerman, ed., *The Economics of Nonprofit Institutions: Studies in Structure and Policy*, Oxford University Press, New York, 154–8.

MAUSER E., 1993, *Comparative Institutional Behaviour: The Case of Day Care*, PhD thesis, University of Wisconsin-Madison.

PAULY M., 1987, 'Nonprofit firms in medical markets', *American Economic Review*, 77(2), 257–62.

— and Satterthwaite, M. (1981) 'The pricing of primary care physicians services: a test of the role of consumer information', *Bell Journal of Economics*, 12, 488–506.

PRESTON A. E., 1988, 'The effects of property rights on labour costs of nonprofit firms: an application to the day care industry', *Journal Industrial Economics*, 36(3), 337–50.

ROOMKIN M. and WEISBROD B., 1994, 'Managerial compensation in for-profit and nonprofit hospitals: is there a difference?', Working Paper, North Western University.

ROSE-ACKERMAN S., 1986, 'Altruistic nonprofit firms in competitive markets: the case of day care centers in the United States', *Journal of Consumer Policy*, 9(3), 291–310.

SCHIFF J. and WEISBROD B., 1991, 'Competition between for-profit and nonprofit organisations in commercial activities', *Annals of Public and Cooperative Economics*, 62, 619–40.

STEINBERG R., 1993, 'Public policy and the performance of nonprofit organisations: a general framework', *Nonprofit and Voluntary Sector Quarterly*, 1, 13–31.

WEISBROD, B., 1977, *The Voluntary Nonprofit Sector: An Economic Analysis*, D. C. Heath and Company, Lexington, MA.

— (1988), *The Nonprofit Economy*, Harvard University Press, Cambridge, MA.

— (1994), 'Nonprofit and proprietary sector behaviour: does institutional form matter?', Working Paper, Northwestern University.

— and SCHLESINGER M., 1986, 'Public, private, nonprofit ownership and the response to asymmetric information: the case of nursing homes', in S. Rose-Ackerman, ed., *The Economics of Nonprofit Institutions: Studies in Structure and Policy*, Oxford University Press, New York, 94–113.

WHITE M. M., 1992, 'Nonprofit recycles find life after Curbside', *Biocycle*, 33(2), 66–8.

YOUNG D. R., 1983, *If Not for Profit, for What?*, Lexington Books, Lexington.

# Part V
# The Behavior of Nonprofit Organizations

Rand Journal of Economics
Vol. 17, No. 4, Winter 1986

# The revealed objective functions of nonprofit firms

**Richard Steinberg***

*Although assertions have often been made about the objectives underlying the behavior of nonprofit firms, there has been no empirical confirmation of these assertions. This article proposes a way to infer a nonprofit organization's objective function by estimating the marginal donative product of its fundraising. Panel data estimates, derived by using Hildreth and Houck's (1968) random coefficients model, suggest that welfare, education, and arts firms are "service maximizers," that health firms are budget maximizers, and that the objective of research firms cannot be ascertained within the family of objective functions considered.*

## 1. Introduction

■ For-profit firms generally seek maximal profits because profits provide income to the owners of the firm. In contrast, although nonprofit firms are allowed to accrue profits under the law, they are legally barred from distributing these profits to the owners of the firm (typically a board of directors). Thus, the objective function cannot be so simply derived in the case of nonprofit firms. Most earlier research on nonprofit firms merely asserted an objective such as prestige maximization, maximization of employee income, redistribution of income, or maximization of a specified quantity/quality tradeoff. (See Hansmann (forthcoming) for a review.) More recently, researchers have analyzed the survivability of various objectives under different regulatory and competitive environments. (See Steinberg (forthcoming) for a review.) Although behavioral implications of the various models have been discussed often, they have not been formulated in a way that would enable researchers to test one theory against another.

In this article I construct an empirical test that enables us to identify a firm's objective within a one-parameter family of plausible objectives. One polar member of this family is budget maximization, in which gross resources are maximized; the other extreme is service maximization, in which the residual available for charitable service is maximized.

Budget maximization was first proposed as a nonprofit objective by Tullock (1971) and Niskanen (1971), and it can be explained in three ways. First, higher managerial salaries and prestige may be associated with a larger budget. Second, self-dealing (purchasing of supplies from firms owned by the manager or directors) may be more lucrative in larger

* Virginia Polytechnic Institute and State University.
I would like to thank Robert Inman, Susan Rose-Ackerman, Henry Hansmann, Jacques Crémer, Thomas Reiner, Julian Wolpert, Dennis Young, Richard Ashley, Alvin Klevorick, and two anonymous referees for helpful comments on previous versions of this work. Burton Weisbrod provided the data. Research was supported by a grant from the Program on Nonprofit Organizations at Yale and through the National Science Foundation's grant to the Metropolitan Philanthropy project at the University of Pennsylvania.

firms. Finally, the firm may be misguided into budget maximization if it hires an external fundraising organization and the contract with this external organization is improperly structured (say, on a cost-plus basis). Weinberg (1980) was the first to propose service maximization explicitly, but it is necessary to attain many of the other objective functions postulated in the literature. For example, a firm interested in some quantity/quality tradeoff (such as a superior education provided to fewer students) would require maximal net resources to accomplish its goal. We can expect service maximization when the board of directors obtains overriding utility from the charitable output of the firm and monitoring costs are low or the manager shares the firm's goals (Steinberg, forthcoming).

Some firms may have mixed motives, for the manager's utility function may include both budget and service levels as arguments. Alternatively, mixed motives could arise as a political compromise among members of the board of directors. We can identify such mixed motives by intermediate values of the parameter defining the family of objectives.

Section 2 indicates how a firm reveals its objective by its behavior. In Section 3 I empirically specify this test and I report the results in Section 4. In Section 5 I discuss alternative specifications and in Section 6 I summarize my results. Details on sample selection criteria, the classification of organizations, and data problems appear in the Appendix.

## 2. Nonprofit objective functions and efficient allocations

■ I assume that nonprofit maximands are members of the following one-parameter family:

$$\psi(F;k) = k(X + C(F) - F) + (1-k)(X + C(F)), \tag{1}$$

where

$k$ = the objective function parameter;
$X$ = exogenous resources available to the firm;
$F$ = expenditure by the firm on solicitation (fundraising); and
$C$ = contributions received by the firm, which are a function of $F$.

When $k$ is zero, the first term drops out, and the maximand is the gross revenue (budget) obtained by the firm. This corresponds to budget maximization. When $k$ is one, the maximand is the net revenue obtained from a fundraising campaign. Since this net revenue is entirely available for service provision, this corresponds to service maximization. Intermediate values of $k$ represent mixed objectives.

Assuming that the contributions function is differentiable with nonnegative first and negative second derivatives, we can characterize interior solutions to (1) subject to the budget constraint,

$$0 \leqslant F \leqslant X + C,$$

by[1]

$$dC/dF = k.$$

Thus, $dC/dF$, which I shall henceforth refer to as the marginal donative product of fundraising, reveals the firm's objective. We can estimate the marginal donative product of fundraising: an estimated value of one reveals a service-maximizing objective, and an estimated value of zero demonstrates budget maximization.

A budget-maximizing firm increases its fundraising expenditure whenever there is a nonnegative marginal donative product, while a service-maximizing firm only increases its fundraising when the marginal returns are at least as great as the marginal expenditures. If

[1] Corresponding results have been derived for more complicated and realistic formulations of the problem by Boyle and Jacobs (1978), Weinberg (1980), Rose-Ackerman (1982), Steinberg (1983, 1985), Weisbrod and Dominguez (1984), and Cullis, Jones, and Thanassoulas (1984). Most of these articles consider only service maximization, but extension to the broader family is straightforward. Under most circumstances, the decision rule remains the same. Exceptions will be noted as they arise.

fundraising is a tool for providing services (rather than an end in itself), then budget-maximizing behavior is surely wasteful.

## 3. Empirical specification

■ My panel data set contains the budgets of 2,202 nonprofit organizations located in four U.S. metropolitan areas (Philadelphia, Los Angeles, Houston, and Minneapolis/St. Paul) for the years 1974–1976, as reported to the IRS. Organizations are classified into five sectors on the basis of the type of service provided. The first sector is public welfare, which, loosely, contains charities. Organizations in this sector are devoted to the care or rehabilitation or legal protection of groups such as children, animals, the poor, minorities, women, criminals, juvenile delinquents, and neighborhoods.

The second sector is health. This comprises hospitals, clinics, mental health groups, and multipurpose organizations, the primary purpose of which appears to be the provision of medical care. Thus, I classified old age homes as public welfare, while organizations providing medical services for the aged are in the health sector. Hospitals provide a special problem, for many of them are also research and teaching institutions. I therefore include hospitals in this category unless research or teaching appears to be the primary purpose of the organization.

The third sector, education, contains private schools ranging from kindergarten through graduate institutions. This sector also includes tutoring programs, special education, and vocational training programs. The fourth sector, arts and culture, includes performing arts groups, museums, zoos, historical societies, and similar groups. The final sector is research. It comprises scientific, medical, and other research-oriented organizations. Further details on sample selection and classification appear in the Appendix.

I hypothesize that organizations in the same sector are likely to share a common objective, and estimate this objective for each sector by determining the sector's (mean) marginal donative product of fundraising. Objectives are assumed to be common within sectors, but distinct among them because organizations within a sector share a common environment, which dictates which objectives can survive, and socialization process, which dictates which objectives are likely to be initiated.

The donative revenue function, which relates contributions received to a firm's expenditures on fundraising, will vary across firms and across time periods. To make the estimation process manageable, I assume a fixed-effects model. That is, I assume that the donative revenue function has a firm-specific intercept (constant across time periods) and a time-specific intercept (constant across firms), while the slope of the revenue function is common across firms.[2] Including firm-specific effects controls for factors such as the organization's ideology, accounting practices, and location. Including time-specific effects controls for such factors as the stage of the business cycle, which affects both the income of donors and the need for the type of service provided, and the value of tax deductions provided to donors in that year. Because the panel is so short, the firm-specific intercepts also control, somewhat, for firm-specific factors that vary slowly over time, such as the demographic characteristics of the potential donor pool drawn on by the firm, characteristics of other firms serving similar needs, and the reputation of the firm.

[2] To test this specification, I performed a joint $F$-test to see whether the firm-specific effects were collectively significant. In the baseline model these effects were significant at better than the .001 level for the health, education, and arts sectors. For welfare, they were significant at about the .15 level, whereas for research, they were significant at about the .07 level. The time-specific effects were never significant, but, as they only used up a single degree of freedom and were theoretically plausible, they were ratained in all reported results. I also estimated regressions (not reported here) in which time-specific effects were excluded, but these results were nearly identical to the reported ones.

In general, we can estimate a fixed-effects model by including a set of $N-1$ spatial dummy variables ($N$ is the number of cross sectional units) and $T-1$ temporal dummy variables ($T$ is the number of years). In the present case it is computationally simpler and equivalent to omit the dummies and to use data in first-difference form because only two years of data are available and lagged effects are included in the model. In first-difference form we should interpret the intercept as an indicator of the trend in donations.

I incorporate lagged effects in my model because of informational and response delays. Fundraising and donating occur over a fiscal year, rather than at a point in time. Thus, it is quite reasonable to assume that solicitations occurring late in the year result in donations in the following year. Although longer lags are theoretically plausible, it was not possible to estimate longer lags with this data set. When fundraising has effects in two years, efficiency requires that

$$\partial C_t/\partial F_t + (\partial C_{t+1}/\partial F_t)/(1+r) = k.$$

For a stable donative revenue function, this is equivalent to specifying that the current and discounted lagged effects of fundraising must sum to $k$. When all variables are specified in nominal terms, it is appropriate to use a nominal discount rate. I select 10%. (Results are not very sensitive to this choice of discount rate.)

I incorporate two other explanatory variables in both current and lagged form—administrative and service expenditures. Administrative expenditures ($A$) are included because donors may regard them as indicators of the efficiency with which their donations are translated into services and because some fundraising may be reported in this category since there are no clear accounting guidelines on how nonprofit firms should classify their expenses. I also include administration because the marginal donative product of administration is itself of interest. If administration served only as an input to revenue production, then the marginal donative product of administration would reveal the objective function in the same fashion as does the marginal donative product of fundraising: a value of one would reveal a service-maximizing objective, while a value of zero would indicate a budget-maximizing goal. But since administration is jointly an input to revenue production and to charitable service production (it is impossible to convert revenues to charitable output without at least some administrative expense), $k$ exceeds the marginal donative product of administration by the unknown value of the marginal charitable output of administration.

I include service expenditures ($E$) for four reasons. First, the size of the organization is a form of advertisement. Larger organizations are more visible and hence more able to secure contributions at any level of fundraising. Second, the model is consistent with certain forms of interdependent utility maximization by donors. A donor is more likely to know personally (and therefore, perhaps, care about) an individual receiving services or working for a nonprofit if that organization serves more clients, and client population is likely to be correlated with $E$. Third, donors, uncertain about the quality or efficiency of a particular nonprofit, may use $E$ as a screening device. Fourth, government grants may be allocated to organizations affecting the greatest number (of both clients and donors) to gain maximal political leverage, and this too is correlated with $E$.

The marginal donative product of service expenditure is also of interest. Regardless of the value of $k$, efficient firms choose a savings rate that sets the marginal donative product of service expenditure equal to zero. When the value exceeds zero, the savings rate is excessive in the sense that a decrease in current savings would allow service expenditure to rise in the current period without falling in any subsequent period.[3]

[3] Although a firm that set the marginal donative product of service expenditure to a positive number by oversaving could spend its saved resources in a future period, it would have fewer resources to spend in at least one period because donations in the initial period would be lower. Steinberg (1983) provides a formal proof of this optimality criterion for the finite-horizon case.

It may seem that fundraising causes charitable service expenditures, and not the other way around, so that $E$ is not an exogenous explanatory variable. Likewise, it may seem that donations cause fundraising, and not *vice versa*. In Section 5 I present several alternative multiequation models in which I allow causality to run both ways, but I believe the more simple, single-equation model is the appropriate one. If a firm chose its fundraising allocation by looking at its service expenditures or donations, its behavior would not be consistent with any objective function in the specified family. One can easily cite examples of higher donations' causing the firm to increase its fundraising activity (because optimism has been induced), but it is just as easy to provide examples of donations' decreasing fundraising activity (because campaign targets have been met). Such stories seem essentially *ad hoc*, and without an objective function (family), we have no hope of deriving an appropriate structural model. The simultaneous equation regressions reported in Section 5 should thus be regarded as exploratory.

In further defense of the single-equation specification, note that $C$, $F$, $A$, and $E$ are not inherently related to each other by a budget constraint. Although contributions are one source of funds, they are not the only source; sales, dues, fees, rentals, and capital gains also provide resources. Further, certain categories of expenditures, principally savings (net addition to endowment) are not included as right-hand-side variables. Finally, the firm can finance its fundraising before receiving donations by tapping its endowment, borrowing, or writing a contingent contract with an external fundraising firm.[4]

If all firms in the same nonprofit industry optimize with respect to the same value of $k$, and allocations are not excessively far from this mark, it is appropriate to estimate a linear functional form.[5] Incorporating firm- and time-specific effects into the model by expressing all data in first-difference form, we have the basic specification:

$$DC_{i,t} = \alpha + \beta_1 DF_{i,t} + \beta_2 DF_{i,t-1} + \beta_3 DA_{i,t} + \beta_4 DA_{i,t-1} + \beta_5 DE_{i,t} + \beta_6 DE_{i,t-1} + \eta_{i,t}, \qquad (2)$$

where the prefix $D$ indicates that the value of the variable lagged one period was subtracted from the value for the indicated time period, where $\eta_{i,t} = \epsilon_{i,t} - \epsilon_{i,t-1}$, with $\epsilon$ the error in the undifferenced equations, and where $\alpha$ is the coefficient on $DYEAR$ (identically 1), and accounts for the year-specific intercepts.

If firms are able to achieve their goals exactly in each time period, then (2) is naturally estimated by ordinary least squares. In that case $\hat{\beta}_1 + \hat{\beta}_2/(1 + r)$ would be an estimate of $k$. But it seems more realistic to assume that firms randomly and symmetrically deviate from setting each marginal product to its optimal value. Then, it is convenient to assume the following stochastic structure:

$$\beta_1 + \beta_2/(1+r) = k + \epsilon_F; \qquad E(\epsilon_F) = 0; \qquad E(\epsilon'_F \epsilon_F) = \sigma^2_F; \qquad (3a)$$

$$\beta_3 + \beta_4/(1+r) = m + \epsilon_A; \qquad E(\epsilon_A) = 0; \qquad E(\epsilon'_A \epsilon_A) = \sigma^2_A; \qquad (3b)$$

$$\beta_5 + \beta_6/(1+r) = n + \epsilon_S; \qquad E(\epsilon_S) = 0; \qquad E(\epsilon'_S \epsilon_S) = \sigma^2_S; \qquad (3c)$$

$$E(\epsilon_{i,t}) = 0 \quad \text{for all } i, t; \qquad E(\epsilon'\epsilon) = \sigma^2 I; \quad \text{and} \qquad (3d)$$

$$F_t, F_{t-1}, A_t, A_{t-1}, E_t, \text{ and } E_{t-1} \text{ are nonstochastic or} \qquad (3e)$$

$$F_t, F_{t-1}, A_t, A_{t-1}, E_t, \text{ and } E_{t-1} \text{ are uncorrelated with all error terms.}^6 \qquad (3ei)$$

[4] Steinberg (1983) considers these complications in a formal model. Although the criterion to determine whether an interior solution is optimal is affected, the decision rule is unaltered for interior optima.

[5] Steinberg (1983) reports results for a number of nonlinear specifications, and finds that estimates are very sensitive to the choice of functional form.

[6] It is reasonable to assume that the regressors are fixed parameters since they are the firm's choice parameters, they are easily controllable, and the data are for individual firms. The weaker condition, (3ei), is sufficient, however, for consistency.

Model (2) supplemented by (3) satisfies the assumptions of Hildreth and Houck's (1968) random coefficients model. Because firms in the same sector are assumed to miss a common objective randomly, it is plausible that all draws in each sector are made from a common distribution function, with zero mean and finite variance. The regressors are the choice variables, so that it is plausible to assume that they are nonstochastic (though noncorrelation with the error terms is sufficient for consistency). In contrast, the indicated linear combinations of the betas are random variables, whose means are the parameters of interest. Thus, $\hat{\bar{\beta}}_1 + \hat{\bar{\beta}}_2/(1 + r)$ is an estimate of $k$, the objective function parameter; $\hat{\bar{\beta}}_3 + \hat{\bar{\beta}}_4/(1 + r)$ is an estimate of $m$, which should be less than $k$ by the marginal charitable output of administration; and, finally, $\hat{\bar{\beta}}_5 + \hat{\bar{\beta}}_6/(1 + r)$ is an estimate of $n$, which should equal zero regardless of the firms' objectives.

To complete the model one must make assumptions about the covariance of $\epsilon_F$, $\epsilon_A$, and $\epsilon_E$. For the "no covariance model," I assume that this covariance matrix is diagonal, since it seems natural that errors in setting $F$ are uncorrelated with errors in setting $A$ and $E$. As an alternative, in the "covariance model" I allow for correlation among these errors.

Two complications arise in estimating the Hildreth and Houck (1968) model—heteroscedasticity and the possible failure of the estimated covariance matrix of the random coefficients to be nonnegative definite.[7] Heteroscedasticity is appropriately corrected by weighted least squares, but a number of estimators for the weights lead to consistent estimates of (2). Following the advice of Judge *et al.* (1985), who consider both theory and Monte Carlo evidence, I use the three-stage estimator they call $\hat{\hat{\alpha}}$ as my weighting variable. I then calculate standard errors in the usual way.

In the "no covariance" case I still have two options when using this weighting variable. In the first option I accept estimates of the weighting variables, even if they imply that the covariance matrix of the random coefficients is not nonnegative definite. This method is denoted as the RC model. In the second option I change negative elements of this covariance matrix to zero in calculating the weighting variable. I denote this procedure as the $RC^+$ model. There is some Monte Carlo evidence (cited in Judge *et al.*) that the second alternative is more efficient in finite samples, especially for samples of less than 50. For sample sizes exceeding 50 both methods were found to be more efficient than ordinary least squares.

In the "covariance" case it is more difficult to guarantee that the covariance matrix for the random coefficients is nonnegative definite because the necessary restrictions constitute a set of nonlinear inequalities. Although a number of *ad hoc* procedures exist for ensuring nonnegative definiteness, none of them has as yet been demonstrated to be superior in finite-sample efficiency to ignoring the restriction. Thus, I make no attempt to impose the restriction here. I denote this procedure as the RCC model.

There are five possible situations in which we cannot interpret the marginal donative product of fundraising as an estimate of the objective function parameter $k$. First, the nonprofit firm may be capital-constrained and thus unable to achieve the allocation that is optimal with respect to its objective function. In a world of perfectly functioning capital markets, optimal fundraising is always self-financing for the family of objective functions considered here.[8] Although external fundraising organizations, which finance campaigns for their clients, exist, it is likely that *ex ante* uncertainty over the returns to a particular campaign precludes the functioning of a capital market that is *ex post* optimal. Thus, there may be some self-financing campaigns that are not undertaken because the contributions

[7] See Judge *et al.* (1985, pp. 806–809, 434–437) for a discussion of appropriate estimation techniques for the Hildreth and Houck (1968) model.

[8] If an interior solution is chosen in model (1), then it must be that $C^* > F^*$ since $\psi \geq 0$ can be achieved by setting $F = 0$. A solution is feasible if and only if $C \geq F - X$. Since $X \geqslant 0$, interior solutions are always feasible. If the interior solution is not chosen, the corner solution is feasible for all organizations able to survive (and therefore for all observable organizations).

come in too late to be used for fundraising. In such cases firms should either devote all available resources to equating the marginal donative product of fundraising and the marginal donative product of administration to a number less than $k$, or should devote no resources to fundraising and administration (again, under the assumption that administration is not an input to charitable output).[9] More precisely, in such cases optimal allocations will satisfy

$$\frac{\partial C_t}{\partial E_t}+\frac{\partial C_{t+1}}{\partial E_t}\bigg/(1+r)=\frac{\partial C_t}{\partial F_t}+\frac{\partial C_{t+1}}{\partial F_t}\bigg/(1+r)-k=\frac{\partial C_t}{\partial A_t}+\frac{\partial C_{t+1}}{\partial A_t}\bigg/(1+r)-k. \tag{4}$$

If condition (4) were not met, the organization could increase net resources by reallocating expenditures to the category with the highest net marginal donative product, where "net" is defined in terms of the objective function parameter.

The second problem occurs when fundraising expenditures affect the value of volunteer labor resources ($V$) as well as contributions. In such a case the marginal donative product of fundraising would fall short of $k$ by the marginal labor value product of fundraising. The situation is even more complicated when $V$ depends on both $F$ and $C$. Then the efficiency test requires $dC/dF$ to be either greater than or less than $k$, depending loosely on whether $C$ and $V$ are complements or substitutes to donors (Steinberg, 1983). Unfortunately, we cannot estimate contributions of volunteer labor. Thus, the model exactly identifies $k$ only when the value of volunteer labor is unaffected by marginal fundraising.

The third problem arises when fundraising is itself an input to the service provided. For example, a group attempting to influence legislation will find that its fundraising campaign will change the political climate and influence legislation as well as provide resources for further lobbying. A lobbyist with a million dollars may be persuasive, but a lobbyist with a million dollars garnered from a million voters' contributions will be far more persuasive. Another example is a group fighting heart disease. If the fundraising literature persuades donors to have their blood pressure checked, then fundraising is an input to service provision as well as a way of obtaining money for service provision.

For such a nonprofit firm we need a more complete specification of the objective function to derive the efficiency condition. We must know whether nonprofit firms care about the indirect benefits conferred on donors as well as the direct benefits conferred on clients. These goals can be essentially identical (as in the lobbying example) or can differ (as in the health care example). If all benefits provided as the result of a fundraising campaign are regarded identically in the objective function, then the problem is formally identical to the case where volunteer labor is endogenous, and efficiency requires that

$$dC/dF+dZ/dF=k, \tag{5}$$

where

$Z = Z(F)$ = the monetary equivalent of benefits conferred as a side-effect of fundraising.

Although $dZ/dF$ can be negative (an antilitter campaign is hardly helped by campaign literature freely dispensed), it would ordinarily be positive. Thus, $dC/dF$ should be less than $k$. Once again, the data do not enable exact testing for the objective function parameter $k$ when $dZ/dF \neq 0$, though this problem is minimal for the set of organizations studied, as few of them have fundraising campaigns that confer obvious side benefits.

A fourth problem affects only the interpretation of the marginal donative product of

[9] If all organizations in each sector have the same revenue function and capital constraint, then $k$ can be identified as the marginal donative product of fundraising minus the marginal donative product of service expenditure or as the marginal donative product of administration minus the marginal donative product of service expenditure. These assumptions seem too strong to be reasonable, however. Thus, the marginal donative product of fundraising and the marginal donative product of administration will underestimate $k$ if the impact of capital constraints is severe.

administration as an estimate of $k$. In some cases laws and regulations may necessitate administrative expenditures in excess of $A^*$. In these cases the marginal donative product of administration will be less than $k$.

Finally, there are two cases in which efficiency requires that fundraising be zero. It may be that the marginal donative product of fundraising is less than $k$ for all nonnegative $F$. Alternatively, there may be a fixed cost and a range of increasing returns. In such a case the net return when the marginal donative product of fundraising equals $k$ may be less than the fixed cost, so that the firm is better off shutting down its fundraising machinery. In both cases $k$ cannot be identified and, indeed, the marginal donative product of fundraising cannot be estimated. We learn nothing about the goals of organizations with zero fundraising; hence, I have excluded organizations with $F = 0$ in each year from the sample.

## 4. Results

■ I estimate the basic model,

$$DC_{i,t} = \alpha + \beta_1 DF_{i,t} + \beta_2 DF_{i,t-1} + \beta_3 DA_{i,t} + \beta_4 DA_{i,t-1} + \beta_5 DE_{i,t} + \beta_6 DE_{i,t-1} + \eta_{i,t},$$

four different ways for the welfare, health, education, arts, and research charitable sectors.

Table 1 reports results estimated by ordinary least squares. Using White's (1980) spec-

**TABLE 1 Baseline Estimates by Sector***

| Variable | Welfare | Health | Education | Arts | Research |
|---|---|---|---|---|---|
| *Intercept* | 5.2659 | 14.136 | 52.006 | −3.5705 | −38.1085 |
| | (19.623) | (48.068) | (99.847) | (13.641) | (309.616) |
| | (16.613) | (29.853) | (81.393) | (9.005) | (68.457) |
| $DF_t$ | .6317 | .1367 | 1.3859 | .5743 | 2.3412 |
| | (.0583) | (.0493) | (.3622) | (.1713) | (1.1666) |
| | (.0809) | (.0550) | (.4070) | (.1583) | (2.0227) |
| $DF_{t-1}$ | .6367 | −.0107 | .2670 | 1.6556 | 5.7334 |
| | (.0687) | (.0586) | (.3958) | (.4815) | (6.6007) |
| | (.0992) | (.0596) | (.3411) | (.6622) | (4.3114) |
| $DA_t$ | .1905 | .1229 | −.1073 | .5150 | .3876 |
| | (.0983) | (.0455) | (.0892) | (.1200) | (.3277) |
| | (.2105) | (.0545) | (.1252) | (.1594) | (.5669) |
| $DA_{t-1}$ | −.0349 | −.0790 | −.0703 | −.2313 | −.0572 |
| | (.1019) | (.0492) | (.0916) | (.3009) | (.2677) |
| | (.2525) | (.0497) | (.1284) | (.3919) | (.3654) |
| $DE_t$ | −.0307 | .0800 | −.0869 | .1584 | .5233 |
| | (.1010) | (.0570) | (.0995) | (.0682) | (.2585) |
| | (.3370) | (.0530) | (.1372) | (.1022) | (.4035) |
| $DE_{t-1}$ | .1126 | −.1765 | .2776 | −.5389 | .6477 |
| | (.1188) | (.0638) | (.0643) | (.1163) | (2.5200) |
| | (.2539) | (.0637) | (.1256) | (.1207) | (2.4324) |
| $\bar{R}^2$ | .5649 | .1570 | .3241 | .6709 | .6670 |
| $F$ | 43.846 | 3.8551 | 14.265 | 24.441 | 10.683 |
| *pr > chisq*** | .0001 | .0631 | .0001 | .2662 | .0009 |
| $N$ | 199 | 93 | 167 | 70 | 30 |

* Standard errors, calculated by ordinary least squares, are in parentheses below parameter estimates. Asymptotic standard errors, estimated by White's (1980) method, are below these.

** The significance level for White's (1980) specification test for homoscedasticity.

ification test, we reject the hypothesis of homoscedasticity at better than the .01 level for three of the five sectors and find some evidence of heteroscedasticity for the other two. Thus, I report consistent standard errors derived by White's method as well as those derived from ordinary least squares. Table 2 reports the relevant marginal donative products, calculated as the sum of current and discounted lagged effects, and a consistent estimate of their standard errors (that accounts for the covariance between the current and lagged coefficients). Under the maintained hypotheses, the marginal donative products of fundraising and administration are each estimates of *k*. But the estimate of the marginal donative product of administration is less reliable because the interpretation of it as *k* requires the two additional assumptions, which we previously mentioned. The estimate of the marginal donative product of administration is best interpreted as a low estimate of *k*, since when either assumption is violated, the marginal donative product of administration falls short of *k*.

The baseline estimates strongly suggest that education and arts firms are service maximizers and weakly suggest that welfare firms are too. Health firms appear to be budget maximizers, while the motive of research firms cannot be ascertained because of the small sample size and concomitant large standard errors. The point estimates imply that a marginal dollar spent on fundraising would bring in an additional $1.21 in contributions to welfare firms, $1.63 to education, and $2.07 to the arts. If these firms were service maximizers, they would choose a level of fundraising that resulted in a marginal donative product of fundraising of one. Hence, welfare, education, and arts firms are engaging in insufficient fundraising relative to this goal, though the shortfall in fundraising is statistically significant only for

**TABLE 2 Efficiency Parameters in Base Case***

| | Marginal Donative Products: | | |
|---|---|---|---|
| Sector | Fundraising | Administration | Service |
| Welfare | 1.2106<br>(.0362)<br>$P\phi$: .0001<br>$P1$: .0001 | .1578<br>(.4110)<br>$P\phi$: .7015<br>$P1$: .0418 | .0716<br>(.4839)<br>$P\phi$: .8825 |
| Health | .1269<br>(.0612)<br>$P\phi$: .0411<br>$P1$: .0001 | .0511<br>(.0289)<br>$P\phi$: .0806<br>$P1$: .0001 | −.0805<br>(.0468)<br>$P\phi$: .0890 |
| Education | 1.6286<br>(.5550)<br>$P\phi$: .0038<br>$P1$: .2591 | −.1712<br>(.1830)<br>$P\phi$: .3509<br>$P1$: .0001 | .1655<br>(.2088)<br>$P\phi$: .4292 |
| Arts | 2.0795<br>(.7368)<br>$P\phi$: .0064<br>$P1$: .1479 | .3048<br>(.3926)<br>$P\phi$: .4404<br>$P1$: .0814 | −.3315<br>(.1874)<br>$P\phi$: .0818 |
| Research | 7.5533<br>(5.7347)<br>$P\phi$: .2068<br>$P1$: .2649 | .3356<br>(.2377)<br>$P\phi$: .1714<br>$P1$: .0103 | 1.1121<br>(1.9950)<br>$P\phi$: .5826 |

* Asymptotic standard errors are in parentheses. $P\phi$ is the probability of falsely rejecting $H_0$: $DX_t + (DX_{t-1}/1.1) = 0$, where $X$ indicates the coefficients on $F$, $A$, or $E$, respectively. $P1$ is the corresponding probability for the hypothesis that the linear combination equals 1. High values of $P\phi$ for $F$ or $A$ are consistent with budget-maximizing behavior. High values of $P1$ are consistent with service maximization. Both types of behavior imply high values of $P\phi$ for $E$.

welfare. In contrast, a marginal dollar spent by health firms brought in only 13¢ of additional donations. Although this marginal donative product of fundraising is statistically significantly greater than zero, its absolute value is close to the value that budget-maximizing firms would obtain.

My theory predicts that the marginal donative product of administration should be lower than that of fundraising by the unknown marginal charitable output of administration, a prediction that is not refuted by the baseline estimates. In each case the estimated marginal donative product of administration was less than that of fundraising.

Finally, my theory predicts that the marginal donative product of service expenditures should be zero regardless of the firms' objectives. This prediction is somewhat borne out by the estimates: in no case was the marginal donative product of service expenditures significantly different from zero at the .05 level. But one can reject the hypothesis that the marginal donative product of service expenditures equals zero at the .10 level for health and arts firms. Thus, one could cautiously conclude that the average health or arts firm undertakes insufficient saving (and consequently incurs excessive current expenditure) relative to the optimal time path.

Heteroscedasticity is implied in the random coefficients model, and it may be present even if the random coefficients model is not appropriate. A powerful test for the type of heteroscedasticity implied by the random coefficients model is the Breusch and Pagan (1979) test, which is also relevant when either the standard deviation or the log of the variance of the dependent variable is a linear function of exogenous variables (Judge *et al.*, 1985, pp. 446–447). The Breusch and Pagan statistics are uniformly significant at better than the .005 level in the baseline model.[10] Since the Breusch and Pagan test appears to be conservative in small samples (Godfrey, 1978; Breusch and Pagan, 1979) because it reports a lower significance level than the true level, the evidence for this form of heteroscedasticity is convincing.

Table 3 reports results from the random coefficients model without covariance (RC). Table 4 presents the results derived by using the random coefficients technique without

**TABLE 3** **Random Coefficients Model without Covariance: Nonnegativity Constraints Unenforced (RC Model)***

| | Marginal Donative Products: | | |
|---|---|---|---|
| Sector | Fundraising | Administration | Service |
| Welfare | .9269<br>(.0531) | 3.9681<br>(.7732) | 1.8496<br>(.3721) |
| Health | .1141<br>(.0542) | .0567<br>(.0368) | −.0854<br>(.0550) |
| Education | 1.5687<br>(.5708) | −.1799<br>(.1489) | .1987<br>(.1352) |
| Arts | 1.8942<br>(.6018) | .7978<br>(.4094) | −.0143<br>(.1912) |
| Research | 7.5533<br>(5.6506) | .3334<br>(.1325) | 1.1456<br>(2.1589) |

* Asymptotic standard errors are in parentheses.

[10] The critical value for the Breusch and Pagan (1979) statistic at the .005 significance level is 18.548 in the baseline model. Homoscedasticity can be rejected if the sample statistic exceeds this critical value. Sample statistics were: welfare 155.69; health 32.74; education 91.93; arts 68.94; and research 41.38.

**TABLE 4** **Random Coefficients Model without Covariance: Nonnegativity Constraint Enforced (RC⁺ Model)***

| Sector | Marginal Donative Products: Fundraising | Administration | Service |
|---|---|---|---|
| Welfare | 1.2443<br>(.0655) | .0163<br>(.1949) | .1195<br>(.2341) |
| Health | .1616<br>(.0770) | .0528<br>(.0374) | −.0658<br>(.0730) |
| Education | 1.5954<br>(.6621) | −.1526<br>(.1664) | .1977<br>(.1557) |
| Arts | 1.9328<br>(.6021) | .7315<br>(.4270) | −.0344<br>(.1940) |
| Research | 7.4456<br>(5.6587) | .3347<br>(.1538) | 1.0568<br>(2.1741) |

* Asymptotic standard errors are in parentheses.

covariance when the *ad hoc* procedure described in Section 3 is used to enforce the nonnegativity constraint ($RC^+$). As noted earlier, there is limited Monte Carlo evidence supporting the superiority of $RC^+$ over RC.

Table 5 reports results from the random coefficients model with covariance (RCC). This model is more flexible than RC or $RC^+$, at a small cost in terms of available degrees of freedom. But since there is no convenient *ad hoc* technique for imposing nonnegative definiteness on the variance-covariance matrix in the RCC case, $RC^+$ would seem to produce more persuasive estimates.

The same general pattern of implied objective functions is produced by the three random coefficients models as by the baseline model. Welfare, education, and arts firms still appear

**TABLE 5** **Random Coefficients Model with Covariance, Nonnegativity Constraints Unenforced (RCC Model)***

| Sector | Marginal Donative Products: Fundraising | Administration | Service |
|---|---|---|---|
| Welfare | 1.1830<br>(.0129) | −.0824<br>** | −.6402<br>(.0867) |
| Health | .2046<br>(.0486) | .0946<br>(.0284) | −.0468<br>(.0248) |
| Education | 1.7459<br>(.4537) | −.4347<br>(.1489) | .1380<br>(.1404) |
| Arts | 3.7237<br>(1.0027) | .4151<br>(.1821) | .2701<br>(.2502) |
| Research | 2.7433<br>(1.4555) | .1756<br>(.0968) | .4106<br>(.5469) |

* Asymptotic standard errors are in parentheses.

** The estimated variance was negative—a possibility with the use of unrestricted estimated generalized least squares.

to be service maximizers, while health firms appear to be budget maximizers. The point estimates for marginal donative product of fundraising range from .93 to 1.24 for welfare, from 1.57 to 1.75 for education, and from 1.89 to 3.72 for arts sector firms. In contrast, the marginal donative product of fundraising ranges from .11 to .20 for health firms. The predominant motive of research firms is still difficult to ascertain from the estimates, but the marginal donative product of fundraising was significantly different from zero in the RCC model.

The finding that health firms, primarily hospitals, act as budget maximizers is perhaps surprising. Nonprofit hospitals must compete with for-profit and government-run hospitals, so that one might expect competitive pressures to eliminate firms that did not maximize the surplus from fundraising. The health market is somewhat special, however, because donations provided only 9% of income, whereas fundraising constituted only 3% of expenditures by such firms in the sample, so that inefficiency in fundraising is less important to this sector. Sales of goods and services provide the bulk of income, and much of this income is provided by third-party payers who were not notably price-conscious during the sample years. Economic rents from sales of goods and services might provide the cushion that allows budget maximizers to survive. These explanations are speculative, and it might be productive in future research to try to rationalize this result with a formal model.

There is less uniformity in the results of the random coefficients models with respect to the marginal donative products of administration and of service expenditures. With one exception (welfare in the RC model) the marginal donative product of administration remained below that of fundraising, so that the random coefficients models generally confirm this prediction of the theory. In contrast to the ordinary least squares estimates, though, the marginal donative product of service expenditures was significantly different from zero at the .05 level in several cases. Welfare was particularly interesting, for the RC model indicates excessive saving, while the RCC model indicates insufficient saving, both at high levels of significance. The $RC^+$ model is regarded as more reliable, and the marginal donative product of service expenditure for welfare firms does not significantly differ from zero here. As before, the random coefficients models indicate that health firms oversave, but this result was only significant in the RCC model. No other estimates of the marginal donative product of service expenditure significantly departed from zero.

Turning to the possibility of excluded-variable bias, note first that some variables omitted from the model have similar impacts on all organizations in the same sector. Sector-specific regressions implicitly control for these effects. As noted before, the individual-effects model estimated here implicitly controls for excluded variables that are constant over time but vary across firms and for excluded variables that are constant across firms but vary with time. Excluded variables that vary across both firms and time are the sources of possible bias here.

Estimates may be upward biased (true marginal donative products are lower than estimated) because of the exclusion of two types of variables: those that, *ceteris paribus,* cause contributions to be higher and are positively correlated with fundraising, or those that reduce contributions and are negatively correlated with fundraising. One such variable is "charitable needs." If need affects giving, and if certain firms within each sector are dominant in meeting this need, then estimates of the marginal donative product of fundraising will be upward biased. For example, if an earthquake struck, only certain social welfare agencies, such as the Red Cross, might help. Donors would be more receptive to solicitation, so that the donative revenue function would become steeper at each level of fundraising. Thus, both the chosen level of fundraising and donations would rise and so would provide the necessary positive correlation. On the other hand, there would be no bias if changes in need affected all firms in a particular sector, for the time-specific intercept would control for such effects.

A similar argument can be made with respect to other variables that shift the donative revenue function, such as an increase in donor income or wealth, receipt of a large (and publicized) windfall grant or bequest, or a change in tastes. For example, if the income of donors to some (but not all) organizations in a sector were to increase, and this caused the slope of the revenue function to increase,[11] then these organizations would increase both their fundraising and their level of contributions. Thus, the excluded shift in income causes an increase in donations and is positively correlated with the increase in fundraising, so that the estimated marginal donative product of fundraising will exceed the true one.

In sum, many excluded variables are implicitly controlled for in the model estimated here, but the possibility of bias cannot be eliminated. The probable direction of bias is toward overstated marginal donative products of fundraising. Thus, the evidence that health firms are budget maximizers is persuasive even when excluded variable bias is considered. The evidence that other firms act as service maximizers is weakened somewhat. Perhaps these organizations are service maximizers. In this case excluded variable bias would explain why the estimated marginal donative products of fundraising exceeded one. But if excluded variable bias is especially severe, the estimated marginal donative product of fundraising may exceed one when the true marginal donative product of fundraising is consistent with budget maximization.

## 5. Alternative specifications

■ In this section I present results for three alternative specifications. First, Table 6 reports the estimates for a random coefficients model that corresponds to the $RC^+$ model of Section 4, but in which I assume that the firm-specific intercepts are random. The year-specific effects remain fixed because there are insufficient sample years to relax this assumption profitably.

The results for this specification seem to tell the same story as the earlier estimates. Once again, welfare, education, and arts firms are service maximizers, while health firms are budget maximizers. In this specification, however, the apparent precision of the research estimates has improved to the point where I can classify these firms as service maximizers.

**TABLE 6 Random Coefficients Model without Covariance: Nonnegativity Constraints Enforced, Firm-Specific Effects Random***

| | Marginal Donative Products: | | |
|---|---|---|---|
| Sector | Fundraising | Administration | Service |
| Welfare | 1.2546<br>(.0714) | .1288<br>(.1253) | .7455<br>(.0684) |
| Health | .1675<br>(.0651) | .0664<br>(.0151) | .0259<br>(.0225) |
| Education | 1.8656<br>(.4318) | −.0508<br>(.0811) | .2581<br>(.0375) |
| Arts | 2.0737<br>(.5214) | .3275<br>(.0476) | .4768<br>(.0759) |
| Research | 1.2833<br>(.4282) | .0262<br>(.0176) | .3166<br>(.0093) |

* Asymptotic standard errors are in parentheses.

[11] Although an increase in donor income would increase the intercept of the donative revenue function as long as giving is a normal good, the effect on the slope is unclear. If higher income individuals become less responsive to solicitation, the function would flatten and the optimizing nonprofit firm would reduce its fundraising at the same time as it increased its donations. In this case, the bias would be in the opposite direction.

The estimates of the marginal donative product of administration follow the same pattern as for the earlier models, but there are some disparities in the estimates of the marginal donative product of service expenditure.

The second and third alternative specifications are designed to eliminate possible endogeneity bias. As noted, if $F$, $A$, or $E$ is determined by $C$, then the firm's behavior is not consistent with any of the objective functions in the specified family. Thus, the next two specifications are necessarily *ad hoc*. The first specification endogenizes $E$ by assuming that it is determined by contributions and two measures of firms' wealth—market value and net worth. I exclude these variables from the donative revenue function, (6a), because donors are less likely to know about wealth variables or to be indirectly affected by them, unlike service expenditures. Once again, I assume fixed firm- and time-specific effects and estimate the model in first-difference form. For simplicity, I also take the slope coefficients to be fixed, as in the baseline model. Thus, the general form of the "endogenous service expenditure model" is

$$DC_{i,t} = \alpha_1 + \alpha_2 DF_{i,t} + \alpha_3 DF_{i,t-1} + \alpha_4 DA_{i,t} + \alpha_5 DA_{i,t-1} + \alpha_6 DE_{i,t} + \alpha_7 DE_{i,t-1} + \eta_{1;i,t} \quad (6a)$$

$$DE_{i,t} = \beta_1 + \beta_2 DC_{i,t} + \beta_3 DC_{i,t-1} + \beta_4 DM_{i,t} + \beta_5 DM_{i,t-1} + \beta_6 DN_{i,t} + \beta_7 DN_{i,t-1} + \eta_{2;i,t}, \quad (6b)$$

where $M$ is the market value of the firm and $N$ is the firm's net worth.

Table 7 reports the results for the endogenous service expenditure model, which was estimated by three-stage least squares. The estimated marginal donative products of fundraising are quite similar to those for the baseline model, so that the implied objective functions are the same. There are no significant differences between the marginal donative products of administration for the baseline model and those in Table 7, but the estimated marginal donative product of service expenditure did change significantly for welfare and health.

In the final model I take fundraising to be endogenous and replace (6b) with an equation explaining fundraising. Thus, the model is:

$$DC_{i,t} = \alpha_1 + \alpha_2 DF_{i,t} + \alpha_3 DF_{i,t-1} + \alpha_4 DA_{i,t} + \alpha_5 DA_{i,t-1} + \alpha_6 DE_{i,t} + \alpha_7 DE_{i,t-1} + \eta_{1;i,t} \quad (7a)$$

$$DF_{i,t} = \beta_1 + \beta_2 DC_{i,t} + \beta_3 DC_{i,t-1} + \beta_4 DM_{i,t} + \beta_5 DM_{i,t-1} + \beta_6 DN_{i,t} + \beta_7 DN_{i,t-1} + \eta_{2;i,t}. \quad (7b)$$

In principle, this model allows us to isolate the independent effect of fundraising on donations when fundraising is partly determined by expected donations. The results reported in Table 8 are somewhat different from those previously reported. In particular, in this model the estimated marginal donative product of fundraising is 1.15 for health firms, which is significantly different from zero but not from one at the .05 level. The significance level of this result is lower in corresponding two-stage least squares estimates not reported here (the point estimate is .9840 with an asymptotic standard error of .5341), but this result nonetheless casts a little doubt on earlier estimates. Results for welfare, arts, and research follow the earlier patterns, but standard errors are somewhat larger; for education, the marginal donative product of fundraising increases dramatically, but so does the standard error.

It may seem somewhat artificial to endogenize one expenditure variable at a time, but in estimates not reported here for a four-equation model, which treated $F$, $A$, and $E$ as endogenous, very large asymptotic standard errors prevented meaningful conclusions about the parameters of interest.

## 6. Summary

■ Received theory does not predict the objective functions underlying nonprofit organizational behavior though a few recent articles make some progress in this direction. (See Steinberg (forthcoming) for a review.) In this article I attempt to uncover empirically the objective functions revealed by the budgetary behavior of such organizations.

**TABLE 7 Endogenous Service Expenditure Model***

| Sector | Marginal Donative Products:** Fundraising | Administration | Service | Statistics*** |
|---|---|---|---|---|
| Welfare | 1.1568<br>(.1064) | −.8153<br>(.5094) | −1.2528<br>(.5223) | $R^2$: .5367 |
| Health | .0938<br>(.0504) | .0419<br>(.0289) | .1883<br>(.0839) | $R^2$: .3118 |
| Education | 1.4973<br>(.6632) | .0268<br>(.2225) | .3504<br>(.2047) | $R^2$: .7031 |
| Arts | 1.8456<br>(.5412) | .0119<br>(.2390) | −.5523<br>(.1696) | $R^2$: .6794 |
| Research | 9.1930<br>(5.5931) | .3662<br>(.1535) | 1.0691<br>(2.1224) | $R^2$: .9973 |

Determinants of Service Expenditures

| Explanatory Variable | Sector: Welfare | Health | Education | Arts | Research |
|---|---|---|---|---|---|
| $E(DC_t)$ | −.1122<br>(.0900) | −2.8966<br>(1.6225) | 8.6581<br>(.9436) | 1.0766<br>(.1958) | −.4023<br>(.2130) |
| $DC_{t-1}$ | .4637<br>(.0893) | .2199<br>(.3757) | 7.9834<br>(.7586) | .1653<br>(.3084) | −3.0768<br>(.8711) |
| $DM_t$ | −.0131<br>(.0305) | −.0503<br>(.0762) | −.5943<br>(.2012) | .0303<br>(.0408) | −.2739<br>(.1895) |
| $DM_{t-1}$ | −.1175<br>(.0197) | .0007<br>(.0180) | −.3245<br>(.0324) | −.0112<br>(.0103) | .3692<br>(.1682) |
| $DN_t$ | −.0003<br>(.0001) | .0002<br>(.0004) | −.0051<br>(.0009) | .0005<br>(.0002) | −.0001<br>(.0002) |
| $DN_{t-1}$ | −4.8E-5<br>(9.7E-5) | −.0002<br>(.0002) | .0006<br>(.0002) | −.0003<br>(.0001) | .0012<br>(.0004) |

* Asymptotic standard errors are in parentheses beneath parameter estimates.
** Third-stage estimates of marginal donative products are reported.
*** $R^2$ is the weighted $R^2$ for the system, and corresponds to an approximate $F$-test on all nonintercept parameters in the system.

The model was designed to estimate the value of the parameter $k$, which characterizes objective functions in a specified family. When $k$ is equal to one, the nonprofit organization acts to maximize expenditure on charitable output (service maximization). When $k$ is equal to zero, the organization acts to maximize its overall budget, even when budgetary increases come at the expense of service cutbacks (budget maximization).

The parameter $k$ is revealed by the value of the marginal donative product of fundraising at current allocations. Though donative revenue functions may differ across organizations (and thus cause optimal budgetary allocations to differ), all organizations sharing a common objective will choose budgets resulting in the same marginal donative product of fundraising, and this is the sense in which an estimate of the marginal donative product of fundraising reveals $k$. To a lesser extent, $k$ is revealed by the marginal donative product of administration, though, as argued, the marginal donative product of administration is lower than $k$ under most circumstances.

**TABLE 8** **Endogenous Fundraising Model***

| Sector | Marginal Donative Products:** Fundraising | Administration | Service | Statistics*** |
|---|---|---|---|---|
| Welfare | 1.4758 (.1684) | −.5353 (.1666) | −.5267 (.1701) | $R^2$: .3251 |
| Health | 1.1467 (.5131) | −.1095 (.0838) | −.0960 (.1353) | $R^2$: .3120 |
| Education | 18.5860 (8.4341) | −.1885 (.4318) | .6682 (.4361) | $R^2$: .7224 |
| Arts | 2.4821 (1.5271) | −.1769 (.5422) | −.3560 (.1744) | $R^2$: .4970 |
| Research | 4.0212 (5.6121) | .1123 (.1160) | 3.9105 (1.6760) | $R^2$: .7105 |

Determinants of Fundraising Expenditures

| Explanatory Variable | Sector: Welfare | Health | Education | Arts | Research |
|---|---|---|---|---|---|
| $E(DC_t)$ | −.2699 (.2172) | −6.2705 (5.6679) | .7414 (.1312) | .2554 (.1038) | 1.9826 (.3475) |
| $DC_{t-1}$ | −.0341 (.1199) | .0044 (1.2192) | .0809 (.0761) | .2590 (.1466) | 3.8182 (1.2033) |
| $DM_t$ | .0248 (.0428) | .0305 (.2686) | −.0135 (.0152) | .0146 (.0201) | .9413 (.2722) |
| $DM_{t-1}$ | .0153 (.0275) | .2344 (.0512) | −.0045 (.0027) | .0134 (.0050) | −.8205 (.2509) |
| $DN_t$ | .0009 (.0003) | −.0007 (.0014) | −.0002 (.0001) | −.0003 (.0001) | −.0013 (.0002) |
| $DN_{t-1}$ | −.0002 (.0002) | −.0002 (.0008) | −2.6E-5 (1.6E-5) | .0001 (3.9E-5) | −.0014 (.0004) |

* Asymptotic standard errors are in parentheses.
** Third-stage estimates of marginal donative products are reported.
*** $R^2$ is the weighted $R^2$ for the system, and corresponds to an approximate $F$-test on all nonintercept parameters in the system.

I estimated marginal donative products from an individual-effects model applied to five nonprofit industries by using a three-year panel data set. I assumed that firms randomly and symmetrically miss their target marginal donative products so that the Hildreth and Houck (1968) random coefficients model was appropriate for the estimation. I obtained similar results by using ordinary least squares and three variants of the random coefficients model: welfare, education, and arts firms act as service maximizers; health firms act as budget maximizers; and the estimates are insufficiently precise to reveal the objective function of research firms.

## Appendix

■ **Sample selection, classification, and data problems.** Data were obtained from IRS files, as compiled by Burton Weisbrod of the University of Wisconsin. An extract matching numerical information from publicly available sections of IRS form 990 (filed by tax-exempt organizations) and descriptive information from the IRS Exempt

Organization Master File were obtained for all filing organizations in four metropolitan areas (Philadelphia, Los Angeles, Houston/Galveston, and Minneapolis/St. Paul) and three years (1974–1976).

The sample included all organizations that met all of the following criteria:

(1) Gross receipts exceeded $10,000 in each year.
(2) Exemption from federal corporate income tax was granted under section 501-c-3 of the tax code, which covers, roughly, charitable, educational, health care, cultural, and research nonprofit organizations to which contributions are deductible on federal personal income taxes.
(3) At least some services were provided to nonmembers (ruling out "clubs"), as determined by an algorithm utilizing three self-reported activity codes.
(4) Tax forms were filed all three years.
(5) The organization had at least one declared nonreligious purpose (as religious sector tax filers are a small and biased sample of all religious nonprofits).
(6) The organization was primarily a service provider, rather than a pass-through such as a foundation or a United Way.

Remaining organizations were classified into six nonprofit sectors on the basis of their self-declared "activity codes." The sixth (miscellaneous) category was not employed in this study because it was too heterogeneous to be confident that a single objective would characterize the sector. Although the classification was at times arbitrary (especially for multiactivity entities), I believe that each sector is adequately homogeneous. Exact details of the selection and classification algorithms are available from the author.

Interpretation of the numerical data is complicated here by four factors:

(1) Precise accounting definitions of the variables were not included with the tax forms and accompanying explanatory materials.
(2) As no taxes are owed, the IRS did not carefully audit many returns. Likewise, it is unclear how much effort was expended by nonprofits to assure that their answers were accurate.
(3) Organizations that left a question blank were recorded by the IRS as having answered the question with a zero. Thus, we cannot distinguish an organization with zero fundraising expenditure from an organization that did not answer the fundraising question.
(4) Inspection of several photocopies of the actual tax forms indicates that occasionally an organization would place all of its expenditures under any one of the three categories (though it was most common to place them in the second or third), along with a footnote explaining that "they could not break down expenditures in more detail" or "see the accompanying audit for a breakdown." Most organizations attempted to answer all three questions, and it is hoped that errors are sufficiently unsystematic so as not to bias econometric results.

The first problem primarily affects the breakdown of expenditures into three categories: fundraising, administration, and service provision. The exact wording of the questions on the tax forms thus becomes critical. Reported income categories on Part I of the form are "gross sales and receipts from all sources other than shown on lines 5 and 6" (line 1), "gross income" (line 4), "gross dues and assessments from members and affiliates" (line 5), and "gross contributions, gifts, grants, and similar amounts received" (line 6). The expenditure categories are "cost of goods sold" (line 2), "cost or other basis and sales expense of assets sold" (line 3), "expenses attributable to amount on line 4" (line 9), "expenses attributable to amount on line 6" (line 10), and "other program related disbursements" (line 11). The accompanying instructions provide little additional guidance. I have interpreted line 1 minus lines 2 and 3 as net income from sales, line 5 as dues, line 6 as grants plus contributions ($C$), line 9 as administrative expenses ($A$), line 10 as fundraising expenditure ($F$), and line 11 as service expenditure ($E$).

It is hard to know the exact impact of the second problem. All organizations might find it politically expedient to underreport fundraising expenditures in each year. Larger organizations are more carefully and frequently audited by independent auditors, though audits may categorize income and expenditures differently from the way IRS tax forms do. The smallest organizations were excluded from the sample, though enough intermediate size organizations remain to make this a problem of unknown importance.

In general, errors in the measurement of independent variables lead to estimated coefficients that are biased toward zero, though this depends on the covariance structure of the measurement errors. Instrumental variable estimates would be a possible remedy, but this data set contains no good instruments. Inspection of estimated residuals leads to a number of suspected erroneous observations, but most of these seem to be due to the false-zero problem, and they were eliminated by the sample restrictions discussed below.

Both of the first two problems are somewhat ameliorated by the first-difference method of estimation. Measurement, underreporting, or classification errors are presumably reasonably constant over the three years analyzed in each organization. Thus, the errors "subtract out" in the differencing process. In addition, the estimated generalized least squares techniques employed to correct for heteroscedasticity somewhat ameliorate the effect of outliers on parameter estimates.

The false-zero problem was quite significant for data from 1970–1973, so that I did not use such data. Responsibility for assuring that 990 forms are completely filled out rests with the district offices of the IRS, and hence enforcement varied with region. Inspection of the data suggests that all four included districts mandated a high degree of compliance by 1974, though some did so somewhat earlier.

The third and fourth problems suggest that certain observations are not credible. To cope with the problem, I excluded observations that seemed likely to be erroneous. But because erroneous observations cannot be identified with certainty, some erroneous observations may remain, while some legitimate observations may have been discarded. Erroneous observations reduce the power of the model, and it is desirable to eliminate as many as possible. But biased results are always possible when the sample selection rule is data-based. In addition, if an excessive number of legitimate observations are eliminated along with the illegitimate ones, standard errors will increase. Any sample selection rule trades off these problems, and three compromises were tried in Steinberg (1983), one of which is used in the present study, and another in this Appendix.

The least restrictive rule in terms of the resulting sample size excluded observations with contributions of zero in any year from 1974 to 1976 and resulted in the "large" sample. This restriction eliminates some, but not all, of the observations likely to be erroneous for either cited reason. If an organization with a fundraising campaign reports zero contributions in three consecutive years, it seems likely that reported figures are inaccurate. If an organization's contributions suddenly increase from zero to a positive level, it seems more likely that the initial zero resulted from nonreporting than from a shift from nondonative to donative status.

A more restrictive rule—again, gauged in terms of resulting sample size—yielded the "medium" sample that I use in the present study. This sample excluded observations in which fundraising, contributions, or administration were reported as zero in all three years. Observations reporting zero contributions the first year, with positive contributions the second, are included here, even though the initial zero may represent nonreporting. This sample restriction is mainly designed to answer the fourth problem, that of organizations' lumping all expenditures into one category. It is harder to believe that an organization had zero administration or fundraising in three consecutive years than to believe that it placed that category of expenditures elsewhere.

The most restrictive rule resulted in the "small" sample. Organizations were excluded if fundraising or contributions were always reported as zero, or if administration was ever reported as zero. It is hard to believe that an organization has zero administrative expenditure even in one year, so that the more restrictive rule was tried.

The small sample was inadequate, and standard errors were enormous. There is, however, no strong reason to prefer the medium sample used in the text to the large sample. Random coefficient models were not estimated on the large sample, but Table A1 reports ordinary least squares estimates (incorporating time- and firm-specific effects) produced by the large sample, results which should be contrasted with those reported in Table 2. Estimates from the large sample suggest the same general pattern of predominant objectives as that produced by the medium sample.

**TABLE A1 Marginal Donative Products from Large Sample***

| | Marginal Donative Products: | | | |
|---|---|---|---|---|
| Sector | Fundraising | Administrative | Service | Statistics |
| Welfare | .6936<br>(.2357) | .4854<br>(.2215) | .3189<br>(.1729) | $\bar{R}^2$: .3390<br>$F$: 43.918<br>$N$: 754 |
| Health | .0939<br>(.0908) | −.0040<br>(.0340) | −.0614<br>(.0639) | $\bar{R}^2$: .1344<br>$F$: 7.435<br>$N$: 374 |
| Education | 1.1188<br>(.7094) | .1746<br>(.1626) | .1626<br>(.1244) | $\bar{R}^2$: .3648<br>$F$: 39.038<br>$N$: 597 |
| Arts | 1.2722<br>(.2449) | .3283<br>(.4138) | 1.5186<br>(.4561) | $\bar{R}^2$: .8272<br>$F$: 115.903<br>$N$: 217 |
| Research | 2.2108<br>(1.9173) | .0987<br>(.0606) | 1.2406<br>(.4342) | $\bar{R}^2$: .6335<br>$F$: 24.241<br>$N$: 122 |

* The baseline model was run with ordinary least squares for the "large sample" defined in the text. Asymptotic standard errors, calculated by the White (1980) method, are in parentheses below parameter estimates.

## References

BOYLE, S.E. AND JACOBS, P. "The Economics of Charitable Fundraising." *Philanthropy Monthly* (May 1978).

BREUSCH, T.S. AND PAGAN, A.R. "A Simple Test for Heteroscedasticity and Random Coefficient Variation." *Econometrica*, Vol. 47 (1979), pp. 1287–1294.

CULLIS, J.G., JONES, P.R., AND THANASSOULAS, C. "Are Charities Efficient 'Firms'? A Preliminary Test of the U.K. Charitable Sector." *Public Choice*, Vol. 44 (1984), pp. 367–373.

GODFREY, L.G. "Testing for Multiplicative Heteroscedasticity." *Journal of Econometrics*, Vol. 8 (1978), pp. 227–236.

HANSMANN, H. "Economic Theories of Nonprofit Organization" in W. Powell, ed., *The Nonprofit Sector: A Research Handbook*, New Haven: Yale University Press, forthcoming.

HILDRETH, C. AND HOUCK, J.P. "Some Estimators for a Linear Model with Random Coefficients." *Journal of the American Statistical Association*, Vol. 63 (1968), pp. 584–595.

NISKANEN, W.A., JR. *Bureaucracy and Representative Government*. Chicago: Aldine-Atherton, 1971.

JUDGE, G.C., GRIFFITHS, W.E., HILL, R.C., LÜTKEPOHL, H., AND LEE, T.C. *The Theory and Practice of Econometrics*, 2nd ed. New York: John Wiley, 1985.

ROSE-ACKERMAN, S. "Charitable Giving and Excessive Fundraising." *Quarterly Journal of Economics*, Vol. 97 (1982), pp. 193–212.

STEINBERG, R. "Two Essays on the Nonprofit Sector." Ph.D. Dissertation, University of Pennsylvania, 1983.

———. "Optimal Fundraising by Nonprofit Firms" in *Giving and Volunteering: New Frontiers of Knowledge*, 1985 Spring Research Forum Working Papers, Washington, D.C.: Independent Sector, 1985.

———. "Nonprofit Organizations and the Market" in W. Powell, ed., *The Nonprofit Sector: A Research Handbook*, New Haven: Yale University Press, forthcoming.

TULLOCK, G. "Information without Profit" in D.M. Lamberton, ed., *Economics of Information and Knowledge*, Baltimore: Penguin Books, 1971.

WEINBERG, C.B. "Marketing Mix Decision Rules for Nonprofit Organizations." *Research in Marketing*, Vol. 3 (1980), pp. 191–234.

WEISBROD, B. AND DOMINGUEZ, N. "Demand for Collective Goods in Private Nonprofit Markets: Can Advertising Overcome Free-Riding Behavior?" University of Wisconsin-Madison, SSRI, Working Paper #8410, April 1984.

WHITE, H. "A Heteroscedasticity-Consistent Covariance Matrix Estimator and a Direct Test for Heteroscedasticity." *Econometrica*, Vol. 48 (1980), pp. 817–838.

# [19]

ELSEVIER Journal of Public Economics 56 (1995) 257–272

# Charity donations in the UK: New evidence based on panel data

Jyoti Khanna[a], John Posnett[b], Todd Sandler[c,*]

[a]*Department of Economics, Colgate University, Hamilton, New York 13346, USA*
[b]*Department of Economics, University of York, Heslington, York Y01 5DD, UK*
[c]*Department of Economics, Iowa State University, Ames, Iowa 50011-1070, USA*

Received October 1992, revised September 1993

**Abstract**

This paper presents a set of panel data estimates for 159 of the most prominent UK charities for the period 1983–1990. In evaluating alternative specifications, we settle on a fixed-effects estimation. Social welfare charities are shown to fund raise short of the point at which net revenues are maximized, whereas health and overseas charities are found to net revenue maximize. Religious charities maximize total revenues. Estimates of price and fund-raising elasticities are presented for charities overall and for four cohorts. For alternative income sources, no evidence of crowding-out is found.

*Key words:* Non-profit sector; Public goods; Panel data

*JEL classification:* L31; H41

## 1. Introduction

In recent years, much attention has been paid by economists to the nonprofit sector. This sector continues to prosper in the UK and serves an important intermediary function by linking donors and recipients of charity aid.[1] Nonprofit firms receive revenues from a host of sources including voluntary donations, government grants, fees, investment income, rents, and sales of commodities. A number of issues have dominated the litera-

* Corresponding author.

[1] See Posnett (1992) for recent trends in the UK.


*SSDI* 0047-2727(94)01421-J

ture. First, there is the question concerning the underlying objective of the nonprofit firms and whether this objective differs among industry groups (e.g., health, social welfare). Second, there is the issue whether public support and other revenue sources crowd out voluntary donations. Third, there is interest in whether donors are discouraged by fund-raising expenditures, since these expenditures reduce the money spent on charity recipients. This article provides further empirical evidence on these important issues.

Using data for the accounting year 1985/86, Posnett and Sandler (1989) showed that 299 of the largest (and most successful) fund-raising charities in the UK maximize their *net revenue* from donations when deciding fund-raising expenditures. This result contrasts with the Weisbrod and Dominguez (1986) study that demonstrated that nonprofits in the US increase their fund-raising expenditures beyond *net* revenue maximization to the point of *total* revenue maximization. In two studies of US charities, Steinberg (1986a,b) showed that nonprofits in the education, welfare, and art sectors tend to maximize net revenue, while the health sector appears to maximize total revenue. Since the publication of Posnett and Sandler (1989), more data have become available for England and Wales, covering the time period from 1983 to 1990.

The primary purpose of the current study is to provide a set of panel estimates for UK charities during 1983–1990, so that we can re-evaluate our earlier finding of net revenue maximization. In fact, this earlier result does not characterize half of the sample charities for the expanded time period, since UK charities in the social welfare sector are found to fund-raise *short* of the point of net revenue maximization, while charities in the religious sector are found to maximize total revenue. Just the health and overseas sectors are shown to net revenue maximize. Moreover, the expanded data set allows us to distinguish among a host of econometric specifications based on alternative pooling techniques. Our statistical findings provide updated estimates of price and fund-raising elasticities for the entire sample and for cohorts of industry groupings. This study also indicates further evidence that alternative revenue sources from government grants and autonomous income activities (fees, sales, and investment income) do not crowd out or reduce voluntary donations.

## 2. Preliminaries

A significant portion of charitable activities in the UK and elsewhere are accounted for by the nonprofit sector.[2] A number of empirical issues

[2] For an excellent treatment of nonprofits, see Weisbrod (1988).

dominated the literature on nonprofits. First, studies examined the stimulative influence of tax deductability on charitable contributions in the US by focusing on the marginal price of giving a dollar, which equals one minus the marginal tax rate. An increase in this tax rate reduces the effective price of giving and should augment giving. Prior to 1989, this literature found the price elasticities of donations to range from 0.9 to 1.4 in absolute value (Clotfelter, 1989, p. 113), thus indicating a significant responsiveness to marginal tax changes. Furthermore, estimated income elasticities were between 0.5 and 0.8 (Schiff, 1989). In some recent panel studies, price elasticities were, however, near zero (see discussion and references in Barrett (1991) and Steinberg (1990)). Jones and Posnett (1991a) uncovered tax-price elasticities for the UK to be insignificantly different from zero. With panel data on households, Barrett (1991) found elastic tax-price elasticities, thus supporting the government practice of tax deductibility.

Second, nonprofit studies concerned the notion of crowding-out, whereby government funding of charities reduces private charitable giving. A wide variety of findings characterized crowding-out. Abrams and Schmitz (1978) discovered that a dollar of federal expenditure on health, education, and welfare reduces private donations by 0.236 dollars in the US. With more recent data, Abrams and Schmitz (1984) estimated crowding-out to be 30 cents on a dollar of state and local social welfare payments. Kingma (1989) found crowding-out to be 15 cents for public broadcasting. In contrast, Posnett and Sandler (1989) uncovered no significant evidence of crowding-out from local and central government grants for UK charities in 1985. Schiff (1985) found the effect on contributions to differ across government levels and by the form of government transfer. Monetary transfers by state government, for instance, crowd out donations to social welfare, whereas noncash transfers by the state government encourage private charitable giving (see Steinberg's 1991 survey for a summary of different effects of government grants).

Third, studies have been interested in the behavior and the underlying objective function of the nonprofit firms. This set of studies moved away from the use of household data and examined voluntary contributions from the viewpoint of the nonprofit firms (Posnett and Sandler, 1989); Schiff and Weisbrod, 1991; Steinberg, 1986a,b; Weisbrod and Dominguez, 1986). When the literature investigated fund-raising expenditure (*FE*), an important distinction was drawn between revenue-maximizing charities and net revenue maximizing charities. A revenue-maximizing charity is interested in pushing fund-raising expenditure to the point where an additional pound of fund-raising efforts brings in zero additional pounds of voluntary donations (*CV*), so that $\mathrm{d}CV/\mathrm{d}FE = 0$. In contrast, a net revenue-maximizing charity increases fund-raising effort until an extra pound of such effort brings in an extra pound of donations, so that $\mathrm{d}CV/\mathrm{d}FE = 1$. Firm or charity-level studies used the charity's characteristics (e.g., the charity's age), its choices (e.g., fund-raising expenditure), and its alternative sources of contributions as the determinants of giving. The current study is in this tradition.[3]

### 2.1. The output price of giving

We follow Weisbrod and Dominguez (1986) and others[4] by defining the implicit price of giving as the cost to the donor, in pounds foregone, of increasing the output of the charity by £1. This price, $p$, is

$$p = (1 - t)/[1 - (f + a)] , \tag{1}$$

where $t$ is the marginal tax rate, and the denominator is the proportion of total expenditure or nonprofit income actually devoted to the provision of charitable output. In Eq. (1), $f$ and $a$ are the proportions of total expenditure used for fund-raising and administration, respectively.[5] This price measure is lagged in the empirical model so that $f$ and $a$ are in terms of lagged fund-raising and administrative spending shares. Our measure represents a "plausible irrationality" (Rose-Ackerman, 1982), whereby donors use average fund-raising and administrative shares instead of marginal shares to calculate price. Steinberg (1986a, p. 347) criticized this price measure because "it confuses marginal and average firm behavior, neglects multiplier effects, and ignores cross-donative responses." He argued that, if the donor is too small to affect the donations of others, then the entire marginal donation provides marginal service regardless of the fund-raising share so that the true price is 1 (p. 352). Nevertheless, we stick with the price measure in Eq. (1), because it allows us to compare our results to earlier studies, and is on average (mean of 1.17) not too distant from Steinberg's preferred value of 1.

Unlike the US, tax deductibility is a much smaller consideration for the UK. During much of our sample period of 1983–1990, tax deductibility requires either a payroll deduction or giving by covenant, whereby a donor must decide a fixed amount of donations for greater than three years. In the

[3] Price elasticity measures in organization-level studies are not expected to be comparable to tax-price elasticities in household studies, since these latter studies use a price measure that ignores fund-raising and administrative expenditure.

[4] Others included Rose-Ackerman (1982) and Posnett and Sandler (1989).

[5] Since there is no acceptable accounting practice for distinguishing adminstration and fund-raising expenditure among charities, the price variable is surely "noisy". This noise is somewhat attenuated because the Charity Aid Foundation computes these variables for our data set from charity accounts, while employing the same convention throughout the sample period. Since these two spending categories enter the price equation in an additive fashion, the size of the price variable is independent of the assignment between expenditure classes.

Charities Aid Foundation's (1991) survey for 1989/90, 11 percent of the respondents made a donation by covenant or by payroll deduction. In our sample, covenants were 9.7 percent of total voluntary donations in 1983; 6.5 percent in 1985; 7.4 percent in 1987; and 5.9 percent in 1990. Moreover, Jones and Posnett (1991b) found that planned giving by bank standing order and deduction from pay represented approximately 14 percent of total giving. The best available evidence therefore suggests that tax deductible donations in the UK in the period to 1990 represented 10–15 percent of total individual giving. Since we do not have comparable tax deductibility data to complement our revenue and expenditure data of UK nonprofit firms, we must compute price as $p = 1/[1 - (f + a)]$. By dropping tax deductibility, our price differs from the true price by a positive random variable. The expected value of the resulting bias for price elasticity, however, is zero.

## 2.2. On crowding-out

The notion that one source of charity revenue may crowd out another is related to the neutrality theorem, associated with the private provision of a *pure* public good.[6] Since many nonprofit charitable firms provide a public good, the theorem *may* be relevant to these institutions. The neutrality theorem indicates that any engineered redistribution of income, say through taxes and government provision, among an unchanged set of contributors will not alter the Nash-equilibrium public good provision. A set of contributors is unchanged when the redistribution policy does not involve a corner solution in which a previous contributor stops contributing or a new contributor begins contributing voluntarily or involuntarily. If a nonprofit firm provides a pure public good and if the government also provides the same good through taxes levied *on the contributors*, then government provision would crowd out private provision on a pound-for-pound basis. The neutrality theorem does not hold if the sources for alternative financing for the public good come, in part, from noncontributors (Bergstrom et al., 1986, theorem 6). Since most government provision is financed via general-fund taxes that impact both contributors and noncontributors, crowding-out will, if it occurs, be partial. In fact, an increase in government grants *can be consistent with an increase* in donations from contributors when a large number of noncontributors are taxed and the presence of government grants increases the appeal of the charity to donors.

Incomplete crowding-out may also result if the charitable activity gives

[6] On the neutrality theorem and its limits of applicability, consult Andreoni (1990), Bergstrom et al. (1986), Cornes and Sandler (1984, 1986), Rose-Ackerman (1986), Steinberg (1987), and Warr (1983).

rise to jointly produced private and public outputs (Cornes and Sandler, 1984, pp. 593–4; Andreoni, 1990). By their nature, autonomous income activities involve the sale of private goods and, hence, would not fully abide by the neutrality theory. If contributors view government grants, autonomous income, and voluntary contributions as nonsubstitutable (see Schiff, 1985, for a model), then neutrality will be partial and crowding-out will be attenuated. Government grants may be nonsubstitutable if they serve as a quality index or else fund complementary items (Rose-Ackerman, 1986; Steinberg, 1991).

## 3. Empirical specification

To test for crowding-out among alternative income sources and to measure the impact of lagged fund-raising spending, we use the following empirical specification for the determinants of current voluntary income (covenants and other donations but excluding legacies):[7]

$$CV_{it} = \beta_0 + \beta_1 P_{i,t-1} + \beta_2 FE_{i,t-1} + \beta_3 AI_{i,t-1} + \beta_4 GG_{i,t-1} + \beta_5 LEG_{it} + \beta_6 AGE_{it} + u_{it}\,, \tag{2}$$

in which $\beta_0$ is a constant, the $\beta_j$'s are coefficients, and $u_{it}$ is the error term for the $i$th charity in year $t$. The first subscript indicates the charity, while the second denotes the time period. The dependent variable in (2) shows the variation in voluntary contributions ($CV_{it}$) received by a charity over time. In (2), the price variable ($P$) captures the standard determinant of demand and is based on the lagged shares of fund-raising and administrative spending. Lagging these values implies that donors must first acquire information on these expense items prior to determining the implicit (average) price of giving. We also lag autonomous income ($AI$) (which includes rents, investment income, fees, and other income) government grants ($GG$), and fund-raising ($FE$) to allow information to accumulate (estimates based on current values of these variables are available from the authors; these results are, however robust to lagging). Since legacies ($LEG$) are often known in advance, we use current values. The charity's $AGE$ since foundation is known in any period and, hence, is not lagged. Presumably, lagged fund-raising spending has two opposing effects on donations: (1) it stimulates demand for the charitable output, much as advertising augments demand for a product, and (2) raises the implicit price of giving and reduces the quantity demanded. The charity's $AGE$ is included as a quality proxy

[7] A specification with current and lagged values of $FE$, $AI$, and $GG$ was rejected in favor of Eq. (2) owing to problems of multicollinearity.

for the stock of goodwill or the degree of familiarity with the nonprofit firm, and is expected to be a positive stimulant. *AGE* is a more accurate measure of the charity's age in the UK data than its counterpart in the US data, since *AGE* truly indicates the date since foundation, not the date of registration as is the case in the US data. The remaining independent variables – government grants (central and local), legacies, and autonomous income – reflect the alternative sources of income for the nonprofit firm, and are included to test for crowding-out. Unlike Posnett and Sandler (1989), the interactive term $FE \times AGE$ is not included, because of the high degree of multicollinearity with the *FE* term (0.97) that it introduces into the equation. Linear and log-linear specifications of the model were tried. The log-linear specification was rejected in favor of the linear model.[8]

The basic source of the data is the detailed record of income and expenditures for the largest and the most successful charities in the UK, published in the Charities Aid Foundation Statistics (1984–1986) and Trends (1987–1992). In choosing a sample size, we wanted to use all of the years of available data (1983–1990) and to include only those charities for which there were no missing data. In the Charities Aid Foundation data set, the size of the sample varies: 200 charities are listed for 1983–1985; 300 for 1986; and 400 for 1987–1990. First, we identified all of the charities that were carried for the entire eight-year period; this includes 178 charities.[9] Second, we eliminated 19 charities for which data were incomplete. This left a sample of 159 charities that includes the largest and most important charities for the UK (e.g., The National Trust, Cancer Research Campaign, Oxfam, Dr. Barnado's, Imperial Cancer Research Fund). The data on income and expenditures are supplemented with information on date of foundation (*AGE*) and the object or activity codes taken from the central register of charities, maintained by the Charity Commissioners. In total there are eight activity codes for charities: health, overseas,[10] religion, benevolent funds, children assistance, elderly, animal, and general welfare. The last five charity codes were combined into a general category of social welfare. Sample size for the four cohorts breaks down as follows: 60 charities in health; 20 in overseas; 20 in religion; and 59 in social welfare.

Table 1 lists the mean and standard deviations for some of the primary variables of this study. These statistics are given for the full sample of 159 charities and the four disaggregated sectors. On average, health and social welfare charities receive 61 and 63 percent of their respective total income in

[8] The log-linear specification was rejected using the $P_e$ test suggested by Davidson and MacKinnon (Greene, 1990).

[9] A list is available from the authors upon request.

[10] Overseas refers to those charities whose recipients are outside the UK. The other categories are self-evident.

Table 1
Sample means (standard deviations in parentheses)

| | *CV*/ total income | *CV*[a] | *P* | *FE*[a] | *GG*[a] | *AGE*[b] | *FE*/*CV* |
|---|---|---|---|---|---|---|---|
| Full sample | 0.68 | 2.89 | 1.17 | 0.44 | 1.39 | 70.11 | 0.138 |
| | (0.26) | (5.10) | (0.11) | (0.96) | (3.61) | (50.17) | (0.15) |
| Health | 0.61 | 1.99 | 1.15 | 0.35 | 1.47 | 56.72 | 0.161 |
| | (0.23) | (2.59) | (0.11) | (0.69) | (3.51) | (41.23) | (0.14) |
| Overseas | 0.86 | 7.18 | 1.14 | 0.74 | 1.65 | 44.56 | 0.075 |
| | (0.19) | (9.91) | (0.10) | (1.36) | (3.10) | (38.60) | (0.09) |
| Religion | 0.85 | 1.410 | 1.18 | 0.09 | 0.0003 | 111.30 | 0.046 |
| | (0.13) | (0.91) | (0.07) | (0.16) | (0.02) | (74.95) | (0.06) |
| Social welfare | 0.63 | 2.87 | 1.19 | 0.54 | 1.69 | 78.54 | 0.168 |
| | (0.28) | (4.71) | (0.10) | (1.13) | (4.32) | (39.91) | (0.17) |

[a] In millions of pounds sterling.
[b] Years since foundation.

the form of voluntary income, while the overseas and religious charities receive 86 and 85 percent of their respective income from voluntary contributions. Donations account for 68 percent of the income for the entire sample; hence voluntary contributions are an important income source for our sample of nonprofits. Although government grants are considerable for social welfare, health, and overseas charities, they are a minimal revenue source for religious charities. The average price of output for the entire sample is £1.17 with the spread across different activity types ranging from £1.14 to £1.19. Statistics on mean efficiency price for the entire sample and period agree with the single-year price of £1.19 found for a sample of 299 charities by Posnett and Sandler (1989). Fund-raising proportions in the UK average at 14 percent for the entire sample. Health and social welfare charities have relatively high fund-raising proportions of 16 and 17 percent, respectively; religious and overseas charities have low fund-raising proportions of 5 and 8 percent, respectively.

Given the time-series data on nonprofit firms, we exploit the additional information by using panel-data estimation techniques to obtain estimators that are more efficient than those based only on time-series or cross-sectional analysis. The additional degrees of freedom provided by panel data reduces the collinearity among explanatory variables and also reduces the bias arising from omitted variables. Results based on temporal cross-sectional data may repudiate results based on time-series or cross-sectional analysis (see Barrett, 1991).

Several reparameterizations of the basic model of charitable donations given in Eq. (2) were tried. The basic assumption underlying these models is that the effect of all excluded (unobservable) variables can be categorized as individual time-invariant and period individual-invariant. Moreover, the individual and/or time heterogeneity arising from these excluded variables can be absorbed into a variable-intercept model (Hsiao, 1986). The first variation of the basic model is, then, to introduce time-invariant charity-specific effects. The presence of charity-specific effects implies that the residual in Eq. (2) can be written as:

$$u_{it} = \mu_i + \epsilon_{it} , \tag{3}$$

where $\mu_i$ is the charity-specific effect and $\epsilon_{it}$ is the remaining error. The expected value of $\mu_i$ depends only on the class, $i$, to which the observation belongs; the other unobservable characteristics, contained in the term $\epsilon_{it}$, are random and in no way depend on the group. In the one-way fixed-effects model, these charity-specific effects are treated as fixed constants over time. This estimator uses only the variation within each group to explain variation in the dependent variable. The specification of this model is given by:

$$CV_{it} = \beta_{0i} + \beta_1 P_{i,t-1} + \beta_2 FE_{i,t-1} + \beta_3 AI_{i,t-1} + \beta_4 GG_{i,t-1} + \beta_5 LEG_{it} + \beta_6 AGE_{it} + \epsilon_{it} , \tag{4}$$

where $\beta_{0i}$ is the intercept peculiar to the $i$th charity.

For the one-way fixed-effects model, inferences are made conditional on the charity-specific effects in the sample. If we generalize the above model and allow the charity-specific effects to be random, then the above formulation has to be changed to one in which the probability distribution of the dependent variable is conditional on the explanatory variables only. The correlation between the individual effects and the other independent variables is ignored, and marginal inferences are made with respect to the population of all effects. This generalized model is called the random-effects model and is a weighted average of the fixed-effects model and a model based on the group means of all variables – the between-group model (Hsiao, 1986). The one-way random-effects specification is given by:

$$CV_{it} = \beta_1 P_{i,t-1} + \beta_2 FE_{i,t-1} + \beta_3 AI_{i,t-1} + \beta_4 GG_{i,t-1} + \beta_5 LEG_{it} + \beta_6 AGE_{it} + \phi_i + \epsilon_{it} . \tag{5}$$

The one-way fixed- and random-effects models take account of only one of the two possible effects that may be present in the data. Besides charity-specific characteristics, there may be factors present in the data peculiar to specific time-periods but that affect the individual units more or less equally. The addition of time effects to the above models changes the disturbance term, so that the residual now consists of three components:

$$u_{it} = \mu_1 + \lambda_t + \epsilon_{it} , \tag{6}$$

where the time effects ($\lambda_t$) may be assumed to be fixed or random, depending on the assumptions regarding the correlation between the included independent variables and the charity-specific and time effects. The two-way model therefore takes account of both time and individual-specific effects on voluntary contributions. Depending on whether the charity and time effects are fixed or random, the two-way specification is analogous to Eqs. (4)–(5), respectively. Also, in the two-way models, we have the additional coefficient on the time-specific effects ($\lambda_t$). Finally, if both time and individual-specific effects are insignificant, then the best specification would be the pooled model in which observations for all charities are combined. This model predicts the same intercept and the same slope parameters for all the charities.

## 4. Empirical results

Table 2 presents results from the five competing models that explain variations in voluntary contributions to charities over time. A series of tests are applied to the above models to choose the "best" representation. The first test involves the hypothesis of fixed and random effects. The assumption underlying the random-effects model is the exogeneity of the unobserv-

Table 2
Parameters estimated from panel-data estimation: UK charities, 1983–1990

| Variable | Pooled model | Panel-data models | | | |
|---|---|---|---|---|---|
| | | One-way | | Two-way | |
| | | Fixed effects | Random effects | Fixed effects | Random effects |
| Constant | 6.63 | – | 3.09 | 12.75 | 3.28 |
| | (7.06) | | (3.87) | (25.42) | (2.59) |
| $P_{t-1}$ | 4.61 | −1.28 | −1.41 | −1.34 | −1.36 |
| | (−5.76) | (−1.95) | (−2.25) | (−2.04) | (−2.08) |
| $FE_{t-1}$ | 4.96 | 2.43 | 2.93 | 2.44 | 2.49 |
| | (37.60) | (17.20) | (22.62) | (17.26) | (17.89) |
| $AI_{t-1}$ | 0.0002 | −0.004 | 0.002 | −0.004 | −0.004 |
| | (0.02) | (−0.26) | (0.15) | (−0.26) | (−0.22) |
| $GG_{t-1}$ | −0.05 | 0.094 | 0.117 | 0.093 | 0.097 |
| | (−1.78) | (2.57) | (3.74) | (2.56) | (2.73) |
| $LEG_t$ | −0.16 | 0.069 | 0.061 | 0.066 | 0.066 |
| | (−5.45) | (1.74) | (1.78) | (1.64) | (1.60) |
| $AGE_t$ | −0.0023 | 0.086 | −0.001 | −0.136 | −0.001 |
| | (−1.35) | (4.01) | (−0.38) | (−0.37) | (−0.15) |
| $Adj\ R^2$ | 0.707 | 0.942 | 0.640 | −0.950 | 0.596 |

[a]Numbers in parentheses are $t$-statistics.
$CV$ is the dependent variable.

able charity-specific effects; in the fixed-effects model, the unobservable effects are correlated with the explanatory variables. These two specifications can be tested using the Hausman (1978) specification test. The test is based on the significance of the difference between a consistent and an efficient estimator under the null hypothesis. With the null hypothesis of no correlation, the random-effects estimator is consistent but inefficient. Under the alternative hypothesis, the random-effects estimator is biased and inconsistent, whereas the fixed-effects estimator is consistent. This test is valid for both one-way and two-way models. The Hausman test statistic for the one-way model is 92.04 ($p = 0.000$) with six degrees of freedom. We, thus, reject the null hypothesis of no correlation between individual-specific effects and the other explanatory variables. For the two-way model, the test statistic is 11.96 ($p = 0.06$) with six degrees of freedom, so that we can reject the hypothesis at the 0.10 level of significance. For both models, the fixed-effects specification outperforms the random-effects model.

The next comparison is a test of the significance of time effects in the two-way model. Given our results from the Hausman test, this then is a test of the two-way fixed-effects model as opposed to the one-way fixed-effects model. Treating the one-way model as the restricted model, we can use the usual *F*-test to choose between the models. With an *F*-value of 1.74 (d.f. = 7, 941), we were unable to reject the one-way fixed-effects model; the cost in the degrees of freedom does not justify use of the two-way model (Greene, 1990).

The final comparison is between the one-way fixed-effects model and the pooled model. This is a test of the same intercepts and slopes for all charities and implies that there are no significant group effects present. An F-test between the restricted pooled model and the one-way model gives a value of 29.02 (d.f. = 158, 948). The pooled model is rejected in favor of the one-way fixed-effects model. The charity-specific effects are, therefore, a significant factor in explaining variation in contributions across charities. Results from the above tests imply that there is compelling empirical evidence to suggest that charity-specific effects, price, fund-raising activities, autonomous income, government grants, legacies, and the age of the charity are important variables in explaining charitable donations to a nonprofit firm.

The price coefficient for the total sample is −1.28 (see Table 2), significant at the 0.10 level. This suggests that as the implicit price of giving rises, through higher fund-rising and administrative expenditures in the previous period, charitable giving decreases in the current period. The associated price elasticity, evaluated at mean price and mean voluntary contributions, is −0.518. Earlier studies based on cross-sectional data have reported charitable giving to be price elastic. Recent US studies, using panel-data estimation techniques, have challenged these earlier results and found price response to be inelastic (see Steinberg, 1990, for a survey of these results). Our price elasticity confirms with results from these recent studies; but again we caution that our price variable differs from these earlier studies.

Lagged fund-raising expenditure has a positive impact on voluntary contributions ($\beta_2 = 2.43$ in Table 2). The positive coefficient is statistically significant with a *t*-statistic of 17.20 and implies that fund-raising encourages voluntary contributions by advertising the output of the nonprofit organization. Only the partial impact of fund-raising activities on voluntary contributions is measured by this coefficient, as it does not include the effect of fund-raising on price. The partial elasticity of fund-raising, $\eta_f$, evaluated at the mean values, is 0.370. Thus, an increase of one percent in fund-raising raises voluntary contributions by about 0.37 percent, ceteris paribus.

A measure of the total effect of lagged fund-raising on current voluntary contributions is important, because it tells us something about the underlying objective function of the nonprofit organization. Nonprofits choose the level of fund-raising expenditures so as to maximize a donation–revenue function (Steinberg, 1986a). The total effect of lagged fund-raising takes account of the direct and indirect effects of fund-raising, and is derived by differentiating (2) with respect to $FE_{i,t-1}$. It is given by

$$\mathrm{d}CV/\mathrm{d}FE_{i,t-1} = \beta_1 \left( \frac{2 \cdot (Tot\ Exp) - FE - Admin}{(Tot\ Exp - FE - Admin)^2} \right) + \beta_2 \,, \tag{7}$$

where *Tot Exp* is lagged total expenditure and *Admin* is lagged administrative expenditure. Using Eq. (7), $\mathrm{d}CV/\mathrm{d}FE_{i,t-1}$ for the entire sample is 2.42 (the expression in the square brackets, $\mathrm{d}P/\mathrm{d}FE$, is extremely small with a value of 0.0003). A value for this marginal impact not significantly different from one implies that nonprofits are net revenue maximizers, since they choose levels of fund-raising so as to maximize their voluntary contributions. A value of the marginal impact of lagged fund-raising not significantly different from zero implies that nonprofits are total revenue (or budget) maximizers, since they drive the beneficial effect of fund-raising to zero. With $\mathrm{d}CV/\mathrm{d}FE_{i,t-1}$ equal to 2.42 with a standard deviation of 0.141, we reject the hypothesis that the fund-raising elasticity is not significantly different from one. This suggests that the nonprofits are neither net revenue nor total revenue maximizers. However, since this marginal value is greater than one, it indicates that nonprofits fall short of net revenue maximization, meaning that there is no evidence of "too much" fund raising associated with the charities in this sample. The associated total fund-raising elasticity ($\eta_F$), evaluated at mean (lagged) fund-raising and mean (current) contribution levels, is 0.368.

Among the alternative sources of income, only government grants and legacies are statistically significant. Both these variables have a positive effect on contributions. There is, therefore, no evidence of crowding-out. In Table 2, a positive coefficient of 0.094 for government grants implies that a £1 increase in government grants raises contributions by 9.4 pence. Empirical evidence from earlier studies ranged from partial crowding-out (negative coefficient with absolute value between zero and one) to crowd-in, with positive coefficients (see Steinberg, 1991). Schiff (1985) found positive coefficients for state and local government grants to nonprofits for non-cash transfers by the state, and for state-level welfare expenditures. Our data does not discriminate between state/local and federal grants to nonprofits. Steinberg (1991) indicated that using aggregate government grants would result in biased crowding-out estimates, because state and local grants are endogenous and may change in response to a change in federal spending on nonprofits. Since we use one-period lagged values for government grants, the estimated coefficients will not be biased. The coefficient on legacies ($\beta_5 = 0.069$) is positive and suggests that such long-term commitments to nonprofits do not crowd-out giving by other donors. Finally, the *AGE* variable is used as a proxy for quality and goodwill on the part of donors for the nonprofit organization. The coefficient is positive (0.086) and is statistically significant at 0.05 level of significance.[11]

Since the one-way fixed-effects model is the representation of the donative function for nonprofits, we estimate this model for the disaggregated data. The four charity cohorts are *health*, *overseas*, *religion*, and *social welfare*. A heteroscedasticity-robust test of parameter constancy across different sectors was done using the Wald test. With the test statistic equal to 64.32, we reject the hypothesis that coefficients are the same across sectors. By disaggregating the data, the significance of the price coefficient falls. Price is no longer an important variable in explaining variations in contributions in any of the four sectors.

The coefficient on fund-raising expenditures has a positive and statistically significant coefficient for health, overseas and social welfare. The partial fund-raising elasticity, $\eta_f$, is 0.223 for health; 0.238 for overseas; 0.02 for religion; and 0.489 for social welfare charities. The total (marginal) effect of fund-raising is calculating using Eq. (7). Charities in the health sector have a value for $\mathrm{d}CV/\mathrm{d}FE_{i,t-1}$ equal to 1.26. At the 0.05 significance level, we are unable to reject the hypothesis of net revenue maximization. For overseas charities, $\mathrm{d}CV/\mathrm{d}FE_{i,t-1}$ equals 2.3 with a standard deviation of 0.803. These charities also appear to abide by the rule of net revenue maximization. For social welfare charities, $\mathrm{d}CV/\mathrm{d}FE_{i,t-1}$ equals 2.6 with a standard deviation of 0.18; consequently, social welfare charities have an objective function that is

[11] The *AGE* variable includes a pure reputation effect and a time trend, so that the coefficient includes both these influences.

Table 3
Fixed-effects model parameter estimates by sectors for UK charities, 1983–1990

| Variable | Health | Overseas | Religion | Social welfare |
|---|---|---|---|---|
| $P_{t-1}$ | 0.0012 | −6.63 | −0.515 | −1.054 |
| | (0.02) | (−1.24) | (−1.26) | (−1.26) |
| $FE_{t-1}$ | 1.27 | 2.31 | 0.311 | 2.602 |
| | (5.37) | (3.02) | (0.75) | (14.42) |
| $AI_{t-1}$ | −0.015 | −0.104 | 0.018 | 0.061 |
| | (−1.45) | (−0.29) | (0.75) | (1.37) |
| $GG_{t-1}$ | 0.176 | −0.085 | 0.425 | 0.055 |
| | (5.31) | (−0.42) | (0.49) | (1.03) |
| $LEG_t$ | 0.214 | 0.942 | 0.502 | −0.015 |
| | (5.61) | (1.84) | (3.72) | (−0.27) |
| $AGE_t$ | 0.074 | 0.143 | 0.076 | 0.078 |
| | (3.88) | (0.97) | (7.54) | (2.45) |
| Adj $R^2$ | 0.934 | 0.921 | 0.948 | 0.952 |

[a]Numbers in parentheses are $t$-statistics.
[b]$CV$ is the dependent variable.

not identifiable as total or net revenue maximization. These charities fund-raise short of the point of net revenue maximization. Religious charities have a marginal impact of fund-raising that is insignificantly different from zero; hence, these charities are total revenue maximizers.

The total fund-raising elasticity ($\eta_F$) is evaluated at the mean (lagged) fund-raising and contribution level for each activity cohort. The associated total fund-raising elasticities are 0.221 for health; 0.236 for overseas; 0.02 for religion; and 0.489 for social welfare. Partial and total fund-raising elasticities do not differ much for our sample, because the price effect in Eq. (7) is so small.

In Table 3, the effect of alternative sources of income varies across charities in different cohorts. Unlike the case where all charities are taken together, at the disaggregated level government grants encourage giving only in the health sector. For other sectors, the coefficient on $GG$ is not significant. The coefficient on legacies continues to be positive at the disaggregated level, except for social welfare for which it is not significant. The coefficient on the $AGE$ variable is positive and significant for health, religion, and social welfare charities.

## 5. Concluding remarks

Based on panel data estimates, this study analyzes the effect of fund-raising, government grants, and alternative sources of income and expenditures on voluntary contributions of nonprofit firms. Posnett and Sandler (1989) used data from a single year for about the same set of charities, and found voluntary contributions to be price elastic and fund-raising inelastic. Moreover, all charities in their study, except those in the religious sector, maximized net revenues. In this study, we use various tests to identify the additional source of variation that explains voluntary contributions. We find charity-specific effects to be a significant factor. Further, we find contributions to be price inelastic and fund-raising inelastic. With the additional information available from several data points on each charity, we find charities as an *aggregate* to be neither total nor net revenue maximizers. Disaggregating the data by activity, however, shows charities in the health and overseas sector to be net revenue maximizers; charities in the social welfare sector do not have an identifiable objective function. Religious charities are total revenue maximizers. At the aggregate and disaggregate level we find no evidence of crowding-out.

## Acknowledgment

The authors are grateful for the comments of two anonymous referees.

## References

Abrams, Burton A. and Mark D. Schmitz, 1978, The 'crowding-out' effect of government transfers on private charitable contributions, Public Choice 33, 29–41.

Abrams, Burton A. and Mark D. Schmitz, 1984, The crowding-out effect of governmental transfers on private charitable contributions: Cross-section evidence, National Tax Journal 37, 563–568.

Andreoni, James, 1990, Impure altruism and donations to public goods: A theory of warm-glow giving, Economic Journal 100, 464–477.

Barrett, Kevin S., 1991, Panel-data estimates of charitable giving: A synthesis of techniques, National Tax Journal 44, 365–381.

Bergstrom, Theodore, Lawrence Blume and Hal Varian, 1986, On the private provision of public goods, Journal of Public Economics 29, 25–49.

Charities Aid Foundation, 1984, 1985, 1986, Charity statistics (Charities Aid Foundation, 1984, 1985, 1986, Charity statistics (Charities Aid Foundation, Tonbridge).

Charities Aid Foundation, 1987, 1988, 1989, 1990, 1992, Charity trends (Charities Aid Foundation, Tonbridge).

Charities Aid Foundation, 1991, Charity household survey 1989/90 (Charities Aid Foundation, Tonbridge).

Clotfelter, Charles T., 1989, Federal tax policy and charitable giving, in: Richard Magat, ed., Philanthropic giving (Oxford University Press, New York).

Cornes, Richard and Todd Sandler, 1984, Easy riders, joint production, and public goods, Economic Journal 94, 580–598.

Cornes, Richard and Todd Sandler, 1986, The theory of externalities, public goods, and club goods (Cambridge University Press, New York).
Greene, William H., 1990, Econometric analysis (Macmillan, New York).
Hausman, J.A., 1978, Specification tests in econometrics, Econometrica 46, 1251–1271.
Hsiao, Cheng, 1986, Analysis of panel data (Cambridge University Press, Cambridge).
Jones, Andrew and John Posnett, 1991a, The impact of tax deductibility on charitable giving by covenant in the U.K., Economic Journal 101, 1117–1129.
Jones, Andrew and John Posnett, 1991b, Charitable donations by U.K. households: Evidence from the Family Expenditure Survey, Applied Economics 23, 343–351.
Kingma, Bruce R., 1989, An accurate measurement of the crowd-out effect, income effect, and price effect for charitable contributions, Journal of Political Economy 97, 1197–1207.
Posnett, John, 1992, Income and expenditure of charities in England and Wales – 1990/91, in: Charities Aid Foundation, ed., Charity trends 1992 (Charities Aid Foundation, Tonbridge).
Posnett, John and Todd Sandler, 1989, Demand for charity donations in private non-profit markets; The case of the U.K., Journal of Public Economics 40, 187–200.
Rose-Ackerman, Susan, 1982, Charitable giving and 'excessive' fundraising, Quarterly Journal of Economics 97, 193–212.
Rose-Ackerman, Susan, 1986, Do government grants to charity reduce private donations? in: Susan Rose-Ackerman, ed., The economics of nonprofit institutions (Oxford University Press, New York).
Schiff, Jerald, 1985, Does government spending crowd out charitable contributions?, National Tax Journal 38, 535–546.
Schiff, Jerald, 1989, Tax policy, charitable giving, and the nonprofit sector: What do we really know? in: Richard Magat, ed., Philanthropic giving (Oxford University Press, New York).
Schiff, Jerald and Burton A. Weisbrod, 1991, Competition between for-profit and nonprofit organizations in commercial markets, Annals of Public and Cooperative Economics 62, 619–639.
Steinberg, Richard, 1986a, Should donors care about fundraising? in: Susan Rose-Ackerman, ed., The economics of nonprofit institutions (Oxford University Press, New York).
Steinberg, Richard, 1986b, The revealed objective functions of nonprofit firms, Rand Journal of Economics 17, 508–526.
Steinberg, Richard, 1987, Voluntary donations and public expenditures in a federalist system, American Economic Review 77, 24–36.
Steinberg, Richard, 1990, Taxes and giving: New findings, Voluntas 1, 61–79.
Steinberg, Richard, 1991, Does government spending crowd out donations? Interpreting the evidence, Annals of Public and Cooperative Economics 62, 519–617.
Warr, Peter G., 1983, The private provision of a public good is independent of the distribution of income, Economics Letters 13, 207–211.
Weisbrod, Burton A., 1988, The nonprofit economy (Harvard University Press, Cambridge, MA).
Weisbrod, Burton A. and Nestor D. Dominguez, 1986, Demand for collective goods in private nonprofit markets: Can fundraising expenditures help overcome the free-riding behavior?, Journal of Public Economics 30, 83–95.

# [20]

## Interdependence of commercial and donative revenues

*Lewis M. Segal and Burton A. Weisbrod*

### Introduction and overview

As Chapter 3 outlines, nonprofit organizations' principal sources of finance are donations and sales. That is, they can generate revenue through some form of contribution, or they may sell products and services. Proxy measures for the former are what the Internal Revenue Service terms "contributions, gifts, and grants," and for the latter, what it terms "program service revenues" (PSRs), which include user fees and revenue from ancillary activites. Since we utilize these data extensively, it is important to be clear that PSRs encompass all sales-generating activities, whether central to the nonprofit's mission or not. Moreover, "mission relatedness" of an activity is determined by the nonprofit and also by the IRS – and these two perspectives may differ. While some activities that generate program service revenues will be treated by the IRS as taxable, because they are unrelated to organization mission, and other activities as related and, hence, not taxable, the nonprofit's own view may differ. It may judge that an activity is not central to its mission even though the IRS considers the income generated nontaxable; similarly, the nonprofit may view an activity as central to its mission even though the IRS determines it to be unrelated.

In the short run, nonprofits have additional sources of revenue – they may receive interest and dividends from investments, and can borrow and draw down assets; but in the long run their financial health depends on their ability to generate donations and to sell services profitably. This chapter asks: Are these two revenue sources – one philanthropic, the other commercial – interrelated? More particularly, does a change in donative revenue – for example, a cut in government grants – influence nonprofits' commercial activity, or vice versa?

We thank the Aspen Institute Nonprofit Sector Research Fund for contributing to support of the research reported here; Ian Domowitz, John Goddeeris, and Richard Steinberg for helpful comments on earlier drafts; and Cecilia Hilgert for assistance with interpreting IRS data. The views expressed here are those of the authors and not necessarily those of the Federal Reserve Bank of Chicago.

We examine the hypotheses that nonprofits' commercial sales activities are mechanisms for financing their principal, tax-exempt mission, and that nonprofits prefer to avoid such activities, engaging in them reluctantly and then only for their profitability. If sales activities are "nonpreferred," there are several testable implications: One, on which we focus, is that those activities are undertaken to a degree that varies inversely with the nonprofit's revenue from the preferred source, donations. If there is aversion to commercial activity, despite its potential financial contribution to the organization's mission, then donations would "crowd out" commercial activities, with decreased donations causing expansion of commercial activity and increased donations diminishing it.

A second testable implication of an aversion to commercial activity is that nonprofits engage in it less than would maximize profit and, hence, less than would maximize revenue to finance their preferred, mission-related activities. Testing this hypothesis is beyond the scope of this chapter, but our results do shed a bit of light on it. One piece of prior evidence is the finding that nonprofits spend less on fund-raising than would maximize their net profitability (Weisbrod and Dominguez 1986; but see also Steinberg 1986). It seems plausible that an aversion to engaging in fund-raising would reflect a larger predisposition to avoid activities that are, themselves, not part of the organization's mission, apart from their net revenue.

If there is aversion to commercial activity, revenue from donations would be preferred to an equivalent sum from profitable sales activity. A plausible conjecture, therefore, is that an exogenous decrease in donations would be offset, but less than fully, by an increase in net, after-tax revenue from commercial activity. To test the magnitude of such crowding out, however, it is necessary to estimate the profitability of commercial sales, the fraction of increased gross revenue from sales that can be used to cross-subsidize mission-related activities. Little is known about the profitability of various nonprofit-sector commercial activities, and meaningful data are unavailable (although Chapter 5 makes a foray into that area).

## Theoretical relationships between revenues from donations and from program services

The relationship between revenue from donations and from commercial activity can take a variety of forms, as Chapter 3 indicates. If nonprofits are indeed averse to commercial activity, donations will crowd out commercial activity, and there will be a negative relationship between the two forms of revenue. There could, alternatively, be a positive relationship, "crowding in," if increased commercial activity is viewed favorably by donors and leads to increased donations. In addition to such interrelations between revenue sources, there could be interrelations between costs: Producing commercial goods and raising donations could be subject to economies of scope. Finally, the two forms of revenue could be independent and unrelated, as would be the case if nonprofits acted as profit maximizers in the commercial markets in order to obtain as much net revenue as possible for support of their missions, and if commercial and mission-related activities were separable in their costs and revenues.

Crowding out of commercial activity by donations is most likely when it involves sale of goods and services that are viewed by the nonprofit's management as most unrelated to the nonprofit's mission – activities engaged in only for their financial contribution. It may also apply, however, to activities that are related to the mission. For example, as Chapter 3 shows, nonprofits frequently, though not always, can demand user fees of the persons they serve in pursuit of their mission. Colleges can charge students tuition, hospitals can charge patients fees, and museums and zoos can charge visitors admission. They may prefer to avoid such user fees, however, lest they inadvertently discourage utilization by persons in the target population (Chapter 4), which would make this revenue-raising source nonpreferred. For-profit firms, by contrast, are presumed to be indifferent among alternative money-generating activities, caring only about the net profitability. Thus, while a private firm would be expected to pursue commercial market opportunities at maximum profit levels, if nonprofits prefer to avoid commercialism they will engage in it reluctantly, whether or not the IRS treats it as taxable and only if the organization cannot obtain "sufficient" donations – in short, only if the net revenue it generates is great enough not only to be profitable (after any tax) but to overcome the disutility of engaging in it.

Contemporary concern about escalating college tuition illustrates the issues and trade-offs. Rising college production costs, not accompanied by offsetting government grants or private donations, have forced choice between retrenchment, on one hand, and raising additional commercial revenue either from user fees or ancillary activities. All are occurring, but along with sharp rises in tuition – "tuition and fees doubling from 1976 to 1994" – has come increasing concern about the effects, including "pricing as many as 6.7 million students out of higher education" (Applebome 1997, A17). In terms of the analytic framework we utilize, public and private donations and grants are the preferred sources of revenue, but their shortfall may have led to increased use of a non-preferred source, user fees. As Chapters 3 and 4 explain, the aversion to user fees as a source of revenue is caused by their negative effect on the target population – in this case, students. This is despite the increased use of price discrimination, in the form of student financial aid, in attempts to minimize the adverse effect of increased tuition on the target population of students.

As the tuition example makes clear, the hypothesis that nonprofits have preferences among alternative revenue sources is separate from legal definitions of "related" and "unrelated" business activities and their differential tax treatment.

For a nonprofit organization there are no tax consequences of obtaining revenue from user fees rather than from donations, although there is a difference to the payers, since donations are tax deductible, at least for itemizers. The nonprofit's preference for donations is the consequence of the hypothesized negative effect of user fees on the organization's mission, not on tax considerations. A mission that encompasses distributional goals, as discussed in Chapers 3 and 4, would cause a nonprofit not to be indifferent between a dollar of revenue from donations and a dollar from user fees.

So, too, a nonprofit may not be indifferent between raising funds through user fees and netting an equal amount through after-tax profit from provision and sale of other, non-mission-related outputs – termed *ancillary* in Chapter 3. Whatever their legal form, and whether or not the IRS applies the Unrelated Business Income Tax (UBIT) to them, these are activities that are seen by the nonprofit as elements outside of its mission, and in some cases incompatible with that mission. Aversion to ancillary activities may reflect a view that commercialism – acting in ways identified with private firms, and thinking about markets and profitability in their terms – detracts from the spirit and goals appropriate to nonprofits. To the extent this is the case, as noted above, there is no necessary identity between what a tax authority, the IRS, treats as unrelated and what the organization leadership regards as not contributing to its mission. Thus, a nonprofit hospital that decides to open a major heart-transplantation unit, which it expects to generate substantial profit, knows that this will be regarded by the IRS as a mission-related activity, and hence nontaxable, even if the hospital would not be establishing that unit were it not for its profitability.

An aversion to commercial activity has the same effect as a tax on it, increasing the effective marginal cost of production and thus decreasing the effective marginal profit from commercial activity. This leads to our central hypothesis:

*Commercial activity in any form – whether involving user fees or expansion into ancillary markets – can be expected to be sensitive to the level of donations, changing inversely to it.*

This chapter examines the microeconometric empirical evidence to determine whether there is a negative causal relationship between donations and commercial activity. We do not study separately revenue resulting from UBIT activities and from untaxed activities, which are aggregated in program services (but see Chapter 5, which does examine some relationships between the two).

During the 1980s the nonprofit sector, as a whole, became increasingly reliant on sales revenue relative to donative revenue. As Table 6.1 shows, "contributions, gifts and grants" (donations) to charitable (501(c)(3)) organizations from both private and government sources declined as a share of total revenue between 1982 and 1993, while the share from program services (sales) grew.

Table 6.1. *Revenues from donations[a] and from commercial activities for charitable 501(c)(3) nonprofits, 1982–93[b] (in billions of constant dollars)[c]*

| Tax year | Donations (CGG) | Total revenues | Component as % of total revenue: Total CGG | Private CGG | Govt. CGG | Program service revenue (PSR) |
|---|---|---|---|---|---|---|
| 1982 | $42.79 | $203.42 | 21.0 | 11.2 | 9.8 | 63.4 |
| 1983 | 46.59 | 231.78 | 20.7 | 10.9 | 9.8 | 65.9 |
| 1985 | 51.83 | 249.43 | 20.8 | 11.3 | 9.4 | 62.6 |
| 1986 | 54.85 | 266.86 | 20.6 | 12.9 | 7.6 | 64.3 |
| 1987 | 54.30 | 273.56 | 19.8 | 11.7 | 8.2 | 68.2 |
| 1988 | 58.38 | 299.79 | 19.5 | 10.9 | 8.6 | 67.5 |
| 1989 | 61.70 | 320.73 | 19.2 | 10.8 | 8.5 | 68.4 |
| 1990 | 64.80 | 332.25 | 19.5 | 10.9 | 8.6 | 70.6 |
| 1991 | 63.71 | 359.54 | 17.7 | 9.8 | 7.9 | 70.3 |
| 1992 | 71.80 | 383.15 | 18.7 | 10.2 | 8.5 | 71.0 |
| 1993 | 70.78 | 390.63 | 18.1 | 9.9 | 8.2 | 71.3 |

[a]Reported to the IRS as "contributions, gifts, and grants" (CGG).
[b]Excluding 1984, for which data are not available.
[c]All dollar values are deflated by the Consumer Price Index for All Urban Consumers (1982–4 = 100).
*Source:* Entries for 1982 and 1983 are derived from Hodgkinson et al., *Nonprofit Almanac 1992–1993*. San Francisco: Jossey–Bass, 1992, tab. 4.5. Entries for 1985–93 are authors' calculations from the IRS, Statistics of Income Division, data tapes.

Of course, revenue, whatever its source, is not equivalent to profit. The true margin of expected net revenue from any source is an important determinant of a nonprofit's choice among revenue sources, but evidence is difficult to obtain. What we expect, but cannot test, is that organization mission will cause differential preferences among potential sources, so that it will not be the case that marginal profitability from all sources will be equated, let alone equated with the opportunity cost of capital.

In our theoretic framework we emphasize this distinction between the nonprofit's preferred and nonpreferred activities: The organization prefers to engage in its mission-related pursuits; it becomes involved in revenue raising, a nonpreferred activity, only as necessary to achieve its mission. Some donations may come to the organization with little or no effort, but such exogenous income may be judged by the nonprofit to be suboptimal and lead it to devote resources to increasing contributions or to profit-making commercial activities. Fund-raising to garner additional contributions and program services to garner sales revenues are quite similar in their goal, which is largely to generate resources that would permit expansion of the mission-related activities. This also is the intention behind user fees, as discussed above.

Seldom is a source of revenue entirely exogenous, entirely independent of organizational effort. We judge, however, that there is a greater measure of such independence with respect to contributions, gifts, and grants (CGG) than for commercial sales revenues. Changes in federal government funding of grants to hospitals, universities, and arts organizations, for example, can dramatically change donative revenue, as has been the case recently with sharply diminished federal grants to the National Endowment for the Arts ("Republican Effort to Eliminate Arts Agency Survives Challenge" 1997) and to public television (see Chapter 13).

In a later section we turn to empirical tests to determine to what extent, if any, nonprofit commercial activity in the form of program service revenue is a response to changes in exogenous revenue from donations. Difficulties emerge as we look for operational counterparts to the concepts of preferred and nonpreferred sources of revenue, and the differential tax treatment of various forms of revenue creates another force affecting organization choice among alternative sources of revenue.[1]

Available data from the IRS Form 990 return (Appendix) provide proxy measures that map (imperfectly) to the aforementioned theoretic concepts: CGG to the preferred, unconstrained revenue sources, and PSR to the nonpreferred revenue sources that involve activities, including commercial sales, sometimes seen by nonprofits as digressions from their missions.

Our concept of a nonprofit's commercial activity encompasses all endeavors that involve a transaction with a consumer paying for output received. Payment, of course, is a matter of degree. A "pure" nonprofit organization is one that finances production entirely through unrestricted donations generated costlessly and distributes its charitable output, at a zero price, to all "deserving" persons: Output is simply given away. This polar case is the ideal for two reasons:

1 Only with a zero price can the organization be reasonably assured that no deserving person is being denied access to its service, although some nonprice form of rationing might be required if the total quantity available is insufficient.
2 Only by remaining free of commercial activity can the nonprofit concentrate its managerial resources on providing services rather than on debates over the appropriateness of engaging in the sale of other goods and services in order to raise money.

[1] "Contributions, gifts, and grants," as reported on the IRS Form 990 information return, sometimes constitute what we would term *sales* – e.g., for the naming of a building at a hospital, college, or community center. At the same time, some revenue reported as sales – "program service revenues" on the Form 990 – has a substantial donative element, as when consumers pay more for a service provided by a nonprofit than they would pay to a for-profit firm.

In the contrasting case, typical of a private firm, the organization receives no donations, gives away nothing, and charges a profit-maximizing price for its output. The distinction between a nonprofit's reliance on donations and on revenue from sales is central to this chapter's focus on whether donative revenue crowds out program service revenue.

Actual nonprofit organizations are arrayed on a continuum in terms of the percentage of revenue they derive from sales. The purely donative nonprofit derives none of its revenue from sales (Hansmann 1980); at the opposite pole are nonprofits that derive all of their revenue from sales. One index based on this finance-source characteristic is the *collectiveness index,* the proportion of an organization's total revenue derived from donations (see Weisbrod 1988 for discussion and application). Table 6.2, based on IRS tax data for charitable nonprofit organizations in 1987, displays a complementary metric: the proportion of total revenue that comes from commercial sources. Its value varies substantially by industry, with health organizations being the most commercial (with sales accounting for 89 percent of total revenue) and community-improvement organizations being the least (only 11 percent).

The more use a nonprofit organization makes of prices to raise revenue, the more it is emulating the private sector; whether such commercial activity takes a form that involves competition with the private sector is another matter. Chapter 1 shows how nonprofits' commercialism takes both forms, and Chapter 9 illustrates well the growing collaboration between universities and private enterprise in scientific research. The current chapter attempts to explain the forces affecting the commercialism of the nonprofit sector – its increased dependence on revenue from sales – independently of whether it involves competition or cooperation with for-profit firms.

We have reviewed, within the context of the multiproduct model presented in Chapter 3, building on James (1983), the reasons for expecting one or another relationship between the level of a nonprofit's commercial activity and its revenue from donations. One analytic perspective indicates that exogenous contributions and commercial activity will be either unrelated or inversely related, depending on the degree to which commercial activity itself, apart from the revenue it generates, detracts from the goals of the nonprofit; but other perspectives suggest positive relationships between donative and commercial revenues. We explore several of these possibilities, including the effects of a change in service provision by other organizations, economies of scope in production, complementarities in revenues, and price rationing of output.

The section on the empirical relationships between donations and sales uses our newly developed panel of tax-return data covering the period 1985–93 for large nonprofit "charitable" – 501(c)(3) – nonprofit organizations. Much of the prior empirical research on the mix of revenue sources used cross-sectional data and focused on a single industry, such as universities (James 1983) or social-service agencies (Schiff and Weisbrod 1991). We examine each of five indus-

Table 6.2. *Percentage of charitable 501(c)(3) nonprofits engaging in unrelated business activity*[a]

| NTEE classification and code | % filing UBIT return[b] | PSR as % of total revenue | No. of observations |
|---|---|---|---|
| Science and technology research institutes, services (U) | 9.3 | 46 | 128 |
| Health – general and rehabilitative (E) | 9.2 | 89 | 3,369 |
| Disease, disorder, medical disciplines (G) | 6.3 | 36 | 167 |
| Arts, culture, and humanities (A) | 6.1 | 27 | 666 |
| Educational institutions and related activities (B) | 4.9 | 56 | 2,040 |
| Community improvement, capacity building (S) | 4.6 | 11 | 488 |
| Religion related, spiritual development (X) | 4.5 | 54 | 234 |
| Human services – multipurpose and other (P) | 3.1 | 41 | 893 |
| Recreation, sports, leisure, athletics (N) | 3.0 | 50 | 183 |
| Mental health, crisis intervention (F) | 2.5 | 43 | 179 |
| Philanthropy, voluntarism, and grant making (T) | 2.3 | 24 | 492 |
| Housing, shelter (L) | 1.9 | 68 | 702 |
| Youth development (O) | 1.2 | 69 | 185 |

[a]The data are an asset-based sample, and the estimates presented are weighted averages based on the sampling weights. However, differences in asset distribution across industries may skew the estimates.

[b]The UBIT return, Form 990-T, is required for all nonprofits that receive at least $1,000 in gross unrelated business income in a given year.

*Source:* Authors' calculations from the IRS, Statistics of Income Division, data tapes.

tries, using a variety of techniques. The panel data permit us to consider time lags and organization-specific effects.

Our findings may be summarized as follows:

1. Aggregate trends for the panel show that although sales revenues are increasing faster than donative revenue, both have increased in real terms. We attempt to determine whether the slower rate of growth in donations caused any part of the increase in commercial activity. We begin by documenting the positive cross-sectional correlations between contributions and sales. Not surprisingly, there is a scale effect such that larger organizations tend to receive larger amounts of revenue from each type of source, donative and commercial. The panel nature of the data lets us control for organization-specific attributes of the nonprofit that do not change over time, including the scale of the organization, its geographic location, and its efficiency.

2. Controlling for organization-specific (fixed) effects, for the full panel of nonprofits, we find a significant negative relationship between donations and

sales revenues, consistent with the theory that nonprofit organizations have an aversion to commercial activity.

3. Taking a longer view, we also examine the relationship by using the change in three-year averages, 1985–7 compared with 1991–3, and again find a strong negative relationship.

4. All of these approaches assume that donations are exogenous, an assumption we relax in two ways. First, we use fund-raising expenditures to remove, or instrument out, whatever portion of donations is within the organization's control. These expenditures prove to be an important influence on donations: Current and lagged values of fund-raising expenditures, in conjunction with firm-specific effects and lagged contributions, explain about a third of the year-to-year variation in donations. Second, we use lagged donations, rather than current donations, as a regressor to explain the extent of commercial activity. These produce some changes but do not alter the overall tenor of our findings. Regression analyses based on log values of the dependent and independent variables, however, reveal substantially smaller results, near zero and even positive for some industries.

5. Finally, we employ a statistical test of causality that allows for a feedback effect whereby variation in sales revenues causes changes in donative behavior, and that also allows both donations and commercial activity to be simultaneously affected by unspecified and unmodeled forces, such as government spending, changes in the economic environment, or changes in need. The perspective presented in Chapter 3 and summarized above portrays nonprofit organizations in two dimensions: the types of services they produce and their sources of revenue, with the two being related. Thus, anything altering the donative revenue that a nonprofit realizes without its having to produce the nonpreferred output would affect the level of commercial activity in the opposite direction. A drop in government grants, such as has affected many of the nonprofit subsectors examined in Part II of this volume, is likely to bring expansion of nonpreferred commercial output, other things equal. That prediction of a negative relationship could be reversed, however, if, as is also noted in Chapter 3, there were more complex interdependencies, so that a change in commercial activity had further effects.

In addition to direct effects of donations on commercial activity, there could also be reciprocal effects, of commercial activity on donations. These would be positive if donors favored nonprofits' self-help, revenue-raising efforts and rewarded them, or negative if donors disapproved of commercial activity.[2]

In addition to revenue interdependencies, there could be cost interdependencies. If the production processes are complementary, an increase in ancillary-

[2] In the latter case, this effect would strengthen the expectation of a negative relationship between donations and sales.

good production will decrease costs for the mission-related outputs, thereby reducing revenue needs. Because of such interdependencies of costs and revenues – about which little is known – an exogenous decrease in donations could have a positive, negative, or zero effect on commercial activity, even if the direct effect we hypothesize is negative. In such cases of interdependent revenues or costs, the effect on the nonprofit of an exogenous change in donations would be to shift the donations function or the cost function for the preferred good. Thus, reality may be more complex than our simple model. No strong prediction can be made.

Little is known regarding whether managers or donors are indifferent as to the nature of the nonprofit's revenue-generating tactics, and whether they generally regard commercial activity as detracting from the organization mission, apart from the revenue generated. Anecdotal evidence, however, suggests that nonprofits do sometimes forgo opportunities to obtain added revenue because they prefer to avoid engaging in those activities. For example, recently Oxford University turned down a gift of $34 million, to establish a new school of business, apparently because it reached a judgment that a business school was incompatible with its mission – that is, "with the historical values of the university"; the view was expressed that "education should prepare people for public service, not profit" (Ibrahim 1996). It is not clear, however, whether such decisions reflect a sense of organization mission or a recognition of effects on other donors.

It is hard to say which set of assumptions about organization objectives, revenue interdependencies, and cost interdependencies is more likely. Moreover, we conjecture that the more likely set differs across industries: Donors to arts organizations, hospitals, colleges, and antipoverty activities need not respond in the same way to increased commercial activity in ancillary markets. Similarly, opportunities for nonprofits to utilize their preferred-good inputs to expand production in ancillary markets may well be more limited in some industries than in others. Day-care centers, for example, employ inputs that are quite specific to use by young children and are in use for much of the day and even evenings, and so appear to have relatively little potential for utilization in ancillary revenue-generating activities. Hospitals are more promising loci for production of ancillary outputs, as they provide services that involve a wide variety of inputs for inpatients and outpatients, health-care related but also involving food preparation, laundry, television rental, and so on, and that have substantial excess capacity.

### *Changes in provision of the preferred service by other suppliers*

The multiproduct model is extendable in several directions that provide further insight into the relationship between contributions and commercial activities.

We consider the case of a nonprofit that is concerned with the aggregate level of provision of the preferred good, not simply with its own production. An exogenous decrease in production by others would raise the marginal utility schedule for the nonprofit's own production, and its desire to increase production.

Would this cause the organization to engage in more commercial activity? Again, the answer depends on whether the commercial activity is a neutral or a nonpreferred activity. A decrease in provision by government agencies or by other nonprofits has essentially identical implications for a specific nonprofit organization as we described for a fall in the organization's revenue from donations. In all these cases the effect is to increase the marginal utility of the nonprofit's preferred output and, hence, to cause it to pursue added revenue more aggressively. Diminished donations, ceteris paribus, reduce production of the preferred good, moving the organization back along its marginal utility schedule to a greater marginal utility of output. A fall in exogenous provision shifts the entire schedule outward, again increasing marginal utility from added output of the preferred good. The result in both cases is an increase in the marginal utility of the preferred output, which could be great enough to overcome the disutility from additional ancillary commercial activity. Thus, we expect such commercial activity to be correlated negatively with a decline in provision by other agencies and organizations. Again, however, this result relies on commercial activity being nonpreferred, and it could be strengthened or weakened by revenue and cost interdependencies, as explained above.

Analogous to a change in other providers' output of the preferred good would be a change in the overall magnitude of social "need" for the nonprofit's services. To see this, consider a nonprofit social service agency that observes an increase in poverty. This would be equivalent to a decrease in other suppliers' – nonprofit or governmental – provision of antipoverty services, and it would increase the willingness of a nonprofit organization to initiate or expand production of profit-generating ancillary goods. As we have noted, it could also increase private donations. If such a simultaneous increase in both sources of revenue occurred, it would not reflect a change in one causing the change in the other, but the simultaneous effect on both revenue sources of the exogenous change in need or in production by others of the preferred good. The point, which becomes important when we turn to the empirical work, is that findings of correlation or, for that matter, lack of correlation, between donations and commercial activity can reflect many plausible scenarios and, hence, are difficult to interpret.

### *Price discrimination in the provision of preferred goods*

Nonprofits' commercial revenue from "sales" can come not only from sales of an ancillary, nonpreferred good, but also, as we pointed out earlier, from fees charged to consumers of the preferred, mission-related good. Thus, a positive correlation between donative and commercial revenue may also result from the increased use of price as a rationing mechanism for preferred goods. Access to preferred goods that are of the private-good type can be rationed by varying price according to recipients' perceived ability to pay, while also taking account of the nonprofit's target consumers – those it seeks to help the most.

Thus, a decrease in, say, government grants could cause nonprofit hospitals to charge private-pay patients more; and colleges could increase their full tuition, collecting more from students with the greatest demand while increasing financial aid to those with more elastic demand, possibly leaving their net prices unchanged. Such price discrimination might be interpreted as a form of non-preferred activity, engaged in reluctantly, at less than profit-maximizing levels, thus being responsive to exogenous changes in revenue. Nonprofits that have distributional goals, seeking to provide the preferred output to particular beneficiaries, can choose to use additional donations to cut prices below marginal cost to their target consumers. (For further analysis of price discrimination by nonprofit firms with distributional goals, see Chapter 4 and Steinberg and Weisbrod 1997.) Recognizing the role of prices and price discrimination of preferred goods is important, for nonprofits' commercial (i.e., private-enterprise-like) activity is not limited to markets for ancillary goods.

Price discrimination cannot be used, however, for preferred goods that are collective in nature. Universities can discriminate in their pricing of education, a private-type preferred good, but cannot do so in their provision of collective goods, such as basic research. Zoos can discriminate in admission fees to viewers, but not in their provision of the collective good, animal species breeding. (For an analysis of commercialism in zoos and aquariums, see Chapter 11.) Nonprofits whose missions are to provide collective goods have little opportunity to charge user fees, and so their options are more limited.

In light of the complexities we have discussed, it is not surprising that our findings, reported in the next section, indicate no simple and consistent pattern. There is considerable variation among industries, some showing negative effects of donations on their commercial activity, but others showing positive effects, and still others showing none. In addition, findings are not entirely robust to alternative specifications. Negative relationships between donations and commercial activity are found in some specifications, although by no means uniformly. The industry studies in Chapters 8–13 further demonstrate the variation in provision of ancillary outputs and in dependence on user fees.

## The empirical relationships between donations and sales

A crude measure of a nonprofit's ancillary activity is its engagement in money-raising activities that the IRS regards as unrelated to their tax-exempt mission, thereby generating income that is subject to the UBIT. Table 6.2 (see the previous section) shows, for 1987, wide variation in the percentage of nonprofits in each industry that reported such income, ranging from 1.2 percent in the youth-development sector to 9.2 percent in the health sector. Our empirical analyses in the next subsection suggest a pattern, but one that varies among industries.

We assembled the panel data used for this study from Internal Revenue Service Form 990 tax returns collected annually between 1985 and 1993. The sampling scheme used by the IRS Statistics of Income (SOI) Division is based on the asset level reported on the nonprofit's tax return. The composition of the SOI sample varies from year to year, with larger (greater asset) nonprofits being more likely to be included than smaller ones. Although the sample varies over time, all organizations with more than $50 million in assets (not controlling for inflation) are included each year. Our analysis uses the "balanced" panel of the 2,679 nonprofit firms observed in all nine years. These large organizations, though only a small percentage of all nonprofits, represent a substantial portion of the total assets and revenue activity in the nonprofit sector.

There are two sources of possible bias from the use of this panel of nonprofits. First, in addition to the fact that nonprofits with low asset levels are underrepresented, only "surviving" organizations are included; that is, organizations that cease to exist or, for any other reason, do not file a return in any of the sample years are not in the panel. Similarly, nonprofits that are "large" (over $50 million in assets) in some year but not in others are excluded from the panel if data for them are not available in the years when their assets fall below the threshold. Nonetheless, the relationship between organizational revenue from sales and from donations (referred to in the IRS Form 990 returns as "contributions, gifts, and grants") is worth examining for this important subset of nonprofits. Our findings will not necessarily be generalizable, however, to the full population of nonprofit organizations, most of which are small. There is, on the other hand, a positive dimension to the limited sample: The focus on large organizations provides a degree of homogeneity that is useful given the limited information available from the tax returns.

Two-thirds of our panel consists of nonprofit organizations involved in health and education activities, as characterized by Independent Sector using their National Taxonomy of Exempt Entities, which has been adopted by the IRS. Table 6.3 presents the industrial distribution of the organizations studied. We analyze first the combined sample of all organizations, and then the nonprofits in each of the five industries for which the panel includes over a hundred organizations – specifically, hospitals (NTEE code E22), which are approximately 70 percent of the health category (code E), and universities (code B43), which are about 40 percent of the education category (code B), along with housing and shelter, human services, and arts, culture, and humanities.

Table 6.3. *Industrial composition of balanced panel of 501(c)(3) tax returns, 1985–93, based on the National Taxonomy of Exempt Entities (NTEE)*

| NTEE classification and code | Frequency | % of sample |
|---|---|---|
| Health – general and rehabilitative (E) | 1,121 | 41.8 |
| Hospitals, general (E22) | (779) | (29.1) |
| Educational institutions and related activities (B) | 643 | 24.0 |
| University or technological institute (B43) | (265) | (9.9) |
| Housing, shelter (L) | 155 | 5.8 |
| Human services – multipurpose and other (P) | 143 | 5.3 |
| Arts, culture, and humanities (A) | 128 | 4.8 |
| Philanthropy, voluntarism, and grant making (T) | 92 | 3.4 |
| Community improvement, capacity building (S) | 89 | 3.3 |
| Science and technology research institutes, services (U) | 37 | 1.4 |
| Youth development (O) | 31 | 1.2 |
| Disease, disorder, medical disciplines (G) | 28 | 1.0 |
| Religion related, spiritual development (X) | 27 | 1.0 |
| Mutual, membership benefit organizations, other (Y) | 21 | 0.8 |
| Animal, related (D) | 20 | 0.7 |
| Mental health, crisis intervention (F) | 20 | 0.7 |
| International, foreign affairs, and national security (Q) | 19 | 0.7 |
| Public, society benefit – multipurpose and other (W) | 19 | 0.7 |
| Recreation, sports, leisure, athletics (N) | 17 | 0.6 |
| Medical research (H) | 16 | 0.6 |
| Employment, job related (J) | 14 | 0.5 |
| Environmental quality, protection, and beautification (C) | 13 | 0.5 |
| Unknown/unclassified (Z) | 12 | 0.4 |
| Social sciences (V) | 6 | 0.2 |
| Public protection (I) | 4 | 0.1 |
| Food, nutrition, agriculture (K) | 2 | 0.1 |
| Public safety (M) | 2 | 0.1 |
| Totals | 2,679 | 99.7[a] |

*Source:* Authors' calculations from the IRS, Statistics of Income Division, data tapes.
[a]Does not equal 100% because of rounding.

The upper portion of Table 6.4 (rows 2–5) presents descriptive statistics on the organizations in the panel at the beginning of the time interval, 1985.[3] All values are in millions of constant dollars, adjusted by the Consumer Price Index (1982–4 = 100). In 1985 the average nonprofit in the panel received $6 million in contributions, gifts, and grants while generating more than five times that

[3] Data are also available for 1982 and 1983, although not for 1984, when the IRS did not take a sample. Because of the missing year, we examine data only for the period beginning with 1985.

Table 6.4. *Descriptive statistics for balanced panel of 501(c)(3) tax returns, 1985–93*

| | Full balanced panel | University or technol. inst. NTEE code B43 | Hospital, general NTEE code E22 | Housing, shelter NTEE code L | Human services – multipurpose & other NTEE code P | Arts, culture, humanities NTEE code A |
|---|---|---|---|---|---|---|
| 1. Number of organizations | 2,697 | 265 | 779 | 155 | 143 | 128 |
| | *1985 average ($)* | | | | | |
| 2. CGG (mil. of 1982–4$) | 6.0 | 24.4 | 1.3 | 0.6 | 3.9 | 7.9 |
| 3. Program service revenue (mil. of 1982–4$) | 32.4 | 53.6 | 57.0 | 4.1 | 5.6 | 3.6 |
| 4. Assets (mil. of 1982–4$) | 87.9 | 222.5 | 73.3 | 18.0 | 20.2 | 48.2 |
| 5. Pct. filed a UBIT return | 23 | 34 | 36 | 5 | 10 | 26 |
| | *1985–93 (% change)* | | | | | |
| 6. Real growth of CGG revenue | 21 | 18 | 38 | 44 | 17 | 9 |
| 7. Real growth of program service revenue | 61 | 38 | 63 | 16 | 50 | 47 |
| 8. Real growth of assets | 53 | 19 | 43 | 22 | 9 | 42 |
| 9. Increase in fraction filing UBIT return | 15 | 25 | 24 | 0 | –1 | 10 |

*Abbreviations:* CGG, Contributions, gifts, and grants; NTEE, National Taxonomy of Exempt Entities; UBIT, Unrelated Business Income Tax.
*Source:* Authors' calculations from the IRS, Statistics of Income Division, data tapes.

– $32.4 million – in program service revenues. The size and relative importance of these revenue sources varies widely by industry: The average hospital is far more commercial, receiving only $1.3 million in contributions but having $57 million in sales revenues. At the other extreme, the average arts organization in our panel received more than twice as much in contributions as in sales revenues. Row 5 of the table displays the fraction of firms filing a Form 990-T tax return, reflecting their receipt of revenue from unrelated business activities. This measure again discloses great variation among industries in their involvement in commercial activity, in this case with unrelated ancillary activities: More than a third of hospitals and universities filed a UBIT return, compared to only 5 percent of the housing and shelter organizations.

Such variation in commercial activity is consistent with our prior view that because of the differing technologies of production in the various mission-focused activities, there would be variation among industries in their potential not only for developing profitable markets for ancillary goods, whether legally related or unrelated, but also in their opportunities to generate revenue from user fees for mission-related activities. At the same time, these findings are also consistent with other models, such as that organization objective functions, including aversion to ancillary activities and to user fees for mission-related activities, differ across industries.

Between 1985 and 1993 the revenue from each of the two principal sources, contributions (i.e., CGG) and sales, increased substantially in constant dollars. Contributions, gifts, and grants to nonprofits in our panel grew by more than 21 percent (row 6), but sales grew 61 percent (row 7), nearly three times as much. There has, indeed, been increasing reliance of nonprofit organizations on commercial activity. Consistent with this view, the fraction of nonprofits filing a tax return for unrelated business activity increased from 23 percent in 1985 to 38 percent eight years later.

This upward growth trend, however, masks variation over time: Although average real contributions grew continuously for our panel of nonprofits, there was variation from year to year in that growth. Moreover, in any particular year many nonprofits did not experience growth, with 40–60 percent of the sample experiencing a decline.

The discussion of the earlier section, "Theoretical relationships between revenues from donations and from program services," suggested that a decline in exogenous donations to a nonprofit organization may cause it to turn, if reluctantly, to increased commercial activities in order to cross-subsidize its preferred activities, implying a negative "crowding out" relationship between donations and commercial activity (see also Chapter 3). Other parts of the analysis, however, suggested a positive, "crowding in" relationship, due to such additional forces as the possible effects of commercial activity on donations and the abil-

Table 6.5. *Regression analysis of balanced panel of 501(c)(3) tax returns, 1985–93*

| Specification[a] | Estimate |
|---|---|
| *Effect on program service revenue of:* | |
| 1. Contributions | 0.76** |
| 2. Contributions, w/ firm effects | –0.09** |
| 3. Contributions, w/ firm and time effects | –0.13** |
| 4. Contributions, w/ firm effects instrumenting for the possible endogeneity of contributions | –0.13** |
| 5. Lagged contributions, w/ firm effects | –0.43** |
| *Effect on log program service revenue of:* | |
| 6. Log contributions[b] | 0.10** |
| 7. Log contributions, w/ firm and time effects[b] | –0.02 |
| *Long-run regression analysis avg. (1991–3) – avg. (1985–8):* | |
| 8. Effect on program service revenue of contributions | –1.05** |
| 9. Effect on log program service revenue of log contributions[b] | –0.02 |
| *Long-run regression analysis omitting zero values, avg. (1991–3) – avg. (1985–8):* | |
| 10. Effect on program service revenue of contribution | –0.73** |
| 11. Effect on log program service revenue of log contributions[b] | –0.02 |
| *Statistical tests for the direction of causality*[c] | |
| 12. Significance of lagged contributions on program service revenue | 0.01 |
| 13. Significance of lagged program service revenue on contributions | 0.40 |

[a]All dollar values are deflated by the Consumer Price Index for All Urban Consumers (1982–4 = 100).
[b]Log–log regression models use zero in place of log(0).
[c]Tests are based on a vector autoregression with firm fixed effects, and two lags of contributions, program service revenue, and fund-raising expenditures. Longer-lagged values are used as instruments.
* Statistically significant at the .10 level.
** Statistically significant at the .05 level.
*Source:* Authors' calculations from the IRS, Statistics of Income Division, data tapes.

ity of the organization to utilize the resources from its preferred goods in the production of ancillary goods.

To test these relationships we apply a more disaggregate, microlevel analysis. We begin by describing the methodology and results for the full panel of organizations in Table 6.5. The panel data permit us to examine changes over time while controlling for unobserved organization characteristics that do not change over time; that is, we employ a "fixed-effect" regression model that takes into account characteristics of each organization that, although not directly observable, are specific to the organization over time.

Our findings indicate that unobserved heterogeneity among organizations is of major importance. Rows 1 and 2 of Table 6.5 present the regression estimates of the effect of a one-dollar increase in contributions on the contemporaneous level of sales, with and without inclusion of a firm-specific component; the results differ significantly and substantially. The regression without the fixed effect estimates that a one-dollar increase in contributions is associated with a seventy-six-cent increase in sales activity – no crowding out effect here. We believe, however, that this estimate reflects scale differences across organizations such that larger organizations receive more revenue, both commercial and donative, than smaller ones. The regression estimate reflects a positive correlation due to scale but does not reflect causality. Inclusion of fixed effects, which we believe to be important, results in a statistically significant negative coefficient on contributions. As implied by the cross-subsidization model with aversion to commercial activity, changes in total contributions are negatively correlated with changes in gross sales revenue.

The negative result for the fixed-effect model in the pooled sample of organizations is robust to a variety of alternative specifications, including the addition of time-trend variables to capture aggregate economic conditions (row 3), the inclusion of fund-raising expenditures in an attempt to deal with the possible endogoneity of donations (row 4), and the use of a one-year lagged independent variable instead of contemporaneous donations to deal with endogeneity as well as effects over time (row 5). Controlling for the endogenous portion of contributions somewhat increases the negative relationship between donations and sales. The coefficient displayed in row 5 of Table 6.5 suggests that a one-dollar decline in exogenous donations causes an increase in commercial activity of forty-three cents, although the profit available to cross-subsidize preferred activities is surely less.

As a further robustness check we estimate the model in logs rather than levels, with (row 7) and without (row 6) fixed effects. These results are much closer to zero, suggesting that large values – which receive relatively less weight in the logarithmic formulation – have significant influence on our estimates, even though the data sample is already limited to organizations with large amounts of assets, and even though we used fixed effects. The log–log model with fixed effects again produces a negative coefficient, but it is not statistically significant. The interpretation of the estimate in row 7 is that a 1 percent decrease in donations causes a 0.02 percent increase in commercial activity.

The effect of changes in contributions on sales activity might well depend not on single-year, transitory changes, but on changes expected to be "permanent." The single-year changes might measure fluctuations that are smoothed across time, which may induce fluctuations in assets rather than sales. Moreover, data for any given year can be misleading, since year-end donations may sometimes be reported in the next year. To address these concerns we use three-year averages of the data in the regression model. That is, for each nonprofit we form the average of gross sales and of contributions for 1985–8 and, again, for 1991–3; then we compute the change in each variable between the two periods, thereby smoothing effects that might result from, say, a large amount of donations arriving either shortly before or shortly after the end of a nonprofit's fiscal year. Row 8 of Table 6.5 presents these estimates based on a specification in levels. The result, again, is strongly negative and statistically significant. However, the log–log specification (row 9) continues to produce a statistically insignificant result.

The difference between the level and log specifications led us to explore the data further. We noted that there were particularly large fluctuations involving transitions to or from zero contributions. For example, the returns for the New England Medical Center Hospital (EIN 042374071) report contribution above $20 million per year for 1985–8, zero contributions for the next two years, and then contribution levels above $40 million for the next three years. Perhaps such zeros are reporting error; perhaps they reflect large transitions of organizations undergoing radical change – we do not know how to explain such anomalies. Moreover, although the Internal Revenue Service scrutinizes tax returns for internal consistency, it does not examine the consistency of the returns over time. In order to reduce the effect of large transitions involving zero contributions, we repeated the long-run analyses, omitting from the estimation of mean contributions any reported zero. Thus, if an organization had two years with positive donations followed by a year with zero, we used the two positive values but excluded the year with the zero contributions. As we expected, the estimates for the effect of contributions on sales are somewhat smaller in absolute value than had been found when the zero observations were included, but they remain largely consistent with the earlier analysis.

Overall, we find somewhat mixed relationships between an organization's donative income and its revenue from sales. For the aggregate sample, Table 6.5 shows that a number of formulations, particularly those employing firm-specific effects, indicate significant, negative relationships (lines 2–5), whereas others, based on log values, show effects that are negative but insignificant (lines 7 and 9) or, in one case, positive and significant (line 6). The differences between relationships observed in levels and in logs are noteworthy. For reasons not well understood, there seem to be larger absolute responses, but smaller percentage responses of sales activity.

Negative relationships in Table 6.5 generally show effects less than unity. At the outset of this chapter we conjectured that when nonprofits use commercial activity to replace lost CGG, they replace them only partially. Moreover, since commercial revenue is only partially profit, the replacement rate is even lower than is indicated by the coefficients on sales. This finding is consistent with the hypothesized aversion to commercial activity, although we cannot be certain as to the influence of cost and revenue interdependencies.

The structural regression models employed thus far assume that causality runs from donations to sales. Explanations put forth in the theory section, however, suggest that even if causation does run in that direction, it could simultaneously run in the reverse direction – fluctuations in commercial revenue affecting donative revenue – or that both variables could be responding to a third variable omitted from the analysis. One way to detect such relationships is to use a system of simultaneous equations to determine whether fluctuations in one variable precede fluctuations in the other, after controlling for all other available information. A statistical model that provides a test of such so-called *Grainger causality* is the panel vector autoregression described in Holtz-Eakin, Newey, and Rosen (1988). Using it, we relate current sales activity to the preceding two years' data on donations, fund-raising, and sales revenue. Separately, there is an equation with donations as the dependent variable and the same set of regressors. All of the data are *first-differenced* – that is, differences between years are used – to remove the firm-level effect we identified as important in the earlier analyses. This transformation, combined with the presence of a lagged dependent variable, produces a correlation between the error term in the regression and the transformed right-hand-side variable that is eliminated using earlier data as an instrument. That is, we regressed the change in sales activity in year $t$ on the changes in sales, contributions, fund-raising, and assets in years $t-1$ and $t-2$ while using the data prior to $t-2$ as instruments.

Using this technique on the data for all industries, we find evidence that contributions statistically cause – that is precede – changes in sales, but sales do not cause contributions. The causality tests in row 12 of Table 6.5 reports the significance level of a joint $F$-test measuring the degree to which lagged contributions are a significant predictor of current sales after controlling for the organizational fixed effect and prior values of all the variables.

### *Industry-specific effects of donations on sales revenue*

Results for five industry subsamples are presented in Table 6.6, which we have limited to the most important specifications. These five subsamples constitute 55 percent of our aggregate sample; the balance consists of nonprofits (shown in Table 6.3) in industries for which samples are quite small.

Our findings for the housing/shelter and arts/culture sectors largely match the aggregate estimates – in our preferred, fixed-effect, formulations (rows 2 and 4) – in both the nonlog and log estimates. The estimates from the log–log specification, insignificant for the combined sample, are negative and statistically significant for the two industries (row 4).

Table 6.6. *Regression analysis by industry of balanced panel of 501(c)(3) tax returns, 1985–93*

| Specification[a] | University or technol. inst. NTEE code B43 | Hospital, general NTEE code E22 | Housing, shelter NTEE code L | Human services – multipurpose & other NTEE code P | Arts, culture, humanities NTEE code A |
|---|---|---|---|---|---|
| *Effect on program service revenue of:* | | | | | |
| 1. Contributions | 0.92** | 2.54** | 0.67** | 1.63** | 0.10** |
| 2. Contributions, w/ firm and time effects | 0.15** | –0.01 | –0.38** | 1.21** | –0.15** |
| *Effect on log program service revenue of:* | | | | | |
| 3. Log contributions[b] | 0.21** | 0.08** | 0.18** | 0.27** | 0.33** |
| 4. Log contributions, w/ firm and time effects[b] | –0.02 | 0.02** | –0.22** | 0.14** | –0.10** |
| *Long-run regression analysis, avg. (1991–3) – avg. (1985–8)* | | | | | |
| 5. Effect on PSR of contributions | 0.34** | 0.78** | –0.43 | 2.95** | –0.23** |
| 6. Effect on log PSR of log contributions[b] | –0.01 | 0.03 | –0.27** | 0.19 | –0.06 |
| *Statistical tests for the direction of causality*[c] | | | | | |
| 7. Significance of lagged contributions on PSR | 0.32 | 0.22 | 0.01 | 0.01 | 0.81 |
| 8. Significance of lagged PSR on contributions | 0.06 | 0.30 | 0.27 | 0.01 | 0.36 |

[a]All dollar values are deflated by the Consumer Price Index for All Urban Consumers (1982–4 = 100).
[b]Log–log regression models use zero in place of log(0).
[c]Tests are based on a vector autoregression with firm fixed effects, and two lags of contributions, program service revenue, and fund-raising expenditures. Longer-lagged values are used as instruments.
* Statistically significant at the .10 level.
** Statistically significant at the .05 level.
*Source:* Authors' calculations from the IRS, Statistics of Income Division, data tapes.

For the other three industries, however, findings are quite different. Between contributions and sales for universities and human-service organizations, we find relationships that are both positive and statistically significant, but the relationship is essentially zero for hospitals (row 2). The log estimates (row 4) are also positive and significant, except for in the case of universities, where there is no significant effect. These three industries comprise 44 percent of our aggregate sample. The fact that we find positive relationships between contributions and sales for them, but negative relationships for the aggregate, indicates that there are many organizations in the panel that exhibit negative relationships in industries where samples were too small to analyze.

The association of increased donations with increased, rather than decreased, commercialization in an industry is not consistent with the simple multiproduct organization model in which commercial activities are disliked. It is consistent, however, with that model if, in those industries, there are economies of scope in production – that is, cost complementarities or complementarities in revenue. As we explained earlier, there is no reason to believe that such interdependencies are equally important across industries. We also noted other circumstances that could elicit a finding of a positive relationship between donations and sales, even if commercial activity is disliked; for example, a reduction in government grants could cause a simultaneous increase in private contributions and commercial activity. There is a clear need to learn more about both cost and revenue interdependencies in nonprofit organizations before it will be possible to state with confidence the effect on commercial activity of changes in some source of donative revenue.

The results of tests of causality from commercial activity to donations also vary by industry. Rows 7 and 8 indicate that fluctuations in donations affect commercial activity in the housing sector, while in the university sector it appears that the driving force is the reverse, from sales to donations. In two industries, hospitals and arts, there is no evidence of causation in either direction, suggesting that both donations and sales are being influenced by a third factor. In another industry, human services, there is evidence of significant causation running in both directions.

## Concluding remarks

The appropriate model for nonprofit behavior remains far from settled. So, too, is an understanding of how nonprofits come to have particular combinations of revenue from donations and from sales of goods and services, and particular combinations of revenue from mission-related and unrelated activities. However, a multigood production model, in which nonprofits determine the extent of activity in several sectors, is promising. Using data for 2,679 nonprofits observed from 1985 to 1993, we estimated a set of structural and reduced-form models that suggest that exogenous declines in donations yield significant increases in commercial activity for some industry sectors but not for others. The results vary considerably by industry, a finding that is understandable in light of differential organization goals as well as differences in interdependencies among revenue opportunities and in cost interdependencies between mission-related and ancillary goods production. Our findings indicate strongly the need for more analyses of output and revenue determination in specific industries where nonprofits play a major role.

Several questions raised during the analysis require further research. First, within our model of nonprofit behavior, contributions are considered exogenous. Relaxing this simplification involves determining the extent to which organizations can influence contributions, including the effect of a nonprofit's commercial activities on willingness of individuals and organizations to give it donations, and the extent to which other unspecified events affect both sales and donations. For example, changes in sources of sales revenue, such as through the adoption of Medicare and Medicaid in the health industry, can affect organization behavior and, in turn, the supply of donations (including volunteer time). Second, a dynamic model of behavior suggests that nonprofits may draw down assets in response to exogenous transitory fluctuations in donations.

Debate over whether government spending on social welfare programs has crowded out private donations, so that current and prospective reductions in government support will lead to increased private donations, illustrates the importance of these issues. In addition, our findings that reduced donations have quite different effects on commercial revenue-raising activity in the higher-education, hospital, arts, housing, and human-services components of the nonprofit sector highlight the danger of generalizing about the responses of the sector, as a whole, to exogenous changes in donations.

# References


Applebome, Peter. 1997. "Rising College Costs Imperil the Nation, Blunt Report Says," *New York Times*, June 18, pp. A1, A17.

Hansmann, Henry B. 1980. "The Role of Nonprofit Enterprise," *Yale Law Journal* 89(5) (April): 835–901.

Hodgkinson, Virginia Ann, Murray S. Weitzman, Christopher M. Toppe, and Stephen M. Noga. 1992. *Nonprofit Almanac 1992–1993*. San Francisco: Jossey–Bass.

Holtz-Eakin, Douglas, Whitney Newey, and Harvey S. Rosen. 1988. "Estimating Vector Autoregression with Panel Data," *Econometrica* 56(6): 1371–95.

Ibrahim, Youssef M. 1996. "We Can't Do Business, the Dons Tell a Big Donor," *New York Times*, November 26, p. A4.

James, Estelle. 1983. "How Nonprofits Grow: A Model," *Journal of Policy Analysis and Management* 2 (Spring): 350–65.

"Republican Effort to Eliminate Arts Agency Survives Challenge." 1997. *New York Times*, June 18, p. A16.

Schiff, Jerald, and Burton A. Weisbrod. 1991. "Competition between For-Profit and Nonprofit Organizations in Commercial Markets," *Annals of Public and Cooperative Economics* 62(4): 619–39.

Steinberg, Richard. 1986. "Should Donors Care About Fundraising?" in Susan Rose-Ackerman (ed.) *The Non-Profit Sector: Economic Theory and Public Policy*. Oxford: Oxford University Press, pp. 347–64.

Steinberg, Richard, and Burton A. Weisbrod. 1997. "To Give or to Sell? That Is the Question: Or, . . . Price Discrimination by Nonprofit Organizations with Distributional Objectives." Working Paper, Department of Economics, Indiana University / Purdue University at Indianapolis, and Department of Economics, Northwestern University.

Weisbrod, Burton A. 1988. *The Nonprofit Economy*. Cambridge, MA, and London: Harvard University Press.

Weisbrod, Burton A., and Nestor D. Dominguez. 1986. "Demand for Collective Goods in Private Nonprofit Markets: Can Fundraising Expenditures Help Overcome Free-Rider Behavior?" *Journal of Public Economics* 30 (June): 83–95.

# Part VI
# Comparing Nonprofit and For-Profit Behavior

# [21]

BURTON A. WEISBROD

# *Institutional Form and Organizational Behavior*

Institutions are the fundamental arrangements through which societies seek to deal with social and economic problems. Thus, it is important to understand the effectiveness of alternative forms of institutions. This chapter focuses on three nongovernmental forms of economic institutions—private firms, church-related nonprofit organizations, and non-church-related nonprofits. The issues and perspectives presented, however, are applicable to the broader array of institutional forms.

I direct attention to two questions: What kinds of differences in behavior should be expected among alternative institutional forms? What evidence is there about comparative institutional behavior, and how should it be interpreted?

Theory and evidence about the virtues and limitations of private enterprise have a centuries-old history, dating back at least to Adam Smith's *Wealth of Nations,* published in 1776. Analysis of the private nonprofit sector, however, is in its infancy. Nonprofit organizations constitute a rapidly growing segment of the U.S. economy, having increased from 309,000 organizations in 1967 to nearly 1 million today, of which some 400,000 can receive tax-deductible contributions (those nonprofits exempt from corporate income taxation under section 501(c)(3) of the Internal Revenue Code), and from 2.3 percent of national income at the close of World War II to approximately 5 percent now.[1] How effective nonprofits are, how their behavior compares with that of private firms, and what society is gaining in return for its many subsidies to nonprofits are increasingly important questions.

Partly in response to the growth of the nonprofit sector, nonprofits are the subject of increased political attention. Tension between nonprofits and private firms has escalated, with charges that nonprofits are guilty of "unfair competition" (U.S. Small Business Administration 1983). Tension is also increasing between nonprofits and governments, as concern over government budget deficits brings closer scrutiny of nonprofits' tax exemptions and deductions (Gaul and Borowski 1993).

At the same time that nonprofits are under growing attack they are being increasingly relied upon to respond to changing economic and social conditions. There is increasing demand for trustworthy institutions as a geographically mobile population and an array of increasingly complex goods pose problems for consumers who seek assurance that they are actually receiving the quality of goods and services they expect. (The chapters by Jane Mansbridge and by Alan Wolfe in this book address the importance of trust, altruism, and

I thank Carolyn Moehling and Kanika Kapur for their research assistance.

1. If the substantial value of volunteer labor—the overwhelming majority of which goes to nonprofits—were counted, the economic importance of nonprofits would be seen to be even greater.

related concepts of public spirit in a world of growing complexity and diversity.)

Still another force increasing attention to nonprofits is an apparent decline in confidence in government and an accelerated search for alternatives. Privatization of social services is a powerful worldwide force today, but there has been little attention paid — by government decisionmakers or by researchers — to the merits and demerits of divestiture to private business firms relative to private nonprofit organizations, let alone to the implications of divesting to a church-related or some other form of nonprofit. The growth of for-profit prisons, for example, has its critics, but the debate has centered on the choice between government and private enterprise (O'Brien 1993; *New York Times* 1994) rather than nonprofits (see, however, Weisbrod 1988).

Two recent events — one in higher education and one in health care — highlight the public policy implications of understanding comparative institutional behavior. First, in 1991 the U.S. Department of Justice brought an antitrust action against the Ivy League universities and the Massachusetts Institute of Technology (MIT) for alleged price fixing in the granting of financial aid to prospective students. The Ivy schools have since agreed to abandon the practice, but MIT has not. It contends that the actions, which it does not deny, promote rather than harm social welfare, in the context of its charitable nonprofit activities. The implicit argument is that although price fixing is undesirable in private, for-profit firms, it should be regarded as desirable when nonprofits (or perhaps only certain nonprofits?) engage in it ("M.I.T. Wins a New Trial in Price-Fixing Case" 1993). The claim is that private firms and nonprofits use price-fixing power in different ways and with different results. The argument, while plausible, has not been subject to careful research, and neither has the implication that some or all antitrust laws ought not apply to all forms of institutions; currently they do.[2]

Second, in 1993 the Clinton administration proposed a health care reform plan that called for hospital mergers to reduce duplication of facilities and reduce costs and prices. Although the prediction that reducing the amount of competition — which hospital mergers within a single community would tend to do — would reduce prices is contrary to basic economic theory, that theory assumes profit-oriented firms. The hospital industry in the United States, however, is heavily dominated by nonprofit organizations. If they achieved greater monopoly power, would they use it to increase prices and profits or to decrease prices and expand socially valuable activities?

In spite of the paucity of theory and of evidence, judgments and assertions about the comparative behavior of private firms and nonprofit organizations abound, and these beliefs give rise to conflicting behavioral predictions and public policy prescriptions. One view is that nonprofit sector behavior is socially preferable. The New York State Moreland Commission, for example, responding to charges of improprieties in the nursing home industry in the mid-1970s, proposed to "phase out proprietary nursing facilities in New York and to substitute nonprofit institutions as the mainstay of the industry" (Temporary Commission 1976). The California legislature prohibited for-profit health maintenance organizations from treating Medi-Cal (the California Medicaid) enrollees (Goldberg 1976) in the early 1970s. The debate about the role of for-profit hospitals relative to nonprofits continues even now, with critics of investor-owned hospitals claiming that the high prices they charge relative to nonprofit hospitals means that their "wave has crested" (Freudenheim 1993). Earlier, though at a more abstract level, Kenneth Arrow conjectured that "in the provision of medical services, profit-making . . . arouses suspicion and antagonism on the part of patients and referring physicians, so they do prefer nonprofit institutions" (Arrow 1963). Such a preference would be justified only if nonprofit status connoted behavior that is systematically different and preferable.

The examples just given come from health care. There are similar views and doubts, however, about the limits to profit seeking in day care (Mauser 1988), prisons (O'Brien 1993; Weisbrod 1988) and in certain legal areas (Mansnerus 1993)[3] — all fields in which output quality is difficult to monitor.

In all these areas, policymakers base their decisions on assumptions about similarities and differences in behavior based on institutional form, and they are doing so despite a research base that, while growing (Ben-Ner and Gui 1991), remains weak. Underlying the debates at both the research and policy levels are two fundamental questions: Can nonprofit organizations, church-related or otherwise, be expected to behave in systematically varying ways compared with other forms of organizations, and if so, is their behavior socially preferable? The case for granting special privileges to nonprofit organizations rests on the belief that they do behave differently — that institutional form does matter — and that the nonprofit form of institution is preferable, in some identifiable conditions. Nonprofits that receive public subsidies are assumed to pursue public interest goals even when doing so deviates from ordinary self-interest considerations.

This chapter focuses primarily on the first of these two issues — the positive question of whether different forms of institutions act differently. That is, if nonprofit organizations, private firms, government agencies, and so forth were confronted by the same opportunities, would they make different

2. Another education case involves the attempt by the state of California to close a number of private, for-profit universities regarded as "diploma mills" (*New York Times*, 1994).

3. Most states continue to prohibit for-profit enterprise, but not nonprofit organizations, that refer clients to private law firms (Mansnerus 1993).

choices?[4] The goals of the chapter are to (1) clarify what it means to ask the question, Does institutional form matter?, (2) identify the dimensions in which divergences can be expected, and (3) examine some evidence on comparative institutional behavior. The question whether institutional form matters cannot be answered unless we explore the effects of institutional form on economic behavior, ceteris paribus. Thus, there are three subsidiary questions we must ask: What is meant by an institutional form? What dimensions of economic behavior does society care about? What variables should be included in the ceteris paribus? Each of these will be examined in turn.

The theme of this chapter is that any organization's decisions reflect the interplay of its goals and the constraints on it. Whenever one or both differ among institutions, behavioral differences will result. Economics research that has attempted to predict and to evaluate the decisions made by various forms of institutions has focused on the role of constraints rather than on organization goals. The principal reason is that constraints appear to be more malleable—more easily observed and more subject to legal and regulatory control. One constraint has dominated economics research on the behavior of forms of institutions other than private enterprise: the freedom of the organization and its manager to generate profit and to reward managers and owners accordingly. The lure of profit, economists assume, motivates all entrepreneurs and managers and fosters efficient decision making by private firms. In contrast, nonprofit organizations and government agencies, whose managers face a nondistribution constraint that legally forecloses benefiting from organization profit or surplus, have been assumed to be insulated from competitive pressures and hence prone to inefficiencies.

The structure of this chapter is as follows: after considering the definition of the term *institutional form,* I delve briefly into a theoretic examination of the types of behavior that are relevant in a comparative study of institutional form. Succeeding sections deal with the issue of which variables should be held constant as we seek to identify the independent effects of institutional form and present some recent empirical findings. Finally, policy implications and directions for future research are discussed.

## DEFINING *INSTITUTIONAL FORM*

A form or type of institution can be defined usefully by its goals or objective function and the set of constraints it faces for achieving its goals.[5] Thus, a nonprofit organization is a different type of institution from a private firm either because the constraints on it differ or because its objectives differ or both. A complete typology of institutional forms would consist of the intersection of the full set of potential constraints and goals. The logical possibilities are vast and have not yet been set forth in a comprehensive fashion.

### Constraints

Some constraints are imposed technologically—by the state of scientific knowledge—but others result from laws, regulations, and codes of social conduct imposed by society. I assume that technological constraints apply equally to all organizations, while legal constraints may differ. In the United States today the legal constraints on nonprofit (sometimes termed tax-exempt) organizations differ from those on private firms in a number of respects: (1) Nonprofits, which have no owners, are legally prohibited from distributing profit to their management. They are not legally prevented from realizing profit, but they may lawfully use profits only to purchase inputs in subsequent periods.[6] This "nondistribution constraint" (Hansmann 1980) is, in effect, a legal restriction on managerial compensation—in all forms, pecuniary or other; it cuts the link between organization profit and managerial income. (2) Nonprofits also face regulatory constraints on their entry and on their financial interactions with for-profit firms.[7] They also benefit, however, from a variety of explicit subsidies, tax benefits, and exclusions from legal constraints that face private firms, and in these respects nonprofits are less constrained. (3) All nonprofits are exempt from federal corporate profits tax. (4) Some are exempt from state and local taxes on property, sales, and profits. (5) Some are eligible for postal subsidies. (6) Some may receive tax-deductible donations.

Nonprofits may also differ from private firms in (7) factor supply markets, in which labor suppliers, including volunteers, may prefer to work for nonprofit organizations, in which case nonprofits face lower supply prices. The two types of firms may also differ in (8) consumer demand; some consumers may prefer to buy from a nonprofit organization—that is, may be willing to pay a higher price to a nonprofit for the same commodity—either preferring to give a donation to the organization through the price paid or believing that the nonprofit provides a good or service that, while ostensibly the same as the private firm's version, is preferable because it has more of certain attributes that are costly for consumers to observe (for example, "tender loving care" in a nursing home).

Only those nonprofits that are eligible to receive tax-deductible contributions—essentially the organizations granted tax-exempt status under section 501(c)(3) of the Internal Revenue Code—receive the subsidies and exemptions

4. The normative question of whether any such differences, if they exist, justify social encouragement of nonprofit organizations—either in the aggregate or in particular activities—will be dealt with only briefly.

5. An organization's objective function is a statement of each of its (perhaps numerous) goals and the relative weight attached to each.

6. Thus, in a one-period model, the nonprofit organization would be seen as being subject to a zero-profit constraint.

7. One indicator of governmental regulatory constraint is that only 70–75 percent of applications for nonprofit, tax-exempt status are approved by the IRS (Weisbrod 1988, table A.2, p. 170).

noted above.[8] I further distinguish between church-related and other nonprofits. They are currently treated identically under the law — that is, the legal constraints on them are the same — but their economic and social behavior may differ because their goals may differ.

*The Nondistribution Constraint.* This restriction on the distribution of profit alters incentives in multiple dimensions. The conventional argument is that it reduces the incentive for efficiency because the manager of a nonprofit organization may not lawfully share in any profit or surplus generated by his or her managerial skills (Alchian and Demsetz 1972). What is less recognized is that the nondistribution constraint has additional effects — it also reduces the incentive to engage in activities that, while privately profitable, are socially inefficient. A legally nonprofit organization has little incentive, for example, to pollute the air or water with waste products in the pursuit of organization profit. Similarly, a nonprofit organization has little incentive to skimp on quality of output or otherwise take advantage of poorly informed consumers.

The nondistribution constraint can also affect the manner of distribution of outputs — that is, to whom outputs go. A profit maximizer has the incentive to sell its goods and services to the highest bidders because that is the route to maximum returns to stockholders and managers. A nonprofit organization, by contrast, with no stockholders but with managers facing the nondistribution constraint, has no financial incentive to provide its output to the highest bidders. If the nonprofit pursues public interest goals, behaving in a manner I have characterized elsewhere as "bonoficing" (Weisbrod 1988), it may provide at least some of its output to consumers who are socially "deserving" but who have little or no ability to pay — for example, scholarships to a school, charity care in a hospital, and free admission to a museum. A testable implication of this line of argument is that private firms, church-related nonprofits, and other nonprofits differ in their utilization of price, as opposed to alternative distribution mechanisms such as waiting lists, to determine access to their services.

The nondistribution constraint has been given central attention in the economics literature on nonprofit organization behavior. Although it is unquestionably significant, its importance has been exaggerated. Nonprofit organizations would not exist if they were not given advantages that offset the disadvantage imposed by the nondistribution constraint. Hence, any variations in behavior between nonprofits and for-profits result not from the nondistribution constraint alone, but from its interactions with all of the aforementioned subsidy and exemption constraints, along with any differences in objective functions.

*Enforceability of the Nondistribution Constraint.* So far I have assumed implicitly that the nondistribution constraint is fully enforced. Enforcement is costly, however, and hence incomplete. To the extent that a constraint is unenforced it may have little effect on behavior.

Determining whether a manager's compensation is a competitive wage, which is legal, or whether it includes a residual profit component, which would violate the constraint, is complex. The IRS required nearly five years to determine whether the nonprofit PTL Ministry paid its president, Jim Bakker, an excessive salary — that is, one that included a distribution of profit. In 1987 the IRS finally decided that the nondistribution constraint had been violated, and it revoked the PTL tax-exempt status "because a substantial portion of P.T.L.'s net earnings went to benefit . . . Bakker." The IRS claimed that between 1981 and 1983 Bakker was paid "nearly one million dollars more than was reasonable" (Weisbrod 1988, 118–19). Although PTL was a large organization, capable of paying such salaries, Krashinsky (in this volume) notes that the nondistribution constraint is especially difficult to enforce when firms are small, as in day care.

There appears to be a logical internal contradiction involving the nondistribution constraint, which contributes to its enforcement problem. The constraint is generally interpreted as permitting a nonprofit organization to pay a manager a wage equal to what the manager could obtain in a competitive private market; the competitive market wage, however, would be a function of the manager's marginal contribution to the firm's profit, and so that wage is a function of organization profit. Yet the nondistribution constraint typically precludes such a profit-sharing compensation contract. (Occasional exceptions have been made to this proscription, but the general restriction remains.)

Because of enforcement costs, managers seeking to maximize profits (and their own income) might organize as legal nonprofits while operating no differently from private firms. These nonprofits — "for-profit firms in disguise (FPIDS)" — could behave like profit maximizers, distributing their outputs no differently, taking no less advantage of their informational superiorities over consumers, and generating no fewer external costs than private firms (Weisbrod 1988).[9]

8. Under current law in the United States, there are twenty-one classes of exempt organizations defined under section 501(c) of the Internal Revenue Code — subsections 501(c)(1)–501(c)(21); these are all exempt from the federal corporate income tax and are subject to the nondistribution constraint. The 501(c)(3) organizations, however, are virtually the only organizations to which one may make a donation that is tax deductible. For data on the numbers of entities that are exempt from federal income taxation under each 501(c) subsection, see U.S. Internal Revenue Service 1991.

9. The question of whether the nondistribution constraint is fully enforced suggests that the constraint is one-dimensional, but it need not be. Indeed, the expense preference or managerial discretion models of nonprofit organization behavior imply that the constraint is two-dimensional. That is, we can think of constraints on the distribution of profit in (a) money form — e.g., as salary, bonus, profit-sharing, etc. — which is fully binding, and in (b) a form such as elaborate office furnishings and lavish expense accounts, which is not binding (Migue and Belanger 1974; Williamson 1964). Legally, there is no such distinction, but en-

Even if the nondistribution constraint were not effective, however, many of the other differences in constraints between legal nonprofit organizations and private firms would remain. The differential subsidies that nonprofits receive would still have effects: Postal subsidies and property tax exemption would still present nonprofits and private firms with different relative input prices, which would cause even the FPIDs to engage in factor substitution; other things being equal, nonprofits, whether they behave like social welfare maximizers or like FPIDs, would utilize the U.S. mail relatively more than would their private firm counterparts and would have input ratios reflecting greater utilization of land and capital, which are subsidized, relative to labor.

**Objective Functions**

Nonprofits and private firms may also behave differently because their objectives differ. Consider the following three cases: Case I—(a) all managers have identical utility functions of the type U = U(Y,S), where Y = managerial income and S = provision of a socially beneficial good to deserving consumers, and (b) private firms are profit maximizers while nonprofit organizations are subject to the nondistribution constraint and its corollary—having to use all its resources to purchase inputs used for its tax-exempt purpose. In equilibrium, managers of private firms would receive greater compensation in the form of Y, and their counterparts in nonprofit organizations would receive greater utility from S; thus, the observed difference in measured financial rewards, Y, would be a compensating differential that offset the differential in S. Differential financial rewards—nonprofit managers receiving less, other things equal—would be observed across types of institutions even in a world in which managers are homogenous.

Case II—(a) all managers have identical utility functions of the type U′ = U′(Y), with only income mattering, and the conditions under (b), above, also hold here. In equilibrium, there should be no systematic difference in managerial incomes across institutional forms. Nonprofits as well as for-profit firms would have to pay equal rewards, and those rewards could be made only in units of Y.

Case III—This involves heterogeneous managerial utility functions, differing in terms of managers' relative valuations of (or marginal rates of substitution between) Y and S—some persons having utility functions as in case I, others as in case II—and the assumptions in (b) holding. Here we might expect systematic sorting of managers between institutional forms to occur. Managers with greater relative valuation of S will be attracted to the nonprofit sector, where the nondistribution constraint—which restricts compensation in terms of Y but not in the forms of S discussed above—is relatively less restrictive than it is for managers who value S relatively less. Managers with bonoficer-type utility functions will gravitate to nonprofit organizations, where they can be hired at lower wages because the organization provides more outputs in form S, which serve to compensate wage differentials.

Evidence on systematic differences in managerial preferences is difficult to find, but there is some. First, it appears that the types of people who gravitate to managerial positions in nonprofit organizations are systematically different in their preferences, particularly in their concerns with considerations broader than their own narrow financial self-interest. On psychological tests, managers who choose and are chosen by nonprofits display greater relative concern with being forgiving and helpful than do their proprietary sector counterparts (Rawls, Ulrich, and Nelson 1975). Second, managers of nonprofits appear to be willing to work at lower rates of pay than they could obtain in the private market, which is consistent with the view that such social benefits (for example, helping the poor or the underinformed)—S in the model presented above—serve as compensating differentials. This was found in a study comparing lawyers' earnings in private law firms and in nonprofit, public interest law firms (Weisbrod 1983), although these findings have been questioned (Goddeeris 1988). Similar variations have been found in a recent study of executive compensation in for-profit and nonprofit hospitals (Roomkin and Weisbrod 1997). The bonoficer model appears to fit organizations run by these nonprofit managers better than the profit-maximizing model, but much more research is needed.

Nonprofits, having no owners but subject to IRS regulatory constraints, may come to have objective functions that reflect the utility functions of managers or trustees or both. Trustees, unlike directors of private firms, typically are selected not by an external group analogous to stockholders, but by either the founding entrepreneur or the sitting group of trustees.[10] No economic theoretic model of the role of nonprofit trustees and their relationship to organization management exists. In the balance of this paper I do not distinguish between trustees and management, instead referring to them collectively as managers. The relationship between nonprofit trustees and their management deserves more attention.

**Two Models of Organization Behavior**

*Profit Maximizer.* A private firm, which I shall also refer to as a proprietary or a for-profit firm, is an institution that can be regarded as having the objective of profit maximization and facing constraints that include the state of technology, consumer demand, factor prices, and legal rules and governmental regulations. This model assumes that there is no nondistribution constraint and no source of revenue other than sale of output—that is, there is no revenue from gifts or donations or if there is, its amount is determined exogenously.

*Bonoficer.* An organization might seek to generate less than maximum profit, while engaging in activities that are

forcement costs may be greater with respect to the latter dimension—another matter deserving further study.

10. Some trustees of nonprofit organizations are selected by a voting process analogous to that of private stockholders. For example, some university trustees are elected by alumni.

socially desirable but unprofitable—for example, supplying information to underinformed consumers rather than taking advantage of its informational superiority or helping the poor or avoiding activities that pollute. Thus, a bonoficer might utilize a production process that is more costly but less environmentally degrading than an alternative or distribute output to certain deserving but impecunious consumers.

The bonoficer and profit maximizer models differ in two significant ways: (a) The bonoficer's objective function includes not only profit but also the provision of services that have social value, while the profit maximizer includes only profit; (b) The bonoficer's revenue constraint reflects the greater availability of revenue from donations, which depend, at least in part, on the organization's actions. In this model, donations—which may be in the form of either money or time (volunteer labor)—are determined partly by the organization's decisions about its socially productive but privately unprofitable activities; in effect, donations are receipts from provision of a collective good.[11] Sales revenues, by contrast, are receipts from provision of private goods.

The bonoficer and profit-maximizer models can be seen as special cases of a more general form of objective function:

$$G = \alpha(\pi) + (1 - \alpha)S,$$

where $\pi$ = organization profit, S = the organization's own provision of services that have social value but are not profitable, and $\alpha$ is a parameter that can range from 0 to 1. For $\alpha$ = 1, we have the pure profit maximizer; $\alpha = 0$ is the pure bonoficer; as an organization's preference for S diminishes relative to that for $\pi$—that is, as $\alpha$ approaches 1, the bonoficer case collapses to the profit-maximizer case; intermediate cases, in which $\partial f/\partial S > 0$ and $\partial f/\partial \pi > 0$, describe the "weak bonoficer."[12] Later I shall examine the possibility that two classes of nonprofits, church-related and other, differ in their relative positions on this spectrum.

To summarize, if nonprofit organizations are bonoficers, their behavior will reflect the combined effects of (a) the nondistribution constraint, which attenuates property rights and hence reduces incentives for efficiency, (b) other legal constraints and subsidies that apply differentially to nonprofits and private firms, and (c) the bonoficing objective function, which encourages production of goods that are suboptimally provided in private markets. A constraint on profit distribution alters incentives generally—not only to be privately efficient but also to engage in activities that are privately profitable but socially inefficient. The net effect of these countervailing forces cannot be determined a priori.

Modeling nonprofit behavior is not likely to be a matter of finding a single model. As Wolfe (in this volume) argues, the multiplicity of the bases for behavior leads to a mixture of motives for altruistic institutions. This inevitably confounds the modeling of a single, comprehensive nonprofit objective function. Further, nonprofits are not necessarily homogeneous in their objective functions, some pursuing narrow self-interest goals consistent with profit maximization, while others pursue broader social objectives (bonoficers). Enforcement of the nondistribution constraint may also vary systematically, being less binding on some nonprofits; for example, regulators may assume that church-related nonprofits have bonoficing objective functions and so require less monitoring.[13]

## WHAT DIMENSIONS OF INSTITUTIONAL BEHAVIOR SHOULD WE CARE ABOUT?

*Efficiency.* Do institutional forms differ in the cost at which they convert inputs into outputs? There have been many attempts to compare production costs, but we are still uncertain about how to measure output. Further, it is questionable whether we should assume that the same forms of output are produced regardless of institutional form. The discussion above emphasized the potential of nonprofits to provide outputs precisely in those forms that are most difficult to measure and value—quality in hard-to-monitor forms, external effects, and distribution to persons other than those with the greatest willingness to pay. Unless adequate attention is given to these dimensions of output, it is quite possible that output will come to be measured in ways that capture most or even all of private sector output but less of the output of nonprofits, thus biasing the comparative efficiency data.

*Taking Advantage of Consumer Informational Deficiencies.* When commodities are complex, so that it is costly for consumers to gauge performance and, hence, for sellers to guarantee the quality of output, organizational form may signal expected behavior because of the interplay of organization objectives and constraints.[14] As noted above, a

11. Nonprofit organizations vary widely in their dependence on donations. Litigation and legal aid organizations received 97 percent of their revenues through donations, while nonprofit sports and athletic organizations received only 4 percent.

12. Note that a legally nonprofit organization that chose to act as a profit-maximizer ($df/dS = 0$)—which could occur in the light of enforcement costs for the nondistribution constraint—would not behave identically to a private firm even though the objective functions were the same, because the constraints on the two would differ. This is the case in which the nonprofit is a for-profit firm in disguise, taking advantage of subsidies but pursuing profit maximization.

13. The level of monitoring can, however, affect the organization's objective function through the managerial/trustee sorting process. Thus, a lower level of regulatory monitoring could attract more profit-maximizer types of managers, thereby turning the organization into something closer to a for-profit-in-disguise. Although nonprofits are not homogeneous, it is not clear that models should be industry specific (for hospitals, see Newhouse 1970 and Pauly and Redisch 1973). For a discussion of tax policy and the objective function, see Eckel and Steinberg 1993.

14. Zeckhauser and Viscusi (1990) have pointed out that in a world of positive costs of obtaining information, it may be efficient to utilize a proxy for information. Specifically, they note that "mandatory requirements may be preferable to . . . information efforts." Institutional form could perform an analogous informational role.

potentially important consequence of the nondistribution constraint—assuming it is enforced—is its blunting of managerial incentive to maximize profits. This is important because organizations that do not pursue maximum profit do not have an incentive to take advantage of their informational superiority over consumers. Because many goods and services are easily evaluated by consumers, it might be expected that the importance of nonprofit as well as government producers will be greatest in markets in which consumers seek trustworthy sellers who will act as if they are effective agents for consumers—perhaps in health care, schooling, and medical research. Even when such complex commodities are involved, however, the fact that consumers vary in their ability to gauge quality suggests that nonprofit and government providers may be especially useful to those consumers who are least well informed—which has been found in recent work on day care facilities (Mauser 1993).

An example of an informational asymmetry would be the rate of injury of children in day care centers. One of the hard-to-monitor dimensions of organization behavior in this industry is the attentiveness of staff in monitoring the youngsters and thereby preventing accidents. Because attentiveness is difficult to observe and accident rate statistics difficult to obtain and to interpret, it would be useful to determine whether institutional form is a useful proxy for such costly-to-monitor variables as attentiveness to accident prevention.

The possible connection between informational asymmetries and institutional form is exemplified in the following. Every commodity may be seen as a bundle of attributes: a given consumer can determine which attributes are present and at what level, at a cost specific to the attribute and consumer. For simplicity, consider each attribute as being one of two types, for any given consumer—either low cost, type I, or high cost, type II; if a consumer is asymmetrically underinformed, it is, by definition, in type II dimensions.[15]

Type II attributes give the seller—whom I assume to be the better informed—the opportunity to chisel or "shave" quality, given consumers' cost of monitoring. If nonprofit, for-profit, and government organizations do behave differently, it might well be in the extent to which they take advantage of opportunities to capitalize on their (type II) informational superiority, especially in situations in which it is costly for consumers to switch to other sellers when unsatisfactory output is detected—for example, in nursing homes. If nonprofits do take less advantage of their informational advantages, they would provide more type II attributes than private firms, other things equal.

*Output Quality.* Another relevant dimension of institutional behavior is output quality as reflected by level of resource inputs. It is true that consumers could learn about the level of any seller's input utilization, but this information can be difficult to obtain. Thus, knowledge of the supplier's institutional form might reveal valuable information on quality. To be sure, however, interpretation of divergences is of critical importance. If institutional form *A* utilizes more units of inputs per unit of measured output—for example, a day of service in a hospital, school, nursing home, or day care center—than does institutional form *B*, that could represent (1) lower quality service by *A*, (2) less needy consumers in *A*, or (3) differential output forms, *A* producing more output in unmeasured dimensions.

*Output Rationing Methods.* Institutional behavior could differ in the means used to distribute output. Two prominent alternatives are price and waiting lists. A profit-maximizing organization would tend to rely on price, increasing it if there is excess demand. This is not to say that private firms never maintain a queue; the key question is whether nonprofits—church-related or not—are more likely to choose to provide their services on a basis other than ability to pay. If nonprofits were better described as bonoficers while private firms placed relatively greater weight on generating profit, then nonprofits would make less use of price to control access and more use of alternative mechanisms such as waiting lists.[16]

As a matter of social policy, we may have a preference, in some industries, for sellers that utilize nonprice distribution techniques rather than providing services to the highest bidders. In the case of human organ transplants, for example, U.S. policy has gone so far as to prohibit the sale of organs; in other industries the optimal solution may be not to prohibit sale altogether but to encourage institutional mechanisms that deploy a variety of distributional mechanisms.

*Generation of External Benefits and Costs.* Insofar as nonprofits are bonoficers, they tend to engage in more activities that provide more external (uncaptured) social benefits and in fewer activities that impose external costs. Although this is an important dimension of output in terms of which private firms and nonprofits might be expected to differ, I shall not examine it further. There is evidence that nonprofit hospitals are more likely than for-profit hospitals to provide services that are unprofitable but that generate favorable social effects—for example, free or low-priced educational programs on drug abuse (Lee and Weisbrod 1977; Shortell et al. 1986).

15. The dichotomization of attributes into two types is an expositional simplification. Each attribute of any commodity can be arrayed on a spectrum from those that are costless to monitor and evaluate to those that are infinitely costly. Moreover, an attribute can be of type I for some consumers and type II for others; I do not deal with this case here, although it may be quite important in explaining the coexistence of for-profit and nonprofit sellers in the same industry.

16. A waiting list is ordinarily thought of as involving the provision of a commodity of given quality through a mechanism that involves waiting time. A related alternative is to reduce quality. For example, a charitable soup kitchen might plan to serve a bowl of soup to each of the *n* persons expected to appear for lunch, but if $2n$ appeared the kitchen might decide that rather than turn away people it would water down the soup.

**WHAT SHOULD BE BOUND UP IN THE "CETERIS PARIBUS"?**

**Regulatory Constraints?**

Whether an organization's institutional form affects its behavior in any specific dimension depends on multiple factors. Institutional form may affect behavior if permitted to do so, but regulatory constraints can preclude that. For example, in the absence of constraints on input utilization—say, a requirement that every nursing home have a registered dietician on the staff—for-profit and nonprofit organizations might choose differently. Similarly, regulatory requirements that all airlines—governmental and private—use particular equipment or serve particular cities (Davies 1971) preclude differential institutional goals from affecting those dimensions of behavior. Still another example involves price regulation; the Medicare Diagnosis Relate Groups (DRG) system of pricing hospital services clearly limits differential pricing policies. In short, if the ceteris paribus includes such exogenous constraints, institutional form may not be permitted to affect certain dimensions of behavior, whereas in the absence of those constraints behavioral differences may be manifest. Mark Schlesinger (in this volume) emphasizes the influence of such external factors as levels of government control in determining the effect of institutional form. The failure to recognize this leads to understating the effects that institutional form would have in the absence of such restrictions and requirements.

**Endogenous Variables?**

Errors will result in estimating the effects of institutional form if endogenous variables—those that are affected by institutional form itself—are held constant. Doing so precludes finding that a particular form of institution has indirect, as well as direct, effects on some dimensions of organization behavior.[17] Although it is well recognized in econometric work that biased estimates result from failure to control for *exogenous* variables that are correlated with both institutional form and the dependent variable under consideration—the omitted variable problem—it is less well recognized that over-controlling is also a source of biased estimates. If the analyst controls for variables that are affected by institutional form, there can be no finding that institutional forms have different effects influencing these variables which, in turn, affect the variables of interest.

An illustration will be useful. In the nursing home industry, a typical nonprofit facility employs more doctors, nurses, and volunteers per one hundred beds than do proprietary homes. The important question is whether these differences are exogenous to institutional form or are results of, say, differential institutional goals. If the latter is so—as seems likely—then such input differentials should not be held constant in the process of estimating the effect of institutional form on, say, consumer satisfaction.

It is common, however, for econometric estimates of the effects of institutional form to hold constant such endogenous variables, and by so doing they fail to estimate correctly the total effects—direct and indirect—of institutional form, obtaining only partial, direct, effects. For example: (1) In a study of government-owned versus privately-owned packaged liquor stores (Simon 1966), the number of off-premise outlets per capita is held constant in the econometric equation even though that number is arguably a consequence of institutional form. (2) In a study of the relative efficiency of governmental and private refuse collection (Savas 1977), the level of service (for example, curbside versus at the residence) is held constant even though level of service may well be a function of institutional form. (3) In studies comparing nonprofit and for-profit hospitals (Lewin, Derzon, and Marguiles 1981; Herzlinger and Krasker 1987), organization case mix is often held constant even though it is arguably a consequence of differential institutional goals.

The overall point is that *institutional form* is a term encompassing a number of dimensions characterizing an organization; the more of these elements that are controlled for in an econometric estimation process, the smaller the probability that the remaining elements, captured by institutional form, will be found to have sizable behavioral effects.

Another illustration of an endogenous variable that is typically held constant is organization size. Concerned about the possible effects of scale economies on organizational efficiency, analysts have generally included size as an explanatory variable in econometric analyses of comparative institutional behavior. By doing so, they treat size implicitly as exogenous to the choice of institutional form. If, however, for-profit, governmental, church-related nonprofit, and other nonprofit organizations pursue dissimilar goals, which, in turn, causes them to choose systematically different sizes, controlling for size would lead to biased estimation of the effects of institutional form.

In the hospital industry, for example, hospital size does vary across institutional form; in one study, the mean nonprofit hospital had 204 beds compared with 155 in the mean for-profit hospitals (Herzlinger and Krasker 1987). The reason for the difference is crucial to the appropriate statistical estimation. If for-profit hospitals are smaller because profit-maximizing behavior causes them to restrict their activities to those that are profitable, and if nonprofits, having access to donations and volunteer labor, can afford to provide unprofitable services, then differential size is a result of institutional form; it should not be controlled for if we are trying to determine the total effect of institutional form, which encompasses effects operating through size—for example, on the variety of services produced.

The issue can be seen as follows. Equation (1) presents a model of the form typically estimated:

17. This section builds on my joint research and unpublished paper written with Elizabeth Mauser 1991.

(1) $Y = a\,W + b\,X + c\,Z + u$,

where Y is a dependent behavioral variable, W is a variable (for example, size) that is endogenous to the institutional form of the organization, X is a binary variable for the organization's institutional form, and Z is a vector of exogenous control variables. The question typically asked is: What is the total effect of X on Y, ceteris paribus?

Equations of form (1) have been estimated for a number of industries, and the effect of institutional form, X, on Y has been estimated as b. If, however, size varies because of, and not independently of, institutional form, then equation (2) would hold:

(2) $W = d\,X + f\,M + e$,

where M is a vector of variables that affect W but not Y directly. If equation (2) holds—if, for example, size is a consequence of variations in organization objective functions and constraints—then the estimate of b from equation (1) will be only the *partial* effect of X on Y, and, indeed, an incorrect estimate of that, given the mis-specification of equation (1). The *total* effect of X on Y is b* in equation (3), which is the sum of b, from (1), and a, from (1) times d, from (2):

(3) $Y = b^*\,X + c^*\,Z + g^*\,M + u^*$.

If equations (1), (2), and (3) are estimated, we can identify both the direct and indirect effects of institutional form because the total effect, b*, can be derived from (3), and *ad*—the indirect effect of X, operating through W—can be estimated from equations (1) and (2). Note that failure to account for indirect effects does not necessarily lead to underestimating of total effects; the total effects need not exceed the partial effects, for the indirect effects can have any sign.

Equations (1), (2), and (3) have been estimated for a sample of hospitals and are summarized here (Weisbrod and Mauser 1991). Our approach is to estimate b from equation (1) and b* from equation (3) in order to determine whether incorrectly treating variables as exogenous—the equation (1) approach—has produced biased conclusions about the total effect of institutional form on one measure of efficiency, cost per patient day.

With the cooperation of Regina Herzlinger, who generously made available the hospital data she utilized with Krasker in 1987, we reestimated their cost equation. They had concluded that for-profit hospitals average 35 percent lower operating cost-per-patient-day.[18] We believe that their estimate of an equation such as (1) is mis-specified, in part because of the endogenous decisions by for-profit hospitals to avoid providing such unprofitable services as obstetric and emergency services.[19] We postulate that the amount of emergency room care provided by a hospital is endogenous to institutional form and, hence, should not be held constant in an estimate of the effect of institutional form on hospital costs. We assume, further, that availability of emergency room services depends on local hospital market conditions as well as on institutional form. If we proxy market conditions by the local wage index, we can estimate equation (3) in our model, allowing the number of emergency room visits to vary endogenously; thus, the coefficient on institutional form captures the total effect of institutional form—the direct effect plus the indirect effect operating through the number of emergency room visits.

When emergency room care is treated as endogenous, we find that the coefficient on the institutional form binary variable indicates that for-profit hospitals have 30 percent lower cost-per-patient-day, compared with the 35 percent differential originally found in the equation (1) estimate by Herzlinger and Krasker. Because equation (2) can be estimated, with the number of emergency room visits as the dependent variable and institutional form and the local wage index as the independent variables, we can separate the effects of institutional form that are indirect—*a* times *d* from equations (1) and (2), which equals +.01—from the direct effect, which is the total effect, b* from equation (3), minus the indirect effect, or −.31. In this illustration, the direct effect of institutional form on cost, operating through size, is relatively small and of opposite sign to the direct effect. Neither of these results, however, is a basis for generalizing. Much more research is needed, in various industries and using various data sets and dependent variables.

All that can be said at present is that more attention needs to be directed, when models are specified and control variables are introduced, to the dangers of over-controlling—holding constant variables that are endogenous to institutional form. Whether one is interested in predicting the behavioral consequences of alternative institutional forms or in making public policy decisions whether to favor one form of institution over another, there is no substitute for careful theorizing about the precise meaning of *institutional form* and for correct specification of the ceteris paribus before proceeding to econometric estimation.

## SOME RECENT EMPIRICAL FINDINGS

This section summarizes a number of empirical tests of behavioral differences between proprietary and each of two types of nonprofit organizations, church-related and other, in two institutionally mixed industries, nursing homes and facilities for the mentally handicapped. Special attention is directed to (1) opportunistic behavior by providers who are

18. For a critique of Herzlinger and Krasker, including comments on the possibility of endogeneity bias, see Steinberg 1987.

19. The director of the perinatology center at New York Hospital-Cornell Medical Center reported that the cost of hospitalization and care for an extremely premature infant—one weighing about 1.5 pounds—was about $90,000 in 1981, a few years preceding the Herzlinger-Krasker data; the state reimbursement covered less than half that cost (French 1981).

more knowledgeable than their consumers about the quality of service being provided; (2) consumer satisfaction with services, especially with those that are difficult to monitor; and (3) the use of waiting lists rather than prices to distribute outputs.[20] The models that are estimated do not force any specific pattern of behavior; they allow differences of any size and direction to be found among the three forms of institutions. If differences are observed, knowledge of a supplier's institutional form would have signal value; they would also have policy relevance once it is decided which behavior is preferred under particular circumstances.

That systematic behavioral differences may not be observed does not imply that institutional form is irrelevant to public policy. It may be that competition drives out all but one form of institution, in which case the industry will not be mixed; or competition may force all surviving forms of institutions to behave in similar ways. It is not necessarily the case that if only one form of institution were permitted in the industry, the choice of form would not matter. In general, competition tends to reduce behavioral differences among organizations having different institutional form; thus, any differences observed tend to understate those that would occur if only one form or another monopolized the industry (Hirth 1993; Wolff and Schlesinger 1992).

Differences among institutional forms in a variety of cost and output dimensions have been examined in a number of mixed industries, but generally not in terms of either type II output dimensions or mechanisms for distributing output. (In the health care sector, see chapter 4 in Gray 1986, and Marmor, Schlesinger, and Smithey 1987; for railroads, Caves and Christensen 1980; for trash collection, Savas 1977; for child care, Krashinsky and Mauser (both in this volume); for airlines, Davies 1971; for international comparisons, Borcherding, Pommerehne, and Schneider 1982; for nursery schools in Austria, Badelt and Weiss 1990; for elementary and secondary schooling, James 1987; Downes 1992; Downes and Greenstein 1993; for worker-owned and corporate plywood cooperatives, Craig and Pencavel 1992. Some of these studies compare private firms with government agencies; others consider private nonprofit providers; the last reference compares types of proprietary firms.)

The rest of this section summarizes some empirical tests of differences in institutional behavior in the dimensions discussed above. Much of the work is ongoing, and this discussion aims merely to offer a flavor of the results obtained.[21]

### Test One: Taking Advantage of Informational Disparities – The Use of Sedatives in Nursing Homes

Residents of nursing homes are in complex states of health.[22] Few patients or families of patients are able to assess the medically appropriate medical care or therapy the patient needs. Thus, any nursing home – for-profit or nonprofit, church-related or other – is typically asymmetrically well informed and hence able to utilize a lower-cost therapy than would be used if the buyer were well informed. The nursing home's actions are observed, but the consumer does not have a sound standard against which to compare the treatment given.

An example of a nursing home's opportunity to capitalize on informational asymmetry to act in its own narrow interest rather than as agent for the patient involves the use of sedative drugs. A nursing home can save money and generate more profit by sedating a troublesome, active patient rather than incurring the greater cost of labor required in caring for such a patient.[23] Consumers have difficulty in determining precisely when the use of such medications is medically justified. The issue is thus whether different goals and constraints faced by proprietary relative to nonprofit nursing homes cause them to make different choices between self-interest in generating profit and consumers' interest in quality care.[24]

Some relevant evidence can be gleaned from a study of the use of sedatives at proprietary and church-owned nonprofit nursing homes (Svarstad, Bond, and Paterson 1984).[25] In 1982–83, a population of 338 newly admitted patients at nine nursing homes was followed for ninety days to determine the extent of variations in the prescribing and utilization of these drugs across homes.

There was, regrettably, no control for medical "need." There is, however, a useful piece of information relative to it: There was no significant difference between the percentages of patients in proprietary and private nonprofit homes who received a sedative prescription from a physician at the time of admission – 36.7 percent versus 33.3 percent, respectively. This suggests that medical need did not vary greatly, although the possibility of degrees of severity of illness cannot be dismissed. These prescriptions permitted nurses to use sedatives on the patients as needed. In sharp contrast, however, with the similarity in percentage of prescriptions, there was a very large and statistically significant difference in the number of dosage units administered to the patients. Proprietary home patients who received sedatives utilized an aver-

20. This section is based heavily on Weisbrod 1996.

21. A thorough discussion of the empirical methodology for most of the following work is in Weisbrod 1996.

22. This discussion is based on Weisbrod 1988, chapter 8.

23. Comments regarding the tradeoff between labor and sedation appeared in the *Wall Street Journal*, which referred to "concerns that such drugs are often prescribed not to treat illness, but simply to sedate troublesome patients" (Winslow 1991), and a *New York Times* editorial, which referred to the view that "the overwhelming majority [of elderly nursing home residents] are restrained or sedated because it makes them easier to handle. . . . State budget officials complained that the new [federal] rules [which restrict the use of drugs and physical restraints] would require more staff." (*New York Times* 1991).

24. I do not assert (or even hypothesize) that there is any significant amount of intentional and medically inappropriate sedating of otherwise active patients. What is involved, at most, are marginal, judgmental decisions.

25. The data in this section were provided to me by Professor Bonnie Svarstad, School of Pharmacy, University of Wisconsin-Madison.

age of 12.5 units of medication per month, compared to 3.0 units in the church-owned nonprofit homes.

Many factors, including differences in the medical needs of patients not captured by the frequency of prescriptions, could explain this disparity in utilization of sedatives. If, however, the explanation is that proprietary homes are more oriented toward increasing profit while the church-owned nonprofits were more bonoficing, then for-profit homes would engage in more substitution of the relatively inexpensive drugs for the more costly labor.

**Test Two: Differences in Input Utilization**

The Survey of Institutionalized Persons (SIP) (U.S. Bureau of the Census 1978) contains data on the quantities of twenty-one kinds of labor used in each of the sampled facilities in the nursing home and mentally handicapped industries. Insofar as these inputs are proxies for quality of outputs that are difficult for consumers to monitor (type II), they can be examined to determine whether forms of institutions differ in their opportunistic behavior.

Differences in labor utilization could exist for reasons other than organization goals. Utilization would differ if, for example, church-related nonprofits attracted labor at lower wages or attracted more volunteer labor; under these conditions, we would expect these nonprofits to utilize more labor even if their goals were no different than those of for-profit firms—provided, of course, that the differential supplies did not result from beliefs about organization goals. It is likely that if such differential labor supply prices do exist, it is because of such beliefs and the preferences of some persons to work for organizations with bonoficing-type goals. Research on such preferences, however, is very limited.

Thus, if input intensities do vary across institutional forms, it will not be possible to pinpoint the source; still, such a finding would suggest, at the least, that institutional form does connote behavior. Moreover, if consumers eventually learn about the consequences of such input variation, they may become differentially satisfied with the quality of services offered by the various types of providers—and this is a testable implication of behavioral differences in type II dimensions that will be discussed below.

I have examined data on institutional utilization of twenty types of paid labor, including MDs, RNs, LPNs, nurse aides, dieticians, teachers, maintenance workers, and administrators. In addition, volunteers were studied, and they were distinguished between volunteers who perform the same twenty activities and volunteers who perform other activities. Controlling for institutional form as well as for the facility's size, monthly charge, and mix of Medicare and Medicaid beds, the regression estimates indicate that *church-related nonprofit homes, compared with proprietary homes, do differ in their labor input utilization.*[26] (1) In the nursing home industry, church-related homes employ significantly (at the .10 significance level or better) more full-time (FT) RNs, dieticians, and maintenance workers per one hundred patient beds and significantly more part-time (PT) nurse aides, maintenance workers, and volunteers (performing work in which there are not paid workers). For all other labor inputs, FT and PT, the estimated utilization is not significantly different between church-related and proprietary homes. Thus, without exception among the forty-one labor groups—twenty FT, twenty PT, and volunteers—investigated, either significantly more is used at church-related facilities than at proprietary facilities or there is no difference in utilization.[27] Not a single labor input, FT or PT, is used significantly more by private firms.[28]

(2) In the mentally handicapped facilities industry, again comparing *church-related nonprofits with proprietary facilities,* we find once more that, ceteris paribus, church-related facilities utilize significantly more of some types of labor—FT LPNs and teachers as well as PT MDs, LPNs, and volunteers.

The magnitude of differences is in many cases substantial as well as significant. For example, church-related nonprofit nursing homes have a predicted utilization of 5.0 FT RNs per hundred beds, compared with 2.6 at proprietary homes; 2.4 FT dieticians compared with 0.6; 17.8 FT maintenance workers compared with 12.4; and 40.7 persons who volunteer at least once per month, compared with 24.3.

Turning to differences between *proprietary homes and other (nonchurch-related) nonprofits,* we find a similar pattern. Controlling for the same variables as above, the nursing home industry exhibits the following: this class of nonprofits uses significantly more of some forms of labor—FT RNs (3.7 vs. 2.7 per hundred beds) and PT MDs (1.2 vs. 0.6), LPNs (2.8 vs. 1.5), nurse aides (7.1 vs. 4.5), maintenance workers (9.8 vs. 4.2), and volunteers (50.0 vs. 24.3)—and again, as with the church-related facilities, every significant difference shows a greater intensity for the nonprofits.

For mentally handicapped facilities, the pattern of labor input behavior is broadly consistent with the pattern displayed by nursing homes. These nonprofits, like their church-related counterparts, utilize significantly more labor than do proprietaries, ceteris paribus, in most labor classes: FT program directors, activity directors, teachers and aides, other professional and technical personnel, maintenance workers, and more PT MDs and volunteers not in the paid occupations. They also employ, by contrast, significantly fewer FT administrators and nurse aides than do proprietary facilities.

26. Tobit-form equations were estimated, in light of the truncation of the numbers of workers at zero.

27. Differences in frequency of volunteering for the twenty types of jobs for which there are paid workers were also examined. The numbers were extremely small, however, even though the numbers of volunteers for other kinds of work were quite substantial. Reasons for such variation in the composition of volunteer labor have not been studied rigorously.

28. Evidence from another institutionally mixed industry, day care, also shows that nonprofit and for-profit providers utilize significantly and substantially different production technologies (Mauser 1988).

The overall pattern remains one of predominantly lower utilization of labor in proprietary facilities.

Much prior research has treated the nonprofit sector as essentially homogeneous. My examination of differences between *church-related and other nonprofits* suggests that understanding the role and behavior of the nonprofit sector requires disaggregation.

Do church-related and other nonprofits behave differently from each other — even though both face the same legal nondistribution constraint? They would if their goals differed or if private market constraints — for example, labor supply or consumer demand — on them differed. (The latter point deserves more attention, for insofar as church-related facilities provide services that are judged by some consumers to be distinct, such facilities enjoy a degree of monopolistic power.) The labor input analyses discussed above provide some evidence, though weak, that the two types of nonprofits do differ in important dimensions. Labor input intensities in church-related nonprofits and proprietary firms tend to differ more than do the input intensities between other nonprofits and proprietary firms. Three differences between the two types of nonprofits are significant — FT LPNs, dieticians, and maintenance workers — and all three show larger intensities at church-related nursing homes. The expected number of FT dieticians, for example, is 2.5 per hundred beds at church-related nursing homes compared with 1.1 at other nonprofit homes, and 0.6 at private facilities, other things being equal. Once more we find a consistent pattern of institutional behavior: every difference between the two classes of nonprofits is either not significant or shows a greater intensity for church-related facilities.

Comparing the two types of nonprofits in the mentally handicapped facilities industry, however, we find little difference. Only one labor input, PT LPNs, has a significantly different estimated utilization rate, with church-related facility utilization being greater (1.5 vs. 0.4). The other factor-intensity differences, both FT and PT, are not significant.[29] Utilization of volunteers is significantly greater at both types of nonprofit nursing homes than at proprietary homes but is not significantly different at the two types of nonprofits.

### Test Three: Differences in Consumer Satisfaction

Input utilization conveys indirect information about outputs in the proprietary and in each nonprofit sector. Consumer satisfaction with various elements of service is another indicator of output quality. Does satisfaction differ systematically across types of institutions, ceteris paribus? Does the generally higher level of labor inputs in nonprofit facilities, and particularly in those that are church-related, translate into higher levels of consumer satisfaction?[30]

If proprietary and nonprofit providers do take differential advantage of their informational superiority, this could be manifested in systematically different levels of consumer satisfaction across forms of institutions. Elizabeth Mauser (in this volume) addresses a similar question in the day care industry by comparing consumer perceptions of institutional differences in quality to actual differences in quality. Interestingly, even though the average quality provided by nonprofits — as measured by experts — was higher than at proprietary institutions, only a quarter of consumers perceived a difference in quality.

The SIP asked family members questions relating to general satisfaction and, separately, satisfaction with buildings and grounds, rooms and furnishing, staff, social activities, and treatment.[31] These measures are likely to capture unobservable, type II attributes of output because type I attributes,

29. Similarly, when data are examined for volunteers in each of the paid labor categories, we find, as we did for nursing homes, that there are few facilities of any institutional form that have such volunteers. The sharply contrasting findings for volunteers performing work for which there are paid workers and other volunteers shed a bit of light on the question of whether volunteers and paid labor are substitutes, complements, or neither. It appears that they are essentially independent inputs, at least where professional (paid) skills are involved.

30. It is beyond the goals of this chapter to examine alternative models of satisfaction, coming to like a complex service, or complaining to a government agency or anyone else (Hirschman 1970). It would be useful, however, to learn more about such processes, given the wide availability of data on satisfaction with and complaints about all sorts of services and conditions such as jobs, public services, social institutions, etc. There would appear to be valuable information in such data, but their interpretation remains unclear (Rubin et al 1993).

One model of complaints (the exercise of "voice") would have them registered whenever a consumer's expectations exceeded realizations. (How expectations are formed is yet another matter.) In this case differential complaint frequencies between for-profit and either church-related or other nonprofit organizations would represent differential disappointment with quality of service. In another model a person would complain whenever he or she judged that doing so would lead to beneficial action and not reprisal. If such a benefit-cost model described the complaint-generating process, interpretation of how complaints (or statements of dissatisfaction) relate to consumers' actual utility levels would be more complex; one form of institution could generate more complaints than another simply because it was more responsive, even if the level of consumer satisfaction with its services was actually higher. In that case, a higher level of complaints would indicate more confidence in an organization, not less gratification from its services.

31. Family members were also asked whether they like or don't like the services provided to their relative. The overall question was, "Do you feel this facility has provided the kind of services and care [the patient] needs?" Only yes and no responses were permitted. Other questions involved specific aspects of the overall service package: "Do you like or dislike the following facilities and services offered by [name of facility]? (1) Building(s) and grounds? (2) Condition of the rooms and furnishings? (3) Treatment services — such as medical, nursing, rehabilitation? (4) Relations with staff? (5) Social activities, things to do? For this set of five services, three responses were possible: "Like it," "Don't like it," and "Don't know/no opinion." The context of these questions, following immediately the one on overall satisfaction, was such that it seems reasonable to interpret them as asking about satisfaction with each of the types of facilities and services.

being observable prior to admission (or purchase), are less likely to be a source of dissatisfaction.

The results from this empirical analysis are strong; every measure of satisfaction is greater for church-related nonprofits than for proprietary facilities. This is so in both industries, and most of the differences are significant.[32] By contrast, levels of satisfaction with other nonprofits and proprietary facilities are essentially indistinguishable. This is further evidence of the lack of homogeneity of the nonprofit sector and the importance of disaggregation.

Differences in satisfaction levels across institutional form, even when significant, however, are not quantitatively enormous. The estimated percentage of respondents satisfied overall with nursing homes is 97 at church-related facilities, 92 at other nonprofits, and 91 at proprietary facilities. Although these differences are relatively modest and not significant, satisfaction with the various service components differs somewhat more, and differences are generally significant statistically. With respect to treatment facilities, for example, estimated satisfaction, controlling for the variables noted earlier, ranges from 92 percent at church-related nursing homes to 87 percent at other nonprofit homes and 80 percent at proprietary homes. At mentally handicapped facilities, satisfaction levels are also generally in the 80 percent or higher range; for buildings and grounds, however, there is a 30-percentage-point difference between the satisfaction level at church-related and for-profit facilities.[33]

### Tests Four and Five: Differences in Distribution of Output

To the extent that nonprofits, church-related or other, are bonoficers or to the extent that they lack the incentive to maximize profit, they would distribute outputs differently from proprietary sellers. Hence, another dimension in terms of which private firms and each form of nonprofit organization might diverge is the mechanism through which output is allocated. A private firm would, presumably, sell its services to the highest bidders and, more generally, to everyone who is willing and able to pay a price exceeding marginal cost. A nonprofit organization, church-related or not, might behave similarly or it might choose to provide outputs to some who are unable or even unwilling to pay, offsetting costs through reduced profit and donated revenues.[34]

Do proprietary firms, church-related nonprofits, and other nonprofits use different mechanisms for determining access to their services? One test is whether they have different price-cost margins. A second way is to find out whether they make differential use of waiting lists. If either church-related or other nonprofits are bonoficers, more motivated than for-profit firms to provide access to some group of deserving consumers, they might sell below full cost or make greater use of such nonprice-rationing mechanisms as waiting lists. On the other hand, if nonprofits of either type are FPIDS, there would, presumptively, be no difference across institutional form in their use of nonprice-distributional mechanisms.[35]

*Test Four: Price-Cost Margins.* SIP data permit estimation of the differences between price and average cost for each facility in the three institutional forms and in both industries. Controlling for facility size[36] and the proportion of its beds that are certified for Medicare and for Medicaid (skilled and intermediate) patients, we find that among nursing homes, the two types of nonprofit facilities have price-cost differences that are a statistically significant $120–$125 lower (in absolute value) than in for-profit homes, ceteris paribus, while among mentally handicapped facilities the differences, also significant, are $55–$105 lower. These differences constitute approximately 19 and 15 percent, respectively, of the mean reported average cost in the two industries. Nonprofit and for-profit facilities do have distinguishable pricing policies. (Differences in the margins between the two types of nonprofits, however, are not significant in either industry.)

*Test Five: Waiting Lists.* The SIP data allow analysis of differential utilization of nonprice-rationing mechanisms among institutional forms. Other variables held constant, are there systematic differences in the use of waiting lists between private firms and nonprofits, and do the two types of nonprofits differ?

In both industries, church-related facilities are significantly and substantially more likely than proprietary facilities to have a waiting list—92 percent and 65 percent, respectively, among nursing homes, and 92 percent and 60 percent, respectively, among facilities for the mentally handicapped, evaluated at the mean values of the explanatory vari-

32. The nursing home equation for rooms and furnishings could not be estimated because the estimated variance matrix is singular.

33. A priori, we might expect differences in satisfaction between nonprofit and proprietary institutions to be greatest for services having the relatively largest type II elements, about which consumers are least well informed at time of admission. Distinguishing between type I and type II attributes of care is complex. Relations with staff and the quality of treatment services might seem to have the largest type II components, being the most difficult to observe prior to admission or to embody in a service contract. However, although some elements of other services such as building and grounds are easy to observe prior to admission (location, for example), others are costly to observe (for example, how suitable the layout of the building is for the uncertain and changing needs of a specific patient).

34. The claim that for-profit firms skim the profitable patients and leave the unprofitable ones for the public and private nonprofit sectors has often been made, particularly in the hospital industry (Ermann and Gabel 1983; Wohl 1984).

35. Even a profit maximizer might find it useful to utilize a waiting list under some circumstances; thus, the key question is not whether there is any utilization of waiting lists but whether there are systematic differences across institutional forms, other things being equal.

36. Earlier I raised a question about the assumption that size was an exogenous variable that should be held constant in the econometric analysis. The matter is complex and as yet unresolved, but I have followed convention in controlling for size, thereby facilitating comparability of these findings with those of prior studies.

ables. A comparison of other nonprofits with proprietary facilities discloses smaller differences; among nursing homes, other nonprofits have an estimated 73 percent frequency of maintaining a waiting list, which is not significantly different from the 65 percent private firm level. At mentally handicapped facilities the corresponding figure for other nonprofits is 69 percent, a difference that is significant though smaller than that between church-related and proprietary facilities. Overall, in both industries, the rankings are identical; church-owned facilities are most likely to have a waiting list, proprietary facilities are least likely, and other nonprofits are intermediate, with most differences significant.

Turning to the length of waiting lists — the number of names listed — my estimates indicate that, after controlling for facility size as well as for the other variables mentioned above, church-related nursing homes have the longest waiting lists and proprietary homes have the shortest. Moreover, church-related facilities' lists are significantly longer than the lists of both proprietary homes and other nonprofits; at the mean values of the regressors, a church-related nursing home is estimated to have forty-eight names on its waiting list, compared with twenty-eight at an other nonprofit and nineteen at a proprietary facility. At facilities for the mentally handicapped, proprietary facilities also have the shortest waiting lists, but none of the differences is significant.

## POLICY IMPLICATIONS AND DIRECTIONS FOR FUTURE RESEARCH

This line of analysis has highlighted a number of potentially critical matters which deserve research attention before public policy action is considered. One is the effect of the nondistribution constraint, especially its separability from the effects of other differences in constraints that accompany it. In particular, I have noted that as long as the private enterprise option with its unrestricted profits and profit disposition is available, no entrepreneur or organizer would ever form a nonprofit organization if doing so meant nothing more than the imposition of a nondistribution constraint. In fact, however, what we actually observe is that along with that constraint comes a variety of offsetting benefits and subsidies; thus, any observed behavior of nonprofit organizations cannot be attributed to the effects of the nondistribution constraint alone. The need for research to separate the various effects and their interactions has barely been recognized.

A second matter involves analysis of the enforceability of the nondistribution constraint. It is difficult, indeed, to determine when a nonprofit organization manager is receiving excessive compensation that is, in effect, an illegal distribution of profit. In addition, although the nondistribution constraint legally applies to compensation in any form, enforcement problems are especially severe with respect to nonpecuniary rewards such as expense accounts and other perquisites.

Another issue deserving research attention is the process of organization goal formation in the nonprofit sector. To some analysts, the behavior of nonprofits is seen as reflecting attempts to surmount the nondistribution constraint for private gain — behavior I have termed that of for-profits in disguise. To others, however, the key element in explaining nonprofit organization behavior and in distinguishing it from private enterprise is its public-serving, charitable, altruistic, or bonoficing goals. What determines the supply of nonprofit sector entrepreneurs with various goals is a largely unanswered question.

Research reported above highlights another issue deserving more attention and involving important public policy implications: Are there differences within the nonprofit sector such that differential enforcement of the nondistribution constraint and differential access to subsidies are warranted? We have found, for example, substantial distinctions between two types of nonprofit organizations — church-related and other — but similar studies would be useful for other institutionally mixed industries and perhaps for other divisions within the nonprofit sector.

Nonprofit organization goals, including their heterogeneity, need to be better understood in order to judge the degree to which assumptions about private sector behavior extend to nonprofits. For example, antitrust laws do not distinguish between private firms and nonprofits — church-related or other; yet a case for such a distinction could be made if, for example, nonprofits use monopoly power in more socially productive ways than do private firms.

An illustration of the relevance of differential institutional goals is the recent governmental proposal to finance the Clinton administration health care plan partly through a federal tax on hospitals (Pear 1993). If for-profit and, say, church-related nonprofit hospitals have differing goals, a change in costs — in the form of a new tax — would tend to have different effects on their behavior, although much would depend on the form of the tax.[37]

Many nonprofit organizations engage in activities that compete with government agencies as well as with private firms. The comparative institutional behavior evidence cited above is limited to the private sector, but it is also important, for public policy purposes, to understand better the comparative behavior of government and private nonprofit providers. Both are subject to the nondistribution constraint, but government organizations have access to tax revenue and are part of a political system, whereas private nonprofits have greater access to private donations but not to tax revenue and are not subject to the same political constraints.

In all these areas there is entwining of interests between

37. This would be true, ceteris paribus. If other constraints differed, however, there could be interaction effects. Thus, a progressive tax on a hospital's gross revenue would have a greater impact on nonprofit hospitals, which are generally larger; and even a proportional tax on a hospital's wage bill would have different effects across types of institutions if labor-capital ratios differed, perhaps as a result of capital subsidies to nonprofits.

policymakers and researchers. What society needs to know is not simply whether institutional form matters, not merely whether private firms, nonprofit organizations, and government agencies act differently, but if they do, in what ways this matters, under what conditions, and for whom.

**REFERENCES**


Alchian, Armen, and Harold Demsetz. 1972. "Production, Information Costs and Economic Organization." *American Economic Review* 62:777–95.

Arrow, Kenneth. 1963. "Uncertainty and the Welfare Economics of Medical Care." *American Economic Review* 53:941–73, at 950.

Badelt, Christoph, and Peter Weiss. 1990. "Specialization, Product Differentiation and Ownership Structures in Personal Social Services: The Case of Nursery Schools." *Kyklos,* Fasc. 1:61–81.

Ben-Ner, Avner, and Benedetto Gui. 1991. "Forward." *Annals of Public and Cooperative Economics* 62, no. 4:469.

Borcherding, Thomas, Werner W. Pommerehne, and Friedrich Schneider. 1982. "Comparing the Efficiency of Private and Public Production: Evidence from Five Countries." *Zeitschrift fur Nationalökonomie,* Supplement 2:127–56.

"California Trying to Close Worthless-Diploma Schools." 1994. *New York Times,* August 31, 38.

Caves, Richard, and Laurits R. Christensen. 1980. "The Relative Efficiency of Public and Private Firms in a Competitive Environment: The Case of Canadian Railroads." *Journal of Political Economy* 88:958–76.

Craig, Ben, and John Pencavel. 1992. "The Behavior of Worker Cooperatives: The Plywood Companies of the Pacific Northwest." *American Economic Review* 82:1083–1105.

Davies, David. 1971. "The Efficiency of Public versus Private Firms, the Case of Australia's Two Airlines." *Journal of Law and Economics* 14:149–65.

Downes, Thomas A. 1992. "Evaluating the Impact of School Finance Reform on the Provision of Public Education: The California Case." *National Tax Journal* 45:405–19.

Downes, Thomas A., and Shane M. Greenstein. 1993. "Understanding the Supply Decisions of Nonprofits: Modeling the Location of Private Schools." Working paper, Center for Urban Affairs and Policy Research, Northwestern University.

Eckel, Catherine, and Richard Steinberg. 1993. "Tax Policy and the Objectives of Nonprofit Organizations." Working paper, Department of Economics, Indiana University/Purdue University at Indianapolis.

Freudenheim, Milt. 1993. "The Hospital World's Hard-Driving Money Man." *New York Times,* October 5, C1.

Gaul, Gilbert M., and Neill A. Borowski. 1993. "Warehouses of Wealth: The Tax-Free Economy." Seven-part series, *Philadelphia Inquirer,* April 18–24.

Goddeeris, John. 1988. "Compensating Differentials and Self-Selection: An Application to Lawyers." *Journal of Political Economy* 96:411–28.

Goldberg, Victor. 1976. "Some Emerging Problems of Prepaid Health Plans in the Medi-Cal System." *Policy Analysis* 55.

Gray, Bradford, ed. 1986. *For-Profit Enterprise in Health Care.* Committee on Implications of For-Profit Enterprise in Health Care, Division of Health Care Services, Institute of Medicine. Washington, D.C.: National Academy of Sciences Press.

Hansmann, Henry. 1980. "The Role of Nonprofit Enterprise." *Yale Law Review* 89:835–99.

Herzlinger, Regina E., and William S. Krasker. 1987. "Who Profits from Nonprofits?" *Harvard Business Review* 65:93–106.

Hirth, Richard A. 1993. "Information and Ownership in the Nursing Home Industry." Ph.D. dissertation, Department of Economics, University of Pennsylvania.

James, Estelle. 1987. "The Public/Private Division of Responsibility for Education: An International Comparison." *Economics of Education Review* 6:1–14.

Lee, A. James, and Burton A. Weisbrod. 1977. "Collective Goods and the Voluntary Sector: The Case of the Hospital Industry." In *The Voluntary Nonprofit Sector,* ed. Burton A. Weisbrod, 77–100. Lexington, Mass.: D. C. Heath.

Lewin, Lawrence S., Robert A. Derzon, and Rhea Marguiles. 1981. "Investor-Owned and Nonprofits Differ in Economic Performance." *Hospitals* 55:52–55.

Mansnerus, Laura. 1993. "Bar Groups are Happy to Find You a Lawyer." *New York Times,* February 27, A30.

Marmor, Theodore, Mark Schlesinger, and Richard Smithey. 1987. "Nonprofit Organizations and Health Care." In *The Nonprofit Sector: A Research Handbook,* ed. Walter W. Powell, 221–39. New Haven: Yale University Press.

Mauser, Elizabeth. 1988. "The Supply of Center-Based Day Care in Massachusetts: Nonprofits versus For-Profits." Department of Economics, Wellesley College.

"M.I.T. Wins a New Trial in Price-Fixing Case." 1993. *New York Times,* September 18, 6.

Newhouse, Joseph. 1970. "Toward a Theory of Nonprofit Institutions: An Economic Model of a Hospital." *American Economic Review* 60:64–73.

O'Brien, Timothy L. 1993. "Private Prison Market Attracts More and More Firms." *Wall Street Journal,* June 10, B2.

Pear, Robert. 1993. "Clinton Scrambles to Find Financing for Health Plan." *New York Times,* September 12, 1:18.

Rawls, James R., Robert A. Ullrich, and Oscar T. Nelson, Jr. 1975. "A Comparison of Managers Entering or Reentering the Profit and Nonprofit Sectors." *Academy of Management Journal* 18:616–23.

Roomkin, Myron, and Burton A. Weisbrod. 1997. "Executive Compensation in For-Profit and Nonprofit Hospitals." Working paper, Department of Economics, Northwestern University.

Savas, E. S. 1977. "Policy Analysis for Local Government: Public Versus Private Refuse Collection." *Policy Analysis* 3:49–74.

Shortell, Stephen, Ellen Morrison, Susan Hughes, Bernard Friedman, James Coverdill, and Lee Berg. 1986. "Hospital Ownership and Nontraditional Services." *Health Affairs* 5(4):97–111.

Simon, Julian L. 1966. "The Effects of State Monopoly on Packaged-Liquor Retailing." *Journal of Political Economy* 74:188–94.

Temporary Commission on Living Costs and the Economy. 1976. *Report on Nursing Homes and Health Related Facilities.* Albany: State of New York.

U.S. Bureau of the Census. 1978. *1976 Survey of Institutionalized Persons*. Current Population Reports, Special Studies, Series P-23, no. 69. Washington, D.C.: Government Printing Office.

U.S. Small Business Administration. 1983. "Unfair Competition by Nonprofit Organizations with Small Business: An Issue for the 1980s." Washington, D.C.

Weisbrod, Burton A. 1983. "Nonprofit and Proprietary Sector Behavior: Wage Differentials among Lawyers." *Journal of Labor Economics* 246–63.

——. 1988. *The Nonprofit Economy*. Cambridge: Harvard University Press.

——. 1996. "Does Institutional Form Matter? Comparing Behavior of Private Firms, Church-Related Nonprofits, and Other Nonprofits." Northwestern University, Center for Urban Affairs and Policy Research.

Weisbrod, Burton A., and Elizabeth Mauser. 1991. "Partial versus Total Effects of Institutional Form: Disentangling Endogenous from Exogenous Variables." Department of Economics, Northwestern University.

Wolff, Nancy, and Mark Schlesinger. 1992. "Changes in Ownership-Related Differences in Hospital Performance in Response to Intersectoral Competition." Institute for Health, Health Care Policy, and Aging Research, Rutgers University.

Young, Dennis. 1983. *If Not for Profit, for What?* Lexington, Mass.: D. C. Heath.

# [22]

## *LESSONS FROM HEALTH ECONOMICS*[†]

# Nonprofit Firms in Medical Markets

*By* MARK V. PAULY*

The medical care industry is characterized by a large market share of output produced in firms which are organized on a not-for-profit basis. The market share of not-for-profit acute care hospitals is especially high, with such firms accounting for 70.3 percent of all beds in 1984, but these firms also exist in nursing homes, in other long-term care, in home health, in out-patient dialysis centers, and in most other parts of the health care industry.

The fact that a firm is not organized with the explicit goal of maximizing profits or stockholders' wealth is, in itself, a reason to be skeptical about the appropriateness of applying the conventional neoclassical models of firms and of markets without qualification. But what sort of qualification is appropriate, and how important is it to make adjustments? Since nonprofit firms selling services directly to consumers characterize other markets as well, the types of answers to this question which have been generated in medical economics provide insights beyond medical care. More importantly, the theoretical and empirical investigation of behavior in such atypical firms itself sheds light on the impact of firm organizational structure and within-firm incentives on firm and market performance in the for-profit sector. There are messages here for the "new industrial organization," as described by Oliver Williamson (1975).

### I. Property Rights Differences Between For-Profit and Nonprofit Firms

There are three major differences in the institutional constraints facing a not-for-profit firm, as compared to the neoclassical for-profit firm. First, not-for-profit firms must look to donations for initial equity capital; they do not have the power to obtain capital in return for the promise of a share of the residual income of the firm. Second, not-for-profit firms are not permitted to pay out as cash dividends any revenues in excess of production costs and cost of debt; residual returns are not alienable. Legal rules even inhibit the ability of managers of the firm to add profits to their salaries *ex post*. Third, not-for-profit firms cannot be sold or liquidated for proceeds to be paid to a set of individual owners.

These institutional differences in the right to transfer wealth have potential consequences for the incentives faced by those who direct the firm. The most obvious difference, and the one that has been subject to the most discussion, is that the "decision makers" who are unable to extract residual income in the form of cash (because of a kind of an attenuation of property rights) will choose to take it in other forms. A related notion is that the inability to sell ownership shares in the firm may lead to a difference in the ability of the firm to obtain large amounts of additional equity capital for capital investment. Differences in tax treatment and requirements to furnish charity care are also important, but will not be discussed here.

[†]*Discussants*: Burton Weisbrod, University of Wisconsin-Madison; Charles E. Phelps, University of Rochester; Roger D. Feldman, University of Minnesota.

*Robert D. Eilers Professor of Health Care Management and Economics, Professor of Public Management and Economics, University of Pennsylvania, and Executive Director, Leonard Davis Institute of Health Economics, 3641 Locust Walk, Philadelphia, PA 19104–6218.

## II. Models of Nonprofit Hospitals

Most of my discussion will refer to hospital ownership structure. There are two, so far rather distinct, strands of analysis in the discussion of the economics of nonprofit hospitals. One set of models has assumed that equity capital has already been obtained, ignored philanthropic motivation, postulated various sets of objectives for the firm, and carefully modeled the maximization of a utility function in those objectives subject to a break-even constraint. Another approach has modeled the role of voluntary donations in the establishment of nonprofit enterprises, but with only a rudimentary behavioral model of production in the enterprise. There is as yet no model which fully integrates the two approaches.

The "objective function" models all postulate an exogenous break-even (or maximum deficit) constraint, but differ in terms of the objectives the hospital is thought to pursue. One set of models postulates that the hospital seeks to maximize the money incomes of a set of decisive agents, particularly the physicians on the hospital's medical staff. Another set of models simply modifies the form in which a nonprofit hospital can pay out profits. The hospital still prices and/or chooses outputs and inputs as would a profit-maximizing firm, but pays "dividends-in-kind" to decision makers (managers or trustees). As Patricia Danzon has noted, "Although the rights to residual profit in a non-profit hospital are not well-defined, profit maximization is nevertheless an appropriate model provided the various claimants can agree on maximizing their joint gain" (1982, p. 38). The third class of models provides an exception to Danzon's conclusion—if output itself yields utility to decision makers, or if something which affects demand (say, "quality") also yields utility to hospital decision makers, then obviously the profit-maximizing price, quality, or output need not be selected.

There are many behavioral models, but little consensus on the appropriate one. One reason for this failure to achieve consensus has to do with the difficulty of distinguishing empirically among theoretically plausible models. The presence of profits in the constraint means that all of the variables which affect profits appear in the comparative statics of each of these models, as, of course, they appear in those of the profit-maximization model. Since the same variables with the same predicted signs show up in all models, it is obviously impossible to distinguish among them on this basis. The only real difference among models is that some include variables which others do not explicitly include. For example, the physician income-maximization model points to dimensions of physician productivity and pricing which may affect what the hospital does. But since other models do not explicitly rule out such influences, no model can be refuted. The heart of the theoretical problem is that the objective function is usually unobservable. Utility always is unobservable, and direct test of whether profit or physician income is at its maximum is usually impossible.

With such "internal" tests known to be inconclusive, the alternative empirical strategy is to compare not-for-profit hospitals, with unknown objectives, to for-profit hospitals whose objectives presumably are known. Detecting differences in behavior and evaluating these differences should shed light on differences in objectives. But what differences should one expect? The physician income-maximization model of the not-for-profit firm implies that, with a given number of medical staff members, the hospital chooses the same levels of output and quality as it would if it maximized money profit. The total price (hospital price plus physician price) is also the same in such a model. Only the division of that price between payments received by physicians and payments received by the hospital potentially differs from the profit-maximization case. The second class of models mentioned above also implies no difference in price, quality, or output between for profit and not for profit firms. Cost would differ, but only because of inclusion of the utility-generating dividends-in-kind in total cost. Only the third model suggest a difference in important aspects of equilibrium. Hence, comparisons of behavior across firm types will display differences only if the third type of model is appropriate, and a finding of no difference would not be surprising.

Much of the motivation for the debate concerning expected differences has concerned the alleged "inefficiency" of the not-for-profit firm because of the attenuation of property rights. Even at a theoretical level, this basic question has not been fully resolved, largely, I believe, because inefficiency in production, in the sense of deviation of resource costs from their theoretical minimum for a given amount and type of output, does not have a well-defined role in models of not-for-profit firms and plays no role whatever in models of for-profit firms.

The inefficiency associated with not-for-profit ownership could be considered to be analogous to a tax. In the conventional analysis of the impact of a pure profits tax on a for-profit firm, the partial-equilibrium conclusion is that such a tax simply reduces rents; it does not cause the firm to deviate from efficient production. One way to look at the "no-cash-payment" rule under which not-for-profit firms must operate is as a kind of inefficient tax, one requiring profits to be paid out in a form which may yield less utility than if they were paid in cash. Particularly in the type of model Danzon outlined, such dividends show up as costs, not as profits. But there is no implication here that there will be inefficiency in production per se. Output is produced with minimum levels of all inputs, and other "costs" are just the accounting implications of dividends-in-kind. Technically, the attenuation of property rights does not lead to inefficiency in production, only to payment of dividends in an inefficient way.

Where characteristics of output, such as quality or volume, yield utility directly, these dividends-in-kind may not be so easily segregated, even conceptually. Nevertheless, none of the utility-maximization models lead to predictions of technically inefficient production, given quantity or quality, and the excessive quality or quantity from the viewpoint of demanders of outputs is just the mirror image of the form of dividends-in-kind.

The real inefficiency therefore arises to the extent that dividends-in-kind are valued less highly by their recipients than would be the cash their cost represents. In the physician-dominated model, at least in a world of certainty and absent administrative costs, there is no inefficiency of this kind. And even in the other models, there would potentially be offsets in cash wages for managers who like "quality," who would choose higher quality as part of their real income even in the profit maximizing form. There is inefficiency only if such managers are overly compensated at the margin in the form of quality or technology.

A test of differences arising from ownership is also made problematic in part because firms of different ownership structures actually do coexist in the same market. Are there certain types of outputs for which certain types of firms are more suitable? The second strand of analysis relates the existence of such firms to certain characteristics of output. Henry Hansmann (1980) has outlined part of the argument. Suppose the quality of output is a positive argument in a nonprofit firm's utility function. Suppose also that some dimensions of quality cannot be observed well by consumers, and that they are aware of this difficulty. Then consumers may prefer to buy such output from not-for-profit firms. In effect, the consumer "sees through" the economic behavior model, identifies the differences in incentives within each type of firm, and chooses that type of firm whose estimated equilibrium value of the unobserved quality level comes closer to the consumer's most preferred option. Neither type of firm is more efficient in some intrinsic sense; each is preferred for a particular type of output or consumer, with the not-for-profit firm possibly sacrificing some productive efficiency in order to assure a quality level closer to what people want. Even this sacrifice need not occur if some managers have a strong enough taste for quality. The not-for-profit form itself is a signal to consumers about which types of firms have managers with a stronger interest in quality.

Given that hospitals of different ownership types can coexist, what would be the expected impact of entry on long-run equilibrium? Obviously competition will constrain the rents that dominant groups can earn, whether these groups are investors, medical staff, or administration and trustees. Morever, while greater competition or other financial pressures will reduce the extent to which members of such groups can get what they want, one should not confuse such external constraints with a change in objectives. For instance, greater competition will compel individual physicians in a physician dominated hospital to be constrained by the medical staff as a whole—in the collective best interest.

Free entry will, as Joseph Newhouse (1970) noted some time ago, force not-for-profit firms to price in long-run equilibrium at the same level as would for profit firms. Other objectives can still be pursued, but only as far as costs equivalent to normal profit on equity capital will allow. The product differentation discussed above will also persist in long-run equilibrium, except that the not-for-profit firm will be forced to produce efficiently whatever quality it chooses.

## III. Donations, Altruism, and Nonprofit Hospital Objectives

Another aspect of the second type of theory is related to the observation that initial equity capital for nonprofit hospitals typically comes from philanthropic donations. There are two issues to be noted here. First, I will review theories of donation, and attempt to integrate them with theories of production. Then I will examine the role of donated equity, and of private not-for-profit hospitals as a whole.

Burton Weisbrod (1977) has provided the most comprehensive theory of nonprofit donations. He argues that donations occur when the government fails to provide collective goods which at least some citizens value more than their cost. Deviations of tax bases from marginal benefit taxes would provide the basis for such donations. The emergence of a not-for-profit *firm* as a recipient of donations can be explained by an argument analogous to Hansmann's explanation of nonprofit output. If donors have difficulty monitoring the quality or quantity of output, or the price or profit levels set by the firm, donations to for-profit firms can be absorbed into profits (see Eugene Fama and Michael Jensen, 1983). In contrast, nonprofit firms may be more likely to use donations for their intended purposes, particularly if the objectives of the firm are consistent with those of the donors.

The quality-monitoring aspects even extend to the physician-dominated form. Surely physicians are in the best position to monitor quality within the hospital, and surely raising hospital capital via donations will, up to a point, be less costly than tapping the conventional capital market. By deviating somewhat from short-run maximization of physician income, and channeling donations to their intended recipients, physicians may be able to attract donations for their hospital. Physicians may also be likely to count hospital quality as part of their real income. Their position in the "trust market" may make them especially suited to be monitors of the use of donations; donors and consumers may then be content to monitor the monitors, and to rely on short-run impediments to profit maximization as a way of constraining the medical staff. It is quite possible that such a strategy may yield larger long-run profits to physicians than would pure profit maximization.

## IV. Empirical Evidence: The Time-Series

The externality-philanthropy view of the not-for-profit hospital provides an interesting perspective on the recent history of such an organizational form. Many people in the medical care industry have bemoaned the recent growth in the share of investor-owned for-profit hospitals (see Arnold Relman, 1980). The actual growth has been less than spectacular. The share of beds in investor-owned hospitals grew, not at the expense of the private nonprofit hospital, but almost entirely by a shrinkage in the share of local government-owned hospitals, and has only increased from 8 percent of beds in 1975 to 10 percent in 1984.

This period corresponds to one in which the relative share of federal government-financed care grew rapidly. In effect, financing of care for low-income or uninsured elderly people was transferred from the voluntary sector to the government. In such an environment it should not be surprising that investor-owned enterprises should grow, especially in expanding markets dominated by cost-based payment. In such markets, it was difficult to mobilize support for new philanthropy when, in principle and in plan, all of the indigent and the medically indigent were to become clients of the government. Thus the relative growth of for-profit firms was a direct response to the erosion of the supply of philanthropic capital. Not-for-profit firms found it difficult to expand or to start, and for-profit firms were able to locate where positive profits could be generated. In this sense, the modest growth of for-profit firms was caused, not by an upsurge of venality, but rather by a substitution of tax-financed charity and private production for the previous vertically integrated solicitation-production combination represented by the not-for-profit firm.

## V. Empirical Evidence: The Cross Section

As noted above, the test of theories of nonprofit firms has to be empirical. There have been many such comparisons. Although they differ in detail, the overall impression is that there is little ownership-related difference in hospital cost given quality, or in quality given bed size, teaching status, and other proxies for type of output. The evidence for nursing homes is less clear. There is obvious specialization by nonprofit nursing home firms in high-quality output, and some evidence that the for-profit firms disappoint those consumers who are poorly informed, as Weisbrod and Mark Schlesinger (1985) have noted.

The one area in which there may be differences between for-profit and not-for-profit hospitals is in price levels. A recent extensive study (Michael Watt et al., 1986) claims to have found differences in charge levels of approximately 17 percent for matched sets of for-profit and not-for-profit hospitals. These differences are reduced to about 10 percent when differences in tax burdens are netted out.

My own impression is that a difference of this magnitude, especially given the failure of other studies (for instance, Frank Sloan and Robert Vraciu, 1983) to find any differential, is not particularly strong evidence for important consequences arising from ownership structure. Since for-profit firms can probably shift equity capital more easily, the main message may simply be that such firms are more likely to be found in markets in which any firm, for-profit or not-for-profit, would charge high prices. There is an important message here: location and production by for-profit firms is endogenous. But no empirical study has taken account of the endogenous nature of ownership structure. This failure renders suspect all of the existing studies attempting to compare prices, profits, and costs between ownership types. Since endogenous for-profit firms are more likely to locate where market conditions permit high profits and prices for any firm, for-profit or not, there is a bias toward finding higher prices in for-profit firms.

One clear message from recent work is that, despite the anomalous character of the not-for-profit form, theory does not predict wide differences in behavior at the level of the market, nor does empirical evidence suggest that large differences do occur. There is however, the potential for wide variations in market structure as measured by ownership shares, even if there is relatively little difference in efficiency, cost, or welfare associated with different forms. Especially if entry is free and consumers somewhat discriminating, relatively small changes in advantages for one organizational form over another can lead to large changes in the share of output produced by not-for-profit relative to for-profit firms. The growth of investor-owned hospitals may be an example of this phenomenon, as is the growth of multi-institutional affiliation in the health care industry.

## VI. The Welfare Economics of Nonprofit Firms

The other major message is that, with free entry and markets that adjust in other ways, there need not be inefficiency created by deviations in ownership forms from the conventional profit-maximizing one. In particular, even ignoring the gains from providing poorly informed consumers with quality closer to their preferred levels, as long as there are sufficiently many managers who place sufficient subjective value on the quality of the output they supervise, there need be no net inefficiency arising from the dividends-in-kind feature of not-for-profit firms. Moreover, gains to poorly informed consumers, who know that they are ignorant and know that the not-for-profit form is better for them, can offset any inefficiency cost even if there are excessive dividends-in-kind. The not-for-profit form may be the second best optimal way of dealing with asymmetric information, exactly as Kenneth Arrow (1963) has suggested. The interesting question is whether this equilibrium with nonprofit firms is (second-best) optimal. Is there an invisible hand which brings such forms into existence when (and only when) they are needed?

There are some potential impediments. The differential tax treatment of for-profit and nonprofit firms may itself cause excessive spread of the not-for-profit form. Even here, one may point to tax subsidies as potential optimal supplements for the public good associated with the externality aspects of not-for-profit firms. In addition, if uninformed consumers do not realize that they are uninformed, things may go awry. Finally, if firms which can somehow pay out profits easily can take on the not-for-profit form, there can be a "lemons" problem in which firms with true not-for-profit motivation are driven out by cleverly disguised imposters. Whether these impediments are significant remains to be seen, but I would not guess that they are.

In my view, the major message from theoretical or empirical work on not-for-profit health care firms is that such ownership differences turn out to be much less important than they might seem. This is especially so where entry is open, but even under imperfect competition nominal ownership structure seems to matter much less than fundamental economic incentives, particularly when the ownership structure itself is chosen in response to those incentives.

## REFERENCES

**Arrow, Kenneth J.**, "Uncertainty and the Welfare Economics of Medical Care," *American Economic Review*, December 1963, *53*, 941–73.

**Danzon, Patricia M.**, "Hospital 'Profits': The Effect of Reimbursement Policies," *Journal of Health Economics*, May 1982, *1*, 29–52.

**Fama, Eugene F. and Jensen, Michael C.**, "Agency Problems and Residual Claims," *Journal of Law and Economics*, July 1983, *26*, 327–50.

**Hansmann, Henry B.**, "The Role of Nonprofit Enterprise," *Yale Law Journal*, April 1980, *89*, 835–901.

**Newhouse, Joseph P.**, "Toward a Theory of Nonprofit Institutions," *American Economic Review*, March 1970, *60*, 64–74.

**Relman, Arnold S.**, "The New Medical-Industrial Complex," *New England Journal of Medicine*, October 23, 1980, *303*, 963–69.

**Sloan, Frank A. and Vraciu, Robert A.**, "Investor-Owned and Not-for-Profit Hospitals," *Health Affairs*, Spring 1983, *2*, 25–37.

**Watt, J. Michael et al.**, "The Comparative Economic Performance of Investor-Owned Chain and Not-for-Profit Hospitals," *New England Journal of Medicine*, January 9, 1986, *314*, 89–96.

**Weisbrod, Burton A.**, *The Voluntary Non-Profit Sector*. Lexington: D.C. Health, 1977.

______ **and Schlesinger, Mark**, "Public, Private, Nonprofit Ownership and the Response to Asymmetric Information," in S. Rose-Ackerman, ed., *The Economics of Nonprofit Institutions*, New York; Oxford: Oxford University Press, 1985, ch. 7.

**Williamson, Oliver**, *Market and Hierarchies*, New York: Free Press, 1975.

# [23]

# Comparing Hospital Quality at For-Profit and Not-for-Profit Hospitals

Mark McClellan and Douglas Staiger

## 3.1 Introduction

Do not-for-profit hospitals provide better care than for-profit hospitals? While many studies have compared care delivered by for-profit and not-for-profit hospitals, these studies have provided relatively little empirical evidence on the performance of not-for-profits and for-profits.[1] The ultimate measure of hospital performance is the impact of its care on important patient outcomes, such as death or the development of serious complications that compromise quality of life. Assessing this impact is very difficult. First, collecting reliable long-term outcome data can be challenging. Second, without comprehensive controls for differences in patient case mix, such measures leave open the possibility that differences between hospitals reflect differences in patient disease severity and comorbidity rather than differences in quality of care. Finally, measures of important patient outcomes are notoriously noisy, due to the small numbers of patients on which they are based and the relative rarity of serious adverse outcomes for most patients. Thus, many policymakers and health care managers have expressed reservations about whether measures of se-

Mark McClellan is assistant professor of economics at Stanford University and a faculty research fellow of the National Bureau of Economic Research. Douglas Staiger is associate professor of public policy at the Kennedy School of Government, Harvard University, and a faculty research fellow of the National Bureau of Economic Research.

The authors thank David Cutler, Karen Norberg, Catherine Wolfram, and seminar participants at the NBER and various universities for their helpful comments. They also thank Dhara Shah and Yu-Chu Shen for outstanding research assistance, and the Health Care Financing Administration and the National Institute on Aging for financial support. All errors are the authors' own.

1. E.g., see Gaumer (1986), Gray (1986), Hartz et al. (1989), Keeler et al. (1992), and Staiger and Gaumer (1995).

rious outcomes are informative enough to identify useful differences in quality of care among hospitals.[2] The problem is particularly onerous for comparisons of quality of care between individual hospitals (e.g., for choosing among hospitals in a given market area).

We readdress the question of assessing hospital quality using longitudinal data sources and methods that we have recently developed (McClellan and Staiger 1997). We discuss the data and methods below. We study important health outcomes—all-cause mortality and major cardiac complications—for all elderly Medicare beneficiaries hospitalized with heart disease in the past decade. Our measures optimally combine information on patient outcomes from multiple years, multiple diagnoses, and multiple outcomes (e.g., death and readmission with various types of complications). As a result, we are able to develop measures that are far more accurate indicators of hospital quality than those previously used in hospital outcome studies. In our previous work, we have shown that these measures far outperform previously used methods in terms of forecasting hospital mortality rates in future years, and in terms of signal-to-noise ratios. Thus, we can expect these measures to enhance our ability to determine whether quality of care differs across hospitals.

After we introduce our data and methods, we present two sets of results. First, we examine how these new hospital quality measures vary across for-profit and not-for-profit hospitals, controlling for other characteristics of the hospital. In addition, we examine how these relationships have changed over our study period. We then examine the experience of three market areas closely: (1) a city in which a few large for-profit and not-for-profit hospitals have coexisted with stable ownership, (2) a city in which a large not-for-profit hospital was purchased by a for-profit chain, and later by another for-profit chain, and (3) a city in which the only for-profit hospital was converted to not-for-profit status.

Based on these new measures of hospital quality, our analysis uncovers a number of interesting differences between for-profit and not-for-profit hospitals. On average, we find that for-profit hospitals have higher mortality among elderly patients with heart disease, and that this difference has grown over the last decade. However, much of the difference appears to be associated with the location of for-profit hospitals: When we compare hospital quality within specific markets, for-profit ownership appears, if anything, to be associated with better quality care. Moreover, the small average difference in mortality between for-profit and not-for-profit hospitals masks an enormous amount of variation in mortality within each of these ownership types. Overall, these results suggest that factors other

2. E.g., see Ash (1996), Hofer and Hayward (1996), Luft and Romano (1993), McNeil et al. (1992), Park et al. (1990), and the sources cited in n. 1.

than for-profit status per se may be the main determinants of quality of care in hospitals.

### 3.2 Background

Comparisons of hospital quality, and of provider quality more generally in health care and other industries, must address three crucial problems: measurement, noise, and bias.

The first problem involves measurement. Without measures of performance, there is no basis for comparing quality of care. One of the major obstacles to research on provider performance is the development of reliable data on important medical processes and health outcomes. For example, a major obstacle to comparisons of different managed care plans today, including for-profit and not-for-profit comparisons, is that many plans simply do not have reliable mechanisms in place for collecting data on the care and outcomes of their patients, especially for outpatient care. While the problem is somewhat less severe for care during an inpatient admission, many hospitals do not have reliable methods for collecting follow-up data on their patients, and health plans do not have mechanisms for tracking patients across hospitals. For example, until several years ago, the Health Care Financing Administration (HCFA) published diagnosis-specific mortality rates for Medicare patients. But because these outcome measures were admission based, they could be favorably affected by hospital decisions about discharging or transferring patients, even though such actions may have no effect or adverse effects on meaningful patient outcomes. We use longitudinal data from the Medicare program linked to complete records of death dates to address the problem of collecting follow-up data on important outcomes for patients. But data limitations exist here as well: Medicare collects no reliable information on the care or outcomes of their rapidly growing managed care population.

The second problem involves noise. Important health outcomes are determined by an enormous number of patient and environmental factors; differences in the quality of medical care delivered by hospitals are only one component. Moreover, most of these outcomes are relatively rare. For example, even for a common serious health problem such as heart attacks, most hospitals treat fewer than 100 cases per year, and death within a year occurs in fewer than one-fourth of these patients. Even though a one or two percentage point difference in mortality may be very important to patients, few hospitals treat enough patients with heart disease in a year to detect such differences in outcomes. While data on other related health outcomes or on multiple years of outcomes might help reduce the noise problem, combining multiple outcome measures raises further complications. Hospital quality may improve or worsen from year to year, and the extent to which different outcomes are related to each other may not be obvious. We develop a general framework for integrating a potentially large number of outcomes over long time periods to address the noise problem. Our methods are designed to distinguish the signal of hospital quality from a potentially large number of noisy outcome measures.

The third problem involves bias. Patient selection may result in differences in outcomes across hospitals for reasons unrelated to quality. In particular, higher quality hospitals are likely to attract more difficult cases. A range of methods, including multivariate case-mix adjustment, propensity scores, and instrumental variables, have been developed to address the selection problem. In this paper, we address the problem by focusing on an illness—heart attacks, and heart disease more generally—for which urgency limits the opportunities for selection across hospitals. A more comprehensive analysis of the selection problem is beyond the scope of this paper. In section 3.6, we discuss some of the further evidence we have developed on the magnitude of the selection bias in our outcome measures.

In the next section, we outline our steps for addressing the measurement problems and noise problems that have complicated comparisons between for-profit and not-for-profit hospitals. Our results follow.

## 3.3 Data and Methods

### 3.3.1 Data

We use the same data as in McClellan and Staiger (1997) for this analysis. Our hospital performance measures include serious outcomes—mortality and cardiac complications requiring rehospitalization—for all elderly Medicare beneficiaries hospitalized with new occurrences of acute myocardial infarction (AMI, or heart attacks) from 1984 through 1994, as well as for all elderly beneficiaries hospitalized for ischemic heart disease (IHD) from 1984 through 1991. To evaluate quality of care from the standpoint of a person in the community experiencing heart disease, we assign each patient to the hospital to which he or she was first admitted with that diagnosis. Our population includes over 200,000 AMI patients and over 350,000 IHD patients per year. We limit our analysis of hospital performance to U.S. general short-term hospitals with at least two admissions in each year, a total of 3,991 hospitals that collectively treated over 92 percent of these patients. In this paper, we focus exclusively on outcome differences for AMI patients, but we use information on IHD patient outcomes to help improve our estimates of hospital quality for AMI treatment.

For each AMI and IHD patient, our mortality measure is whether the patient died within 90 days of admission. In principle, we could use other patient outcomes as well (e.g., death at other time periods or readmission for a cardiac complication). We focus on these two outcomes, and AMI patients in particular, for a number of reasons. First, death is an easily measured, relatively common adverse outcome for AMI, and many acute medical treatments have been shown to have a significant impact on mortality following AMI. Second, AMI cases that are not immediately fatal generally result in rapid admission to a nearby hospital, so that questions of hospital selection of patients are less of a problem for AMI. Finally, we found in a previous study (McClellan and Staiger 1997) that measures of hospital quality based on AMI have a relatively high signal-to-noise ratio and are strong predictors of hospital quality for other outcomes and diagnoses.[3]

For each hospital, we construct risk-adjusted mortality rates (RAMRs) for each year and each diagnosis. These are the estimated hospital-specific intercepts from a patient-level regression (run separately by year and by diagnosis) that estimates average all-cause mortality rates with fully interacted controls for age, gender, black or nonblack race, and rural location. These RAMRs provide the outcome measures on which our hospital comparisons are based.

To describe hospital ownership status and other characteristics, we use data on hospital and area characteristics from the annual American Hospital Association (AHA) survey of hospitals. We use data from the 1985, 1991, and 1994 surveys in this analysis. AHA data are not available for some hospitals, limiting our final sample to 3,718 hospitals.

### 3.3.2 Empirical Methods

Past work comparing quality of care in hospitals has generally relied on a single hospital outcome measure in a given year. For example, to compare quality of care at two hospitals, one would simply calculate the estimated RAMR and the precision of the estimate for each hospital, and assess whether the difference in the RAMRs is statistically significant. The limitation of this approach is that the standard errors are often quite large.

Alternatively, one can combine information from all the outcome measures available for a given hospital (e.g., other years, other patients, other outcomes for the same patients) in order to more precisely estimate a hospital's current quality. This is the approach taken in McClellan and Staiger (1997). We briefly outline the method below.

Suppose we observe AMI_DTH90 and IHD_DTH90. These are noisy estimates of the true hospital intercepts that are of interest:

$$\text{AMI\_DTH90}_{it} = \mu^{1}_{it} + \varepsilon^{1}_{it},$$

3. In particular, McClellan and Staiger (1997) also consider performance measures for ischemic heart disease and for a patient's quality of life following a heart attack (the occurrence of hospital readmission with congestive heart failure, ischemic heart disease symptoms, and recurrent heart attack).

$$\text{IHD\_DTH90}_{it} = \mu^2_{it} + \varepsilon^2_{it},$$

where $\mu$ is the true parameter of interest (the hospital-specific intercept in the 90-day mortality equations), $\varepsilon$ is the estimation error, and we observe each outcome for $T$ years. Note that $\text{Var}(\varepsilon^1_{it}\ \varepsilon^2_{it})$ can be estimated, since this is simply the variance of regression estimates.

Let $M_i \equiv \{\text{AMI\_DTH90}_i, \text{IHD\_DTH90}_i\}$ be a $1\times(2T)$ vector of the $T$ years of data on each outcome, and let $\mu_i \equiv \{\mu^1_i, \mu^2_i\}$ be a $1\times(2T)$ vector of the true hospital intercepts. Our problem is how to use $M_i$ to predict $\mu_i$. More specifically, we wish to create a linear combination of each hospital's observed outcomes data in such a way that it minimizes the mean square error of our predictions. In other words, we would like to run the following hypothetical regression:

$$(1)\quad \mu_{it} = \{\text{AMI\_DTH90}_i, \text{IHD\_DTH90}_i\}\ \beta_{it} + \upsilon_{it} \equiv M_i\beta_{it} + \upsilon_{it},$$

but cannot, since $\mu_i$ is unobserved and $\beta$ will vary by hospital and time.

Equation (1) helps to highlight the problem with using a single year's RAMR as a prediction of the true hospital-level intercept. Since the RAMR is estimated with error, we can improve the mean square error of the prediction by attenuating the coefficient toward zero, and this attenuation should be greater for hospitals in which the RAMR is not precisely estimated. Moreover, if the true hospital-specific intercepts from other outcomes' equations (e.g., other years, other patients) are correlated with the intercept we are trying to predict, then using their estimated values can further improve prediction ability.

In McClellan and Staiger (1997), we developed a simple method for creating estimates of $\mu_i$ based on equation (1). The key to the solution is noting that to estimate this hypothetical regression (e.g., get coefficients, predicted values, $R^2$) we only need three moment matrices:

$$\text{(i)}\qquad E(M_i'M_i) = E(\mu_i'\mu_i) + E(\varepsilon_i'\varepsilon_i),$$

$$\text{(ii)}\qquad E(M_i'\mu_i) = E(\mu_i'\mu_i),$$

$$\text{(iii)}\qquad E(\mu_i'\mu_i).$$

We *can* estimate the required moment matrices directly as follows:

1. We can estimate $E(\varepsilon_i'\varepsilon_i)$ with the patient-level ordinary least squares (OLS) estimate of the variance-covariance for the parameter estimates $M_{it}$. Call this estimate $S_i$.

2. We can estimate $E(\mu_i'\mu_i)$ by noting that $E(M_i'M_i - S_i) = E(\mu_i'\mu_i)$. If we assume that $E(\mu_i'\mu_i)$ is the same for all hospitals, then it can be estimated by the sample average of $M_i'M_i - S_i$.

Finally, it helps to impose some structure on $E(\mu_i'\mu_i)$ for two reasons. First, this improves the precision of the estimated moments by limiting the number of parameters that need to be estimated. Second, a time series structure allows for out-of-sample forecasts. Thus, we assume a nonstationary first-order vector autoregression (VAR) structure for $\mu_{it}$ $(1 \times 2)$. This VAR structure implies that $E(\mu_i'\mu_i) = f(\Gamma)$, where $\Gamma$ are the parameters of the VAR. These parameters can be estimated by generalized method of moments (GMM); that is, by setting the theoretical moment matrix, $f(\Gamma)$, as close as possible to its sample analog, the sample average of $M_i'M_i - S_i$. For details, see McClellan and Staiger (1997).

With estimates of $E(\mu_i'\mu_i)$ and $E(\varepsilon_i'\varepsilon_i)$, we can form estimates of the moments (i)–(iii) needed to run the hypothetical regression in equation (1). By analogy to simple regression, our predictions of a hospitals true intercept are given by:

$$(2) \quad \hat{\mu}_j = M_i E(M_i'M_i)^{-1} E(M_i'\mu_i) = M_i[E(\mu_i'\mu_i) + E(\varepsilon_i'\varepsilon_i)]^{-1} E(\mu_i'\mu_i),$$

where we use our estimates of $E(\mu_i'\mu_i)$ and $E(\varepsilon_i'\varepsilon_i)$ in place of their true values. We refer to estimates based on equation (2) as "filtered RAMR" estimates, since these estimates are attempting to filter out the estimation error in the raw data (and because our method is closely related to the idea of filtering in time series).

### 3.4 National Estimates

One common method of comparing quality of care across hospitals is to run cross-section regressions using a quality measure such as RAMR as the dependent variable and using hospital characteristics such as patient volume, ownership, and teaching status as independent variables. In this section, we investigate the extent to which using a filtered RAMR as the dependent variable affects the inferences that can be drawn from such regressions. A priori, we would expect that using the filtered RAMR (as opposed to the actual RAMR in a given year) would improve the precision of such regression estimates because the dependent variable is measured with less noise. The gain in efficiency is likely to be particularly large for smaller hospitals, since the RAMR estimates in any single year for these hospitals have the lowest signal-to-noise ratio.

Figure 3.1 illustrates this difference between filtered and actual RAMRs by plotting each against volume using data from 1991. Throughout the remainder of the paper we focus on RAMRs based on 90-day mortality among Medicare AMI admissions (although the filtered estimates incorporate the information from 90-day mortality among IHD admissions as well). Keep in mind that the unit for the RAMR measures is the probability of death, so that a RAMR of 0.1 means that the hospital had a mortality rate that was 10 percentage points higher than expected (e.g., 30 percent rather than 20 percent).

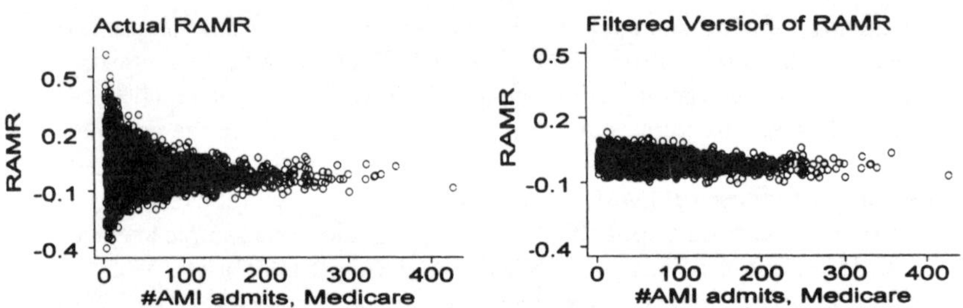


**Fig. 3.1 The relationship between risk-adjusted mortality rates (RAMRs) and patient volume using actual versus filtered RAMR**
*Note:* Based on 90-day mortality for Medicare AMI admits.

There are two interesting features of figure 3.1. First, the filtered RAMR estimates have much less variance than the actual RAMR estimates, particularly for smaller hospitals. This is the result of two distinct effects. Most importantly, the filtered estimates for small hospitals are relying more heavily on data from other years and other diagnoses, and this improves their precision. In addition, the filtered estimates assume the actual RAMR estimates for small hospitals have a very low signal-to-noise ratio, and therefore attenuate them back toward the average (similar to shrinkage estimators).

A second interesting feature of figure 3.1 is that the relationship between outcomes and volume is much more apparent in the filtered data. High-volume hospitals clearly seem to have lower mortality. Thus, these filtered RAMRs appear to be a useful tool for uncovering quality differences across hospitals.

Table 3.1 provides regression estimates that further suggest that these filtered RAMR estimates improve our ability to uncover differences in quality across hospitals. This table contains coefficient estimates from regressions of RAMR estimates (either actual or filtered) on dummies for ownership (for-profit and government, with not-for-profit the reference group), a dummy for being a teaching hospital, and the number of Medicare AMI admissions in the given year (in hundreds). Since volume is potentially endogenous (and since Medicare volume is a crude proxy for total volume), we also report estimates from regressions that do not control for volume. The table contains estimates for 1985, 1991, and 1994. The regressions using actual RAMRs are weighted by the number of Medicare admissions, while the regressions using filtered RAMRs are weighted by the inverse of the estimated variance of each hospital's filtered RAMR estimate.

As one would expect, the regressions based on the filtered RAMR yield much more precise coefficient estimates. The standard errors in regres-

**Table 3.1 Regression Estimates of the Relationship between Hospital Characteristics and the Risk-Adjusted Mortality Rate (RAMR) Based on 90-Day Mortality for AMI Admits (3,718 hospitals)**

| | 1985 | | | 1991 | | | 1994 | | |
|---|---|---|---|---|---|---|---|---|---|
| | Actual RAMR | Filtered Version of RAMR | | Actual RAMR | Filtered Version of RAMR | | Actual RAMR | Filtered Version of RAMR | |
| Number of Medicare admits in AMI (100s) | −0.0178<br>(0.0022) | −0.0153<br>(0.0010) | | −0.0148<br>(0.0018) | −0.0143<br>(0.0009) | | −0.0093<br>(0.0014) | −0.0110<br>(0.0007) | |
| Government | 0.0151<br>(0.0033) | 0.0104<br>(0.0012) | 0.0148<br>(0.0012) | 0.0219<br>(0.0033) | 0.0120<br>(0.0013) | 0.0178<br>(0.0013) | 0.0169<br>(0.0033) | 0.0109<br>(0.0012) | 0.0156<br>(0.0013) |
| For-profit | 0.0016<br>(0.0043) | 0.0030<br>(0.0016) | 0.0061<br>(0.0016) | 0.0115<br>(0.0038) | 0.0071<br>(0.0016) | 0.0100<br>(0.0016) | 0.0102<br>(0.0038) | 0.0087<br>(0.0015) | 0.0115<br>(0.0015) |
| Teaching | −0.0031<br>(0.0033) | 0.0022<br>(0.0014) | −0.0066<br>(0.0014) | −0.0047<br>(0.0030) | −0.0039<br>(0.0014) | −0.0111<br>(0.0014) | −0.0083<br>(0.0028) | −0.0047<br>(0.0013) | −0.0102<br>(0.0013) |

*Note:* Standard errors are given in parentheses. Regressions using the actual RAMR weight by the number of AMI admits. Regressions using the filtered RAMR weight by $1/\sigma^2$, where $\sigma$ is the standard error of the estimated RAMR.

sions using the actual RAMRs are two to three times larger than the corresponding standard errors from regressions using the filtered RAMR. For example, using actual RAMR estimates in 1985, mortality in for-profit hospitals is estimated to be 0.16 percentage points higher than in not-for-profit hospitals. But the standard error for this estimate is so large (0.43 percentage points) that the difference would have to be near a full percentage point before we could be confident of a real difference in mortality. In contrast, using filtered RAMR estimates in 1985, mortality in for-profit hospitals is estimated to be 0.30 percentage points higher than in not-for-profit hospitals and this difference is borderline significant because of the much smaller standard error.

More generally, the coefficients in the regressions using filtered RAMRs are precise enough to uncover a number of interesting facts. For-profit hospitals have higher mortality than do not-for-profits (by 0.30 to 1.15 percentage points depending on the year and specification). Government hospitals have higher mortality and teaching hospitals lower mortality than do not-for-profit hospitals. These differences are larger in specifications that do not control for volume, because (1) government and for-profit hospitals tend to be smaller than average, while teaching hospitals tend to be larger than average, and (2) there is a strong negative relationship between volume and mortality. For example, in 1985 we estimate that an additional 100 Medicare AMI admissions was associated with 1.5 percentage points lower mortality.

The most striking finding in table 3.1 is the apparent change in the coefficients between 1985 and 1994. In the specifications using the filtered RAMR, the coefficient estimates for for-profit and teaching hospitals rise by roughly half of a percentage point in absolute value between 1985 and 1994. At the same time, the coefficient on volume fell in absolute value by about half a percentage point.

These regression estimates suggest that the filtered RAMR can be a useful tool for uncovering general relationships between mortality and hospital characteristics. Based on the filtered data, three facts are clear: (1) there is a negative relationship between volume and mortality, (2) for-profit hospitals and government hospitals have higher mortality than not-for-profit hospitals, while teaching hospitals have lower mortality, and (3) between 1985 and 1994, mortality differences increased between for-profit and not-for-profit hospitals, and between teaching and nonteaching hospitals.

These findings are generally consistent with the existing literature, although our estimates tend to be more precise. Studies examining a variety of patient populations and outcomes measures have found that higher volume is associated with better patient outcomes.[4] Comparisons by ownership and teaching status, to the extent they have found any differences,

4. See Luft et al. (1990) for a fairly comprehensive study of the volume-outcome relationship.

have found not-for-profit and teaching hospitals to have better patient outcomes.[5] The most novel of our findings is that these differences have widened over the last decade. This decade has been a period of rapid change in hospitals, spurred by dramatic changes in the way that both government and private insurers pay for hospital care. The extent to which these market changes might explain the growing differences in hospital mortality is an important area for future research.

## 3.5 A Tale of Three Counties

### 3.5.1 The Sample

If the filtered RAMR helps to compare hospitals at the national level, can it also help at a more micro level? One important use for any measure of hospital quality is to compare individual hospitals within a given market. In this section, we look more closely at the mortality performance of particular hospitals in three counties. Our goals are (1) to learn whether these quality measures are able to identify meaningful differences (and changes over time) in mortality among hospitals in a given city; and (2) to explore whether these patterns in mortality could be attributed to for-profit ownership or other factors affecting the market. At the same time, by going to the county level and focusing on a fixed group of hospitals, we are able to address some of the general results discussed in section 3.4 from a "case study" perspective.

The three counties were chosen on the following basis. First, since we wanted to compare individual hospitals (but not too many hospitals) we limited our search to counties with 2–10 hospitals in our sample. In order to focus on for-profit hospitals, the county had to have at least one for-profit hospital and one other hospital with an average of at least 50 Medicare AMI admissions per year from 1984 to 1994. Within this subset we considered three categories of counties:

Case 1: No change in for-profit ownership over the study period
Case 2: At least one hospital converted into for-profit over the study period
Case 3: At least one hospital converted away from for-profit over the study period

Within each category we eliminated counties that were obviously not distinct markets (e.g., the suburbs of Miami). Finally, we chose the county that had the highest average volume in its primary hospitals.

The resulting counties all contain relatively isolated midsized cities. To preserve the confidentiality of individual hospitals, we refer to each hospital according to its rank in terms of AMI volume between 1984 and 1994.

5. See the sources cited in nn. 1 and 2.

Case 1 contains a small southern city with four larger-than-average hospitals. The largest (hospital 1) and smallest (hospital 4) are for-profit hospitals, both affiliated with the same for-profit chain. Hospital 2 is government run, while hospital 3 is a not-for-profit. Relative to the other two cases, this city had experienced rapid growth in population and income during the 1980s and has a high number of hospital beds per capita. The population is somewhat older, less educated, and less likely to be white, with 10–20 percent enrolled in HMOs by 1994.[6]

Case 2 contains a midsized midwestern city with three larger-than-average hospitals and one very small hospital (hospital 4). Hospitals 1, 3, and 4 are not-for-profit. Hospital 2 was a not-for-profit until the mid 1980s, at which time it was purchased by a large for-profit chain. The ownership of hospital 2 was transferred to a different for-profit chain in the early 1990s. Relative to the other two cases, this city had average growth in population and income during the 1980s and has a low number of hospital beds per capita. The population has higher income and is somewhat younger, more educated, and more likely to be white, with 10–20 percent enrolled in HMOs by 1994.

Case 3 contains a midsized southern city with five larger-than-average hospitals. Hospitals 1, 2, and 4 are not-for-profit. Hospital 3 was initially government owned, and hospital 5 was initially for-profit. Both hospital 3 and hospital 5 converted to not-for-profit status in the late 1980s. Relative to the other two cases, this city had low population growth during the 1980s. Otherwise, this city has fairly average population characteristics with 10–20 percent enrolled in HMOs by 1994.

### 3.5.2 Evidence on Quality in Each County

In keeping with the exploratory nature of this analysis, figure 3.2 simply plots the RAMR (left panel) and filtered RAMR (right panel) annually from 1984 to 1994 for each hospital in case 1. Note that the vertical scale differs between the two plots (in order to preserve the detail of the filtered RAMR plot). Figure 3.3 plots this data slightly differently. Each panel corresponds to a hospital, and plots the actual RAMR along with the filtered RAMR and its 90 percent confidence band. Confidence bands for the actual RAMR are too large to fit on the figure. A horizontal line denoting the RAMR at the average hospital in our sample is added to each panel for reference. The data for case 2 are similarly plotted below in figures 3.4 and 3.5, and for case 3 in figures 3.6 and 3.7.

For case 1, it is impossible to detect quality differences across the hospitals or over time based on the actual RAMR (see the left panel of fig. 3.2).

6. Information on each city/county comes from the *County and City Data Book* for 1988 and 1994. Information on HMO penetration in each county was provided by Laurence Baker, based on his calculations using HMO enrollment data from InterStudy.

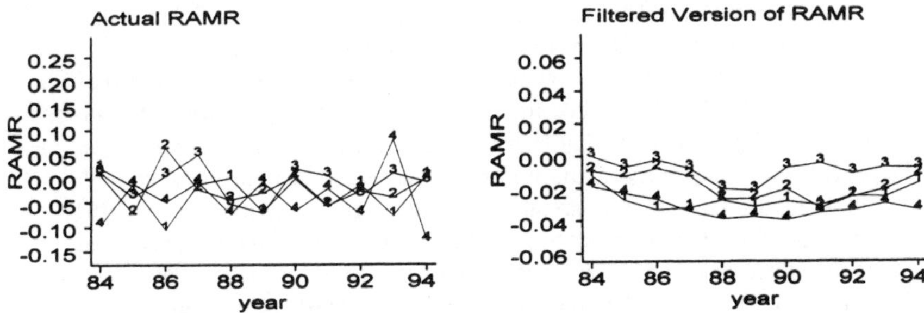


**Fig. 3.2 Trends in risk-adjusted mortality rates (RAMRs) for case 1 (a mid-sized southern city)**

*Note:* Left panel based on actual RAMR and right panel based on filtered RAMR. (Note that the vertical scale of the two panels differs.) The hospitals are ranked from largest (1) to smallest (4) according to their number of Medicare AMI admissions from 1984 to 1994. Hospitals 1 and 4 are for-profit hospitals and are affiliated with the same chain. Hospital 2 is government owned, while hospital 3 is not-for-profit.

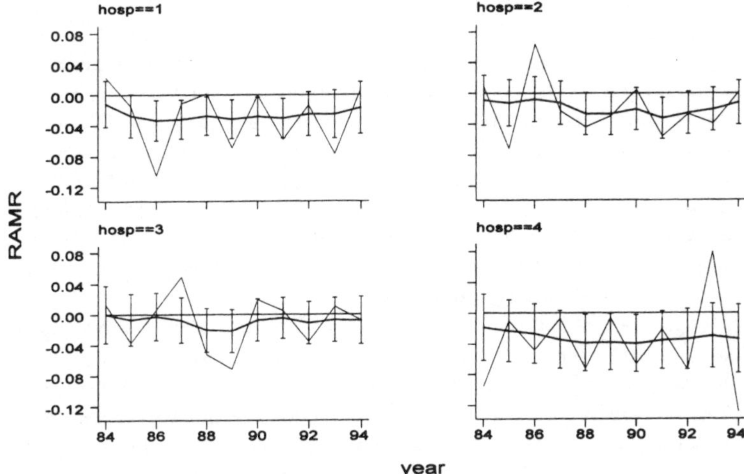


**Fig. 3.3 Trends for case 1 in actual (*thin line*) and filtered (*thick line with 90 percent confidence bands*) RAMR by hospital**

*Note:* The straight horizontal line denotes the RAMR at the average hospital in our national sample (RAMR = 0 by definition). For description of the hospitals, see the note to fig. 3.2.

Obviously, the problem is the variability in the actual RAMR: Even the largest hospital (1) experiences year-to-year changes in its actual RAMR of over five percentage points.

In contrast, the filtered RAMR is much more stable and displays three interesting features. First, the for-profit hospitals (1 and 4) have, if anything, lower mortality than the other hospitals in the market. The fact that the smallest hospital also has the lowest filtered RAMR seems surprising, but this may be the result of its affiliation with hospital 1 (recall that they are members of the same chain). A second interesting feature of the filtered data in figure 3.2 is that every hospital appears to experience an improvement in mortality of about one to two percentage points in the mid-1980s relative to other hospitals nationally. Although it is beyond the scope of this paper, an interesting topic for further research is the analysis of the cause of this general improvement in quality of care in this area.[7] Finally, it is notable that the range of filtered RAMR estimates, while much larger than the differences estimated between the average for-profit and not-for-profit in table 3.1, are still relatively compressed. Based on national data, we estimated (McClellan and Staiger 1997) that the standard deviation across hospitals is around four percentage points for the true hospital-specific intercepts for 90-day mortality.

Figure 3.3 plots each hospital's data separately and adds 90 percent confidence bands to the filtered RAMR (thick line with vertical bars). The horizontal line at RAMR = 0 represents the national average in that year, so when the confidence bands lie entirely below or above this line, it is likely that the hospital is, respectively, better or worse than average. Relative to the size of the confidence bands, there are not large differences either across these hospitals or over time. Hospital 1 (the large for-profit) is the only hospital that is consistently better than the national average, and this seems to be consistent with its general status in the community.

Thus, the overall picture for case 1 seems to be one of fairly homogeneous quality, perhaps slightly above the national average. There are hints of improvement over time and of better quality in the for-profit hospitals, but there are no dramatic differences.

As figure 3.4 illustrates, case 2 is quite different. The only similarity is that it is impossible to detect quality differences across hospitals or over time based on the actual RAMR data plotted in the left panel of the figure. Using the filtered RAMR, there is a clear ranking of quality across hospitals that roughly corresponds to size. The largest hospital (a not-for-profit) consistently has the lowest mortality, while hospital 4 (a very small hospital) has the highest mortality. The difference in mortality between the largest and smallest hospital is substantial, from six to over eight percentage points. These differences are large even relative to the 90 percent confidence bounds for the filtered RAMR (see fig. 3.5). As in case 1, the hospital that we identify as having the lowest mortality is recognized in the community as the leading hospital.

Hospital 2 is of particular interest because it was taken over by a for-

7. Recall that the RAMR measures mortality relative to the average hospital, so this improvement does not simply reflect the downward national trend in heart attack mortality rates. Mortality in these hospitals improved relative to the national average over this time.

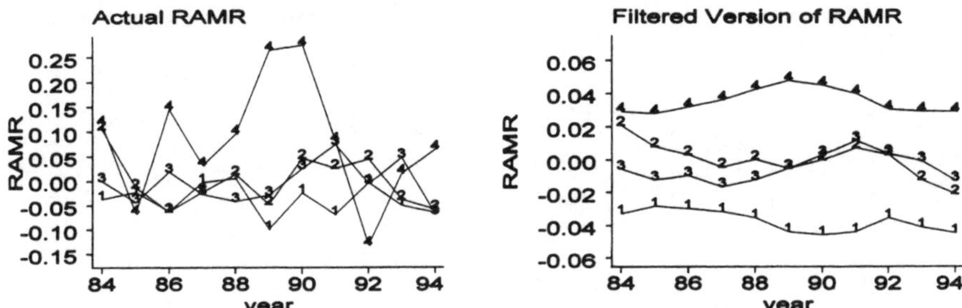


**Fig. 3.4 Trends in risk-adjusted mortality rates (RAMRs) for case 2 (a mid-sized midwestern city)**

*Note:* Left panel based on actual RAMR and right panel based on filtered RAMR. (Note that the vertical scale of the two panels differs.) The hospitals are ranked from largest (1) to smallest (4) according to their number of Medicare AMI admissions from 1984 to 1994. Hospital 4 is quite small. Hospitals 1, 3, and 4 are not-for-profit hospitals. Hospital 2 was a not-for-profit that was purchased by a for-profit chain in the mid-1980s, and then by a different for-profit chain in the early 1990s.

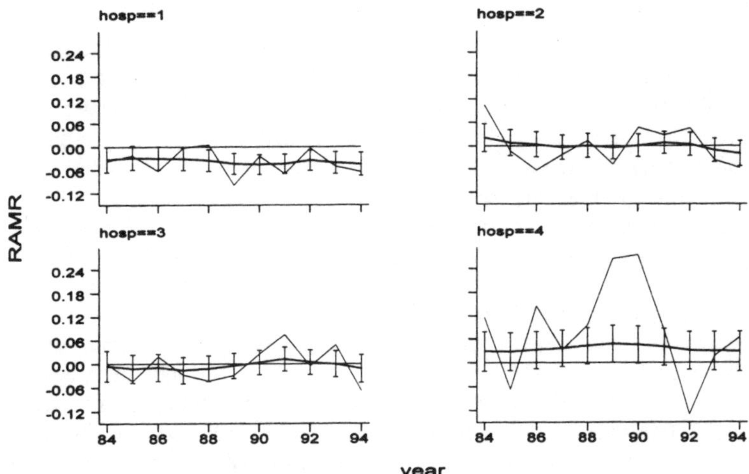


**Fig. 3.5 Trends for case 2 in actual (*thin line*) and filtered (*thick line with 90 percent confidence bands*) RAMR by hospital**

*Note:* The straight horizontal line denotes the RAMR at the average hospital in our national sample (RAMR = 0 by definition). For description of the hospitals, see the note to fig. 3.4.

profit chain in the mid-1980s and then became part of a different for-profit chain in the early 1990s. Around both of these ownership changes, there is a notable decline in the hospital's filtered RAMR of about two percentage points. In fact, it is the only hospital in case 2 that has an apparent trend (downward) in its mortality, going from being worse than average to better

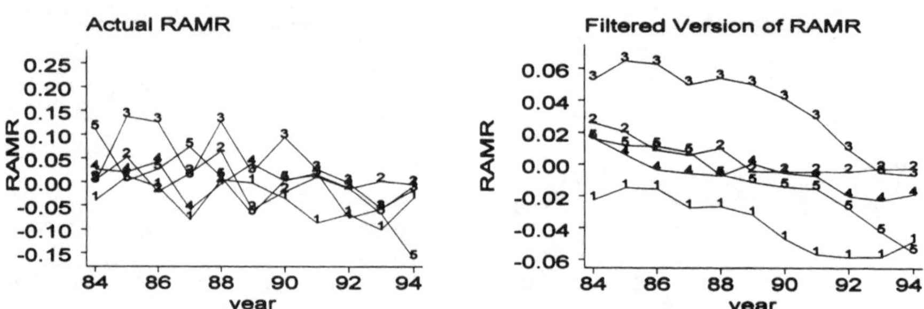


**Fig. 3.6 Trends in risk-adjusted mortality rates (RAMRs) for case 3 (a mid-sized southern city)**

*Note:* Left panel based on actual RAMR and right panel based on filtered RAMR. (Note that the vertical scale of the two panels differs.) The hospitals are ranked from largest (1) to smallest (5) according to their number of Medicare AMI admissions from 1984 to 1994. Hospitals 1, 2, and 4 are not-for-profit hospitals. Hospital 3 was initially government owned and then converted to not-for-profit status in the late 1980s. Similarly, hospital 5 converted from for-profit to not-for-profit status in the late 1980s.

than average. While it is not clear that the change in ownership per se led to these improvements, it is at least suggestive that this may be the case.

The overall picture for case 2 seems to be one of more diversity of quality, although fairly average quality overall. The purchase of a hospital first by one and then another for-profit chain seemed, if anything, to improve quality. However, the purchased hospital is still not clearly any better than the national average in terms of mortality.

Case 3 presents yet another situation (see figs. 3.6 and 3.7). Again, there is a wide range of quality across hospitals in this area, with the range in filtered RAMR of five to eight percentage points (see fig. 3.6). There is a clear downward trend in mortality occurring in this area, which is even seen in the actual RAMR (although the actual RAMR is still very noisy). Using the filtered RAMR, each of the hospitals in this area experienced a decline in mortality of between two and eight percentage points. Hospital 1, the largest not-for-profit, had the lowest mortality throughout almost the entire period. Hospital 3, which converted from government to not-for-profit in the late 1980s, clearly had the highest mortality initially but also experienced one of the largest declines by 1994. Hospital 5, which converted from for-profit to not-for-profit in the late 1980s, had the largest mortality decline of all five hospitals to the point where it had the lowest filtered RAMR in the area in 1994.

Thus, the overall picture for case 3 is one of rapidly improving quality in the area as a whole. At the same time, the for-profit and government hospitals converted to not-for-profit and had the most dramatic quality improvements in the area.

There are two common themes across all of these cases. First, filtered

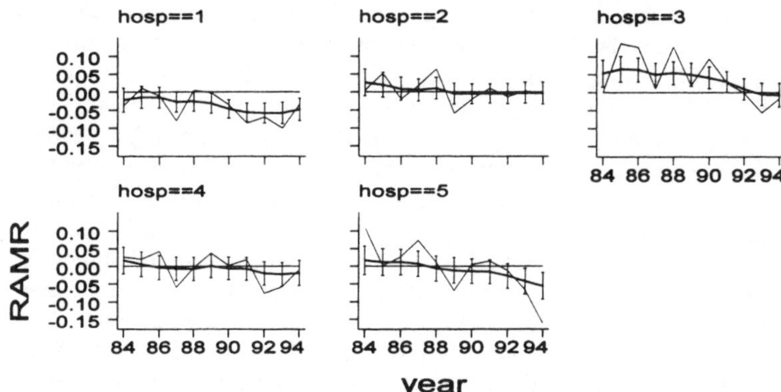


**Fig. 3.7 Trends for case 3 in actual (*thin line*) and filtered (*thick line with 90 percent confidence bands*) RAMR by hospital**

*Note:* The straight horizontal line denotes the RAMR at the average hospital in our national sample (RAMR = 0 by definition). For description of the hospitals, see the note to fig. 3.6.

RAMRs appear to be a useful tool for analyzing quality of care differences across hospitals and over time. More importantly, our microlevel evidence from these specific cases is not consistent with the common belief (supported by our aggregate regressions) that for-profit hospitals provide lower quality of care. In two of our three markets, for-profits appeared to be associated with higher quality of care: Hospitals that were for-profit throughout our study period tended to have lower mortality rates, and changes to for-profit status were associated with mortality reductions.

What might explain this apparent conflict between the case-study evidence and the aggregate cross-section evidence, which showed a poorer performance overall for the for-profits? Some of the explanation may come from the way in which we chose our case studies, relying on areas with relatively large for-profit hospitals that were perhaps likely to represent "flagship" hospitals in their communities. These features may not be representative of the market status of a typical for-profit hospital.

One possible explanation for these results could be that for-profit hospitals selectively locate in areas with low quality (see, e.g., Norton and Staiger 1994). Thus, the aggregate evidence would tend to find that for-profit ownership was correlated with lower quality, while within their markets, the for-profit hospitals could provide higher quality (as in case 1) or at least improve quality in the hospitals they acquire (as in case 2). This explanation would also imply that for-profit hospitals would tend to leave markets in which the quality was rising (as in case 3). If the cross-section correlation is being generated by location, then we would expect within-county differences between for-profit and not-for-profit hospitals to be smaller than across-county differences. In fact, when we include county-level fixed-effects in the regressions from table 3.1, the estimated mortality difference between for-profit and not-for-profit hospitals falls by roughly half. Thus, it appears that at least some of the difference in quality is generated by the different location patterns of for-profit hospitals.

Why might for-profit hospitals tend to locate in areas with low hospital quality? One possible reason would be a relationship between poor hospital management and lower quality of care. Poorly managed hospitals might make attractive takeover targets for for-profit chains, but as a by-product, the for-profits would tend to enter markets with low quality of care. Alternatively, patients may demand high-quality care in some markets, either because of demographic factors such as high income or because of an existing high-quality hospital in the market (e.g., a teaching hospital). If providing such high-quality care results in lower patient margins, then for-profits would be less likely to locate in these areas.

These speculative explanations are based on the results of only a few market case studies. We will leave a more systematic exploration of this question to future work. Clearly, however, a final important conclusion of this research is that the "average" differences in mortality between for-profit and not-for-profit hospitals—or among any other general system for classifying hospitals, such as bed size—account for only a small share of the variation in outcomes across hospitals. Many not-for-profit hospitals are below average, many for-profit hospitals are above average, and these relationships vary enormously at the market level. More extensive market-level analyses using the methods we have developed to evaluate quality could yield new insights into these complex relationships.

## 3.6 Conclusion

In this paper, we have summarized new methods for evaluating the quality of care of for-profit and not-for-profit hospitals. These methods address two of the major problems that have limited the value of previous hospital quality assessments: measurement of important outcomes, and the high level of noise in these measures. In McClellan and Staiger (1997), where we describe these techniques in more detail, we also present evidence on a third major problem: bias in the hospital comparisons because of unmeasured differences in case mix across hospitals. We use detailed medical chart review data to show that hospital performance measures for heart attack care that account for patient disease severity and comorbidity in a much more extensive way are highly correlated with the measures we report in this research. In other words, our measures with limited case-mix adjustment provide reasonably good predictions of hospital performance in terms of measures based on detailed case-mix adjustment. Our results to date on the bias problem are by no means conclusive; hard-to-measure patient factors may differ systematically across hospitals, particularly for less acute conditions than heart attacks. At a minimum, however, by providing relatively precise measures of hospital performance for important dimensions of hospital quality of care, our approach allows further research to focus on this final key problem.

The results of our analysis provide a range of new insights for policy issues related to for-profit and not-for-profit hospital ownership. On average, the performance of not-for-profit hospitals in treating elderly patients with heart disease appears to be slightly better than that of for-profit hospitals, even after accounting for systematic differences in hospital size, teaching status, urbanization, and patient demographic characteristics. This average difference in mortality performance between for-profits and not-for-profits appears to be increasing over time. However, this small average difference masks an enormous amount of variation in hospital quality within the for-profit and not-for-profit hospital groups. Our case-study results also suggest that for-profits may provide the impetus for quality improvements in markets where, for various reasons, relatively poor quality of care is the norm. Understanding the many market- and hospital-specific factors that contribute to these variations in hospital quality is a crucial topic for further research. Using the methods and results developed here, such detailed market analyses can be based on rather precise assessments of differences in hospital performance, rather than on speculation necessitated by imprecise or absent outcome measures.

## References

Ash, A. 1996. Identifying Poor-Quality Hospitals with Mortality Rates: Often There's More Noise Than Signal. *Medical Care* 34:735–36.

Gaumer, G. 1986. Medicare Patient Outcomes and Hospital Organizational Mission. In *For-Profit Enterprise in Health Care,* ed. B. H. Gray, 354–84. Washington, D.C.: National Academy Press.

Gray, B. H. 1986. *For-Profit Enterprise in Health Care.* Washington, D.C.: National Academy Press.

Hartz, A. J., H. Krakauer, E. M. Kuhn, M. Young, S. J. Jacobsen, G. Gay, L. Muenz, M. Katzoff, R. C. Bailey, and A. A. Rimm. 1989. Hospital Characteristics and Mortality Rates. *New England Journal of Medicine* 321:1720–25.

Hofer, T. P., and R. A. Hayward. 1996. Identifying Poor-Quality Hospitals: Can Hospital Mortality Rates Detect Quality Problems for Medical Diagnoses? *Medical Care* 34:737–53.

Keeler, E. B., L. V. Rubenstein, K. L. Kahn, D. Draper, E. R. Harrison, M. J. McGinty, W. H. Rogers, and R. H. Brook. 1992. Hospital Characteristics and Quality of Care. *Journal of the American Medical Association* 268:1709–14.

Luft, H. F., D. W. Garnick, D. H. Mark, and S. J. McPhee. 1990. *Hospital Volume,*

*Physician Volume, and Patient Outcomes.* Ann Arbor, Mich.: Health Administration Press Perspectives.

Luft, H. F., and P. S. Romano. 1993. Chance, Continuity, and Change in Hospital Mortality Rates. *Journal of the American Medical Association* 270:331–37.

McClellan, M., and D. Staiger. 1997. The Quality of Health Care Providers. Working paper. Stanford University, Stanford, Calif.

McNeil, B. J., S. H. Pedersen, and C. Gatsonis. 1992. Current Issues in Profiling Quality of Care. *Inquiry* 29:298–307.

Norton, E. C., and D. Staiger. 1994. How Hospital Ownership Affects Access to Care for the Uninsured. *RAND Journal of Economics* 25:171–85.

Park, R. E., R. H. Brook, J. Kosecoff, J. Keesey, L. Rubenstein, E. Keeler, K. L. Kahn, W. H. Rogers, and M. R. Chassin. 1990. Explaining Variations in Hospital Death Rates. *Journal of the American Medical Association* 264:484–90.

Staiger, D., and G. Gaumer. 1995. Price Regulation and Patient Mortality in Hospitals. Working paper. Harvard University, Cambridge, Mass.

U.S. Department of Commerce. Bureau of the Census. 1988. *County and City Data Book.* Washington, D.C.: U.S. Government Printing Office.

———. 1994. *County and City Data Book.* Washington, D.C.: U.S. Government Printing Office.

# [24]

# Pricing and rationing by nonprofit organizations with distributional objectives

*Richard Steinberg and Burton A. Weisbrod*

## Introduction

The growing commercial activity of nonprofit charities, hospitals, educational institutions, arts organizations, day-care centers, nursing homes, and religious organizations has led many to question the legitimacy of the nonprofit designation and the concomitant tax and regulatory advantages conferred upon the sector. As noted in Chapter 1, if nonprofit organizations are engaging in commercial activity, it is easy to regard them as simply "for-profits in disguise" (Weisbrod 1988); however, there are many varieties of commercial activity. This chapter focuses on the ways in which nonprofit organizations and private firms can be expected to differ in their use of various pricing and other mechanisms through which their goods and services are distributed. We emphasize the potential importance of distributional goals to nonprofits – that is, their concern about reaching certain target populations – and suggest that insofar as they have distributional concerns they will use allocation mechanisms (pricing practices, waiting lists, and the like) differently and have different effects on clients and others, compared with private firms.

Economists and other social scientists have looked at many aspects of nonprofit organization behavior, but we are unaware of any research that has examined the array of alternative allocation mechanisms employed by nonprofits, let alone their relationships to organization missions. Thus, our most important purpose is to provoke researchers, practitioners, and other readers to look across industry boundaries and particular allocation methods to refine understanding of the distribution of goods and services by nonprofit organizations – not only what nonprofits do, but for whom they do it. We leave to future researchers the

We thank Lisa Whitecotton and Daniel Delany for research assistance, Kirsten Grønbjerg, Robert Coen, Wesley Lindahl, and participants at Northwestern University's colloquium on the commercial activities of nonprofit organizations for helpful suggestions. Steinberg acknowledges support from the Indiana University Center on Philanthropy and from the Andrew W. Mellon Foundation.

task of making our hypotheses more precise and performing appropriate empirical tests, but we focus on hypotheses likely to prove testable in practice. Much of what we have to say applies equally well to allocation decisions by government agencies, even though our focus is on private nonprofit organizations.

Nonprofit organizations and governmental agencies generally espouse goals other than profit maximization, such as fairness, redistribution, trustworthiness, public-goods provision, advocacy, education, preservation of values, accessibility, social innovation, empowerment, participation, and promoting individual expression. Profit maximization could provide a means to these ends, perhaps guiding the allocation decisions of a museum shop that sells T-shirts, a fund-raising campaign, or other ventures designed to raise revenue for the nonprofit's preferred, mission-oriented services. Sometimes these other purposes are accomplished as a side effect of profit maximization. For example, for-profit firms must consider their reputations for fair and honest dealings if they are to keep their customers. Sometimes, competitive pressures are such that the only alternative to profit maximization is bankruptcy. However, nonprofit organizations and governmental agencies, motivated by other goals, often appear to allocate their outputs persistently in a manner that does not maximize profits.

Some organizations legally defined as nonprofit may seek to maximize profits derived from some but not all of their activities. Other organizations legally defined as nonprofit may seek to maximize profits derived from all activities, and thus function as for-profits in disguise. The purpose of this chapter is to characterize nonprofit departures from profit-maximizing behavior.

In the next section we delineate the varieties of fee schedules, nonprice requirements, and use of purchasing incentives, and present hypotheses regarding differences in the use of these mechanisms between nonprofit and profit-maximizing organizations. In a later section we outline the effects of allocation mechanisms on an organization's clientele, in order to develop corollary hypotheses about the consequences of the differential allocational or distributional processes.

## The varieties of nonprofit allocation

How are an organization's outputs allocated among potential consumers? For-profit firms use price as the primary allocation mechanism: A price is posted, those willing and able to pay the price receive the good or service, and the price is bid up or down to the point where every potential consumer willing to pay for it is able to purchase the product. Monopolistic for-profit firms select a higher price and produce a lower quantity, but still satisfy consumers' desired purchases at the selected price. For-profit firms also employ various forms of price discrimination, complex pricing mechanisms, and, more rarely, nonprice rationing mechanisms. The unifying principle governing all these allocation techniques is the quest for profits. Profit maximization implies that a perfectly price-discriminating firm would charge each consumer his or her reservation price – providing that the firm's marginal cost can be covered – although the cost of determining that price limits its use. Auctions, tournaments, intertemporal price discrimination, nonlinear pricing that varies with the quantity purchased, and rationing by waiting all represent profit-maximizing responses under imperfect information. Do nonprofits use these mechanisms differently from private firms?

Nonprofit organizations certainly use prices, although perhaps in a different fashion. Organizations in both sectors employ a variety of complex pricing schemes that include sliding-scale fees and other forms of price discrimination, multipart prices with separate access and usage charges, nonlinear prices with caps and deductibles. They also use nonprice allocation mechanisms such as waiting lists, restrictive eligibility requirements, recruiting and marketing techniques, lotteries, and quality dilution.

Table 4.1 catalogs the variety of allocation mechanisms we discuss and summarizes our hypotheses about differences between their use by nonprofit and for-profit organizations. Because of the variety of goals, outputs, environments, and constraints facing different kinds of nonprofit organizations, our hypotheses should be understood as pertaining to nonprofits in general, although not to all of them. Variations within the nonprofit sector in the use of these output-distribution mechanisms would provide further guidance for future research seeking to test our hypotheses.

The simplest distributional mechanism is uniform pricing, of the textbook variety, where consumers are offered the opportunity to purchase any quantity of a good or service at the same price per unit and this price is the same for all consumers. Nonprofit organizations often employ such uniform pricing, particularly for those activities that generate "unrelated business income" (income generated from the sale of goods and services unrelated to the organizational mission). A natural working hypothesis would be that nonprofits employ uniform pricing under the same circumstances and in the same way as profit-maximizing firms. For-profit firms employ it when, given informational and other constraints, this practice would maximize the financial surplus eventually distributed to owners. Nonprofits may employ it for unrelated goods when this practice would maximize the financial surplus available to further the organizational public-goods or redistributional mission, or the private agendas of those in control of the organization. Profits are a means to an end in both cases, although the ends differ. As Chapter 3 shows, the public-serving nonprofits may seek to maximize profits in markets for some goods in order to finance their mission-related activities.

However, Schiff and Weisbrod's 1991 adaptation of James's 1983 model suggests that unrelated business activities are disfavored in organizational utility, so that when uniform pricing is used, nonprofits will underproduce unrelated goods and services relative to the profit maximizer (see Chapter 3). Thus, any empirical test of this hypothesis would need to specify which activities are disfavored or nonpreferred by which nonprofit organizations.

*Sliding-scale fee schedules* are a form of price discrimination in which consumers pay different prices per unit based on observable characteristics of the client (such as income, family size, age, or the severity of the client's dysfunction) rather than on the particular costs of serving that consumer. Sliding scales are used by both nonprofit and for-profit sellers, and they are common in day care for children, mental-health services, church and synagogue membership charges, and professional-society dues. Similar practices appear in other industries under a variety of names. For example, college financial aid granted on a need basis creates a sliding scale for net-of-aid tuition. Diverse copayment rates on health insurance create price discrimination in net health-care costs to patients, based partly on observable consumer characteristics. Special prices for students or retirees at museums and on public transit systems are other instances of price discrimination equivalent to a sliding scale.

Nonprofit organizations that are concerned with the consequences of their allocation mechanism would ordinarily choose an income-based fee schedule, with high-income consumers paying higher fees. Profit-maximizing organizations would also offer income-based fees (when income is the best feasible proxy for consumer willingness to pay), because this way they could raise prices for some without losing other customers who could be profitably served. In this respect, nonprofit and for-profit sliding-scale fees would look quite similar. However, the lowest price selected by a nonprofit that had distributional objectives would often fall below the marginal cost of serving this group, whereas profit maximizers would select a lowest price at or above marginal cost (Steinberg and Weisbrod 1997). The fact that nonprofit organizations provide services free of charge to consumers who will never become paying customers supports this hypothesis, although one needs to distinguish voluntary free care from charity care required by regulators and from care purchased and paid for by third parties such as government.

Sometimes price discrimination by nonprofits is tied simply to consumers' stated willingness to pay more, and to no other characteristic. For example, many nonprofit organizations have membership categories (supporting member, patron, etc.) that charge different fees but provide essentially the same service (or provide token added benefits that do not appear to justify the higher fees). In effect, the consumer is mixing a donation and a purchase. Supporting memberships do not count as donations under the tax laws insofar as there is an exchange of value, but because the value received by the consumer is unaltered by the consumer's selection of a membership category, these memberships combine donation with purchase, thereby constituting what amounts to

Table 4.1. *Nonprofit use of allocation mechanisms*

| Allocation mechanism | Examples | Hypotheses about nonprofit departures from profit-maximization |
|---|---|---|
| *Price* | | |
| Uniform pricing | | Nonprofits and for-profits use uniform prices identically for those outputs unrelated to the nonprofit mission (except for disfavored activities). |
| Sliding-scale fees (interpersonal price discrim.) | Day care; Mental health care; Professional-society dues; Net-of-financial-aid tuition | Nonprofits more likely to price-discriminate and to choose a lowest price that is below the marginal cost of serving their customers. |
| Voluntary price discrim. (when eligibility for particular prices cannot be verified by the seller) | Supporting-member dues; Donations to arts orgs.; National Public Radio; Volunteering | Nonprofits use extensively. The practice is not generally feasible for for-profits (except in cases where the volunteer can control, at least in part, who benefits from her contribution, as in for-profit day care). |
| Intertemporal price discrim. | Free-entrance days | Nonprofits more likely to use this for those who will never be profitable to serve. |
| Noncash payments | Habitat-for-Humanity pricing (fees plus "sweat equity") | Nonprofits may require partial payment in the form of labor or in-kind. For-profits stick to cash. |
| *Nonprice* | | |
| Waiting lists | Day care; Nursing homes; Colleges, universities | Nonprofits more likely to use waiting lists. For-profits more likely to react to persistent excess demand by expanding capacity or increasing price. |
| Eligibility reqmts. | University admissions ("merit"); Fraternal societies; Religious orgs.; Work-shelters for the handicapped; Food pantries | Nonprofits more likely: (1) to use requirements poorly or negatively correlated with willingness to pay; (2) to restrict eligibility to those who cannot pay. For-profits more likely: (1) to use requirements positively correlated with willingness to pay; (2) to use eligibility requirements to establish a niche market. |
| Externally imposed eligibility reqmts. | Meet govt. contracting reqmts.; Conform with tax/regulatory reqmts. | Nonprofits more likely to construe requirements broadly for unprofitable clients and narrowly for profitable clients. |
| Quality dilution and opportunistic quality sharing | Soup kitchens; Homeless shelters; Museums and zoos; Worker training | Nonprofits more likely to hold excess capacity in order to avoid quality dilution. For-profits more likely to dilute quality in cases of contract failure. |
| Product bundling | Museums; Colleges, universities | Nonprofits more likely to bundle "merit goods" in pursuit of paternalistic objectives. For-profits more likely to bundle in pursuit of profit. |
| Recruiting target populations | Hospital location; School field-trips to museums | Nonprofits more likely to target mission-related populations regardless of expected future profitability. |

voluntary price discrimination. Donations in general constitute a form of voluntary price discrimination because each donor determines the size of contribution (Hansmann 1981a; Ben-Ner 1986; Spiegel 1995); the same holds for donations of volunteer time.

We hypothesize that sliding scales and voluntary price discrimination are more common in nonprofit than for-profit organizations for three interrelated reasons. First, there is more scope for a sliding scale when the range of consumers is broad, as it is for nonprofits that serve persons unwilling or unable to pay marginal costs. Second, consumers are more likely to reveal their willingness to pay truthfully when dealing with a nonprofit because they know that when revelation causes them to pay a higher price, that price is supporting a mission they support rather than lining a stockholder's pockets (Ben-Ner 1986). Third, the redistribution accompanying the use of sliding-scale fees sometimes constitutes the nonprofit's mission, rather than serving merely as a means for raising revenue to accomplish some other mission.

Other forms of interpersonal price discrimination are based on occupancy rates and other such production-cost factors rather than on consumer characteristics. In the for-profit world, this kind of price discrimination is common whenever marginal costs are markedly lower than average costs. Commercial airlines, hotels, and movie theaters discriminate by varying prices seasonally or by day of week or time of day, in order to fill empty space, furthering their profits. The key question is whether nonprofits price-discriminate in order to achieve other, nonfinancial goals. If nonprofits employ first-come, first-served opportunities or waiting lists rather than higher prices to adjust to peak-level demand, these forms of price discrimination would be evidence of nonfinancial goals.

Nonprofits, like for-profit firms, employ various forms of intertemporal price discrimination. Performing-arts groups discriminate over time when they distinguish advance ticket prices from at-the-door prices. We have no hypothesis regarding sectoral differences in this practice. However, some nonprofit museums charge admission fees but waive them intermittently on a regular basis, offering, for example, Free Tuesdays. Totally free admission, even on an occasional basis, appears to occur more typically in the nonprofit sector. For-profits sometimes offer promotional prices and free samples in an effort to convert these consumers to paying customers, but rarely do they offer free services targeted to those who will never pay the marginal costs of provision.

Sometimes nonprofit organizations require consumer or user fees in nonmonetary forms, such as labor or a mixture of cash and other forms of payment. For example, Habitat-for-Humanity, a nonprofit devoted to providing low-income housing, requires its customers to pay in both cash and labor ("sweat equity"). This type of pricing is uniquely well suited to nonprofits. For-profits could certainly benefit from labor supplied by their customers but prefer them to pay exclusively in the form of cash because it can be used to hire more efficient workers. In contrast, nonprofits may prefer this "inefficient" payment scheme when it directly supports some part of the organizational mission (e.g., encouraging self-help) as well as supplies resources (e.g., labor, materials, and money for advancing the housing-construction mission).

Nonprice allocation mechanisms, while sometimes combined with positive prices, may also serve to allocate a good or service that is given away at a price of zero. Most obvious is rationing by waiting, through either explicit queuing or the use of waiting lists. We hypothesize that nonprofits are more likely to use waiting lists, whereas for-profits are more likely to react to persistent excess demand by expanding capacity and/or increasing the price. Evidence supporting this hypothesis for the nursing home and mentally handicapped facility industries is presented in Weisbrod (1988, 1998).

When a nonprofit gives goods away or sells them at a price below that which would clear the market, it often specifies formal eligibility requirements that serve to ration the available output. Consumers may be required to provide evidence (or at least assert) that they meet eligibility standards involving income, wealth, family size, gender, religious affiliation, political persuasion, age, employment status, disability, or the like before they are eligible to receive the good or service. Sometimes organizations define their own criteria for determining eligibility for service; other times the eligibility criteria are defined by a contracting government agency. In either case, nonprofit and for-profit organizations may differ in the forms of eligibility requirements and the ways they are implemented, insofar as their organizational goals are distinct. We consider, in turn, the cases of internally and externally selected eligibility rules.

When the organization freely chooses its eligibility criteria, we hypothesize that nonprofits are more likely to use requirements that are poorly (or negatively) correlated with the consumer's willingness to pay, and may even restrict eligibility to those who are unable to pay. Profit maximizers use eligibility requirements to extract more consumer surplus through price discrimination: "Super saver" airline fares restricted to those who stay Saturday night are an attempt to fill seats with those who would not pay higher fares, while allowing the airline to charge more to those – largely business travelers – willing to pay more. Discounts by hotels and car-rental firms to American Association of Retired Persons (AARP) members are another attempt to use eligibility requirements to segment the market. Eligibility requirements are used by profit maximizers as screens for generally unobservable willingness to pay; they allow firms to price-discriminate without incurring the public-relations backlash and threat of antitrust suits that would accompany a more direct attempt at perfect price discrimination across individuals.

Nonprofits may also use eligibility requirements to raise additional revenue by capturing more consumer surplus – using the revenues to finance managerial perks or to cross-subsidize other, mission-related outputs; or they may use such requirements to further the organizational mission directly, by reaching out to particular target populations. Thus, nonprofits, we hypothesize, differ from for-profits in the nature of eligibility requirements, defining their target clientele so as to further their social mission directly rather than to maximize profit. Nonprofits often provide services only to the poor, to persons of a particular religion, ethnicity, or age, or to the most severely afflicted. Overall, insofar as they differ from for-profits in their goals, they will employ restrictions that are well correlated with mission but less well correlated with consumer willingness to pay. Unfortunately, it is difficult to test this hypothesis cleanly because profit maximizers also might use requirements that are poorly correlated with individual willingness to pay. In the case of for-profits, standards poorly correlated with individual willingness to pay are not instruments for advancing a social mission but part of a strategy to establish a niche market by appealing to snobbery, class interests, ethnicity, and the like. Eligibility requirements that serve to differentiate the product provide some monopolistic power to the seller, and so enhance profits.

When government agencies contract with nonprofits or private firms to provides services such as home health care or primary-school management, it is typically the agencies who specify eligibility requirements. For example, Smith and Lipsky (1993, 142–3) cite the case of emergency shelters in Massachusetts that are obligated by government contractors to serve the "most disadvantaged" first. Nonprofits and for-profits may differ, however, in the faithfulness with which they implement these requirements. This is important because it is difficult and expensive for the government contractor to determine whether the clients served by an external agent actually are the most disadvantaged or meet other (possibly subjective) contract criteria. We hypothesize that sectoral differences in behavior will depend upon whether the target population can be served profitably under such conditions. If clients cannot be served profitably, nonprofits pursuing social goals will be less likely than for-profits to take advantage of their informational superiority to interpret the contractually imposed eligibility requirements in a fashion that restricts access; if, instead, clients *can* be served profitably, nonprofits would be more likely to interpret eligibility requirements in a fashion that permits access only to the contractor's intended target clientele. Profit maximizers will tend to use their inevitable discretion by operationalizing eligibility requirements in ways that further profits, declaring "borderline" clients eligible if serving them would be more profitable than serving more disadvantaged persons, declaring them ineligible otherwise. If a contract specifies more than one fee class, profit maximizers would place clients in the most profitable fee class they can get away with. For example, Medicare payments to hospitals depend on the Diagnosis Related Group (DRG) in which a patient is placed. Even before the system was introduced in October 1983, computer software programs had been developed to determine the highest-paying DRG consistent with a given patient's specific conditions and diagnoses. Through the years that followed, the phenomenon of *DRG creep* – the drift of patient classification by hospitals into higher-priced diagnostic groups – was observed (Steinwald and Dummit 1989). It remains unclear, however, whether opportunism is the source of this phenomenon.

Whether this discretionary behavior differed between nonprofit and for-profit hospitals is also not clear. In general, nonprofits are thought to be more trustworthy contractees, reducing the need for the contractor to monitor and enforce contract compliance (Ferris and Graddy 1991) or to engage in lengthy negotiations over contract terms (DeHoog 1984). On the other hand, the nonprofit mission (serving clients) may conflict with the government-agency mission (keeping costs down while appearing to the electorate to be handling the social problem), and in these cases nonprofits would be less appealing to the contractor. In the case of Medicare, if a nonprofit hospital feels that certain costly procedures are medically desirable for a particular patient, it might place that patient in a more lucrative DRG rather than provide those procedures at a loss or prescribe less costly treatment. For-profit hospitals might prefer to place the patient in a lower-priced DRG that is more consistent with government guidelines and not attempt to provide the more expensive procedures.

A third form of nonprice allocation is *quality dilution*. For example, a soup kitchen faced with unexpectedly large demand may thin its "gruel"; a homeless shelter may line the floors with somnolent souls; a hospital may put three patients in a room designed for two, or place patients on gurneys in corridors; and a college may increase its student–faculty ratio. We hypothesize that nonprofits have output quality as a goal, and so are more likely to hold excess capacity in order to avoid quality dilution in times of unexpectedly high demand. This prediction is consistent with the theory presented in Holtman (1983). In contrast, for-profits may dilute quality even when demand is as predicted in order to cut costs and increase profits. This occurs when there is contract failure – where, owing to either the circumstances under which the good is provided or the nature of the good, the consumer is unable to verify that the quality of the product is at the promised level (Hansmann 1980).

Some nonprofits employ product bundling, requiring purchasers of one product also to purchase other products. Thus, a homeless shelter may require residents to obtain psychological or addiction counseling; a parochial school may require students to attend religious services, buy a school uniform, and do volunteer work. For-profits also employ product bundling, but do so in order to enhance profits rather than fulfill a social mission. James (1986) argues that a desire to inculcate values and tastes lies behind the decisions to found an educational, health, or social-service agency and to organize it as a nonprofit. She uses the example of religious organizations:

[T]he object is not to maximize profits but to maximize religious faith or religious adherents, and schools are one of the most important institutions of taste formation or socialization. Similarly, hospitals are a service for which people will have an urgent need at times, and so constitute a good way for religious groups to gain entry. The nonprofit form is chosen because the main objective is often not compatible with profit-maximizing behavior. For example, religious schools, set up to keep their members within the fold, may have to charge a price below the profit-maximization level in order to entice the largest numbers to enroll. (p. 155)

Sometimes nonprofits go beyond product bundling, preferential pricing, and eligibility restrictions in order to solicit actively the participation of target populations. Thus, nonprofit hospitals are more likely to locate in low-income areas (Pauly 1987), and museums negotiate with schools to arrange field-trip visits.

## Effects of nonprofit allocation

In this section, we characterize the broader impact of nonprofit price and nonprice allocation practices on customers and donors. As summarized in Table 4.2, we hypothesize that nonprofit behavior produces a different division of economic value between consumers and producers and among consumers; a different allocation of the risk that the product will cost more (or be of lower quality or quantity) than anticipated; a different self-selection among potential consumers; a different signal to consumers and donors; and different incentives to economize on resource consumption.

Market activities generate economic value divided between that received by producers (producer surplus) and consumers (consumer surplus). *Producer surplus* is the difference between revenues received and the (variable) cost of production; *consumer surplus* is the difference between consumers' willingness to pay and their outlays of time and money for the product in question.

In the for-profit world, total surplus is determined and divided so as to provide the largest piece of the "surplus pie" to the owners of the firm. Sometimes (as in uniform pricing by a for-profit monopoly), the pie is made smaller as a side effect of providing a larger piece to the producer, but the size of the producer piece (in absolute terms, not as a share) is maximized. Profit-maximizing firms would be unconcerned with the distribution of either output or consumer surplus among different types of client unless consumers were to rebel strongly against perceived unfairness. This sort of consumer reaction would reduce the equilibrium size of the piece given to producers, but producers would still act to maximize the size of their piece. In contrast, nonprofits often care about the allocation of surplus even when sales revenue would be unaffected or negatively affected by the nonprofit's pursuit of its concept of equity. We hypothesize that nonprofits are more likely to expand consumer surplus at the expense of producer (or even total) surplus.

Table 4.2. *Effects of nonprofit distributional mechanisms*

| Effect of allocation mechanism | Hypotheses about differing effects of nonprofit and profit-maximizing behavior |
|---|---|
| *Dividing total surplus* | |
| Between consumers and producers | For-profits maximize producer surplus. Consumer surplus is provided only insofar as it enhances producer surplus.<br>Nonprofits are more likely to expand consumer surplus at the expense of producer (or even total) surplus. |
| Among consumers | For-profits do not care except insofar as the distribution of consumer surplus affects producer surplus.<br>Nonprofits are more likely to consider fairness and distribution in the design of their allocation, cost-sharing, and pricing mechanisms. |
| *Allocating risks* | For-profits bear risk only when there is a compensating increase in return.<br>Nonprofits are more likely to bear the largest feasible share of risk, regardless of compensating financial returns, in order to ensure that their clients are not harmed. |
| *Screening* | For-profits use mechanisms designed to uncover those with highest ability and willingness to pay.<br>Nonprofits are more likely to use mechanisms designed to uncover those with greatest "need" (as in addictions treatment or child-abuse prevention), those who are most worthy (say, because they appear to be pious), or those with high willingness but not ability to pay.<br>For-profit mechanisms are also designed to deter those who would be most costly to serve (cream-skimming).<br>Nonprofit mechanisms are less likely to deter high-cost clients; on the other hand, nonprofits are more likely to use exclusionary screens for noncost reasons (e.g., to deter those who are poorly motivated). |
| *Providing a signal of trustworthiness* | |
| To consumers and clients | Nonprofits are more likely to use waiting lists and highly selective eligibility requirements to signal their quality.<br>For-profits are more likely to use high prices to signal quality. |
| To donors and grantmakers | Nonprofit use of fees depends upon the preferences of major funders regarding provision of seed money vs. operating support. |
| *Providing an incentive to economize on resource consumption* | Nonprofits are less likely to use high prices and more likely to use non-price mechanisms to provide incentives for consumers to economize on the use of nonprofit outputs.<br>Nonprofits often use token fees to signal the importance of economizing. |

The possibility that at least some nonprofit social-service agencies occupy a middle ground has been presented by McCready (1988), who considers their use of *Ramsey pricing*. This is a self-financing approach, in which user fees are set so as to maximize the size of the pie, and is therefore intermediate to profit maximization (expanding producer surplus at the expense of total surplus) and some nonprofit notions of equity (expanding consumer surplus at the expense of total surplus). It would finance reductions in price for some nonprofit outputs by increasing prices for other, revenue-generating outputs. Whether the price of a particular output is increased or decreased depends upon whether the quantities of desired purchases by consumers and desired sales by producers are very sensitive to price. Price-sensitive outputs would be priced below marginal cost, whereas insensitive outputs would be priced above marginal cost. Ramsey pricing is designed neither to accomplish redistributional goals nor to treat some outputs as more mission-related than others; but it does differ from profit-maximizing pricing in that it results in a larger total of consumer plus producer surpluses.

Nonprofits may also be concerned with the distribution of surplus among consumers, seeking "fairness" for its own sake, apart from revenue implications. We hypothesize that nonprofits are more likely than for-profit firms to articulate and implement notions of fair distribution in their choice of pricing and nonprice rationing mechanisms. One notion of fairness sometimes employed is the "fair share of cost" notion, usually implemented as equal division of the costs of providing a collective good. Lohmann (1980) notes:

> This method of fee collection is most appropriate for short-term projects or projects in which clients form a closely knit group whose unity is reinforced by such "sharing." . . . [This method] may be of greatest interest to those involved in community organization and group work activities, in which the collection of fees on an occasional basis for specific projects may be the only fund-raising activity necessary. Senior citizens groups taking bus tours, youth groups planning parties, and social action groups planning demonstrations or protest marches may best be handled using the fair-share-of-cost method. (p. 86)

Other notions for fair nonprofit pricing borrow from the literatures on tax equity and bargaining fairness. Prices, like taxes, may be thought fair if they are proportional to either the benefits received or the consumer's ability to pay. *Horizontal equity* (equal prices for similarly situated consumers) may also be thought to be important and to constrain nonprofit patterns of price discrimination and market segmentation. We are unaware of any nonprofits that specifically seek to implement formal notions of bargaining fairness (see, e.g., Moulin 1988; Young 1994), but clearly the potential is there.

Although some nonprofits are particularly concerned with fairness, others distribute their outputs in a manner contrary to their stated mission. Favoritism, nepotism, kickbacks, self-dealing, and other abusive power relationships can govern nonprofit allocation, particularly when allocation criteria require subjective judgments on the part of the nonprofit employee. There is more scope for such abuse in the nonprofit sector because nonprofits are not subject to financially motivated takeover bids that limit abuse among for-profits. On the other hand, insofar as nonprofit managers and board members are dedicated to the organizational social mission, this provides an internal check on abuse (Handy 1995).

The choice of fee (or other rationing) structures also affects the allocation of risk. For example, a daily fee – say, on hospital care – places all the financial risk that the inpatient stay will be unexpectedly lengthy on the consumer, whereas a fee based on completion of a specified task (such as the DRG-based system for reimbursing hospitals for their Medicare patients) places all the risk on the provider. It would be worthwhile to explore whether nonprofits differ from other organizations in their proclivities to accept or shift risk. There is little extant theory to turn to for predictions, but much would seem to turn on two factors: First, differences in organizational goals are likely to prove important. Those nonprofits that desire to serve target populations regardless of ability to pay would seem to be more likely to bear this risk than for-profits or other sorts of nonprofit. Second, budgetary flexibility is likely important. Those nonprofits that receive substantial unrestricted donations would seem to be more able to bear risk. At the same time, the higher costs of borrowing because of nonprofits' inability to sell shares of stock might make them less willing to bear risk (Hansmann 1981b).

Profit-maximizing organizations are not directly concerned with the composition of clientele, caring only insofar as the client mix affects aggregate net revenues. Abstracting, for the moment, from any differences in the costs of service provision to various clients, the most desirable are those with the greatest willingness to pay for the service in question (or those who can attract other clients of this kind). When willingness to pay is not directly observable, which is typically the case, the price mechanism can serve as a screen to distinguish those with highest demand. Thus, nonprofits may use pricing for the same reason that for-profits do: to generate revenue from those who can pay (Moran 1985).

Even with identical desires to distinguish among consumers on the basis of willingness to pay, nonprofits with distributional objectives would differ from profit maximizers in their choice of fee structures: Profit-maximizers would select fees that are as close as possible to the consumer's reservation prices, whereas distributionally concerned nonprofits would screen the same consumers but generally charge them lower prices (Steinberg and Weisbrod 1997); such nonprofits would forgo some revenue in order to advance their overall goals, balancing their pursuit of distributional goals with their revenue needs.

Consumer willingness to pay results from both the consumer's preferences for a particular good or service and that consumer's ability to pay. When two consumers have the same *ability* to pay, differences in *willingness* to pay reflect preferences; however, in general one cannot distinguish whether someone who is willing to pay a large sum is wealthy and relatively unconcerned with the cost or is of modest means and greatly desires the good or service. Nonprofits sometimes care about the intensity of want or need, apart from wealth, whereas profit-maximizers always care about the willingness-to-pay composite. Sliding-scale fees based on income allow nonprofits to screen on the basis of innate preferences by correcting for differences in purchasing power, as Oster (1995) explains:

> It is common practice . . . for private schools to require that even the most indigent student pay at least a small fraction of tuition. This practice helps to sort among parents and identify those families with the highest value on education. (p. 99)

Price serves a screening function whether or not the nonprofit wishes to serve those with the greatest willingness to pay. Soup kitchens, for example, are more concerned with hunger than ability to pay. If the need for a subsidized meal is observable, price does not have to serve this screening function – the combination of price, or some other rationing device, and eligibility restrictions would be sufficient. However, if the nonprofit desires to serve those with an important but unobservable characteristic – for example, "true need" – price is at best an imperfect screen, most useful if the unobservable attribute is correlated with willingness to pay. At worst, price may be counterproductive: Any price that is sufficiently low to allow low-income households to purchase the good or service will also attract higher-income households that do not need a subsidized price. As a result, absent stigma and other social/psychological factors, price screens will fail to distinguish the target population reliably. In this case, additional or alternative screens might be used – for example, locating the soup kitchen in a run-down neighborhood will keep away the nonpoor looking for a free lunch at the same time it provides a convenient location for the needy.

Having a waiting list, whether for admission to a nursing home or for supper at a soup kitchen, may be another effective device for sorting out consumers when the organization's goal is not profit maximization but aiding a particular target population (Nichols, Smolensky, and Tideman 1971). People who are willing to wait are showing the intensity of their preferences and the availability of alternatives, and the nonprofit may wish to serve persons for whom alternatives are poor. The problem is to get people to reveal their true circumstances. A soup kitchen can give food away at no charge, but its budget constraint and distributional goal require it to try to target the poor and only the poor; since they generally have low opportunity costs of time, waiting in line helps to sort out those who are most in need, for they are the ones most likely to be willing to wait. In the case of nursing homes, willingness to be on a waiting list for admission provides some basis for sorting prospective patients who are willing and able to pay a higher price from those whose incomes are more limited. Thus, although either a waiting line or a waiting list is inefficient given a goal of profit maximization, they may be efficient insofar as nonprofits' objective functions include distributional goals.

The possibility that the screening, or demand-revelation, function of price will be counterproductive is highlighted by two examples. Titmuss (1971) noted the problem with using consumer payments for blood to compensate blood donors. Blood markets suffer from informational asymmetry problems: Even persons who had reason to believe their blood was tainted by hard-to-detect infectious diseases – hepatitis was the focus at the time – could profit nonetheless from the sale of their blood because buyers were unable to distinguish "good" blood from "bad." If, argued Titmuss, blood money were prohibited, then only altruists, who presumably would not wish to inflict their diseases on others, would supply their blood. A second example of the limitation of price as a screening mechanism involves drug and alcohol treatment centers and those persons who deny their addiction problems. Charging them fees would be counterproductive, all else held equal, because those in denial would be least willing to pay for treatment.

The effectiveness of the screening function of fees for organizations in either sector depends on the behavior of competitors, both non- and for-profit. In either sector, a high fee cannot be used to screen for high-willingness-to-pay clients unless competitors follow suit. The same is true for nonprofits that use willingness to pay as a screen for some other characteristic that concerns them. For example, a graduate department of economics concerned with output quality, not monetary profit, might wish to admit the "best" students regardless of willingness to pay. Presumably those who could use a graduate education as a springboard to a highly successful career would be willing to pay more than others, all else being equal, but aid offers from actively competing schools would bid up the required amount of aid, generate rents for the student, and thereby eliminate any department's ability to use high fees as a successful screen for the student's supply price.

Another aspect of screening that deserves mention is *cream skimming*, where organizations seek to serve the most profitable clients. For example, when the government contracts with a private job-placement and training agency, a profit maximizer paid on the basis of the number of persons it places has an incentive to screen out hard-to-place clients. Similarly, cream-skimming insurance companies try to screen out those who drive dangerously, and cream-skimming hospitals have a profit-related incentive to screen out poor and uninsured patients. Nonprofits, if they pursue broader public-interest goals and especially if they have distributional goals that favor the poor, would differ from for-profits in their propensity to cream-skim. It is not obvious, however, in which direction they would differ. If the nonprofit hospital accepts more low-cost, insured patients and receives reimbursement that does not distinguish, within Diagnosis Related Group, low- from high-cost patients, it obtains more net profit that can be applied to the treatment of other target-group patients or toward furthering some other element of the nonprofit mission, such as community health education. In any case, in unregulated-price markets, competitive pressures may force all providers to attempt to cream-skim, although this same competition will drive prices down to marginal costs, depriving all competitors of profit from low-cost patients.

The allocation mechanism chosen sends signals to consumers and others as to the quality of service. If an organization thrives after maintaining a higher price than its competitors, it is signaling to prospective consumers, by its survival, that other customers find the product to be of higher quality than the competitor's. We hypothesize that nonprofits are less likely to use price as a signal of quality because use of this kind of signal conflicts with their distributional objectives. Instead, nonprofits are more likely to use waiting lists or highly selective eligibility requirements as a signal. We have no reason to believe either approach would more reliably convey information about quality to consumers, but do hypothesize that different modes of signaling are employed by the two sectors.

Allocation mechanisms also provide a signal to third-party funders (private donors, grant makers, and governments) about the social value of service provision, as Dan Delany (personal communication, 1996) explains:

> The fee and wait-list combination [chosen by an alternative health center for people with AIDS] . . . signaled a level of legitimacy for a service that had not been viewed as such for some time. Clients willing to pay, even after waiting in excess of a year for service, was a powerful statement to fellow service providers, government officials charged with delineating funding priorities, and other funding sources.

The choice of allocation mechanisms also signals to third-party funders the organization's competence and philosophy. The choice of fee structures signals the funded nonprofit's managerial competence and degree of commitment to move towards self-sufficiency, which many funders value. On the other hand, allocation mechanisms may signal an organizational insensitivity to need. When a soup kitchen charges fees, funders may question the organization's commitment to serving the needy, the quality of its management, or the kitchen's long-term stability. Thus, we hypothesize that nonprofit use of fees depends upon the preferences of major funders and the nature of the service provided. (The potential effect of user fees on donations was noted in Chapter 3.)

The ability of any organization to contribute to the public interest in efficiency and distributional equity depends on the actions of both the organization and its customers, patients, or clients. Consumers should have reason to restrict their use of costly services, to seek less costly alternative modes of service delivery, to take preventive actions that reduce their need for services, and to devote effort toward being a "good" client on whom agency efforts will not be wasted. The high fees charged by profit maximizers provide consumers with a reason to economize in all these ways, even though it is no part of the profit-maximizer's profit-making mission to help society in this way. Nonprofits whose distributional concerns make them averse to high fees would not have this automatic beneficial side effect of solving these "moral hazard" problems. Thus, some nonprofits temper their distributional concerns and charge token fees, and others provide efficiency-inducing incentives through nonfee mechanisms. David E. Mason (personal communication, 1996) provides an example:

> [T]he Laubach Literacy organization . . . published teaching and reading materials . . . , trained volunteer tutors, and conducted adult literacy programs . . . in 17 countries. . . . Though the money paid by those who used the reading material was so insignificant that the central office reaped virtually no income from it, we always charged a token fee. We found the learners took better care of the material, and attached a value to it because the fee was required.

In the same vein, fees can induce effort on the part of a third-party payer rather than the client. Private education, where the parents are the third party, provides an example (Oster 1995):

> [Private-school fees] also help to insure that parents have some "stake" in their children's education, so that price plays an ideological role as well. Given the extent to which education has been increasingly seen as a collaborative effort between parents and schools, some pricing may be quite important. (p. 99)

Although user fees usually provide positive efficiency-inducing incentives to clients and third parties, there are dangers. Lohmann (1980) points out that, in the field of mental health,

> [t]he use of strong-arm tactics in the collection of past-due accounts . . . would be considered inappropriate. . . . One mental health agency . . . has largely solved this problem by linking payment of fees to the clinical context: reluctance to pay fees is interpreted as a non-cooperative attitude on the part of the client, and the issue is taken up by the clinical staff. Such an approach, however, may strike some as taking unfair advantage of client vulnerabilities. Certainly, it can be seen that significant tensions can arise between the "helping" thrust of an agency and its need for fee revenue. (pp. 81, 89)

## Conclusion

Nonprofit organizations and for-profit firms both engage in commercial activities, charging fees for services provided. Some analysts, policymakers, and mass media conclude from this observation that commercial nonprofits are simply for-profits in disguise – a conclusion that is premature. Unlike for-profits, nonprofits have a variety of distributional and other "bonoficing" objectives, and they operate under different legal constraints, so that they may set their prices (and design their nonprice allocation mechanisms) on a different basis. In this chapter, we have illustrated a wide variety of ways in which distributional goals might be pursued, each suggesting a testable implication. Our tests are informal and, we hope, suggestive, but they call for formal testing and interpretation. A balanced assessment of the commercial activities of nonprofit organizations requires analysis of the magnitude of differences between nonprofits' and for-profits' pursuit of distributional objectives, a judgment regarding the social value of pursuing distributional goals through nongovernmental organizations, and evaluation of alternative means of pursuing these objectives.

We do not assert, nor have we demonstrated, that nonprofits differ from private firms in their concern for how outputs are distributed among beneficiaries. All nonprofits are not the same, any more than all private firms are. Nonprofits may not behave the same way in all markets, perhaps acting differently in ancillary-goods markets, where the focus is on revenue generation, than in their use of user fees for their target populations, where revenue generation may be balanced with distributional considerations. The distinctions we have discussed in this chapter are intended as conjectures that call for testing. It is important to determine whether, and under what conditions, nonprofits are effective mechanisms for expressing complex social goals involving output distribution.

# References

Ben-Ner, Avner. 1986. "Nonprofit Organizations: Why Do They Exist in Market Economies?" in Susan Rose-Ackerman (ed.), *The Economics of Nonprofit Institutions: Studies in Structure and Policy*. New York: Oxford University Press, pp. 94–113.

DeHoog, Ruth Hoogland. 1984. *Contracting Out for Human Services: Economic, Political and Organizational Perspectives*. Albany, NY: State University of New York Press.

Ferris, James M., and Elizabeth Graddy. 1991. "Production Costs, Transaction Costs, and Local Government Contractor Choice." *Economic Inquiry* 29: 541–54.

Handy, Femida. 1995. "Reputation as Collateral: An Economic Analysis of the Role of Trustees of Nonprofits," *Nonprofit and Voluntary Sector Quarterly* 24(4): 293–306.

Hansmann, Henry B. 1980. "The Role of Nonprofit Enterprise," *Yale Law Journal* 89(5) (April): 835–901.

1981a. "Nonprofit Enterprise in the Performing Arts," *Bell Journal of Economics* 12: 341–61.

1981b. "The Rationale for Exempting Nonprofit Organizations from the Corporate Income Tax," *Yale Law Journal* 91: 54–100.

Holtmann, A. G. 1983. "A Theory of Nonprofit Firms," *Economica* 50: 439–49.

James, Estelle. 1983. "How Nonprofits Grow: A Model," *Journal of Policy Analysis and Management* 2 (Spring): 350–65.

1986. "Comment," in Susan Rose-Ackerman (ed.), *The Economics of Nonprofit Institutions: Studies in Structure and Policy*. New York: Oxford University Press, pp. 154–8.

Lohmann, Roger. 1980. *Breaking Even: Financial Management in Human Service Organizations*. Philadelphia: Temple University Press.

McCready, Douglas. 1988. "Ramsey Pricing: A Method for Setting Fees in Social Service Organizations," *American Journal of Economics and Sociology* 47: 97–110.

Moran, R. Allen. 1985. "Queues: The Economic Theory of Screening and Human Service Productivity," *Southern Economic Journal* 52(2): 492–8.

Moulin, Hervè. 1988. *Axioms of Cooperative Decisionmaking*. Cambridge: Cambridge University Press.

Nichols, Donald, Eugene Smolensky, and T. Nicolaus Tideman. 1971. "Discrimination by Waiting Time in Merit Goods," *American Economic Review* 61(3): 312–23.

Oster, Sharon. 1995. *Strategic Management for Nonprofit Organizations*. New York: Oxford University Press.

Pauly, Mark V. 1987. "Nonprofit Firms in Medical Markets," *American Economic Review* 77(2) (October): 257–62.

Schiff, Jerald, and Burton A. Weisbrod. 1991. "Competition between For-Profit and Nonprofit Organizations in Commercial Markets," *Annals of Public and Cooperative Economics* 62(4): 619–39.

Smith, Steven Rathgeb, and Michael Lipsky. 1993. *Nonprofits for Hire: The Welfare State in the Age of Contracting*. Cambridge, MA: Harvard University Press.

Spiegel, Menahem. 1995. "Charity without Altruism," *Economic Inquiry* 33(4): 625–40.

Steinberg, Richard, and Burton A. Weisbrod. 1997. "To Give or to Sell? That Is the Question: Or, . . . Price Discrimination by Nonprofit Organizations with Distributional Objectives." Working Paper, Department of Economics, Indiana University / Purdue University at Indianapolis, and Department of Economics, Northwestern University.

Steinwald, Bruce, and Laura A. Dummit. 1989. "A Hospital Case-Mix Change: Sicker Patients or DRG Creep?" *Health Affairs* (Summer): 35–47.

Titmuss, Richard. 1971. *The Gift Relationship: From Human Blood to Social Policy*. London: Allyn & Unwin.

Weisbrod, Burton A. 1988. *The Nonprofit Economy*. Cambridge, MA, and London: Harvard University Press.

1998. "Institutional Form and Organization Behavior," in Walter W. Powell and Elisabeth Clemens (eds.), *Private Action and the Public Good*. New Haven: Yale University Press, pp. 69–84.

Young, H. Peyton. 1994. *Equity in Theory and Practice*. Princeton: Princeton University Press.

# [25]

# Whither the Nonprofit Wage Differential? Estimates from the 1990 Census

Laura Leete, *Willamette University*

This article provides new estimates of the nonprofit/for-profit wage differential in the U.S. economy. Using observations on 4.1 million private-sector employees from the 1990 census, I find either zero or slightly positive economy-wide wage differences between nonprofit and for-profit employees in a standard earnings equation format. Significant wage differentials are found at the disaggregated occupation and industry level and provide a basis for testing hypotheses explaining nonprofit/for-profit wage differences.

## I. Introduction

Scholars of the nonprofit sector have long since identified unique characteristics of this portion of the economy. From product characteristics to market structure to objective function, nonprofit organizations are hypothesized to function quite differently from their profit-maximizing counterparts. These differences have been found to extend into the labor market in a number of cases. Several authors have hypothesized differences in either the wage-setting conditions or mechanisms of nonprofit organizations, such that wages paid there should vary from those

The author gratefully acknowledges financial support from the Cleveland Foundation and the Mandel Center for Nonprofit Organizations for this and related projects. This work greatly benefited from comments and suggestions by Neil Bania, Patricia Beeson, Bruce Kingma, Mark Schweitzer, Brad Smith, Rich Steinberg, Dennis Young, participants in seminars in the Department of Economics and the Mandel Center at Case Western Reserve University, and members of the First Annual Workshop in Nonprofit Economics. Robert Ioffe provided expert and patient research assistance.

[*Journal of Labor Economics*, 2001, vol. 19, no. 1]

0734-306X/2001/1901-0005$02.50

paid in comparable for-profit organizations. In the past, little data has been available identifying workers from the nonprofit sector separately from those in the for-profit sector. Thus, the nonprofit wage differential has been estimated only with limited data or only in limited occupations and industries.

This paucity of information exists despite the fact that nonprofit organizations account for both a significant and a growing share of U.S. employment. In 1990, there were approximately 1.1 million nonprofit organizations in the United States with about 9.3 million paid (full-time equivalent) employees. Between 1977 and 1990, the number of nonprofit organizations in the United States increased by 22%; nonprofit employment rose 44%. Nonprofits often dominate human and social services aspects of our economy at a time when both output and employment is shifting increasingly toward functions such as health care, child care, and education. Nonprofit organizations account for 51% of all hospitals, 32% of clinics and other health care organizations, 49% of all colleges and universities, 23% of vocational schools, and 59% of social service organizations. Increasingly, services previously provided by government agencies are now delivered through nonprofit organizations.[1]

In this article, I attempt to redress the existing information gap and shed light on the relationship between the nonprofit sector and the labor market in the United States. Many previous authors have examined differences in pay between the nonprofit and for-profit sectors without taking into account differences in occupations, industries, or worker characteristics (e.g., Mirvis and Hackett 1983; Johnston and Rudney 1987). In examining pay differences here, I will not consider such gross differences in pay. Instead, I will look only at those differences between nonprofit and for-profit organizations that are apparent between comparable workers within comparable occupations and industries, as these categories are typically measured in the literature on wages and labor markets. In the existing literature, explanations for such wage differences fall into two broad categories. In the first, broadly referred to here as the donative-labor hypothesis, nonprofit firms produce a different good or a different quality of good than their for-profit counterparts in the same (measured) industries and occupations. Nonprofit workers derive utility from the nature of the good produced and are thus willing to accept a lower (compensating) wage. The second set of explanations accounts for differences in pay between nonprofit and for-profit organizations that are producing otherwise identical products, and pay differences are attributed to a variety of either observable or unobservable differences in the characteristics of nonprofit and for-profit firms, workers, or their jobs. In

[1] Figures from Young and Steinberg (1995) and Salamon (1992).

these cases, nonprofit wages could be either higher or lower than for-profit wages for comparable workers, depending on the nature of the differences being pinpointed.

Using data from the 1990 census on 4.1 million individuals employed in the private sector, I estimate nonprofit/for-profit wage differentials for the U.S. economy as a whole and separately for highly disaggregated occupation and industry categories. I find a wide range of both positive and negative nonprofit wage differentials across detailed occupation and industry categories that sum to an economy-wide average that is nearly zero. I test implications of the donative-labor hypothesis and find only some evidence consistent with the application of this hypothesis alone. Instead, the pattern of nonprofit wage differentials across disaggregated occupations and industries is suggestive of a number of forces affecting nonprofit wages simultaneously.

In Section II below, I review the existing theories of wages in the nonprofit wage sector and develop a model that illustrates their relationship to available data. In Section III, I describe my data and empirical methodology. In Section IV, I present aggregated and disaggregated estimates of the nonprofit wage differential in the United States, compare them with the findings of previous authors, and conduct various tests of the donative-labor hypothesis. In Section V, I discuss problems of misspecification and misclassification error, and the possible endogeneity of nonprofit status. In Section VI, I offer some concluding comments.

## II. Models

As suggested above, explanations of for-profit/nonprofit wage differences fall into two major categories. The first category covers the cases in which the goods produced by nonprofit and for-profit workers have different properties. These ideas, all variants of the donative-labor hypothesis, are attributable to the work of Hansmann (1980), Preston (1989), Rose-Ackerman (1996), and Frank (1996). While each author offers a slightly different rationale and formulation, in each case individuals accept lower pay from a nonprofit organization in return for assisting with production in which the worker finds intrinsic value. According to Preston, this lower pay is equivalent to a monetary donation to an organization producing public goods. Frank views it as a compensating differential in return for work that is more morally palatable. Alternately, Rose-Ackerman notes that ideologues may accept lower pay in return for the guarantee that their efforts are helping to achieve their idealistic goals and are not lining the pockets of for-profit stockholders. Hansmann suggests that it is a result of a sorting mechanism through which employees more interested in the production of quality services than in financial gain signal this to nonprofit organizations. The variants put forth by both Hansmann and Rose-Ackerman are particularly applicable to the case in which nonprofit organizations are formed because of information asymmetries and consumers take nonprofit status as an indicator of either product quality or integrity along ideological lines.

Variants of this hypothesis have sometimes been put forth in order to explain lower nonprofit wages across industries, contrasting nonprofit work in one industry with for-profit work in another. Frank suggests that individuals view working as stockbrokers as less morally palatable than working in substance-abuse prevention. Preston suggests that nonprofit differentials might disappear when examined in sufficiently detailed industries. For any of these hypotheses to explain nonprofit/for-profit wage differences within the same detailed, measured industry classification, nonprofit and for-profit firms must produce either different products or, as emphasized by Hansmann, a different quality of product. For example, nonprofit and for-profit television-broadcasting firms share the same detailed industry classification, but each produces distinctly different programming with different levels of social externality. For-profit movie houses and nonprofit theatres produce a different product for different audiences and hire employees working toward different ends, yet they share the same industry classification. In addition, the means of distributing a final product can be considered its distinguishing characteristic. Legal services provided gratis to the poor and indigent may be identical in content and quality to legal services sold to better-off paying customers. The redistributive nature of the former, however, imbues it with public good content lacking in the latter.

The second class of explanations of nonprofit/for-profit wage differences generates differences in pay based on fundamentally different conditions within nonprofit and for-profit firms producing identical output. These differences may or may not be inherent in nonprofit status and could be either positive or negative. A number of authors suggest reasons why nonprofit wages might be higher than comparable for-profit wages: Rose-Ackerman (1996) points out that in industries in which nonprofit and for-profit organizations compete, nonprofit organizations are generally larger. As is well known, larger organizations typically pay higher wages, perhaps because of their ability to exploit economies of scale (Brown and Medoff 1989). Feldstein (1971), Shackett and Trapani (1987), Borjas, Frech, and Ginsburg (1983), and Preston (1989) have all suggested that freedom from tax, regulatory, or profit-maximizing pressures allows nonprofits to distribute rents to workers. Feldstein offers a precursor to Akerlof's (1984) "gift-exchange" rationale for why they might do so, which in turn is suggestive of efficiency-wage arguments. Borjas et al. (1983) argue that because nonprofits are constrained from accumulating a surplus, there is less incentive for them to minimize costs. Alternately, a positive or negative nonprofit wage differential could result from unobservable (to the researcher) differences in working conditions, worker characteristics, or both. Firm and worker differences may be correlated if different work environments or corporate cultures cause workers with different traits to self-select differentially into the two sectors.

Finally, Ito and Domain (1987) suggest an application of the efficiency-wage hypothesis (Yellen 1984) to the nonprofit sector that could fall into either class of explanations offered above. They argue that efficiency wages might be more prevalent in nonprofit settings because of the nature of the output in the sector and the difficulty of monitoring worker effort there. This explanation requires that nonprofit and for-profit firms produce different products. Alternately, however, one might argue that even when producing the same product, nonprofit and for-profit firms might organize production differently, leading to the use of efficiency wages in one setting and not the other (as suggested by Feldstein's argument above).

## Modeling Nonprofit/For-Profit Wage Differences

In order to relate these various theories to empirical estimates of the for-profit/nonprofit wage differential, I develop a simple model of wage determination. This is used to decompose the various influences on nonprofit/for-profit wage differences and to demonstrate how the estimated nonprofit/for-profit wage effect could vary both in sign and in magnitude across different industries and occupations. In a standard model of wage determination, workers are assumed to derive utility from their compensation and from other nonpecuniary job characteristics.[2] While there is undoubtedly an extensive range of nonpecuniary job characteristics, I will summarize them here in the context of the literature on nonprofit workers and their jobs. Preston, Frank, Rose-Ackerman, and Hansmann all express a similar notion that the nature of the output produced enters the utility functions of workers. Thus, I specify that workers derive positive utility from the perceived intrinsic value (IV) of work and suggest that this notion captures the variants put forth by all four authors.

Thus, the utility that an individual worker derives from a particular job can be specified as

$$U_{ij} = U(W_{ij}, \mathrm{IV}_{ij}, \mathrm{OJC}_j, \mathrm{IJC}_j), \tag{1}$$

where $U_{ij}$ is the level of utility of the $i$th worker on the $j$th job, $W_{ij}$ is their log wage, $\mathrm{IV}_{ij}$ is the level of intrinsic value they perceive on the job, and $\mathrm{OJC}_j$ and $\mathrm{IJC}_j$ are other nonpecuniary characteristics of the job that are

[2] Because of data limitations here, I will only consider wages.

associated with its occupation and industry, respectively.[3] The function U is increasing in both $W$ and IV, but could be either increasing or decreasing with respect to the components of OJC and IJC. Individuals maximizing their utility subject to a standard budget constraint will then exhibit the following labor-supply function:

$$\mathrm{LS}_{ij} = f(W_{ij}, \mathrm{IV}_{ij}, \mathrm{OJC}_j, \mathrm{IJC}_j). \quad (2)$$

A standard derivation of labor demand would yield the following:

$$\mathrm{LD}_{ij} = g(W_{ij}, \mathrm{HC}_i, R_j, D_j, \mathrm{RD}_j), \quad (3)$$

where $\mathrm{LD}_{ij}$ is the quantity of labor demanded from workers with characteristics of the $i$th worker in the $j$th job, $\mathrm{HC}_i$ is human capital of the $i$th worker, $\mathrm{R}_j$ is represents regional economic conditions where the job is located, $\mathrm{D}_j$ represents discrimination (based on nonproductivity related characteristics) by the employer, and $\mathrm{RD}_j$ represents conditions that lead to the distribution of rents to workers.[4] The intersection of labor supply and demand yields a market-equilibrium wage determined by some function

$$W_{ij} = h(\mathrm{IV}_{ij}, \mathrm{OJC}_j, \mathrm{IJC}_j, \mathrm{HC}_i, R_j, D_j, \mathrm{RD}_j). \quad (4a)$$

A log-linear example of such a function is

$$W_{ij} = j + k\mathrm{IV}_{ij} + l\mathrm{OJC}_j + m\mathrm{IJC}_j + n\mathrm{HC}_i + o\mathrm{R}_j + p\mathrm{D}_j + q\mathrm{RD}_j. \quad (4b)$$

Most elements of this equation are straightforward. However, the conditions that lead to the distribution of rents to workers (RD) requires some further elaboration. The distribution of rents requires both the ability to accumulate rents and conditions that would lead to the distribution of rents to workers. The ability to accumulate rents could stems from factors such as industry competitiveness ($C$), firm efficiency ($E$), firm size ($S$) (via economies of scale), or the tax-exempt status of nonprofits (NP). The likelihood that such rents are shared with workers comes from conditions that would facilitate gift-exchange or efficiency wages ($G$), unionization (UN) or the nondistribution constraint implicit

[3] A fourth category of nonpecuniary job characteristics could be added here: those that are idiosyncratic and characteristic of neither the detailed occupation and detailed industry. However, this term is omitted here for simplicity.

[4] The assumption that labor demand follows the same structure in nonprofit and for-profit firms is relaxed below.

in nonprofit status. Thus, rents shared with a given worker can be expressed as some function of these variables:

$$\mathrm{RD}_j = a + b\mathrm{NP}_j + cC_j + dE_j + eS_j + f\mathrm{UN}_j + gG_j. \tag{5}$$

Combining equations (4b) and (5) yields a final wage equation:

$$\begin{aligned} W_{ij} = (j + qa) + k\mathrm{IV}_{ij} + l\mathrm{OJC}_j + m\mathrm{IJC}_j + n\mathrm{HC}_i + oR_j + pD_j \\ + qb\mathrm{NP}_j + qcC_j + qdE_j + qeS_j + qf\mathrm{UN}_j + qgG_j. \end{aligned} \tag{6}$$

If $\Delta x$ represents the average nonprofit/for-profit difference in variable $x$ across the economy, then the average difference in wages between nonprofit and for-profit workers can be expressed as

$$\begin{aligned} W_{\mathrm{NP}} - W_{\mathrm{FP}} &= \Delta W \\ &= qb + k\Delta\mathrm{IV} + l\Delta\mathrm{OJC} + m\Delta\mathrm{IJC} + n\Delta\mathrm{HC} + o\Delta R \\ &\quad + p\Delta D + qc\Delta C + qd\Delta E + qe\Delta S + qf\Delta\mathrm{UN} + qg\Delta G. \end{aligned} \tag{7}$$

In the context of equation (7), the different variants of the donative-labor hypothesis can be expressed as the requirement that both $k < 0$ and $\Delta\mathrm{IV} > 0$. That is, workers will accept lower wages in jobs that, in their minds, produce intrinsic value of one kind or another ($k < 0$), and the average intrinsic value of work is higher in the nonprofit sector ($\Delta\mathrm{IV} > 0$). Hypotheses that specify that nonprofit and for-profit workers earn different wages while producing the same products can be summarized as suggesting that $\Delta\mathrm{IV} = 0$, while other element(s) of equation (7) are nonzero. Previous authors have generally abstracted from nonprofit/for-profit differences in human capital ($\Delta\mathrm{HC}$), regional locations ($\Delta R$), discrimination levels ($\Delta D$), or unionization levels ($\Delta\mathrm{UN}$), interpreting these as control variables. The view that nonprofits accumulate rents and distribute them to workers because of either their tax-exempt status or the nondistribution constraint can be summarized as the requirement that both $q > 0$ and $b > 0$. Feldstein's suggestion that nonprofit firms would be more likely to pay higher wages to their workers as a philanthropic act (and other applications of the gift-exchange or efficiency wages) can be interpreted as the condition that both $qg > 0$ and $\Delta G > 0$. Working conditions that systematically vary across sectors would be interpreted as nonzero values for $\Delta\mathrm{OJC}$ and $\Delta\mathrm{IJC}$ and their associated coefficients. The difference in characteristics between sectors could either be intrinsically related to nonprofit status in some fashion or simply be correlated with it.

## Empirical Estimation

Empirical estimation of any nonprofit-wage effect is complicated by the fact that adequate measures are not available for the intrinsic value of a job, occupation- and industry-related job characteristics, industry competition, firm efficiency, firm size, unionization, or conditions leading to efficiency wage or gift exchange. Instead, we can only proxy for these variables using occupation, industry, and nonprofit status. Let OCC and IND represent sets of dummy variables representing detailed occupation and industry categorizations. Then proxies for the unobserved variables can be specified as

$$\text{OJC} = r_3\text{OCC}; \tag{8a}$$

$$\text{IJC} = s_2\text{IND}; \tag{8b}$$

$$\text{IV} = t_1\text{NP} + t_2\text{IND} + t_3\text{OCC}; \tag{8c}$$

$$C = u_2\text{IND}; \tag{8d}$$

$$E = v_1\text{NP} + v_2\text{IND}; \tag{8e}$$

$$S = w_1\text{NP} + w_2\text{IND}; \tag{8f}$$

$$U = x_1\text{NP} + x_2\text{IND} + x_3\text{OCC}; \tag{8g}$$

and

$$G = y_1\text{NP} + y_2\text{IND} + y_3\text{OCC}. \tag{8h}$$

Using these proxies, equation (6) becomes

$$\begin{aligned} W = {} & (j + qa) + (kt_1 + qb + qdv_1 + qew_1 + qfx_1 + qgy_1)\text{NP} \\ & + (kt_2 + qcu_2 + qdv_2 + qew_2 + ms_2 + qfx_2 + qgy_2)\text{IND} \\ & + (lr_3 + kt_3 + qfx_3 + qgy_3)\text{OCC} + n\text{HC} + oR + pD. \end{aligned} \tag{9}$$

In this specification, the estimated nonprofit coefficient subsumes multiple effects that are related to the nonprofit nature of the enterprise. These include the effect of the intrinsic value of work (both the general "payment" for intrinsic value, $k$, and the nonprofit/for-profit difference in the level of intrinsic value between jobs in the same [measured] occupation and industry, $t_1$), the direct effect of nonprofit status on rent distribution ($qb$), and the effect on rent distribution (holding occupation and industry

**Table 1**
**Predicted Sign of Components of the Nonprofit Wage Effect**

| | Effect of Intrinsic Value (1) | Effect of Direct RD (2) | Effect of Nonprofit Status on Rent Distribution | | | |
|---|---|---|---|---|---|---|
| | | | Efficiency (3) | Firm Size (4) | Unionization (5) | Gift Exchange (6) |
| From equation (4b) | $k < 0$ | $q > 0$ | $q > 0$ | $q > 0$ | $q > 0$ | $q > 0$ |
| From equation (5) | ... | $b > 0$ | $d > 0$ | $e > 0$ | $f > 0$ | $f > 0$ |
| From equation (8a–h) | $t1 > 0$ | ... | $v1$ ? | $w1 > 0$ | $x1 < 0$ | $y1 > 0$ |
| Complete effect | $kt1 < 0$ | $qb > 0$ | $qdv1$ ? | $qew1 > 0$ | $qfx1 < 0$ | $qgy1 > 0$ |

constant) of nonprofit/for-profit differences in efficiency ($qdv_1$), firm size ($qew_1$), unionization ($qfx_1$), and gift exchange ($qgy_1$). Whether the sum of these effects is positive or negative is indeterminate and could vary considerably by occupation and/or industry. These effects are decomposed and their expected signs are shown in table 1.

Among the underlying coefficients, those from equations (4b) and (5) capture the effect of a given variable on wages. At least a priori, one might expect these to be constant across subsectors of the economy. However, the coefficients estimated from equations (8a) through (8h) are estimates of the nonprofit/for-profit difference in the level of a particular variable. This will reflect the difference for whatever subset of individuals is included in the estimation. Therefore, among the complete effects, only the effect in column 2 of table 1 might be expected to be constant across all occupations and industries.

To date, empirical examination of nonprofit pay differences has occurred in limited contexts only. The results are as varied as the theories that precede them. Preston (1989) found up to 15% lower wages for white-collar nonprofit workers. Preston (1988) found higher wages for nonprofit day-care workers, while Borjas et al. (1983) found little difference between wages in nonprofit and for-profit nursing homes. Weisbrod (1983) found that nonprofit lawyers earn 20% less. Leete (1993) found professional staff in nonprofit residential care facilities to have 36% higher wages than comparable staff in for-profit facilities.[5]

While many of the authors discussed above have sought an all-encom-

[5] Shackett and Trapani (1987) looked at a sample of all workers. However, their indicator for nonprofit status was actually an indicator for working in hospitals or educational services only. They did not include other industry controls. Thus, their results are not comparable to the others discussed here.

passing explanation of nonprofit wages, their work taken together suggests a variety of influences on wage-setting mechanisms across nonprofit and for-profit organizations. In addition, an examination of the nonprofit sector shows great diversity of use of the nonprofit form.[6] It is not difficult to imagine that the varying conditions required by these hypotheses could be satisfied differentially across different occupations and industries. Indeed, Preston (1989) suggests that the donative-labor hypothesis might lead to negative wage differentials in some industries and that the lack of regulatory pressures might lead to positive wage differentials in others. Similarly, Hansmann (1980) allows for a variety of outcomes depending on a variety of influences on nonprofit firms. This view, of multiple influences and outcomes, is consistent with the empirical evidence accumulated in the literature to date and, as discussed below, with the findings presented in this article.

## III. Data

The data set used here is the Five-Percent Public Use Microdata Sample (PUMS) of the 1990 census. This includes a sample of 4.1 million individuals employed in the private sector, of whom 8.5% work in the nonprofit sector. This data was self-reported by individuals receiving the "long form" survey of the census. Sector of employment was identified by asking individuals if they were an employee of "a private for-profit company . . . , a private not-for-profit tax-exempt or charitable organization, local government, state government, etc."[7] Government employees are eliminated from the sample, and individuals who answer "private not-for-profit tax-exempt or charitable organization" are coded as being nonprofit workers. Responses were checked for consistency with answers to questions on employer name, location, industry, and occupation. As part of the consistency check, data processors could use a directory of company names to identify the correct industry code and legal form of an organization. They could then recode the answer to the "class of worker" question accordingly (implications of misreporting of nonprofit status will be discussed below).

In addition to type of employment, the PUMS reports individual's wage and salary income for 1989, three-digit occupation and industry of employment, weekly hours of work, number of weeks worked, and individual characteristics such as age, education (including type of degree held), gender, race, area of residence, language fluency, and disability

[6] See, e.g., Salamon (1992), Salamon and Anheier (1996), James and Rose-Ackerman (1986), and Rose-Ackerman (1996) for good overviews.

[7] An appendix is available from the author with the exact wording of this question and the accompanying instructions.

**Table 2**
**Means of Dependent and Independent Variables by Sector**

| Variable | For-Profit % | Nonprofit % |
|---|---|---|
| Ln(hourly wage 1989) | $M$ = 2.23 | $M$ = 2.27 |
| Years of potential experience (age − education level − 6) | $M$ = 19.9 | $M$ = 21.8 |
| Female | 43.9 | 66.6 |
| Not fluent in English | 3.1 | 1.3 |
| Average hours worked per week, 1989 | 40.6 | 37.9 |
| Working < 10 hours per week, 1989 | 1.8 | 3.8 |
| Working < 25 hours per week, 1989 | 9.8 | 16.5 |
| Average weeks worked, 1989 | 45.1 | 45.1 |
| Working < 13 weeks, 1989 | 5.7 | 5.1 |
| Race: | | |
| White | 81.5 | 83.8 |
| African-American | 9.4 | 9.5 |
| Hispanic | 3.4 | 2.5 |
| Asian | 2.6 | 2.4 |
| Other | 3.2 | 1.9 |
| Educational attainment: | | |
| No school | .8 | .4 |
| Nursery school | .0 | .0 |
| Kindergarten | .0 | .0 |
| Grades 1–4 | .8 | .3 |
| Grades 5–8 | 4.0 | 2.0 |
| Grade 9 | 2.5 | 1.1 |
| Grade 10 | 3.7 | 1.7 |
| Grade 11 | 3.6 | 1.7 |
| Grade 12, no diploma | 3.8 | 2.0 |
| High school graduate or GED | 35.2 | 21.7 |
| Some college, no degree | 20.5 | 17.6 |
| Associate degree, occupational program | 3.8 | 5.2 |
| Associate degree, academic program | 2.9 | 4.2 |
| Bachelor's degree | 13.5 | 22.6 |
| Master's degree | 3.0 | 12.6 |
| Professional degree | 1.5 | 3.7 |
| Doctorate | .4 | 3.1 |
| $N$ | 3,822,413 | 323,548 |

NOTE.—Data include private-sector workers who are not disabled or enrolled in school.

status. Hourly wages are imputed as annual wage and salary income divided by weeks multiplied by weekly hours worked in 1989. Government workers are eliminated from the sample so that the comparisons made are strictly between for-profit and nonprofit workers. Restrictions keyed to student and disability status and to the number of weeks and hours worked are tested below.

Sample means of the variables used are reported in table 2 by nonprofit status. Nonprofit workers average higher hourly wages; are more likely to be part-time, female, and fluent in English; and they have on average more years of potential labor-market experience (defined as age minus years of education minus six). The racial mix in the nonprofit sector is slightly more white, and educational levels are higher. All of these characteristics are as expected, given the preponderance of white-collar, service-sector occupations in the nonprofit sector.

## IV. Findings

### The Economy-Wide Nonprofit Wage Differential

In this section, I reproduce estimates made by previous authors of an economy-wide nonprofit-wage differential and investigate the relationship between those estimates and the more detailed information available in the 1990 PUMS data. The most comprehensive estimates of the nonprofit-wage differential to date are those made by Preston (1989) for workers in managerial and professional, and clerical and sales occupations. Preston found nonprofit-wage differentials for workers in managerial and professional, and clerical and sales occupations to range from approximately −6% to −15% using data on 8,312 individuals from the 1979 Current Population Survey (CPS).[8] Unlike the 1990 PUMS, however, the CPS did not include direct information on the nonprofit/for-profit status of a worker's employer. Preston inferred this information from the industry of employment. For estimation purposes, workers were assigned to the nonprofit sector if they worked in a detailed census industry category identified by Rudney and Weitzman (1984) as having at least two-thirds of total employment in the nonprofit sector. Workers in industries with a "small but significant number of nonprofit employees" were eliminated from the sample.[9] Workers in all other industries were designated as being in the for-profit sector.

Preston estimated an equation of the form

$$W_i = \alpha + \beta(CS_i \times NP_i^c) + \delta(MP \times NP_i^c) + \gamma MP_i + \eta \mathbf{X}_i, \qquad (10)$$

where $NP^c$ is the constructed variable indicating nonprofit status, CS is a dummy for clerical and sales workers, MP is a dummy for managerial and professional workers, and **X** is a vector of controls that includes dummy

[8] These approximate percentage differences are taken from coefficients on dichotomous variables in semi-log wage equations. It should be noted that in this context, the true percentage differences should be calculated as *e*(Calculated Coefficient) − 1 (see Halvorsen and Palmquist 1980), if the calculated coefficient is a consistent estimate of the true coefficient. If it is not, a less biased approximation is supplied by Kennedy (1981). It is exp[Calculated Coefficient − ½ Var(Calculated Coefficient)] − 1.

[9] The eliminated industries are radio and television broadcasting and cable; security, commodity brokerage, and investment companies; theaters and motion pictures; lodging places, except hotels and motels; miscellaneous entertainment and recreation services; nursing and personal care facilities; legal services; research, development, and testing services; and miscellaneous professional and related services.

**Table 3**
**Comparison of Results with Preston (1989)**

| | Findings from Preston (1989)[a] (1) | PUMS with Preston Methodology[a] (2) | PUMS with Actual Nonprofit Variable[a] (3) | PUMS Demographic and Human Capital Controls[a] (4) |
|---|---|---|---|---|
| Nonprofit × clerical/sales | −.0608** | −.0853*** | −.0747*** | −.0653*** |
| | (.0243) | (.0021) | (.0023) | (.0023) |
| Nonprofit × managerial/professional | −.1524** | −.1976*** | −.2142*** | −.1987*** |
| | (.0171) | (.0015) | (.0017) | (.0017) |
| CPS variables: | | | | |
| Managerial/professional | Yes | Yes | Yes | Yes |
| Female | Yes | Yes | Yes | Yes |
| Black | Yes | Yes | Yes | |
| Years schooling | Yes | Yes | Yes | |
| Potential experience | Yes | Yes | Yes | Yes |
| Potential experience$^2$ | Yes | Yes | Yes | Yes |
| Union | Yes | | | |
| Urban | Yes | Yes | Yes | Yes |
| Region controls (4) | Yes | Yes | Yes | Yes |
| PUMS variables: | | | | |
| Race (5) | | | | Yes |
| Female × race | | | | Yes |
| Education (17) | | | | Yes |
| Not fluent | | | | Yes |
| Female × not fluent | | | | Yes |
| Female × potential experience | | | | Yes |
| Female × potential experience$^2$ | | | | Yes |
| Female × years schooling | | | | Yes |
| Race × not fluent | | | | Yes |
| Race × potential experience | | | | Yes |
| Race × potential experience$^2$ | | | | Yes |
| Race × education | | | | Yes |
| MSA/PMSA (367) | | | | |
| Part-time status | | | | |
| Female × part-time | | | | |
| Race × part-time | | | | |
| Three-digit occupation | | | | |
| Three-digit industry | | | | |
| Three-digit occupation/industry | | | | |
| *N* | 8,312 | 2,405,790 | 2,405,790 | 2,405,790 |
| Adjusted $R^2$ | N.A. | .290 | .289 | .305 |

SOURCES.—Column 1 data are from Preston's findings from the Current Population Survey (CPS), 1979; Anne E. Preston, "The Nonprofit Worker in a For-Profit World." *Journal of Labor Economics* 7 (October 1989): 438–63. All other data are from the Public Use Microdata Sample (PUMS), 1990.

NOTE.—Data include managerial and professional, and clerical and sales workers only. Standard errors are given in parentheses. N.A. = not available.

[a] Sample restrictions: selected industries.

[b] Sample restrictions: none.

[c] Sample restrictions: no students or disabled.

* Significant at .05 level.

** Significant at .01 level.

*** Significant at .001 level.

continued over

variables for female, black, location in an urban area, region, union status, and years of education. The estimated coefficients β and δ are the estimated log wage difference between nonprofit and for-profit wages for clerical and sales workers, and for managerial and professional workers, respectively, and should reflect the underlying determinants of nonprofit wages detailed in equation (9).

In order to reproduce Preston's work, I estimate equation (10) from the

| PUMS Location Controls[a] (5) | PUMS Occupation Controls[a] (6) | PUMS Industry Controls[a] (7) | PUMS Full Equation[a] (8) | PUMS Full Equation[b] (9) | PUMS Full Equation[c] (10) |
|---|---|---|---|---|---|
| −.0580*** | −.0664*** | .0060* | −.0056 | −.0074* | −.0003 |
| (.0023) | (.0023) | (.0027) | (.0029) | (.0029) | (.0033) |
| −.1767*** | −.0249*** | .0006 | .0095*** | −.0014 | −.0038 |
| (.0017) | (.0021) | (.0022) | (.0023) | (.0022) | (.0024) |
| Yes | | | | | |
| Yes | Yes | Yes | Yes | Yes | Yes |
| Yes | Yes | Yes | Yes | Yes | Yes |
| Yes | Yes | Yes | Yes | Yes | Yes |
| Yes | Yes | Yes | Yes | Yes | Yes |
| Yes | Yes | Yes | Yes | Yes | Yes |
| Yes | Yes | Yes | Yes | Yes | Yes |
| Yes | Yes | Yes | Yes | Yes | Yes |
| Yes | Yes | Yes | Yes | Yes | Yes |
| Yes | Yes | Yes | Yes | Yes | Yes |
| Yes | Yes | Yes | Yes | Yes | Yes |
| Yes | Yes | Yes | Yes | Yes | Yes |
| Yes | Yes | Yes | Yes | Yes | Yes |
| Yes | Yes | Yes | Yes | Yes | Yes |
| Yes | Yes | Yes | Yes | Yes | Yes |
| Yes | Yes | Yes | Yes | Yes | Yes |
| | Yes | Yes | Yes | Yes | Yes |
| | Yes | Yes | Yes | Yes | Yes |
| | Yes | Yes | Yes | Yes | Yes |
| | Yes (206) | Yes (206) | | | |
| | | Yes (226) | | | |
| | | | Yes (19,567) | Yes (20,610) | Yes (19,832) |
| 2,405,790 | 2,405,790 | 2,405,790 | 2,405,790 | 2,577,575 | 2,094,749 |
| .323 | .361 | .376 | .382 | .381 | .364 |

1990 PUMS data, with all sample restrictions and variable definitions as specified by Preston (with the exception of the inclusion of a variable for union status that is not available on the PUMS data).[10] This procedure

[10] The definitions of "managerial and professional" and "clerical and sales" workers used here are based on 1980 census occupation classifications.

generates a sample of 2,405,790 individuals. My results are compared with Preston's in table 3. Column 1 shows Preston's findings from the 1979 CPS: a nonprofit differential of −.061 for clerical and sales workers, and of −.152 for managerial and professional workers. The same equation estimated from the 1990 PUMS generates very similar results, shown in column 2: −.085 for clerical and sales, and −.198 for managerial and professional workers. The equation is then estimated again substituting actual nonprofit status reported in the 1990 PUMS for Preston's constructed nonprofit variable, and the results are shown in column 3. The nonprofit differentials are only slightly changed. Thus, Preston's constructed variable for nonprofit status does not perform too differently from the status of nonprofit workers as reported on the PUMS.[11]

Further estimation with the PUMS data, however, does alter the interpretation of the results. Because Preston's constructed nonprofit variable was a function of industry, industry controls were not included in the estimation. Furthermore, the sample size and availability of information in the CPS limited the number of controls included. To test the effect of further controls from the PUMS, equation (10) is modified to

$$W_i = \alpha + \beta(CS_i \times NP_i) + \delta(MP \times NP_i) + \eta \mathbf{Z}_i, \qquad (11)$$

where $\mathbf{Z}$ is successively redefined to include controls for gender, race, lack of fluency in speaking English, part-time work status (less than 25 hours per week), 17 categories of educational attainment and type of degree earned, potential experience and potential experience squared, location controls for 367 urban and rural areas, and detailed occupation and industry controls (first as three-digit occupation and industry controls and then as controls for 47,189 occupation/industry interactions).[12] In

[11] Following Preston, I also estimate eq. (2) on a sample of white males alone, in order to minimize variation in uncontrolled labor quality, and find similar results. Of course, Preston's estimates and the estimates made here involve data collected 10 years apart. Any differences could be attributable to changes in nonprofit/for-profit–wage differences that occurred between 1979 and 1989. However, that I nearly replicate Preston's 1979 results using 1989 data suggests that this is not the case.

[12] Dummy variables represent each separate census metropolitan statistical area/primary metropolitan statistical area (MSA/PMSA) as well as the non–MSAs/PMSAs of each state. The 47,189 occupation/industry interactions consist of the nonempty intersection of 490 occupation and 234 industry identifiers. The equation including 47,189 occupation/industry controls is estimated using SAS version 6.12 for Windows. The GLM procedure is used, using the ABSORB option for both occupation and industry. Thus, the equation is estimated in deviations form, where each observation for an individual variable is calculated as the deviation from the occupation/industry cell mean. The SAS then reports all calculated ordinary least squares (OLS) coefficients except the (implicit) coeffi-

addition, interaction terms are added for gender with race, and for gender and race each separately with language fluency, education, potential experience and part-time work status. Using this specification, I also investigate the addition of industries excluded by Preston, the elimination of part-time workers, and the limitation of the sample to those who were not enrolled in school and who did not report having a disability that limited their ability to work.[13]

As the controls included in **Z** are successively added in columns 4 through 8 of table 3, the results diverge from Preston's. The nonprofit-wage differential for clerical and sales workers drops from −.085 when Preston's methodology is used to a statistically insignificant −.006 in the fully specified equation. Similarly, the nonprofit-wage differential for managerial and professional workers drops from −.198 to (a still statistically significant) .01. In the case of clerical and sales workers, the biggest change in the coefficient occurs when detailed industry controls are added to the equation (col. 7 of table 3). In the case of managerial and professional workers, the introduction of detailed occupation controls has the largest influence. In columns 9 and 10 of table 3, I alter the sample restrictions, first eliminating the restriction on industries included and then eliminating students and disabled workers from the sample. Neither change significantly alters the findings, however.

Managerial and professional, and clerical and sales workers account more than three-quarters of the workers in the nonprofit sector. To extend the analysis to the entire economy, however, I repeat the analysis using observations for all workers. I also look at full-year/full-time workers, white- and blue-collar workers, and one-digit occupation groups separately.[14] I alter the equation to estimate one economy-wide nonprofit effect. The equation becomes

$$W_i = \alpha + \beta \mathrm{NP}_i + \eta \mathbf{Z}_i. \tag{12}$$

The results are presented in table 4.[15] There is no statistically significant nonprofit-wage differential across all workers, full-time/full-year work-

cients on the occupation/industry cell. A typical estimation requires about 15 minutes on a Pentium II computer with a 266-megahertz processor, 128 megabytes of RAM, and approximately 700 megabytes of hard-disk work space.

[13] The inclusion of disabled workers may particularly influence results with regard to nonprofits: the severely disabled clients of "sheltered workshops" in the nonprofit sector who earn some pay will bias nonprofit wages downward.

[14] Here 1990 census occupational classifications are used to define occupation groups.

[15] Coefficient estimates for the fully specified economy-wide equation are available from the author.

**Table 4**
**The Nonprofit-Wage Differential, Economy-Wide and by Occupational Subgroup**

| | All Occupations | | White-Collar Workers | | | Blue-Collar Workers | | | | |
|---|---|---|---|---|---|---|---|---|---|---|
| Variable | All (1) | Full-Year/ Full-Time Workers Only (2) | All (3) | Managerial and Professional (4) | Technical, Sales, and Administrative (5) | All (6) | Service (7) | Farm, Forestry, and Fishing (8) | Precision, Craft, and Repair (9) | Operators, Fabricators, and Laborers (10) |
| Nonprofit | −.0005 | .0001 | .0013 | −.0089*** | .0109*** | −.0022 | .0347*** | −.0216 | −.0464*** | −.0582*** |
| | (.0015) | (.0016) | (.002) | (.003) | (.003) | (.003) | (.004) | (.018) | (.007) | (.006) |
| Three-digit occupation/ industry interaction | Yes (47,189) | Yes (43,575) | Yes (22,394) | Yes (9,760) | Yes (12,406) | Yes (24,566) | Yes (3,159) | Yes (429) | Yes (9,265) | Yes (11,050) |
| $N$ | 4,145,608 | 2,972,558 | 2,237,614 | 923,128 | 1,314,486 | 1,907,994 | 473,564 | 99,180 | 549,643 | 785,607 |
| Adjusted $R^2$ | .357 | .435 | .363 | .320 | .304 | .295 | .183 | .125 | .270 | .250 |

SOURCE.—Data from the Public Use Microdata Sample (PUMS), 1990.
NOTE.—Data include private-sector workers who are not disabled or enrolled in school. Standard errors are given in parentheses.
* Significant at .05 level.
** Significant at .01 level.
*** Significant at .001 level.

ers (34 or more hours per week and 40 or more weeks per year), or white- or blue-collar workers as a whole.[16] These results mask an array of both positive and negative significant effects for the underlying one-digit occupation groups. The nonprofit-wage effect for managerial and professional workers and for technical, sales, and administrative workers are statistically significant and close to −0.01 and +0.01, respectively. Among blue-collar workers, there is a positive and significant effect for service workers, and negative and significant effects for precision, craft, and repair workers, and for operators, fabricators, and laborers. The significant effects among blue-collar workers are larger in magnitude, ranging from 0.035 to −0.058.

The range of effects across occupation groups reflects the multiple underlying elements of the nonprofit-wage differential detailed in equation (9) and the fact that they are expected to vary by occupation or industry. For instance, the negative effect for blue-collar workers might reflect a lower unionization rate ($w_1 < 0$) among nonprofit workers, while the negative effect for managerial and professional workers might reflect a higher level of intrinsic value in those jobs in nonprofit organizations ($t_1 > 0$) coupled with a labor donation ($k > 0$).

Of course, the inclusion here of very detailed occupation and industry controls raises the possibility that a nonprofit/for-profit differential is simply being absorbed by occupation/industry effects in cells that represent exclusively nonprofit or for-profit workers. This effect is relatively small, however. When I limit the sample to the 10,432 occupation/industry cells in which both sectors are represented (3.6 million individuals) the nonprofit log wage difference is −.0006. When the sample is limited further, to the 1,585 occupation/industry cells in which there were at least 10 workers in each sector (2.4 million individuals), the estimated log wage difference is still close to zero, only .006. Raising the cutoff to 50 workers from each sector per cell (1.6 million individuals) raises the estimated difference to .011. The results from the second and third restrictions are statistically significant at the .001 level.[17]

The finding of an economy-wide nonprofit-wage differential that is close to zero or slightly positive is at odds with the perception of a large negative wage difference put forth by a number of previous authors (e.g., Preston 1989; Mirvis and Hackett 1983; Johnston and Rudney 1987). The wage differences estimated by Preston for white-collar workers appear to

[16] Equation (12) is also estimated separately for those working at least 10 hours per week, and for those working at least 10 hours per week and at least 13 weeks per year. The resulting estimates of the nonprofit effect are little changed. They are .0005 and .0022, respectively (and are not statistically significant).

[17] The $t$-statistics for these estimated coefficients are −.38, 3.45, and 8.01, respectively.

**Table 5**
**Nonprofit Differentials for Selected Industries: Comparison with Previous Authors**

| | Registered Nurses (COC 95) in Nursing Homes (CIC 832) | | | Day-Care Centers (CIC 862) | | | Lawyers (COC 178) in Legal Services (CIC 841) | | |
|---|---|---|---|---|---|---|---|---|---|
| | Borjas et al. (1983)[a] (1) | PUMS (1990)[b] (2) | PUMS (1990)[b] (3) | Preston (1988)[c] (4) | PUMS (1990)[b] (5) | PUMS (1990)[b] (6) | Weisbrod (1983)[a] (7) | PUMS (1990)[b] (8) | PUMS (1990)[b] (9) |
| Nonprofit | church: .0005<br>other: .0208 | −.0154<br>(.017) | .0017<br>(.0173) | FIDCR: .05–.10*<br>other: −.007–.030 | .0702***<br>(.0099) | .0597***<br>(.0100) | −.2000* | −.2779***<br>(.0433) | −.2189***<br>(.0432) |
| Region | Yes | Yes | | Yes | Yes | | | | |
| MSA/PMSA | | | Yes (357) | | | Yes (366) | | | Yes (360) |
| Urban | Yes | Yes | | | | | | | |
| Female | Yes | Yes | Yes | Yes | Yes | Yes | Yes | Yes | Yes |
| Race | Yes | Yes | Yes | Yes | Yes | Yes | Yes | Yes | Yes |
| Female × race | Yes | Yes | Yes | | | Yes | | | Yes |
| Not fluent | | | Yes | | | Yes | | | Yes |
| Years schooling | Yes | Yes | Yes | Yes | Yes | Yes | Yes | Yes | Yes |
| Potential experience[d] | Yes | Yes | Yes | Yes | Yes | Yes | Yes | Yes | Yes |
| Potential experience$^2$ | Yes | Yes | Yes | Yes | Yes | Yes | Yes | Yes | Yes |
| Part-time status | | | Yes | | | Yes | | | Yes |
| Three-digit occupations | N.A. | N.A. | N.A. | Yes (5) | Yes (135) | Yes (135) | N.A. | N.A. | N.A. |
| Other LF quality measures[e] | Yes | | | Yes | | | Yes | | |
| Female × part-time | | | Yes | | | Yes | | | Yes |

continued over

| | (1) | (2) | (3) | (4) | (5) | (6) | (7) | (8) | (9) |
|---|---|---|---|---|---|---|---|---|---|
| Female × not fluent | | | Yes | | | Yes | | | Yes |
| Female × potential experience | | | Yes | | | Yes | | | Yes |
| Female × potential experience$^2$ | | | Yes | | | Yes | | | Yes |
| Female × years schooling | | | Yes | | | Yes | | | Yes |
| Race × part-time | | | Yes | | | Yes | | | Yes |
| Race × not fluent | | | Yes | | | Yes | | | Yes |
| Race × potential experience | | | Yes | | | Yes | | | Yes |
| Race × potential experience$^2$ | | | Yes | | | Yes | | | Yes |
| Race × years schooling | | | Yes | | | Yes | | | Yes |
| $N$ | 3,310 | 6,073 | 6,073 | 1905 centers | 21,503 | 21,503 | 790 | 16,323 | 16,323 |
| $R^2$ | .441 | .126 | .252 | | .133 | .190 | .457 | .059 | .142 |

SOURCES.—George J. Borjas, H. E. Frech, III, and Paul B. Ginsburg, "Property Rights and Wages: The Case of Nursing Homes," *Journal of Human Resources* 18 (Spring 1983): 231–46; Anne E. Preston, "The Nonprofit Worker in a For-Profit World." *Journal of Labor Economics* 7 (October 1989): 438–63; the Public Use Microdata Sample (PUMS), 1990; and Burton A. Weisbrod, "Nonprofit and Proprietary Sector Behavior: Wage Differentials among Lawyers," *Journal of Labor Economics* 1 (July 1983): 246–63.

NOTE.—COC = Census Occupation Code; CIC = Census Industry Code. Standard errors are given in parentheses. N.A. = not available.

[a] Reference year: 1973–74.

[b] Reference year: 1989.

[c] Reference year: 1976–77.

[d] "Actual experience" is measured in the Borjas et al., Preston, and Weisbrod studies.

[e] See text for details.

* Significant at .05 level.

** Significant at .01 level.

*** Significant at .001 level.

be largely attributable to occupation and industry effects that could not be identified separately from nonprofit effects with available data. Of course, nonprofit status, industry, and occupation are by no means independently determined. This endogeneity and its implications for the analysis of nonprofit wages will be discussed below.

The findings here could be interpreted to mean that there are no wage differences between nonprofit and for-profit jobs once industry and occupation of employment are accounted for. This interpretation would run counter to all of the theoretical arguments in the existing literature. Furthermore, studies of individual sectors provide evidence of significant wage differences between nonprofit and for-profit organizations in particular occupations or industries. The economy-wide finding here could represent an average of differentials that occur with different strengths and magnitudes across different occupations and industries. To investigate this possibility I turn to a disaggregation of the nonprofit-wage differential.

## Differentials Disaggregated

A few authors have looked closely at the nonprofit-wage differentials for particular industry and occupation groups. Borjas et al. (1983), Weisbrod (1983), and Preston (1988) have each used specialized survey data with detailed information on worker qualifications, working conditions, and organizational structure of particular occupations and industries (registered nurses in nursing homes, lawyers in legal services, and workers the day-care industry, respectively). These studies are replicated here as closely as possible using the PUMS data. The summary of these comparisons is shown in table 5. Whether replicating the original equation or using the full set of variables available in the PUMS, the PUMS-based comparisons are remarkably close in each case.

Having found support for previous estimates of the nonprofit-wage differential in several detailed occupations/industries, I now turn to an investigation of wage differentials across all detailed industries. To do so, I estimate a modified version of equation 12 separately for three-digit industries in which both the nonprofit and for-profit sectors are represented.[18] The distribution of differentials estimated for 91 three-digit industries is shown in figure 1.[19] Statistically significant nonzero differ-

[18] These are estimated for industries in which there are at least 50 observations in each sector and in which at least 1% of total employment is nonprofit. To create a more parsimonious specification, education is represented as a continuous variable representing years of education only, and MSA/PMSA location identifiers are replaced by dummy variables for states and an urban/rural dummy variable identifier. Industry controls are eliminated.

[19] The employment-weighted average of these estimated differentials is −.038.

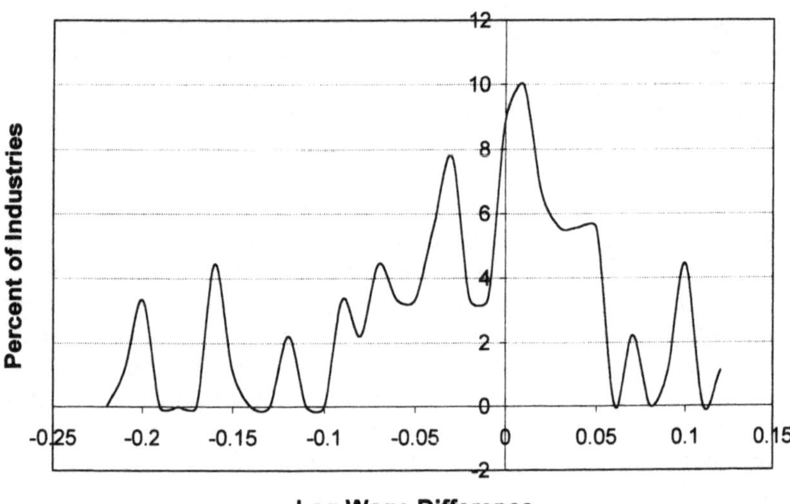


FIG. 1.—Distribution of nonprofit-wage differentials estimated by industry (91 industries with > 50 observations and > 1% of employment in each sector). Author's calculations from 1990 U.S. census data (Five-Percent Public Use Microdata Sample).

entials were estimated for 34 industries.[20] These nonzero log wage differentials, sorted by percent nonprofit, are shown in table 6 and range from −.213 to .095. The economic importance of these results varies, however. Among these 34 industries, only 17 have a nonprofit employment density of 5% or more. Among these 17, about half of the nonprofit/for-profit differentials are positive and about half are negative; about half exceed 5% in absolute value, while half fall between 1% and

The economy-wide differential estimated from the comparable equation run on individuals only in these 91 industries is .003 ($n$ = 3,737,304, $t$ = 1.85). The difference in results is attributable to the fact that in the separate industry equations, returns to all variables vary by industry, whereas in the economy-wide equation, differences between industries are restricted to intercept differences only.

[20] The sample size for the industry equations estimated here range from 1,725 (vocational schools) to 299,911 (construction). As noted by Leamer (1978), rising sample sizes lead to ever-smaller standard errors. Thus, the larger the sample size, the higher the threshold should be set for determining statistical significance. By leaving the threshold here at the .05 level, I cast the broadest net for industries with nonzero estimated differentials. Industries with significant nonprofit employment for which statistically insignificant differentials were estimated include offices and clinics of health practitioners, vocational schools, residential care facilities with nursing, libraries, museums, art galleries and zoos, and social services, not elsewhere classified.

**Table 6**
**Nonprofit Log Wage Differentials Estimated by Industry**

| Industry | Estimated Nonprofit Log Wage Differential | *t*-statistic | Adjusted $R^2$ | Total Observations | % Nonprofit |
|---|---|---|---|---|---|
| Logging | −.213 | −2.69 | .165 | 7,724 | .012 |
| Wholesale trade: apparel, fabrics, and notions | −.207 | −2.37 | .356 | 5,984 | .011 |
| Retail trade: miscellaneous | −.203 | −9.59 | .176 | 21,000 | .072 |
| Manufacturing: miscellaneous wood products | −.202 | −2.55 | .257 | 6,950 | .010 |
| Telephone communications | −.169 | −9.27 | .328 | 51,523 | .015 |
| Manufacturing, not elsewhere classified | −.163 | −5.71 | .317 | 33,123 | .016 |
| Legal services | −.163 | −7.60 | .298 | 43,628 | .025 |
| Radio and television broadcasting | −.162 | −7.24 | .312 | 16,531 | .050 |
| Wholesale trade: scrap and waste materials | −.151 | −2.23 | .228 | 5,893 | .018 |
| Manufacturing: newspaper publishing and printing | −.125 | −3.45 | .301 | 21,412 | .014 |
| Manufacturing: printing and publishing, except new | −.093 | −6.05 | .277 | 60,888 | .026 |
| Job training and vocational rehabilitation | −.093 | −3.17 | .292 | 2,422 | .653 |
| Manufacturing: miscellaneous | −.092 | −2.02 | .306 | 15,968 | .012 |
| Personnel supply services | −.082 | −3.27 | .236 | 20,400 | .043 |
| Utilities, n.e.c. | −.079 | −2.45 | .348 | 3,691 | .063 |
| Landscape and horticultural services | −.078 | −2.31 | .133 | 22,253 | .021 |
| Construction | −.072 | −6.22 | .226 | 299,947 | .011 |
| Theaters and motion pictures | −.064 | −2.82 | .217 | 14,910 | .128 |
| Electric light and power | −.055 | −4.80 | .322 | 27,393 | .071 |
| Real estate, including real estate finance | −.051 | −3.42 | .181 | 73,421 | .041 |
| Manufacturing: apparel and accessories | −.047 | −1.90 | .305 | 49,949 | .011 |
| Research, development, and testing | −.037 | −3.40 | .377 | 17,474 | .203 |
| Miscellaneous entertainment and recreation services | −.031 | −2.50 | .168 | 31,774 | .129 |
| Elementary and secondary schools | −.023 | −4.52 | .236 | 72,433 | .634 |
| Savings institutions, including credit unions | −.022 | −2.07 | .401 | 11,697 | .213 |
| Nursing and personal care facilities | .022 | 3.50 | .282 | 60,120 | .194 |
| Banking | .028 | 2.44 | .445 | 90,222 | .020 |
| Colleges and universities | .048 | 6.99 | .337 | 35,436 | .627 |
| Insurance | .049 | 6.29 | .330 | 101,616 | .057 |
| Hospitals | .049 | 18.87 | .370 | 171,612 | .437 |
| Day-care services | .065 | 6.54 | .148 | 21,505 | .354 |
| Laundry, cleaning, and garment services | .086 | 1.99 | .178 | 18,209 | .012 |
| Bus service and urban transit | .095 | 4.49 | .156 | 12,279 | .083 |
| Educational services, n.e.c. | .119 | 4.28 | .112 | 4,988 | .385 |

NOTE.—Industries with 50 or more employees and over 1% employment in each sector. Estimated differentials are significant at the .05 or higher.

5% in absolute value. Interestingly, the majority of industries with the largest nonprofit concentrations (over 10%) fall into the latter group.[21]

## Hypothesis Testing

This variation in the nonprofit-wage differential across industry (and comparable estimates across occupations) allows for some tests of the donative-labor hypothesis. The interpretation and validity of these tests is limited, however. For each industry, the estimated differential is an estimate of $(kt_1 + qb + qdv_1 + qew_1 + qfx_1 + qgy_1)$ from equation (9), where $t_1$, $v_1$, $w_1$, $x_1$, and $y_1$ are industry-specific nonprofit/for-profit differences in the intrinsic value of work, organizational efficiency, firm size, unionization levels, and gift-exchange conditions, respectively. Variants of the donative-labor hypothesis pertain only to the first term, $kt_1$. Thus, finding evidence in support of the hypothesis requires not only that $kt_1$ be negative when appropriate but also that it not be cancelled by other possible positive terms in the equation. Alternatively, other negative terms in the equation could lend unearned support to the hypothesis. Thus, the findings here must be interpreted with caution.

Preston (1989) has argued that the donative-labor hypothesis has two testable implications: First, because homogeneity of organizational purpose might be greater *within* detailed industry categories than *across* broader aggregations, one would expect smaller nonprofit-wage differentials at the detailed industry level. Second, Preston hypothesized that one might expect workers with more control over and contact with public good production to donate more labor. Thus, controlling for industry, one would expect the nonprofit-wage differential estimated by occupation to be more negative in white-collar occupations (and occupations with traits such as responsibility and control) than in blue-collar occupations. In addition, I propose that public-good-intensive organizations might be expected to receive both more public support of their operations as well as more labor donations. Thus, one might expect share of revenue from public sources (donations and government grants) to be related to donations of labor.

The estimates made here do not conform to the first of these implications. The magnitude of industry-specific nonprofit differentials tends to increase, not decrease, as industries are disaggregated.[22] Of course, as will be apparent in some examples discussed below, one can argue that the

[21] Comparable estimates are made for each three-digit occupation as well. Statistically significant coefficients range from −0.43 to 0.50. A table of these estimates is available from the author.

[22] This is also true for estimates derived from intermediate levels of industry aggregation (one- and two-digit levels), which are not shown here.

industry classifications used here are still insufficiently detailed to allow for an appropriate test of this implication.

As shown in table 4, the pattern of nonprofit-wage differentials is not entirely consistent with Preston's second conjecture either. Wage differentials are not consistently negative for white-collar workers, nor are they consistently more negative for white-collar workers as compared with blue-collar workers. A second approach to testing Preston's second conjecture is to estimate nonprofit-wage differentials by detailed occupation and to relate these differentials to occupational characteristics.[23] Occupational characteristics are derived by England and Kilbourne (1988) from the *Dictionary of Occupational Titles,* fourth edition (U.S. Department of Labor 1977).[24] Indicators were chosen to reflect occupational characteristics associated with decision-making, autonomy and responsibility. The variable GED (General Educational Development) measures amount of formal education required, PEOPLE measures the level of complexity at which workers in an occupation must deal with people, and SJC measures adaptability to making generalizations, evaluations, or decisions based on sensory or judgmental criteria. In addition, blue-collar characteristics of a job are captured by SVP (Specific Vocational Preparation), which measures the amount of on-the-job training required, and OUT, indicating whether a job is performed outdoors. Finally, the variable PEOPREF measures the percent of workers in an occupation whose (detailed) job category requires a preference for "working for the presumed good of people." If workers donate labor to the production of public goods, one would expect occupations with high values of PEOPREF to be associated with more donated labor. Similarly, if workers who have more contact with the final production of services or those with more decision-making responsibility are more likely to donate labor, then one might expect the variables PEOPLE and SJC to also be negatively associated with the nonprofit-wage differential in an occupation.

The estimated coefficients are not shown here but are available from the

[23] Amemiya (1978) and Hsiao (1986, p. 151) provide justification for this type of two-stage methodology. Estimates of nonprofit wage differentials are derived for each three-digit occupational classification in the same fashion as industry differentials were derived above.

[24] These variables are available in Inter-University Consortium for Political and Social Research (ICPSR) dataset 8942. They are constructed by England and Kilbourne from *Dictionary of Occupational Titles* (1977; DOT) job-characteristics data as follows: dichotomous scores indicate whether a particular detailed DOT job category has a certain characteristic. England and Kilbourne use a special sample from the 1970 census coded with both 1970 and 1980 census occupation codes to construct employment-weighted averages of these scores for the 1980 census occupation codes. I convert 1980 census occupation codes to 1990 census occupation codes for use here.

author. All statistically significant coefficients have the opposite sign of what one would expect under the donative-labor hypothesis. Those occupations that require more dedication to working for the presumed good of people, more complex dealings with people, or more judgment making are associated with more positive nonprofit-wage differentials. Those who work outdoors have more negative nonprofit-wage differentials. The coefficients on GED and SVP have the expected signs (negative and positive, respectively) but are not statistically significant.[25]

A final approach to testing Preston's second conjecture is to look at the relationship between educational level and labor donation. Within a given occupation and industry combination, if more highly educated employees are more likely to experience control over and contact with the public good nature of nonprofit production, then one would expect nonprofit-wage differentials to be more negative for the highly educated and less negative (or perhaps zero) otherwise. This variation by education level within job may particularly help capture some of the nuances of occupational definition that are missed in the three-digit occupational classification scheme. In a modified version of equation (12), I estimate separate nonprofit-wage differentials for each of the 17 levels of educational attainment. These results are shown in table 7 and differ for white- and blue-collar workers. Among white-collar workers, statistically significant differentials are positive among those with education at the associates-degree level or below and negative for those with bachelors, masters, and professional degrees. The negative differential is particularly large for the professional degree group (−.113). The pattern is somewhat opposite among blue-collar workers, with negative and significant differentials only for those with education at the high-school-graduation or some-college (no degree) level and rising positive differentials among those with higher levels of education. These results are consistent with the donative-labor hypothesis if it is interpreted as applying only to white-collar workers.

The third implication put forth above is also tested here: under the donative-labor hypothesis, one might expect organizations with a high share of revenue from public sources (donations and government grants) to also receive the most donated labor and thus to have the most negative nonprofit-wage differentials. Data on sources of revenue for nonprofit organizations is obtained from the U.S. IRS Form 990. The Form 990

[25] The results discussed here are weighted by the number of nonprofit employees in an occupation. However, eliminating weights or weighting by the total number of employees in an occupation does not alter the findings. Results including additional controls for the race and gender composition of occupations and median occupational income (with the idea that labor donations might be related to ability to donate) are not shown here, but they do not alter the findings.

**Table 7**
**Nonprofit Wage Differentials by Education Level**

| Education Level | All Workers | White-Collar Workers | Blue-Collar Workers |
|---|---|---|---|
| No school | .056** | .085* | .049* |
| Nursery school | .307* | .641* | .190 |
| Kindergarten | .073 | .037 | .036 |
| Grades 1–4 | .037 | .182** | .015 |
| Grades 5–8 | .037*** | .101** | .012 |
| Grade 9 | .011 | .004 | .010 |
| Grade 10 | .029** | .054** | .018 |
| Grade 11 | .003 | .005 | .006 |
| Grade 12, no diploma | .003 | .033** | −.014 |
| High school graduate or GED | −.001 | .016** | −.017*** |
| Some college, no degree | −.006* | .005 | −.018** |
| Associate's degree, occupational program | .047*** | .054** | .058*** |
| Associate's degree, academic program | .028*** | .032** | .035* |
| Bachelor's degree | −.013*** | −.014** | .004 |
| Master's degree | −.001 | −.011** | .071** |
| Professional degree | −.093*** | −.113** | .188*** |
| Doctorate | .026** | .004 | .287*** |

SOURCE.—Data from the Public Use Microdata Sample (PUMS), 1990.
NOTE.—Data include private-sector workers, no student or disabled workers.
* Significant at .05 level.
** Significant at .01 level.
*** Significant at .001 level.

sample provides data on revenue sources and NTEE (National Taxonomy of Exempt Entities) industry codes for a stratified sample of 12,448 nonprofit organizations for 1988 (see Segal and Weisbrod 1998). The NTEE codes are mapped into Standard Industry Codes (following Smith 1992) and then to census industry codes. The share of revenue from each source for each census industry category is calculated and matched with the nonprofit-wage differentials estimated separately for each industry from the 1990 census data.[26] Because the IRS data on nonprofit organizations represents relatively few industries, the final sample is limited to 35 detailed census industry categories accounting for 88.8% of total nonprofit employment. The nonprofit-wage differentials for these industries are regressed on revenue share information; the results are available from the author. They provide little additional support for the donative-labor hypothesis. Neither of the coefficients on donations or government support are statistically significant, although the coefficient on private donations is negative.

[26] The results shown are for an equation estimated with industry nonprofit employment as the weight. However, results from the unweighted equation or weighted by industry total employment are largely unchanged.

## Discussion

The simple tests conducted here only support the donative-labor hypothesis along one dimension—with respect to differentials by education level for white-collar workers. However, these tests take this one explanation for nonprofit-wage differentials in isolation. The lack of broader support for this hypothesis may point, not toward its complete rejection, but to the possibility that it is only one of several forces leading to wage differences between the nonprofit and for-profit sector. These forces may combine with varying degrees and intensities across industries, a possibility that is not captured in the empirical work here.

Observations of negative differentials in legal services, broadcasting, publishing, theaters and movies, entertainment, elementary and secondary schools, job training and vocational rehabilitation, and research development and testing, are cases where variants of the donative-labor hypothesis could be a dominant factor in determining the nonprofit-wage differential. The products produced by nonprofit lawyers generally have a distinct public good or redistributive aspect lacking in those produced by for-profit lawyers. Similarly, nonprofit organizations in broadcasting, publishing, theatres and movies, entertainment, and research development and testing, typically operate for different purposes than, and produce different products from, their for-profit counterparts. This is also the case with nonprofit job training and vocational rehabilitation centers, and nonprofit schools, which serve a different clientele than their for-profit counterparts. In these nonprofit organizations, individuals may accept lower wages in return for work in which they find more intrinsic value á la Frank, Preston, or Rose-Ackerman. The wage differential need not be related to the nonprofit form of organization per se, only to the product produced and, in many cases, the public good content of the product produced. Thus, the nonprofit-wage differentials estimated for these industries may spring more from the lack of refinement in our industry classification scheme than from anything else.

In a second set of industries, differences between nonprofits and for-profits may have more to do with differences in product quality than differences in the product itself. According to Hansmann (1980), nonprofits in the area of social, medical, and educational services fall into the class of nonprofits formed due to information problems. Quality of service here is difficult to observe, as is quality of performance of individual employees. The nonprofit form of organization may be both a solution to these problems and a signal to the consumer of such a solution.

While Hansmann suggests that such conditions might lead to lower pay for nonprofit managers (interested more in quality of service than in profits), there are other possible outcomes. Efficiency wages could be used to elicit higher quality output in the nonprofit sector. Alternately, employees who are "higher quality" along unobserved dimensions may be hired to produce higher-quality output. These latter explanations are consistent with the higher pay that we observe among nonprofit providers of hospitals, nursing and personal care facilities, day-care centers, colleges and universities, and other educational services.

In other industries, a difference in product or quality of product is less obvious. Employment at nonprofit electric light and power utilities, telephone companies, and urban transit providers reflects the historical fact of rural electric and telephone cooperatives, urban bus cooperatives, and the like.[27] Similarly, the nonprofit form of organization in the insurance industry is an historical legal anomaly. The products produced here by nonprofits and for-profits are most likely indistinguishable. Instead, the nonprofit form was a historical response to market failure or legal requirements. In these cases, nonprofit-wage differentials may proxy for differences in market or work conditions (including firm size or location) that are incidental to their nonprofit status. In other industries, nonprofit organizations may be dominated by worker or consumer cooperatives. For example, this may be the case in wood-product manufacturing and scrap- and waste-material wholesalers, among others. The nonprofit-wage differences here may reflect the different working conditions inherent in these firms with their different ownership and control structures.

## V. Considerations

### Model Specification

Could the industry nonprofit-wage differentials observed here be an empirical anomaly resulting from model specification? Two types of possible misspecification come to mind. In the first case, if one or more demographic groups receive differential returns and that group (or groups) has an above- or below-average concentration of employment in the nonprofit sector, a lack of proper controls will lead to a bias in the measured returns to nonprofit employment. This type of misspecification should not influence the results here, however. In all equations estimated here, multiple interaction terms are included for race and gender with other key explanatory variables (education, experience, part-time status, and language fluency). Thus, any differences in returns to demographic groups should be captured in these interaction terms and not gain expression through the nonprofit variable.

Alternately, misspecification could take a second form. If returns to

[27] While Hansmann (1980, p. 835) makes clear the legal distinction between cooperatives and nonprofits, employees of cooperatives are included among nonprofit employees in the census data used here.

one or more independent variables vary between nonprofit and for-profit organizations and the means of these independent variables also vary by industry, this will generate a range of nonprofit-wage differentials by industry that are related to the differences in the industry means of these variables. To investigate this possibility, I estimate wage equations separately for each of 91 industries with sufficient nonprofit and for-profit observations; returns to key independent variables are allowed to vary by nonprofit status. This equation is specified as

$$\ln W = a + b\mathbf{X} + c\mathbf{Y} + d\text{Nonprof} + e\text{Nonprof} \times \mathbf{Y}. \tag{13}$$

The variables included in the vector **Y** are gender, race, gender/race interactions, potential experience (and potential experience squared), and education. The remainder of the variables included in the vector **Z** in equation (12) are included here as the vector **X**.[28] In this specification, the industry nonprofit differentials, no longer limited to being intercept terms, depend on the level of **Y** at which they are measured. Using overall means from the whole sample of individuals (in 91 industries), a nonprofit/for-profit–wage differential for each industry can be calculated:

$$\text{NPFP}_i^O = \hat{d}_i + \hat{e}_i\bar{Y}^O, \tag{14a}$$

where the subscript $i = 1, \ldots, 91$ indicates industry, $\hat{d}$ and $\hat{e}$ are OLS estimates of coefficients specified in equation (13), and $\bar{Y}^O$ represents the variable means for the overall sample. Alternately, the calculation can be based on the industry level means ($\bar{Y}_i$), resulting in

$$\text{NPFP}_i^I = \hat{d}_i + \hat{e}_i\bar{Y}_i. \tag{14b}$$

If industry variation in means were responsible for industry variation in nonprofit wage differentials, then one would expect the variance of the nonprofit-wage differentials across industries to be lower when they are calculated as $\text{NPFP}_i^O$ than when they are calculated as $\text{NPFP}_i^I$. This is not the case, however. The means and variances of the two sets of calculations are virtually the same, with the variance of $\text{NPFP}^O$ slightly greater than that of $\text{NPFP}^I$, implying that the industry differences are not simply a result of differences in industry means of explanatory variables.[29]

[28] With modifications as noted in n. 18 above.

[29] I do not calculate a Oaxaca (1973) decomposition here as that provides an explanation of the sources of nonprofit/for-profit–wage differences within an industry, while here we are interested in the source of variation in nonprofit/for-profit differences between industries.

## Misclassification Error

Another possible source of error in the work here is the self-reported nature of nonprofit status. In self-reported data such as the PUMS, the extent to which people correctly answer regarding the nonprofit status of their employer is subject to question. The trade association representing nonprofit organizations, Independent Sector, has argued that the 1990 census severely undercounted nonprofit employees as a result of misreporting (Hodgkinson et al., n.d.). They report, from an analysis of independent data sources, that the nonprofit sector's share of the labor force is closer to 10.8% than to the 8.9% they estimate from the PUMS.[30] If Hodgkinson et al. were correct, and nonprofit status were commonly misreported, the wage differences estimated here from the PUMS would be biased.[31]

The evidence here, however, suggests that misreporting may not be so serious. In the comparisons above of lawyers, nursing homes, and day-care centers, the PUMS closely replicated estimates made from more detailed industry surveys, which did not rely on self-reporting of nonprofit status. Preston (1989, 1990) has found comparable results with data that is and is not self-reported. Nevertheless, to allow for the possibility that such a bias could exist, I investigate the algebraic relationship between the actual and estimated shares of for-profit and nonprofit employees in the economy based on the assumption that Hodgkinson et al. are correct. If the reporting error for nonprofit employees were as high as 75%, the estimated nonprofit differential would be about one-fifth the magnitude of the true differential. However, given the small size of the estimated economy-wide differential of −.0005, the actual differential is probably still not much more than −.00265. While larger than the estimated figure, this is still very close to zero.[32]

## Endogeneity

Another consideration is that of the endogeneity of nonprofit status, to either other organizational characteristics or to industry itself. Nonprofit

[30] The difference between the 8.9% that they estimate from the PUMS and the 8.5% estimated in this article is attributable to differences in sample selection.

[31] Aigner (1973) shows that to the extent that observations are misclassified, the magnitude of observed differences between them in measured variables will be dampened. This is because the *observed* values for each group will *actually* be drawn from *both* groups of observations. This effect is particularly strong when one group is very small relative to the other and the observations from the smaller group are easily swamped by a small number of misclassifications from the larger group.

[32] The full details of this derivation are discussed in an appendix available from the author.

status or conversion from one status to another may not be independent of other firm characteristics. In turn, wage levels may also be determined by these same characteristics. If these were not controlled for, then any observed relationship between nonprofit status and wages would simply be a reflection of underlying correlations between wages and organizational characteristics. This does not seem to be the case here at the economy-wide level (since the coefficient on nonprofit status is close to zero). However, if the strength and direction of such effects varied significantly by industry, this could account for the patterns observed here within particular industries.

Alternately, one might think of industry and nonprofit status as being jointly determined by the nature of the product produced. If wages are in turn a function of both industry and nonprofit status, this would introduce multicollinearity on the right-hand side of the equation (leading to increased variance of the estimated coefficients, but leaving the estimates themselves unbiased). This does not appear to be the case, however. The standard error of the estimated nonprofit coefficient rises only somewhat as industry controls are added to equation (12), from 0.0013 to 0.0015. This increase does not account for the loss of statistical significance of the estimate, which drops by an order of magnitude when industry controls are introduced. Of course, this issue would not effect the estimates made at the detailed industry level.

Finally, there is a more profound question that relates to the endogeneity of industry, nonprofit status, *and* wages. If all three are jointly determined by the nature of the product produced (or something else) then the underlying model and issues are quite different from those presented here. Ideas along these lines have not been fully developed in the literature, but could be important. If this were the case, the coefficients estimated here on nonprofit and industry controls would be subject to both the issues of spurious correlation and multicollinearity discussed above. More important, if this were the case, a very different underlying model of wage determination in the nonprofit sector would be needed to truly elucidate theoretical and empirical understanding of the wages structure.

## VI. Summary

Estimates of nonprofit/for-profit–wage differences made here from 1990 census data expand on the previous work of Preston (1988, 1989), Borjas et al. (1983), and Weisbrod (1983). After including detailed controls, there does not appear to be a single economy-wide nonprofit-wage effect, even after allowing for considerable misclassification error in the nonprofit indicator itself. This finding is robust to concerns of multicollinearity and equation specification. There do appear to be significant differences between nonprofit and for-profit wages within particular occupations and industries, however. In particular, the findings here are consistent with previous work done at the detailed industry level but are not consistent with the *economy-wide* application of the donative-labor hypothesis or with any one hypothesis that implies a uniformly positive or negative nonprofit-wage differential. Instead, the patterns found here are indicative of the differential application of a variety of forces across industries. Hansmann (1983), Preston (1989), and others provide a number of competing suggestions for the determination of nonprofit wages in a way that is consistent with the findings here.

While the simple tests employed here lend only some evidence to the donative-labor hypothesis posed in isolation, future research should focus on more sophisticated specifications that allow for testing of multiple hypotheses at the same time. Doing so would require more detailed data on product characteristics, firm characteristics and working conditions by both industry and sector. This might include more information on firm size and productivity, unionization rates, and personnel policies, as well as indicators of the public good content and redistributive nature of products produced. Furthermore, additional careful and detailed industry studies, following the lead of Weisbrod (1983), Borjas et al. (1983), and others, may provide additional insight as to the sources of these observed wage differences at the detailed industry level.

## References

Aigner, Dennis J. "Regression with a Binary Independent Variable Subject to Errors of Observation." *Journal of Econometrics* 1, no. 1 (March 1973): 49–59.

Akerlof, George A. "Gift Exchange and Efficiency-Wage Theory: Four Views." *American Economic Review* 74 (May 1984): 79–83.

Amemiya, Takeshi. "A Note on a Random Coefficients Model." *International Economic Review* 19 (October 1978): 293–96.

Borjas, George J.; Frech, H. E., III; and Ginsburg, Paul B. "Property Rights and Wages: The Case of Nursing Homes." *Journal of Human Resources* 18 (Spring 1983): 231–46.

Brown, Charles, and Medoff, James. "The Employer Size Wage Effect." *Journal of Political Economy* 97 (October 1989): 1027–59.

England, Paula, and Kilbourne, Barbara. *Occupational Measures from the Dictionary of Occupational Titles for 1980 Census Detailed Occupations.* Data set 8942. Ann Arbor, MI: Inter-University Consortium on Political and Social Research, 1988.

Feldstein, Martin S. *The Rising Cost of Hospital Care.* Washington, DC: Information Resources Press, 1971.

Frank, Robert H. "What Price the High Moral Ground?" *Southern Economic Journal* 63 (July 1996): 1–17.

Halverson, Robert, and Palmquist, Raymond. "The Interpretation of Dummy Variables in Semilogarithmic Equations." *American Economic Review* 70 (June 1980): 474–75.

Hansmann, Henry B. "The Role of Nonprofit Enterprise." *Yale Law Journal* 89 (April 1980): 835–901.

Hodgkinson, Virginia A.; Weitzman, Murray S.; Noga, Steve M.; and Gorski, Heather A. *National Summary: Not-For-Profit Employment from the 1990 Census of Population and Housing.* Washington, DC: Independent Sector, n.d.

Hsiao, Cheng. *Analysis of Panel Data.* Cambridge: Cambridge University Press, 1986.

Ito, Takatoshi, and Domain, Dale. "A Musical Note on the Efficiency Wage Hypothesis—Programmings, Wages and Budgets of American Symphony Orchestras." *Economics Letters* 25 (1987): 95–99.

James, Estelle, and Rose-Ackerman, Susan. *The Nonprofit Enterprise in Market Economics.* New York: Harwood Academic, 1986.

Johnston, Dennis, and Rudney, Gabriel. "Characteristics of Workers in Nonprofit Organizations." *Monthly Labor Review* 110 (July 1987): 28–33.

Kennedy, Peter E. "Estimation with Correctly Interpreted Dummy Variables in Semilogarithmic Equations." *American Economic Review* 71, no. 4 (September 1981): 801.

Leamer, Edward. *Specification Searches: Ad Hoc Inference with Nonexperimental Data.* New York: Wiley, 1978.

Leete, Laura. "Assessing Wages and the Problem of Turnover in Nonprofit Child Welfare Agencies." Research report. Cleveland: Case Western Reserve University, Mandel Center for Nonprofit Organizations, October 1993.

Mirvis, Philip H., and Hackett, Edward J. "Work and Work Force Characteristics in the Nonprofit Sector." *Monthly Labor Review* 106 (April 1983): 3–12.

Oaxaca, Ronald. "Male-Female Wage Differentials in Urban Labor Markets." *International Economic Review* 14 (October 1973): 693–709.

Preston, Anne E. "The Effects of Property Rights on Labor Costs of Nonprofit Firms: An Application to the Day Care Industry." *Journal of Industrial Economics* 36 (March 1988): 337–50.

———. "The Nonprofit Worker in a For-Profit World." *Journal of Labor Economics* 7 (October 1989): 438–63.

———. "Women in the White-Collar Nonprofit Sector: The Best Option or the Only Option?" *Review of Economics and Statistics* 72 (November 1990): 560–68.

Rose-Ackerman, Susan. "Altruism, Nonprofits, and Economic Theory." *Journal of Economic Literature* 34 (June 1996): 701–28.

Rudney, Gabriel, and Weitzman, Murray. "Trends in Employment and Earnings in the Philanthropic Sector." *Monthly Labor Review* 107 (September 1984): 16–20.

Salamon, Lester M. *America's Nonprofit Sector: A Primer.* New York: Foundation Center, 1992.

Salamon, Lester M., and Anheier, Helmut K. *The Emerging Nonprofit Sector: An Overview.* New York: St. Martin's, 1996.

Segal, Lewis M., and Weisbrod, Burton A. "Interdependence of Commercial and Donative Revenues." In *To Profit or Not to Profit: the Commercial Transformation of the Nonprofit Sector*, edited by Burton A. Weisbrod, pp. 105–27. New York: Cambridge University Press, 1998.

Shackett, Joyce R., and Trapani, John M. "Earnings Differentials and Market Structure." *Journal of Human Resources* 22 (Fall 1987): 518–31.

Smith, Bradford. "The Use of Standard Industrial Classification Codes to Classify the Activities of Nonprofit, Tax-Exempt Organizations." Working Paper no. 19. San Francisco: University of San Francisco, Institute for Nonprofit Organization Management, November 1992.

U.S. Department of Labor, *Dictionary of Occupational Titles*, 4th ed. Washington, DC: U.S. Government Printing Office, 1977.

Weisbrod, Burton A. "Nonprofit and Proprietary Sector Behavior: Wage Differentials among Lawyers." *Journal of Labor Economics* 1 (July 1983): 246–63.

Yellen, Janet L. "Efficiency Wage Models of Unemployment." *American Economic Review* 74 (May 1984): 200–5.

Young, Dennis R., and Steinberg, Richard. *Economics for Nonprofit Managers.* New York: Foundation Center, 1995.

# Part VII
# Public Policy

# [26]

# COMPETITION BETWEEN FOR-PROFIT AND NONPROFIT ORGANIZATIONS IN COMMERCIAL MARKETS*

by

Jerald SCHIFF

*Fiscal Affairs Department*

*International Monetary Fund*

and

Burton WEISBROD

*Center for Urban Affairs and Policy Research*

*Northwestern University*

## Introduction

Competition between nonprofit and for-profit firms, while not a new phenomenon, has become the focus of increased interest in recent years. Nonprofit organizations (NPOs), faced with declining support from government and unable to increase private giving significantly, appear to have increasingly turned to commercial activities[1] traditionally performed by for-profit firms. This growing inter-sectoral competition has, however, been subject to relatively little economic analysis. Those economists that have examined the competition be-

---

* This paper was completed prior to the time that Schiff joined the Fund, and the opinions expressed do not necessarily reflect those of the IMF.

1 By "commercial" we mean output that is sold directly to consumers, as opposed to being financed, at least in part, by donations, and that provides no significant external benefits.

tween nonprofit and for-profit firms have focused primarily on the issue of whether the various tax and other advantages received by nonprofits[2] provide them with unfair advantages[3]. Congressional hearings (House Ways and Means Committee, June-July 1987) have also provided a forum for debate over this issue of "unfair competition".

In this paper, we examine an NPOs decision of whether or not to undertake commercial activities in competition with for-profit firms, and show how government tax and spending policies will influence this decision. We specifically consider the impact and desirability of current tax advantages offered to NPOs engaged in commercial activities, and conclude that inefficiencies introduced by the preferential treatment of nonprofits engaged in commercial activities may be more important than any inequities brought about by such treatment. These inefficiencies are of two types: (1) commercial activities which do not generate external benefits are subsidized, and (2) subsidies to the activities of NPOs that do provide external benefits are based on the ability of organizations to generate commercial profits, and so cross-subsidize their primary nonprofit activities, rather than on external benefits generated by the nonprofit activities.

The model, based on James (1983), hypothesizes that nonprofit managers receive disutility from commercial activities, but may nevertheless engage in them in order to cross-subsidize their preferred nonprofit activities. Approaching the behavior of the NPO in this way sheds light on several issues not addressed by more standard models. For instance, we predict that cutbacks in government support for a nonprofit organization would cause the NPO to pursue commercial profits more vigorously, and present evidence to support this view. On the other hand, the typical model, which does not allow for the NPOs distaste for commercial activities, would predict that nonprofits would always attempt to maximize profits from commercial activities, regardless of the level of support received from government. In addi-

2 Nonprofit organizations in the United States do not pay corporate income tax unless income is generated by an activity that is unrelated to the organization's tax-exempt purpose (see text for discussion). In addition, nonprofits are generally exempt from state and local property taxes as well as some sales taxes. They also receive various other advantages, such as lower postal rates.

3 For exceptions, see Hansmann (1981, 1989), Rose-Ackerman (1982) and Steinberg (1988).

tion, we provide a plausible explanation for the coexistence of NPOs and for-profit enterprises in the same industry; previous analyses have either ignored this issue, or presented explanations with a "knife-edge" quality.

We present our model of the behavior of an NPO in Section 1, and extend it to consider long-run equilibrium in a nonprofit industry. In Section 2, we present econometric evidence in support of the model. Following that, in Section 3, we examine competition between nonprofit and for-profit firms, and consider the impact and desirability of preferential tax treatment of NPOs. We close with a discussion of policy implications in Section 4.

## 1 A Model of The Nonprofit Firm

There is no consensus among economists regarding the objective function of NPOs. Because the nondistribution constraint[4] legally prohibits a nonprofit firm from distributing profits to its owners, the firm is generally not modelled as a profit-maximizer. Among the hypothesized maximands in the literature are disguised profits (discretionary spending), output quantity and quality and various inputs, such as staff size[5]. The objective function we employ, to be described below, allows us to focus specifically on a nonprofit organization's choice between producing the output for which it received its tax-exempt status – which we refer to as its "nonprofit" output – and a "commercial" output[6].

Assume that an NPO – which we identify with its "manager" – has a well-defined objective function defined over its various activities. In this model, the firm can produce either nonprofit or commer-

4 See Hansmann (1981) for a discussion of the non-distribution constraint.

5 For instance, Mique and Belanger (1974) model nonprofit bureaus as maximizers of an objective function defined over discretionary spending and output. Newhouse (1970) hypothesizes a nonprofit hospital that maximizes a combination of output quality and quantity. Williamson (1964) views nonprofits as maximizers of staff size.

6 The output referred to as "commercial" may be legally tax-exempt. We use the terminology to distinguish between the activity for which the NPO received tax-exempt status and other, perhaps related, activities. For instance, a university bookstore might be legally exempt, but for the purposes of this model, it would be considered commercial.

cial output. Commercial output is sold at an exogenous market price, $p$, while nonprofit output is financed by donations, and perhaps by profits from commercial activity. In addition to producing output, NPOs can spend some of their resources soliciting for donations. We assume that the nonprofit manager receives positive utility from producing the nonprofit output, but negative utility from engaging in commercial activity. This is consistent with the claim of nonprofit organizations that the output for which they receive tax-exempt status provides their *raison d'être* and that they view their commercial activities as, at best, necessary evils.

The objective function is maximized subject to the constraint that the firm break even[7]. We write the NPO's maximization problem as:

Maximize $U(z, x)$ subject to

$$D(z, x, S) + px - C(z, x) - S = 0$$

where $z$ is the exempt output and $x$ is a commercial good that the nonprofit may sell at exogenous market price $p$. We assume, as noted, that $Uz > 0$, but $Ux \leq 0$.

Donations, $D$, may come either from private sources – largely individuals, but also foundations and corporations – or from government, e.g. in the form of grants. Donations are assumed to potentially depend on both exempt and commercial output levels as well as solicitation expenditures, $S$. It is assumed that $Dz \geq 0$, $Ds \geq 0$ and $Dx \leq 0$. We might expect donations to fall as the commercial output of a nonprofit organization increases since, in a world of imperfect information, donors may view the fact that an organization engages in commercial activity as a signal that the quality of nonprofit output is low. Concern is sometimes expressed that engaging in commercial activities causes nonprofits to "lose sight of their charitable mission".

The firm's cost function, $C(z, x)$, is specified as a joint cost function in order to allow for economies of scope. For example, universities may be able to produce certain types of research more cheaply than for-profit firms because universities produce the research jointly with graduate instruction.

7 A surplus may be accumulated in any given period, but in the long run all revenue must be spent. Thus, in a single period model, the firm must break even.

## 1.1 Comparative Static Results

Previous analyses of nonprofit competition with for-profit firms have generally assumed that the nonprofits behave as profit-maximizers in the commercial activity. The implications of the model presented here are, however, quite different. First order conditions imply that, because the nonprofit manager receives positive utility from producing the nonprofit output, the firm will produce its nonprofit output beyond the profit-maximizing level, to the point at which $Dz + Uz/\lambda = Cz'$ where $\lambda$ is the marginal utility of income. On the other hand, the organization will take less than full advantage of the profit-making potential of the commercial activity, both because the manager dislikes producing commercial output ($Ux \leq O$) and because donations may be adversely affected by commercial activity ($Dx \leq 0$). The NPO will produce $x$ to the point at which $p + Dx + Ux = Cx$ using profits earned to cross-subsidize exempt activity[8]. So, for instance, if a museum views sales of postcards at its shop as a less preferred commercial activity, it will sell fewer than the profit-maximizing number of cards. However, it may sell some postcards to generate revenues for preferred artistic activities[9].

It can be shown[10] that, in the context of this model,

$\partial z/\partial D > 0$, $\partial x/\partial D \leq 0$, $\partial z/\partial p > 0$, and $\partial x/\partial p$ either > or < 0. This implies, first, that changes in government policies that affect donations to NPOs, either directly or indirectly, will influence the extent of nonprofit competition with for-profit firms. The fall in $D$ acts, in effect, as an inward shift of the nonprofit manager's budget constraint, causing the organization to pursue less favored revenue sources. While the profits earned from increased commercial activities will be used to cross-subsidize nonprofit output, $x$, these profits will not fully offset the decline in $D$. In particular, the reductions in government support of the nonprofit sector in the 1980s would be expected to increase this competition[11].

---

8 The objective function could be expanded to include discretionary spending (i.e. disguised profits); in this case some of the commercial profits would be diverted to such spending.

9 Another example, offered by James (1979), the subsidization by universities, from profits earned from undergraduate education, of research and graduate education.

10 For a derivation of this and following results, see James (1983) or Schiff and Weisbrod (1986).

11 Salamon and Abramson (1985) report, e.g., that excluding Medicare and Medicaid, nonprofits lost \$49.5 billion in federal government support between 1982 and 1985.

The Tax Reform Act of 1986, which reduced subsidies to charitable donors – by reducing marginal tax rates and the number of itemizers, and by eliminating the deduction for charitable contributions by non-itemizers – would be predicted to have had a similar effect[12].

Another implication of this model is that price or cost changes in the commercial market may lead to "perverse" responses by nonprofit firms. A rise in the price of the commercial good (or a fall in the cost of producing the commercial good) may, by allowing greater profit per unit of $x$, induce the nonprofit firm to partly avoid the distasteful activity by cutting back on production of $x$. Profits from sale of $x$ will, however, rise, allowing output of $z$ to rise as well.

The comparative static results also indicate that a nonprofit organization will solicit for donations to the point at which $Ds = 1$; i.e. it will solicit in order to maximize net revenue raised[13]. Exogenous changes in donations may influence solicitation expenditures, as they do commercial activities, although the direction is uncertain. If a reduction in government grants, e.g., increases the marginal productivity of soliciting, *Ds*,' then soliciting will increase with cuts in *D*. However, if *Ds* falls with reductions in *D*, solicitations would fall.

### 1.2 Entry and Exit by Nonprofits

Thus far, we have simply considered the behavior of a single NPO. However, just as the existence of profits in the for-profit sector will induce entry, so should changes that make the nonprofit sector relatively more attractive induce entry into that sector[14].

Ignoring, for now, the possibility of "mixed industries" containing both nonprofit and for-profit firms, we can view entrepreneurs as choosing between entering either the nonprofit or proprietary sector. Suppose that all potential nonprofit entrepreneurs are identical.

12 Tax payments on unrelated business income have increased from $39 million in 1985 to $127.9 million in 1990 (unpublished data, Internal Revenue Service, Statistics of Income). Note, however, that this may reflect, in part, increased compliance rather than simply increased commercial activity.

13 Steinberg (1986) finds that, for three of the five nonprofit industries examined, Ds is not significantly different from 1, as the model predicts. Weisbrod and Dominguez (1986), however, find that NPOs appear to solicit beyond the point at which $Ds=1$.

14 For a more detailed analysis of long-run equilibrium in a nonprofit industry, see Schiff (1988).

They will enter the nonprofit sector if $U(z, x)$ exceeds the reservation utility level available in the for-profit sector, $U^*$, which will depend on the level of profits available[15]. If there is free entry into the nonprofit sector, then, long run equilibrium will occur when $U(z, x) = U^*$. Any change that reduces the ability of nonprofits to produce their exempt output, or increases their reliance on commercial activities – such as a fall in government support or a change in the tax treatment of donations by individuals – will lead to exit from the sector.

## 2 Empirical evidence

### 2.1 Data and Methodology

We turn now to examine econometric evidence regarding the behavior of nonprofit organizations in general and, specifically, the response of NPOs to exogenous shifts in their budget constraints. Utilizing tax returns (IRS Form 990) from the over 11,000 NPOs active in the social services sector[16] for at least one year between 1973 and 1976[17], we estimate equations for two categories of revenue received by these organizations: contributions, gifts and grants (CONTR) and sales and other receipts, such as investment income (SALES). Utilizing the zip code of each organization, we matched each observation with the state in which it is located, allowing us to estimate the impact of changes in various categories of state and local government expenditures on revenues received by NPOs. In addition, a third equation was estimated, in which the observations were the 50 states and the dependent variable was the total number of nonprofit social welfare organizations (ORGS).

15 It is consistent with our description of the NPO objective function to assume that the potential nonprofit entrepreneur would also receive disutility from producing commercial output in the for-profit sector as well. That is, $U^*$ should be a function of $x$ as well. We return to this point when we consider mixed industries, below.

16 We consider the social services sector to include NPOs aiding specifically the poor, handicapped or otherwise needy. The definition does not include, e.g., ordinary hospitals and schools, but would include schools for the blind.

17 All nonprofits were required to file Forms 990 if their revenue exceeded $5,000 for the year.

The government spending variables included in each equation were: cash transfers to individuals (CASH), vendor payments to private agencies for provision of social services (VENDOR), other state welfare spending (WELFARE), and local welfare spending (LOCWELF). In addition, the following explanatory variables were included in the CONTR and SALES equations: age of the organization AGE), solicitation expenditures (SOLEX), tax-deductible status (DEDUCT), mean household income in the state (INCOME), a proxy for the mean price of a contribution in the state (PRICE), state population (POP), percent of population over 65 (POP65) and under 18 years old (POP18), percent below poverty (POOR), and the number of competing social service NPOs in the state (ORGS). In the ORGS equation, the same variables, other than the organization-specific ones, were included.

While the data covers four years, the regression analysis uses values averaged over the four year period. This approach is employed for several reasons; first, because NPOs are not required to file a tax return for a given year by a particular date, returns from two NPOs in the same calendar year can encompass different time periods. In addition, the dependent variables CONTR and SALES take on a value of zero for a significant portion of observations[18]. Thus, Tobit estimation appeared to be a reasonable methodology to employ[19]; given the truncated nature of the data, it would be difficult to utilize the panel data to estimate a fixed-effects model with consistent estimates[20]. The ORGs equation is estimated by ordinary least squares.

Of particular interest here is the impact on NPOs in the social welfare sector of an exogenous shift in their budget constraints[21]. We proxy such a shift by changes in government purchases of social services from nonprofit social welfare agencies, VENDOR. We interpret such revenues as representing payment for the preferred, nonprofit, output and view cuts in such payments as exogenous to any single NPO. We would predict, based on the analysis above, that a cut in VENDOR would reduce social services provided by the nonprofit

18 For the four-year averages, CONTR took on a zero value for 38 percent of the observations, SALES 29 percent.

19 Note that it was impossible to determine how many of the zero values for the dependent variables actually represented missing data. Our methodology implicitly assumes that all zeros were true zeros, rather than missing data.

20 See Heckman and .Macurdy (1980) for a discussion of this issue.

21 For discussion of other results, see Schiff and Weisbrod (1986).

sector, and increase total commercial sales by the sector. In addition, the number of NPOs providing social services should fall, as reduced ability to provide nonprofit output, and increased reliance on commercial activities would make the nonprofit sector a less attractive alternative.

## 2.2 Results

The regression results largely bear out our expectations (see Appendix Table 1 for complete results). We turn first to the SALES equation, to examine the effect of a change in VENDOR on commercial activities. To interpret the results, it is important to recognize that VENDOR is aggregated at the state level, while SALES is at the organization level; i.e. we are estimating the impact of a change in state spending for vendor payments on a given NPO's sales. In addition, the SALES variable includes both sales to government – vendor payments – by a given NPO *and* sales of commercial output. The regression results indicate that VENDOR has only a small, and statistically insignificant, impact on total SALES – including vendor payments and commercial sales – by a typical NPO. This suggests that NPOs compensate for lost preferred revenue by taking more complete advantage of the potential for commercial sales. The coefficient on VENDOR implies that a reduction in vendor payments to social welfare NPOs of 10 percent, or $225 million in one year[22], leads to only a small reduction of approximately $20 million in total sales by the nonprofit sector[23]. Thus, it appears that NPOs increase other sales, a proxy for commercial activity, by approximately $205 million. This result is consistent with the view that commercial activity provides disutility for NPO managers, so that they pursue commercial sales only when more preferred revenue sources dry up.

Our analysis above suggests that following the decline in VENDOR, total output of the preferred nonprofit good should decline, notwithstanding the increased commercial activity. We proxy total nonprofit output by the revenue available to finance such output –

---

22 VENDOR includes payments under the Medicaid program, most of which go to organizations not included in the definition of the social welfare sector used here. An estimated 74 percent of VENDOR went to Medicaid during the period 1973-76; our estimate of the impact of a cut in VENDOR assumes that any reduction in payments would affect Medicaid in the same proportion.

23 This takes into account the indirect effect of VENDOR on SALES through the induced change in the number of organizations, ORGS.

vendor payments and private donations received plus profits from commercial sales, which are available for cross-subsidization. The coefficient on VENDOR in the CONTR equation is positive and significant, and indicates that the 10 percent decline in VENDOR ($225 million) would cause an additional fall in contributions received by the nonprofit sector of some $14 million[24]. Separate data on profits from commercial sales are not available but if even if we assume, for illustrative purposes, that profits are a rather high 20 percent of sales, the increase in cross-subsidy would be only $40 million. Thus, the offset to the $225 million loss in vendor payments is quite small – on the order of 15 percent – even though commercial sales appear to increase quite dramatically[25].

The reduction in financing for preferred nonprofit output and the increased reliance on commercial sales appears, as predicted, to make the sector less desirable for nonprofit entrepreneurs. The coefficient on VENDOR in the ORGS equation is positive and significant, and indicates that the 10 percent cut in VENDOR would reduce the number of social welfare nonprofits by 180, or approximately 2 percent[26]. However, even after the exit takes place, the remaining NPOs appear to be worse off than before the reduction in vendor payments; the regression results indicate that commercial sales increase, while revenues for nonprofit output – vendor payments, private donations and cross-subsidies from commercial profits – fall for the typical NPO. We would have expected exit to continue until the remaining NPOs were as well off as before any exogenous cut in vendor payments.

24 This fall in private donations as a result of the fall in Vendor payments may be due to the fact that government support of a nonprofit is seen by donors as an assurance that the nonprofit is of high quality. For a discussion, see Rose-Ackerman (1981) and Schiff and Weisbrod (1986).

25 It is possible also that the level of solicitation expenditures could also respond to changes in the level of vendor payments; this would affect further the level of resources available for provision of nonprofit output. In separate regression results, not reported here, VENDOR is estimated to have a negative but insignificant effect on solicitation expenditures.

26 Another interpretation of this result is that in states that have large nonprofit sectors, the government is able to rely more heavily on vendor payments.

## 3 Competition Between For-Profit Firms and NPOs

We have hypothesized that NPOs enter commercial industries in order to earn profits to cross-subsidize their nonprofit activity. This model has a number of implications for the efficiency and equity of nonprofit competition with for-profit firms in commercial markets. We turn now to examine more closely this issue of competition across institutional forms.

In order to examine the outcome of competition between for-profit firms and NPOs in commercial markets, we must describe the objectives of the two types of organizations. We have already described the NPO as receiving disutility from producing commercial output, $x$. It is typically assumed, on the other hand, that proprietary firms are profit-maximizers, so that their utility is unaffected by the type of output produced. In order to motivate the assumption that NPOs and for-profit enterprises have different objectives in the commercial market, imagine that there are two types of potential entrepreneurs, in unlimited supplies, one of which gets disutility from producing commercial output, and the other of which does not[27]. We would expect, in this case, that the for-profit sector, which is the locus of most commercial activity, would be dominated in long-run equilibrium by those who receive no disutility from producing $x$, as they would be willing to accept a lower rate of profit than would those with a distaste for commercial activity. That is, we would simply not expect to see nonprofits in commercial markets, and there would be no issue of "unfair competition". This, in fact, is the case in the typical commercial industries.

This analysis must be modified, however, to account for two factors that help to explain the existence of NPOs in commercial markets; first, that nonprofits have various tax advantages relative to proprietary firms and, second, that there may be complementarities in production or consumption between the nonprofit output produced by an NPO and its commercial good.

### 3.1 The Impact of the Tax Subsidy for Nonprofits

We focus here on the nonprofit subsidy in the form of exemption from corporate income tax. This exemption is not unrestricted; any profits from activities that are "unrelated" to the organization's ex-

27 More generally, one could imagine a continuum of potential entrepreneurs, with differing degrees of disutility from commercial activity.

empt purpose are subject to the unrelated business income tax (UBIT), which has a structure similar to the corporate income tax. However, we assume for the purposes of this analysis that the commercial activity of nonprofits receives the same preferential tax treatment as its exempt activity.

This is a close approximation to reality, for several reasons. First, compliance with the unrelated business income tax (UBIT) is believed to be poor[28]. Second, courts have generally given a broad interpretation to the "relatedness test", allowing much commercial activity to receive tax advantages. Third, there are a number of important exceptions to the UBIT, such as activities carried out for the convenience of a nonprofit's members. Finally, even if an activity is unrelated, ambiguities regarding the allocation of costs between exempt and non-exempt activities allow substantial avoidance of tax. In 1990, only 38,861 NPOs, or approximately 4 percent of all NPOs, claimed unrelated business income[29].

What is the impact of the preferential tax treatment of nonprofits engaged in commercial activities? Ignore, for now, the possibility of for-profit firms competing with NPOs in either the nonprofit or commercial markets. Since the corporate tax is generally viewed as either a tax on capital in the corporate sector[30] or a tax on corporate profits[31] we can view the nonprofit exemption from corporate taxation as an implicit subsidy to either nonprofit capital or profits.

Although pure profits taxes (or subsidies) are usually presumed to have no effect on output and prices, this would not be the case in the nonprofit sector. An exemption from a profits tax in the commercial industry would have an effect analogous to that of an increase in the price of the commercial good, discussed above. On the one hand, making commercial activity more profitable would, ignoring its disutility to nonprofit managers, increase such activity. On the other hand, the tax exemption allows nonprofits to produce any given level of nonprofit output at a lower level of production of the distasteful commercial good. The net effect is uncertain. The output of the

28 See Goodspeed and Kenyon (1988).
29 Unpublished data, Internal Revenue Service, Statistics of Income. Note, however, that commercial income earned by for-profit subsidiaries of NPOs are taxable, but would not be recorded as unrelated business income.
30 See, e.g., Harberger (1962).
31 See, e.g., Stiglitz (1973).

nonprofit output, however, will unambiguously rise in response to the increased profitability of commercial activity. The tax exemption would induce entry into the nonprofit sector although, in the absence of competition from for-profit firms, profits in the commercial activity could remain positive in long-run equilibrium; since NPOs have a distaste for producing commercial output, the existence of positive profits does not ensure further entry. If, alternatively, we view the tax exemption as a subsidy to capital in the nonprofit sector, commercial output could again either rise or fall, nonprofit output would increase and entry would occur. Profits may again be positive in the long-run[32].

Now suppose that entry into the commercial industry is opened to for-profit firms, which are subject to corporate tax. Whether these proprietary firms would be able to enter the x industry and earn positive profits, and so drive out NPOs, would depend on: (1) the size of the tax advantage enjoyed by NPOs, and (2) the extent to which commercial activities are distasteful to nonprofits. If tax advantages were small relative to the disutility of commercial activities for NPOs, then the profits available to potential for-profit entrants would be large compared with the size of the subsidy to nonprofits, and the industry would come to be dominated by for-profits. If, however, tax advantages were large and nonprofits were almost indifferent to engaging in commercial activities, NPOs dominate. However, the closer to completely indifferent the nonprofit managers were to commercial activity, the closer to zero would profits be driven by nonprofit entry; NPOs will act much like proprietary firms in commercial markets. A combination of strong distaste for commercial activities combined with large tax advantages would be necessary to allow substantial commercial profits to be earned by nonprofit firms, in long-run equilibrium.

## 3.2 Tax Advantages and "Unfair Competition"

We have argued that for-profit firms may, in some cases, be driven out of commercial activities in which nonprofits operate, due to differential tax treatment. In addition, long run equilibrium may be characterized by nonprofit capital owners earning positive profits. Whether, however, this situation is one of "unfair competition" or not is another matter. Note, first, that if capital is mobile between the nonprofit and for-profit sectors, then the long run impact of a subsidy

32 Other results, e.g. on the incidence of the tax, will differ depending on whether the UBIT is viewed as a tax on capital or profits.

to capital in the nonprofit sector should be to increase the return to capital in both sectors, much as the incidence of the corporate income tax is thought to fall on all capital. By this view, capital owners in the for-profit sector are better off with the nonprofit tax exemption than without it[33].

However, while capital owners as a whole may be made better off, it is plausible that those proprietary firms may be harmed that were initially engaged in commercial activities later taken over by tax-preferred nonprofits. Imagine for-profit firms in an industry in long-run equilibrium without tax preferences for nonprofits. Now suppose nonprofits are granted tax exemptions. If the for-profit firms are driven out – by no means a certainty, as discussed above the for-profit capital owners will be forced to find other uses for their capital. If they were initially earning positive profits, these capital owners will be made worse off, but it is difficult to see this as unfair. On the other hand, if they were initially earning zero profits, they will likely be no worse off in the new long-run equilibrium.

Note that one at least theoretic possibility is that the for-profit firms will take on the nonprofit form to receive the tax exemption. In many cases, however, this would not be a realistic alternative, since the commercial activity would receive an exemption only if undertaken in conjunction with some other primary activity for which the organization received exempt status. We would not, for instance, expect for-profit bookstores to become universities in order to compete with nonprofit university bookstores.

For-profit capital owners may have legitimate complaints regarding unfair competition when one considers adjustment costs. It may be difficult to move capital, particularly human capital, from one industry to another and the costs involved may be seen as an unjust burden. However, as Rose-Ackerman (1982) points out, if the possibility of nonprofit competition was considered, upon entry, by for-profit firms in an industry, then claims of unfair competition lose much of their strength, even if exiting the industry proves costly.

### 3.3 Tax Advantages and "Inefficient Competition"

Perhaps more important than any harm imposed on for-profit firms are the inefficiencies introduced into commercial activities by nonprofit tax advantages, if these advantages allow nonprofits to

33 This point is also made by Goodspeed and Kenyon (1988).

expand into commercial industries. These inefficiencies are of two basic types, one involving the commercial activity, the other the nonprofit activity[34].

The first sort of inefficiency arises from the fact that the tax exemption, which is designed to subsidize the production of the nonprofit good – which presumably generates external benefits – has the effect of also subsidizing commercial output, which presumably does not. Thus, we might expect the tax exemption to lead to the provision of more than the socially optimal level of commercial output. If the tax exemption allows NPOs to drive for-profit firms from an industry, then the price of the commercial good must be lower as a result of the exemption, implying that the exemption has increased commercial output. Note that, while the price of the commercial good may be lower even at a lower level of nonprofit production, since the tax exemption lowers production costs for nonprofit firms, this would imply that consumers would be rationed. In this situation for-profit enterprises could sell at a higher price to those closed out of the nonprofit market. In fact, this may help to explain the co-existence of NPOs and for-profit firms in a given market.

The second inefficiency is due to the fact that the tax exemption for the commercial activity leads to a less than optimal subsidy to the exempt activities of nonprofits. Nonprofit output should, in a first best world, be subsidized such that the marginal external benefit is equated across organizations. However, since NPOs in our model engage in commercial activities in order to cross-subsidize nonprofit activities, the tax exemption provides subsidies that increase with the ability and willingness of an organization to engage in profitable commercial activities. This need not bear any relationship to external benefits provided. Bittker and Rahdert (1976) argue that the commercial activities of nonprofits should not be taxed because all profits must eventually be used to produce the nonprofit output. Our argument suggests that, even if this is the case, granting tax advantages to nonprofits may not be desirable, as there may be more efficient ways to subsidize charitable output.

34 For other discussions of the inefficiencies arising from tax preferences given to nonprofits, see Hansmann (1989) and Clotfelter (1988).

### 3.4 Complementarities in Production and Consumption[35]

Our analysis thus far assumes that NPOs and for-profit firms produce commercial goods at the same cost and for which consumers are willing to pay the same price. Both assumptions may be relaxed.

One possibility is that, due to the non-distribution constraint, NPOs have less incentive to produce efficiently, and so will exhibit higher costs than for-profits for any given type of output. In this case, any inefficiency involved in subsidizing nonprofit commercial activity would be exacerbated. However, it is quite plausible that NPOs may produce certain outputs more cheaply than do for-profits, due to complementarities in production, and it may be precisely those commercial activities in which we find nonprofits.

Complementarities in production – economies of scope – occur when it is cheaper to produce commercial good $x$ when nonprofit good $z$ is being produced by the same firm than to produce $x$ alone. Universities, for instance, may find it cheaper to produce applied commercial research than do for-profit firms because the universities can use low-cost graduate student labor, or because research is a joint product with other university activities, such as faculty scholarship. In this case, it is not the nonprofit form per se, but the relationship between exempt and commercial output that is key. Commercial research firms would, in effect, need to form a university, or merge with one, to enjoy the same economies of scope. Some recent joint ventures between commercial biotechnology firms and universities are consistent with such an expectation.

Economies of scope, then, may help to explain the pattern of commercial activity by NPOs. Such activity is not distributed randomly across industries. Hospitals do not go into steel production and social welfare agencies do not form airlines. Rather, they engage in commercial activities in which they may have advantages. Rose-Ackerman (1982) has argued that repealing the UBIT would have the effect of spreading nonprofit commercial activity across industries rather than concentrating them in the "related" industries. She argues that this would lessen any unfair impact on for-profit businesses. However, if economies of scope are an important determinant of a nonprofit's choice of commercial activity, then such "spreading" is not likely to occur.

---

35 For further discussion, see Weisbrod (1988), chapter 6, Steinberg (1988) and Hansmann (1989).

Nonprofits might dominate a commercial activity, even in the absence of tax advantages, if there are, in fact, economies of scope. For-profit firms, unable to enter the nonprofit industry, would also find themselves at a cost disadvantage in the commercial industry. Economies of scope do not, however, offer a rationale for subsidizing the commercial activities of nonprofits. Such a subsidy would not be necessary, since nonprofits would out-compete for-profit firms without tax advantages, and would still be inefficient, unless the activity generated external benefits.

One case in which it might be efficient to offer a subsidy to commercial activities of NPOs arises if they enjoy economies of scope, but face barriers to entry in the commercial industry. In this regard, Hansmann (1981) notes that the inability of nonprofits to raise equity capital may limit the growth of nonprofits.

Complementarities in consumption occur when consumers are willing to pay more for $x$ when it is produced or sold jointly with $z$ than when it is produced or sold alone. This might be due, for instance, to convenience of location-university bookstores, for instance, may be able to charge higher prices than other bookstores. A nonprofit affiliation may also act as brand name advertising-e.g. Planned Parenthood condoms[36]. Again, such complementarities imply that nonprofits may dominate a commercial industry even without tax advantages, but do not provide a rationale for preferential tax treatment.

### 3.5 Mixed Industries

This analysis has suggested that commercial activities will tend, in the long run, to be dominated either by tax-advantaged NPOs or for-profit firms. However, NPOs engaged in commercial activities typically co-exist with for-profits.

There are several possible explanations for this co-existence. One is that these industries are not in long-run equilibrium and that, if ever reached, this equilibrium would indeed be characterized by a single institutional form in each industry. A second explanation is that long-run equilibrium is characterized by the tax-advantaged NPOs earning just enough profit to make the distasteful commercial activity worthwhile, while for-profits in the same industry, without the subsidies, earn approximately zero economic profits. There is, unfortunately, little evidence on the relative rates of profit for

36 See Skloot (1987) for this example.

nonprofits and for-profits in the same commercial industries. In any case, this explanation has a "knife-edge" quality to it which is not particularly appealing. Third, it is likely that in at least some of the industries, nonprofit and for-profit firms are producing differentiated goods; in some sense, then, they are not really in the same industry.

This paper provides another potential explanation of mixed industries, which relies on -the negative utility provided to NPO managers by producing commercial output. As noted above, this disutility implies that even in the case in which NPOs can out-compete for-profit firms (i.e. charge a lower price) they may be unwilling to meet the entire demand for commercial output at the market price. In this case, for-profit enterprises may meet the excess demand, albeit at a higher price.

## 4 Conclusions and Policy Implications

We model NPOs as maximizing an objective function defined over preferred "nonprofit" output and distasteful "commercial" good. Nonprofits compete with for-profit firms in commercial markets, in order to cross-subsidize the nonprofit activities. NPOs increase (decrease) their commercial activities when private or government donations fall (rise). They may also respond to price changes in the commercial markets in a perverse manner. We argue that tax subsidies provided to nonprofits can cause inefficiencies in both the commercial and exempt industries.

The primary policy tool for dealing with nonprofit competition in commercial activities is the unrelated business income tax, or UBIT. Nonprofits are required to pay corporate tax on income from activities not "substantially related" to their exempt activity. However, as noted, most nonprofit commercial income goes untaxed, and this may lead to inefficiencies. One way of attempting to avoid this would be to strictly employ the relatedness test as it currently stands. For an activity to be "substantially related" it must, according to IRS regulations, "contribute importantly" to the accomplishment of the exempt purpose. Thus, it is not sufficient that the commercial activity contribute in some way. Courts have, however, interpreted "contribute importantly" in a rather loose manner[37]. In any case, even if the relatedness test was stiffened, inefficiencies would remain. Recall that, even in the case in which there are complementarities in production or consumption, there is no obvious rationale for subsidization of commercial output.

Alternatively, a "commerciality" test might be substituted for the current relatedness test[38]. This has the conceptual advantage of potentially eliminating subsidization of commercial output, although defining "commercial" is not likely to be much easier than defining "related" has been.

The current policy debate over the UBIT has been conducted in isolation from other issues involving the nonprofit sector, and this is unfortunate. Taxing more of the commercial income of NPOs would lead to a reduction in nonprofit revenue and production of the output for *which* the nonprofits are presumably granted tax-exempt status. Nonprofit leaders argue that their organizations have already lost much of their government support, and that removing the commercial source of revenue would cripple them further. However, if the levels of certain nonprofit outputs are less than socially optimal, more efficient alternatives to nonprofit expansion into commercial markets should be sought. For instance, a tax on commercial profits could be combined with additional government subsidies directed to the exempt activity, or increased incentives for private donations. Each of these options likely involves some inefficiencies in practice; policy-makers need to compare the distortionary effects of various policy options to determine the second-best optimum.

## REFERENCES

BITTKER Boris and RAHDERT George, 1976, "The Exemption of Nonprofit Organizations from Corporate Income Taxation", in *Yale Law Journal*, 85, 301-351.

BENNETT James and RUDNEY Gabriel, 1987, "A Commerciality Test to Resolve the Commercial Nonprofit Issue", in *Tax Notes,* September 14, 1095-1098.

CLOTFELTER Charles, 1988/89, "Tax-Induced Distortions in the Voluntary Sector", in *Case Western Reserve Law Review*, 39, 633-694.

37 See, e.g., St. Luke's Hospital of Kansas City v. U.S., 80-2 USTC 9533 (W.D. Mo. 1980). Performance of routine laboratory tests for nonhospital patients of doctors on the hospital staff was ruled in that case to be related.

38 Bennett and Rudney (1987) suggest this.

COPELAND and RUDNEY Gabriel, 1986, "Business Income of Nonprofits and Competitive Advantage: Part One, in *Tax Notes,* November 24, 747-756.

GOODSPEED Timothy and KENYON Daphne, 1988, "The Economic Effects of the Tax-Exemption Granted Nonprofit Firms and the UBIT", unpublished draft, Office of Tax Analysis, U.S. Treasury.

HANSMANN Henry, 1981, "The Rationale for Exempting Nonprofit Organizations from Corporate Income Taxation", in *Yale Law Journal,* 91, 54-100.

——, 1989, "Unfair Competition and the Unrelated Business Income Tax", in *Virginia Law Review* 75, pp. 605-635.

——, 1980, "The Role of Nonprofit Enterprise", in *Yale Law Journal,* 89, 835-899.

HARBERGER Arnold, 1962, "The Incidence of the Corporation Income Tax", in *Journal of Political Economy,* 70, 215-240.

HECKMAN James and MACURDY Thomas, 1980, "A Life Cycle Model of Female Labor Supply", in *Review of Economic Studies,* 47, 47-74.

JAMES Estelle, 1978, "Product Mix and Cost Aggregation: A Reinterpretation of the Economics of Higher Education", in *Journal of Human Resources,* 13, Spring, 157-186.

——, 1983, "How Nonprofits Grow", in *Journal of Policy Analysis and Management,* Spring, 350-365.

MIQUE Jean-Luc and BELANGER Gerard, 1974, "Toward a general Theory of Managerial Discretion", in *Public Choice* 17, 27-43.

NEWHOUSE Joseph, 1970, "Toward a Theory of Nonprofit Institutions", in *American Economic Review,* 60, 64-75 .

ROSE-ACKERMAN Susan, 1980, "Do Government Grants to Charity Reduce Private Donations?", in *Nonprofit Firms in a Three-Sector Economy,* Michelle White, (ed.), Washington D.C., Urban Institute Press.

——, 1982, "Unfair Competition and Corporate Income Taxation", in *Stanford Law Review,* 34, 1017-1039.

——, 1987, "Ideals versus Dollars: Donors, Charity Managers, and Government Grants", in *Journal of Political Economy* 95.

SALAMON Lester and ABRAMSON Alan, 1985, "Nonprofits and the Federal Budget: Deeper Cuts Ahead", in *Foundation News,* March-April, 48-54.

SCHIFF Jerald, 1986, "Expansion, Entry and Exit in the Nonprofit Sector: The Long and Short Run of It", Program on Non-Profit Organizations (Yale University), Working Paper Number 111.

——, and WEISBROD Burton, 1986, "Government Social Welfare Spending and the Private Nonprofit Sector: Crowding Out, and More", November, unpublished.

SKLOOT Edward, 1987, "Enterprise and Commerce in Nonprofit Organizations", in Walter Powell, editor, *The Nonprofit Sector: A Research Handbook,* New Haven, CT.: Yale University Press, 380-396.

STEINBERG Richard, 1988, "Fairness and Efficiency in the Competition Between For-Profit and Nonprofit Firms", Program on Nonprofit Organizations, Yale University, Working Paper Number 132, June.

——, 1986, "The Revealed Objective Function of Nonprofit Firms", in *Rand Journal of Economics,* 17, Winter, 508-526.

STIGLITZ Joseph, 1973, "Taxation, Corporate Financial Policy and the Cost of Capital", in *Journal of Public Economics,* 2, 1-34.

WEISBROD Burton and DOMINGUEZ Nestor, 1986, "Demand for Collective Goods in Private Nonprofit Markets: Can Fundraising Expenditures Help Overcome Free-Rider Behavior?", in *Journal of Public Economics,* 30, June, 83-96.

WEISBROD Burton, 1988, *The Nonprofit Economy*, Cambridge, MA.: Harvard University Press.

WILLIAMSON Oliver, 1964, *The Economics of Discretionary Behavior: Managerial Behavior in a Theory of the Firm,* Englewood Cliffs, N.J.: Prentice Hall.

# [27]

# Commercialism among nonprofits: Objectives, opportunities, and constraints

*Estelle James*

## Introduction

Earlier chapters in this book provide a comprehensive picture of growing commercialism among nonprofit organizations. *Commercialism* is defined to mean the degree of reliance on sales revenues rather than donations or government grants, the production of goods for sale that compete with goods produced by for-profit organizations, collaborations and partnerships with for-profits, and, ultimately, conversion into for-profits. The book attempts to answer the questions: Is commercialism increasing? If so, why and so what? Should it be encouraged or discouraged by public policy? Is growing commercialism good because it allows nonprofits to flourish and grow, or bad because it makes them more like for-profits? Here I contrast the arguments set forth in this book with a contrary hypothesis about nonprofit behavior and why it appears to be changing. I review the evidence provided to see which view of the nonprofit world is most consistent with the facts, and discuss some of the public-policy implications.

The book depicts nonprofit organizations as having different and more altruistic objective functions than for-profits, which lead them to engage in commercial activities marginally and reluctantly, in order to cross-subsidize their preferred noncommercial activities, when other revenue sources such as donations and subsidies are not available. In fact, this is a point of view that I have espoused in the past, and I believe it is consistent with long-standing behavior in some organizations, such as universities.

However, the contrary hypothesis that I shall examine here is stimulated by empirical observations in this book, indicating that the most dramatic growth in commercialism has occurred in situations where institutional or legal constraints on sales revenues were lifted, revealing large new opportunities. Non-

*Editor's note:* After the studies in the preceding chapters were completed, we invited Estelle James, a distinguished contributor to the literature on the nonprofit sector, to write an overview chapter presenting her perspective on our work.

profits responded enthusiastically to the new opportunities, without much evidence of reluctance. It is unclear whether the large "potential profits" thereby generated were used to cross-subsidize loss-making, public-consumption goods or were simply plowed back as investments to generate more profit-making goods; the contrary hypothesis predicts that the latter effect will dominate in many cases. Declines in donations, in some industries analyzed in this volume, seem to be a consequence rather than a cause of the increased reliance on sales. These empirical observations suggest that constraints and large opportunities, rather than altruistic objectives and cross-subsidization, play an important role in explaining the limited commercialism of nonprofits in the past and its striking emergence in some industries in recent years. When constraints are removed and large new opportunities for profit-making present themselves, nonprofits may behave very much like for-profits.

## The theory of nonprofit organizations and cross-subsidization

The starting point for my discussion is the assertion (which I call the *conventional hypothesis*) that nonprofits have nonpecuniary altruistic objectives. They exist to provide public (collective) goods and to distribute quasi-public goods in ways that are different from market distribution – that is, to redistribute real income via free or low-price access to goods and services that generate external benefits. These objectives lead to pricing policies that differ from those of for-profits. (See Chapter 3 for a theoretical discussion of possible differences.)

How are these goods financed, given that consumers cannot be excluded from the consumption of public goods, and nonprofits do not want to rely on the price mechanism even in cases where it is technologically feasible? In part through donations, by recipients of the consumer surplus or the external benefits who receive a "warm glow" by acting altruistically. Donations, it is well known, are limited by the free-rider problem and by the difficulty potential donors have in monitoring the effects of their donations. Nonprofit status (i.e., the nondistribution constraint) helps solve the monitoring problem by reassuring donors that their contributions will, in fact, be spent on services rather than simply on increasing profits that are distributed to the firm's owners. The choice of nonprofit managers whose objectives coincide with those of the donors provides additional reassurance. Tax deductibility of donations helps solve the free-rider problem, by decreasing the after-tax cost of the donations.

Government subsidies to nonprofit organizations are important additional sources of revenue. When government grants and private donations decline, the nonprofit is forced to become commercialized, to survive. Commercialization is said to be nonpreferred by nonprofits, because it involves producing goods they dislike, or charging prices that limit the consumption of goods they do like (Chapter 4). Thus, when other discretionary funds are available, commercialization stops below the profit-maximizing point. The theory of cross-subsidization hypothesizes that when other revenue sources become less available, nonprofits will become more commercialized in order to generate a larger profit, which they can use to finance their provision of preferred public and quasi-public goods. This book argues that commercialism has been increasing in the nonprofit sector over the past two decades for this reason, and examines in detail several industries dominated by nonprofits to document this claim.

In evaluating a theoretical argument, it is useful to have a countertheory against which to test it. As a countertheory, then, we might hypothesize that pecuniary rather than altruistic objectives dominate the decisions of many nonprofits. These "false" nonprofits – which Weisbrod (1988) referred to as "for-profits in disguise" – may maximize profits that they then distribute in disguised form (as higher wages and perks), or they may maximize revenues that lead to power and prestige for their managers. They are lured into the nonprofit sector by the tax and subsidy advantages that they gain therefrom. If these advantages decline, the disadvantages (loss of access to equity capital) may dominate and lead to an exodus from the nonprofit sector.

Further, nonprofit managers and donors may have different interests. If nonprofit managers are primarily interested in revenues, they may limit their commercial activities because they fear that donations will fall if they appear to be self-supporting. The operative factor here is not the disutility of commercial activities, but their negative impact on other sources of funds. If large new opportunities open up – for example, due to technological, institutional, or legal changes that enable the price system to work – the gain in sales revenue may far outweigh the possible loss in donative revenues, and nonprofits may eagerly embrace the new opportunities. We may then see commercialism increase dramatically and nonprofit behavior that is very much like that of for-profits.

Thus, whereas the conventional, cross-subsidization hypothesis emphasizes the differences in objectives between for-profits and nonprofits, views commercialism as a source of disutility, and sees increases in commercialism as a response to declining donations and grants, the counterhypothesis emphasizes the similarities in objectives between nonprofits and for-profits, downplays the importance of disutility, sees donations as responding to sales rather than vice versa, and underscores the key role played by the removal of institutional and legal constraints in opening up new sales opportunities and expanding commercialism. The next section of this chapter examines the empirical evidence to see which of these views receives more support.

## The evidence

The great value of this book is that it provides detailed empirical evidence from many industries that allow us to explain and evaluate the growing commercialism among nonprofits.

In Chapter 6, one of the chapters that cuts across industries, Segal and Weisbrod ask: Did the slower growth rate of donations over the past decade cause increased reliance on sales revenues? Their first answer is positive. Using panel data (a pooled cross section with lags) from the Forms 990 of nonprofits for 1985–93, they demonstrate that (next year's) sales revenues increase significantly when the growth rate of donative revenues declines. However, as they note, this specification assumes that donations are exogenous. When they use a vector autoregression model that allows for simultaneous determination of donations and sales, they find that sales influence donations, rather than vice versa. When the data are disaggregated by industry, the correlation between sales and donations is positive for some – most notably hospitals and universities – and negative for others.

On the whole, I find this unconvincing evidence of cross-subsidization based on preferred versus nonpreferred goods. Rather, the simultaneous-determination model is consistent with the idea that revenue-maximizing nonprofit managers will charge a lower price than they would if they viewed donations as exogenous; that is, their reluctance to rely on sales revenue may stem more from its expected impact on donations than on its disutility to them – a possibility noted in Chapter 3. The zero or positive relationship between sales and other revenue sources seems to exist primarily in multiproduct industries, where donations may be targeted to goods where price finance still does not work and cross-subsidization from the more profitable goods is not expected.

Chapters 7 and 8 describe in detail the decline in economic and legislative advantages for nonprofits that have led to increased commercialism in the health industry. Initially nonprofits had a secure place in this industry, justified by the expectation that they would provide charity care, better-quality service, and other socially useful activities through donations and cross-subsidization. Health care has long been given as a key example of an industry where consumer information is limited, trust is a substitute, and nonprofits were more likely to be trusted by consumers than were for-profits. As a result, the industry has been dominated by nonprofits, which have enjoyed numerous tax and subsidy advantages. For example, according to the Health Maintenance Organization Act of 1973, only nonprofits were eligible for federal subsidies, and nonprofit hospitals have long benefited from special tax exemptions. However, direct federal subsidies to HMOs ended in the early 1980s, and the tax advantages of Blue Cross and Blue Shield and hospitals gradually eroded over time, especially during the 1980s.

Even more important – and possibly explaining this change in public policy – the growth of health insurance, through private coverage, Medicare, and Medicaid, ensured that most people could pay for medical services. In other words, institutions developed that enabled price finance to work, even for the poor, thereby diminishing the redistributive rationale for nonprofits. The advent of medical insurance, which was strongly supported by hospitals, makes cross-subsidization and the provision of charity care by nonprofits less critical. Not surprisingly, donations fell drastically in response to insurance, evidence that as institutions change so that the good in question can be privatized, donors will take their money elsewhere. This diminishes the comparative advantage of the nonprofit sector. Total revenues of hospitals increased, however, implying that the gains from insurance and sales far outweighed the loss from donations. (Consistent with this observation, for-profit hospitals tend to avoid areas where uninsured people live, whereas nonprofits are more likely to survive in these areas).

In recent years, employers and government have sought cheaper and more predictable health-care arrangements. Competition among both nonprofits and for-profits – in the context of prospective payment systems, the setting of price limits by Medicare and Medicaid, the increasing use of HMOs and preferred providers, and negotiations between insurance companies and hospitals – meant that although costs were covered, there was little surplus left for discretionary spending and cross-subsidization.

As a result of these forces, numerous studies show that (with the exception of the small group of teaching hospitals) nonprofit and for-profit hospitals coexist and behave in very similar ways with respect to quality of service, degree of uncompensated care (minimal), and efficiency. Indeed this coexistence and similarity, largely stemming from a common reliance on third-party price finance, may have led to the diminution of public-policy privileges for nonprofits described above. Consequently, the rationale for remaining nonprofit appears to be disappearing – that is, the disadvantages of the nonprofit form (lack of access to equity capital) outweigh the advantages – and we are currently observing a wave of conversions, asset sales, and contracting-out arrangements, from nonprofits to for-profits, among the Blues, HMOs, and hospitals. Nor have I seen much evidence of reluctance as to conversion in these organizations; in fact, the managers are often major beneficiaries – evidence for the counter-theory.

The other major change in balance between nonprofits and for-profits has occurred in the biotech area, where the lines between nonprofit-university research and for-profit applications have become increasingly blurred. Chapter 9 describes the many changes in federal policy that set the stage for these developments. Legislation in 1980 allowed universities to retain the patent rights to discoveries stemming from federally funded research, a right that had previously been denied to them. After 1984 these property rights could be transferred (sold) to others, including for-profits. Legislation in 1986 permitted universities and firms to collaborate without fear of antitrust litigation. In 1989 the opportunities for licensing of university research and other intersectoral collaboration were further expanded. In 1993 defense-related research was opened up to commercialization. New NSF programs encourage or require university–industry cooperation. Corporations are used to evaluate the technical merits of proposals, including the feasibility of commercialization and marketing as key points in the evaluation process.

In this case, as in the health industry discussed above, public-policy changes probably were not exogenous; rather, they were probably an endogenous response to changing economic circumstances. After the cold war ended, and as international trade and capital movements expanded, public policy toward research has been driven by the belief that U.S. corporations were losing out in global economic competition, and that we could avoid this by developing new technologies, which requires a shift from basic to applied research. In the past, with the United States dominating the world economy, it was expected that domestic firms would capture most of the benefits of basic research; but as other countries have grown in economic power, this assumption is no longer valid. Instead, Japan, Korea, and other emerging countries may be expected to appropriate some of the benefits of our basic research. Under these conditions the U.S. government has less incentive to invest in basic research, and more incentive to shift its focus to the applied level, where the benefits are narrower and more likely to be captured by domestic firms; and this is exactly what has happened, as legal constraints changed to permit and encourage applied research.

Fortuitously, the computer and biotech (genetics and pharmaceuticals) industries were on the verge of major breakthroughs, poised for commercial development of scientific discoveries. As research in these industries generated huge potential profits, universities seized upon the new opportunities for pecuniary benefits. The result: a proliferation of alliances between industry and the academy, an upsurge in licensing, cooperative R&D agreements, and joint research consortia. Nineteen percent of university research and a much larger share in the biotech area is now carried out in close linkage with industry. Key faculty members move back and forth between industry and university laboratories, and small start-up firms, spun off from universities, are often led by present or past faculty members. Universities get an increasing share of their income from patents, licenses, royalties, equity in these start-up companies, and research agreements with private industry. A large and growing share of university research is now financed by private rather than public sources. In the life sciences, private support is greater than public support; but in this case public and private funding sources appear to be complements rather than substitutes. For example, the upsurge in university patenting and university share of total patents that has occurred over the past decade has attracted private funds, but most of the discoveries originated in NSF- and NIH-funded research projects.

Three key points are especially worth noting: First, the changing university behavior is due to changing public policies – in particular, the removal of constraints that closed off key avenues of commercialization to nonprofit universities, at a critical moment in time, permitting large new opportunities to open up. Second, these changing public policies are themselves an endogenous response to changing perceptions of the (domestic) economic benefits from basic versus applied research. Third, the universities responded enthusiastically. Though some concerns have been raised about the conflict between the academic value of free and open information versus the commercial motive for keeping information secret, on the whole universities (particularly the life-science parts of universities) aggressively pursued for-profit alliances and modes of behavior once the legal barriers came down. There is little evidence of disutility here, nor any indication that private funding of the life sciences allowed other university resources to be allocated elsewhere, as a form of cross-subsidization (e.g., profits from applied biotech research likely has not found its way to humanities libraries). I regard this as further evidence for the counterhypothesis.

In contrast to health and higher education, in other industries commercialism is moving at a much slower pace and with fewer changes in underlying economic conditions and legal constraints. Chapter 12 finds that, among art museums, sales revenues have increased, but only in proportion with other revenues. As government and foundations have supported capital investment, special exhibitions, and outreach programs, the maintenance and normal operating expenses that they generate must be covered from elsewhere, and museums have turned to admission fees and sales from auxiliary operations for this purpose. Still, the proportion of revenues from sales has remained roughly constant, as commercial and donative sources have increased at similar rates.

Chapter 10 describes complementarity between membership contributions and sales, but possible substitution between sales and donations, in the social-service industry. Although many managers of social-service nonprofits feel a pressing need to generate additional resources because government funding for these activities has been cut, commercial activities are approached with caution owing to a possible loss of reputation and donations. Are these activities frowned upon because they generate intrinsic disutility, or because they may reduce other funding sources; that is, does a utility-maximizing or revenue-maximizing objective shape the nonprofits' behavior? We cannot respond with certainty, given the possibilities of cross-subsidization on the one hand and negative interactions among funding sources on the other hand, as Chapter 3 noted. However, we do observe that to minimize crowd-out, managers look for commercial activities that are a natural outgrowth of their primary missions: The American Lung Association and the American Cancer Society accept sponsorship from companies selling products that seem consistent with good health, AARP endorses (for a fee) insurance companies that are said to provide good service to senior citizens, and so on.

We also observe that membership fees for social-service nonprofits are kept low – to increase member numbers and hence the organization's political clout and its market for commercial sales. In this case, membership fees and sales revenues are complementary because most sales are to members. Again, this behavior is consistent with maximization of either revenue or utility.

Econometric evidence provided in Chapter 11 seems most consistent with the utility-maximization and cross-subsidization hypotheses. Zoos charge prices below the profit-maximizing levels; that is, they operate in the inelastic part of their demand curves, to keep admissions high and reach low-income groups. Sales of nonpreferred, ancillary goods (animal rides, souvenirs, food, parking) by zoos has grown as donations have decreased since the 1970s. Although similar behavior might be predicted for revenue maximizers in the face of strong and increasing crowd-out, zoos generally seem to fit the conventional model.

Further evidence both of cross-subsidization and the importance of constraints is found in Chapter 13 on public broadcasting. Initially public TV was not supposed to engage in commercial activity; indeed, freedom from the demands of advertisers was its raison d'être. However, since 1981 public broadcasting stations have been permitted to sell services and products, as new legislation removed old constraints and opened the door to commercialism. Rules on corporate sponsorship have eased, and further easing is under consideration. Simultaneously, government grants to public broadcasting have declined. As a result of these forces, we observe growing partnerships with for-profits, fundraising and membership drives, sales of broadcast time to corporate sponsors, and provision of auxiliary services (CDs, transcripts). It is difficult to disentangle whether the removal of constraints or the increased financial pressure for cross-subsidization is the greater motivating force for commercialism; probably the two interacted, creating greater opportunity and greater need at the same time.

As in the social-service industry, public broadcasters fear that advertising and other forms of commercialism may crowd out public and private donations, and they shape their sponsors' messages and other sales techniques to minimize this negative effect. I suspect we shall see much more commercialism in this industry as legal restrictions continue to be lifted.

As in the health and education industries, changing public policy in public broadcasting may be seen as an endogenous response to changing technology and institutions – in this case the advent of cable TV, which enabled the price mechanism to work better, hence undercutting the rationale for government grants and private donations to public TV. In the days before cable, pricing could not be used because exclusion of viewers was not technologically feasible, and commercial TV was financed by advertisers interested in maximizing consumption of their products. Strong preferences for a particular type of programming by small groups of people were ignored by these advertisers because it would not increase their sales. Public broadcasting, financed by government grants and private donations, was supposed to overcome this market failure.

After the advent of cable TV, this small group could finance its preferred type of programming by paying a high fee to a cable producer, undercutting the rationale for grants and donations. Cable TV allows strong specialized tastes to be catered to, since it converts a nonexcludable good into an excludable good for which intensity of preference can be registered via the price people are willing to pay. Thus, the economic rationale for subsidizing public TV and for limiting its commercialism has declined in the past two decades, and the subsidies and constraints have likewise declined. The quest for organizational survival has led public TV to seek other (nonprice, noncable) financing sources, and these are likely increasingly to rely on commercialism directed toward a niche audience.

In sum, the industries where commercialism has been most rampant, as manifested in partnerships, mergers, and conversions, are also industries where (1) institutional or technological change has made exclusion and price financing more feasible and/or (2) tax and subsidy advantages to and constraints upon nonprofits have been lifted since the early 1980s. The removal of constraints makes it possible for nonprofits to act more like for-profits; the reduction in tax and subsidy advantages makes it advantageous for nonprofits to convert to for-profit status; and the feasibility of price finance enables both legal and behavioral conversion between the two sectors. Indeed, we observe all these instances, particularly in the health industry and the university-biotech arena. Moreover, these occurrences are all consistent with the counterhypothesis, which views many (but, of course, not all) nonprofits as quite willing to react opportunistically to changing incentives and constraints in order to maximize revenues or disguised profits, rather than as being driven by nonpecuniary altruistic objectives reluctantly to undertake commercial activities. Furthermore, in all these cases public policies may be viewed as an endogenous response to changing economic conditions and institutions that make it desirable and feasible to shift the balance from public to private goods.

At the same time, less dramatic increases in commercialism observed in museums, social-service organizations, zoos, and public broadcasting are more consistent with the conventional hypothesis that nonprofits commercialize and cross-subsidize when they are driven to do so by a reduction in public or private donations. In these cases, underlying institutions and constraints have not changed so as to produce discontinuous changes in behavior. Commercialism in these industries continues to be slowed by the disutility it creates and by the fear that sales revenues may drive out donations: It is impossible to disentangle these two effects.

## Public-policy implications of commercialism

Why do we care about commercialism among nonprofits? Why is it worth writing a book about this topic? Should special privileges given to nonprofits be withdrawn as nonprofits become more like for-profits? To answer these questions it may be useful to recount the reasons why public policy creates a special legal category for nonprofits and gives them special tax and subsidy advantages in the first place.

### *Tax and subsidy advantages: Why do they exist and should they be removed?*

Historically, most nonprofits were religious organizations that started schools, hospitals, and mutual-benefit organizations to serve their members better and maintain their loyalty. From a political-economy perspective, they may have received special tax treatment because of their political power and (especially in the United States) because of our legal strictures to maintain a separation between church and state.

As society became more secular, so too did these organizations; but they remained concentrated in areas (education, health, social-service charities) where externalities are thought to exist and where the price mechanism could not be relied upon to achieve optimal results. Indeed, this book asserts – but does not prove – that nonprofits exist to provide public goods and to expand consumption of quasi-public goods to groups that otherwise could not afford to purchase them. Subsidies and tax privileges to nonprofits may be given to encourage donations and to overcome the free-rider problem that exists where exclusion and pricing are not possible.

In other countries direct government payment for these services is common, but in the United States indirect subsidy via tax advantages is more likely – possibly because as a heterogeneous society we cannot reach a consensus on which goods and services to subsidize. Thus we decentralize that decision and subsidize via matching grants to organizations that receive "votes" in the form of donations.

Public policy earmarks these privileges only for organizations that agree not to distribute their revenues to private owners in the form of dividends or capital gains, because the government cannot observe the detailed behavior of many decentralized organizations. Just as the nonprofit form may be taken as a proxy of trustworthiness by private donors, so too it may be regarded as less likely to abuse its subsidies (thereby causing a political scandal) by public donors. However, organizational form is only a second-best proxy for what we would really like to observe. Indeed, if "for-profits in disguise" are enticed into the field by the existence of tax privileges and subsidies, it may be a third-best proxy.

Given this background, increased commercialism of or sales by nonprofits enables them to pursue their altruistic mission better by providing revenues, which should please both public and private donors. However, balanced against this are a number of problems it creates or new situations it underscores. First, it may signal that the service provided by nonprofits can now be financed by the price mechanism, due to new technologies and institutions, so public and private donations are no longer needed. In this case, private donations are likely to diminish over time, as donors shift their money to other areas where they are less dispensable. Since donations are diminishing, tax exemption for philanthropy does not pose a new public-policy problem, but other tax privileges may merit reconsideration. If benefits can be captured by prices, why should income- and property-tax exemption be offered?

Second, the increased emphasis on sales revenues may attract more "for-profits in disguise" into the sector – and may lead "real" nonprofits to hire new types of managers, with training, background, and objectives similar to those in the for-profit sector. These managers may be equally likely as for-profit managers to cheat the consumer or donor with respect to output characteristics that are not readily observable. In effect, true nonprofits may be turned into "for-profits in disguise" as a result of the managerial selection process, without full cognizance of this fact by the organization and without a deliberate decision having been made. Further, the psychological theory of cognitive dissonance suggests that attitudes follow behavior – so even if values were not pecuniary to begin with, they would gradually become so as managers are expected to meet monetary goals and are evaluated according to their success in doing so. In that case, the generation of commercial revenues may become an end in itself, and nonprofit status is no longer a reliable signal for trustworthiness or for the desire to "do good" – which were the rationales for tax privileges and public subsidies in the first place.

Additional policy questions are raised in this volume about the justification for and possible abuse of income-tax exemptions for nonprofits when auxiliary-good production is large. Chapter 5 shows that nonprofits with unrelated business income (UBI) report lower general and administrative expenses on their Forms 990 than those without UBI. This suggests that a large share of their general expenses are attributed to their unrelated business (UB) activities, thereby sheltering the UBI from taxes even though these activities are not supposed to be tax exempt. One might expect that, for similar reasons, buildings with large depreciation potential would be treated as costs of the UB rather than of the nonprofit. (The nonprofit does not need these costs to shelter its regular income, which is automatically tax exempt.) These costs may be true joint costs that cannot be disentangled between the nonprofit and UB, or they may be costs that could in principle be disentangled but cannot readily be monitored. In the latter case, this attribution means that the government gets less tax revenue from the UB activities than it "should," and other firms or households must be taxed more as a result.

Nonprofits also benefit from property-tax exemption. Chapter 5 shows that nonprofits tend to engage in commercial activities disproportionately in states where these tax rates are high, giving them a large comparative advantage over for-profits. For example, property used partially for UBI generation, particularly property without large depreciation potential, may be counted as nonprofit property that is exempt from property tax, thereby enabling nonprofits to undercut for-profits producing similar goods, distorting the choice of organizational form, and further reducing tax revenues.

In general, when one organization engages both in profit-making and nonprofit activities, producing both public and private goods, it is natural to try to segment the income and cost flows between the two so as to maximize the value of the tax exemptions. This is particularly problematic for public policy if the nonprofits cannot be counted on to use the resulting revenues, via cross-subsidization, for socially useful purposes. Since the value system in nonprofits may itself change as commercialism increases, for the reasons given above, it may be that such exemptions should gradually be withdrawn once the commercial activities of an organization exceed a specified point.

### *(When) Should special constraints apply to nonprofit behavior?*

Besides these questions as to the tax privileges of nonprofits, this book raises questions about whether and under what circumstances special legal constraints should apply. This issue is most clearly exemplified by the case of biotech research at universities, where constraints on commercial behavior were previously strong but have recently been substantially weakened. The rationales for the constraints were, presumably, the potential conflict between profit-making behavior and public-good-maximizing behavior, and an unwillingness to rely on nonprofit status alone to resolve this conflict in the public interest.

In the past, when federally funded basic research was carried on at universities, results could not be patented and were regarded as open information, published in scientific journals and freely discussed at scientific meetings, as soon as (or even before) they were validated. In contrast, privately funded applied research was more likely to be carried on at industrial laboratories, and results were patented before they were made public. As the constraint on university patents was removed, the line between these two types of research has become blurred, and the public–private good conflict has reemerged.

Patents are a compromise between the efficiency value of making information readily accessible once it is exists and the need to provide incentives to incur the costs that generate this information in the first place. The institution of patents may increase research funding, but it also directs that funding into areas where benefits can be appropriated and marketed within a reasonably short time, even if other areas such as basic research are more promising from the long-run, global perspective. Government grants to universities, together with the nonprofit university value system, solved the investment problem without patents and therefore allowed the efficiency gains from more open access and a broad, long-run perspective. Increased scarcity of government grants (relative to demand) combined with removal of constraints on patenting rights introduced this conflict into academia. Although the commercialization of scientific discoveries via patents makes more resources available for research, it directs the nature of the research toward the short and medium term, and runs the risk of limiting the utilization of research results.

Moreover, under the new set of incentives, the allocation of university resources is likely to be strongly influenced by the profitability of outputs. For example, disciplines with commercial prospects may be given priority over those without, rather than basing these judgments on educational criteria. A larger share of university resources and faculty time may be devoted to the business rather than to the science of research and development. Faculty members whose research may lead to profitable patents or licenses, or collaborations with private industry, may be more likely to be hired and tenured than others; therefore, they have an incentive to concentrate on these areas. Although access to grants has always been a factor in resource-allocation decisions at universities, the grants supposedly were awarded according to basic scientific merit; but now commercial profitability plays a stronger role. In effect, the removal of constraints on the commercial activities of universities has shifted the trade-off between public and private research goods in favor of the latter. Have we chosen the right mix? Is this shift in values good for academia and for the economy in the long run? This is the public-policy issue raised as legal constraints are lifted and commercialism increases.

### *Conversions: How can society's interests be protected?*

The most extreme form of commercialism occurs, as Chapter 7 showed, when nonprofits convert to for-profit status, as has been occurring most notably among HMOs, hospitals, and the Blues in the health industry. Presumably conversion occurs when the advantages of for-profit status outweigh the advantages of nonprofit status. This may be socially desirable if price finance is now so widely feasible that a public good has been turned into a private good, if access to equity capital is important in order to expand facilities, and if donations are no longer a large potential source of revenue. The danger is that the decision makers may take into account only the gains to them personally, rather than the gains and losses to society as a whole. For example, if a group of insiders purchases at a low price nonprofit assets that have been accumulated out of tax-exempt donations over the years, and if they cut the public services of the new organization in order to maximize their profits, this may be a case where society as a whole has lost. Alternatively, if a foundation is set up with the proceeds of the asset sales, and management is turned over to people without a social commitment but who earn high salaries and perks, this may be another example of a social loss. Several instances of this sort are reported in this volume. Conversions thus raise issues around who should be permitted to buy and under what procedures (e.g., Should competitive open bidding be required?), how the nonprofit's assets should be valued, how society should be compensated, and who should manage the compensation funds.

## Conclusion

Over the past two decades subsidies to many nonprofit organizations have fallen while the need for their services has grown due to government cutbacks. The growing commercialism among nonprofits is often attributed to these two factors: The conventional theory of nonprofit behavior spelled out earlier predicts that they will rely increasingly on sales revenues to cross-subsidize their preferred public goods as public and private donations fall. This volume provides several empirical examples from the museum, social-service, zoo, and public broadcasting industries consistent with this hypothesis. Though commercialism can lead to abuses of tax privileges (e.g., through cost shifting), these may be minor and correctable in comparison with the gains in nonprofit services.

However, in the health and university-biotech industries, where the most dramatic examples of commercialism have occurred, including extensive partnerships with and conversions into for-profit firms, the driving force seems to have been more basic changes in underlying institutional and economic conditions. Moreover, perhaps as a consequence of these underlying changes, the whole set of legal privileges and constraints faced by nonprofits has changed in these industries. Widespread medical insurance permits full pricing for hospital services, and special legal privileges for nonprofits thereafter decline; global competition puts greater emphasis on applied over basic research, and this leads to the removal of legal proscriptions on the rights of universities to patent the results of federally funded research. These basic changes alter in a discontinuous way the incentives of organizations to enter or stay in the nonprofit sector and the behavior of those organizations that do remain. In particular, we see little evidence of a reluctance to commercialize or of the use of sales revenues for cross-subsidization in these cases.

It appears that marginal and global changes in commercialism may have quite different causes and effects. A diminution in other revenue sources or an increase in perceived need may explain marginal changes in commercialism, given the underlying set of economic, institutional, and legal constraints – consistent with the cross-subsidization hypothesis. However, they do not explain discontinuously large changes in commercialism. These may be due, instead, to dramatic changes in constraints and the opening up of new sources of sales revenues; the disutility from profitable activities and the cross-subsidization of loss-making activities become far less important to nonprofits under these circumstances. This suggests that pecuniary objectives may never have been far from the surface. When faced with large new opportunities for commercialism, many nonprofits seem quite willing to shed their altruistic cover and assume the values and behavior of for-profits.

Given that sales revenues appear to crowd out donations, tax exemptions for contributions automatically become less important under these circumstances. However, public-policy issues are raised concerning:

1 the use of an organization's legal status to determine eligibility for income- and property-tax exemptions and other privileges in situations where nonprofits and for-profits produce similar goods and/or share similar values; and
2 the conditions for converting from nonprofit to for-profit status once assets have been accumulated out of tax-exempt revenues.

In both cases the policy goal should be to ensure that public resources are indeed being used to provide public rather than private goods and to promote social rather than personal welfare – even though these categories are admittedly ambiguous and imprecise.

## References

Weisbrod, Burton A. 1988. *The Nonprofit Economy*. Cambridge, MA, and London: Harvard University Press.

# [28]



# Organizational Choices for Public Service Supply

James M. Ferris and Elizabeth Graddy
University of Southern California

This article investigates the nature of the service production choice of local governments. The incentives and constraints embedded in different organizational forms—public, nonprofit, and for-profit organizations—have implications for both production and transaction costs of various production options. Based on a national sample of local governments providing health services, choices among internal public production, external public production, nonprofit, and for-profit production are examined. A nested logit model is utilized to examine the impact of production and transaction costs of alternatives, the number of producers of each alternative, and the characteristics of the jurisdiction that determine the importance of production and transaction costs characteristic to the jurisdiction. The empirical results indicate that the public organization choices (internal and external) have unobserved components of utility in common, as do the private organizational choices (nonprofit and for-profit). This suggests that decisionmakers recognize the public–private distinction in their supply decisions.

## 1. Introduction

Organizational theories suggest that the different incentives and constraints embedded in public, nonprofit, and for-profit organizational forms can result in different behaviors and outcomes. Such differences are likely to affect the production and transaction costs of service delivery and, thus, be of considerable importance to local government decision-makers who are considering contracting the production of local public services.

Under contracting arrangements, the government finances the service, but contracts with an external supplier for its delivery. Analyses of the contracting choice have focused on the advantages of internal versus external production (e.g., Ferris and Graddy, 1988; Stein, 1990). However, the production decision facing local governments is more complex than a simple dichotomous choice between internal and external production. The providing government faces an array of external options for production, including contracts with other governments, contracts with for-profit firms, and contracts with nonprofit organizations.[1] But it is not at all clear how these decision-makers view

1. In this article, we use the terms "for-profit firms" and "nonprofit organizations" in refer-

these organizational distinctions. Are local government officials cognizant of the relative advantages among the organizational choices or do they simply view the decisions as one of public versus private production?

This article investigates the nature of the service production choice that local governments make among four alternatives: internal public production, contracted public production, contracted nonprofit production, and contracted for-profit production. We consider whether these four alternatives are viewed as distinctive, or whether decision-makers in some sense group them into public or private alternatives.

To address this, we explore the organizational choices of local governments in providing three types of health services: hospital, substance abuse prevention and treatment, and mental health. In Section 2 we discuss the relationship between organizational form and service delivery costs and develop a model of organization choice for the supply of publicly provided goods and services. In Section 3 we present the empirical analysis: the data, the model and variable specifications, and the estimation results. In Section 4 we consider the implications of our findings.

## 2. The Organizational Choice Model

Governments consider alternative organizations to deliver publicly provided services because they are interested in containing service delivery costs.[2] This interest in efficiency is motivated by conflicting pressures on local governments—citizen demand for services coupled with their rejection of tax increases and a concurrent reduction in federal revenue sharing.[3] Service delivery costs include transactions costs (contract writing and monitoring costs) as well as direct service production costs. Thus, local governments must consider both production-cost efficiencies and transaction-cost efficiencies in making a production choice. The incentives and constraints embodied in the different organizational choices (internal public, external public, nonprofit, and for-profit) have implications for both types of costs (see Ferris and Graddy, 1991).

ence to privately controlled organizations. Publicly controlled corporations or nonprofit organizations represent very different supply arrangements that typically involve off-budget activities and rely on private financing to some degree.

2. Although Donahue (1989) raises the possibility that contracting may be a mechanism to cut back service levels, he offers some empirical support for this efficiency assumption in his review of a Touche Ross privatization survey. A large majority of responding city managers reported their motive for considering contracting out was to lower service delivery costs.

3. We assume that the provision decision is independent of the production decision. Estimates of the price elasticity of local spending indicate that demand is relatively price inelastic. Studies using micro data report an elasticity close to 0 and those relying on community-level data report an elasticity typically in the range of 0.2 to 0.5 (Bergstrom, Rubinfeld, and Shapiro, 1982). These empirical findings suggest that the cost savings that organizational choices might achieve are unlikely to have a substantial stimulative effect on the level of service provision, and thus lend support to our assumption of the independence of the provision and production decisions of local governments.

Production efficiencies are determined by scale economies, managerial incentives, and input flexibility. Scale economies imply decreasing costs up to some minimum efficient size level. If jurisdictions are located such that services can be aggregated, then an external supplier may be able to attain lower per-unit production costs. This scale advantage is available to any external supplier that can produce the aggregated service level, whether public or private. Managerial incentives developed in the private sector are more conducive than those in the public sector to realize production costs savings, because for-profit and nonprofit organizations can redeploy surpluses.[4] The incentives are probably strongest in for-profit organizations with their profit motive, but nonprofits need surpluses to cross-subsidize (James, 1986). Input flexibility is also greater in the private sector, which is not subject to civil service or public budgeting systems. For-profit organizations have an additional flexibility advantage over nonprofits due to their ability to raise financial capital through the issuance of stock.

Transaction costs are incurred by efforts to reduce the agency problems inherent in contractual relationships.[5] If a local government contracts with an external producer, transaction costs are incurred in determining the capacity of the bidders to produce the service according to the specifications of the contract, in writing a contract that defines and measures the service output, and in monitoring the agent to determine if the contracted service meets specified quantity and quality standards. These costs are incurred regardless of organizational form, but their magnitude is likely to vary by organizational type and with the nature of the service. The public and the nonprofit sectors should generate lower contract specification and enforcement costs than for-profit organizations because the incentives for opportunistic behavior are presumably reduced by the lack of a profit motive. This distinction is especially important in instances where contract writing is complicated (e.g., under changing citizen preferences or cost conditions) and monitoring is difficult (e.g., with intangible outputs) (see Weisbrod, 1988). Transaction costs should be lowest with internal production.[6]

Therefore, no one organizational form appears to dominate in terms of achieving service delivery efficiencies, but rather each presents different trade-offs between production and transaction costs.[7] For example, for public

4. The lack of property rights to residuals in public organizations leaves public managers with no incentive to minimize costs. Indeed, they have a motive to create slack, since it gives them resources with which to meet their own objectives.

5. Williamson (1985) differentiates two types of transaction costs: governance and measurement. Governance costs derive from the role of governance structures on potential conflicts between parties to a contract. Measurement costs derive from the difficulties posed by performance and attribute ambiguities that are associated with product or service production. Although the two types of transaction costs are interrelated, measurement costs are the most critical to organization choice in public service supply.

6. Of course this does not mean there are no transaction costs involved in internal production. We simply assume these costs are smaller within an organization than across organizations.

7. Empirical studies comparing costs across organizational forms have focused on production

services with complex outputs, internal production should offer lower transaction costs (because internal monitoring is less difficult) but higher production costs (because the public organizational form has the least efficient managerial incentives and the least input flexibility) than the alternatives. In contrast, for-profit production is likely to entail higher transaction costs (due to the stronger incentives for opportunism and thus greater need to monitor) but lower production costs (due to stronger managerial efficiency incentives and greater input flexibility). The organizational choice thus depends on how the local government weighs these two components of service delivery costs.

Production costs tend to be more visible since they are associated with the inputs required to produce the service and, thus, are more easily measured. Consequently, their impact on government expenditures is more direct and observable. Transaction costs, on the other hand, are more subtle. They are usually reported as part of general administrative costs and are not typically tied to the delivery of a specific service. This makes them more difficult to identify and quantify. In fact, when such costs are recognized, they are often allocated by formula rather than by actual experience. Nevertheless, transaction costs can be substantial, particularly when outputs are intangible. In this case, contract specification and monitoring become more difficult and this translates into higher transaction costs. Indeed, the desire to maintain accountability could generate transaction costs that outweigh the production cost savings of contracting.

The relative importance of these two types of service delivery costs to local government decision-makers are affected by the local political and fiscal context. For example, if a government has fiscal problems, the desire to cut the more visible production costs may dominate concerns about the quantity and quality of service outputs that generate transaction costs. In this fiscal context, the production-cost efficiencies of potential producers become more important. On the other hand, if citizens place a high priority on maintaining the quantity and/or quality of a public service, governments may be forced to ensure that all dimensions of service outputs are maintained by any potential producer. This would raise the relative importance of the transaction-cost differences across organizational form in organizational choice.

The number of suppliers across the organizational options also affects the organizational choice. The choice set for public service suppliers varies by service. For example, there are a large number of nonprofit suppliers in the social services, but few in public works. The number of service suppliers in a market area, regardless of distribution over the choice set, also affects the degree of competition among potential producers. Although organizations

costs. Numerous studies indicate that private production is less costly than public production (see Borcherding, Pommerehne, and Schneider, 1982; Boardman and Vining, 1989). Evidence comparing for-profit and nonprofit suppliers, however, is less conclusive. In the much studied hospital industry, Wilson and Jadlow (1982) and Robinson and Luft (1985) found that for-profit hospitals had lower costs than nonprofits, but Watt et al. (1986) found no relationship between ownership and cost. There is much less information on the costs of other services.

differ with respect to constraints and incentives, competition has a salutary effect on the costs of all organizational forms.[8] Other things being equal, service delivery costs should be lower in jurisdictions with a large number of suppliers.

The organizational choice is thus affected by the characteristics of jurisdictions as well as the production- and transaction-cost characteristics of the alternatives. More precisely, each local government has utility ($U$) for the outputs of each alternative ($j, j = 1$ for internal public, 2 for external public, 3 for private nonprofit, and 4 for private for-profit) that is a function of the characteristics of the alternative and of the jurisdiction. We can divide the utility of each alternative into a deterministic and a stochastic component:

$$U_j = V_j + \varepsilon_j, \tag{1}$$

where $V_j$ is a function of observed characteristics and $\varepsilon_j$ are the unobserved components of utility. The decision-maker subscript is suppressed for convenience.

## 2.1 Choice Probabilities

If we assume the $\varepsilon$ in Equation (1) are distributed independently and identically according to the extreme-value distribution, then the probability that the $j$th alternative will be chosen is

$$P_j = e^{V_j} / \sum_{m=1}^{4} e^{V_m} \qquad \text{for all } j. \tag{2}$$

Equation (2) is a multinomial logit model, the most common specification of discrete choice models (McFadden, 1974). This model provides a computationally convenient form for the choice probabilities, but has an important drawback: the "independence from irrelevant alternatives" (IIA) property. This property states that the ratio of the probabilities of choosing any two alternatives is independent of the attributes of any other alternative in the choice set.

The IIA property of logit models derives from the assumption that the unobserved components of utility are independently and identically distributed. A logit estimation assumes that $\varepsilon_j$ and $\varepsilon_k$ are uncorrelated (for all $j \neq k$), thus any factor the researcher does not observe that affects the utility of alternative $j$ is assumed not to affect the utility of alternative $k$. This assumption is likely to be violated if two alternatives are close substitutes for each other.

Consider the implications of the IIA property for our model. If one of the four production choices available to local governments is removed, the proba-

8. For example, Mehay and Gonzalez (1985) find that public organizations that produce police services for their own governmental units as well as compete to supply such services for other governmental units have lower production costs than public organizations that produce services only for their own jurisdiction.

bility of choosing the other three alternatives would increase. The important question is by how much each would increase. For example, if there are no nonprofit suppliers and the probabilities of choosing internal and external public production increase by the same amount, then the internal and external public choices have the IIA property. If, however, the for-profit probability goes up by more (or less) than the other two choices, then its ratio to either is not unchanged with and without the nonprofit choice, and the IIA property does not hold.

We hypothesize that both types of public organizations have unobserved components of utility in common with each other but not with the private organizations, and that both types of private organizations have unobserved components of utility in common with each other but not with public organizations. This means the IIA property cannot be assumed to hold for all pairs of alternatives in our model.

Therefore, use of the multinomial logit model would be inappropriate. If, however, we partition the alternatives such that IIA holds within subsets, then we may use the GEV (generalized extreme value) or nested logit model. Thus, we partition the four choices into two nests: a public organization nest that includes the internal and external public choices, and a private organization nest that includes the nonprofit and for-profit choices. The nesting is represented in Figure 1.

The unobserved components of utility in Equation (1), $\varepsilon$, are now assumed to be distributed as generalized extreme value, with all $\varepsilon$ within each nest correlated, but with no correlation across nests. If we denote the nests as $k$ (where $k$ = PUB,PRIV), then the choice probabilities are described by the following nested logit model:[9]

$$P_{kj} = \frac{e^{V_{kj}/\lambda}\left(\sum_{m=1}^{2} e^{V_{km}/\lambda}\right)^{\lambda-1}}{\sum_{k=1}^{2}\left(\sum_{m=1}^{2} e^{V_{km}/\lambda}\right)^{\lambda}}, \tag{3}$$

where $\lambda$ (or more precisely $1 - \lambda$) is a measure of the correlation of unobserved utility within the next.

It is useful to rewrite this joint probability as

$$P_{kj} = P_{j/k} \cdot P_k \tag{4}$$

where $P_{j/k}$ is the conditional probability of a local government choosing organization $j$, given that it has chosen nest $k$, and $P_k$ is the probability of choosing nest $k$.

9. The development and interpretation of the nested logit model relies on McFadden (1978) and Train (1986).

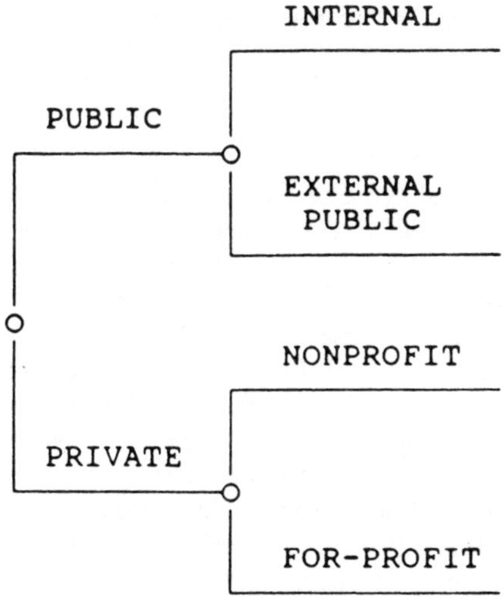


Figure 1. Nesting structure of logit model.

Thus, we can specify Equation (3) with three submodels: the marginal probability of the choice between public and private organizations ($P_k$); the conditional probability of the choice between internal and external public, given that public is chosen ($P_{j/\mathrm{PUB}}$); and the conditional probability of the choice between nonprofit and for-profit, given that private is chosen ($P_{j/\mathrm{PRIV}}$).

We begin by decomposing the deterministic portion of Equation (1) into the following linear-in-parameters specification:

$$V_{kj} = \alpha'\mathbf{N}_k + \beta'\mathbf{A}_{kj} \tag{5}$$

where **A** is a vector of observed characteristics that vary both by alternative and by nest, **N** is a vector of observed characteristics that vary only by nest, and $\alpha$ and $\beta$ are parameter vectors.

Based on McFadden (1978), the conditional probability of choosing an organization given a nest is

$$P_{j/k} = \frac{e^{\beta'\mathbf{A}_{kj}}}{e^{I_k}}, \tag{6}$$

where $I$ defines the "inclusive value"[10] and is

$$I_k = \log \sum_{j=1}^{2} e^{\beta'\mathbf{A}_{kj}} \tag{7}$$

10. Intuitively, $I_k$ denotes the average utility the decision-maker can expect from alternatives within nest $k$ (Train, 1986: 69).

The choice between the public and private nests is given by

$$P_k = \frac{e^{\alpha' \mathbf{N}_k + \lambda I_k}}{e^{\alpha' \mathbf{N}_{\text{PUB}} + \lambda I_{\text{PUB}}} + e^{\alpha' \mathbf{N}_{\text{PRIV}} + \lambda I_{\text{PRIV}}}}. \quad (8)$$

The nested logit model is estimated by maximum likelihood. The sequential procedure is to estimate the parameters $\beta$ from Equation (6), calculate the values $I_k$, and then estimate $\alpha$ from Equation (8) with the inclusive value included as an explanatory variable.[11]

McFadden (1978) shows that a sufficient condition for a nested logit model to be consistent with stochastic utility maximization is that the coefficient of the inclusive value, $\lambda$, lies in the unit interval. More precisely, if the estimated $\lambda$ is between 0 and 1, the resulting choice probabilities are consistent with utility maximization. If $\lambda > 1$, then the choice probabilities *may* be consistent with utility maximization, but only within the ranges of observed data. If $\lambda < 0$, the probabilities are *inconsistent* with utility maximization (Train, 1986: 236). Thus, an estimated $\lambda$ outside the unit interval will be viewed as evidence of a specification error.

Tests of significance applied to the coefficient of the inclusive values can be used to test the IIA property. If $\lambda$ equals 1, there is no correlation among the unobserved components of utility for alternatives within a nest, and the model reduces to the multinomial logit. Thus, if the estimated $\lambda$ is significantly different from 1, this is evidence that the IIA property does not hold. Alternatively, if it is not significantly different from 1, then the multinomial logit model applies to all the alternatives in the choice set, and a nested specification is unnecessary.

## 3. Estimation

We estimate our model of organizational choice using data on the production choices of a cross-section of U.S. cities that provide health services—hospital services, substance abuse prevention and treatment programs, and mental health programs. We chose these services because the health care industry is one of the few where local governments are likely to have all four organizational options.[12] In addition, these three services vary in terms of the "intangibleness" of their outputs and thus the transactions costs associated with their

11. The use of this sequential estimation strategy does *not* mean that the decision-maker is making a sequence of choices. The nested logit model assumes the decision-maker makes one choice from the set of available alternatives.

12. The possibility exists that the number and type of suppliers are endogenous to the model, that is, local government contracting choices may affect the number and organizational form of suppliers. Given the structure of the health care industry, this should not cause estimation problems. The relative role of local governments in health services provision is minor. In 1985, governments accounted for 42 percent of all health care expenditures (U.S. Bureau of Census, 1988). Local government's share of public expenditures was 41.6 percent of total government expenditures. But the great majority of local government health delivery is done through countries rather than cities. Cities are responsible for approximately 6.7 percent of total health care expenditures. This suggests that, in the context of city decisions about health care producers, endogeneity is not likely to introduce any significant bias into the parameter estimates.

delivery (particularly the writing and monitoring of contracts). For example, hospital services are relatively well defined and easy to measure, while mental health and substance abuse prevention and treatment services have less tangible outputs that are difficult to measure.

### 3.1 Data

Information collected by the International City Management Association (1982b) in 1982 provides the organizational choices of local governments. Based on survey responses to questions about the services cities provide and the associated production arrangements, we are able to ascertain whether a service is produced through one of the local government's own agencies, contracted with another government, contracted with a nonprofit organization, or contracted with a for-profit firm. We obtained information on community-level characteristics from the *1983 County and City Data Book* (U.S. Bureau of the Census, 1984), *Significant Features of Fiscal Federalism, 1982–83* (Advisory Committee on Intergovernmental Relations, 1984), and the *1983 American Hospital Association Guide to the Health Care Field* (AHA, 1983).

Of the 471 cities with complete data,[13] 189 cities provide one or more of the three local health services considered here. Ninety-one cities provide hospital services; 107 provide mental health services; and 152 provide substance abuse prevention and treatment services. For our purposes, an observation is the provision of one of the three services. Thus, our data set contains 350 observations.

The characteristics of the sample jurisdictions as of June 1, 1980, can be summarized as follows. The mean population size of the cities is 140,989 (standard deviation = 296,676). Ninety-one percent of these cities are within a Standard Metropolitan Statistical Area (SMSA); 67 percent are run by a professional city manager; and 60 percent operate under a fiscal limitation, that is, legal limits on tax rate or tax assessment. The mean public-employee salary in these cities is $12,257 (standard deviation = $2,456), compared to $13,432 for private-sector service employees (standard deviation = $2,937). The mean number of public employees is 1.43 per 100 residents (standard deviation = .96). The mean number of households under the poverty level is 11.57 percent (standard deviation = 5.6). Finally, among the hospitals providing the services in our sample, a city's public hospitals have on average 5.95 beds per 1,000 population (standard deviation = 15.50) and its private hospitals have 44.30 beds per 1,000 population (standard deviation = 33.71).

### 3.2 Empirical Specification

Consider now the empirical specification of the three submodels—the choice between public and private organizations, between internal and external pub-

13. Since the County and City Data Book only contains information on cities with populations over 25,000, jurisdictions with populations less than 25,000 were dropped from our sample, and the reader is cautioned against drawing inferences from this analysis for small cities.

lic organizations, and between for-profit and nonprofit ones. The determinants of these choices are the production- and transaction-cost characteristics of the alternatives, the number of producers of each type, and the characteristics of the jurisdictions that determine the importance of production- and transaction-cost characteristics to the jurisdiction.

The last group of variables requires some elaboration. Recall that a fundamental property of logit models is that only the difference in the utility of choices (not their level) can affect the choice probabilities. This implies that a variable that does not vary over alternatives cannot affect the choice probabilities. Since we believe that jurisdictional characteristics affect the organizational choice, these variables must be specified as interacting with variables that vary over alternatives. Jurisdictional characteristics are thus interacted with dummy variables that reflect the three choice submodels: private versus public, external public versus internal public, for-profit versus nonprofit. In the three submodels, the dummy variables have a value of 1 for private, external public, and for-profit, and 0 otherwise.

3.2.1 Production-Cost Variables. The organizational alternatives differ in production costs due to managerial incentives, input flexibility, and scale economies. We specify differences in managerial incentives with an ordinal variable, *Efficiency Incentives*, that assumes a value of 1 for internal, 2 for external public, 3 for private nonprofit, and 4 for private for-profit. This categorization reflects the implications of the literature on the production-cost efficiencies of the four organizational options considered. This variable becomes a dummy variable in each of the three submodels, reflecting the stronger incentives for efficiency in for-profit over nonprofit organizations, in external public over internal organizations, and in private over public organizations.[14] Decision-makers sensitive to costs are likely to prefer organizations with strong managerial incentives to decrease production costs; this would be reflected with positive coefficients.

Input flexibility also distinguishes public and private organizations. Civil service systems constrain managerial discretion with respect to labor decisions. One manifestation of this is the difference in labor costs, and this difference is captured with *Labor Costs*. *Labor Costs* equals the mean public salaries in the jurisdiction for public organizations and the mean private-sector service salaries in the jurisdiction for private organizations. Local governments providing health services, which have a large labor-cost component, should be influenced by the relative labor costs of the organizational alternatives. They are likely to find organizational forms with lower labor costs more attractive. Thus, we expect the labor-cost coefficients to be negative.

14. This specification prohibits the addition of constants to the estimating equations. It would be preferable to have a more precise measure of efficiency, but in the absence of such data, specifying organizational differences in efficiency is preferable to omitting an efficiency measure. Note, however, that if there are nonefficiency characteristics of the organizational forms that affect choice and these are not captured by other variables in the model, then they will distort the interpretation of the *Efficiency Incentives* dummies.

Scale economies differentiate internal and external options. Small jurisdictions may seek external suppliers to capture these economies. Jurisdiction population, *Population*, is included to capture this preference. *Population* is formed by multiplying the 1980 jurisdiction population by the public/private dummy variable and by the external-public/internal-public variable. The expected coefficient is negative since small jurisdictions may need to use external public or private organizations to obtain scale economies. Scale economies are not expected to differentiate the two private organization types.

We capture the interest of the local government in production-cost savings with a government-form variable and a measure of fiscal limits. The government-form variable, *Manager Form*, reflects whether the local government is administered by a professional manager. *Manager Form* is formed by multiplying a dummy variable that has a value of 1 if the city has a manager-council form of government and a 0 otherwise by the public/private dummy variable. The manager-council government form is assumed to be more sensitive to cost efficiency because of their professional and nonpartisan orientation, in contrast to the more political orientation of the mayor-council form (Zax, 1985). If this is true, city managers should prefer private organizations with their greater efficiency incentives. Thus, we expect a positive coefficient.

The variable *Fiscal Limits* indicates the existence of legal limits on taxing. The importance of reducing production costs should be greater in communities with tax limits. Therefore, *Fiscal Limits* is formed by multiplying a property-tax-limit dummy by the public/private dummy variable and by the for-profit/nonprofit dummy variable. Jurisdictions with fiscal limits may need the expected production-cost savings of private organizations compared to public ones and of for-profit organizations compared to nonprofit ones.

Transaction-Cost Variables. Transaction costs are generated by the writing and monitoring of contracts. Monitoring costs depend on the characteristics of both the service and the supplying organization. Contracts for services with intangible outputs are difficult to monitor, and thus monitoring costs should be a more important consideration in contracting intangible services than tangible services.

The variable *Monitoring Costs* captures the interactive effects of service and organizational form on monitoring costs. This variable assumes its highest value for an intangible service contracted with a for-profit organization, the next highest value for an intangible service contracted with a nonprofit or external public organization, the third highest value for a tangible service contracted to any external organization, and the lowest value for any service produced internally. Thus increasing values of *Monitoring Costs* represent increasing monitoring costs. We expect the coefficient to be negative. Local governments should prefer the lower monitoring costs of internal production compared to external public, of public production compared to private, and of nonprofit production compared to for-profit.

The strength of the jurisdiction's preferences about service provision and quality determines its willingness to incur transaction costs. In communities where the service constituency is vocal and influential, issues of perceived commitment to service provision and of maintaining service quality are likely to be of greater importance to the decision-maker. The primary constituency of local health services is the poor. We capture constituency preference with the interactive variable *Poor*. *Poor* is formed by multiplying the percentage of the jurisdiction's 1980 population with income below the poverty level by the public/private dummy variable, the internal-public/external-public dummy variable, and by the nonprofit/for-profit dummy variable. We expect negative coefficients since jurisdictions responsive to service constituencies should prefer producers viewed by the constituency as more committed to service delivery (internal over external, public over private, and nonprofit over for-profit). Public producers reinforce the perceived commitment to public provision of the service. Nonprofit organizations, with their historical record and commitment to providing health services to the poor, are expected by service constituents to provide both better access and higher-quality services than for-profit suppliers.

Jurisdictions may also be influenced by their public employee unions. Public employees should resist the use of private producers. We capture this influence with the interactive variable *Public Employees*. *Public Employees* is formed by multiplying the percentage of public employees per 100 residents by the public/private dummy variable. Public employees, aside from influencing the cost conditions of local government through bargaining, also affect local government decisions through their strong interest and involvement in local politics (Zax and Ichniowski, 1988). Jurisdictions with a high percentage of public employees are likely to face strong opposition to using private producers for health service delivery; thus, we expect a negative coefficient.

3.2.3 Choice-Set Variables. All jurisdictions do not face the same producer choice set. Ideally we could form each jurisdiction's choice set based on the available suppliers of each service. Unfortunately, data do not exist on all the external suppliers of our sample services. As a proxy, we use two measures of supplier availability. The American Hospital Association collects data on the hospitals that provide the three services in our sample. This source differentiates public and private producers and nonprofit and for-profit ones. Thus, we define the variable *Beds* as the number of beds in hospitals providing the service in each jurisdiction by organizational type.

A second choice-set variable, *SMSA*, is included to capture the option of jurisdictions located within SMSAs to cross jurisdictional boundaries to obtain external producers. This control is needed since *Beds* is jurisdictionally defined. *SMSA* is formed by multiplying an SMSA dummy variable (1 if the jurisdiction is located within an SMSA, 0 otherwise) by the public/private dummy variable and by the internal-public/external-public dummy variable.

3.2.4 Summary. To summarize, the production-cost variables are *Efficiency Incentives*, *Labor Costs*, *Population*, *Manager Form*, and *Fiscal Limits*. The transaction-cost variables are *Monitoring Costs*, *Poor*, and *Public Employees*. The choice-set variables are *Beds* and *SMSA*.

The three submodels are specified as follows. The conditional probabilities of choosing an organization given a nest are:

$$P_{j/\text{PUB}} = f[\textit{EfficiencyIncentives,Population,Monitoring Costs,Poor,SMSA}], \text{ where } j = \text{Internal,External Public} \quad (9)$$

$$P_{j/\text{PRIV}} = f[\textit{EfficiencyIncentives,Fiscal Limits,Monitoring Costs,Poor,Beds}], \text{ where } j = \text{Nonprofit,For-profit} \quad (10)$$

with the functional form $f$ described by Equation (6).

The choice between the nests is

$$P_k = g[\textit{EfficiencyIncentives,Labor Costs,Population, ManagerForm,Fiscal Limits,MonitoringCosts,Poor, PublicEmployees,Beds,SMSA}], \text{ where } k = \text{Public,Private} \quad (11)$$

with the functional form $g$ described by Equation (8).

### 3.3 Results

The results are presented in Table 1, with the standard errors corrected for the use of estimated inclusive values.[15] We consider first the Level 2 model—private versus public, and then consider the Level 1 models—external public versus internal, and private for-profit versus private nonprofit.

The value of the coefficient on the inclusive value in the private/public choice model, .18, lies within the unit interval. This indicates that the empirical model is consistent with the assumption that local governments make utility-maximizing organizational choices. In addition, this coefficient estimate is significantly different from 1.[16] This indicates that, as expected, the two public organizations have unobserved components of utility in common, and the two private organizations have unobserved components of utility in common. Thus the IIA property does not hold across the four alternates, and the nested specification is necessary.

Consider now the determinants of organizational choice in the Level 2 model. The choice between public and private organizations is driven by four variables. As expected, cities with a manager form of government prefer the lower production costs of private organizations, and jurisdictions with more public employees prefer public organizations. Contrary to expectations, cities under property tax limits prefer public organizations. Finally cities within SMSAs prefer public organizations. This presumably reflects the greater availability of external public producers to these cities.

The results of the Level 1 models reveal distinctions within each nest as well. In the public-sector nest, small cities use external public suppliers over

15. The software used was LIMDEP version 5.1.

16. A Wald test revealed a $\chi^2$ of 3.09 with a probability level of .08.

Table 1. Nested Logit Estimates of Organizational Choice

| Variables | Level 1: External Public (= 1) or Internal (= 0) | Level 1: For-Profit (= 1) or Nonprofit (= 0) | Level 2: Private (= 1) or Public (= 0) |
|---|---|---|---|
| Production-cost variables | | | |
| *Efficiency incentives* | −0.88 | 1.15* | 1.96 |
| | (1.11) | (0.52) | (1.23) |
| *Labor costs* | — | — | −0.023 |
| | | | (0.029) |
| *Population* | −0.041** | — | −0.0037 |
| | (0.013) | | (0.0071) |
| *Manager form* | — | — | 0.70** |
| | | | (0.26) |
| *Fiscal limits* | — | 0.28 | −0.94*** |
| | | (0.37) | (0.28) |
| Transaction-cost variables | | | |
| *Monitoring costs* | 0.37 | −2.45*** | 0.11 |
| | (0.45) | (0.38) | (1.72) |
| *Poor* | 0.082* | −0.045 | 0.045 |
| | (0.040) | (0.037) | (0.037) |
| *Public employees* | — | — | −0.27* |
| | | | (0.14) |
| Choice-set variables | | | |
| *Beds* | — | .000052 | .0000032 |
| | | (.00019) | (.0000027) |
| *SMSA* | 0.61 | — | −1.17* |
| | (0.79) | | (0.52) |
| Inclusive Value | — | — | 0.18 |
| | | | (0.47) |
| Log-Likelihood | −179.54 | | −221.64 |
| Restricted (Intercepts only) Log-Likelihood | −242.60 | | −242.60 |
| $\chi^2$ | 126.12*** | | 41.92*** |

Note: Standard errors (in parentheses) are corrected for use of estimated inclusive values. Asterisks denote significance in two-tailed tests. Probability levels are: *$p < .05$, **$p < .01$, ***$p < .001$.

internal production to capture scale advantages, as expected. Jurisdictions with larger proportions of their citizens in poverty also use external public suppliers over internal production. This result is contrary to our expectations and may reflect a dual role for the poverty measure. Jurisdictions with a high proportion of their population in poverty are obviously poor, and their need to reduce service delivery costs is acute. External public production offers a cost-saving option that may not be as threatening to service constituents as contracting with the private sector. External public production is still public production, with its implied assurance of continued public provision and thus access.

In the private-sector nest, decision-makers value the stronger efficiency incentives of for-profit organizations relative to nonprofit organizations. In addition, the results also indicate that local decision-makers value the lower monitoring costs of nonprofit organizations relative to for-profit organizations. This underscores the trade-offs that decision-makers confront in making organizational choices for service production.

## 4. Conclusion

Local government decision-makers face a variety of organizational choices in the production of local services. In evaluating their options, they consider both the production-cost and transaction-cost implications. This examination of the actual production decisions of local governments that provide health services indicates that decision-makers differentiate between public and private alternatives. There are unobserved public characteristics that cause the two public organization options to be closer substitutes for each other than either private organization form would be, and there are unobserved characteristics of the two private organizations that cause them to be closer substitutes for each other than either public organization would be. The results thus suggest that decision-makers recognize the public/private distinction in their organizational choices.

The determinants of their choice between public and private organizations and between the alternatives within these groups are based on the hypothesized factors. Scale economies differentiate between external and internal public organizations, and efficiency incentives and monitoring costs differentiate between for-profit and nonprofit private organizations. Managerial preferences for private organizations and public employee opposition to them help define the choice between public and private organizations.

These results support the idea that local government decision-makers believe the private sector offers cost-saving advantages over the public sector. This finding is consistent with the common perception of the inefficiency of public bureaucracies. Of course, whether local decision-makers are acting on faith or facts cannot be discerned in this study.

Finally, the importance of monitoring costs in differentiating the nonprofit and for-profit organizations is interesting in light of evidence that the actual behaviors of private nonprofit and for-profit health care organizations have converged over time as they have come to depend on the same funding sources (see Ferris and Graddy, 1989). Better information on production- and transaction-cost differences will be needed before empirical studies can inform government decision-makers about the trade-off in service delivery costs between these two private organizational forms.

## References

Advisory Commission on Intergovernmental Relations. 1984. *Significant Features of Fiscal Federalism, 1982–83*. Washington, D.C.: Advisory Commission on Intergovernmental Relations.

American Hospital Association (AHA). 1983. *American Hospital Association Guide to the Health Care Field*. Chicago: American Hospital Association.

Bergstrom, Theodore, Daniel Rubinfeld, and Perry Shapiro. 1982. "Micro-Based Estimates of Demand Functions for Local School Expenditures," 50 *Econometrica* 1183–1206.

Boardman, Anthony E., and Aidan R. Vining. 1989. "Ownership and Performance in Competitive Environments: A Comparison of the Performance of Private, Mixed, and State-owned Enterprises," 32 *Journal of Law & Economics* 1–33.

Borcherding, Thomas E., Werner W. Pommerehne, and Friedrich Schneider. 1982. "Comparing the Efficiency of Private and Public Production: The Evidence from Five Countries," Supplement 2 *Journal of Economics* 127–156.

Donahue, John. 1989. *The Privatization Decision*. New York: Basic Books.

Ferris, James, and Elizabeth Graddy. 1988. "Production Choices for Local Government Services," 10 *Journal of Urban Affairs* 273–89.

———, and ———. 1989. "Fading Distinctions Among the Nonprofit, Government, and For-Profit Sectors," in V. Hodgkinson and R. Lyman, eds., *The Future of the Nonprofit Sector*. San Francisco: Jossey-Bass.

———, and ———. 1991. "Production Costs, Transaction Costs, and Local Government Contractor Choice," 29 *Economic Inquiry* 541–54.

International City Management Association. 1982. *Alternative Approaches for Delivering Public Services*. Washington, D.C.: International City Management Association.

James, Estelle. 1986. "How Nonprofits Grow: A Model," in S. Rose-Ackerman, ed., *The Economics of Nonprofit Institutions*. New York: Oxford University Press.

McFadden, Daniel. 1974. "Conditional Logit Analysis of Qualitative Choice Behavior," in P. Zarembka, ed., *Frontiers in Econometrics*. New York: Academic Press.

———. 1978. "Modelling the Choice of Residential Location," in A. Karlqvist et al., eds., *Spatial Interaction Theory and Residential Location*. Amsterdam: North-Holland.

Mehay, Stephen, and Rodolfo Gonzalez. 1985. "Economic Incentives under Contract Supply of Local Government Services," 46 *Public Choice* 79–86.

Robinson, James C., and Harold S. Luft. 1985. "The Impact of Hospital Market Structure on Patient volume, Average Length of Stay, and the Cost of Care," 4 *Journal of Health Economics* 333–56.

Stein, Robert. 1990. *Urban Alternatives: Public and Private Markets in the Provision of Local Services*. Pittsburgh, Pa.: University of Pittsburgh Press.

Train, Kenneth. 1986. *Qualitative Choice Analysis*. Cambridge, Mass.: MIT Press.

U.S. Bureau of the Census. 1984. *County and City Data Book, 1983*. Washington, D.C.: Department of Commerce.

———. 1988. *Statistical Abstract of the United States*. Washington, D.C.: Department of Commerce.

Watt, J. Michael, Steven C. Renn, James S. Hahn, Robert A. Derzon, and Carl J. Schramm. 1986. "The Effects of Ownership and Multihospital System Membership on Hospital Functional Strategies and Economic Performance," in H. Gray, ed., *For-Profit Enterprise in Health Care*. Washington, D.C.: National Academy Press.

Weisbrod, Burton. 1988. *The Nonprofit Economy*. Cambridge, Mass.: Harvard University Press.

Williamson, Oliver. 1985. *The Economic Institutions of Capitalism*. New York: Free Press.

Wilson, George W., and Joseph M. Jadlow. 1982. "Competition, Profit Incentives, and Technical Efficiency in the Provision of Nuclear Medicine Services," 13 *Bell Journal of Economics* 472–82.

Zax, Jeffrey. 1985. "Economic Effects of Municipal Government Institutions." Working Paper No. 1675, National Bureau of Economic Research, Cambridge, Mass.

———, and Casey Ichniowski. 1988. "The Effects of Public Sector Unionism on Pay, Employment, Department Budgets, and Municipal Expenditures," in R. Freeman and C. Ichniowski, eds., *When Public Sector Workers Unionize*. Chicago: University of Chicago Press.

# Name Index

## The International Library of Critical Writings in Economics

1. Multinational Corporations
   *Mark Casson*
2. The Economics of Innovation
   *Christopher Freeman*
3. Entrepreneurship
   *Mark Casson*
4. International Investment
   *Peter J. Buckley*
5. Game Theory in Economics
   *Ariel Rubinstein*
6. The History of Economic Thought
   *Mark Blaug*
7. Monetary Theory
   *Thomas Mayer*
8. Joint Production of Commodities
   *Neri Salvadori and Ian Steedman*
9. Industrial Organization
   *Oliver E. Williamson*
10. Growth Theory
    (Volumes I, II and III)
    *R. Becker and E. Burmeister*
11. Microeconomics: Theoretical and Applied (Volumes I, II and III)
    *Robert E. Kuenne*
12. The Economics of Health
    (Volumes I and II)
    *A.J. Culyer*
13. Recent Developments in Macroeconomics
    (Volumes I, II and III)
    *Edmund S. Phelps*
14. Urban and Regional Economics
    *Paul C. Cheshire and Alan W. Evans*
15. Modern Public Finance
    (Volumes I and II)
    *A.B. Atkinson*
16. Exchange Rate Economics
    (Volumes I and II)
    *Ronald MacDonald and Mark P. Taylor*
17. The Economic Value of Education: Studies in the Economics of Education
    *Mark Blaug*
18. Development Economics
    (Volumes I, II, III and IV)
    *Deepak Lal*
19. The New Classical Macroeconomics
    (Volumes I, II and III)
    *Kevin D. Hoover*
20. The Economics of the Environment
    *Wallace E. Oates*
21. Post Keynesian Theory of Growth and Distribution
    *Carlo Panico and Neri Salvadori*
22. Dynamic Labor Demand and Adjustment Costs
    *Giorgio Galeazzi and Daniel S. Hamermesh*
23. The Philosophy and Methodology of Economics (Volumes I, II and III)
    *Bruce J. Caldwell*
24. Public Choice Theory
    (Volumes I, II and III)
    *Charles K. Rowley*
25. Evolutionary Economics
    *Ulrich Witt*
26. Economics and Psychology
    *Shlomo Maital and Sharone L. Maital*
27. Social Choice Theory
    (Volumes I, II and III)
    *Charles K. Rowley*
28. Non-Linear Dynamics in Economic Theory
    *Marc Jarsulic*
29. Recent Developments in Experimental Economics
    (Volumes I and II)
    *John D. Hey and Graham Loomes*

30. Monopoly and Competition Policy (Volumes I and II)
*F.M. Scherer*
31. The Economics of Technical Change
*Edwin Mansfield and Elizabeth Mansfield*
32. The Economics of Exhaustible Resources
*Geoffrey Heal*
33. The Economics of Institutions
*Geoffrey M. Hodgson*
34. The Economics of Transport (Volumes I and II)
*Herbert Mohring*
35. Implicit Contract Theory
*Sherwin Rosen*
36. Foundations of Analytical Marxism (Volumes I and II)
*John E. Roemer*
37. The Economics of Product Differentiation (Volumes I and II)
*Jacques-François Thisse and George Norman*
38. Economic Growth in Theory and Practice: A Kaldorian Perspective
*John E. King*
39. Markets and Socialism
*Alec Nove and Ian D. Thatcher*
40. Recent Developments in the Economics of Education
*Elchanan Cohn and Geraint Johnes*
41. The Theory of Inflation
*Michael Parkin*
42. The Economics of Location (Volumes I, II and III)
*Melvin L. Greenhut and George Norman*
43. Financial Intermediaries
*Mervyn K. Lewis*
44. The Political Economy of Privatization and Deregulation
*Elizabeth E. Bailey and Janet Rothenberg Pack*
45. Gender and Economics
*Jane Humphries*
46. Macroeconomics and Imperfect Competition
*Jean-Pascal Bénassy*
47. Labor Economics (Volumes I, II, III and IV)
*Orley C. Ashenfelter and Kevin F. Hallock*
48. The Economics of Altruism
*Stefano Zamagni*
49. The Economic Analysis of Rent Seeking
*Robert D. Tollison and Roger D. Congleton*
50. Economics and Biology
*Geoffrey M. Hodgson*
51. The Economics of Ageing
*John Creedy*
52. Fiscal and Monetary Policy (Volumes I and II)
*Thomas Mayer and Steven M. Sheffrin*
53. The Economics of Information (Volumes I and II)
*David K. Levine and Steven A. Lippman*
54. Transaction Cost Economics (Volumes I and II)
*Oliver E. Williamson and Scott E. Masten*
55. Agricultural Economics
*George H. Peters*
56. International Debt (Volumes I and II)
*Graham Bird and P. Nicholas Snowden*
57. Economics and Discrimination (Volumes I and II)
*William A. Darity, Jr*
58. Business Cycle Theory
*Finn E. Kydland*
59. International Trade (Volumes I and II)
*J. Peter Neary*
60. The Money Supply in the Economic Process
*Marco Musella and Carlo Panico*

61. Small Firms and Economic Growth (Volumes I and II)
*Zoltan J. Acs*
62. Producer Cooperatives and Labor-Managed Systems (Volumes I and II)
*David L. Prychitko and Jaroslav Vanek*
63. Ethics and Economics (Volumes I and II)
*Alan P. Hamlin*
64. The Economics of the Family
*Nancy Folbre*
65. The Economics of Training (Volumes I and II)
*Orley C. Ashenfelter and Robert J. LaLonde*
66. Chaos Theory in Economics: Methods, Models and Evidence
*W. Davis Dechert*
67. General Equilibrium Theory (Volumes I, II and III)
*Gérard Debreu*
68. Economic Growth: Theory and Evidence (Volumes I and II)
*Gene M. Grossman*
69. Long Wave Theory
*Christopher Freeman*
70. The Economics of Communication and Information
*Donald M. Lamberton*
71. The Foundations of Public Finance (Volumes I and II)
*Peter Jackson*
72. The Theory of the Firm
*Mark Casson*
73. The Economics of Uncertainty (Volumes I and II)
*John D. Hey*
74. The Economics of Global Warming
*Tom Tietenberg*
75. The Development of Ecological Economics
*Robert Costanza, Charles Perrings and Cutler Cleveland*
76. Economic Growth in the Long Run: A History of Empirical Evidence (Volumes I, II and III)
*Bart van Ark*
77. The Economics of Productivity (Volumes I and II)
*Edward N. Wolff*
78. The Economics of Population: Key Modern Writings (Volumes I and II)
*Julian L. Simon*
79. Political Business Cycles
*Bruno S. Frey*
80. Cultural Economics: The Arts, the Heritage and the Media Industries (Volumes I and II)
*Ruth Towse*
81. Law and Economics (Volumes I, II and III)
*Richard A. Posner and Francesco Parisi*
82. Independent Central Banks and Economic Performance
*Sylvester Eijffinger*
83. Culture, Social Norms and Economics (Volumes I and II)
*Mark Casson*
84. Industrial Policy and Competitive Advantage (Volumes I, II and III)
*David B. Audretsch*
85. The Economics of Housing (Volumes I and II)
*John M. Quigley*
86. Economic Demography (Volumes I and II)
*T. Paul Schultz*
87. Trade and the Environment: Economic, Legal and Policy Perspectives
*Alan M. Rugman and John J. Kirton with Julie A. Soloway*
88. The Economics of Fiscal Federalism and Local Finance
*Wallace E. Oates*
89. Price Theory and its Applications
*Bernard Saffran and F.M. Scherer*

90. Women in the Labor Market (Volumes I and II)
*Marianne A. Ferber*
91. Market Process Theories (Volumes I and II)
*Peter Boettke and David Prychitko*
92. Input–Output Analysis (Volumes I, II and III)
*Heinz Kurz, Erik Dietzenbacher and Christian Lager*
93. Mathematical Economics (Volumes I, II and III)
*Graciela Chichilnisky*
94. The Foundations of Regulatory Economics (Volumes I, II and III)
*Robert B. Ekelund, Jr.*
95. The Economics of Marketing
*Martin Carter, Mark Casson and Vivek Suneja*
96. Service Industries in the Global Economy (Volumes I and II)
*J.R. Bryson and P.W. Daniels*
97. Economic Justice (Volumes I and II)
*Giorgio Brosio and Harold M. Hochman*
98. Foreign Exchange Intervention: Objectives and Effectiveness
*Sylvester C.W. Eijffinger*
99. Economic Anthropology
*Stephen Gudeman*
100. Consumer Theory
*Kelvin Lancaster*
101. The Economics of Famine
*Jean Drèze*
102. Microeconomic Theories of Imperfect Competition
*Jean J. Gabszewicz and Jacques-François Thisse*
103. The Economics of Executive Compensation (Volumes I and II)
*Kevin F. Hallock and Kevin J. Murphy*
104. The Foundations of Long Wave Theory (Volumes I and II)
*Francisco Louçã and Jan Reijnders*
105. The Economics of Commodity Markets
*David Greenaway and C.W. Morgan*
106. Corporate Governance (Volumes I, II, III and IV)
*Kevin Keasey, Steve Thompson and Mike Wright*
107. Economic Welfare: Concepts and Measurement (Volumes I and II)
*John Creedy*
108. Economic Forecasting
*Terence C. Mills*
109. Recent Developments in Game Theory
*Eric S. Maskin*
110. The Economics of Increasing Returns
*Geoffrey Heal*
111. The Economics of Corruption and Illegal Markets (Volumes I, II and III)
*Gianluca Fiorentini and Stefano Zamagni*
112. The Economics of Price Discrimination
*George Norman*
113. The Economic Theory of Auctions (Volumes I and II)
*Paul Klemperer*
114. The Economics of Regional Policy
*Harvey W. Armstrong and Jim Taylor*
115. Economic Integration and International Trade
*Carsten Kowalczyk*
116. The Political Economy of Science, Technology and Innovation
*Ben Martin and Paul Nightingale*
117. The Economics of Science and Innovation (Volumes I and II)
*Paula E. Stephan and David B. Audretsch*
118. Innovation, Evolution of Industry and Economic Growth (Volumes I, II and III)
*David B. Audretsch and Steven Klepper*

119. The Economics of Energy
(Volumes I and II)
*Paul Stevens*
120. Privatisation in Developing Countries
(Volumes I and II)
*Paul Cook and Colin Kirkpatrick*
121. The Economics of Tourism
(Volumes I and II)
*Clem Tisdell*
122. The Economics of Unemployment
(Volumes I, II, III and IV)
*P.N. Junankar*
123. Privatisation and Corporate Performance
*David Parker*
124. Income Distribution
(Volumes I, II and III)
*Michael Sattinger*
125. International Finance
(Volumes I and II)
*Robert Z. Aliber*
126. Welfare Economics
(Volumes I, II and III)
*William J. Baumol and Charles A. Wilson*
127. The Theory of Trade Policy Reform
*Carsten Kowalczyk*
128. The Economics of Defence
(Volumes I, II and III)
*Keith Hartley and Todd Sandler*
129. The Economics of Property Rights
(Volumes I and II)
*Svetozar Pejovich*
130. Gender and Development: Theoretical, Empirical and Practical Approaches
(Volumes I and II)
*Lourdes Benería with Savitri Bisnath*
131. The Economics of Politics
(Volumes I and II)
*Dennis C. Mueller*
132. Economic Theory and the Welfare State (Volumes I, II and III)
*Nicholas Barr*
133. The Regulation and Supervision of Banks
(Volumes I, II, III and IV)
*Maximilian J.B. Hall*
134. The Political Economy of Monetary Union
*Paul De Grauwe*
135. The Economics of Sport
(Volumes I and II)
*Andrew Zimbalist*
136. The Economics of Advertising
*Kyle Bagwell*
137. Regulation, Economics and the Law
*Anthony I. Ogus*
138. The Economics of Barter and Countertrade
*Rolf Mirus and Bernard Yeung*
139. The Economics of Technology Transfer
*Sanjaya Lall*
140. The Political Economy of Development
(Volumes I, II and III)
*Amitava Krishna Dutt*
141. Macroeconomics and the Environment
*Mohan Munasinghe*
142. Happiness in Economics
*Richard A. Easterlin*
143. Speculation and Financial Markets
(Volumes I and II)
*Liam Gallagher and Mark P. Taylor*
144. Public Procurement
(Volumes I and II)
*Sue Arrowsmith and Keith Hartley*
145. The Economics of Intellectual Property
(Volumes I, II, III and IV)
*Ruth Towse and R.W. Holzhauer*
146. Forecasting Financial Markets
(Volumes I and II)
*Terence C. Mills*
147. The Economics of Labor Unions
(Volumes I and II)
*Alison Booth*

148. New Developments in Exchange Rate Economics
(Volumes I and II)
*Lucio Sarno and Mark P. Taylor*

149. Long Term Trends and Business Cycles
(Volumes I and II)
*Terence C. Mills*

150. The Economics of Language
*Donald M. Lamberton*

151. The Economics of Migration
(Volumes I, II, III and IV)
*Klaus F. Zimmermann and Thomas Bauer*

152. Cost–Benefit Analysis
*Arnold C. Harberger and Glenn P. Jenkins*

153. The Economics of Budget Deficits
(Volumes I and II)
*Charles K. Rowley, William F. Shughart II and Robert D. Tollison*

154. Alternative Theories of the Firm
(Volumes I, II and III)
*Richard Langlois, Tony F. Yu and Paul Robertson*

155. The Distribution of Tax Burdens
*Don Fullerton and Gilbert E. Metcalf*

156. International Financial Integration
(Volumes I and II)
*Sylvester C.W. Eijffinger and Jan J.G. Lemmen*

157. The Economics of Structural Change
(Volumes I, II and III)
*Harald Hagemann, Michael Landesmann and Roberto Scazzieri*

158. The Economics of Poverty and Inequality
(Volumes I and II)
*Frank A. Cowell*

159. The Economics of Schooling
(Volumes I and II)
*Eric A. Hanushek*

160. Intra-Industry Trade
*Peter J. Lloyd and Herbert G. Grubel*

161. Economic Analysis of Regional Trading Arrangements
*Richard Pomfret*

162. The Principal Agent Model: The Economic Theory of Incentives
*Jean-Jacques Laffont*

163. The Economics of Business Strategy
*John Kay*

164. Recent Developments in Transport Economics
*Kenneth Button*

165. The Economics of Higher Education
*Clive R. Belfield and Henry M. Levin*

166. Constitutional Political Economy
(Volumes I and II)
*Stephan Voigt*

167. Economics and Religion
(Volumes I and II)
*Paul Oslington*

168. The Economics of Conflict
(Volumes I, II and III)
*Todd Sandler and Keith Hartley*

169. Cognitive Economics
(Volumes I and II)
*Massimo Egidi and Salvatore Rizzello*

170. Comparative Law and Economics
(Volumes I, II and III)
*Gerrit de Geest and Roger Van Den Bergh*

171. Personnel Economics
(Volumes I and II)
*Edward P. Lazear and Robert McNabb*

172. Empirical Industrial Organization
(Volumes I and II)
*Paul L. Joskow and Michael Waterson*

173. Multinationals and Public Policy
(Volumes I and II)
*Stephen Young*

174. Complexity in Economics
(Volumes I, II and III)
*J. Barkley Rosser, Jr.*

175. Time in Economic Theory
(Volumes I, II and III)
*Stefano Zamagni and Elettra Agliardi*

176. The Economics of Affirmative Action
*Harry J. Holzer and David Neumark*

177. Recent Developments in Environmental Economics
(Volumes I and II)
*Michael Hoel*

178. The Economics of Natural Hazards
(Volumes I and II)
*Howard Kunreuther and Adam Rose*

179. Recent Developments in Growth Theory
(Volumes I and II)
*K. Daron Acemoglu*

180. The Political Economy of Environmental Regulation
*Robert N. Stavins*

181. The Economics of Nonprofit Enterprises
*Richard S. Steinberg*

Future titles will include:

Recent Developments in Urban and Regional Economics
*Paul C. Cheshire and Gilles Duranton*

The Economics of Public Private Partnerships
*Darrin Grimsey and Mervyn K. Lewis*

The Psychology of World Equity Markets
(Volumes I and II)
*Werner De Bondt*

The Economics of Crime
(Volumes I, II and III)
*Isaac Ehrlich and Zhiqiang Liu*

New Developments in Economic Sociology
(Volumes I and II)
*Richard Swedberg*

New Economic Geography
*J. Vernon Henderson*

The Economics of Deflation
(Volumes I and II)
*Pierre L. Siklos*

The Economics of Networks
*Michael L. Katz and Carl Shapiro*

The Economics of Contracts
*Lars A. Stole*

Spatial Economics
*Masahisa Fujita*

Recent Developments in Labour Economics
*John T. Addison*

Institutions and Economic Performance
*Masahiko Aoki*

Imperfect Competition, Nonclearing Markets and Business Cycles
*Jean-Pascal Bénassy*

The International Monetary Fund and the World Economy
*Graham Bird and Dane Rowlands*

International Taxation
*Richard M. Bird and Michael Smart*

The Economics of Knowledge
*Robin A. Cowan*

Path Dependence
*Paul A. David*

Recent Developments in Economic Methodology
*John B. Davis*

The Economics of the Mass Media
*Gillian Doyle*

The Economics of Gambling and National Lotteries
*William R. Eadington*

The Economics of Transfer Pricing
*Lorraine Eden*

Recent Developments in International Trade Theory
*Rodney E. Falvey and Udo Kreickemeier*

Financial Crises
*Douglas Gale and Franklin Allen*

The Economics of Association Football
*Bill Gerrard*

The Economics of Innovation Policy
*Bronwyn Hall*

Islamic Finance
*M. Kabir Hassan and Mervyn K. Lewis*

The Economics of Vouchers
*Caroline M. Hoxby*

The Economics of Free Trade
*Douglas A. Irwin and Arvind Panagariya*

The Economics of Organisation and Bureaucracy
*Peter M. Jackson*

Computational Economics
*Kenneth L. Judd*

Feminist Economics
*Mary C. King, Ann Mari May and Diana L. Strassman*

Cooperation, Competition and Collusion: The Economic Theory of Incentives
*Jean-Jacques Laffont*

The Phillips Curve
*Richard G. Lipsey and Robert Leeson*

The Economics of Biotechnology
*Maureen McKelvey and Luigi Orsenigo*

The Economic Role of the State
*Steven G. Medema*

Open Economy Macroeconomics
*Norman C. Miller*

Innovation and Economic Development
*Lynn Mytelka*

Forms of Capitalism: Comparative Institutional Analyses
*Ugo Pagano and Ernesto Screpanti*

The New Evolutionary Economics
*Jason Potts and Kurt Dopfer*

The Economics of Public Utilities
*Ray Rees*

The Economics of Modern Business Enterprise
*Martin Ricketts*

New Developments in Public Choice
*Charles K. Rowley, Robert D. Tollison and William F. Shughart*

Recent Developments in International Investment
*Alan M. Rugman*

Cartels
*Stephen Salant and Margaret Levenstein*

The Economics of the Hidden Economy
*Vito Tanzi*

The Economics of Leisure and Recreation
*Clem Tisdell*

Recent Developments in Evolutionary Economics
*Ulrich Witt*